JAMES DEAN

TOMORROW NEVER COMES

James Dean became a legend, worldwide.
This book tells how he did it.

COMMEMORATING THE 60TH ANNIVERSARY OF THE
DEATH OF JAMES DEAN
(FEBRUARY 8, 1931-SEPTEMBER 30, 1955)

ANOTHER EXAMPLE OF BLOOD MOON'S AWARD-WINNING
ENTERTAINMENT ABOUT HOW AMERICA INTERPRETS ITS
CELEBRITIES.

WWW.BLOODMOONPRODUCTIONS.COM

JAMES DEAN

TOMORROW NEVER COMES

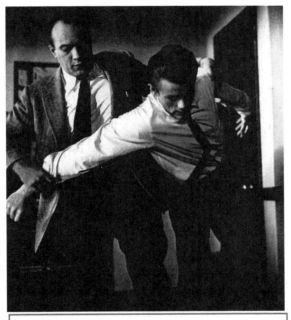

A MYTH-SHATTERING TALE ABOUT AMERICA'S
OBSESSION WITH CELEBRITIES.

DARWIN PORTER &
DANFORTH PRINCE

JAMES DEAN

Tomorrow Never Comes

Darwin Porter and Danforth Prince

www.BloodMoonProductions.com

Manufactured in the United States of America

ISBN 978-1-936003-49-5

Front cover design by Richard Leeds (Bigwigdesign.com)
Back cover design by Tiffany Voorhees

Distributed worldwide through National Book Network
(www.NBNbooks.com)

1 2 3 4 5 6 7 8 9 10

A Word About Phraseologies

Since we at Blood Moon weren't privy to long-ago conversations as they were unfolding, we have relied on the memories of our sources for the conversational tone and phraseologies of what we've recorded within the pages of this book.

This writing technique, as it applies to modern biography, has been defined as "conversational storytelling" by *The New York Times,* which labeled it as an acceptable literary device for "engaging reading."

Blood Moon is not alone in replicating, "as remembered" dialogues from dead sources. Truman Capote and Norman Mailer were pioneers of direct quotes, and today, they appear in countless other memoirs, ranging from those of Eddie Fisher to those of the long-time mistress (Verita Thompson) of Humphrey Bogart.

Some people have expressed displeasure in the fact that direct quotes and "as remembered" dialogue have become a standard—some would say "mandatory"—fixture in pop culture biographies today.

If that is the case with anyone who's reading this now, they should perhaps turn to other, more traditional and self-consciously "scholastic" works instead.

Best wishes to all of you, with thanks for your interest in our work.

Danforth Prince
President and Founder
Blood Moon Productions

PREVIOUS WORKS BY DARWIN PORTER
PRODUCED IN COLLABORATION WITH BLOOD MOON

BIOGRAPHIES

Bill & Hillary, *So This Is That Thing Called Love*

Peter O'Toole, *Hellraiser, Sexual Outlaw, Irish Rebel*

Love Triangle, *Ronald Reagan, Jane Wyman, & Nancy Davis*

Jacqueline Kennedy Onassis, *A Life Beyond Her Wildest Dreams*

Pink Triangle, *The Feuds and Private Lives of Tennessee Williams, Gore Vidal, Truman Capote, and Famous Members of their Entourages.*

Those Glamorous Gabors, *Bombshells from Budapest*

Inside Linda Lovelace's Deep Throat, *Degradation, Porno Chic, and the Rise of Feminism*

Elizabeth Taylor, *There is Nothing Like a Dame*

Marilyn at Rainbow's End, *Sex, Lies, Murder, and the Great Cover-up*

J. Edgar Hoover & Clyde Tolson
Investigating the Sexual Secrets of America's Most Famous Men and Women

Frank Sinatra, *The Boudoir Singer. All the Gossip Unfit to Print*

The Kennedys, *All the Gossip Unfit to Print*

Humphrey Bogart, The Making of a Legend *(2010)* , and
The Secret Life of Humphrey Bogart *(2003)*

Howard Hughes, *Hell's Angel*

Steve McQueen, *King of Cool, Tales of a Lurid Life*

Paul Newman, *The Man Behind the Baby Blues*

Merv Griffin, *A Life in the Closet*

Brando Unzipped

Katharine the Great, *Hepburn, Secrets of a Lifetime Revealed*

Jacko, His Rise and Fall, *The Social and Sexual History of Michael Jackson*

Damn You, Scarlett O'Hara, *The Private Lives of Vivien Leigh and Laurence Olivier*
(co-authored with Roy Moseley)

FILM CRITICISM
Blood Moon's 2005 Guide to the Glitter Awards
Blood Moon's 2006 Guide to Film
Blood Moon's 2007 Guide to Film, *and*
50 Years of Queer Cinema, *500 of the Best GLBTQ Films Ever Made*

NON-FICTION
Hollywood Babylon—It's Back! and **Hollywood Babylon Strikes Again!**

NOVELS
Blood Moon,
Hollywood's Silent Closet,
Rhinestone Country,
Razzle Dazzle
Midnight in Savannah

OTHER PUBLICATIONS BY DARWIN PORTER
NOT DIRECTLY ASSOCIATED WITH BLOOD MOON

NOVELS
The Delinquent Heart
The Taste of Steak Tartare
Butterflies in Heat
Marika *(a roman à clef based on the life of Marlene Dietrich)*
Venus *(a roman à clef based on the life of Anaïs Nin)*
Bitter Orange
Sister Rose

TRAVEL GUIDES

Many Editions and Many Variations of *The Frommer Guides, The American Express Guides, and/or TWA Guides, et alia* to:

Andalusia, Andorra, Anguilla, Aruba, Atlanta, Austria, the Azores, The Bahamas, Barbados, the Bavarian Alps, Berlin, Bermuda, Bonaire and Curaçao, Boston, the British Virgin Islands, Budapest, Bulgaria, California, the Canary Islands, the Caribbean and its "Ports of Call," the Cayman Islands, Ceuta, the Channel Islands (UK), Charleston (SC), Corsica, Costa del Sol (Spain), Denmark, Dominica, the Dominican Republic, Edinburgh, England, Estonia, Europe, "Europe by Rail," the Faroe Islands, Finland, Florence, France, Frankfurt, the French Riviera, Geneva, Georgia (USA), Germany, Gibraltar, Glasgow, Granada (Spain), Great Britain, Greenland, Grenada (West Indies), Haiti, Hungary, Iceland, Ireland, Isle of Man, Italy, Jamaica, Key West & the Florida Keys, Las Vegas, Liechtenstein, Lisbon, London, Los Angeles, Madrid, Maine, Malta, Martinique & Guadeloupe, Massachusetts, Morocco, Munich, New England, New Orleans, North Carolina, Norway, Paris, Poland, Portugal, Provence, Puerto Rico, Romania, Rome, Salzburg, San Diego, San Francisco, San Marino, Sardinia, Savannah, Scandinavia, Scotland, Seville, the Shetland Islands, Sicily, St. Martin & Sint Maarten, St. Vincent & the Grenadines, South Carolina, Spain, St. Kitts & Nevis, Sweden, Switzerland, the Turks & Caicos, the U.S.A., the U.S. Virgin Islands, Venice, Vienna and the Danube, Wales, and Zurich.

BIOGRAPHIES

From Diaghilev to Balanchine, The Saga of Ballerina Tamara Geva

Lucille Lortel, The Queen of Off-Broadway

Greta Keller, Germany's Other Lili Marlene

Sophie Tucker, The Last of the Red Hot Mamas

Anne Bancroft, Where Have You Gone, Mrs. Robinson?
(co-authored with Stanley Mills Haggart)

Veronica Lake, The Peek-a-Boo Girl

Running Wild in Babylon, Confessions of a Hollywood Press Agent

HISTORIES

Thurlow Weed, Whig Kingpin

Chester A. Arthur, Gilded Age Coxcomb in the White House

Discover Old America, What's Left of It

CUISINE

Food For Love, Hussar Recipes from the Austro-Hungarian Empire,
with collaboration from the cabaret chanteuse, Greta Keller

AND COMING SOON, FROM BLOOD MOON

Donald Trump, The Man Who Would Be King
Lana Turner, Hearts and Diamonds Take All
Rock Hudson, Erotic Fire

WITH ACKNOWLEDGMENTS TO A CAST OF HUNDREDS OF OTHER PLAYERS,

THIS BIOGRAPHY OF JAMES DEAN IS DEDICATED TO STANLEY HAGGART, ROGERS BRACKETT, ALEC WILDER, & WILLIAM BAST

WITH SPECIAL THANKS TO EARTHA KITT & GERALDINE PAGE

BLOOD MOON
Productions, Ltd.

Contents

the same roles and the same lovers. How Newman stepped into Jimmy's shoes, post-mortem.

BLOOD
MOON
Productions, Ltd.

A HOOSIER FARMBOY

WANDERS ALONG HOLLYWOOD'S BOULEVARD OF BROKEN DREAMS

The "Live Fast, Die Young" Rebel Asserts, "Live as if You'll Die Today"

THE SYMBOL OF MISUNDERSTOOD YOUTH,
A LITTLE BOY LOST AND IN SEARCH OF HIMSELF,
REMAINS FOREVER YOUNG

"A young man must be courageous in the bedroom. Try anything—life's too short to worry about what's perverted."

—James Dean

"How big is your cock, dah-ling?"

—Tallulah Bankhead to James Dean

James Dean was twenty years old, a UCLA dropout, and without any real cash. The year was 1951, and the July 4th holiday was about to bring business in Hollywood to a halt

The dingy low-rent apartment he occupied at 1216 North Edgemont had peeling paint and "hot and cold running cockroaches" (Jimmy's words).

His friend, Ted Avery, also a struggling actor, supported himself working as an usher at CBS. He let Jimmy sleep on his sofa while his wife was away. The arrangement was temporary, and Jimmy needed to find another place to sleep and hang out...and soon.

Los Angeles: The corner of Sunset Blvd. at Vine in the 1950s.

That morning, Avery and Jimmy shared some cups of coffee, the only edible thing they could find in their otherwise empty kitchen cabinets.

The previous evening, Jimmy had consumed the last edible object remaining in their larder, dried oatmeal from Quakers. After boiling it on the stove, he mixed it with the remains of a sticky-looking jar of marmalade, the only thing left in their refrigerator.

Money (the lack thereof) was a problem, and Avery suggested that Jimmy should get a job as a means of keeping their meager household afloat. The acting gigs each had managed to attract seemed like memories from the distant past.

Avery, an expert at rope tricks, had taught Jimmy some of his tricks and techniques, suggesting that they might help him get cast in some B westerns. Jimmy practiced and quickly learned the techniques, which he later used after his casting in *Giant.* Sometimes, at the Santa Monica Pier, the two friends would put on a show—donations appreciated. Dressed in borrowed cowboy outfits, reminiscent of a young Gene Autry and Roy Rogers, they twirled lariats like Will Rogers, Jr.

Avery had heard of a job that had become available at Ted's Auto Park, an outdoor parking facility adjacent to the CBS television studios, near the intersection of Gower and Sunset Boulevards.

Although the job paid only a dollar an hour, plus tips, Jimmy learned that some guys could make as much as $200 a week on the side, hustling tricks—at least the better looking and better endowed young men. He also was told that a lot of producers, directors, and radio and TV stars, even big screen actors and actresses, parked their cars at Ted's.

"Sometimes an attendant gets an acting job—if you get my drift—through somebody he meets in a parking lot," Avery claimed.

"I'm drifting," Jimmy said. "Count me in. When those queers get a look at me in my tight jeans and T-shirt, they'll cream in their pants."

An hour later, after telling Avery goodbye on the pavement in front of Ted's Auto Park, Jimmy headed for its office, which was housed in a plank-sided shed that evoked a boxcar on a railroad. Apparently, the establishment's founder and namesake (Ted) had long ago departed. Instead, Jimmy faced Bill Homburg, a beefy, burly bear of a man who spoke English with a distinctive German accent. Seven years ago, he had fought in World War II. Jimmy didn't need to ask which side he'd been on.

Jimmy pounded the unforgiving streets of Los Angeles in the 1950s with dreams of replacing Marlon Brando.

Using his male flash and as much charm as he could muster, Jimmy tried to entice Homburg into giving him a job. He even told the boss what a great driver he was, which was a far stretch. "My lifelong dream is to park cars for the big shots."

"That means you want to be an actor," Homburg said.

"You nailed it. I plan to take Hollywood by storm. Move over, Marlon!"

"You'll fit in well here," Homburg predicted. "All my guys want to be actors. I hope you're not averse to the casting couch."

"Nope," Jimmy answered.

"You look like queer bait to me," Homburg said. "I only hire guys who look like queer bait. So I guess I'll hire you. You've got to show up at seven every morning, and don't be late, fucker. The pay is a dollar an hour, plus tips, which can be anything. It depends on how much..."

"How well I park cars," Jimmy interjected.

"That, too."

After the interview ended, with the promise of a new job beginning in the morning, Jimmy continued his walk along Sunset Boulevard, that boulevard of broken dreams, with renewed confidence. Nonetheless, his growling stomach told him that tomorrow was a long way off.

Making a fast decision, he headed for Santa Monica Boulevard, which he'd been told was the best place for a good-looking kid who needed to make cash really quick.

***

3

Since it was still early in the day, the "buyers and sellers" along Santa Monica Boulevard were not yet out in full force. That happened in the late afternoon before businessmen headed home to their wives and kids. After dark, denizens of the Los Angeles night emerged.

Jimmy knew that although he didn't have the best body on the street, his expressive face had always been a winning feature. When asked about his appeal, he said, "I'm a babe for the younger set." At that time, not many young men referred to themselves as a "babe."

Although he was thin, he had an obviously developed musculature. He seemed to evoke a self-awareness that few actors of his day had, except for Brando and Montgomery Clift. He didn't want to be classified with the pretty boys of the 1950s, especially Tab Hunter, Robert Wagner, or the ultimate narcissist, Tony Curtis.

A UCLA dropout with acting ambitions, here's James Dean from his college days.

His hair color was compared to that of an almond, brownish but with blonde highlights from the California sun. Supple, Cupid-like lips were surrounded by the delicate skin of an angular face. His sleepy, "bedroom eyes" hinted at the potential for adventure.

Many young men who had never thought of themselves as homosexual found themselves drawn to Jimmy. Exuding a femininity that existed harmoniously with his masculinity, he suggested androgyny. At times shy and awkward, he looked out at the world through horn-rimmed glasses. He was a brooder, rarely indulging in small talk.

Sometimes, he cocked his head to one side and—with a Chesterfield dangling from his lips— stood slightly hunched over with his eyes squinted. Often, his hands were stuffed into his front pockets. He was invariably dressed in blue jeans with a white T-shirt, setting the style for young men in the 1950s.

George Beaume, a casual acquaintance at the time, sensed a poetry in Jimmy. "He had this mysterious gaze and could look at his fellow actors without really seeing them. He existed in his own space, his own world. You'd see the sudden tensing of his face, which reeled from one emotion to another like a sinking ship. You'd sometimes hear him laugh, although his voice had a demonic ring. In contrast to his shyness, he could also become preening proud, the cock of the walk. It all depended on what was happening to him that night. If hurt by someone or brutally put down, he'd look like a lost little boy tearing at your heartstrings. I truly didn't know what to make of him. But I sensed there was something *there.*"

As he loitered on the sidewalk beside Santa Monica Boulevard, a short man in his late thirties or forties, dressed in a suit, walked by and gave Jimmy a casual but interested glance before moving on. He'd strolled only about twelve feet before he turned around and came back.

"Aren't you Jerry Burns from Cleveland, Ohio?" he asked Jimmy.

"Cut the shit, man," he answered. "It'll cost you twenty."

"I don't usually pay that much, but okay, I guess." He signaled an oncoming taxi.

As Jimmy piled into the back seat with him, the man, who had introduced himself as Frank, gave an address in West Hollywood.

They were driven to an upmarket apartment house with a doorman. As Jimmy and Frank walked past the doorman, Frank told him, "That new television set of mine is acting up. I've brought a repairman. Unless television gets better, it'll never replace radio."

"Yeah," the doorman said with a knowing smile.

The elevator stopped on the eighth floor, and Jimmy was directed into an ocean-view apartment with plush carpeting.

"How about a drink?" Frank asked.

"Too early in the day for me, man," Jimmy said. "I haven't got all day. Let's get on with it."

"How romantic!" Frank said sarcastically.

"I'm not selling romance," Jimmy said. "I go for girls. Can I have the twenty upfront?"

The man showed Jimmy the bedroom, where he removed a bill from his wallet. "Get undressed." He had become a commander.

Seductively, Jimmy removed his T-shirt before taking off his boots. Then his jeans came down. He wore no underwear. He tossed his jeans onto the floor and, fully naked, lay down on the bed, closing his eyes.

Frank seemed to devour him as it became obvious that Jimmy was conjuring up images that had nothing to do with the man who serviced him.

The act itself took no more than four minutes. After that, Jimmy jumped out of bed, asking if he could use the shower.

There, under the streaming water, he lathered his chest and crotch. Suddenly, Frank pulled back the curtain. "I want to watch you shower," he said.

"It'll cost you another five," Jimmy said.

"Okay," the man said.

Under Frank's penetrating gaze, Jimmy didn't want to prolong the shower. After he'd finished, he stepped out and was handed a large bath towel.

Within five minutes, he was at the door, holding out his hand for that extra five-dollar bill.

"Thanks for coming," Frank said. "That's known as a *double entendre.*"

"Whatever," Jimmy said, heading toward the elevator and the street.

***

At last, and with money in his pocket, Jimmy strolled along Santa Monica Boulevard to Barney's Beanery, where he ordered two cheeseburgers and a bowl of chili, all for $1.65. He devoured the food under a misspelled sign, "FAGOTS STAY OUT."

The dive was famous, and he'd wanted to go there for a long time. Since it was founded in 1927, it had attracted such stars as Clara Bow (*"The It Girl"*), Jean Harlow *("The Platinum Blonde"),* and such matinee idols as Clark Gable and John Barrymore.

The big names no longer came here. Surrounding Jimmy were mostly out-of-work actors attracted to the place by its 50¢ hamburgers.

Stuffed, Jimmy pondered what to do for the rest of the day. Should he give some of his just- earned dough to Avery or should he spend it on himself, perhaps paying a photographer to create some portraits as enticement for prospective casting directors. He quickly decided that Avery's fiscal needs—including his rent money—would have to wait.

From a phone booth, he placed a call to Beverly Wills, the daughter of the highly successful *comedienne,* Joan Davis. Beverly was starring as Fluffy Adams, a second banana in the CBS radio comedy, *Junior Miss.* She had plenty of money of her own; whenever she went out with Jimmy, she always picked up the tab. In Jimmy's words, "Guys who look like me shouldn't have to pay."

She was one of the so-called "Hollywood brats," pampered teenagers who had movie stars for parents.

Hardly a beauty, Beverly was not exactly ugly. She made up for any deficiency by her bright, bubbly personality and her sense of fun and humor. She lived in a mansion in Bel Air, next door to the director, Alfred Hitchcock.

Jimmy was indecisive about pursuing a romance with Beverly, figuring at times that he should be spending his nights in the bed of a big-time director or producer who might advance his acting career. And whereas Davis would do nothing for him, Beverly, in contrast, had tried to get work for him through Hank Garson, the director of *Junior Miss.* She had asked him to cast Jimmy in a small

Beverly Wills...dating Jimmy and picking up the tabs.

6

part, and, after acquiescing, he had agreed to meet him backstage the following day.

"This sullen young man showed up, and I felt he looked a bit like Frank Sinatra," Garson said. "I asked him to stand in front of a microphone and read some lines for me so I could check out his voice—after all, this was radio. But his reaction shocked me: He told me, 'Go fuck yourself! I don't do readings!' Then he stormed out. What a prick!"

Jimmy didn't fare well with other directors either, most of whom considered his five feet eight inches "too short."

To one director, Jimmy angrily asked, "How in Hell can you measure acting in inches?" Then he suggestively grabbed his own crotch with a line that effectively ended his audition: "I'll show you some inches, faggot."

Several other directors told him, "You're not pretty enough, and you don't have a good enough build. If you looked like Tab Hunter or Tony Curtis, we might hire you. But you don't."

To each of these casting directors, Jimmy uttered the same reaction: "Fuck you, asshole!"

***

Seventeen-year-old Beverly invited Jimmy over right away. He was happy to learn that her mother wasn't at home. Davis didn't like Jimmy—in fact, she detested him. And he didn't like her style of acting —"If that's what it's called." She'd been successful as a B-movie actress and later as a leading star in radio comedy. Jimmy had seen only one of her movies, *If You Knew Susie* (1948), in which she had co-starred with her lover at the time, Eddie Cantor.

> Jimmy hooks up with the kind-hearted daughter of a famous actress, Joan Davis, depicted above with Jim Backus in a publicity shot for what became her best-known role, the TV sitcom conceived to compete with *I Love Lucy, I Married Joan*.

Davis was currently preparing the launch of a TV sitcom, *I Married Joan*, in which she would play the manic wife of a mild-mannered community judge, Jim Backus. CBS wanted a show similar to its big hit, *I Love Lucy*, which had premiered in 1951, starring Lucille Ball and her womanizing, real-life hus-

Joan Davis in the 1948 film that made her famous.

band, Desi Arnaz.

Two weeks earlier, Jimmy had met Backus for a dinner at the Davis manse. *[Ironically, Backus would later be cast as Jimmy's apron-stringed father in Rebel Without a Cause.]* Jimmy had been introduced to Beverly when he was rooming with William Bast, who later became an author and writer-producer for film and television. At the time, Bast had been dating Beverly, slipping into her bedroom, right down the hall from her mother's, for lackluster attempts at intercourse.

Within a few weeks, Jimmy had lured Beverly away from his roommate.

At first, she had not been impressed with Jimmy, as she'd relate in a posthumous article for *Modern Screen*, published in March of 1957 and ludicrously entitled "I Almost Married James Dean. Who Am I?"

Beverly's mini-memoir of her encounters with James Dean appeared alongside this feature on Kim Novak in March of 1957.

"*I thought he was pretty much of a creep until we got to this picnic and then all of a sudden, he came to life. We began to talk about acting and Jimmy lit up. He told me how interested he was in the Stanislavsky method, where you not only act people, but things, too.*

'*Look,' said Jimmy. 'I'm a pine tree in a storm.' He held his arms out and waved wildly. To feel more free, he impatiently tossed off his cheap, tight, blue jacket. He looked bigger as soon as he did, because you could see his broad shoulders and powerful build. Then he got wilder and pretended he was a monkey. He climbed a big tree and swung from a high branch. Dropping from the branch, he landed on his hands like a little boy, chuckling uproariously at every little thing. Once in the spotlight, he ate it up and had us all in stitches all afternoon. The 'creep' had turned into the hit of the party.*"

Jimmy arrived by taxi (a rare luxury for him at the time) at Joan Davis' Bel Air mansion, with its pool, bar, and tennis court. He was glad that except for the cook preparing an elaborate dinner for a special guest that evening, Beverly was alone in the house.

She immediately led him to her bedroom for a session of heavy necking. He stopped short of intercourse because he wasn't in the mood.

Two hours later, Davis arrived and somewhat frantically set about getting things in order for her dinner party. She found Jimmy sitting in an armchair in her living room with his left leg dangling over an armrest. He was munching on an apple and listening to music on the radio.

She showed her disappointment at how sloppily he was dressed, telling him that he'd better leave because within the hour, Tallulah Bankhead would be arriving for drinks and dinner.

Beverly interjected, "But I've invited Jimmy to stay for dinner!"

Davis looked acutely disappointed before heading into the kitchen to see how dinner was coming along. Jimmy had already bonded with the cook, an obese woman from Alabama. Her name was Odessa, and as time went by, she frequently prepared Jimmy's favorite dish, pot roast, whenever he stayed for dinner. Knowing that he had very little money, Odessa would leave foodstuff for a week in Jimmy's car parked in the driveway outside.

Very grand, very formidable, very funny, and very debauched: Tallulah Bankhead, as depicted in Jean Cocteau's 1947 Broadway production of *The Eagle Has Two Heads*. It flopped.

Although Bankhead's arrival created excitement throughout the Davis household, to Jimmy, she was only a name, vaguely connected to Broadway. He'd never seen her in anything.

Currently, she was starring in a radio variety show, *The Big Show* (1950-52), a ninety minutes program that was broadcast every Sunday night. As mistress of ceremonies, Bankhead entertained big-name stars, including Marlene Dietrich and Ethel Merman. Davis was a regular on her show. Sometimes, Bankhead would sing, her signature songs including "Bye Bye Blackbird," and "Give My Regards to Broadway."

The moment Bankhead barged through the door, she took center stage. Jimmy had never met a woman like her. After Davis introduced her to Jimmy, she immediately asked: "How big is your cock, *Dah-ling*?"

Then she plopped down on the sofa, demanding "a bourbon and branch water. Go easy on the branch water."

Throughout the dinner, Jimmy was mesmerized by the bigtime star. She was a formidable presence, still showing some of her

Immensely powerful in show-biz promotions after World War II, Bankhead was MC of one of Radioland's most popular shows. Jimmy reacted to her instinctively.

Here, she's participating in a staged reading with Laurence Olivier ("Heathcliff") and Vivien ("Scarlett O'Hara") Leigh.

faded beauty of the 20s and 30s. Davis seemed upset that she was showing more attention to Jimmy than she did to her.

Tallulah summoned Odessa from the kitchen and ordered her to sit down at the table with her. Both women shared tales of their native Alabama.

Tallulah kept ordering bourbon. "I drink today, *Dah-lings*, as the world knows. But when I arrived in New York, Daddy warned me to stay away from men and booze. But he didn't warn me about cocaine and women."

"Incidentally, *Dah-ling*, don't believe that shit about cocaine being habit-forming. It's not. I've been snorting it for years."

At times, she talked about sex. "I've tried many varieties. The conventional position I found claustrophobic. All the other positions give me a stiff neck or lockjaw."

Three hours later, in bidding Jimmy good night, she wetly kissed him on the lips. "I haven't had so much fun, *Dah-ling*, since the night I went down on Hattie McDaniel."

Later that night, Jimmy described Bankhead to his roommate, Avery.

"Tallulah is a *prima donna* bitch with a succulent, scarlet-painted mouth. It was a kind of living thing, with a mind of its own. They gave me a hard-on. All evening long, I wanted to get up from the table and stick my erect cock between them. That would have silenced her."

Bankhead and Jimmy were destined to meet months later in Manhattan, although they would never work together.

Jimmy Meets His Substitute Father/Mentor With Incest on His Mind

The next morning at seven o'clock, Jimmy showed up at Ted's Auto Park, adjacent to CBS's Studios. If parking cars provided a means of meeting power brokers in Hollywood, he'd park cars. "I'm sure I'll be discovered. With my good looks and talent, I'm bound to be noticed."

"Modest, aren't you?" Avery said.

"I've got nothing to be modest about," Jimmy said. "If you don't believe in yourself, no one else will,"

"That makes sense," Avery said.

When he reported to work on his third morning, a Saturday, Jimmy was frustrated that no one had really given him a second look so far. But his luck was about to change.

A shiny new Buick, painted emerald green and ivory, pulled into the parking lot. Out stepped a tall, curly haired man, who appeared in his mid-thirties.

He was immaculately dressed in a midnight blue suit and red tie with the most expensive pair of leather shoes Jimmy had ever seen on a man. "Probably, unborn lamb," Jimmy later recalled.

With his canny awareness, Jimmy knew he was being checked out from crotch to face and back to crotch.

As he later recalled, "I was sorta pissed off. He was checking me out like a slab of meat. I'd come to Hollywood to be a great actor—not just like Brando, but like Montgomery Clift, John Garfield, only better. I resented having to sleep my way up the ladder. Perhaps I could have been fired, but I said something I shouldn't have."

Rogers Brackett, in a CBS publicity shot...radar eyes for a pretty face.

"I hope you're satisfied that I'm good enough to eat."

"Don't be a smart ass," said the owner of the Buick. "I was checking you out because I'm always searching for a star of tomorrow."

"Yeah, right," Jimmy said. "Every parking attendant on the lot has heard that line."

"In my case, I mean it," the man said. "You've got something. I don't know what."

"I know what I've got," Jimmy said. "A cock you want to suck."

"Maybe that's so. But I bet you've got talent, too. The truly gifted artist is always arrogant, as Joan Crawford said to John Garfield in *Humoresque.*"

"What are you? A casting agent? A talent scout?"

"I'm a producer. I might cast you in one of my shows. That is, if you truly have talent, other than being an arrogant little prick."

"Listen, mister, I'm the best god damn actor in Hollywood if given a chance. And my prick's not so little."

"My name's Rogers Brackett. What's yours?"

"James Dean, and don't you forget it," he answered. "You can call me Mr. Dean."

"I'll catch you later," Brackett said. "You think you're too big for your breeches, but I can cut you down to size."

"We'll see about that," Jimmy said, walking away, taking the parking ticket to Homburg's office. "Who is that guy?" he asked his boss." Anybody important or just a wise guy?"

"He's Rogers Brackett. He produces the weekly radio show, *Alias Jane Doe.* It stars Lurene Tuttle."

"So he's a real producer after all," Jimmy said.

"Why do you want to know?" Homburg asked. "Did the fucker come on to you?"

"Not at all," Jimmy lied. "He's definitely straight."

"Like hell he his," Homburg claimed. "He's a chicken hawk. Sucked off half the young guys on my lot."

A few hours later, Brackett returned, signaling Jimmy to retrieve his Buick.

After giving him a final lookover, Brackett got behind the wheel of his car, where he handed Jimmy a five-dollar bill, the biggest tip he'd ever received. A lot of men gave him only a quarter.

Attached to the bill was a paper clip with his calling card, listing his phone number and address.

"I'll expect you at eight tomorrow night," Bracket said. "I'll have Chasen's cater a dinner for us. That's the best restaurant in Los Angeles."

"What makes you think I'll show up?" Jimmy asked.

"I've seen that gleam in your eye," Brackett said. "You know I'm the man who'll make you a star."

"You'll make me all right."

"Our meeting today may be historic, an event like Professor Higgins encountering Eliza Doolittle."

"I don't know who in the fuck they are, but I'll take your word for it."

"Don't be late," Brackett said. "I don't want to sound too melodramatic, but it may be your date with destiny."

"If you say so, guy."

***

Jimmy had a hunch he could get a job out of Rogers Brackett. He showed up at his apartment on time, in his battered old Chevy that had a full tank of gas. With the money he'd made the following afternoon, he had more than enough to fill up his gas tank, since he'd need it to drive into the Hollywood Hills, above Sunset Strip.

Before his departure, Jimmy had asked questions about Brackett, learning that he was known "as the Oscar Wilde of Hollywood." He was a true child of Tinseltown, seemingly known to half the people in the industry.

He'd been born in Culver City, virtually on the doorstep of Metro-Goldwyn-Mayer. He father was Robert Brackett, an early partner of Louis Selznick. Rogers himself had worked for Louis' son, David O. Selznick. Jimmy also found out that Brackett was employed by the powerful advertising agent, Foote, Cone, & Belding.

Parking his car, Jimmy stepped out into the fashionable Sunset Plaza Drive. After he rang the bell, Bracket opened the door wearing a red silk robe.

His living room was outfitted in a color scheme of chartreuse and royal purple, a daring combination pioneered by Brackett's close friend, Stanley Mills Haggart, an interior designer.

After pouring him a drink, Brackett led him out onto his panoramic terrace, with its view over Los Angeles. The city lay before him like a gigantic carpet of lights.

"I've got a dream," Jimmy said.

"And what might that be?" Brackett asked.

"I want to conquer this fucking town and make it mine."

"A noble ambition, my dear," Brackett said. "Perhaps I'll help you." He put his arm around Jimmy's slim waist. The doorbell rang. "That's dinner from Chasen's. I ordered three of Elizabeth Taylor's favorite dishes. I call her the Princess. Perhaps I'll introduce her to you someday."

"Hell, man, Elizabeth Taylor and I will one day star together in a big budget movie."

After dinner, Jimmy thanked his host for treating him "to the best meal I've ever had."

Over drinks on the terrace, Brackett told him he'd like to take him to two parties that upcoming weekend—one of them a pool party on Saturday at agent Henry Willson's house.

"You've got to meet him. He's a power broker who can make a young man's career: Guy Madison, Rory Calhoun, Rock Hudson, John Derek, Robert Wagner."

"I'd like to go," Jimmy said. "But I've never heard of this Willson."

"You will," Brackett said.

"Then on Sunday, I'd like to invite you to this gathering at the home of George Cukor, the director. Surely, you've heard of him"

"Vaguely," Jimmy said.

"Katharine Hepburn and Spencer Tracy, and a lot of other big names, will be there. I'll introduce you around."

"Meeting all these big shots is one thing, getting a job is quite another."

"Depending on how the evening goes, I can get you a job on my CBS radio program, *Alias Jane Doe.* I'm in charge of casting for my ad agency. The show stars Lurene Tuttle. She plays a reporter who disguises herself to get the scoop, then publishes her revelations under the byline of Jane Doe. Madison Musser is the love interest."

[Brackett delivered on his promise, casting Dean in four episodes. They aired in 1951, on July 28, August 11, September 15 and 22, for which he was paid $56.99 per show.]

"Unless you're bullshitting me, it sounds like you're okay."

By eleven o'clock, it was getting late, and Jimmy had to be on the parking lot the next morning at seven o'clock.

Brackett rose from his seat and took Jimmy's hand. "How about retiring to my bedroom?"

"Okay, but what's the deal?" Jimmy asked. "Do I fuck you, or do you fuck me? Or else a sixty-nine?"

"A combination of all three," Brackett said, leading the way.

Jimmy Meets the Pretty Boys of Henry Willson's Adonis Factory

In 1950s Hollywood, when the "Adonis Factory" of Pretty Boys flourished, Henry Willson was a starmaker. In time, he created first names to hawk—Troy, Rock, Cal, Rod, Dial, Clint, or Touch, among others. He represented such clients as Robert Wagner, Guy Madison, Rory Calhoun, and Tab Hunter, though he was mainly known for having discovered Rock Hudson.

Willson's Saturday afternoon pool parties had become notorious. The mistress of these parties was Truie Delight, a devoted follower of the black evangelist Father Devine. She seemed to ignore all the homosexual couplings going on around her, concentrating instead on the food and drink. She prepared simple barbecues of foot-long hot dogs, hamburgers with all the fixings, and corn on the cob served with creamy butter melting in the hot California sun. There were many jokes about her tasty potato salad. The gays claimed it was creamy because Truie had scooped up and added all the semen collected from the pool house during the previous week's party and added it as a secret ingredient.

Truie also made the drinks, serving them to aging movie and TV executives along with a bevy of gorgeous guys, each of them wearing the briefest of bikinis to show off their assets. Willson didn't allow total nudity, however. That was reserved for the rooms upstairs and for the privacy of the poolhouse.

Brackett drove Jimmy, wearing jeans and a T-shirt, to Willson's residence on Stone Canyon Drive. After they were ushered inside, Jimmy felt he was within a sea of male beauty, interspersed with about a dozen older men still dressed in suits.

The biggest and beefiest attraction that afternoon was Clint Walker, a giant of a man who stood 6'6". He'd been a security guard and a nightclub bouncer before Willson discovered him and aggressively promoted him to casting directors as a western hero. As his agent described Walker, "His muscles stretched from Hollywood & Vine to Times Square, but his dick is even longer."

"I look like a pre-teen compared to him," Jimmy whispered to Brackett.

14

Clint's competition was muscleman Steve Reeves, a devotee of the "Pecs Before Talent" school. His titles from bodybuilding competitions included "Mr. Pacific," "Mr. America," "Mr. World," and ultimately, "Mr. Universe." Willson wanted to help him break into movies, and before the end of the decade, Reeves would be featured as the focal point of Hercules movies, sometimes known as "spaghetti sword-and-sandals pictures." Although presumably straight, he was willing to sell up-close-and-personal access to his muscles to male clients.

At one of Henry Willson's parties, Jimmy met heartthrob and muscle man, "I'm big all over," Clint Walker.

Finally, Brackett took Jimmy over to introduce him to Willson, who was licking some of Truie's barbecue sauce off his fingers. To Jimmy, he was grotesquely ugly, with wide hips resting on short legs, and a hawkish nose with a bulbous lower lip often curled into a pout. Like the popular Broadway columnist, Dorothy Kilgallen, Willson had no chin. Frank Sinatra called Kilgallen "the chinless wonder," and Willson "son of chinless wonder."

Willson had for a time evoked the epicene appearance of director Vincente Minnelli, once married to Judy Garland. In time, however, as he put on weight, he came to resemble the famous silhouette of Alfred Hitchcock. Jimmy had seen the director on occasion walking up his driveway, as Hitchcock lived next door to Jimmy's on-again, off-again girlfriend, Beverly Wills.

Steve Reeves appears in his most famous role, *Hercules (1957)*. "I'm straight, but my muscles are for sale."

Jimmy impatiently endured the gay banter between Willson and Brackett, which turned him off.

"I tell my straight actors, if there are any left in Hollywood, that sucking a cock is not much different from sucking on a woman's nipple. Sucking cock is a hell of a lot more sanitary than a guy burying his face in a woman's smelly snatch. I also tell them not to have sex in their dressing room before appearing on camera. It shows up on the screen."

Finally, he turned to Jimmy and didn't disguise his bluntness. "Do you like to fuck or get fucked?"

"Jimmy does everything wanted and needed," Brackett interjected.

Looking Jimmy up and down like a male slave on an auction block, Willson said, "Before the sun sets a few times over the Pacific, I'll find that out for myself."

Jimmy wandered off, but an hour later, Willson cornered him. "Rogers wants me to represent you, make you a star, as I've done to so many others.

Leading Hollywood talent agent Henry Willson with his major client and "discovery," Rock Hudson.

He says you've got a lot of talent. But I need to determine that for myself."

"And how do you plan to do that, Mr. Willson?"

"Come over Tuesday night for a private audition. Around eight o'clock. I don't use a casting couch, contrary to popular belief. I audition an actor in my king-sized bed. Don't panic. I know I'm no beauty. I won't even take my clothes off, but you will. Jaybird naked in the center of my bed."

"Again, don't panic. I don't expect you to do anything to me. I'm the best cocksucker in town. If you wish, I'll take you only from the neck down."

"I'm looking forward to it," Jimmy said. "Just thinking about it is giving me a boner."

"That's my boy," Willson said, patting Jimmy's cheek. "Now I've got to talk to Rock...excuse me."

Jimmy had no intention of ever showing up at Willson's house again.

About ten female guests were at the party, but they left before six o'clock. Brackett told Jimmy the "gang bangs" occurred after dark.

En route to the bathroom, Rock Hudson stopped and introduced himself to Jimmy. He was attired in a white bikini that displayed his considerable endowment. "I think every guy here today is after me. You got a crush on me too?"

Jimmy was offended, but Brackett had warned him to be polite to Hudson. Willson was predicting that he would soon be the biggest male star in Hollywood.

"From what I've seen here today, you're the hottest thing since God created Adam," Jimmy said.

"Let's get together," Hudson said. "I'll have Henry hook us up."

"It's a deal," Jimmy said. He later told Brackett, "Hudson is one stuck-up asshole."

"Yes, but what a delectable rosebud it is," Brackett replied.

After meeting Hudson, Jimmy was anxious to leave the party. He motioned to Brackett, who signaled that he needed to finish his discussion with some producer.

Suddenly, as the evening shadows fell, a charming, handsome, charismatic young man stood before Jimmy. There was something about his presence that was magnetic. He stared with a certain longing into Jimmy's blue eyes.

"I thought it would never happen," the man said. "I've met my soul mate. They call me 'The Black Star,' even though I'm lilywhite. Who are you?"

"Polaris."

"I knew it. I seek out his North Star every night," the man said.

"You've found him."

"I know you're here with someone else tonight, and I am too. I promised Rock I'd go home with him. But I'd rather be going home with you."

"Ditto."

"By the way, I'm John Carlyle. You can call me Johnny."

"Johnny, how about letting James Dean here eat your flesh like a cannibal?"

"Blood raw or well done?"

Carlyle reached into the pocket of his slacks and removed a piece of paper, which he stuffed into the right side picket of Jimmy's jeans, probing deeper, and lingering a bit longer, than was necessary.

"How is Willson promoting you?" Jimmy asked.

"As the next Montgomery Clift. And you?"

"As the untouchable—except for you."

***

[When Jimmy didn't show up the following Tuesday night, Willson developed an antagonism for him that lasted for years after Jimmy's death in a car crash.

In the future, whenever Jimmy's name was mentioned, Willson weighed in with his opinion. "That Dean bullshit wouldn't have lasted. He was too arrogant, too narcissistic. If you ask me, he was Hollywood trash."

"I advise all my actors not to emulate his acting style. By 1957, he'd be pounding the pavement looking for a job. All doors would be closed to him. By then, he would have been universally despised.]

John Carlyle..."the next Montgomery Clift."

Ask Jimmy:

IN LIEU OF A CASTING COUCH,
DIRECTOR GEORGE CUKOR PREFERS A KING SIZED BED

Arriving at Cukor's palatial "castle" on Cordell Drive in West Hollywood, Jimmy—with Brackett at the wheel—was impressed. The director lived in a large white house with a high wall enclosing an orange grove. To one side of the house was an Olympic swimming pool.

Beside the pool, Cukor was hosting a lavish Sunday buffet for some twenty guests, none of whom Jimmy recognized. Brackett had told him that Cukor was friends with such big name stars as Greta Garbo and Cary Grant.

However, within minutes, two of the world's most recognizable faces came onto the patio. Katharine Hepburn appeared on the arm of Spencer Tracy, who seemed to be recovering from a hangover. She was rather boyish, dressed in a pair of white slacks. She wore no makeup to cover her bad skin. When Jimmy was introduced, she said, "Welcome to Hollywood, dear boy. You'll have a hard time hanging onto your virginity in this town."

Tracy gave a knowing smirk. "Perhaps he's already lost it."

Brackett fitted in perfectly with this chic crowd, but Jimmy felt out of place and wandered off by himself into the large terraced garden with its Italian statues, many of them male nudes. The ivy-covered walls gave a sense of privacy, one reporter referring to the setting as "a bachelor's pleasure dome."

When he grew bored, he went into the main house, finding it empty. The furnishings were a strange combination of antiques not well blended with post-war modern. He knew little about art, but Cukor had identified the artists, whose names were engraved on gold-plated plaques on the lower edge of each of the painting's frames. They included Picasso, Toulouse-Lautrec, and Salvador Dalí.

Eventually, he wandered down a portrait gallery to the bathroom. *En route*, he saw replicas of the smiling faces of Claudette Colbert, Olivia de Havilland, Vivien Leigh, Laurence Olivier, Garbo, Joan

Platonic Lovers and "Switch-Hitters": Spencer Tracy with Katharine Hepburn in *Without Love* (1945).

Crawford, Norma Shearer, and Rex Harrison.

At the end of the hall, he came upon a bronze portrait bust of Tallulah Bankhead, whom he'd recently met. Cukor had helmed her in *Tarnished Lady* (1931).

He had apparently seen Jimmy enter his house, and he decided to come in after him, as he was always nervous having strange young men wandering among his treasures. There had been thefts in the past from hustlers.

As Jimmy emerged from the toilet, he encountered Cukor in the portrait gallery. "You're the Dean boy, right? A friend of Rogers?"

Director George Cukor, as he looked around the time he met James Dean

"You've nailed me."

Cukor followed Jimmy into the main living room, where he looked around proudly at his treasures. "This is my showcase," he told Jimmy. "It's perfect for me. Billy Haines was my decorator, but I've added my personal touches as well.

"Never heard of him, but then, I'm not much up on decorators."

"Billy was Old Hollywood, the Silents. A big star until Louis B. Mayer kicked him off the lot because he wouldn't give up his lover, Jimmy Shields."

"At least he found a new profession," Jimmy said. "I hear many of those biggies in the Silents ended up on bad days. Alcoholics, whatever."

"Or whatever...." Cukor said.

"I know Rogers has to report early in the morning to CBS. Why don't you come by at ten tomorrow for breakfast?"

"I'd like that," Jimmy said. "For all I know, you might cast me as the lead in your next picture. I'm the greatest."

"That remains to be seen. But there is a part in my next picture, *The Actress,* that calls for a young actor to play the love interest of Jean Simmons. Spence is the star."

"I'll do it," Jimmy said. "See you tomorrow morning at ten. Perhaps you'll find out how talented I really am."

"That is my desire."

***

The next morning, Jimmy arrived at Cukor's with a sore ass. Rogers had wanted to fuck him, and he didn't really like it. But he figured he'd better get used to being invaded.

His old Chevy pulled up in the driveway. After he rang the doorbell, a

Japanese houseboy directed him out to the pool patio where Cukor was already serving breakfast to another young man. As Jimmy approached, he was startled to see that it was John Carlyle, "The Black Star" himself, in a bathing suit.

Although Carlyle had given him his phone number at Henry Willson's party the week before, Jimmy had not had time to call.

At first, Cukor seemed shocked that Jimmy knew Carlyle. "I don't know why I'm surprised," he sighed. "All you pretty boys seem to know each other as David *knew* Bathsheba. If I had been a pretty boy, I could have climbed the Hollywood ladder so much quicker. After all, pretty boys make up their own rules as they go along."

The chatter over breakfast was filled with Hollywood gossip, which Jimmy devoured along with a big breakfast. Cukor bragged about the success of *Born Yesterday,* which he'd directed. It had won a Best Actress Oscar for Judy Holliday, beating out Gloria Swanson for *Sunset Blvd.,* and Bette Davis for *All About Eve.* "I'm currently directing Spencer and Katharine in *Pat and Mike,*" he said.

Carlyle's eyes lit up when he told Jimmy that Cukor was going to remake *A Star Is Born,* with Judy Garland in a comeback role. "George here has virtually guaranteed me a part in it."

Jimmy was jealous, but figured he should not mention that Cukor might cast him in *The Actress,* Tracy's next film.

After breakfast, Cukor suggested his two good-looking guests strip for a skinny dip in his pool. "Don't bother with bathing trunks. All of us are men."

Both Carlyle and Jimmy realized that this was Cukor's not-so-subtle attempt to appraise their bodies, especially their genitals. Each actor was also eager to see the other entirely nude.

With their clothes off, Cukor obviously liked what he saw. So did Carlyle and Jimmy appreciate the sight of each other's nudity, which they would explore more fully at some future moment.

Like a protective hen, Cukor seemed to hover over his pool, hawkeyeing their frolicking in the water. Finally, when he'd had enough of that, he yelled "CUT," as if he were directing one of his pictures.

He gave each of them a large white bath towel to wrap around their nude bodies before directing them to his bedroom. Despite the size of his sprawling house, only one of its rooms was configured as a bedroom, as Cukor—with the exception of the hustlers who shared his bed—never wanted to house overnight guests,

From within its precincts, Cukor ordered both of the young actors to lie down. Cukor pulled off his shirt but retained his trousers. Moving above them on the bed, he fondled their balls until they were fully erect.

As he went down on them, Jimmy and Carlyle began to kiss each other rather passionately. Cukor was thorough in his work, going from one young man to the other until he brought both of them to a spectacular climax. Jimmy didn't say anything, but Carlyle pronounced it "the most exquisite orgasm I've ever experienced."

"Nothing like surrendering yourself to a man who knows how to handle you guys," Cukor said. Then he ordered both of them to the shower before entering it himself. When they emerged, after having soaped each other's bodies, two one-hundred dollar bills—one for each of them—was waiting for them on Cukor's bed.

The director was in his living room pacing up and down, looking at the clock. He told Jimmy that he wanted to discuss something privately with Carlyle, and he asked Jimmy to walk down the hill to the cottage that lay on his grounds. Inside, he said, he'd find Spencer Tracy, and that he should help him get dressed for a two o'clock meeting with Ruth Gordon, who had written the screenplay for *The Actress.* "He'll be late if you don't."

"You mean...I mean...you want me to wake up Tracy and get him dressed?" Jimmy asked, astonished.

"Exactly," Cukor said. "Spencer will love it. His door is always unlocked. Just walk right in and do whatever you have to do."

"See you guys later," Jimmy said, heading with trepidation out into the garden and down the hill.

***

Spencer Tracy was like a movie god to Jimmy, who always claimed that, "He made acting look so easy, when it's not."

Rumored to be cantankerous, demanding, and difficult, Tracy intimated Jimmy. The idea of waking him up from a drunken stupor and helping him get dressed was beyond his comfort level. Yet he didn't want to defy Cukor's command.

He'd heard all the legendary gossip about Tracy and Hepburn—that he was an incorrigible drinker involved in a platonic relationship with Hepburn, and that Hepburn was a lesbian, at least with young women with perfect skin.

Outside the cottage, Jimmy hesitated before testing the doorknob. He found it unlocked, as Cukor had predicted. Stepping inside the living room, he called out, "Mr. Tracy," but his voice wasn't very loud.

The door to Tracy's bedroom had been left open. He peered inside to discover the actor sprawled nude on top of the bedcovers. He had obviously plopped down there the previous evening when he was drunk. Permeating the room was the distinctive smell of urine.

21

"Mr. Tracy," Jimmy said again, his voice growing louder. Finally, Tracy stirred, slowly, rising up from his pillow and confronting Jimmy through blurry eyes. "Hell, didn't I pay you for last night?"

Jimmy assumed that Tracy had mistaken him for a hustler from the night before. He explained that he'd been sent by Cukor to get him ready for his two-o'clock meeting with Ruth Gordon to discuss the script for his upcoming movie, *The Actress.*

Tracy got out of bed and hobbled to the bathroom. Fifteen minutes later, he was in the kitchen making coffee. Jimmy had read that Hepburn claimed that Tracy made the best coffee in the world. After tasting it, Jimmy agreed, although he wasn't one to judge, having sampled a steady diet of some of the worst coffee in some of the sleaziest diners in Los Angeles.

Over coffee, and a bit prematurely, Jimmy told Tracy that Cukor might offer him the role of Jean Simmons' boyfriend in their upcoming movie. This seemed to pique the aging actor's interest.

Within twenty minutes, a fully dressed Tracy was walking up the hill to Cukor's manse. "Kid, I like you. I hope you get the part. I've got the script in the cottage. If you'll call me some night this week, we'll go over it, and I'll rehearse you." He handed Jimmy a card. "My private number's on the back."

Jimmy knew this was a come-on, but he agreed to call him.

When they reached Cukor's door, Tracy shook Jimmy's hand. He noticed that John Carlyle's car was already gone.

"Okay, kid, I'll look forward to your call." Before going inside, he looked back at Jimmy, who at first thought he'd misunderstood his final remark.

"I just hope your mother in the hospital didn't tell some god damn doctor to cut off your foreskin."

***

When Jimmy arrived for work the next morning at Ted's Auto Park, Bill Homburg called him into his ramshackle office. "Why didn't you show up for work yesterday morning?"

"I was sick," Jimmy lied.

"Couldn't you have called in? We were short-staffed. You're fired! Here's your back pay in cash."

Jimmy counted the bills for his dollar-an-hour job. "There's not much cash here. I think you're cheating me."

"You didn't earn much. Also, I learned you dented George Burn's fender. The cheapskate wants us to pay."

"Won't you give me another chance?"

"Get the hell out of here."

22

Once again, out on the street, Jimmy was in a quandary. What to do? The money from Cukor would pay his living expenses for a while, but not for long.

He decided it was time to make up with William Bast, his former roommate, who was working next door at CBS as an usher.

James Dean & William Bast

TOGETHER ON A ROLLER-COASTER THROUGH TINSELTOWN— PASSIONS, BETRAYALS, RECKLESS COMPULSIONS, EARLY STRUGGLES

The same age as Jimmy, but less good-looking, William Bast was a struggling young actor who also wanted to write. Over time, he had evolved into Jimmy's best friend, but their relationship was destined to be turbulent, and sometimes violent.

For a time in 1951, they had shared an apartment together, a studio on the top floor of a modest apartment complex built around a courtyard on Tenth Street in Santa Monica.

It was a charming little aerie decorated in what Bast defined as the "Santa Fe-cum Mexican style with hand-painted Aztec design motifs."

The rent was seventy dollars a month, and they were hoping to make the payment, plus food costs, based on whatever Jimmy could make at odd jobs. Bast worked for twenty dollars a week.

Bast had met Jimmy when they studied drama together at UCLA. At the time, Jimmy was unhappy housed within the Sigma Nu fraternity house. Likewise, Bast had been sleeping on a bunk bed within one of the university's dormitories.

He had not been impressed with Jimmy's performance in a student production of *Macbeth*. It has opened at Royce Hall on November 29, 1950. After watching the performance, Bast told his friends, "This guy performed the role of Malcolm with the most dreadful Indiana accent, a terrible farm boy twang. He couldn't pronounce Shakespeare, couldn't get his tongue around it."

"I thought he was a Hoosier shit-kicker not too long ago slopping the hogs. His knobby knees stuck out beneath his kilt, and he had bad posture."

When Jimmy was introduced to Bast, he told him,

William Bast...was he a friend or foe to Jimmy? Bast could never decide.

"Getting cast in Macbeth has been the biggest thrill of my life."

Although he may have been secretly attracted to Jimmy, Bast did his best to conceal it. He later told two of their friends, "I think he's a very stupid boy for his age. And there's something weird about him. I can't figure out what it is."

Eventually, the two struggling actors found common ground in their love of the theater. Once, at the Santa Monica Pier, when both men had each had a few beers, they stood side by side at an open urinal. Years later, Bast recalled, "I found myself staring at his dick, and I wanted it. But somehow, I was too afraid to make an overture. After all, it was 1950. We both were keeping up a macho front and talking about girls."

When Bill Bast first hooked up with Jimmy, his greatest acting challenge, till then, had been his involvement in a 1950 college production of *Macbeth*. In it, Jimmy is depicted above, right.

One day, Jimmy approached Bast and told him that he'd been kicked out of his lodgings within the Sigma Nu fraternity house. At a beerfest, one of the brothers had called him a faggot because he was a theater arts major. Enraged, Jimmy had attacked him, hitting him with a large glass ashtray. Even though the blow had practically knocked him out, Jimmy had continued to pound his head, even after he'd fallen on the floor. After pulling Jimmy off the man, two fraternity brothers kicked him out of the building. He returned the next morning and packed his lone suitcase.

Jimmy suggested that he and Bast should pool their resources and rent an apartment together.

Eventually, they moved into a small penthouse. It contained a tiny bedroom with just enough space for a double bed. Bast had assured the landlady that one of them would sleep on the sofa. That was not the case—they each wanted the comfort of a bed.

Bast would later confess that sometimes in the middle of the night, he would feel Jimmy's erection pressing against his body, but that nothing sexual transpired between them during the early stages of their apartment share. That would come later.

Dazed and confused, Bast experienced mixed emotions. As he expressed later, "I was jealous of Jimmy, but strangely attracted to him as well. He often paraded around the apartment in the nude, and, on looking back, I was turned on but didn't want to admit it."

After two weeks of living with Jimmy, Bast concluded that he was a manic-depressive. Sometimes, he'd go for two or three days before speaking, just sulking and keeping to himself. Then he'd emerge from this self-isolation and become the life of the party.

Actually, Bast interpreted some things about Jimmy as rather pompous. "The only greatness for a man is immortality," Jimmy told him.

His major at UCLA was Theater Arts, but he began to miss classes, and eventually dropped out completely.

According to Bast, "At times, this little Indiana farmboy had such inner strength, such self-assurance, such dedication, and, most of all, a streak of independence. He told me he wouldn't 'kiss ass to get a job,' but I suspected he was doing just that—or rather getting his ass either kissed or fucked by all those gay directors and producers, even stars."

"In spite of this brave façade, he would break down and become a little boy lost—afraid, insecure, battered, and bruised by a world he found increasingly hostile. As Bette Davis once told me, 'Hollywood is not for the weak of heart. It's the land of the tarantula.'"

In his battered old Chevy, a gift from his estranged father, Winton Dean, Jimmy drove from studio to studio to appear at "cattle calls" with dozens of other aspiring actors. He couldn't afford to buy trade papers, but he read them at newsstands, writing down the addresses and details in a little red notebook he carried. He desperately wanted to make a screen test, but received no offers.

After a casting call, he'd return, deeply disappointed, to their apartment. When days would pass without any casting calls to attend, he'd sink into despair. During those periods, he often spent the night wandering around Santa Monica or going into Hollywood. On most of those occasions, he'd return to the penthouse at dawn, sleeping throughout most of the day.

Actor Gregory Bottoms remembered him at the time. "He wasn't well groomed, often dirty and unshaven, wearing soiled clothes. He looked like he didn't have a friend in the world, really beaten by life. But he'd save and put on his one good pair of slacks and a freshly ironed white shirt when he'd go on those casting calls. When there were no casting calls, he let himself go. He looked like a bum."

According to Beverly, "Jimmy could go through a whole alphabet of emotions. In a single night, when he couldn't get an acting job, which was often the case, he was bitter about everything and everybody. I hated to see him so blue and depressed. He made me depressed. He told me he hoped to die early so he wouldn't have to face the even more horrible bitterness of growing old. Yet when he was happy, he was the most lovable and fun person to be around, always cutting up and playing games to amuse people. Once, when he'd eaten some bad Mexican food, and had a lot of gas, he upset the guests at my mother's house by letting farts, telling people he was imitating a skunk. The guy was outrageous."

Jimmy's favorite time with Beverly involved driving north with her along the coastal road. He liked the breezes from the Pacific flowing into the car.

At secluded spots, he would sometimes take her down to a moonlit beach for seductions. He would later brag to male friends, mostly acquaintances, about "what a ladykiller I am. I gave my girlfriend a knifing penetration last night with her legs wrapped around my back. I filled her with my thundering ramrod. Our loins crashed together to the sound of ocean waves."

An actor friend, Steve Alexander, was skeptical. "Did you read that in one of those illegal porn novels? Shall I go on with your description? 'Your balls swung freely against her creamy thighs, as your cock continued to hammer on relentlessly, vibrating for a small eternity.' You see, I can make up stuff like that, too!"

"Fuck you, shithead!" Jimmy said before storming off.

On the nights he stayed home, Bast claimed that Jimmy demonstrated a certain artistic flair, creating whimsical mobiles for their sparsely furnished apartment. He also experimented with drawings and clay sculpture, and he asked Bast to pose nude for him. His roommate agreed. Bast later suspected that in sculpting his body, Jimmy spent a long time staring at his penis.

At the time, Bast was dating Beverly Wills. He had become involved with her through his work as an usher at CBS during her gig there in a radio comedy series, *Junior Miss.*

Bill and Jimmy often double-dated, Jimmy escorting a spunky brunette from Texas, Jeanetta Lewis. He'd met her through her stint as the wardrobe mistress for a production of *Macbeth* at UCLA. She had developed a crush on Jimmy during the short run of that student production.

Since the two men didn't have any money for dating, they often spent the evenings at the Bel Air mansion of Beverly's mother, Joan Davis. "Jimmy seemed to be eating all the time," Beverly said.

The quartet enjoyed the pool parties, barbecues, and dinners lavishly provided by Davis, who at the time was at the peak of her financial success as an actress.

For entertainment, these "theatrical amigos," as they called themselves, performed together in scenes from plays.

Jimmy shocked the young women with excerpts from a copy of Henry Miller's *Tropic of Cancer*, which had been smuggled in from Paris. *[Censors had banned it in the United States at the time.]* "Jimmy seemed to have selected only the most pornographic passages, and Beverly was shocked," Bast said.

Meanwhile, Jimmy continued sketching. Spanish matadors were a favorite subject of his pen-and-ink drawings. He was fascinated by what he called their tight "toreador pants."

"His drawings were rather crude," Bast said, "but I wish I had saved them. They'd be worth a fortune today. He always drew the bullfighters with enormous endowments hanging halfway down to their knees. He told me that he'd read that Ernest Hemingway advised bullfighters to stuff their crotches if they didn't have natural endowments."

He was fascinated by the subject of death, especially sudden death, as when a matador could be struck down in his prime. He'd read Hemingway's *Death in the Afternoon.* "He was intrigued by death in general," Bast said. "One of his most macabre drawings depicted skeletons dancing in a graveyard."

"One night, Jimmy displayed his latest artistic creation to Bast, Beverly, and Jeanetta. It was a sculpted clay candleholder that evoked a vagina. According to Bast, "It was 'living art,' as Jimmy called it. He lit a candle for us and slowly let the hot wax drip into the *faux* vagina. The girls were horrified, and I found it revolting."

A highlight of their double-dating occurred when Davis threw a birthday party for some of the elite of the "Hollywood brats," the pampered children of movie stars and/or young actors and starlets with solid connections. Jimmy was photographed with a young Debbie Reynolds, whom he would see a lot more of when he began to date actress Pier Angeli, one of Reynolds' best friends.

The talented starlet had just completed her involvement in *Three Little Words* (1950), an MGM musical starring Red Skelton and Fred Astaire.

As part of the entertainment for her daughter's party guests, Davis had hired a national archery champion for a bow-and-arrow exhibition. At one point, Jimmy came up to him and, in a reckless, highly dangerous decision, asked the archer to shoot an apple off his head in a style corresponding to the legend of William Tell. On learning of the request, Davis intervened and put a stop to it, then asked Jimmy to leave the party.

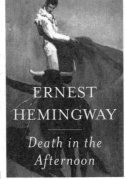

***

The rent on their apartment was coming due, and neither Bast nor Jimmy had enough money to pay it. Awakening Jimmy one morning, Bast virtually demanded that he to accompany him to CBS Studios, where he could get him a job as an usher, even though it paid only

Ernest Hemingway's ode to the art of bullfighting reinforced several of Jimmy's lifelong obsessions.

twenty dollars a week. Sometimes, one of the big stars would give an usher a five-dollar bill for running some special errand.

Bast told Jimmy that he'd get to meet some really major entertainers, citing Jo Stafford, the Andrew Sisters, Bing Crosby, Steve Allen, Eve Arden, Lucille Ball, Dinah Shore, Jack Benny, George Burns, and Gracie Allen. Stars such as those showed up regularly at CBS for its Lux Radio Theater, replicating for radio the roles they had previously crafted on the screen. CBS also produced big musicals, hiring such singers as Rosemary Clooney or Mario Lanza.

At CBS, Bast introduced Jimmy to his boss, a flamboyant creature named Sylvester Divan III. Behind his back, his ushers referred to him mockingly as "Miss Divine." He reminded Jimmy of the actor, Franklin Pangborn, a player who built a career on roles calling for a character who was fussy, effete, effeminate, and—by implication—gay.

After appraising Jimmy from head to foot, Divan hired him. Then he accompanied him to a dressing room with racks of blue uniforms with elaborate gold braid. Appraising his body size, he selected a pair of trousers saying, "I'm sure this will fit." Then, with a raised eyebrow, he continued, "I never failed to guess a man's size."

The *double entendre* was not lost on Jimmy.

"Looks like a monkey suit to me," Jimmy said.

"Try it on—don't argue, dearie."

"Right here, right now?" Jimmy asked.

"And why not?"

"I'm not wearing any underwear," Jimmy said.

"Don't worry about that," Divan told him. "Yours wouldn't be the first cock I've seen."

"I bet," Jimmy answered, sarcastically.

"Don't get smart with me, young man," Divan said, "if you want this job."

Provocatively, like a stripper, Jimmy slipped off his shoes and took off his pants, slowly exposing his penis. Then, within full view of Divan's leering gaze, he stepped into the uniform. "It sort of fits. Maybe a little tight in the crotch, wouldn't you say?"

"Cocky fellow, aren't you?" Divan said.

"And why not?" Jimmy said. "As you've seen, I've got a cock. So why can't I be cocky?"

We'll discuss that later," Divan said, "Come on, I'll show you the ropes. You pretty boys always have it made. You can get whatever you want just by dangling those wares you have between your legs."

Fussy, fussy, Franklin Pangborn...a lookalike for Jimmy's lecherous boss, "Miss Devine."

***

Two nights later, outfitted in his monkey suit, Jimmy was treated to one of the most memorable nights of his life.

One of the biggest shows at CBS was the Bing Crosby show. Its namesake had invited Judy Garland to come onstage and sing, knowing that she was in a depressed state, having recently been fired by Louis B. Mayer from the musical, *Annie Get Your Gun,* in which she'd been replaced by Betty Hutton. The story had generated embarrassing and unwelcome headlines in newspapers across the country.

Even though, jimmy was technically supposed to be on duty, Bast had procured him an otherwise unoccupied seat on the front row of the balcony, where he'd be partially obscured behind a curtain in case Divan began looking for him.

Bast had been assigned to escort Garland to her dressing room. She was accompanied by her ugly husband, a rather gruff Sid Luft.

In both photos above, clients line up for radio shows hosted within either the CBS Television Studios (top photo), or at its nearby annex, the Lux Radio Theater.

Jimmy, till he walked out, worked as an usher.

This was her first public appearance since she'd been axed by her longtime studio, MGM.

Crosby came out and opened the program in his usual casual style, singing two of his favorite numbers. But it soon became obvious that the audience—a full house with standing room only—was waiting for Garland. As Bast had told Jimmy, "All the world rushes to see a train wreck."

After Crosby announced her appearance, there was a long, awkward moment. No Garland.

Then suddenly, she appeared. Members of the audience went wild, delivering a standing ovation. She was dressed entirely in black, as if in mourning, which in a kind of way she was. To Jimmy, she resembled a pale, pathetic little creature, looking gaunt and tiny

After her entrance and her recognition of the audience's applause, she ventured toward Crosby for a "kiss-kiss," looking as if on the verge of collapse.

He extended a steady hand. The loud cheers seemed to revive her, injecting her with a new kind of energy.

"Somehow, Judy seemed to come alive," Jimmy later told Bast.

As she began to sing, Jimmy was moved by the power of her voice. She belted out "Rock a-bye My Baby to a Dixie Melody," and in doing so, over-powered the audience with emotion.

The night was hers. Many songs later, at the end of her performance, the audience went a bit insane, standing and cheering wildly as Garland exited from the stage for the continuation of her life's troubled journey.

"We loved her, and she loved us," Jimmy later told Bast.

As ironic as it seemed, in just two short weeks, Jimmy would be in a bed-room with Garland and another man—not Sid Luft.

***

With Beverly paying for the gasoline, Jimmy, in his Chevy, liked to race up the coastal highway at ferocious speeds. She was always urging him to drive more slowly and less dangerously, but he told her he needed the speed to feel alive.

Those who knew him called him "the Road Terror of Malibu."

"When he was behind the wheel, there came a transformation in his face," she recalled. "He had this demonic look about him. I came to feel he wanted to kill himself and take me along with him. A kind of Romeo and Juliet thing."

One night, when he was moving faster than a hundred miles an hour, they heard the wail of a police siren. Jimmy didn't slow down until she screamed at him.

He gradually brought the car to a standstill as the police closed in on him. "I'll need all my male charm to get out of this."

Before a cop appeared at his window, he turned to her. "You're lucky. This pig copper saved your life. Tonight was the night I planned to take you, me, and this car to a watery grave."

No longer an *ingénue*, Judy Garland, as she looked around the time Jimmy applauded her wildly during an (unauthorized) break from his job as an usher at CBS.

Chapter Two

How, One by One, the Emerging Hustler,

JAMES DEAN,

Shacked Up with the A-List Legends of Hollywood

Spencer Tracy, Clifton Webb, Joan Crawford,
George Cukor, Walt Disney, Judy Garland

"You know, I've had my cock sucked by some of the big names of Hollywood"
—James Dean

"I think the main reason for living in this world is discovery and diversity in sexual conquests. Why tie one hand behind your back?"
—James Dean

James Dean was given a ticket for speeding, which required an appearance before a judge and which called for a ten-dollar fine. He ignored the ticket as well as three more warnings. The fine was increased to twenty-five dollars. He received a notice from the courthouse in Van Nuys that unless he paid the fine, his driving license would be revoked. There was even a threat of a possible jail sentence.

He told William Bast, his roommate, that he feared going to jail. "A good looker like me would get his lilywhite ass pounded nightly from every black stud in there."

His hearing before the judge was set for ten o'clock one morning. Before he was called, he sat and listened to the trial of a Mexican fruit picker charged with being a Peeping Tom looking in windows where the shades or Venetian blinds weren't drawn. The laborer was sentenced to one year in prison.

After Jimmy's appearance before the judge, he said, "I faced a judge who must have looked like Torquemada at the Spanish Inquisition. I'd read about him. I knew His Honor would be a tough sell."

Facing the judge, Jimmy later claimed that he delivered an Academy Award-winning performance. He went into his Little Boy Lost act, even though the judge sternly lectured him on both speeding and ignoring warnings about the ticket.

Jimmy threw himself upon the mercy of the court, claiming that he needed the money for food. He said he would be homeless within the week, and that every day, he'd searched for a job. "I was wrong, and I admit it. It'll never happen again. I'm desperate."

The judge decided to go easy on the struggling actor. "He seemed to melt," Jimmy recalled.

The fine was reduced to five dollars, and the judge warned that he didn't want to see Jimmy in his courtroom again.

Leaving the courthouse, Jimmy had a smirk on his face. He told Bast, "I put one over on that judge."

Later, however, when he showed up for work at CBS, his charm didn't work with Sylvester Divan III. Called into Divan's office, Jimmy learned there were casting couch requirements even for acquisition of a low-paying job as an usher. Divan revealed that he required his favorite ushers to visit him one night a week at his apartment. The usher who had that duty on Thursday night had been fired, and Divan wanted Jimmy to replace him for appearances at weekly intervals at Divan's apartment in West Hollywood.

Divan was crudely blunt as was his style (or lack thereof). "I want you to use my succulent lips and mouth like some pussy. If you can keep it in and go for a second round, then you get an extra five a week."

Jimmy was revolted by the mere presence of his soon-to-be ex-boss. "Your mouth makes me want to throw up," he said. "You're nothing but faggot slime."

Divan's made-up face looked shocked before flashing anger. "All the other boys do what I want."

"I'm not one of your other boys, and I'll never be that."

"Then get the hell out of this building. You're fired! And leave the uniform!"

"You're welcome to this fucking monkey suit!"

After changing back into his street clothes, Jimmy walked past the sneering fussbudget and was back on the street again.

He knew there were other ways to hustle a buck.

Jimmy Dances for Pepsi-Cola
And Meets a Future Lover

At UCLA, Jimmy had made friends with James Bellah, the son of the novelist James Warner Bellah. His new friend was an expert in fencing, wanting to become "the next Errol Flynn." Jimmy was intrigued about learning the art of swordfighting, and Bellah agreed to give him lessons "in case dueling comes back."

One afternoon, after a fencing lesson, Bellah told him about a Pepsi-Cola commercial being cast. Its director wanted to hire a group of teenagers for twenty-five dollars a day plus a box lunch. Filming was to take place on December 13, 1950 at Griffith Park in Los Angeles.

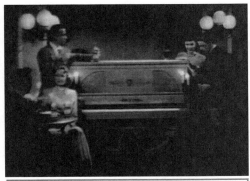

Jimmy wanted the job and went with Bellah to meet Ben Alcock, who was directing the commercial for Pepsi. Ironically, and unknown to Jimmy at the time, Alcock was a close friend of Rogers Brackett.

In wardrobe, Jimmy was given a blazer and white flannel slacks to wear. He was to stand with clean-cut consumers clustered in a group beside a jukebox, collectively

An image captured from James Dean's first television appearance. It was a commercial for Pepsi. He's depicted above on the far right, just before the clip moves on to show him interacting happily, catalyzed by Pepsi, hip but wholesome, with the other actors.

singing "Go get a Pepsi for that Pepsi bounce!"

Flashing a smile, Jimmy clapped his hands and snapped his fingers, a signal for the teens to start dancing.

He was introduced to Beverly Long, an attractive blonde, who recalled, "All of us were drinking Pepsi. At one point, we were going round and round on this carousel, having a blast. Then an announcer is heard urging teens "to buy Pepsi because it's the best. Buy Pepsi by the carton!"

Jimmy had lunch with this pretty blonde, telling her that he planned to go to New York to become a serious actor. That was the beginning of a harmless flirtation.

Nick Adams as The Rebel (of a different sort)

[A far more significant relationship began that day when Jimmy met Nick Adams, a bisexual actor who had also been cast in the commercial. Nick came on rather strong to Jimmy, but he was reluctant to get too deeply involved. That would come later and more intensely.

Nick invited Jimmy out that night, but was turned down. Before leaving the set, Nick urged Jimmy to call him, and made sure that Jimmy had all the details he needed to stay in touch.

In a surprising future development, both Beverly and Nick would eventually be cast with Jimmy in Rebel Without a Cause.*]*

Roddy McDowall

Makes Love to "John the Apostle"

Jerry Fairbanks was the producer of the above-noted Pepsi commercial. He was impressed with Jimmy and told Alcock, "The kid is clearly the star. He has something."

As months went by, more and more professionals in the industry kept saying that Jimmy "had something," although without being able to define it.

Fairbanks had also been designated as the executive producer of an upcoming inspirational/religious film, *Hill Number One*, and he invited Jimmy to audition for a role. Jimmy was more than willing. and Fairbanks asked him the next day if he'd show up to meet the film's director, Arthur Pierson.

He didn't want to, but Jimmy read for Pierson and for one of its consultants and contributors, Father Patrick Peyton. Collectively, they agreed to cast him in the minor role of John the Apostle, incarnated as a character in the film, supposedly for transmission of spiritual inspiration and instruction.

[Hill Number One, set in a U.S. Army camp during the Korean War, is the story of a chaplain who arrives to find the soldiers demoralized. He tells them that the hill they are storming used to be known as Calvary. The storyline then switches to flashback, relaying the story of Jesus' crucifixion and resurrection. Jimmy—wearing a djellaba that looked like it had been borrowed from a high school drama production—played John the Apostle. The other actors, also in robes inspired by the Bible, resembled burly, bearded linebackers. When Jimmy donned his headdress, he evoked a desert sheik.]

Some fifty actors had been signed for this religious epic, including many name stars such as Joan Leslie, Gene Lockhart, Leif Erickson, Regis Toomey, and Roddy McDowall.

The teleplay was to be broadcast on the Family Theater on March 25, 1951, where it would reach an audience of forty-two million viewers, the largest number of people ever to watch a James Dean film at one time.

That night, Jimmy told Bast, "I find my lines sickening. They're so fucking phony. I have to say such crap as 'Rejoice! He has risen as He promised!'"

As director, Pierson had little time for him, but Jimmy sought him out when he learned that he had helmed Marilyn Monroe in one of her first films, *Dangerous Years* (1948) for Fox. Cast opposite the star, William Halop, Marilyn had played a waitress, Evie, in a little down called Gopher Hole. She worked in this jukebox joint, a gathering place for rowdy teenagers.

When Jimmy asked about Marilyn, Pierson admitted that he was surprised at how fast her star had risen, claiming that Fox had fired her after the end of filming.

"She was heartbroken," Pierson said. "She told me she didn't want to make films to earn big money. I remember her exact words: 'I want to become a famous movie star so that everyone will love me. That way, I'll be surrounded by love and affection, something I've never had before.'"

"One day, I'll meet her," Jimmy predicted. "I'll give her more love than she can handle."

Jimmy, looking biblical, or *faux-biblical*, alongside David Young, in Hill Number One.

* * *

Jimmy enjoyed meeting Ruth Hussey,

whose bright, sophisticated delivery saved many a film. He'd seen her in *The Philadelphia Story* with Katharine Hepburn, Cary Grant, and James Stewart.

He brought Hussey a cup of coffee. "Oh, darling," she said, "thank you." She spoke about the vagaries of being a film star. "Save some money on the way up, because you'll need it during your descent. I guess I was always destined to play second stringers. I'm fading from films now—hence, appearing in this turkey. Guess what's coming up for me? I've been asked to play Jerry Lewis' mother in *That's My Boy*. Yes, the never-great Ruth Hussey is reduced to that indignity for a paycheck."

Roddy McDowall, former child star, as he appeared, all grown up and connected to every underground scene in Hollywood, in the late 1940s.

As fellow cast members, Jimmy and McDowall were attracted to each other. As he'd later admit to Bast, "Roddy and I sucked each other's cocks. He's got me beat. Really well hung. He's very likable, but a bit of the nervous type."

The former child star had been known to perform auto-fellatio at private gay parties. "The two of us one night went to this mansion in Beverly Hills, where we put on an exhibition for guests," Jimmy confided to Bast.

***

When *Hill Number One* was shown on TV, Jimmy's first fan club was formed at the Immaculate Heart School in Los Angeles. It would be the first of many fan clubs established during his lifetime and beyond the grave.

Bast accompanied Jimmy to one of its meetings, which consisted mostly of impressionable girls ages fourteen to sixteen.

"Jimmy was thrilled at this adulation," Bast said. "An honest-to-God fan club. I was his chaperone at this lovefest. He was as nervous as hell."

"When we arrived at this hall in the Los Feliz district, Jimmy got out of the car and turned to me. 'Let's go in and face the jailbait.'"

There were about twenty girls waiting inside, each with an autograph book. Jimmy signed all of them and gave each of the girls a beaming smile. "He looked dreamily into their eyes, making them swoon, as he checked out their budding breasts," Bast said.

Jimmy Stars in an Exhibition

AT A PARTY HOSTED BY CECIL BEATON FOR BRITISH GAYS

Although largely devoid of details, the story of Jimmy's occasional performances at private sexual exhibitions has been documented in books before, including a mention in one edition of *The Hollywood Babylon* series.

As he confessed to his roommate, William Bast, Jimmy performed in a sexual exhibition with Roddy McDowall, whom he'd met while filming *Hill Number One.* After their brief fling, Roddy suggested that "for a lark," they perform before some members of the cream of the crop of British expatriates, living in or else visiting Hollywood.

Cecil Beaton, the famous designer, photographer, and author, was staying in a mansion in Beverly Hills. He was throwing a party only for those "born and bred in Britain."

It took some persuasion, but apparently, Roddy finally convinced Jimmy to perform a sex act with him in front of Beaton's mostly celebrated guests. Cary Grant was rumored to have attended the exhibition.

Beaton was an intimate friend of some of the most distinguished people on earth, including Picasso, Jean Cocteau, Winston Churchill, Laurence Olivier, and André Gide. He was known for his affair with Greta Garbo, and he also photographed members of the Royal family, including Queen Elizabeth.

Roddy and Jimmy arrived early at Beaton's rented manse. He was one of the most talkative men Jimmy had ever met. "Welcome to this *nouveau riche* home," Beaton said. "It's the ultimate statement in Hollywood vulgarity—that's why I love it so. When in Hollywood, why not wallow in vulgarity?"

As the three men talked over drinks, whereas the British-born Roddy chatted amicably with Beaton, Jimmy had little to say.

"I have seduced women but I infinitely prefer men," Beaton said. "I've gone from Gary Cooper to Marlene Dietrich. Women have their place. I love to dance with them, including the Duchess of Windsor. At

Cecil Beaton, depicted in the unatttributed photo (probably a self-portrait) above, was the most arts-connected and avant-garde photographer in Europe. When he came to Hollywood on a "getting to know you" visit, he rented a house and threw some parties..... Jimmy was part of the entertainment.

intimate parties, I've also danced and kissed the duke."

"I like to talk to women about plays, gowns, fashion," Beaton continued. "I'm particularly interested in their lovers—take Porfirio Rubirosa, for example. He has one of those enormous octaroon cocks."

"My time in Hollywood is made more endurable because I have my own octoroon cock upstairs," Beaton claimed. "He used to be a boxer. He's not the first black boxer who's made love to me. He is built to the point of monstrosity. God should put a limit on penile measurements. The penis can be just too gross in some instances.'

Before his guests arrived, Beaton took Jimmy and Roddy into a studio, where he asked them to strip so he could photograph each of them in the nude—"Only for my private collection, darlings, no one else will see them."

Details of that night became known only because author Christopher Isherwood attended, and later revealed what happened to such friends as Tennessee Williams, Gore Vidal, and ultimately, Truman Capote, who virtually broadcast it to everyone on his grapevine.

According to Isherwood, about thirty guests were shown into the master bedroom where Jimmy and Roddy were lying nude under a spotlight on a king-size bed. Otherwise, the room was in darkness.

The bodies of both Roddy and Jimmy were met with sighs of approval. Slowly, the two young men began to make love to each other. A wild sixty-nine was followed by Jimmy sodomizing Roddy.

After the voyeurs filed out, Jimmy and Roddy put back on their clothing and went downstairs to have drinks with their flirtatious voyeurs, some of whom tried to line up dates with them.

When Jimmy discussed the exhibition with Bast, his roommate wanted more details, but didn't get them.

All that Jimmy told him was this: "I wanted the fucking limeys to see what an all-American boy, born and bred in the cornbelt of Indiana, looked like. I'm suntanned all over, as you know. That really turned them on. Those Brits don't get enough sunshine in their country. All of them have lily-white bodies. When they get to Hollywood, they really go for suntanned boys."

He did add one final comment: "Roddy and I should have been paid."

Grand and gay literary chic... Christopher Isherwood attended a Los Angeles "exhibition" for British expatriates

38

How Two-Timing Jimmy Ended, Violently,
Two Separate Romances with Young Women

When Bast was working nights at CBS, he sometimes asked Jimmy—who at the time was unemployed—to retrieve Beverly Wills and, as a chauffeur, to transport her to script sessions or to parties.

Over a period of the next ten days, she began an affair with Jimmy. For a while, Bast didn't have a clue. To keep up appearances, Jimmy and Beverly continued to double date with Bast and Jeanetta Lewis.

Beverly later recalled this secretive time in their lives. "After getting fired at CBS, he tried to get an acting gig and continued to show up at cattle calls, hoping for a job. Nothing was happening. However, he often had money, but he never told me how he got it. Later, rumors surfaced that he was hustling. I didn't want to think about that."

"Often, he was horribly depressed, almost suicidal. He told me, 'The world just doesn't understand me—it never will.'"

One night, Beverly met with Bast and opted to tell him the truth. "You're not going to like this," she said, "but Jimmy and I have fallen in love. Please forgive me. But these things happen. Neither of us would do anything to hurt you."

He responded in anger. "You mean he has time to fit you into his busy schedule?"

"Don't be hurtful," she cautioned. "We're serious. There's talk of marriage."

"I don't think Jimmy and I can go on living together in the penthouse," he said. "There'd be two of you making love in our double bed while I listen to the sounds from the sofa, nearby."

Later, he confessed that he didn't really care that Beverly had abandoned him for Jimmy. What he didn't tell her was that he'd met Paul Winston (called "Craig" in his memoirs), and that he was falling in love with him. He described Winston as a "Nordic knockout, a blonde, blue-eyed and *muy simpatico* Marine, twenty-four years old. He had a gentle smile, an intimate voice, and a compelling air of sensitivity about him." Hailing from Minnesota, he was stationed at the Camp Pendleton Marine Base, in nearby San Diego County.

Unknown to Bast, Jimmy was continuing to date Jeanetta Lewis, although seeing her less frequently, of course. Sometimes, he'd just arrive at her apartment, even as late as two o'clock in the morning, after he dropped off Beverly at her mother's mansion.

One night, Bast was wandering along the Pacific Palisades when he decided to drop in on Jeanetta. He wanted to discuss the new situation between Jimmy and Beverly. Perhaps she could console him over the loss of his two friends.

When he told her what was going on, she exploded. "That two-timer! What a jerk! That asshole has been stringing me along."

He was surprised to learn that Jimmy was still dating her and often slept over at her apartment.

The couple talked until dawn, as Jeanetta urged Bast to move out of the penthouse. "Jimmy is bad for the both of us."

By mid-morning, she drove him to Mar Vista, about two miles from the Pacific. There, Bast answered an ad and decided to rent a small studio at 12623 Green Avenue. The rent was reasonable, and he decided he didn't need a roommate.

He called his landlady to notify her that he would no longer be responsible for the rent. It was up to Jimmy to pay it by himself.

Jeanetta joined him on the drive back to the penthouse to lend moral support as he was packing his clothing. Apparently, the landlady had already informed Jimmy of this new development in his living arrangement.

Bast later remembered, "Jimmy was waiting for me downstairs. I'd never seen him so furious. He denounced me as 'a dirty little snake.' I tried to calm him down, but he lunged for my throat and started to choke me."

Seeing what was happening, Jeanetta ran toward the two men and tried to break up the fight. She screamed at Jimmy, "You'll kill him!"

Momentarily, Jimmy got control of himself, but within a minute, he'd turned on Jeanetta. "So Billy Boy is fucking you now?"

"What do you care, you little creep?" she said. "You're a god damn liar. A fucking jerk."

With his anger still bubbling, he balled up his fist and slammed it into her face. Blood spurted from her nose.

Regaining his breath, Bast feared a neighbor would spot them and call the police. Using all his diplomatic skills, he managed to usher them both back into the penthouse so Jeanetta could stop her bleeding.

Once inside, she rushed to the bathroom. The sounds that emerged made both men realize that she was vomiting.

Suddenly, Jimmy was apologetic. "I was an animal," he admitted. "Don't leave me."

"It's over," Bast said. "I'm packing my things and heading out. I don't want to see you again."

Jimmy left the apartment and went and stood by Jeanetta's car parked by the sidewalk. He stood there an hour, waiting to them to come down. With her freshly washed face, she walked by him without speaking.

In contrast, Bast shook his hand. "It's been great, kid. We've had our moments."

Jimmy didn't say anything, but looked forlorn through teary eyes.

Bast later admitted, "It was time for me to leave and get on with my life. I knew that temporarily, at least, Beverly would pay the rent for Jimmy if he didn't make it hustling. Some nights, he didn't return home alone, and I knew he was pursuing 'a source of revenue,' to put it in its most polite terms."

"Another reason for me to leave was that I was starting to fall in love with him myself until my Marine came along. The god had sent him directly from Valhalla."

Rogers Brackett had flown to New York for a three-week visit, but had phoned Jimmy, even holding out the suggestion that he might want him to move in with him. Jimmy knew he couldn't see Beverly every night and return to a home with Brackett, too, so a decision would have to be made.

In the meantime, he needed money, and he was determined to contact some of his new connections, such imposing figures a George Cukor and Spencer Tracy. He also wanted to call John Carlyle, just for fun.

The time had come for a showdown with Beverly. That summer, she had moved north to Paradise Cove to stay with her father and his new girlfriend. One night, she threw a beach party for her coven of "Hollywood brats." Jimmy was invited and told to bring his appetite, because there would be a pig barbecue on her father's oceanfront terrace. She informed him that she'd even hired a four-piece band from Laguna Beach.

As Beverly remembered it, "Jimmy arrived with a chip on his shoulder. It was like he was spoiling for a fight." Two hours later, after Jimmy refused to dance with her, a "Beach Boy Adonis" (her words) asked her to dance.

"I guess we were dancing too close," she said. "He was in a bikini and was rubbing up against me. I was trying to make Jimmy jealous. At any rate, he came up to the young man and grabbed hold of one of his breasts, pinching it as tight as he could.

"Get away from her, you faggot. I'll black both of your eyes."

"I tried to keep the boy from striking Jimmy," she said. "He stormed off the terrace and headed down the beach. When I caught up with him, he called me a whore and slapped my face. I fell over in the sand. I knew it was over for us. That's why I later wrote that piece about why I didn't marry Jimmy Dean."

41

A Drunken Spencer Tracy Seduces Jimmy,

Who Steals His Wallet

Jimmy called Spencer Tracy, who remembered him and chastised him a bit for not calling sooner. The aging actor agreed to meet him at one o'clock the following afternoon at George Cukor's house.

After Jimmy drove there, the Japanese houseboy directed him to the pool area, where Tracy was lounging in the sun.

"Hi, kid," he called to him. "Come on over."

Jimmy later admitted that he was rather tongue-tied but Tracy put him at ease with his friendly banter. Occasionally, he drank from a flask. "George rarely stocks wine or booze. The cheap bastard. I have to bring my own whenever I visit."

Although Jimmy hoped that he might talk about Katharine Hepburn, with whom he was famously linked, a slightly drunk Tracy began discussing his wife, the former actress Louise Treadwell. He said he'd been to visit her that morning to spend time with his daughter, Susie, and his son, John. It was with a sense of despair that he told Jimmy that John had been born deaf. "Imagine living in a world where you could never hear the birds sing."

Jimmy had long ago learned that all gay men didn't dress up like drag queens. He'd been around Hollywood long enough to know that several very macho figures of the silver screen, including Gary Cooper, had had a gay past.

To him, Tracy was the most macho man on the screen, with a quiet masculinity that contrasted with the swagger of John Wayne.

By 3:30PM, when Cukor still had not appeared on the terrace, Tracy suggested that he and Jimmy walk down the hill to Tracy's cottage "for a little privacy." Jimmy, of course, knew what he had in mind.

As Jimmy would later recall to Rogers Brackett, he had never known a man who held his liquor as well as Tracy. His preferred beverage was scotch.

Since Jimmy was hungry, he asked if he could go into the kitchen and whip up something for a late lunch. "Help yourself. She usually leaves some foodstuff for me." Jimmy assumed "she" meant Hepburn.

Spencer Tracy, an anguished Catholic, appropriately cast as Father Flanagan, an influential priest specializing in the rehabilitation of juvenile delinquents, in *Boys Town* (1938).

Tracy was right. The refrigerator was well-stocked, and included a roasted chicken. He took it out and sliced off some of the breast, which he later mixed up with some salad greens. He brought two heaping plates into the living room, where, to his surprise, Tracy devoured his share. "I haven't eaten anything all day," he said. "Sometimes, I can make it through an entire day relying only on liquid nourishment."

By 8PM, Jimmy became anxious to get on with the action, since he had made other plans for the evening.

Jimmy knew what Tracy wanted, but the actor seemed reluctant, almost shy, to introduce the subject of sex. "Let's go into the bedroom, Mr. Tracy," he said.

Tracy looked surprised, but rose from his armchair, and then plopped down onto the bed. Jimmy seemed to want to get the sex act over with and be on his way. In full view of Tracy, he stripped off his clothes and climbed onto the bed beside him.

Suddenly, Tracy began to weep uncontrollably. "I don't like who I am," he sobbed. "I hate my life. That's why I drink so much. To escape."

"I held him tightly, like a baby," Jimmy later recalled to Brackett. "This strong character on the screen was like a helpless little boy. Since I knew what he wanted, I took his hand and placed it between my legs."

"His hand moved over to my groin, and then he began nibbling at my foreskin—that bit of skin fascinated him. Although he finally got around to taking the whole cock, it was clear to me, for some strange reason, that he was a devotee of foreskin."

After the sex act, both men fell asleep. Tracy took Jimmy in his arms. As he drifted off, he whispered, "Don't leave me. Don't ever leave me!"

In the early morning hours, Tracy woke up and stumbled out of bed. Only a small lamp on the nightstand illuminated the room. He couldn't seem to find his way to the bathroom, so finally, he gave up, pissing in the corner of the bedroom. Then he returned to the bed.

Jimmy couldn't go back to sleep, so he decided to leave. Very quietly, he got up and retrieved his clothing. In the living room, Tracy's wallet was on the coffee table. It contained two one-hundred dollar bills and a few one- and ten-dollar bills. Jimmy took the two hundreds, leaving the remainder of the money for the actor, in case he needed it for his eventual migrations to the bank or perhaps to the studio.

He never expected to see Tracy again. Nor did he want to. Only that morning, he'd read in *Variety* that Cukor had cast Anthony Perkins as Jean Simmons' boyfriend in *The Actress*, leaving him to conclude that he wouldn't be working on that picture with Tracy as its major star.

Tracy was a sad, forlorn person, cursed with a depression that seemed to reside within him. It mirrored Jimmy's own bouts of morbidity. He and Tracy did not belong together.

Jimmy made his way up the hill to Cukor's home, entering the open door that led to the kitchen. The Japanese houseboy was preparing breakfast for his boss.

`The director was nowhere to be seen. Spotting Jimmy, the boy said, "Good morning, Mr. Dean fellow. Mr. Cukor asked me to give you a letter." Then he handed him a letter that had been resting on the kitchen table. "Thanks," Jimmy said. "I'll read it later. Tell him I'm sorry he decided to cast Perkins instead of me."

En route to his penthouse, Jimmy still hadn't read the letter. He was still thinking about Tracy, and something he'd said.

Tracy had asked him, "Do you know what happens to old actors in Hollywood? What will happen to me one day? Me, as well as Jimmy Stewart, Clark Gable, Bogie. Our only public appearances will be at funerals."

Was Walt Disney a Homosexual?

"OH WALT, SAY IT ISN'T SO!"

—*MICKEY MOUSE*

Back at his penthouse, Jimmy read the note from Cukor, who apologized for having cast Anthony Perkins instead of himself in *The Actress*.

"I want to make amends," wrote Cukor. "If you'll come over tonight, I'll introduce you to one of the biggest names in Hollywood. I've already alerted him to the fact that you'd be ideal as the hero of one of his big-budget movies. More than anyone, this gentleman can make you a star."

Arriving at eight o'clock that evening in blue jeans and a white T-shirt, Jimmy was ushered into Cukor's living room as the director was bidding farewell to a very tense Katharine Hepburn.

"Just because I have to fight for my independence as a woman, you're against me—just like a man. Even Spence is on your side."

"My dearest darling Kate," Cukor said. "We'll shoot the scene tomorrow as I've set it up. You can't overrule your director. Instead of objecting to everything I want, you should listen, for a change. It'll do

Portrait of a Diva:
Katharine Hepburn

you good."

"You should be nice to me," she said. "After all, I'm a star."

"You're more than that," Cukor said. "You're a spoiled, rotten bitch."

Hepburn stormed out of the living room, brushing past Jimmy without a word.

"Forgive that outburst," Cukor said, apologetically. "Come on in and sit down beside me. I'll have my boy get you a drink."

"She was really, really mad," Jimmy said. "I'd be afraid of her."

"I'm about the only one who'll stand up to her. When John Huston made *The African Queen* with her, he told me he feared that the movie-going public wouldn't be able to tell Kate's scaly skin from that of a crocodile."

Jimmy was shocked at such a harsh appraisal, but said nothing.

"Is your producer friend here?" Jimmy asked, anxious to change the subject.

"Don't be impatient," Cukor said. "He'll be here soon. He's a very busy man."

At 9PM, in walked Walt Disney, the creator of Mickey Mouse, Dumbo, Cinderella, Donald Duck, and Snow White. Although he knew very little about him, Jimmy recognized him at once. In the 1950s, very few members of the American public knew anything about the producer. Some biographers would later designate him as "Hollywood's Prince of Darkness."

An anxiety-ridden, chain-smoking alcoholic and lifelong anti-Semite, Disney was also a special informant for the FBI in Hollywood, routing out communists and "subversive Jews" during the Joseph McCarthy era.

According to dozens of sources, he was also a homosexual. After his death, he would be outed by several underground newspapers.

Throughout his life, Disney was plagued with what one biographer called "his sexual inadequacies." That might explain, if these rumors are true, what caused him to turn to virile young men to provide him with sexual pleasure, which he could not provide, except in rare instances, to women.

Based on Disney's fast appraisal of his body, Jimmy just assumed that the producer approved of him. "I think Jimmy here looks like a clean-cut, All-American boy," Disney said to Cukor, right in front of Jimmy.

He quickly responded, "Looks can be deceiving, Mr. Disney."

"A boy with spunk," Disney said. "I like that."

During the first hour of their conversation, Jimmy realized that Disney and Cukor had a jocular but very

Anti-semitic guardian of show-biz' Family Values: Walt Disney

competitive relationship. At one point, Cukor turned to Jimmy and said, "Ask Walt to tell you about his honeymoon with Lillian. She found out that he liked to look into garbage cans and watch maggots devour rotting meat. "

"At least I wasn't fired from *Gone With the Wind* because Clark Gable didn't want a cocksucker directing him."

"Too late," Cukor said. "I sucked Gable's little cock back in 1929."

"Did Walt tell you that Leni Riefenstahl wasn't Hitler's favorite filmmaker? Walt was! *Snow White and the Seven Dwarfs* was Der Führer's *favorite movie.*"

"No person in Hollywood can be blamed for the fan base he attracts," Disney said, defensively.

Before the two men took Jimmy upstairs, Disney seemed to want a final assurance from Cukor that Jimmy would be very discreet.

"Please understand," Disney said, lighting up another cigarette. "If word got out that I patronized hustlers, my empire might crumble. Mothers might not let their kids see my movies."

Jimmy was insulted. "Mr. Disney, I'm not a hustler. I'm an actor, and a god damn good one at that."

"I'm sure you are, dear boy," Disney said to him.

"Before their departure upstairs, Disney seemed to blame Cukor for hooking him up to the hustler scene to which he'd become addicted.

As Cukor later told Jimmy, "Blaming me is like a drug addict blaming the dealer who got him hooked."

Perhaps to make him jealous and to torment him a bit, Jimmy later revealed to Brackett some of the most intimate details of his brief life as a hustler. He was particularly adept at bragging how he had become linked to the rich and famous without any assistance from Brackett's connections.

He didn't exactly give a "blow-by-blow" encounter of the night he spent with Cukor and Disney, but he did claim that both men kept most of their clothes on. He had "every inch of my body devoured by ravenous mouths. I've never been so drained in my life."

When Brackett quizzed him about Disney possibly featuring him in one of his upcoming movies, Jimmy had to admit the truth: After those moments of passion, Cukor never returned any of his phone calls. Likewise, Disney never contacted him, and there is no record that Jimmy was ever considered for a role in one of Disney's family-oriented films.

***

William Kern, a journalist who wrote under the pseudonym "Bill Dakota," was the editor of *The Hollywood Star*, a gossip tabloid that was a hot seller during the 1970s. Dakota seemed to have the inside scoop on anything transpiring within gay Hollywood.

His most notorious edition (Volume 1, no. 4) appeared in 1976. It carried the red-letter, front-page headline: WALT DISNEY WAS HOMOSEXUAL—EDITOR REVEALS FACTS!

When that paper hit the newsstands along Hollywood Boulevard, it outsold *Playboy* and every other publication. It is reasonable to say that the first major outing of Walt was the talk of the town at every dinner party and in every bar that night.

The editor even went to a notary public and signed a sworn statement, replicated on that edition's front page, that the events he revealed about Walt were true. The article revealed that he had been paid to have sex with Walt. Dakota's experience with the creator of Mickey Mouse was given further credence by other men who testified to having had the same experience.

Even though the term "outed" had not been coined at that time, Walt Disney, creator of Mickey Mouse, was officially "outed," becoming one of the first of many stars—both male and female—who would be outed in the years to come. In the immediate aftermath of Walt's death, the underground press in Hollywood—much of which was produced on old-fashioned mimeograph machines without a lot of design savvy—went into overdrive. Hustlers came forth and described the details of their paid encounters with Walt.

Although the various sources derived from widely varied backgrounds, a pattern emerged. According to several of these allegations, Walt rarely, if ever, requested that the young man remove his clothes. "I was subjected to a quick blow-job, paid a hundred-dollar bill, and shown to the door as quickly as possible," said hustler Ralph Ferguson. "For me, it was easy money. Walt was known in the hustler world as a good mark."

Over the years, insights into the marriage of Walt and his wife, Lillian, have remained largely a closely guarded secret. What she knew of her husband's nocturnal activities, if anything, is not known. Obviously she might have been suspicious. Walt often didn't come home at night. He used the excuse that he was working late at the studio and was sleeping over.

He was rumored to have maintained different apartments in the Greater Los Angeles area, which he rented under assumed names. It was alleged that he entertained paid hustlers there. One of the many "male madams" of Hollywood supplied him with a discreet group of young men, often out-of-work actors.

Clifton Webb

Jimmy placed a call to John Carlyle, that actor he'd had sex with at George Cukor's home. He wanted to spend a night alone with Carlyle, but instead, he got a surprise invitation. Carlyle suggested that both of them meet that evening at Clifton Webb's house for an eight o'clock dinner. The actor lived in a pink stucco house on Rexford Drive in Beverly Hills.

Jimmy accepted the invitation with a sense of adventure, based on a vague idea of what was in store for him.

A black manservant showed Jimmy into the house, directing him down the foyer to the living room, where Webb and Carlyle were already having drinks. Carlyle rose and hugged Jimmy, but Webb remained seated, extending his hand and holding Jimmy's paw an extra-long time. "You're everything John said you'd be," Webb said, appraising him.

He was impressed with the décor and taste of the house, which, Webb asserted, had once been owned by director Victor Fleming.

Webb had launched his Broadway career as a singer-hoofer. He'd achieved screen fame portraying the dandified Waldo Lydecker in Gene Tierney's *Laura* (1944), for which he was later nominated as a Best Supporting Actor.

In the words of critic Barry Monush: "Webb was everybody's favorite prissy snob—dapper, dryly critical of others, and oh-so-pleased with himself. He was usually raising a nose, looking down with superiority at some other, less confident character, and tossing off a witty *bon mot* or insult with the sting of a wasp."

Jimmy was surprised by the sudden appearance of an elegantly dressed woman who looked to be in her 80s. Webb said, "This is my beloved mother, Maybelle."

Jimmy found that her mannerisms, fluttering eyelids, and tantalizing lisp evoked an earlier part of the century. He also noticed that she wore far too much rouge, and that her dress appeared to have been fashionable in 1930.

Over dinner, she did most of the talking,

Clifton Webb with Barbara Stanwyck in *Titanic* (1953)...Both of them were competing for Robert Wagner.

48

treating her son with an imperial *hauteur*, ordering what he could and could not eat. Apparently, in her heyday, she'd been a feisty, high-kicking dancer.

She did not seem embarrassed by her son's "auntie-like effeminacy" (Jimmy's words). At one point, she told the table, "Many mothers with homosexual sons kick them out of the house. I would never do that. To me, the greatest loss a mother can suffer is when her son leaves the house to marry another woman."

"Maybelle, darling, you know I will never do that."

The purpose of the evening became all too clear after Webb escorted Maybelle up the stairs to bed. Carlyle whispered to him, "Clifton wants us to go to his bedroom and put on a show. He sometimes gives blow jobs, but mostly he's a *voyeur*. Also, a director. He insists on directing the sex act."

"I'm short of cash," Jimmy said.

"He'll give us $150 each, which is good because I need money for gas and rent, not to mention food."

"Okay, we'll put on a show for the creep, and we'll have some fun ourselves."

Later, when Jimmy described the night to Brackett, he left out most of the details, except to say, "John and I got so carried away that at one point, we forgot that Webb was in the room."

Over the next few weeks, Webb called Jimmy back on three different occasions without Carlyle. "He never took off his clothes, but the guy has a suction pump for a mouth," Jimmy told Brackett.

Apparently, Webb's experience with Jimmy was frequently repeated with other young men for sale. Scotty Bowers, in *Full Service,* his *exposé* of underground Hollywood, wrote that he often supplied tricks for the veteran actor.

Bowers recalled that Webb's mother, Maybelle, fully understood what was happening whenever Webb headed for the bedroom with his *beau du jour.* "The mother would start behaving like a brooding, clucking hen and say, 'Now, now, boys, don't misbehave.'"

Webb, with his man of the moment, usually spent fifteen or twenty minutes alone with him, and would then reappear. According to Bowers, "Maybelle liked me. She often scurried over to me and whispered in my ear, "Oh, Scotty, thank heavens for you, darling. You make my Clifton so happy, you know."

Scotty Bowers, one of Hollywood's most "connected" hustlers and pimps.

***

49

Webb became a mentor and great supporter of Jimmy's film career. He even began to supply columnists with items about him. He spoke to Dorothy Kilgallen, an entertainment columnist in New York. She printed one of Jimmy's first news items:

"Clifton Webb is playing star-builder. His protégé is James Dean, who just snapped up one of the leading roles in John Steinbeck's East of Eden. *Young Dean might be described roughly as having the Marlon Brando style of dungarees and a T-shirt instead of a blue serge suit."*

In Hollywood, Webb found Hedda Hopper a much more difficult sell. The gossip maven had already met Jimmy. A public relations man from Warners had arranged for them to meet in the commissary for an interview, claiming that Jimmy was a genius on film.

"To believe the press agents, every boy in a dirty shirttail and blue jeans is a genius, emerging from Lee Strasberg's Actors Studio in New York," Hopper claimed. "Ninety-nine times out of a hundred, the gangling lad is like a dream brought on by eating *Port Salut* cheese too late at night. If you wait long enough, it goes away."

Jimmy showed up for the interview looking like a dirty garage mechanic. He ordered three cheeseburgers medium rare and only muttered something instead of answering Hopper's questions.

The walls of the commissary, where Hedda had rendezvoused with Jimmy, were decorated with publicity pictures of Warner Brothers' stars. He looked up into the smiling face of Ronald Reagan.

Rising suddenly from his chair, he spat upon the picture, then removed a handkerchief from his back pocket to wipe away the spittle.

Then he sat down again and began to devour his second cheeseburger. Hopper rose from the table and walked out of the commissary, composing what she was going to write in the next day's column about this uncouth actor who had insulted her.

When *East of Eden* was filmed, her friend, Clifton Webb, called her, praising Jimmy's performance, and urging her to see the film.

"I've already met Mr. Dean," she responded, "and wild horses couldn't drag me to a picture he made."

Webb finally convinced her to call director Elia Kazan with a request to set up a private screening for

Hedda Hopper...forgiving Jimmy's previous sins.

her. Reluctantly, she attended the screening, and later reported that she was spellbound.

"I couldn't remember ever having seen a young man with such power, so many facets of expression, so much sheer invention as an actor," she wrote. "I phoned Jack Warner and asked him if I could interview Dean at my home."

Two days later, Jimmy arrived at her door, wearing a charcoal suit, a black shirt and tie, along with heavy riding boots. This time, he was polite and cordial to the columnist, winning her over with his manly charm.

From then on, and throughout the remainder of his short career, Hedda Hopper became one of his most avid supporters. In print, she pronounced him one of the brightest stars in Hollywood. All his past sins were forgiven.

"Jimmy later told William Bast," I don't care for Hopper at all. She's not my kind of dame. But I decided it's better for her to write good shit about me in her column than attack me."

Webb continued to support and praise Jimmy's acting. Writing in *New York Magazine,* actor William Redfield said, "The rumors were rife that James Dean was Clifton Webb's *protégé.* That always struck me as odd, because Jimmy, in his manner, did not appear to be a homosexual. But of course, that often happens. And I don't think he was exclusively gay. What exactly went on between Webb and Dean I don't know, although I imagine it took a sexual form."

"They Say I'm a Practicing Homosexual,
But I Say I'm Perfect."
—Cole Porter

On their first real date together—that is, one without a voyeur or a "john" hiring them—John Carlyle took Jimmy to a car dealership to show off his new purchase, an Oldsmobile in midnight blue. He'd bought it on an easy installment plan. Within the dealership, he went on to suggest that Jimmy should consider replacing his beat-up old Chevy, which had developed some loud muffler problems.

Although Jimmy pretended to be impressed with the Olds, it's almost certain that if and when he opted for a replacement, it would be something faster and sportier.

Once the papers were signed, Carlyle was free to drive away. That's when he told Jimmy that he could not drive and wanted to be taught.

Impulsively, he invited Jimmy to Lake Arrowhead, where a cabin had been made available to them. Once there, they'd have time for driving lessons, and for other activities too.

Jimmy rose to the challenge of orchestrating some driving lessons, but warned Carlyle, "You'll never be a race car driver. Your favorite part of a car is the god damn brake."

[Later, back in Los Angeles, Clifton Webb asked Jimmy how the driving lessons were progressing. Carlyle, with Jimmy as his instructor, was practicing on the secluded offshoot streets of Brentwood and Bel-Air.

Facetiously, Jimmy told Webb that Carlyle had run over only two children. "Fortunately, they were very little and didn't damage the tires."]

After Jimmy and Carlyle's arrival at Lake Arrowhead, they bought some provisions for the cabin's cramped kitchen. Then they went for a swim and settled into their cabin for "Love in the Afternoon."

Carlyle would later write a memoir, from which the editors, right before publication, cut fifty pages based on the advice of the publisher's lawyers. In the expurgated section of that memoir, he claimed that he and Jimmy were most compatible in bed. "Both of us gave as much as we got. We were neither a top or a bottom, but versatile in all acts. Actually sixty-nine was our favorite figure in arithmetic. Both of us were ready for anything in the hay, except it left us so drained, we didn't have much energy left for lake sports."

For dinner on their first night, Carlyle had accepted an invitation to the elegant vacation home of the heir, J. Watson Webb, Jr. *[No relation to Clifton Webb]*, whose stone-and-timber home overlooked the north shore of the lake. His art-collecting family had left him a fortune, but, as he admitted, "Just for fun, darlings, I once worked as a film editor at Fox."

He told Jimmy and Carlyle that he was involved in pre-production of a new film at Fox entitled *Don't Bother to Knock,* starring Marilyn Monroe, Richard Widmark, and Anne Bancroft.

As a Hollywood gossipmonger, he rivaled both Hedda Hopper and Louella Parsons, spewing out revelations that neither of these peddlers in print could publish.

"Did you know that Fred Astaire once seduced a nine-year-old boy?" he asked his guests. "That Cary Grant was arrested in the men's room of a department store going down on a young man who worked in the men's clothing department?"

He also provided information that Jimmy didn't really want to hear. "Did you know that Tyrone Power and Monty Woolley actually eat shit sandwiches?"

"The other month, the world's favorite matador, Luís Miguel Dominguin, came for a visit,"

J. Watson Webb...privy to gossip too dangerous to print.

Webb said. "My guests wanted to see the scars on his body caused by bulls in the ring. Luís was very accommodating. He pulled off his clothes and let my guests examine his scars. All those hands on that magnificent body of his produced an erection. The inevitable happened."

"Watson was a very dear friend, but he could be mischievous," Carlyle said. "He fed Jimmy and me this delectable beef dinner. Only after it was over, he told us it was horsemeat. Jimmy went outside to vomit."

***

Back in the Los Angeles area, a very different party invitation arrived. Clifton Webb called with an invitation to a Sunday afternoon pool party at the pink palazzo home of composer Cole Porter. Clifton and Porter had been friends since they'd worked together on the ill-fated Broadway show, *See America First* in 1916.

At the last minute, Webb fell ill, but called Porter, who claimed he'd be delighted to "entertain your two young friends, especially if they are as handsome as you say, without you."

Carlyle felt secure enough behind the wheel to drive to Brentwood, although Jimmy noticed that the right fender of his Olds had been dented. Blaming Jimmy, Carlyle claimed. "You didn't teach me to park right."

In the foyer of the "pussy pink" (Carlyle's term) manse, Porter's black butler/manservant showed them inside. In addition to working for Porter, he maintained other pursuits which included occasional gigs as a jazz musician in Hollywood. Carlyle had informed Jimmy that Porter "has a fondness for black meat. On occasion in New York, he visits this male bordello in Harlem."

Emerging from the powder room in the mansion's ground-floor hallway was none other than Joan Crawford, whom Carlyle had already met at a previous party. She was as formidable off screen as on. After kissing her on both cheeks, Carlyle introduced her to Jimmy.

"I'm in awe, Miss Crawford," he said. "You gave such a great performance in *Mildred Pierce,* although I had a hard time believing you were ever a waitress."

"What Jimmy meant is that an elegant lady like you belongs only in satin gowns and ermine," Carlyle said.

"I have an earthy side, too," Crawford said. "Why don't you two good-looking guys drop over tomorrow night at eight? We'll go swimming in my pool. Don't bring your bathing trunks. You won't need them."

Cole Porter..."It Was Just One of Those Things."

53

When she saw hesitation on Jimmy's face, she said, "Don't worry about it. It doesn't matter to me. Only the other night, I had a wonderful time with Rock Hudson. We 'went to heaven' in my poolhouse. I told him, 'just imagine I'm Clark Gable. After that, we managed very well."

[Crawford had silly euphemisms she used—usually to describe sex acts or body parts— throughout the course of her life. They included references to intercourse as "going to heaven," and to her breasts as "ninny pies."]

She reached into her purse and handed her card Carlyle. On its back, she had handwritten her private phone number. "Got to go, kids. Tonight, the real thing, Clark Gable, is coming over."

After she'd gone, Jimmy told Carlyle, "Stars out here don't waste much time getting to the point, do they?"

"They're too busy and, with such heavy demands on their time, they don't bother with a lot of small talk."

At the pool, a fully dressed but immobilized Cole Porter looked like some rich potentate overlooking his array of good-looking muscle men.

Later, in his memoirs, Carlyle wrote, "He was propped up on a raised dias by the pool. Each muscleman guest appeared more striking than the one beside him. After two rounds of daiquiris, Mr. Porter's butler lowered the dias to carry his crippled master to an outdoor table, where an elegant lunch was served to the slightly woozy collection of Adonises."

After the long lunch, Porter's butler carried the composer into his elegantly furnished and thick-carpeted living room. The other guests filed in, the bathers with large bath towels wrapped around their otherwise nude bodies. The hired entertainment of the afternoon was about to begin.

Word had spread that "Mr. Universe" (Steve Reeves) had been hired— through his agent, Henry Willson— to stage an exhibition. At the time, Willson, was trying to get Reeves a movie role in some epic, Hercules-inspired movie. In the meantime, the title holder was hustling rich gay men for sex or else staging private shows.

Jimmy had already met Reeves at Willson's party, the event to which he'd been escorted by Rogers Brackett early in their relationship.

Reeves appeared before the appreciative audience wearing a robe. He soon removed it to reveal a posing strap that was almost transparent. For about half an hour, he demonstrated various muscleman

A publicity photo of Steve Reeves...Available for sexual exhibitions.

54

poses and some of the exercise techniques that kept his body in a rigorously maintained state of perfection.

Then, Porter called out for him to remove his posing strap. Seemingly expecting that to happen, and accompanied by loud clapping, the muscleman took it off, then walked around the room, allowing his fans to feel his body, especially what was dangling between his legs. Jimmy would later define it as a "shameless exhibition," but Carlyle reminded him, "Steve has got something to show off."

After he made the rounds of the room, Reeves displayed a full erection, thanks at least to some extent to all those hands manipulating his body. Then, from a position in the middle of the room, he masturbated for his audience. When he was finished, the most aggressive of his fans moved in "to clean up with their tongues" (Carlyle's words).

Carlyle later wrote: "to avoid the competition I was certain to lose over who would stay over for dinner, I chose not to linger."

Jimmy felt the same way. "I'm not in the same league as these musclemen. No one is going to crown me Mr. Universe."

On his way out the door, Carlyle assured Jimmy, "But you have other charms."

"I hope you're eager to enjoy them later tonight," Jimmy said. "All of that has made me horny."

In 2006, Carlyle would publish a memoir, *Under the Rainbow: An Intimate Memoir of Judy Garland, Rock Hudson, & My Life in Old Hollywood,* with a foreword by Robert Osborne of Turner Movie Classics.

Although its publisher *[Da Capo press published it in 2007]* promoted it as a book detailing his many love affairs, including those with Marlon Brando, Rock Hudson, and Jimmy, the sections on his involvement with Brando and Jimmy were removed as part of a last-minute decision.

However, many people at the publishing house read his description of making love to Jimmy.

Carlyle's agent, Henry Willson, had seen the first draft of his client's tell-all memoir and had had a copy made. He later leaked some of the passages of the sections that were later cut to the underground *exposé* press and to gay friends. One passage that was expurgated included his description of making love to Jimmy:

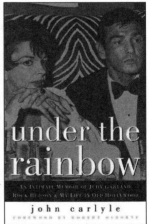

"He could lie for hours in my arms as I kissed him, bit gently into his neck, and sort of nibbled on all parts of him. He liked that a lot. He had a very smooth, un-

muscled body and liked to be devoured. His curved buttocks were his chief asset, and he had silken pubic hair that he like me to pull on with my teeth. As I explored his body, his flesh prickled with tender excitement."

"After I did all that, he would suddenly yell out, 'Take me! Make me yours! When it was over, he just wanted to lie in my arms and fall asleep."

"My fear was that he was falling in love with me, and I didn't want that. At the time, I was one of the pretty boys of Hollywood. My phone was ringing off the wall."

"Jimmy wanted us to be together and live like a couple. I wasn't ready for that. Guess what? I was dating him, but was also slipping around and fucking Rock Hudson and Marlon Brando."

"And did I tell you that Jimmy and I seduced Judy Garland one night, all three of us in the same bed? Judy in time became my sometimes lover and greatest companion, the star of my memoirs. It all began with a party one night at the home of Clifton Webb."

AFTER HER AFFAIRS WITH BARBARA STANWYCK AND CLARK GABLE,
Joan Crawford Maneuvers Jimmy Into a Three-Way

In the 1950s, Joan Crawford, facing a long drawn-out career decline as she aged, began to date younger men. She had three dates with Rock Hudson and also had a brief fling with Hudson's lover, the handsome, well-built actor, George Nader. At the time, Nader and Hudson were having a fling of their own, which later evolved into a lifelong friendship. Crawford always told her *confidantes*, "Rock's big attraction is the fat baby's arm between his legs."

On the night that followed the party at Clifton Webb's house, Crawford welcomed Carlyle and Jimmy into her immaculate home in Brentwood, where all the white living room upholsteries were covered in plastic. That afternoon, it had rained slightly, and she asked the young men to remove their shoes in case they were tracking in mud. As she directed them toward her patio, Jimmy whispered to Carlyle. "I think Crawford has a foot fetish."

The sky that night was clear and lit with a full moon that illuminated the swimming pool. Spotlights encircled her terrace. Although her invitation had not specifically included dinner, there were platters of cold food resting on her bar. Both men ate heartily, especially Jimmy.

Although at times she took a great interest in other people and sometimes helped them financially, she appeared self-enchanted on the night she entertained Carlyle and Jimmy.

She did take the time, however, to learn what she had suspected: That both of them wanted to be movie stars. Jimmy asserted that more important than status as a star was his burning desire to be an actor, even if it meant abandoning Hollywood for New York.

"Acting on the stage would terrify me," she said. "I'm strictly a movie queen. Even in the dim light, her steely eyes focused on each of them, as if sizing them up. "You're both good lookers and in Hollywood, that sure helps—I should know. Of course, I've seen many a gorgeous man or woman come and go—mostly go. They arrive daily at the train station, with their broad shoulders and Greek god profiles. But they need more than that to get ahead. They've got to have a keen intelligence beneath their shock of unruly hair."

She looked both of them up and down once again. "I have this instinct: I can tell just by meeting a wannabe actor if he has what it takes to make it."

"And what's your verdict of us?" Jimmy asked. "Do we have it or not?"

"Forgive my bluntness, but one of you does, the other doesn't. I'll not tell you which is which. Only one of you will rise to the top. The other will end up pumping gas in San José or else serving beer to the musclemen of Venice Beach. There's also the chance that one of you might end up a rich man's toy."

"Do you believe that the casting couch works for a young man like it does for a beautiful girl?" Carlyle asked.

"The casting couch might lead to a role in the beginning, but it won't make you a star. I was accused of lying on the casting couch back in the 20s. To that I always said: 'The casting couch is better than the cold, hard floor.'"

"Facing up to your disappointments can also make you a star," she claimed. "I'll tell you the secret of my success on the screen. I've used my personal disappointments—and they've been horrendous—to bring life to the characters I play in the movies."

Before she'd finished her fifth vodka, she seemed to wander down memory lane. She told them terrible stories about her abuse at MGM, but also spun some amusing tales.

She discussed her brief affair with movie cowboy icon Don ("Red") Barry. "He was very short except in one department. At first he overwhelmed me with gifts, including a diamond necklace worthy of Marie Antoinette and a white mink coat more suited to Lana Turner. Our ro-

Portrait of Joan...Always lusting for the new boy in town.

mance ended soon. The day after I said goodbye, I got a visit from a jeweler and a furrier who arrived pounding on my door. It seems that Red had never paid for these trinkets, and they wanted them back."

She asked Jimmy which actor on the screen he most admired. Although Jimmy's admiration for Marlon Brando might have been the answer most of his latter-day fans might have expected, in this single instance, in a departure from his norm, he said, 'John Garfield.'"

"I got to know John when we starred together in *Humoresque*," Crawford declared. "When I was introduced to him, I extended my hand. Instead of shaking it, he pinched my breast instead. That was the beginning of a brief fling."

"Do you think that the press treats you fairly?" Carlyle asked.

"Of course they do, my dear," she said sarcastically. "That's why they depict me as having this iron will—a gutsy bitch, an aggressive broad, and a man-eating dame. Perhaps the press confuses me with my screen image."

"To keep up that image, I'm always searching for the right script. A *Mildred Pierce* script is rare. I almost lost that one. Michael Curtiz, that Hungarian shit, wanted Bette Davis. When she said no, he asked Barbara Stanwyck who also turned him down. In the end, he had to settle for Oscar-winning Joan Crawford."

Once again she concentrated on Jimmy and Carlyle, asking if either of them had ever been married or been seriously committed to someone. Both of them denied any such previous involvement.

"I don't recommend marriage," she said. "I was a failure at it. My last husband was an actor, Phil Terry, all six feet one, a former football player weighing 175 pounds. He was certainly good-looking but he spent most of our marriage fucking Robert Taylor instead of me."

"That didn't surprise me," she said. "Most actors in Hollywood are at least bisexual if not homosexual. When I was dating Jeff Chandler, I found that he was also dating Rock Hudson. I indulged Jeff in his cross-dressing fantasy. Sometimes, he wanted to go out with me dressed in full drag. Of course, we had to go to obscure joints. He'd wear a gown, a big red wig, a diamond necklace, and those so-called Joan Crawford fuck-me high heels. I felt like I was making love to myself."

"Gays dominate the industry, and I've always adored working with them and, on occasion, loving them. Lesbianism isn't bad either—at least you don't get pregnant. When I meet a man, I have this uncanny ability to determine his bedmanship, even before auditioning him. I can forgive a gay man for turning me down. A straight man, never! I hold grudges."

Finally, after three more vodkas, she rose on wobbly feet. "Gentlemen, I have an early call, so let's adjourn to my bedroom upstairs and get on with the war games, meaning men *vs.* woman."

Days later, Jimmy would provide a blow-by-blow description to Rogers Brackett. But when Clifton Webb grilled him, he supplied only the most meager of details. In reference to that night, Webb later told gossipy Cole Porter, "I think that whereas John Carlyle actually screwed Crawford, she gave James Dean a blow-job."

Jimmy did provide one tantalizing detail directly to Webb. "I won't be visiting Miss Crawford again. I can't abide bad breath."

REPEATING HIS PENCHANT FOR SEDUCING BOYS IN HOLLYWOOD
Alfredo de la Vega
(A CLOSE FRIEND OF NANCY REAGAN)
Entertains James Dean

One night at one of Clifton Webb's parties, Jimmy was introduced to the actor's friend, Alfredo De La Vega. He was an elegant Mexican aristocrat, the son of a wealthy family who had fled to points north of the Mexican border during the Mexican Revolution of 1910. Eventually, they settled in Los Angeles, where they began to purchase real estate with the gold they'd hauled away with them.

In their new world, they acquired prestige and influence. Soon, they became known for their elegant dinners and parties. On any given night, they entertained the Gary Coopers, the Clark Gables, and/or such famous compatriots as Dolores Del Rio.

They also contributed to political campaigns and developed influence with Republicans, including Ronald Reagan and Nelson Rockefeller.

In time, Alfredo became an escort of First Lady Nancy Reagan during her early years in the White House. He was also seen dining with her and her good friend, Betsy Bloomingdale.

In Alfredo's younger days, when he first met Jimmy, he had a reputation as a serial seducer of the pretty young men of Hollywood. His list of sexual conquests, some arranged through agent Henry Willson, included Guy Madison, Rory Calhoun, George Nader, Rock Hudson, Steve Reeves, John Derek and, later, Troy Donahue.

After his introduction to Jimmy, the real estate mogul invited him two nights hence to his lavish apartment in a building he owned. Alfredo said he would have his limousine pick him up at seven o'clock and deliver him there.

Jimmy later reported the details of the evening to William Bast. "Sitting in that apartment, I thought I'd hit pay dirt. This was the kind of life I deserved instead of some tired old farm in Indiana. His living room was filled with nude statues of young men, including a replica of Michelangelo's *David.*"

"Wherever I looked, his wealth was on display—the oriental carpets, the antiques, the crystal, the paintings, the Salvador Dalís and Picassos. Dinner was prepared by a Japanese chef. Kobe beef, the best I've ever been served. The finest wines. I drank too much."

"At the end of this magnificent dinner fed to a starving boy, Alfredo told me it was time we got better acquainted. He claimed he couldn't really develop a friendship with a young man until he'd tasted his essence."

"It brings me closer to a beautiful boy such as yourself when I taste everything, and I mean, everything. Every young male beauty has a different taste and smell. There is no part of a man on whom I don't lavish my adoration. Every inch of him, including those hidden inches that are waiting to burst forth in all their glory."

"Consider me as dessert," Jimmy said, as he followed Alfred to his bedroom. There, he was instructed to strip and to climb onto the bed.

"He lived up to his stated desire," Jimmy told Bast. "There wasn't a part of me he didn't taste from my big toes to my earlobes. And oh yes, plenty of 'essence' too."

What had really impressed Jimmy was the array of five custom-made sports cars in rainbow colors parked in Alfred's garage. The Mexican proudly showed them off to Jimmy and even let him get behind the wheel of one of them for a drive up the coast.

"I figured that if I became his boy, he'd give me the privilege of driving any of those cars any time I wanted," Jimmy told Bast. "I also suspected he'd give me a big weekly allowance. I was thinking of asking for five hundred dollars every Saturday."

"Like Joan Crawford predicted, either Carlyle or I might end up as some rich man's toy. That way, I could pursue an acting gig if I wanted to or else spend my days riding around in those cars."

Jimmy stayed the night and left after breakfast at ten the following morning. Before leaving, there had been no offer, so he asked Alfredo if he could call him again.

"My dear boy," he answered. "Every hour away from you will be unbearable until I hear that wonderful, seductive voice of yours."

At that point, Jimmy thought he was exaggerating. He waited an entire day before phoning him, only to be told by the butler that De La Vega had flown to Acapulco with Merle Oberon with no plans to return.

"By then, it was obvious to me that Alfredo did not plan to adopt me,"

Jimmy told Bast.

He later talked about Alfredo to Webb, knowing what good friends they were. "I should have warned you," Webb said. "Once Alfredo has had a young man, he wants to move on to his next seduction. I nicknamed him 'The Mexican Conquistador.' He might have invented the slogan, 'So many men, so little time.'"

[Jimmy died years before the night of September 26, 1987, when Alfredo was shot four times in his upper chest at his West Hollywood apartment at 1285 N. Crescent Heights Boulevard. Only the night before, he'd attended a birthday party for Nancy Reagan.

Homicide found no forced entry, and detectives believed that some hustler might have assassinated him, since he was known for bringing strings of young men to his residence.

His close friend was the strikingly handsome actor John Gavin, who was also of partial Mexican descent. (The rest of his gene pool was Irish.) Gavin told the press, "Alfredo was like an uncle to me, and I'm terribly saddened to hear of his brutal death. He had many friends and he loved life and the social whirl. He was in great demand in Hollywood. He will be mourned by so many."

ANOTHER THREE-WAY. THIS TIME IT'S

Over the Rainbow...with Judy Garland

John Carlyle lost the opportunity to describe yet another major development in his life with Jimmy when its details were removed from the final version of his memoir, *Under the Rainbow.* It centered around the time they were invited to one of Clifton Webb's formal parties. "We were the most shabbily dressed bums there, but coasted by on our good looks and male charm," Jimmy recalled.

In an article in *Ladies' Home Journal,* Judy Garland, the guest of honor, remembered the evening and wrote about her encounter there with Marilyn Monroe, a rising starlet at the time.

"Marilyn followed me from room to room. 'I don't want to get too far from you,' she told me. 'I'm scared. I told her, 'We're all scared. I'm scared, too.' That beautiful girl was frightened of loneliness, the same thing I've been afraid of all my life."

Fortunately, Frank Sinatra arrived at Webb's party, and he managed to lure Monroe away from Garland for the night. The highlight of the party was when Garland sang a medley of her favorite songs, including *Over the Rain-*

bow. Listening intently to this impromptu concert were about seventy-five guests, two of whom included Jimmy and Carlyle.

The singer was accompanied on piano by Roger Eden, an associate producer for Arthur Freed. During the course of the evening, she sang songs by Cole Porter, Gershwin, and Warren.

During her concert, Webb's black poodle "adopted me and wouldn't leave my side," Jimmy later said. "Watching Judy sing was one of the highlights of my life."

When it ended, after all the congratulations had been expressed, Garland for a moment was left alone. That's when Carlyle led Jimmy over to introduce themselves. After some pleasantries, Carlyle announced, "George Cukor has promised me a role in your upcoming *A Star Is Born.*"

"Oh, we'll be working together," Garland exclaimed. "I'm delighted to hear that, darling!"

"Unfortunately for me, my scene is with James Mason, not with you."

"In that case, we'll get together for a cuddle off screen," she said.

"I'm looking forward to *that*," Carlyle responded, flirtatiously.

It soon became clear to the two men that Garland had arrived at the party alone, without a husband or lover to escort her.

"Could we take you home, Miss Garland?" Jimmy asked. "A pretty little thing like you should not be out at night wandering the streets alone."

Later, in Garland's living room, the intimate trio talked, laughed, and joked until around two o'clock in the morning, consuming a full package of cigarettes. Carlyle put his cigarette and hers into his mouth at the same time, and then lit them both, a scene he'd stolen from Paul Henreid and Bette Davis in *Now, Voyager.*

By three o'clock the following morning, Carlyle and Jimmy had piled onto her upstairs bed for a sexual romp. Jimmy would later try to relay a blow-by-blow description to Rogers Brackett, although he claimed, "I don't really remember who did what to whom. Judy gave us some pills, after popping a few herself."

Jimmy did remember one of Garland's lines in bed: "I've had it with mass adoration. What I need is one-on-one love."

"In our case," Jimmy said, "Call it two-on-one love."

At around eleven o'clock the following morning, the two men were huddled together in bed, sleeping off their drunk of the night before. Unexpectedly, a large glass ashtray hit both them in the head. "It was a rude awakening," Jimmy said.

Standing nude at the bottom of the bed, an angry, hung-over Garland confronted them with: "Do you fuckers really love me, or are you just pretending because I'm Judy Garland?"

"We love you, Judy," Jimmy said. Rubbing his forehead, Carlyle chimed in. "I love you, too, Judy, now that you didn't kill me with that god damn ashtray."

"You guys had better not be bullshitting me," she said. "I've got to warn you: I have one *helluva* temper."

Then, impulsively, Garland ran screaming from the bedroom, heading down the hallway. Perhaps fearing she would harm herself, a nude Carlyle ran down the stairs after her, ending up on the floor of the living room, where she had fallen down on the carpet.

By the time a fully clothed Jimmy made it to the living room, Garland and Carlyle were lying together in a tangled mess, giggling and rolling over together.

At that point, Jimmy decided it was time he got out of that household. He headed toward the front door and walked for miles, pondering the events of the previous night.

Months later, Cukor came through with his promise and cast Carlyle in a role in *A Star Is Born.* At the age of twenty-three, he was assigned the role of an assistant director in a "movie-within-a-movie."

Carlyle's character was supposed to be directing James Mason, Garland's husband, "Norman Maine" in the movie, but—as dictated by the script—the fading star was drunk and unable to pull off a swashbuckling scene in a pirate adventure inspired by roles associated with Errol Flynn.

Jimmy went alone to see a sneak preview of *A Star Is Born* in a movie house in Huntington Park. He was one of the few people who ever got to see Carlyles's brief appearance. In its final release, Carlyle's scene was cut from the movie, much to his disappointment.

When Jimmy later encountered Carlyle, the somewhat embittered actor told him, "A star was not born, a star was cut."

Although Carlyle and Jimmy, as lovers, drifted apart, Jimmy was able to arrange a small role for his friend in his upcoming movie, *A Rebel Without a Cause.*

During its filming, Jimmy stood on the sidelines watching chain-smoking Nicholas Ray direct Carlyle and other young actors in a scene from *Rebel.* The scene took three nights to shoot, and it was bitter cold on the night of filming.

Carlyle's girlfriend in the scene was Kathryn Grant, who would soon go on to marry Bing Crosby.

"I remembered placing my trembling hands around a Dixie cup of coffee to keep them warm," Carlyle said. "I was shaking so bad I couldn't get a car in gear during one scene. Dennis Hopper crouched down under the gears, out of camera range, and helped me lurch forward."

"When I later bolted from the driver's scene, I had one line to deliver. I was not only frozen, but mortified. I flubbed my line with Kathryn. Ray fired me that night. He told me that if some director ever needed an actor to play a wooden Indian, he should cast me."

Although humiliated, he took his firing in stride. "After all," he told Jimmy, "I came to Hollywood to become a movie star, not an actor."

***

Years later, Carlyle would meet Garland again and begin a roller-coaster friendship that included sex. He later called it the highlight of his heterosexual life. She proposed marriage to him, but he held her off, while still maintaining the friendship. She'd married a gay husband before, so it was familiar turf to her.

One night, she told him, "You're not going to rid of me."

But he did.

***

Once again in pursuit of his vagabond lifestyle, Jimmy was awakened by the ringing of his phone. It was Rogers Brackett, the TV director had returned to Los Angeles after completing a project for his ad agency in New York.

"I've missed you, Hamlet," Brackett told him. "In New York I could think of no one else."

"Glad you're back," Jimmy said. "Welcome."

"I want to see you tonight. It's very urgent."

"That means you've got a job for me," Jimmy said.

"That, too, but I've also got a personal offer to make to you. I want you to move in with me."

"You mean, let you have exclusive property right to my dick?" Jimmy asked.

"Something like that..."

Chapter Three

A TV PRODUCER AT CBS "ADOPTS"
A KID FROM THE STREET,

JAMES DEAN,

SHOWING HIM OFF
AS A TROPHY TO THE HOLLYWOOD ELITE

*Jimmy's Tryst in Jack Benny's Dressing Room
and a Flurry of Subsequent of Affairs*

SCHTUPPING WITH HEDY LAMARR AND BARBARA PAYTON

It was a rainy Thursday night when Jimmy packed his meager belongings into his old Chevy and drove to the luxurious apartment of Rogers Brackett on Sunset Plaza Drive. His car almost stalled as he headed along the inclined road that meandered uphill to the Hollywood Hills from the nightclub-studded Sunset Strip. Actually, as he was to learn that night, the apartment was a sublet from William Goetz. *[Goetz was a film producer and studio executive and one of the founders of what was eventually renamed 20th Century Fox. Brackett later informed Jimmy that Goetz was married to Edith Mayer, daughter of MGM's Louis B. Mayer. Jimmy met Goetz casually one afternoon when he came by to check on his property. Since Jimmy didn't know who he was, he let one of his remarks ("you should be in pictures") go by unchallenged.]*

A skilled chef, Brackett had prepared a lavish dinner for Jimmy as a gesture of welcome into his new living quarters. Jimmy had told his friends that he'd occupy a separate bedroom, but the small garden apartment had only one bedroom, and it contained a double bed.

Jimmy wanted his freedom, but even before he opted to move in, he had known what to expect. The question that had not been asked was how often he'd have to put out.

Brackett, who later worked for Grey Advertising in Manhattan, told Jimmy that he loathed the commercially oriented job he had. "I do it for a paycheck, and for no other reason. My true love is the ballet, the theater, concerts. I'm the cultural type."

The dinner he'd prepared was spectacular and, as Brackett later admitted, the sex was sensational. "It was a two-way, reciprocal street."

The next morning over breakfast, in reference to his new, glamorous address, Jimmy said, "I like living here. It makes me feel superior to be looking down on the city and its dreary residents. It's like living on some magic carpet high in the sky."

As part of their living arrangement, Brackett was quick to produce acting jobs for Jimmy. He got him a gig in *Alias Jane Doe,* the radio show, and another in *Stars Over Hollywood* for CBS Radio, a production that had been staged and promoted by Brackett's employer, the advertising agency, Foote, Cone, and Belding. *Stars Over Hollywood* had been broadcast most Saturday mornings since 1941, featuring such second-tier stars as Ann Rutherford, who had played Vivien Leigh's younger sister, Careen O'Hara, in *Gone With the Wind* (1939). Alan Hale, Sr., a beefy, hearty actor with a bushy mustache, was also a regular.

One afternoon, Jimmy was introduced to Basil Rathbone. He found the actor suave, imperious, and grandly self-satisfied, evoking some aspects of Clifton Webb. To Jimmy, Rathbone was the definitive screen version of Sherlock Holmes. That night over dinner, Jimmy confessed to Brackett. "Did you know that Rathbone is secretly gay? He made a pass at me."

"And what did you do?"

"I told him to catch me later."

Brackett began to expand Jimmy's cultural horizons, introducing him to some of his favorite writers, including André Gide, Jean Cocteau, and Shakespeare. One night the two of them sat through a performance of *Hamlet* together.

Brackett had never seen Jimmy so mesmerized by a literary work. When it was over, Jimmy asserted, "I feel it is my destiny to play Hamlet on the stage."

Wes D. Gehring, a professor of film history, wrote that themes associated with *Hamlet* were replicated in Jimmy's screen persona in *East of Eden,* "playing the most uncertain of characters attempting to resolve situations that have fathers at their centers. In fact, one might also interpret the morose, brooding Hamlet as a possible catalyst for Dean's decisions as they related to his interpretation of his *angst*-ridden character."

On the social circuit, Brackett escorted Jimmy to many of Hollywood's social venues and introduced him to his friends. Alec Wilder, the composer, later said, "Rogers took this Indiana farm boy, used to slopping the hogs, and introduced him to a world of culture and sophistication. Jimmy would always remain that farm boy in his heart, but with a more cutting edge as time went by."

Some of Brackett's friends were completely turned off by Jimmy. One of them was Leonard Spiegelgass, an aggressive homosexual who was a Hollywood player and the powerful story editor at Metro. "The boy was not housebroken. I'd installed this expensive new beige carpet, and he tracked in mud. He was a chain smoker, and he dropped ashes on my carpet. At one point, he jumped up and announced, 'I've got to take a piss. Where's the fucking john?' He unzipped and had his dick half way out before he left the living room. I considered him toxic, but Rogers thought him the hottest thing since he'd once sucked off Lex Barker, Lana Turner's Tarzan. I had planned to seduce the kid, but he was such a turn-off, I kicked him out into the rainy night."

Ironically, Spiegelgass's sister, Beulah Roth, befriended Jimmy. She'd been a speechwriter for Franklin D. Roosevelt and Adlai Stevenson, and was married to the photographer, Sanford H. Roth, who later also became a close friend of Jimmy's.

One Sunday afternoon during their time together in Hollywood, Brackett escorted Jimmy to the rented Malibu cottage of Miles White, who, for a period of twenty-five years, had been the top costume designer of Broadway musicals. He had designed the wardrobes for Rodgers and Hammerstein's first two Broadway hits, *Oklahoma!* and *Carousel*. He had also designed clinging and/or glittering on-stage garments for Carol Channing, Tallulah Bankhead, Bette Davis, and Lena Horne.

White later remembered Jimmy's visits. Like Brackett, he referred to him as "Hamlet."

"I was on the West Coast designing costumes for the Civic Opera House and also for the circus, Barnum & Bailey. During each of his visits, Hamlet sat in the corner, nursing a Bud and not saying a damn thing. I found him very hostile."

Miles White, the leading costume designer on Broadway, was not impressed by Jimmy's hustler approach. "He wanted me to help get him cast in either *Oklahoma!* or *Carousel*."

One weekend, when Brackett had business in San Francisco, he didn't invite Jimmy to go along. To White's surprise, Jimmy showed up that Sunday alone. He was drunk.

"Rogers must have told him that movie versions of *Carousel* and *Oklahoma!* were in the works," White said. "Jimmy was particularly interested in playing the (leading) role of Curly in *Oklahoma!*, with a dubbed voice, of course, for the singing parts. He also thought he'd be ideal in the role of the irresponsible carnival barker in *Carousel*. He wanted me to recommend him."

"I listened to his pitch—suddenly he'd found a voice—but he didn't impress me then or now. Other actors, notably Gordon MacCrae, were far better suited for the role, and Gordon could sing."

At one point, when Jimmy thought he was not going over with me, he stood up in my living room and unzipped his jeans. I couldn't believe it. He pulled out his dick. 'If you get me just one of those roles, you get this.' Then he shook his dick at me. I ordered him out of the house. I never told Rogers about that Sunday afternoon."

***

One of the most important show biz moguls that Brackett introduced to Jimmy was Ralph Levy, a pioneer in early TV comedy shows.

Levy had tried to launch himself into show business way back in 1946, when he answered a "cattle call" audition for the role of a chorus boy in *Annie Get Your Gun*. From that early failure, he rose, over a period of only eight years, to a position as director of Mary Martin in a Rodgers & Hammerstein musical on Broadway.

Later, Levy migrated from the theater to the emerging medium of television, producing *The George Burns and Gracie Allen Show* and the highly successful *Jack Benny Show*. In time, he'd produce *The Bob Newhart Show,* and direct such stars as Red Skelton, Lucille Ball, Ed Wynn, and Edgar Bergen. He also directed A-list film stars, including Marlon Brando, Shirley Jones, David Niven, and Doris Day. Later, his career included key involvements in *The Beverly Hillbillies, Petticoat Junction, Green Acres,* and *Hawaii-Five-O.*

When he could, Levy hired Jimmy as an extra on *The Alan Young Show,* an entertainment venue that had begun as a situation comedy on the radio, and eventually evolved, by 1951, into a major-league TV variety show, eventually winning some Emmy awards. Jimmy approached its MC, Alan Young, directly and asked if he could use his influence to snag a speaking role. Young told Jimmy, "I'll get back to you, kid." Of course, he never did.

Levy always had frequently stated that Jack Benny—who appeared frequently on his show—was a marvelous man—and that he was privy to many aspects of Benny's secret life. As Levy's friend, Brackett later said, "To put it bluntly, Levy pimped for Benny. Even though Benny *schtick* included a sort of gag gay comedy act, American

Jack Benny in *(upper photo)* a comedy schtick celebrating his "39th" birthday and *(in lower photo)* in drag.

TV viewers usually assumed he was straight. After all, he'd been married to Mary Livingston since 1927. Yet throughout his career in show biz, Benny maintained a secret preference for delivering blow-jobs to good-looking guys."

Brackett went on to assert, "Although he played a miser on TV, in private life, Benny was very generous, giving these guys a hundred-dollar bill, big money back then. As I found out later, Levy delivered Jimmy one afternoon to Benny's dressing room for a quickie. I later forced Jimmy—if he wanted to go on living with me and paying his bills, to reveal the truth."

In the TV comedies that Levy helped administer, he really couldn't use an actor like Jimmy. However, he did make several phone calls to help him get jobs in the theater after Jimmy moved to New York City.

Death in the Afternoon

(JIMMY DREAMS OF BECOMING A MATADOR)

Jimmy had become hooked on the art and mystique of bullfighting during his childhood in Indiana. James DeWeerd, a local preacher who fell in love with the young boy, sparked his interest in the sport by showing him home movies he'd taken in Mexico of bullfighters in the ring.

Jimmy's future director, Nicholas Ray, later tried to explain the young actor's fascination with bullfighting: "There was the ritual, the matador's inescapable endurance test, the challenge of proving himself, and there was the physical grace of the bullfight itself, almost like a ballet. All of this intrigued Jimmy to the point that it almost became an obsession."

When Brackett became aware of Jimmy's interest in bullfighting, he invited him for at least three weekend visits to Mexicali.

En route to points south of the (U.S.) border, Brackett complained about Jimmy's driving loudly protesting that he was going too fast. A speed demon, Jimmy ignored his lover's pleas to slow down.

In Mexicali, both Brackett and Jimmy became swept up in festive moods, attending the bullfights and drinking too much tequila.

By chance, Brackett ran into an old friend, Budd Boetticher, a film director known mainly for his low-budget westerns, many of them starring Randolph Scott, the former lover of Cary Grant. A bullfight *aficionado*, he had worked as the

Budd Boetticher next to a poster displaying his passion, bullfighting. He gave Jimmy a "magic talisman," the blood-soaked matador's cape once owned by...

the celebrated American matador, Sidney Franklin, depicted in 1937 with Ernest Hemingway. Franklin is demonstrating a bullfighter's maneuver with a cape that's very similar to the one Jimmy received as a gift and talisman of good luck from Budd Boetticher.

technical director of the wildly popular bullfighting film, *Blood and Sand* (1941), starring Tyrone Power as a matador.

Boetticher was in Mexicali working for John Wayne Productions, shooting *The Bullfighter and the Lady,* which featured such B-rated actors as Robert Stack and Gilbert Roland, a fading Latin lover of yesterday.

Boetticher was said to be gay, and he was mesmerized by Jimmy, arousing Brackett's jealousy. Jimmy and the director managed to sneak away for some time together. Boetticher invited him to his hotel suite where he gave Jimmy a most precious gift, the blood-soaked cape of Sidney Franklin. As a matador, Franklin had the unique distinction of being born a Jew in Brooklyn. Ernest Hemingway helped fan Franklin's legend through praise for his "intelligent valor," facing death in the afternoon.

From within his hotel suite, Boetticher asked Jimmy to try on a flamboyantly pink "suit of light" designed in the tight-fitting style worn by matadors. Jimmy could hardly pull himself into the very tight garments.

Boetticher assured Jimmy that although no bullfighter could compete with the size of the genitals of the bulls they appeared with, matadors wore their pants that way as "proof of their manhood." Hemingway had advised bullfighters who were not particularly well-endowed to stuff their crotches.

It was later assumed—but never verified by Brackett—that the director performed fellatio on Jimmy after he undressed in his hotel suite.

After one of their trips to Mexicali, *en route* back to Los Angeles, Brackett and Jimmy engaged in a lovers' quarrel. At one point near Laguna, Jimmy braked the car and jumped out, racing toward the beach. As Brackett recalled, "I was furious at him, so I drove off, even though I knew he'd left his wallet in the back seat. Two days later, he managed to make it back to Hollywood looking worse for wear. I didn't ask what he'd been up to. We survived our first big quarrel and resumed our life together."

During their next trip to Mexicali, Jimmy and Brackett were accompanied by actor David Wayne and his wife, the former Jane Gordon.

According to Wayne, "All that Jimmy talked about was bullfighting, even though Rogers told me he wanted to be an actor. I finally got him talking about acting when I told him that I was one of fifty applicants who had been granted membership in the newly formed Actors Studio in Manhattan. He told me he'd go to New York one day to try to get into the Actors

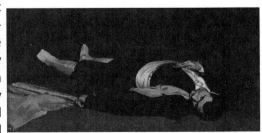

Death of a Toreador (1864), by Edouard Manet, interpreted by some (including Jimmy) as a celebration of the heroism of sudden, unexpected death.

Studio himself.

Wayne also said that Jimmy seemed to forgot about bullfighting when he learned that he would soon be appearing in a movie, *As Young As You Feel* (1951) with Marilyn Monroe.

[In a short time, Wayne would go on to star with Monroe in three more films, more than any other actor. They included We're Not Married *(1952);* O'Henry's Full House *(1952); and* How to Marry a Millionaire *(1953).]*

In Mexicali, sitting above the bullfighting arena between Wayne and Brackett, Jimmy was mesmerized by his view of the matador, Carlos Arruza, performing brilliantly in the ring.

Jimmy later purchased a copy of his favorite painting, Manet's *Dead Bull-fighter, [a.k.a. The Dead Toréador, painted around 1864]* referring to it as "The Dance of Death."

Throughout the rest of his life, Jimmy carried around Sidney Franklin's blood-soaked cape wherever he went. It became something of a security blanket for him. In a series of apartments, he tacked the cape onto a wall, often as the room's only decoration.

Sometimes, he even wore it, draping it casually over his left shoulder. In New York, in one of his more daring escapades, he treated oncoming cars as if they were the bull in a ring. Once or twice, he was lectured by a police officer, although never arrested, despite its obvious dangers as a pastime.

The Truth About That Nude Picture Showing Jimmy, With a Full Erection, in a Tree

During Jimmy's time with Brackett, he posed for one of the most controversial sets of nude photos in the history of Hollywood movie stars. One day, he stripped and posed naked after climbing a tree, at one point exhibiting himself with a full-blown erection. For years, Brackett carried a copy of the blurry snapshot in his wallet, showing it to his friends. Some of them reported that eventually, after it was lost, he wept.

Many biographers have disputed that it was Jimmy depicted in these candid shots, published long before the technology of "doctoring" photographs (through computer programs such as Adobe's PhotoShop) became widely available.

Among Jimmy's biographers, the full frontal, fully erect nude of Jimmy was first published in *Boulevard of Broken Dreams,* a biography written by Paul Alexander, a former reporter for *Time* who had also written two books on

Sylvia Plath.

Another chronicler of Jimmy's life, John Gilmore, claimed that the young man depicted in the tree was not Jimmy. "The image isn't even close," he was quoted as saying.

Perhaps he should look again. The image not only resembles Jimmy, it's a dead-on likeness.

Brackett, who was perhaps the most experienced judge of Jimmy's genitals, insisted that the nudes were real, "not only the erection, but the testicles. I spent quite a few months nesting there, so I think I'm qualified to identify them."

John Willis of *Theatre World* also provided authentication. Founded by David Blum in 1945, the magazine, published annually, was widely regarded as the pictorial and statistical "book of record" for virtually everything associated with the American Theater.

X-rated Jimmy

Willis took over the editorship of *Theatre World* after Blum. He claimed that the nude photos of Jimmy had been snapped by Earle Forbes, the magazine's staff photographer. "There was a very exhibitionistic quality in Jimmy," Willis said. For a while, Forbes was one of the world's premiere photographer of male nudes. Some of his work was eventually published in a book entitled *Reed Messengill's Uncovered—Rare Vintage Male Nudes*.

Willis also claimed that both Forbes and Blum not only owned a collection of Jimmy's nudes, but also nudes of other young performers, many of them posed before their subjects became famous. Among those cited by Rose included actors Rock Hudson and Warren Beatty, along with singers David Bowie, Elvis Presley, David Cassidy, and Jim Morrison.

The Bad and the Beautiful

Jimmy Dreams of a Screen Debut Dressed Only in His Underwear ...and of Stealing Kirk Douglas from Lana Turner

Brackett had many friends in Hollywood, but in many ways, the gay writer, George Bradshaw was his closest companion.

When both Bradshaw and Brackett were on the West Coast together, it became something of a tradition to spend Sunday afternoons with each other, sharing observations and catching up on the latest gossip.

From the beginning, Jimmy was rude, erratic, and rebellious around Bradshaw. Once, when Brackett was in a huddle with Bradshaw in the kitchen, both men heard Jimmy call out: "FIRE!"

Bradshaw rushed into the living room to discover a Queen Anne armchair on fire. Brackett was right behind him with a pitcher of water, which he used to douse the flames. Bradshaw thought he'd set the fire on purpose, despite Jimmy's apologies and assertions that he'd accidentally set fire to the chair with his cigarette.

Of course, Brackett was ready and willing to pay for the damages.

During their drive together from Bradshaw's back to Hollywood, Brackett lectured Jimmy like a stern father. "Do you really have to test my love by performing one outrageous stunt after another? You have my love, god damn it. So quit pulling this shit. The next thing I know, you'll be smashing up my car."

When Bradshaw talked to Brackett the next day, the writer said, "Naturally, you're invited over Sunday for brunch, but do you have to bring Jimmy with you?"

"Please understand that I'm afraid NOT to bring him. I don't trust him wandering around Los Angeles by himself on a Sunday afternoon. Who knows what trouble he'll find?"

"Okay, but I'll have the fire department standing by."

Jimmy's negative attitude about Bradshaw changed completely after he heard that the author was working on a Class A movie script entitled *Tribute to a Bad Man,* whose plot revolved around three betrayals catalyzed by the manipulations of a Hollywood producer. There was a small role in it that called for a sullen but exceedingly handsome young man. Bradshaw told Brackett. "I had your Jimmy in mind when I created this pivotal scene."

[After additional input from Charles Schnee, Bradshaw's original title was later changed to The Bad and the Beautiful. *A campy showcase forever after associated with the life and legend of Lana Turner, it was directed by Vincente Minnelli and released in 1952.*

That week, instead of adhering to their usual Sunday afternoon schedule, Brackett took Jimmy to Bradshaw's home on a Monday night, because Brackett wanted to meet Lana Turner, who had agreed to show up there at around

8PM. He knew many stars in Hollywood, but had never met Lana, who was one of his all-time, most fixated-upon favorites.

That Monday night at Bradshaw's, Brackett and Jimmy were each eagerly awaiting Lana's arrival, who didn't appear until 9:30PM. She had been driven to Bradshaw's house by an anonymous, shadowy-looking male escort who refused to join the gathering, opting instead to remain within her car, parked outside.

She politely accepted "gushing tributes" from both Jimmy and Brackett, as if it were her due. At one point during their conversation, she expressed her dislike of the leading men emerging from Hollywood of the 1950s, notably Marlon Brando and Monty Clift. "Give me Clark Gable or Robert Taylor any time, especially that handsome devil Tyrone Power. Errol Flynn was a darling, and I just adored John Hodiak, not to mention Victor Mature!"

Honey, don't fail to mention your Tarzan, Lex Barker," Bradshaw said. "Talk about sex appeal!"

"There were problems with him I don't care to discuss," she said, stiffly, changing the subject.

Lana had read the first draft of Bradshaw's film script, and she was thrilled with her role of Georgia Lorrison. "I think it might be my greatest part to date. For the daring car scene alone, when I leave the home of my lover who has betrayed me, I'll probably get an Oscar if I can pull it off. MGM kicked out poor Judy Garland, but I want to hold my own. Incidentally, I saw Judy two days ago. She's a pathetic little thing. Fired from *Annie Get Your Gun*. I think it's all downhill for her from now on, but not for me."

"Judy was good for my ego. She told me her greatest desire in life was to be Lana Turner. She said that compared to me, she was a polliwog, a tadpole on its way to becoming a frog."

At one point, Lana seemed to take notice of Jimmy, who was flattered by her attention. "Don't tell me: You want to be an actor?" she asked. "Please, not another Brando

Lana Turner and Kirk Douglas in a scene from *The Bad and the Beautiful* that, based on censorship standards of its day, was "shockingly erotic."

The first draft of the script had Lana discovering that her lover, as played by Kirk, also had a male lover, to be played by James Dean.

clone."

"Hell, no!" he said. "I have my own style and technique. I can act rings around Brando and make an audience actually understand what I'm saying."

"Good for you, dear heart." Within minutes after a final drink, Lana was ready to leave. "I've got a hot date waiting for me in the car. I would have invited him in, but I didn't want you guys to go ape-shit over him and steal him from me for the night."

*   *   *

The following Sunday afternoon, according to their ritual, Brackett and Jimmy were back at Bradshaw's home. This time, Bradshaw read a scene to them through which Jimmy might make his screen debut. "Can you imagine a guy like me making love on screen to Lana Turner?" Jimmy asked.

"Let's not get ahead of ourselves," Bradshaw cautioned. He outlined the scene for them, and it was, indeed, a dazzling one. For the first time, and against the Production Code, he wanted to blatantly depict homosexuality on the screen.

In his draft of the script, Georgia Lorrison, as played by Lana, arrives unexpectedly at the home of director Jonathon Shields (to be portrayed by Kirk Douglas). She confronts him in his foyer to demand an explanation and/or apology for his failure to escort her, as had been pre-arranged, to a premiere.

During their confrontation, a shadowy, mostly undressed male figure suddenly appears at the top of the stairs, having just emerged, it's made clear, from Shields' bedroom. It's a handsome young man clad only in a pair of boxer shorts. Without uttering a word, he stares enigmatically, perhaps with a sense of triumph, down at Lana.

"If Jimmy is assigned the part," Bradshaw predicted, "the girls will swoon and the gay men will go crazy."

Although Jimmy was vastly intrigued, Brackett suspected and feared that the scene would never pass the scrutiny of the censors.

"You won't have any spoken dialogue," Bradshaw said. "But your defiant face will show it all. You'll portray the man who stole the (male) lover of Lana Turner, one of the most desirable women on the planet."

Walter Pidgeon

INTRODUCES JIMMY TO SEX WITH HIS LONGTIME COMPANION
TOGETHER, THEY SEDUCE THE YOUNG ACTOR

Before Bradshaw headed back to New York, the cast of *Tribute to a Badman (aka, The Bad and the Beautiful)* had been approved by producer John Houseman. Vincente Minnelli, Judy Garland's former husband, had cast the major roles. In addition to Lana and Kirk Douglas, other leading actors included Walter Pidgeon, Dick Powell, Barry Sullivan, and Gloria Grahame.

Motivated in part by politics associated with the studio, Bradshaw hosted a cocktail party to which he invited the stars along with the film's producer and director. Lana had an important engagement that night and didn't show up, but the rest of the distinguished guests did.

Brackett had informed Jimmy that Minnelli was gay and that he would probably come on to him. That was more or less what happened, although the director's time was for the most part monopolized by his stars.

During the party, Jimmy got to spend at least twenty minutes with Houseman, who was not gay, but seemed genuinely interested in the young man as an actor. "Let me know how I can reach you. There's a picture coming up that might be ideal for you. And don't think that is some bullshit line. I like women. I really know of a role in an upcoming movie that you might be ideal for, but you'll have to pass a screen test."

Jimmy had been in Hollywood long enough not to be shocked at what transpired at parties there. But later, he was nonetheless surprised when Pidgeon engaged him in a long conversation on the oceanfront terrace.

Pidgeon? Gay? Could it be? It certainly appeared that way to Jimmy. Pidgeon asked if Jimmy could come to the address he provided on the upcoming Friday night at around 9PM. "I want to talk to you about your career."

Jimmy decided to do something impulsive. Pidgeon, even though his career was in decline, was one of the most influential stars in Hollywood. As a kid, he'd seen those Pidgeon and Greer Garson movies, including *Mrs. Miniver* (1942).

Before they parted, Jimmy kissed the veteran actor passionately on the lips. "That's so you won't forget me."

"I'll count the hours until we meet again."

***

Jimmy, as was his way, later confessed details of his sexual encounter with Walter Pidgeon to Brackett. Perhaps he had two reasons: One to make his spon-

Greer Garson with Walter Pidgeon in the hugely influential *Mrs. Miniver*, one of the greatest tear-jerking propaganda films to emerge from the early days of World War II.

sor/lover jealous, and perhaps also to prove that he could inaugurate contacts with major stars all on his own.

Hedda Hopper once labeled Pidgeon as "the only guaranteed straight man in Hollywood, and I'm not using the expression in the comedic sense."

The Canadian actor's homosexuality was whispered about by the elite of Hollywood and once came to the attention of that homophobe, Louis B. Mayer at MGM.

But public or written exposure of Pidgeon's gay life has been rare. A notable exception occurred when Hollywood's "star fucker," Scotty Bowers, published his memoirs, *Full Service,* in 2012. The book was reviewed twice in *The New York Times* and received the endorsement of such skeptics as Gore Vidal.

Bowers serviced both male and female stars. He opens his book with a description of his seduction by Pidgeon at the home of his longtime lover, Jacques Potts, a milliner to the stars. Despite the status of Potts and Pidgeon as lovers, Pidgeon was married to Ruth Walker, whom he'd wed in 1931.

The following Friday, after a rendezvous at their designated location, Pidgeon drove Jimmy up Benedict Canyon in Beverly Hills to a spacious, elegantly furnished home. He told Jimmy that the house had been built by Harold Lloyd, the famous comic actor of the silent screen in the 1920s.

Potts was at the door to greet "Pidge," as he called him. He kissed his lover before turning to appraise their conquest. Then he smiled his approval. "Dear boy," he said to Pidge. "You sure know how to pick 'em. This kid is impressive, indeed."

Jimmy resented being treated like a "piece of meat," as he'd later tell Brackett, but decided to go along with the act for the money.

After being offered a drink, Jimmy was invited out onto the terrace that encircled a heart-shaped swimming pool. Since it was a hot night, Pidgeon suggested he might like to take a dip, informing Jimmy that he didn't need to wear a swim suit since Pott's servant wasn't scheduled to arrive until morning.

As Jimmy later confessed, "I sort of got off on the attention and compliments they gave me. When I emerged from the pool, both men had undressed, and they toweled me off."

In the bedroom, each was a skilled oral artist, taking their turns with me while they jerked off. At the climax of the evening, Pidge "topped Potts as I was invited to watch," Jimmy said.

It appears that Jimmy, during the next few weeks, made a total of three more visits to Lloyd's former mansion. The sexual routine was the same except on one occasion, when Jimmy arrived with fellow actor/hustler Nick Adams, with whom he was living at the time, during a period when Brackett had relocated in Chicago.

Although both Potts and "Pidge" found Jimmy the cuter of the two, much attention and praise was heaped on Adams' exceptional endowment. Jimmy later claimed, "I watched both men work Nick over at the same time, and it was some workout. Nick and I each left with a hundred-dollar bill in of our pockets."

***

Regrettably for both Bradshaw and Jimmy, Vincente Minnelli rejected Bradshaw's first screenplay and even changed the title to *The Bad and the Beautiful.* Charles Schnee was called in to drastically revise it, and in 1952, the *film noir* would win five Oscars out of six nominations.

In the rewrite, Jimmy's possible role was rewritten and the gender of the interloper emerging from Douglas' bedroom was changed from male to female. Minnelli cast the emerging starlet, the sultry brunette, Elaine Stewart, into the role.

Even though he never appeared in a film scene with Lana, Jimmy's fascination with the blonde goddess continued.

Years later, when he was in the process of searching for a place to live in West Hollywood, his prospective landlord, David Gould, showed Jimmy the master bedroom of a fully furnished house for rent.

The previous tenant of 1541 Sunset Plaza Drive, had been Lana Turner. "She slept in this very bed—and never alone," Gould claimed to Jimmy.

"I'll sign the lease," Jimmy said. "I'll be sleeping in Lana's bed myself. And never alone!"

***

Jimmy would later dismiss and eventually, abandon "all of Brackett's social whirl of gossipy queens and cocktail party chatter. It was pure hogwash. There were two favorite topics, depending on one's sexual preference. 'How big is his cock?' or 'What size are her tits?' I grew bored by many of Rogers' friends. I was treated like a court jester, ready to perform at any minute, preferably with my pants down. I'm not just some dick to suck or rosebud to plug. I've got talent. I want to make it on my merits as an actor—not as some good-looking Hollywood stud hustling his ass."

Years later, on the set of *Rebel Without a Cause,* he would reflect with director Nicholas Ray about this period of his life . "Behind Roger's back, these jerks would invite me to dinner on their luxurious oceanfront terraces. After a few drinks, their greedy little hands would be closing in on my dick. I knew that if I kept this up, the year would be 1975, and I would be some aging ex-pretty boy waiting tables or pumping gas. In Hollywood, they drain you to the last drop and then you're discarded as yesterday's toy."

"Now that I'm a star, I've got these jerks—many of them out of work today—by the balls."

Brackett was hip and well-informed about which stars were gay "or used to be gay."

Jimmy was shocked to learn that such macho icons as Gary Cooper and John Wayne, during their early days, were known to lie on the casting couch.

He and Brackett became regulars at The Club, a watering hole which attracted gay men late at night to its darkened precincts on Hollywood Boulevard.

Jimmy invited his university friend from his days at UCLA, James Bellah, to Brackett's apartment. Bellah later recalled, "This ad agency guy flew into the living room on gossamer wings. When he went to the kitchen to get us some ice, I turned to Jimmy and said, 'What the hell? This guy is queer as a three-dollar bill.'"

"So what?" Jimmy responded, defiantly.

One night, Jimmy asked Brackett to go with him to see Marlon Brando perform in the filmed (1951) version of Tennessee Williams' *A Streetcar Named Desire.* It would mark the eighth time that Jimmy had seen the movie.

According to Brackett, "Although he would never admit it, Jimmy was mesmerized by the screen acting of Marlon Brando, who would loom so large in his future. The two actors were very much alike, although Jimmy would almost slug you if you ever compared him to Brando. I think he was also strongly attracted sexually to Brando. It was like a schoolgirl crush that grew more serious until he actually stalked Brando at night."

"Unlike the lies I've transmitted to many an interviewer, in which I stated that I hooked up with him because I believed in his talent, from the beginning, when I first met him in that parking lot, I wanted to get in the kid's pants. He was just my type, real cocky."

"I didn't admire all that Method acting crap and that Brando posturing, but Jimmy certainly did. One night I found him imitating Brando in front of the mirror."

"A lot of people have referred to our affair as a father-son relationship, that is,

Marlon Brando, as Stanley Kowalski in Tennessee Williams' *A Streetcar Named Desire,* mesmerized James Dean.

Elia Kazan, who directed both actors, said, "Marlon as Apollo is driving the Sun Chariot. But he's looking back to see an even brighter ball of fire on the distant horizon."

if I'd fathered Jimmy when I was only fifteen. If it were father and son, then it was pure incest from the beginning."

As William Bast later claimed, "Jimmy was eager to learn. He sapped the minds of Brackett's friends as a bloodsucker saps the strength of an unsuspecting man."

To his straight friends, Jimmy dismissed his arrangement with Brackett "as a meal ticket."

It was around this time that Jimmy became worried that he'd be drafted into the Army, fighting in a war for South Korea. Harry S Truman had upped the draft quotas in the summer of 1950.

Jimmy had been contacted by his Selective Service Board in Grant County, Indiana. He showed Bracket their letter that night, wondering if he should inform the board that he was a conscientious objector.

Brackett had another idea. A few days later, he took him to a gay psychiatrist (Dean J. Taylor of Canada) whom he'd met at a party.

After a long session with Jimmy, at which Brackett sat in, Taylor, for a fee, agreed to write a letter to the Selective Service Board of Indiana on behalf of Jimmy. In his claim, he stated that "James Dean is a hopeless psychotic, DO NOT GIVE THIS YOUNG MAN A FIREARM."

Bracket had left the room an hour before the end of Jimmy's interview with Taylor. Jimmy later informed Brackett "I had to prove to the good doctor that I was indeed a homosexual."

"And how did you do that?" Brackett asked.

"That's for you to imagine."

Later, thanks mostly to Taylor's intervention, Jimmy was classified 4-F.

It has been suggested that Jimmy did not need to resort to evasive tactics to avoid being drafted into the Army. After an eye examination, because of his severe nearsightedness, he was pronounced "all but blind." That defect alone seemed enough to have justified his designation as 4-F._

***

Scotty Bowers either tricked with or supplied handsome members of his former Marine Crops to a bevy of Hollywood stars, including Charles Laughton (who ate shit sandwiches), Tyrone Power (a fellow Marine), Errol Flynn, Spencer Tracy, George Cukor, Randolph Scott, Cole Porter (who was known to have blown twenty Marines in one night), Rock Hudson, and Noël Coward.

As Bowers related in his memoirs, he even sold himself to such unlikely persons as J. Edgar Hoover and the Duke of Windsor. He also supplied carefully screened young women to Katharine Hepburn and the Duchess of Windsor.

He knew many of the handsome young movie stars of the 1950s, usually servicing them himself before supplying them with a steady stream of "tricks" for sale.

Bowers had only one encounter with Jimmy Dean, and he wasn't impressed at all, as he'd later relay in his memoirs. Sometimes, Bowers found work moonlighting as a bartender at private parties, as he did one night at the home of the Brazilian millionaire, Ozz Francesca, who maintained a strange friendship with Jimmy that was never fully explored. Francesca was gay, sharing his home with his understanding wife and their daughter. For a while, he reigned in Hollywood circles and was known for hosting some of the most lavish, star-studded parties in town.

At one party that Bowers worked, the guests were formally dressed. Jimmy showed up in blue jeans and a white T-shirt. Bowers remembered him "moping around the room, puffing on a cigarette and looking decidedly bored and gloomy."

At Francesca's party, Jimmy, according to Bowers, displayed the same anti-social behavior he presented during visits to the homes of Brackett's friends.

At one point, Jimmy dropped his lit cigarette on Francesca's heirloom Persian carpet and crushed it out with his foot. Bowers rushed to clean it up.

Later, at the bar, Jimmy demanded a glass of champagne. Opening a bottle of Dom Perignon, Bowers poured a glass of bubbly into a tulip-shaped, rose-colored glass.

Jimmy took only one sip of it before making a face as if he'd swallowed slop, and poured the contents of the glass onto the carpet. "Bartender, serve me something else, and it'd better be drinkable this time!"

Bowers later dismissed Jimmy "as a prissy little queen, moody and unpredictable. He had a few romantic flings with women, but from all reports, he was essentially gay."

One of Bower's major sources of information was one of his clients, Monty Clift, who had had a sexual involvement with Jimmy in New York. Bowers found Clift "another temperamental, moody queen with a surprisingly vicious tongue."

Unlike Jimmy, Clift was exclusively gay, but none of the tricks that Bowers sent over pleased him. "The guy's prick was an inch too long, or an inch too short. His hair was not parted properly, or his feet were too small, his toes too long, there was always something wrong. Monty was never satisfied."

Bowers also found Jimmy's friend, Roddy McDowall "excessively fussy and hard to please."

Both Jimmy and Bowers, at different times, also tricked with actor Anthony Perkins, who was engaged in a long-term relationship with Tab Hunter, although he constantly cheated on his lover. Bowers admitted that, "I tricked with him myself on numerous occasions, but Tony, like Monty, was very fussy, always demanding to be fixed up with 'someone different.'"

In his memoirs, Jimmy was the only movie star that Bowers actually despised. He seemed to have gotten on with all the other big names at the time.

He wrote, "It was only a matter of time before Jimmy did himself in. He was his own worst enemy."

***

Jimmy and his former roommate, William Bast, had recovered from the feud that had begun when Bast had decided to move out of their shared apartment. They agreed to meet over a bowl of chili at Barney's Beanery. Jimmy won Bast over by flashing his charm school smile and saying, "Let's tongue kiss and make up. I'll suck yours if you'll suck mine."

"Are you sure you're referring to tongues?" Bast asked jokingly. The two men embraced and sat down to eat.

Barney warned them, "There will be no man-hugging in my dive."

Bast later reflected that Jimmy's life with Brackett had changed him a lot. "He had acquired more polish, seemingly overnight, or at least learned the rudimentary rules of social behavior. But as I was soon to find out, he could still revert to his bad boy image."

"The shitkicker from Indiana was on the way to becoming an urban sophisticate," Bast claimed. "I don't want to exaggerate too much. Noël Coward he would never be. But suddenly, he was showing off by talking about French Impressionists, Colette, the Cubists, literature, the brilliance of Stravinsky. My country boy had also joined that hideous array of name-dropping Hollywood. He could drop quite a few: Jack Benny, Walter Pidgeon, Clifton, Webb, Cole Porter, Joan Crawford, Judy Garland, Lana Turner. I was jealous...I mean, really, really jealous."

En route with Bast to Brackett's apartment, Jimmy farted three times. "It was that second helping of chili," he claimed.

Brackett was "in residence," as he called it, and Bast later recorded his negative impression of the ad agency producer. "Brackett struck me as an arch, foppish villain out of a Dickens novel or a naughty Max Beerbohm dandy. His unusually long neck supported an avian head, on the thin beak of which was perched large, horn-rimmed glasses, giving him a somewhat owlish look. It took little time for Jimmy to fall prey to this chicken hawk. I think that if it has been Dracula himself, with Hollywood connections, Jimmy would have been a voluntary blood donor. I might have considered a Sugar Daddy myself—but never this Wicked Bitch of the East."

Indecent Exposure

How Jimmy Met and "Made It" with Goddess-turned-Prostitute, Barbara Payton

One Saturday when Brackett had an appointment with some client and didn't want to drag Jimmy along, Jimmy and Bast agreed to drive down to Laguna together for a day at the beach. For the first time since Bast had known him, Jimmy had two-hundred dollars in his wallet. Perhaps to show off his new wealth, Jimmy invited Bast to a chic fish restaurant with a swimming pool and rooms to rent upstairs.

The figure of a beautiful blonde caught Jimmy's eye. It was the notorious actress, Barbara Payton, who was wearing the bottom half of a very small polka dot bikini. *[aka, a "cache-sexe" ("sex hider" or a very small triangular-shaped garment designed to barely conceal the genitals.)]* Everything else she had was on ample display.

Perhaps to impress Bast with his heterosexual credentials, Jimmy surveyed Payton from top to bottom, claiming, "The hot bitch has more body than a Renaissance Madonna. I'm going to the car to get my sketch pad."

Back with his pad, Jimmy approached Payton, and she seemed flattered to pose for him. From a distance of twenty feet, Bast witnessed their interchange, although Jimmy did not invite him over.

Within the hour, Jimmy disappeared with Payton, heading for a room she'd rented above the restaurant.

The rooms upstairs opened onto balconies that overlooked the pool. At one point, Jimmy appeared "stark raving nude for about a minute on one of the balconies," according to Bast. "A ripple went across the crowd as Jimmy showed off his junk to the voyeurs below."

By five o'clock, Jimmy once again joined Bast beside the pool. He claimed he had to clear out of Payton's room because she'd gotten her calendar mixed up and had invited both of her lovers, Franchot Tone and Tom Neal, to Laguna at the same time. She'd told Jimmy she didn't know which one she wanted to get rid of. "Joan Crawford and Bette Davis always called Franchot 'The Jawbreaker" and Tom is known as 'Donkey Dong.' So you see what a difficult choice it is for me to make."

Jimmy later bragged to Bast that "Blondie is one

Barbara Payton before her decline and collapse. "I am not ashamed," she stated in a memoir.

in a million. An hour or two with her is like a month with any other broad. She's not only got a great body, but the bitch knows how to use it in bed. She's electrifying. I'm totally satisfied from my nostrils to my little toe. She has a sexual technique that must have been developed over two-thousand years."

Later that night, back in Los Angeles, Jimmy asked Brackett, "Just who in hell is this actress floozie, Barbara Payton? Someone told me she's a movie star."

Before the night was over, Jimmy ended up knowing more about Payton than he really wanted to handle.

[Payton, "the brassy blonde with a hooker heart" flashed briefly across the movie screens of the early 1950s before she devolved into an alcoholic, drug-addicted prostitute. Marlon Brando, her former lover, once referred to her as "Hollywood's Number One Trollop."

Still young and beautiful at the time Jimmy seduced her, Payton had drifted from the cold winds of Minnesota to the warm beds of such A-list players as Howard Hughes and Gregory Peck. She was graced with sky-blue eyes and a fair complexion that revealed her Norwegian ancestry.

Hollywood's most sexually motivated attorney, Greg Bautzer, once said, "You have never been given a blow-job until you've been on the receiving end of Barbara's skilled mouth and tongue. I've been blown by the best of them— Lana Turner, Judy Garland, Joan Crawford, Marlene Dietrich—you name 'em. Barbara takes top prize."

Hughes once told his pimp, Johnny Meyer, "Payton will do anything in bed—and I mean anything. If you want to piss in her mouth, that's okay with blondie."

Payton had been the Queen of the Tabloids between 1950 and 1952. The single most scandalous movie star ever to emerge from the placid 1950s, Payton dumped her husband in the late 40s and headed for Hollywood determined to make it big. "If a blonde with absolutely no talent like Lana Turner can become a movie star, then I know I can too," she announced to anyone interested.

When her test at RKO didn't work out, she ended up as a carhop at Stan's Drive-In at the corner of Sunset Boulevard and Highland Avenue. Hustling tips and peddling chocolate milkshakes and blood-letting hamburgers, she also did another type of hustling on the side.

The riches from her nocturnal activities allowed her to buy an expensive wardrobe. Soon she was seen at all the posh clubs, including the Trocadero, Ciro's, and El Mocambo. She was hailed as "the Queen of the Night."

Her love nest on Cheremoya Avenue was paid for in 1949 by none other than the much-married Bob Hope. When the comedian refused to give her an additional $5,000 a week in "spending money," she threatened to blackmail him in exchange for her silence. Hope settled what was called "a huge sum of money" on her, but she went through all her new loot in just three months, claiming, "I have expensive tastes."

A.C. Lyles, the movie producer, once claimed that "Payton never had an itch she didn't scratch." Minor actor Mickey Knox recalled that she'd kept him in bed for three days and nights, all in one stretch. "I had to crawl out of that dump on my hands and knees. What a workout! What a pussy!"

She even got involved with James Cagney, who secured her a contract at Warner Brothers for $5,000 a week. He put her in Kiss Tomorrow Goodbye (1950). The film had hardly been released before she was swallowing Gary Cooper's mighty sword near the sound stages of Dallas while taking in $10,000 a week. Suddenly, she was seen around town with the classy New York actor, Franchot Tone, who had been married to Joan Crawford in the 1930s. Tone was twenty-two years older than Payton, and he lavished expensive gifts on her, including jewelry.

During her affair with Tone, Payton also fell for rock-jawed Tom Neal, a sort of dime store John Garfield. Almost sadistically, Payton played one man against the other and would eventually marry each of them, thereby creating two of the shortest marriages ever recorded in Hollywood history.

Neal learned about Payton's involvement with Tone, and on the night of September 13, 1951, emerged from the bushes outside Payton's apartment and attacked Tone, smashing his nose and breaking one of his cheekbones. Tone was rushed to the hospital with a brain concussion and remained in a coma for eighteen hours. Morning newspapers headlined this "Love Brawl" across the world.

In time, Payton would descend into the status of a drunk on Skid Row. She moved deeper and deeper into heroin addiction and—among other professions—became a lesbian-for-hire. She ended up a broken down and snaggle-toothed whore working Santa Monica Boulevard, jumping inside the cars of strangers and giv-

One of the most notorious love triangles of the 1950s spun around Franchot Tone (top photo), along with Barbara Payton and Tom Neal.

As the usually elegant Tone ungraciously described his marriage (1951-1952) to Payton, "I went from Joan Crawford and Bette Davis to a blonde whore."

ing fast blow-jobs for ten dollars while her clients kept the motor running.

In February of 1967, Payton, unconscious, was found in the parking lot of Thrifty's Drug Store in Hollywood. At first, sanitation workers thought that her reclining body was a bag of trash. She'd been living on the streets for the past three months. She was rushed to Los Angeles County General Hospital.

After her release from the hospital, she went to stay with her parents, both of whom were also alcoholics. In May of 1967 her mother found her slumped over a toilet. Her daughter was dead. An autopsy revealed that she'd died of a heart attack and liver failure just six months shy of her 40th birthday.]

Jimmy Studies Method Acting with James Whitmore

"THE POOR MAN'S SPENCER TRACY"

Their friendship renewed, Bast enticed Jimmy into taking acting lessons from James Whitmore from premises on the upper floor of the Brentwood Country Mart, a shopping area at 26th Street and San Vicente Boulevard near the boundary between Santa Monica and Los Angeles.

Whitmore was not a Hollywood pretty boy, but a serious actor with a stocky build, a rather gruff personality, and a reputation as a blunt conversationalist.

As regards roles he was considered suitable for, some Hollywood talent agents described him as "the poor man's Spencer Tracy," and "a less expensive Spencer Tracy type."

He preferred acting on stage to working in Hollywood movies, but, as he admitted when he moved to the West Coast, "a paycheck comes in handy."

Before meeting Whitmore, Jimmy had seen him in the 1949 World War II drama, *Battleground,* in which Whitmore had played a battle weary, tobacco-chewing Army sergeant.

[For his role in Battleground, *Whitmore won an Oscar nomination as Best Supporting Actor. He also starred with Marilyn Monroe in* The Asphalt Jungle *(1950), and with Nancy Davis in* The Next Voice You Hear *(also 1950). He would later play a dumb thug in the movie versions of* Kiss Me Kate *(1953), and Gloria Grahame's grizzled father in* Oklahoma! *(1955).]*

In a classroom with about a dozen dedicated actors, male and female, Jimmy interpreted Whitmore as a stern teacher, suggesting that it

James Whitmore, depicted above in *Battleground,* evolved into a noteworthy acting coach, exposing Jimmy to the tenets of "The Method."

took "blood, sweat, and tears" to become a successful actor. "Don't go into acting seeking movie star fame or glory. For every Marilyn Monroe, there are ten thousand other dyed blondes taking the train back to the Middle West, hoping to find a husband who'll let them be a housewife. There's personal gratification in acting, supreme gratification, in fact, but it will cost you plenty to obtain it."

At first, Jimmy did not impress Whitmore at all. The older actor found him "shy and very introverted. He never volunteered to act out any scene before the class, always holding back, giving nothing of himself. But in time, he began to open up a bit, and came to sense that he possessed a great talent, though masked behind all his neurotic behavior."

During the weeks that followed, when Whitmore saw actual demonstrations of Jimmy's acting talent, he urged him to abandon Hollywood and head for New York. There, he could seek work on the stage and in the burgeoning TV industry that was turning out dramas by the day. Before the film sets and production facilities of most television shows had moved to the West Coast, the early TV industry was based in Manhattan. Jimmy later confided to Brackett and others what happened when Whitmore asked Bast and Jimmy to perform an improvised scene in front of the class.

Jimmy's assignment involved the portrayal of a poor college student who had stolen a valuable watch. Bast would portray a jeweler who had been warned by the police to be on the lookout for a young man who might fit Jimmy's description, who would arrive with a (stolen) watch with intention of getting it repaired so that he could then sell it for a lot of money.

The task of the character played by Bast involved detaining Jimmy's character "at any cost" until the police could arrive. In the ensuing struggle over the watch, Bast denounced Jimmy as "a pompous bastard" and accused him of being "a nearsighted little son of a bitch." [This line in the script echoed what the two men had said one night in a fight over Jimmy's failure to pay half the rent on the penthouse they shared.]

Suddenly, without meaning to, and in front of the class, Bast and Jimmy got into an onstage wrestling match that turned violent. At one point, Jimmy was on top of Bast, staring into his eyes as he choked him.

Bast later recalled, "Those were the eyes of a killer staring down at me. All of our past conflicts seemed to bubble up in Jimmy. It was no longer an actor's improvisation. This was serious."

It appeared to Whitmore that if he didn't intervene, Jimmy would choke Bast to death.

Later, as Jimmy related to Brackett, "In my worst moment, I couldn't control myself and I almost suffocated Bast. Now I've got to confess something. I'm not proud of this—in fact, I'm ashamed—but that act of violence against him gave me a raging hard-on."

In 1955, Jimmy discussed his workshop experience in Whitmore's classroom with a reporter for *Seventeen* magazine. "I learned a lot from him. One thing he said helped me more than anything. He taught me the difference between acting as a soft job and acting as a difficult art. Another thing, he warned me never to be caught acting."

"Whitmore opened my eyes. There is always someone in one's life—at least there should be—who opens your eyes so that you can see for the first time. For me, it was definitely Whitmore. He told me to go to New York, and he was right. That's when things started to happen for me. He also changed my life forever by giving me a letter of introduction to *[the famous director]* Elia Kazan.

Only weeks before his untimely death, Jimmy once again extolled the importance of Whitmore in his life as an actor, ignoring any mention of the spade work of Rogers Brackett.

Brackett's composer friend, Alec Wilder, knew why. "The kid lived in terror as he became famous that his homosexual life would be exposed. He didn't want the world to know he'd been some plaything to some older, male, TV producer."

* * *

Whereas he'd been deeply impressed with the dramatic potentialities of *Hamlet,* Jimmy became even more enthralled with the symbolism of *The Little Prince,* a copy of which had been provided to him by Brackett.

The original French-language classic by Antoine de Saint-Exupéry became Jimmy's Bible. He read it and reread it, and soon was quoting lines from it.

One of his favorite excerpts from it was: "*Love does not consist in gazing at each other, but in looking outward together in the same direction.*" To anyone willing to listen, Jimmy maintained that the novella contained "some of the most profound observations of the human condition ever written. It shows how life really should be lived."

[Penned as a French-language novella or "adult fable" in 1943 The Little Prince *(aka Le Petit Prince) is the third most translated book in the world, and was voted in France as the best book of the 20th Century. Translated into 250 languages, it has sold more than 150 million copies, with an annual sales*

A post World War II best-seller, translated from the French. It influenced James Dean more than any other book he ever read.

rate of two million a year. Styled as an arch and artful children's book, it focuses on its author's wistful conclusions about human existence and love. Emotional "truths" are expressed by a fox to an isolated and highly spiritual alien child (*The Little Prince*) whom the author/narrator discovers wandering in a desert:

> *On ne voit bien qu'avec le cœur. L'essentiel est invisible pour les yeux.* ("One sees clearly only with the heart. What is essential is invisible to the eyes.");
> *Tu deviens responsable pour toujours de ce que tu as apprivoisé.* ("You become responsible, forever, for what you have tamed."); *and*
> *C'est le temps que tu as perdu pour ta rose qui fait ta rose si importante.* ("It is the time you have lost for your rose that makes your rose so important.")

Jimmy became obsessed with turning *The Little Prince* into a movie, although Brackett warned that the novella, in part because of its abbreviated symbolism and poetic brevity, would be difficult to adapt into a screenplay. Jimmy wanted to play the aviator who counsels and guides a young boy who wants to learn about life.

To pacify Jimmy, Brackett made some queries at CBS and learned before the end of the same day that film rights to the novella had been purchased by Hedy Lamarr, the sultry brunette screen goddess from Vienna, hailed in some quarters as "the most beautiful woman in the world."

Jimmy had been enthralled by Lamarr's performance as the exotic temptress in *Samson and Delilah* (1949), the steamy and campy Cecil B. De-Mille epic co-starring Victor Mature.

Behind Brackett's back, Jimmy was continuing his sessions with the psychiatrist, Dr. Dean Taylor. The Canadian was counseling him without expectation of payment, in return for Jimmy unzipping after an hour of pouring out his troubles.

After one of their sessions, the doctor told him that he had to hurry and get cleaned up and that Jimmy had to leave. "I'm seeing Hedy Lamarr at five o'clock."

Jimmy was stunned by the news. It was the equivalent of one of those weird coincidences that happen within the context of a Charles Dickens novel. As instructed, Jimmy left Taylor's inner office, but remained in the doctor's waiting room, with his secretary, for Lamarr's arrival.

Outfitted in a black suit with mauve accessories, Lamarr made a glamorous entrance fifteen minutes later. She walked past Jimmy as the secretary escorted her into Taylor's inner office.

As Jimmy remained in place for an hour, he flirted with the impressionable young girl behind the desk. He got her to agree to introduce him to Lamarr when she emerged from the psychiatrist's inner office. He told her that he was a great fan of the glamorous star, and that he wanted her autograph. He also agreed to go out on a date with the rather unattractive secretary.

Later, after Taylor uncovered how Jimmy had maneuvered, he said, "I'm not surprised that Hedy found Jimmy enticing. I've never known her to turn down the amorous attention of any handsome young man. She's oversexed."

Among other reasons, Lamarr was consulting a psychiatrist because of conflicts associated with her career. Although *Samson and Delilah* had been a worldwide hit, she had recently made two flops in a row—*A Lady Without a Passport* (1950) and *Copper Canyon* (also 1950), in which her best scenes weren't caught on film—i.e., episodes within the shrill and brittle feud she maintained throughout production with her leading man, Ray Milland, who detested her.

Long without an MGM contract, and in the process of visibly aging, Hedy's career options were narrowing. She expressed her rampant fears that she'd end up "on Poverty Row," chained to a dwindling roster of low-budget, badly scripted potboilers, or—even worse—ignored forever.

It is not known exactly what Jimmy said to Lamarr after she emerged from her session with Taylor. He obviously delivered his pitch about bringing *The Little Prince* to the screen, and perhaps exaggerated the influence and intentions of Brackett, who might, he insinuated, be willing to produce it.

Lamarr seemed to find Jimmy very appealing, as he focused upon her the full power of his manly charm and sex appeal. She agreed to receive him at her residence that evening at eight o'clock.

In the only suit he owned, he arrived on her doorstep exactly at eight. He was ushered into her living room by a butler. Lamarr had carefully and artfully arranged herself on a sofa.

He was stunned by her glitzy appearance. She wore a full-bodied, off-the-shoulder turquoise gown that had been designed by Edith Head for her performance in *Copper Canyon.*

Over drinks and dinner, there were only small references to *The Little Prince.* Lamarr was the most self-enchanted actress in Hollywood, or so Jimmy believed, knowing that competition for that label was stiff.

Two views of Hedy Lamarr: *lower photo,* in *Copper Canyon* (1949), the last film she'd made before meeting Jimmy. Her career was in decline.

91

She expressed numerous complaints: "I'm tired of hearing that people adore me for my beauty. I want to be adored for myself, for the person who inhabits my soul. My beauty has lever led to my finding love."

"I may be the world's most beautiful woman, but I was a disappointment to my parents. They wanted a boy. My father was a very large man, and very ferocious. One time, I wore this red ribbon in my hair, thinking it would please him. It did not. I learned he hated bows. He beat me severely."

Her main concern was that she was moving into "the dangerous years" for a woman in Hollywood. She had been born in 1913 in Vienna, and now was living in America in the '50s. "Many Hollywood actresses commit suicide at this time in their lives. They can't stand the emotional strain of a fading career."

"I can get you involved in bringing *The Little Prince* to the screen," Jimmy promised. "You still have the rights, don't you?"

"Indeed I do," she said. "But I must warn you. I may look like a delicate hot-house flower, but I'm one strong negotiator. You must tell your producer friend that I don't sell my rights cheaply."

Jimmy didn't return to Brackett's apartment until 2AM. He didn't tell Brackett or Bast what had transpired with Lamarr. It was obvious that she had seduced him, as she had many other young men and even women. If legend is to be believed, she had even been seduced by Adolf Hitler, defining him afterward as "under-endowed and with only one testicle."

Months later, when *The New York Journal-American* announced that Lamarr was arriving in New York, Jimmy did tell Alec Wilder that he'd been sexually intimate with the star. "She was a *femme fatale* all right. Very demanding in bed. Very hard to satisfy. I pictured her as the Black Widow spider."

"My God," Wilder said. "I don't know about the Hitler thing, or even the Mussolini claim, but I know of some of the other men who have preceded you into *La Lamarr's* boudoir: Howard Hughes, Charles Boyer, Errol Flynn, Chaplain, Clark Gable, David Niven, and Senator John Kennedy."

To Jimmy, she confessed that the men in her life had ranged from a classic case of impotence—a Texan, no less—to a whip-wielding sadist who enjoyed sex only after he tied her up.

***

Although Brackett reported that he was shopping *The Little Prince* to potential movie producers, Jimmy didn't believe him. This led to a brutal fight, during the heat of which Jimmy stormed out of the apartment and disappeared for two days.

"You could have found a producer if you'd wanted to," Jimmy said to

Brackett accusatorily after he returned. "You just want to keep me tied to you so I can't become a star myself."

[The Little Prince *finally made it to the screen in 1974 as a British movie directed by Stanley Donen, and it did not include an onscreen appearance from Hedy. The role of the aviator, so ferociously coveted by Jimmy, was assigned to Richard Kiley after Richard Burton rejected an offer to play it. The young prince was portrayed by Steven Warner. The musical score by Alan Jay Lerner and Frederick Lowe was not particularly memorable.*

Meanwhile, Hedy had devoted her time to other pursuits, including another painful bout of plastic surgeries, and endless rewrites of a screenplay co-authored with Christopher Taaj. Entitled Untamed, *it was about a Viennese* femme fatale *who become romantically involved with a brutal Teutonic dictator until he discovers that she is a Jewess. For her description of this European goddess, she surprised a reporter by saying that for inspiration, she had drawn upon the persona of four different American movie stars—Judy Garland, Montgomery Clift, Marilyn Monroe, and James Dean.*

"I'll sure have to wait and see how you combined those four all-American stars into a European femme fatale," *the newsman had queried.*

"An artist sometimes draws inspiration from the strangest sources," Lamarr responded.]

AN ANGUISHED, ALIENATED SCENE WHEREIN

Jimmy, With His Gay Patron, Visits His Father

Rogers Brackett was anxious to meet Winton Dean, Jimmy's estranged father, so one Sunday afternoon Jimmy drove his "surrogate" father figure, Brackett himself, to the modest Dean home in Reseda, California, north of the campus at UCLA , which Jimmy had briefly attended.

The ostensible goal of the visit involved hauling away mementos from Jimmy's schoolboy days in Indiana. Winton had stored boxes of his son's memorabilia in a leaky woodshed in his backyard.

Later, Brackett recalled that visit to Winton's home, where he lived with his wife, the former Ethel Case. To Brackett, the home evoked his favorite novel about Hollywood, Nathaniel West's *Day of the Locust.* In Jimmy's former bedroom was a small, caged, colony of chinchillas, which the Deans were raising to eventually sell for their fur.

Jimmy and Brackett tried to make small talk with Winton, but both the son and the visitor found him unwilling to communicate. The hostility between father and son was too apparent, and it became clear from the two or three remarks he made that Winton suspected that "something perverted" was going on between Jimmy and his older "roommate."

"As for Ethel, she disappeared into the kitchen and didn't come out even to tell Jimmy goodbye," Brackett said.

***

On another occasion, Jimmy drove William Bast to visit his father and step-mother. "Two less responsive creatures I have seldom encountered," Bast recalled. He found Ethel "mousy and shy, Winton reserved and monosyllabic."

Bast later wrote that he felt sorry for Jimmy, "as he twisted himself in knots trying to please his father."

He also suggested that Jimmy performed a virtual tap dance for his father. "We smelled something good that Ethel was cooking in the kitchen, but we were offered only a cup of coffee. Both of us were hungry."

Bast claimed that he found Winton "a dreadful, stupid, uncaring father. He was awful with his son, even when he became successful. Instead of taking pride in Jimmy's sudden fame, Winton was jealous of his achievements."

Jimmy complained to his father about his transportation, explaining how hard it was to move around Los Angeles in search of a job. Two weeks later, Winton delivered a battered 1939 Chevy, which had otherwise been sitting, unused, in his garage, long ago replaced with a newer vehicle.

Gradually, over a period of months, both Bast and Brackett managed to elicit some meager biography from Jimmy about his childhood years in Indiana.

***

Jimmy's father, Winton, had been born into a Quaker family which had settled in Indiana in 1815. A tall, very taciturn man, Winton worked as a dental technician at a local veterans' hospital in Marion.

Born into a Methodist family, Mildred Wilson was Jimmy's mother, the daughter of a factory worker. Short and a bit plump, she was rumored to be part Indian, as evidenced by her complexion and black eyes. Quiet and sensitive, given to daydreaming, she played the piano and often escaped to books.

Jimmy was born six months after his parents' marriage, on February 8, 1931. They lived as a family together at the poetic-sounding Seven Gables apartment complex in Marion, Indiana, which is about seventy miles north of Indianapolis.

Mildred was fond of poetry, citing Lord Byron as her favorite. She decided to name her newborn James Byron in honor of that poet.

The Dean family moved frequently, and Jimmy was a very unhealthy child,

94

suffering from frequent vomiting, rashes on his skin, diarrhea, nosebleeds, and other maladies. Their causes were unknown. However, it was later speculated that Mildred painted every apartment they moved into, using paint that contained dangerous toxins which may have been the reason for Jimmy's chronic bad health.

He was four years old when his family moved to Greater Los Angeles, living in Santa Monica while Winton worked at the local hospital.

As Jimmy grew up, he became a stubborn child. Winton believed in "bare butt" spanking, hoping to force his rebellious son to behave. That didn't work. Years later, a psychiatrist who examined Jimmy in Los Angeles suggested the possibility that his taste for being spanked by his sexual partners in advance of anal penetration had originated with his father's harsh discipline.

When he was old enough, Jimmy entered the public school system. Noticing that her son had an artistic bent, Mildred saved up money for violin and tap-dancing lessons for her young son. When news of that reached his classmates, bullies beat him up after school and called him a sissy.

Jimmy later confessed to Alec Wilder that "My father married my mother only because he knocked her up."

Theirs was not a compatible marriage, and each of the two spouses had very different interests and tastes. Based on her interest in the arts, Winton contemptuously referred to his wife as "my little bohemian." He constantly lectured her that by cuddling Jimmy and encouraging him to learn dance techniques and to play the violin, "You're turning him queer."

Tragedy struck in July of 1940 when Mildred, who had been suffering for months from ovarian cancer, suffered a painful, lingering death. In twisted reasoning, Jimmy interpreted his mother's death as a rejection of him.

His father shipped him back to Indiana, where he went to live with Marcus and Ortense Winslow. (Ortense was Winton's sister.) They emerged as kindly guardians of the troubled youth, and welcomed him to their 178-acre farm outside Fairmount, Indiana. Jimmy was assigned his own bedroom within a large white house dating from the turn of the 20th Century.

***

Aboard the train, on his ride back to Indiana, then nine-year-old Jimmy slipped into the baggage car that was carrying the coffin and the body of his mother. Prying open the lid of the coffin containing her body, he clipped a lock of her hair and carried it in his wallet throughout the remainder of his own short life.

Within eighteen months of his mother's death and Jimmy's departure from his father's California home, Winton was drafted into the U.S. Army in the wake of the surprise December of 1941 Japanese attack on Pearl Harbor.

Throughout the rest of his life, Jimmy suffered from the loss of his mother. On the set of *Rebel Without a Cause,* he told Natalie Wood, "God played a dirty trick on me, taking my mother from me. That led to my father abandoning me."

He told another co-star, Dennis Hopper, that he used to sneak out of the Winslow household late at night and cry at his mother's gravesite. "I would demand that she answer me and tell me why she left me when she was only twenty-nine years old. Sometimes, I fell sobbing onto her grave. I would cry out, 'I need you! I want you back!'"

During Jimmy's adolescence in Indiana, he decided one summer that he wanted to be a trapeze artist, and began practicing trapeze acrobatics in the family barn in Fairmount. During one of his improvised "rehearsals," he lost his balance and fell, knocking out his two front teeth.

His father was due for a visit in two weeks. During his time in Indiana, he fashioned a removable bridge for his son. Forever after, as a joke, whenever Jimmy wanted to portray a snaggle-toothed hillbilly, he removed the bridge and shocked whomever he happened to be dating at the time.

Later on, even when he became a movie star and could afford expensive dentistry, Jimmy preferred to keep the removable front teeth crafted by his father.

He was graduated from Fairmount High School in May of 1949, where he had excelled in sports. By June of that year, he'd packed up his meager belongings and headed for Los Angeles.

He rode the Greyhound bus, a transit requiring four days and nights. As he later recalled, "I was propositioned by at least five guys, usually when I went to take a leak. But I didn't accept any of their offers."

For a while, he lived with Winton, who, upon his arrival in California, greeted him rather coldly at the door. Ethel, his stepmother, wasn't at all welcoming. Winton had married Ethel Case in 1945, right after his discharge from the military.

Jimmy and Ethel took an instant dislike to each other.

Even though he tried to get close to Winton, he never could. The years had made his father even more distant than before. When Jimmy confided that he wanted to become an actor, Winton dismissed the dream, defining all actors as "faggots. At least you'll get your cock sucked frequently if you go into the movie racket. That's how handsome young actors break into the business, or so I heard."

During his stay with Winton and Ethel, Jimmy enrolled in the nearby Santa Monica City College, a two-year junior college. But he wasn't happy there, and didn't fit in.

When he transferred to the campus at UCLA, he moved out of Winton's house and found lodging at the Sigma Nu fraternity residence, where he was a pledge. After a few weeks, he was kicked out.

He would never return to Winton's home, and his father never welcomed him back. Jimmy grew increasingly uncomfortable during his infrequent reunions, which usually lasted less than an hour.

When he played his roles in *East of Eden* and *Rebel Without a Cause,* he claimed, "I've lived these parts. I know about father-son alienation."

Fixed Bayonets

JIMMY MAKES AN INGLORIOUS MOVIE DEBUT
"DOLING OUT DEATH TO LITTLE YELLOW MEN"

At a chance meeting at a Hollywood cocktail party, Rogers Brackett spoke to an acquaintance, Isabelle Draesmer, an agent who booked actors into movie roles. Privately, he contemptuously referred to her as "small fry," but she was willing to take on new, untested actors and often found bit parts for them in films.

She had known Brackett casually for several years, and trusted his judgment, based on his far-flung experience within the film colony. He claimed, "James Dean is the hottest undiscovered male star in Hollywood."

"It sounds like you're in love with him," she said with a smirk.

"Perhaps I am."

The following day, a spruced-up Jimmy arrived at Draesmer's modest office at 8272 Sunset Boulevard. She, too, was impressed with him, and by that afternoon, following a lunch, she signed him as a client of her agency.

She said, "He had some hidden talent. Of that, I wasn't sure, what it was, exactly, but it was something. I was aware that his farm boy diction, technique, and posture needed to be vastly improved. Yet I sensed he was a possible new Monty Clift, whom I'd first seen perform on the stage in New York."

She telephoned a photographer friend of hers, Wilson Millar, who agreed to take publicity shots of Jimmy for her to send out to casting directors.

The next day, Jimmy arrived at Millar's studio at 2060 North Highland Avenue, where, as he later claimed to Brackett, "I got the once over of my life. I didn't strip for him, but I felt he has X-ray vision."

"Dean was a handsome boy," Millar later said. "Not your typical Hollywood pretty boy of the '50s. In profile, he looked better. Full frontal, he was just another good-looking kid, of which there were thousands hounding casting offices. Frankly, I thought his eyes were too close together. He was near-sighted and tended to squint."

"I thought he might find a minor role or two as a juvenile. His mouth intrigued me, as he had perfect lips. I asked him what kind of movie star he'd like to be. He surprised me when he claimed he wanted to be turned into a male Marilyn Monroe. Later, I heard he'd used that line on others. To say it again, his sex appeal definitely stemmed for the movement of that succulent mouth."

Draesemer went to work "hustling Rogers' boyfriend," as she phrased it. Within a week, she managed to land him a very small part in *Fixed Bayonets!*, a 1951 war drama directed by Samuel Fuller for 20th Century Fox. Coincidentally, Fuller was a friend of Brackett's.

The movie was set during the first brutal winter of the Korean War (1950-1953), just after that country's invasion by Red China. The grimy tale involved the fate of a lone forty-eight man platoon. The picture starred Richard Basehart and Gene Evans.

Cast in the uncredited role of "Doggie," a sentry, Jimmy appears only briefly, near the end of the film. His brief role was later whacked a bit, but he still made the final cut. In the original sequence, he runs up to Lieutenant Gibbs (Craig Hill) and squats beside him. "Lieutenant," he says. "I think I hear them coming. Could it be the rear guard, huh?" He then cocked his rifle.

Many sources claim that Jimmy's appearance was completely cut, and it's true that many movies were later edited (i.e., "shortened") for release on television. Jimmy may not have been recognizable, since the film was shot at night, his face was blackened, and he wore a helmet.

After his scenes were filmed and completed, through the interventions of Brackett, who used his link to Fuller, Jimmy lingered on the set for three extra days with the hope that the director might need him in another scene.

When Brackett came on set to visit him, he introduced Jimmy to the film's star, Richard Basehart, who agreed to accompany them to lunch in the studio's commissary. Basehart had been cast as the sensitive Corporal Denno, who had an in-

Jimmy avoided the actual draft, but ended up as a foot soldier on screen in *Fixed Bayonets!* His helmeted face appeared for about a minute.

nate aversion for taking responsibility for the lives of his men. His character says, "I can take an order, but I can't give one."

Previously, Basehart had starred with Valentina Cortese in *The House on Telegraph Hill* (1951) and had married her. He told Jimmy and Brackett that he and his new wife wanted to play the leads in an upcoming production of Tennessee Williams' *Orpheus Descending.*

"I'm willing to take off my boxer shorts for Tennessee if he'll give us the roles. Valentina claims I have Grade A government-inspected meat."

Jimmy was surprised at the actor's frankness, and suspected that perhaps he was joking. Later, Jimmy would learn that many actors often spoke that provocatively during unguarded moments.

After lunch, Brackett brought Jimmy over to meet Fuller, who was a cult director, hoping he might have a future role for his *protégé*. After they chatted a bit, Jules Buck, an influential producer, arrived on the scene. He, too, was introduced to both Brackett and Jimmy.

Among other achievements, Buck had been the cameraman for John Huston, shooting film for some of Huston's wartime documentaries, including *The Battle of San Pietro* (1944).

But instead of focusing on Jimmy, Buck told them that he had opted to relocate to Paris. In time, he would launch his own film production enterprise, Keep Films, in England with his "exciting new star," Peter O'Toole. Eventually, Keep Films turned out entertainment that included O'Toole performing in *Becket* (1964), *Lord Jim* (1965), and Woody Allen's *What's New, Pussycat?* (also 1965).

For his movie debut, Jimmy was paid $44. The check was sent to Draesemer, who deducted her ten percent. He later told friends, "I played Doggie, doling out death to little yellow men."

When the movie was released, the cantankerous critic, Bosley Crowther of *The New York Times,* wrote: *Fixed Bayonets!* was a tribute to the U.S. Infantry, but it is something less than inspired."

During his first dinner with Draesmer, Jimmy told her he'd had to face two hard choices. "I wanted to do what was best for my career. I could marry Joan Davis' daughter (Beverly Wills), or I could move in with Rogers, our chicken hawk. Joan hated me, and Beverly could do nothing for me. But Rogers is a producer, if only a minor one, but he knows everyone who's ever farted in Tinseltown."

"But with Rogers, it'll be a sing-for-your supper deal," Draesmer said.

"I can keep him at bay if he comes at me with his tongue hanging out," he said. "Besides, there's a second bedroom."

Let's be honest with each other," she said. "I've been to his apartment for a party. There's only one bedroom with a double bed."

"So be it," he answered. "Let's change the subject. That wasn't much of a part in *Fixed Bayonets!*. What juicy part have you got in store for me next?"

His agent later recalled, "No one ever denied that Jimmy was anything but an opportunist. In that regard, he had something in common with a female star, Marilyn Monroe. I predicted those two would eventually make movies together and create box office magic. What a pair! Alas, their candles gave off a magic glow that would not last the night."

***

Jimmy's next role was not for the big screen, but for what was called at the time "the little black box": Television.

Draesemer sent him over to meet with Frank Woodruff, the writer, director, and producer of a TV drama for the Bigelow Theater Series. He spent only ten minutes with Jimmy before casting him in an uncredited role for which he would be paid $45 for a day's work.

The drama was entitled *T.K.O. (Technical Knock Out)*, scheduled for release in the autumn of 1951.

Its plot focused on a teenage boy, played by Martin Milner, a young actor who would go on to greater fame thanks to his pivotal role in the hit TV series, *Route 66*. In *T.K.O.*, he portrayed a boxer fixated on paying for an expensive operation his father desperately needed.

Hanging out on the set, Jimmy talked with Milner. He had seen him in the 1947 classic, *Life With Father*, a film that starred William Powell and Irene Dunne.

Jimmy didn't appreciate Powell or Dunne's acting style at all, but he was intrigued by one of the film's young co-stars, Elizabeth Taylor. He boasted to Milner, "One day I'm going to fuck that beautiful little wench."

Also cast was Regis Toomey, who, although he was not Jimmy's type of actor, impressed him with a contest he had won. In 1941, when he starred in *You're In the Army Now*, he scored the record for the longest screen kiss in cinematic history, an osculation that lasted three minutes and five seconds. The female object of his affection was Jane Wyman, who had recently divorced Ronald Reagan.

Even though his role in *T.K.O* was minor, Jimmy alerted *The Fairmount News* back in Indiana that he was in the show. His family and friends tuned in. The role was so small that some TV viewers in Fairmount didn't even notice when Jimmy appeared on the small screen.

He never saw the completed film. By the time it aired as a TV show in Los Angeles, Jimmy had already left the city.

Lauren Bacall

BOGIE GETS VIOLENT WITH JIMMY

Months after Jimmy died in 1955 and right before his own death in 1957, Bogie told his closest friend, Spencer Tracy, "Did you know I once made a movie *[it was released in 1952]* with that little prick, James Dean? *Deadline—USA.*"

Fresh from his triumph in *The African Queen* (1951), with Katharine Hepburn, Bogie signed for the story of a crusading newspaper editor. *Deadline—U.S.A.* had been written by Richard Brooks, who was also the director, and set for release by 20th Century Fox. Brooks hired Jimmy for a bit part.

Bogie's leading lady in the film—hardly anyone's romantic interest—was Ethel Barrymore, the *grande dame* of the American theater. Bogie had once starred with her brother, Lionel Barrymore, in *Key Largo* (1948).

Jimmy followed his bit part in *Fixed Bayonets!* with an even smaller role in *Deadline—U.S.A.* Others in the cast, each a well-known name, included Kim Hunter, Ed Begley, Martin Gable, Paul Stewart, and Jim Backus, who would later play Jimmy's father in *Rebel Without a Cause* (1955).

Jimmy had a nonspeaking role, appearing only briefly in a scene set in a busy press room as one of the newspaper workers. The scene was filmed in the press room of the *New York Daily News. Deadline—U.S.A.* has since been praised as one of the best films about the newspaper industry ever made.

Some sources claim that Jimmy never appeared in *Deadline.* However, when Fox digitalized and re-released the picture, its promoters hired Humphrey Bogart's biographer, Darwin Porter, the co-author of this book, to narrate the behind-the-scenes events of the film as an added bonus included on the CD. Porter specifically points out the footage within the film devoted to pre-fame Jimmy, whose face was immediately recognizable.

Jimmy was never formally introduced to Bogie on the set, and he was awe struck by the veteran actor, secretly admiring his talent and envying his great fame. He closely observed Bogie from a distance. Jimmy's custom of hanging out on a movie set after the completion of his brief footage had by now become a tradition.

Humphrey Bogart with Lauren Bacall in *To Have and Have Not,* the film that made them famous as a screen team. Their subsequent marriage would not be as idyllic as their onscreen romance.

He was there the afternoon that Bogie lashed out at Brooks. Bogie had just learned than upon orders from Darryl F. Zanuck, Brooks had first offered his role as a crusading newspaper editor to Richard Widmark, who had rejected it. Then, Brooks offered the part to Gregory Peck, who had also rejected it.

"Here I am, a fucking Oscar winner, and I'm given sloppy seconds," Bogie shouted before storming off the set.

After his departure, Jimmy overheard Brooks talking to Ed Begley and Martin Gabel.

According to Brooks, as transmitted through Begley, "*Deadline* probably marks the beginning of the end for Bogie. He looks like shit. He's not the same man we loved. He's arrogant and grumpy, and he shows up without knowing his lines. He's very sarcastic to other actors, all except to Miss Barrymore, whom he treats with the respect she deserves."

It wasn't until months later that Jimmy was actually introduced to Bogie. Their first "official" encounter was both explosive and disastrous.

On the set of *East of Eden,* Merv Griffin arrived at around noon for a reunion with Jimmy, whom he had always been attracted to ever since they'd lived in adjoining apartments at the seedy Commodore Arms Hotel in Los Angeles. After Jimmy's patron, Rogers Brackett, was transferred to Chicago, Jimmy moved in with Nick Adams, a fellow actor dreaming of stardom but down on his luck. Brackett left Jimmy no money, and Nick was out of work, so Nick suggested that both of them turn to hustling.

As a gay young man himself, although with more money than either Jimmy or Nick, Griffin was "a buyer in the meat market," as Jimmy rather crudely described it. "Flash a twenty-dollar bill at either Nick or me, and we get a hard-on."

Griffin, on the set of *East of Eden,* was hoping for some repeat action, but he quickly found that Jimmy was no longer in a position where he needed to hustle. Playing the lead in *East of Eden,* Jimmy, by then, had already—after a long struggle—achieved stardom.

Griffin sat with Jimmy for about fifteen minutes, gossiping and smoking during the lunch break.

Looking up, Griffith spotted two figures approaching them. One was Bogart, the other Solly Biano, head of casting at Warner Brothers. Under his breath, Griffith whispered, "I hope Solly does more for your movie career than he did for mine."

Ignoring Griffin, Solly introduced Bogie to Warners' rising young star, although Jimmy avoided making eye contact with Bogie. Solly had thought that Bogie and Jimmy might hit if off because both of

Merv Griffin in 1945 as a sports announcer and radio personality

them were graduates of the "I Don't Give a Fuck" school of acting.

During part of his time on the set that morning, Bogie had stood on the sidelines, concealing himself and watching Jimmy perform in a scene.

"I hear you're the hot new rebel of Hollywood," Bogie said. "I remember when they said the same thing about me. Welcome to the Rebel Club."

Jimmy took the extended hand of the screen legend, still refusing to make eye contact.

Bogie complimented him on his technique, but Jimmy continued to stare at his feet, still not speaking.

"They tell me you're great, kid," Bogie said to him.

"Yeah," Jimmy said. "So they say, whoever the fuck *they* are. As if I give a god damn rooster's asshole what people think of me."

That was too much for Bogie. He grabbed Jimmy by the lapels of his jacket and yanked him around. "Look me in the eye, you little cocksucker! When I talk to you, show me some respect. You're just another stupid punk with skid marks on your underwear. Another Brando clone. Just what Hollywood doesn't need. In two fucking years from now, you'll be gone and forgotten." He shoved Jimmy back, nearly knocking him down.

Looking perplexed, Griffin stood with Solly as Bogie stormed off the set.

Jimmy watched him go, with contempt on his face, even though he had always admired Bogie. Perhaps it had all been an act on his part to conceal his idol worship. "I never saw *Casablanca,* and I never intend to." Actually, he'd seen the film three times, and it had always been his favorite.

"I hear that Mr. Bogart plays a queer who ends up with Claude Rains in the final reel, not Ingrid Bergman."

Then Jimmy turned and walked away. Griffin would never see him again. But Jimmy would suffer through two more unfortunate encounters with Bogie.

***

[When stardom came, Jimmy no longer patronized his former hangout, Googies and instead, became a client of the chic Villa Capri, where the stars dined. One evening, he arrived at the restaurant accompanied by Lili Kardell, a nineteen-year-old Swedish actress.

Sitting two tables away were Bogie and Frank Sinatra with three male companions. To razz Jimmy, Sinatra called the waiter over and ordered him to deliver milk and crackers to "Baby Jimmy."

Bogie quickly scribbled a note: "Dear Punk, next time try combing your hair with an actual comb, not a dishrag!"

Jimmy would have a final run-in with Bogie, one even more violent than first introduction.]

Making Movies with Dean Martin & Jerry Lewis

JIMMY'S OFFSCREEN SHENANIGANS WITH JOHN BROMFIELD

Sailor Beware (1952) was a loosely equivalent remake of the hugely popular 1942 movie musical, *The Fleet's In,* that had starred Dorothy Lamour and William Holden.

In spite of a weak script and stale jokes, *Sailor Beware* did better box office than Gary Cooper's *High Noon* and MGM's *Singin' in the Rain,* which later was hailed as the best musical ever made. *Sailor Beware* was built around the onscreen antics of Jerry Lewis and Dean Martin, then the number two box office attraction in America.

Once again, Jimmy was disappointed with his small role, but it was a larger part than he had been given in *Fixed Bayonets!.* Playing a "corner man" for Lewis' boxing opponent, Jimmy was featured in several minutes of screen time, mostly in the background, but only one line of dialogue.

On his first visit to the set of *Sailor Beware,* the cast and crew attended a studio breakfast paid for by the producer, Hal B. Wallis. Jimmy was perhaps the only member of the cast who found Lewis and Martin funny that morning. The comedic duo ran around the film set pouring pancake syrup over everybody's head, including Jimmy's. Production was delayed for two hours that morning while everybody showered.

During the shoot, Lewis paid no attention to Jimmy, although he later claimed, "I discovered the boy," after Jimmy became a famous star.

Although Jimmy was needed on the set for three days of shooting, he convinced the film's director, Hal Walker, to let him hang out afterwards, asserting, "I want to see how movies are made."

"OK, kid," Walker said, "but don't get in the damn way or I'll kick you out on your ass."

A footnote in Hollywood history, Walker, who hailed from Iowa, is known mainly for helming some early Dean Martin/Jerry Lewis films. He's even better known for directing Bing Crosby and Bob Hope in their famous road pictures during their (cinematic) travels to Bali, Morocco, and Zanzibar.

Jimmy was on the set when Betty Hutton appeared on Walker's arm. She had signed for a cameo role as Martin's girlfriend, a character named "Hetty Button." She'd had a supporting role in the wartime version of the film, *The Fleet's In.*

An unfunny, exhibitionistic, neo-slapsticking, caper

She had recently scored big triumphs, first in *Annie Get Your Gun* (1950), in which she'd replaced Judy Garland and consequently faced a hostile cast and crew; and in Cecil B. DeMille's *The Greatest Show on Earth* (1952). Yet her career was heading for a nosedive, and, to Jimmy, she seemed to be coming unglued. Walker introduced him to Hutton, who seemed to clutch him. When the director was called away, she continued to cling to Jimmy, whispering to him, "I'm afraid." He noticed that she was trembling. "Hold onto me. Don't let me go. God help me!"

This embarrassing moment for Jimmy continued for about four minutes before Walker returned for her. She immediately transferred her emotional dependence to Walker, not even looking back at Jimmy.

That night he told Rogers Brackett, "If that's what big stardom does for you, count me out!"

Two days later, Jimmy got to witness the star of the picture, the Parisian actress, Corinne Calvet. In postwar France, she had become the country's number one pinup girl, although she had originally studied criminal law at the Sorbonne. Her mother was a distinguished scientist, who played a part in the development of Pyrex glass.

As a regular patron of Paris' famously artsy Left Bank café, *Les Deux Magots,* Calvet held her own in animated conversations with Jean-Paul Sartre and Jean Cocteau.

American audiences came to know her when she played opposite sexy Burt Lancaster in *Rope of Sand* (1949). Privately, she cut a seductive path through Hollywood's forests of studly men, seducing the likes of Errol Flynn, Tyrone Power, Jimmy Stewart, and John Barrymore, Jr., among others.

All of this was accomplished despite her marriage at the time to John Bromfield, considered by his admirers as the sexiest man in Tinseltown. This hunk of beefcake was known to bestow his favors on both men and women.

Jimmy stood with Bromfield as both of them watched Calvet emote in a scene from *Sailor Beware*

Tragi-Funny Lady: Betty Hutton

Two views of the French sex kitten, Corinne Calvet.

Lower photo: With her errant husband, pinup hottie, John Bromfield.

with Dean Martin. Jimmy and Bromfield seemed to size each other up, and, as events would later prove, they liked what they saw. Their flirtation was interrupted by the sudden appearance of Wallis on the set. From a concealed position behind the camera, he'd been watching Calvet and Martin during the filming of their love scene.

He stepped forward and yelled, "Corinne, I told you I don't allow my actresses to wear falsies."

Her French temper flared. "I'm not wearing them," she shouted back at him.

"Go to your dressing room at once and remove those god damn fake tits!"

"Are you calling me a liar?" she asked. She walked toward him and, in front of Jimmy and her husband, who stood nearby, she took Wallis' hand and placed it inside her brassiere. Does that convince you they are for real?"

Then, without saying a word, Wallis stormed off the set. As he was leaving, Martin yelled "Bravo!"

Bromfield whispered to Jimmy, "Let's get the fuck out of here. I've seen enough for one day. I'm sure when the scene is over, Martin will take my wife to his dressing room to fuck her."

Outside the sound stage, Bromfield directed Jimmy to two motorcycles, which he had borrowed. He asked Jimmy to ride with him into the Hollywood Hills. "We'll stop for lunch somewhere."

Over sandwiches, Jimmy learned that he'd been a tuna fisherman and that he'd been discovered by that notorious Hollywood agent, Henry Willson, whom Jimmy had already met. "He examined all my body parts," Bromfield candidly admitted. "I was also introduced to his second prize, Rory Calhoun. Rory and I are just coming down from a white heat affair. Rory's a *love 'em and leave 'em* kind of guy. He seduces as many women as he does men."

Jimmy never discussed any of the details of his brief fling with Bromfield. However, he did tell William Bast, "That Corinne Calvet is one god damn lucky French gal."

The following day, Jimmy faced the cameras himself, playing one of two managers of an amateur Navy boxer, who must face Lewis in the ring. In one scene, Jimmy massages his boxer as he listens to Lewis boast that he's won one hundred and one previous bouts in the ring. Of course, this is all comedic bluff. Jimmy delivers his one line to his own boxer: "That guy's a professional."

He conspires with the other manager to bring in the sailor's older professional brother to face Lewis in the ring. Entirely by accident, Lewis knocks out the pro and wins the bout.

Although he had nothing more to say, Jimmy can be seen in the background climbing in and out of the boxing ring as the action unfolds. He is dressed in a white T-shirt and slacks, with a towel wrapped around his neck.

Jimmy Submits to a "Physical" from Vince Edwards

(TV's Future Dr. Ben Casey)

Jimmy never saw Bromfield again, but on his final day on the set, he met another actor, equally handsome and well built. He was billing himself as Vincent Edwards, later as Vince Edwards. Eventually, he became a household name thanks to the role he played of Dr. Ben Casey in a popular TV series (1961-1966).

Both actors were bisexual. The Brooklyn-born Edwards was three years older than Jimmy. A top-rate swimmer, he had been part of the U.S. Ohio State University swim team that won the U.S. National Championships.

When Jimmy met him, he was about to sign with Paramount Pictures for his major film debut in *Mister Universe* (1951). According to Bast, to whom Jimmy revealed his fling with Edwards, Jimmy was both attracted to Ed-

The whacky, campy 50s. Two views of heartthrob John Bromfield.

top photo: in *Revenge of the Creature* (1955); *lower photo:* Beefcake fiesta with Tab Hunter

wards and jealous of him at the same time. Edwards appeared to be heading for film success much faster than Jimmy.

He was not particularly modest, telling Jimmy, "I studied at the American Academy of Dramatic Arts, but I think I can make it big in the movies based on my looks alone."

Unlike Jimmy, Edwards had been assigned a private dressing room. After meeting Jimmy, he invited him there during a luncheon break.

Once inside, Jimmy had to take a leak, heading to Edwards' cramped little bathroom. Over the toilet hung a full frontal nude of the actor, revealing his well-muscled body and endowment.

Back in the dressing room, Jimmy became more flirtatious with Edwards. As he was undressing, Jimmy moved in. "I've already gotten a sneak preview of what I'm going to get."

"Oh that!" Edwards said. "I was photographed for an arts style class. The male nude, you know."

"Mighty impressive physique," Jimmy said, weaving himself into Edwards' arms.

[Two days later, when Jimmy returned to the set where he was not needed, he spotted Edwards and approached him, whispering, "Thanks for showing a guy a good time. You're one hot dude."

"Fuck off, faggot! Edwards said. "Get out of my face or I'll slug you."

Later, Jimmy learned that he'd approached the wrong Edwards. Vince had a twin, Anthony Edwards.]

Sailor Beware was the fifth cinematic teaming of Jerry Lewis and Dean Martin. Jimmy overheard Lewis bragging about their conquests of women. "All the broads are crazy for Deano," Lewis said. "Even Marilyn Monroe. Actually, I've fucked more women than Deano, but most of them want to burp me."

Ironically, later, both Martin and Jimmy would pursue the same actress, Pier Angeli.

Brackett claimed, "From Jimmy, Angeli heard talk of love. But Lana Turner set me straight on Martin. He was romantic at night, all wine and candlelight. But come the dawn, all a gal got was a pat on the ass and a promise 'to see you around, kid.'"

Sailor Beware marked the first time that Jimmy's name appeared in *The Hollywood Reporter* under "castings." Jimmy later told Bast, "My acting, if that is what it was called, mostly involved standing around looking at Lewis go through a lot of crazy antics. At one point, he pretended to be punch drunk and cauliflower brained."

Where Jimmy's future was concerned, the most important contact he made on the set was with another struggling young actor, Dick Clayton. He admitted he didn't have much talent as an actor, and decided he was going to become a theatrical agent instead.

"You interested in signing on as my first client?" he asked Jimmy.

Clayton was told by Jimmy that he planned to go to New York to seek stage work. "In that case, I want to set you up with an agent, Jane Deacy. She's not the biggest but she's one of the best agents."

Jimmy wrote down all the details. "I'll call her for

Two views of Vince Edwards, a.k.a., Dr. Ben Casey. "I'm a grower, not a show-er."

you and recommend you as a client," Clayton promised.

"Great!" Jimmy said. "Soon, I won't have any more need for Isabelle Draesemer."

Ironically, in just a few short months, Clayton was working as an talent agent for the Famous Artists Corporation, and in that capacity, signed Jimmy on as a client for the duration of 1954 and 1955.

Clayton later was quoted as saying, "Jimmy seemed very vulnerable when I met him, very impressionable, with this little boy lost puppy dog look. We were friendly, but something in his attitude made me pull back. I figured he wasn't the type of boy you hugged."

Draesemer's later claim to fame involved her "discovery" of James Dean, thus guaranteeing her a footnote in Hollywood history.

Like James Whitmore, she, too, encouraged Jimmy to move to New York, even though it meant losing him as a client. She also coached Buddy Ebsen and Hugh O'Brien to stardom.

After swearing all her life that she'd never marry an actor, she wed the B-picture cowboy star, Tex Terry, and retired to Indiana, Jimmy's home state.

With her husband, she opened Tex's Longhorn Tavern in the state's famous Parke County, known for its collection of covered bridges. Until her death, she was always willing to talk about Jimmy to out-of-state tourists, relaying her version of that famous teenage boy from Indiana who wandered into her office so long ago.

Rock Hudson vs. James Dean

How a Hollywood Feud Originated as a Hot Trick

Jimmy's last Hollywood film before his relocation to New York City via Chicago was *Has Anybody Seen My Gal?* When he signed for a bit part within it, it was entitled *Oh Money, Money.* It was the best of a lackluster group of Hollywood films in which he would briefly appear before he hit the bigtime.

The 88-minute color film, released in the summer of 1952, was the first in which Jimmy uttered a complicated line of dialogue from a position in the foreground of the frame.

Helmed by Danish-born director Douglas Sirk, *Has Anybody Seen My Gal?* starred Piper Laurie in the lead, with Rock Hudson and Charles Coburn getting second billing. Also featured was child actress Gigi Perreau, whose chief rival was Natalie Wood, Jimmy's future co-star.

In her memoirs, *Learning to Live Out Loud,* Laurie claimed that she was rather embarrassed to be billed over Coburn, an Oscar-winning actor. She also alleged that "He had this tic about pinching women's bottoms, and if you were female and under one hundred and five, you had to give him wide berth."

She also said that at the time she was unaware of "the young boy who sat at the end of the counter in a drugstore scene." Years later, her uncle called from New York after watching the movie in its TV release. "Did you know you were in a movie with James Dean?"

That was her first awareness of that. By that time, Jimmy was well on his way to becoming Hollywood legend.

As for Rock Hudson, Laurie admitted that she was unaware of his gender preference when they starred together. "There was no chemistry between us. He never made a pass at me. I just assumed I wasn't his type."

In contrast, Jimmy was well aware of Hudson's sexual preference, having flirted with him at a party at the home of Hudson's gay (and predatory) agent, Henry Willson. Hudson recognized Jimmy and invited him for lunch. He was filled with gossip, telling Jimmy that he'd heard that Laurie had had an affair with Ronald Reagan.

Jimmy would be appearing in a television drama with Reagan within a few months.

Over sandwiches, Hudson seemed bitter at Universal for awarding star billing to Laurie and for arranging for studio publicists to promote her career more aggressively than his. "They claim that she bathes in milk every day and that she dines on flower petals as a means of protecting her luminous skin. What bullshit!"

Like Jimmy, Laurie in time, would tire of making bad films in Hollywood and would retreat to New York to study acting and to seek work on the stage and in television.

After lunch, Hudson invited Jimmy to his dressing room, since he wasn't needed on the set. The invitation from the tall, handsome actor was blunt: "I like to fuck and get fucked. How about it, Kid?"

"You're on, Big Boy," Jimmy said. He'd later give a blow-by-blow description of his sexual encounter to William Bast.

Usually, men came on to Jimmy during his early appearances in Hollywood. An exception was Lynn Bari, a co-star in the film. She was seventeen years his senior and found Jimmy very attractive. At this stage in her declining career, she'd been reduced to portraying matronly characters rather than the *femmes fatales* she'd been known for in the late '30s and '40s.

During World War II, the sultry, statuesque brunette, once known as "the Scarlett O'Hara of Virginia," was the nation's second most popular pinup girl, ranking just under Betty Grable. Bari had played man-killers in some 150 films for Fox.

After hanging around the set for days, Jimmy was called for his scene. He had tried unsuccessfully to get Sirk to notice him, but he had seemed more intent on promoting Hudson, who had been cast as Laurie's soda-jerk boyfriend.

Sirk told Coburn that he found it amusing that Hudson towered over Laurie. "Rock looks great in his raccoon coat."

Two years later, Sirk would cast Hudson in a remake of Lloyd Douglas' novel, *Magnificent Obsession,* in a role that interacted, romantically, with the Oscar-winning Jane Wyman, the former Mrs. Ronald Reagan. Like Laurie, Jane was unaware of Hudson's sexual preference and made the mistake of falling in love with him.

Before facing the camera, Jimmy heard Sirk's direction: "Act superior and offhand."

The director approved Jimmy's red bow tie, his 1920s-era college sweater, his straw boater, and his white trousers.

In an extended interlude, Jimmy comes into the drugstore where Coburn is working as a soda jerk. Jimmy says, "Hey, gramps, I'll have a choc malt, heavy on the choc, plenty of milk, four spoons of malt, two scoops of vanilla ice cream, one mixed with the rest and one floating."

Coburn snaps back, "Would you like to come in on Wednesday for a fitting?"

Sirk shot the scenes three times until he got it right. At the end, he ignored Jimmy, but complimented Coburn as "the perfect Frank Capra curmudgeon."

Later, Coburn invited Jimmy for coffee. The young actor learned that the older actor had been born in Macon, Georgia, in 1877. He confessed to Jimmy that, "I have the hots for Nancy Davis." At that time, she had not yet married Reagan.

Coburn also told Jimmy that he had been cast in the 1953 *Gentlemen Prefer Blondes.* "I'm faced with a hard choice," he said. "Do I chase after busty Jane Russell or go for that bleached blonde thing, Marilyn Monroe?"

With his work finished, Jimmy tallied up his total receipts for his brief appearances in three separate films. They came to $300.

His romance with Hudson lasted on and off for about ten days. Roddy McDowall, who came to know Jimmy quite well in New York, claimed, "Rock and Jimmy started out as lovers, but in time, they became bitter enemies. There was a lot of jealousy on Jimmy's part. He would have given anything to be Rock Hudson."

Years later, Hudson was asked if he'd met Jimmy during the making of *Has Anybody Seen My Gal?.* "Yeah, I ran into the kid. He had a very small role with slicked back, wavy hair, very neatly combed. That's all I remember."

Actor Nick Adams had a different memory. Late one afternoon, Adams had arrived at Hudson's home at five o'clock. He'd been hired as a staff member attending the bar—shirtless, of course—at a seven o'clock gay male cocktail party. He was ushered into the living room, where it was understood that he'd be setting up the bar.

"To my surprise, both Rock and Jimmy were sitting on his thick carpet, jaybird naked. They were spreading some kind of foul-smelling lotion into their crotches. It seems that each guy had a bad case of the crabs."

***

Rogers Brackett and his sophisticated mother, Tess, were very close. She was fully aware of her son's homosexuality, and never chastised him for it. During his Hollywood months with Jimmy, Brackett took him over to his mother's home in Culver City at least once a week for dinner.

One night, Brackett informed Jimmy that he was packing up and moving out of Hollywood. His employers had temporarily transferred him to Chicago for some short-term assignments, with the understanding that after that, he be permanently relocated to Manhattan.

He promised to send for Jimmy in Chicago after he settled in. His announcement led to a bitter fight, with Jimmy accusing his patron, "You'll never send for me. You'll meet some other good-looking guy in a parking lot—and that will be that."

As a parting gift, Jimmy asked Brackett for $2,000 to tide him over until he could find more work in films. Brackett refused, claiming he need all his cash on hand to get reestablished—first in Chicago, then in New York.

"I may be a producer for CBS, but the job doesn't pay that much."

On his final day in Los Angeles, when Brackett had to report to CBS to close down his office, Tess arrived at his apartment to assist her son in packing up his possessions, since he would not be returning to the rented apartment.

Later that afternoon, she heard Jimmy sobbing in the bathroom. The door was half open.

She knocked on it, calling out to him, "What's the matter? Can I help?"

"I'm afraid!" he shouted at her. "Afraid of being left alone. All my life, I've been abandoned. And now this!"

Chapter Four

TWO REBELS, JIMMY & NICK ADAMS, BECOME
HOLLYWOOD HUSTLERS,
SNARING, AMONG OTHERS, MERV GRIFFIN

Jimmy Poses for Photographers—Nude

ON A RETURN VISIT TO INDIANA, JIMMY RESUMES HIS AFFAIR WITH THE PRIEST WHO MOLESTED HIM

In New York, "The Little Prince" Tackles Tallulah Bankhead, TV Drama, Peggy Lee, and a Sexy Brunette (Dizzy Sheridan)

After failing at a movie career in Hollywood during the 1950s, an Irish-American from California, Merv Griffin (1925-2007), evolved into TV's most powerful and richest mogul, eventually winning 17 Emmy Awards for *The Merv Griffin Show*, a durable daytime staple that attracted 20 million viewers daily.

Behind the scenes, Griffin became known for his Midas touch, developing two of Hollywood's most popular game shows, *Jeopardy!* and *Wheel of Fortune*.

He had first entered the entertainment scene as a boy singer with Freddy Martin's band in the 40s.

He had long been known in the industry as a closeted gay. He married only once—it was unsuccessful—but he did produce an exceptional son from his ill-fated union.

Most of Jimmy's fans never knew about his involvement with Griffin. The

Two views of Merv Griffin in Knoxville, Tennessee, promoting his 1953 movie, *So This Is Love*, co-starring Kathryn Grayson. In the lower photo, he signs autographs for his adoring fan club members.

struggling actors met as neighbors in Los Angeles within the seedy Commodore Garden Apartments, when their respective careers were going nowhere. In the beginning, their trysts were sexual, for which Griffin, who had more money than Jimmy, paid his fellow actor fifty dollars per session.

At the time, Jimmy was sharing his modest studio at the Commodore Garden with another struggling actor, Nick Adams. Nick had wanted to get intimate immediately, but Jimmy had held him off until his financial situation worsened. Hard up, he accepted Nick's invitation to move in with him.

One night, Nick and Jimmy met Griffin under unusual circumstances. Griffin had stumbled across Errol Flynn, who had passed out in the courtyard of Commodore Gardens. No longer the swashbuckling matinée idol he'd been in the 30s and '40s, this once perfect specimen of manhood had become dissipated after a reckless life of debauched adventures. Motivated by financial troubles, he'd checked into the Commodore. Recognizing him at once, Griffin attempted to carry him back to his apartment. At that moment, after a night of hustling along Santa Monica Boulevard, Nick and Jimmy approached.

After helping the hustlers tuck the fading star into bed, Griffin observed the two young men more closely, finding one of them particularly handsome and appealing. He extended his hand. "Hi, I'm Merv Griffin."

"This here is James Dean, and I'm Nick Adams," the taller of the two said. "We've seen you around."

"Sorry we didn't say 'hi' before," Jimmy said. He looked at the body passed out on the bed. "If I didn't know better, I'd say that was Errol Flynn—or what's left of him."

Jimmy and Nick seemed impatient to leave, but Griffin invited them for a drink at sundown in the courtyard the next day.

Nick Adams met James Dean in 1950, when they appeared together in a Pepsi-Cola commercial for TV. He is seen above as Johnny Yuma in his hit TV series, *The Rebel.*

Although they arrived late, both actors showed up for that drink the next day with Griffin. He was amazed at their candor. All of them shared their various dramas in trying to find acting gigs in L.A.

"Let's be truthful with the man," Jimmy said. "We want to be actors. But right now, we might list our profession as hustlers."

"I see," Griffin said. "Are you referring to pool hall hustling, or do you mean love for sale?"

"More like dick for sale," Jimmy said.

Years later, on his way to becoming a famous Hollywood player, Griffin described his encounters with the young actor to several of his gay friends, notably Roddy McDowall, who also knew Jimmy.

Griffith summed him up: "A slouching stance, youthful rebellion in faded jeans, a cigarette in the corner of a kissable mouth, alienation, even outright hostile at times, and the most angelic face I've ever seen on a young man."

This Dean guy is going to be a big star," Griffin predicted. "I have this feeling about him. But he's got a lot of weird habits. He'll smoke a cigarette so far down that it'll burn his lips. Yes, actually burn them with intent. He gets off on being burnt. He confessed that to me as a hustler, and for a fee, he'll let a john crush a lit cigarette onto his butt. But he won't allow his chest or back to be burnt in case he has to strip off his shirt for the camera—that is, if he ever gets a role."

"The first time I was with him, even before I had sex with him, he pulled down his jeans and showed me cigarette burns on his beautiful ass. Strange boy. But I adore the kid."

That night, Griffin was invited into Nick and Jimmy's apartment. Jimmy wore a white Mexican shirt and new jeans, the gift of an admirer who had taken him to a clothing store. As Griffin recalled, "The whole studio smelled like the inside of a dirty laundry bag. Yet there was a sexual tension in the air."

To Griffin's surprise, he spotted a hangman's noose hanging from a hook on the ceiling "That's waiting for me if I decide to commit suicide," Jimmy told him.

Griffin didn't know if he were joking or if he really meant it.

As Jimmy put on a pot of coffee, Nick stripped down for a shower. Dangling his penis in front of Griffin, he said, "Now you know why I'm called 'Mighty Meat' along the Strip."

After he'd showered, Nick emerged with a towel around his waist. "Being a struggling actor is like having to eat a shit sandwich every day," he said. "It's kiss ass..." Then he paused: "Sometimes literally. You wait for the next job, not knowing if you're going to get it or not. Trying for a gig and having to compete with a hundred other starving actors. Congratulating your best friend when he got the job instead of you." He glanced furtively at Jimmy and continued. "Waiting outside that producer's door. Even worse sometimes, getting invited inside and having to submit to a blow job from some disgusting piece of flesh. And then losing the job to the guy he planned to cast all along. Trying to get a gig is half the job of being an actor. Take it from me."

As the evening progressed, Griffin was amazed that Nick was "tooting his own horn," sometimes at the expense of Jimmy. There was definite competition between the two actors. It was as if Nick sensed that Jimmy had far better looks and more talent than he did.

A future biographer, Albert Goldman, summed up Nick Adams: "He was forever selling himself, a property which, to hear him tell it, was nothing less than sensational. In fact, he had very little going for him in terms of looks, talent, or professional experience. He was just another poor kid from the sticks who had grown up dreaming of the silver screen."

Right in front of Jimmy, Nick claimed that his friend would cater to kinkier offers from johns along Santa Monica Boulevard than he would. "I turn down a lot of sick queens, but Jimmy here will go for anything. One night, this weirdo wanted to eat my shit. I told him to 'fuck off,' but Jimmy went off with the creep in his car."

"Why not?" Jimmy asked with a devilish bad boy look. "I hadn't taken a crap all day."

Years later, Griffin confessed to McDowall and to other gay friends, "Before I finished with them, I had to borrow five-hundred dollars to pay the freight, but it was worth every penny. Nick had the bigger endowment, but Jimmy was better at love-making. It was the best sex I've ever had, even if I did have to pay for it."

***

Later, to Griffin's surprise, he ran into Jimmy on the 20ᵗʰ Century Fox lot, where he was working as an uncredited extra.

Jimmy bonded with Griffin like a long-lost buddy, reminiscing about their encounters at the Commodore Garden Apartments. At five o'clock that afternoon, both of them headed for a drink at the tavern across the street. After his second vodka, Jimmy confessed to Griffin that he'd abandoned hustling and that he planned a move to New York in pursuit of TV and stage work.

No mention was made of Nick Adams.

Since work as an extra paid so little, and because acting gigs were so infrequent, Jimmy confessed that he'd devised a new way to make money: "I pose for nude photographs, sometimes with an erection. I've had a lot of copies made, and I sell them for twenty-five dollars each. It beats hustling, and no one even touches me, except perhaps the photographer. Not bad, huh?"

"Sounds like a great way for an out-of-work actor to make some extra cash, unless those nudes come back to haunt you after you make it big as a movie star."

"Like I give a god damn about that," Jimmy said. "I've set up a session with this photographer in Los Angeles. I've got a posing session at nine tonight. Wanna come with me?"

"I'd love to," Griffith said. "There's more that a bit of the *voyeur* in me."

"The pictures this session are for a private collector."

Later that evening, outside the photographer's studio, Jimmy removed his denim shirt and blue jeans. He wore no underwear. He handed his apparel to Griffin for safekeeping. "I like to arrive at the doorstep 'dressed' for action." Then he chuckled at his own comment.

At the door, the shocked photographer hustled the two men inside. "I've got two Eisenhower Republican old maids living upstairs. They might see you and have a heart attack. I don't want those old biddies to know what goes on in here."

During the shoot, Griffin assisted the photographer, fetching a glass of water or holding the spotlight. But mostly he stared with fascination at the subject.

As a nude model, Jimmy had no inhibitions. At one point, he grabbed a prop from a previous shoot, a black lace mantilla abandoned by a female model's posing. He plucked a red rose from a vase, grasping its stem with his teeth.

"This may be too girlish a pose for your client." The photographer warned, but he snapped the picture anyway.

117

At the end of the session, Jimmy put back on his clothes, and then rejected the photographer's invitation for a three-way with Griffin.

Back on the street again, Griffin asked, "What's next?"

"I want to go back to your place and fuck you," Jimmy said.

"A man after my own heart."

The pictures that Jimmy posed for that night are now in private hands, and considered a valued collector's item.

Competing for the Singing Cowboy Role in Oklahoma!

Jimmy Beats Paul Newman,
But Then They Both Lose to Gordon MacCrae

Until its final casting was defined and publicized, Jimmy clung to the hope of starring as Curly McLain in the film version of *Oklahoma!* (1955). When he heard that Fred Zinnemann had been named as its director, he got in touch with him and requested an audition.

"I've got to be frank with you," he told Jimmy. "I'm considering Paul Newman for the role, even though he can't sing. I can always dub a soundtrack afterwards."

"I can't sing a whole lot, but I sure as hell can act the role of Curly better than any other god damn actor in Hollywood," Jimmy said.

He was very persuasive and enticed Zinnemann into testing him out. The director had seen pictures of Jimmy and thought that from a physical standpoint, he'd be ideal for the role.

When Jimmy arrived at the director's snobby hotel, he was almost ejected from the lobby. The staff behind the desk later claimed, "He showed up looking like a cowboy wino."

He wasn't allowed to pass through the lobby, but was directed to the rear service entrance, where he rode the freight elevator up to Zinnemann's suite.

Zinnemann was impressed with Jimmy's rendition of the "Poor Jud is Dead" number alongside the veteran actor Rod Steiger, who had also been cast.

Later, Griffin called Jimmy about getting together for a drink. *[Unknown to Jimmy, Griffith had also been lobbying for the role of Curly, even though Zinnemann was insisting on a Paul Newman type.]*

Griffin, a talented singer in his own right, concealed from Jimmy how much he had wanted the role. When he had met with Zinnemann, the director had rejected Griffin for the role, but suggested that he could arrange for him to be in a movie called *The Alligator People* instead. "Would you allow makeup to transform you into an alligator?"

Griffin had rejected the offer and headed for the door.

Over a drink with Griffin, Jimmy boasted that Zinnemann had told him that his tryout was one of the best auditions the director had ever witnessed.

The role Jimmy wanted but wasn't destined to get. *Center figures*: Gordon MacRae as Curly, Shirley Jones as his bride.

"And your singing?" Griffin asked. "You can sing?"

"I'm not sure yet, but if I can pull off the role of Curly, I might become a singing star in other musicals."

Eventually, Zinnemann opted against Jimmy, instead offering the role to Frank Sinatra, who rejected it. The director finally settled on Gordon MacCrae, an actor and an accomplished singer.

As a result, the public never had to sit through Jimmy belting out a rendition of "Oh, What a Beautiful Morning."

***

As early autumn fell across Los Angeles in October of 1951, Jimmy prepared to leave the city. He told William Bast, "My dreams of becoming a movie star have been bashed." He revealed that he was going to Chicago to join Rogers Brackett, who had been temporarily stationed there by his ad agency. "After that, I'm heading for stardom on Broadway, but I don't have a lot of money."

Bast learned that although Brackett had arranged and paid for his train ticket to New York, with a stopover in Chicago, he had given him only a hundred dollars in spending money. "He likes to keep me on a tight leash. I certainly don't have one cent left from my work as a movie extra."

Bast met with Jimmy for a farewell bowl of chili at Barney's Beanery. His former roommate found Jimmy in a depressed mood. "You can knock your fucking brains out in Tinseltown. If you're lucky, you'll occasionally get $44 a day working as an extra in some shit movie. There's got to be more of a future for me than that."

"With Brackett, you'll be singing for your supper again," Bast warned.

"A gig's a gig," Jimmy responded.

"I'm not performing for Rogers anymore," Jimmy claimed, although Bast did not find that statement convincing. "If I can't make it in show business on talent alone, then I don't want to be in it at all."

119

Bast had been made aware of the inner conflicts Jimmy had faced about selling his body. In a memoir, he speculated, "Surely, being kept had to produce some kind of internal conflict in this Quaker-bred Indiana farm boy."

Bast recalled a shocking scene he'd secretly witnessed which seemed to demonstrate Jimmy's inner conflicts about renting his charms to any passerby on the street.

He had awakened one night at around 2AM, when he still shared the penthouse with Jimmy. Quite by chance, he looked out the window down onto the street scene below. There, he spotted Jimmy sitting on a bus bench, lit by a street lamp. To Bast, Jimmy was obviously cruising, waiting for a john to pull up in his car and offer him money in return for sexual favors.

Bast stayed glued to the window. Within a few minutes, a Cadillac stopped. The male driver called out to Jimmy, who rose from the bench and headed toward the car. Bast expected him to get in and ride away.

Instead, as he approached its open window, Jimmy pulled out a flick knife and seemed to threaten the driver, who stepped on the gas and sped away.

After that, Jimmy returned to their penthouse. Bast quickly retreated to the bedroom and pretended to be asleep. He didn't want him to know that he'd witnessed the scene below.

Back at Barney's Beanery, Jimmy looked around the room at the many out-of-work actors who had managed to scrape together enough money for a bowl of Barney's dubious chili.

Suddenly, Jimmy's face lit up. "I've got this great idea. I'll go to New York and find us a place to live. Why don't you follow me? We'll be two struggling actors trying to make it in the cultural capital of the world, where our talents are sure to be appreciated."

"That might not be a bad idea," Bast said. "Let's keep in touch after you get there. When you have an address, send it to me. I'll respond at once."

After more talk and more plans, the two men retreated to the sidewalk, where they warmly embraced for a farewell. "I hope that faggot-hating Barney isn't watching," Jimmy said. Then he kissed Bast on both cheeks and headed out into the fading afternoon, toward his new life.

Later that evening, after Bast had returned to his modest studio, he could hear the shouts of the spectators across the street, roaring from the American Legion Stadium, where a violent wrestling match was being staged between a white giant and a black giant.

Missing Jimmy, he fell asleep listening to the roar of the crowd. "Break his neck! Tear the fucker apart!"

Unhappy, and In Chicago

JIMMY ENJOYS A BRIEF FLING WITH A MARRIED STARLET
WHO CHALLENGED THE HOLLYWOOD PRODUCTION CODE

It was in Chicago that Brackett made his debut into the field of television. His decision was partially based on references in *The Hollywood Reporter* about the challenges confronting radio from the emerging media of "the little black box."

One of his first duties involved supervision of a show for kiddies entitled *Meadow Gold Ranch.* He told Jimmy, "If you can't beat 'em, join 'em. Television is the medium of the future, and you should seek work in TV dramas being filmed in Manhattan."

"But I want to become a movie star," Jimmy protested.

"Why not a TV star?"

After his arrival in the Windy City, Jimmy entered the lobby of The Ambassador East, one of the most expensive hotels in Chicago. Dressed in jeans, he had draped Sidney Franklin's blood-soaked matador's cape over one of his shoulders. After registering himself into Brackett's room, his battered suitcase was carried onto the elevator by a smartly uniformed bellhop, who Jimmy claimed "looked like a dead ringer for John Derek."

Whereas with Bast, he had maintained the pretense that his relationship with Brackett was no longer sexual, Brackett told a different story. "I don't think Jimmy was in the door for more than ten minutes before I had his clothes off. The pickings for me in Chicago had been lean, and I was hungry. Sex in the morning, sex when I came in from the office, and sex after retiring to bed. The kid told me I exhausted him."

Jimmy seemed lost in the vast sprawl of Chicago and stayed mostly within the hotel room, not wanting to wander alone on his own.

During his fourth evening in town, a guest arrived at their hotel room. It was David Swift, a respected director, screenwriter, animator, and producer. He would later recall his introduction to Jimmy: "I knocked several times before this young man slowly opened the door and peered out. I think Rogers was in the shower. The kid had on this tattered old matador's cape and seemed to be rehearsing an imaginary bullfight. Instead of telling me who he was, he shouted '*TORO! TORO!*' I thought he might be insane."

Suddenly, having wrapped a robe around himself, Brackett was in the room, pushing Jimmy aside. "It was then that I learned that this crazy guy was James Dean, and that he was this actor wannabe," Swift said.

He had arrived to accompany his friend, Brackett, and Dean to the Chicago production of the controversial play, *The Moon Is Blue*. It starred Swift's young and attractive new wife, actress Maggie McNamara. In a previous production that starred Barbara Bel Geddes, it had been a hit on Broadway, where it had been attacked for its "light and gay treatment of seduction, illicit sex, chastity, and virginity."

Jimmy found the play candid and exciting and enjoyed its frank discussions about sex. He was charmed by McNamara's performance and told her so backstage after the performance.

Over thick Chicago steaks, as Swift renewed his friendship with Brackett, McNamara and Jimmy got to know each other. Swift informed everyone that he was developing a TV sitcom, *Mister Peppers,* scheduled for transmission on NBC during the summer of 1952. Its star was Wally Cox.

Maggie McNamara, as she appeared on the cover of *Life* magazine in April, 1950.

[As a gossipy footnote, Swift claimed that Cox was the lover of Marlon Brando. That information fascinated Jimmy. It was perhaps the first time he'd heard that Brando was bisexual.]

McNamara, a New Yorker, had been a teen fashion model and had appeared on the April, 1950 cover of *Life* magazine. She said that producer David O. Selznick had seen the magazine

...and years later, as she starred in an episode of *The Twilight Zone* ("RingaDing Girl").

cover and had offered her a movie contract. "I turned it down. I'm not ready for movies yet."

Whereas Swift had not been particularly impressed with Jimmy, he later admitted, "For Maggie and Jimmy, it was instant love. My wife just adored him and practically wanted to adopt him and make him part of our household."

During the days ahead, while Brackett and Swift were otherwise occupied, McNamara and Jimmy set out to explore Chicago together during the daylight hours. According to Swift, "I know I should have been jealous, but Rogers assured me that Jimmy was one hundred percent homosexual. I later learned that was not true."

Jimmy told Bast that on three different afternoons, he returned with McNamara to the suite she otherwise occupied with Swift. "We made love, and I was really into her."

Bast speculated that "Jimmy was eager to establish his heterosexual credentials after all the gay sex he'd had. He also told me that they didn't spend as much time exploring the glories of Chicago. Instead, they talked for hours, plotting their future careers. The two lovebirds really seemed into each other. I don't think Swift and Brackett had a clue."

"Whether it was true or not," Bast continued, "Jimmy also told me that when the time came for him to say goodbye to McNamara, her final words to him were, 'I should have married you instead of David. You and I are kindred souls."

[Eventually director Otto Preminger would cast McNamara as the female lead, alongside William Holden and David Niven, in the 1953 film version of The Moon Is Blue. *The movie challenged the censorship provisions of the Production Code of its day and was consequently banned in several states, including Maryland, Ohio, and Kansas. Preminger appealed the ban all the way to the Supreme Court and won his case. The ban was overturned, and* The Moon Is Blue *became credited as instrumental in weakening the influence of censorship in the film industry.*

For her role in it, McNamara was nominated for an Oscar as Best Actress of the Year. She later appeared in the romantic drama, Three Coins in the Fountain (1954), *and also played the lead opposite Richard Burton in a biopic* Prince of Players *(1955) about the mid-19th-century Shakespearean actor Edwin Booth.*

Her career, however, was in serious decline by the mid-1950s, offers for acting jobs only sporadic. Preminger claimed that "Maggie suffered greatly after becoming a star. Something went wrong with her marriage to David Swift. She had a nervous breakdown."

Her last appearance was with the silent screen great, Lillian Gish, on The Alfred Hitchcock Hour *in 1964. After that, she faded from public view and worked as a typist until her death on February 18, 1978.*

She was found dead on the sofa of her New York apartment, having overdosed on sleeping pills.]

Childhood Memories Come Flooding Back

JIMMY RETURNS TO FAIRMOUNT

Before establishing a life for himself in New York, Jimmy told Brackett that he wanted to return to Fairmount, Indiana, to visit his family, especially his aunt and uncle, Ortense and Marcus Winslow, who had reared him as a little boy after his mother died.

Brackett, who remained behind, bought him a round-trip ticket from Central Chicago to the train depot at Marion (Indiana), where it was understood that the Winslows would meet his incoming train.

As he rode the rails, many memories of his boyhood in the 1940s came racing back.

At this point in his life, Jimmy had not yet made any of his legendary films, nor had he yet taken Hollywood by storm. But in a short time, he would become the most famous alumnus of Fairmount. Unlike Marilyn Monroe and Elvis Presley, he had not been born into poverty. As a teenager on a Midwestern farm, he had led a comfortable middle-class life.

His Aunt Ortense remembered him as "a pretty boy, fair-skinned, rosy-cheeked, with ruby red lips. His mother always dressed him real cute until he finally adopted his own style: Blue jeans, a white T-shirt, and boots."

His first train ride to Fairmount had transpired in 1940, as part of his 2,000-mile "funeral cortège" from Los Angeles aboard "The Challenger." His grandmother, Emma Dean, had accompanied him, along with the embalmed corpse of his dead mother, Mildred. It had traveled within a sealed coffin, within a car otherwise devoted to luggage.

Years had passed since his post-graduation departure from the Winslow homestead. Whereas the family's ownership of its 14-room farmhouse had survived the Great Depression, many of their neighbors had lost their homes through foreclosures by greedy banks.

The Winslows had always been warm-hearted guardians.

In this small Hoosier town of 2,700, Jimmy as a boy raced along maple-shaded Main Street, a thoroughfare lined with staid, matronly, white-painted Victorian homes with moss-green shutters. He remembered the scene as reminiscent of a Norman Rockwell cover for *The Saturday Evening Post.*

Route 9 connected Fairmount with Marion, ten miles to the north, where Jimmy had lived, temporarily, with his parents.

Now, with Brackett far away in Chicago, Jimmy settled once again for a reunion with the Winslows and the circumstances of his childhood.

Within a reasonable time after his arrival, Jimmy left the house and headed for the Rexall Drugstore, where he ordered a chocolate malt. Ironically, something akin to that had been choreographed opposite Charles Coburn during his one big scene in the movie, *Has Anybody Seen My Gal?*

As a farm boy during his childhood, Jimmy had been taught to perform daily chores—feeding the chickens their grain, sweeping out the barn, collecting freshly laid eggs, milking cows, and helping with the spring planting. Marcus had even purchased a pony for him to ride through the fields. In summer, he fished for carp in a nearby creek.

At the local public schools, he was bright and intelligent, but often didn't listen in class and rebelled against doing homework. He earned mostly Cs and Ds on his report card.

When he had turned fifteen, his uncle got him a summer job in a nearby factory that canned tomatoes. "I earned ten cents an hour and felt like a character in a John Steinbeck novel," Jimmy later said.

Later, his uncle bought him a motorcycle, a model from Czechoslovakia. Once he was safely away from the sightlines of anyone watching from his uncle's farm, he stepped on the gas, navigating around "Suicide Curve" at full throttle. Many accidents, including two deaths, had been suffered within recent memory by motorists who did not maneuver their way around the curve.

Jimmy's fascination with motorcycles would continue throughout the rest of his life. One of his female classmates complained, "We learned to get out of Dean's way when we heard him roaring in on that damned motorcycle. Sometimes, he seemed to be trying to run over us. He was very reckless. His accidental death was often predicted."

Before he graduated from high school, Jimmy reached his full height of 5'8", weighing 140 pounds.

In spite of his small stature, he excelled at sports, particularly basketball. His coach claimed that "The boy often had to jump three feet in the air, but he got the ball in the hoop. His playmates nicknamed him, 'Jumping Jim.' In fact, he became our champion player, in spite of the fact that he also had to wear glasses because he was nearsighted."

"He broke his glasses faster than I could buy him a new pair," said Marcus.

Jimmy also took up pole vaulting and excelled at that sport, too, although he quickly tired of it.

His mother, Mildred, had been the first to notice his artistic flair. In Fairmount, he had often wandered down by the creek or in the meadows, sketching landscapes and still lifes. When not preoccupied with that, he hurled himself into track and field pursuits.

Jimmy Dean: High school basketball team member, despite his myopia.

***

No one would have more influence on Jimmy than the

125

local Methodist pastor, Dr. James DeWeerd, who was viewed locally as a hero. Evoking Billy Graham, he combined dramatic rhetoric delivered with the flair of an actor.

Shortly before his fifteenth birthday, Jimmy developed a strong crush on the reverend, who seemed responsive to the needs of this cute adolescent. In his early thirties, the Wesleyan minister was known for his charisma and histrionics in the pulpit.

DeWeerd had traveled widely in Europe and had once studied in England at Cambridge University. During World War II, he'd served as an army chaplain. After a serious injury, he was awarded a Purple

Jimmy's child-molesting priest, James DeWeerd

Heart for rescuing some fellow soldiers from a fire set by the Nazi *Luftwaffe*.

Jimmy was fascinated by DeWeerd's war wounds. Shortly after they met, the pastor removed his shirt and let Jimmy inspect his scars.

He could almost put his fist into the scarred hole in DeWeerd's stomach. As he later confessed to Bracket. "I got sexually excited trying to put my fist into that hole."

Not everyone in Fairmount succumbed to DeWeerd's spell. Some of the older boys called him "Dr. Weird" or "Miss Priss." At the time, homosexuality was almost never mentioned. Instead, the pastor was defined as "eccentric" rather than queer, a widely adopted synonym for homosexual back then.

DeWeerd was known to round up a carful of the high school's top athletes and drive them to the neighboring hamlet of Anderson. There, he would watch them strip down and swim naked in the YMCA's swimming pool. He often invited the better-endowed and/or more receptive ones to his elegantly furnished home, where he lived with his mother, Leila DeWeerd, an aging schoolteacher.

At the time, homosexuality was interpreted as "worse than communism." One basketball player was alert to DeWeerd's sexual preference. Years later, he told a reporter that "the good pastor was always in the locker room checking out our stuff as we wandered down the corridor, bare-ass, to the shower room. Some of the guys knew of his interest and soaped themselves up a bit in the shower, so that they could produce a partial hard-on for this preacher man."

"He gave many of us blow-jobs back then," the athlete claimed. "That was a good thing for some of us because gals didn't put out much until marriage."

Jimmy would later describe the Reverend DeWeerd to William Bast, remembering him as a handsome man and rather stocky. "He had a jovial laugh and was very kind, very loving, and his blue eyes forgave me, regardless of what I had done." He also recalled the pastor's rather full and sensuous lips.

"He put those lips to work on me, exploring every inch of my body," he confessed to Bast. "Every crevice. I lost my virginity to him."

The doctor did more than just seduce young Jimmy. He imbued him with a philosophy of life, telling him, "The more things you know how to do, and the more you experience, the better off you'll be—and that pertains to sexuality as well."

DeWeerd was the most cultured man in Fairmount. He introduced Jimmy to yoga, the bongo drums, Shakespeare, and Tchaikovsky. He also introduced him to car racing and bullfighting.

An *aficionado*, DeWeerd showed Jimmy movies of the bullfights he'd filmed in Mexico City, Seville, and Toledo, Spain. He also had a private collection of nude pictures of well-endowed bullfighters, something that probably affected Jimmy's life-long fascination with bullfighting.

DeWeerd also taught Jimmy how to drive. One of their shared highlights involved an excursion to the "Indy 500" races in Indianapolis. There, DeWeerd introduced him to the ace driver "Cannon Ball" Baker. According to Marcus, "When he got back home, the boy discussed nothing but car racing for days at a time."

Jimmy was at the DeWeerd house for dinner three or four nights a week, the Winslows putting up no objection to the frequency of those visits. After the pastor's mother retired for the evening, Jimmy and DeWeerd would read to each other or listen to classical music.

In September of 1956, DeWeerd granted an interview to *The Chicago Tribune*. "Jimmy was usually happiest stretched out on my library floor, reading Shakespeare and other books. He loved good music playing softly in the background., Tchaikovsky was his favorite."

What DeWeerd didn't tell the newspaper was that after his mother was safely asleep, he invited Jimmy to his downstairs bedroom and watched as he stripped down. He always said, "I want you naked for this workout."

As Jimmy later confessed, "He paid lip service to me. There wasn't a protrusion or hole that he missed."

Sometimes, after they'd made love, Jimmy would lie in DeWeerd's bed and indulge in what he called "spiritual talks."

The pastor said, "All of us are lonely and searching. But, because Jimmy was so sensitive, he was lonelier and he searched harder. He wanted the final answers, and I think I taught him to believe in a person's immortality. He had no fear of death because he believed, as I do, that death is merely a control of mind over matter."

"On the darker side, Jimmy was a moocher. He tried to get as much from you as possible, and if he didn't consider you worth anything to him, he immediately dropped you."

The editor of *The Fairmount News,* Al Terhune, later wrote: "Jimmy was a parasitic type of person. He hung around DeWeerd a lot, picked up his mannerisms, and absorbed all he could."

DeWeerd may not have been Jimmy's only homosexual contact as a teenager in the process of discovering himself. Two years after Jimmy died, a fellow schoolmate from Fairmount spoke to a reporter who was researching the screen legend's boyhood. Married and the father of two, the former athlete did not wish to be named. But he recalled seeing Jimmy behind the wheel of an emerald green- and cream-colored Chrysler New Yorker.

At one point, the schoolboy was introduced to the owner of the car, Jimmy's new friend, a master sergeant in the U.S. Air Force.

Jimmy was said to have met him at a street fair in Marion. The schoolmate remembered the military man as good looking and well built, with a blonde crewcut. "He sure didn't look queer to me. He was very masculine. He was frequently seen with jimmy, who was always behind the wheel driving the guy's car around Fairmount. He visited Jimmy on many an occasion, but usually they drove off together to Marion, or so I was told. That town had a hotbed motel on the outskirts."

Jimmy later told Brackett and composer Alec Wilder that "some Air Force guy introduced me to sodomy. DeWeerd preferred lip service."

He also told Bast, "Penetration at first hurts like hell until you get to lie back and enjoy it—even demand it."

***

It appears at some point that Jimmy began to worry that he was a homosexual. He had shown little interest in girls before. "He wasn't popular with the girls," said Sheila Wilson. "He later looked great in the movies, but back then, we were drawn to Tab Hunter and later, to Robert Wagner. They were real cute. Jimmy wore heavy glasses and he was too short for me. When he peered at me, I felt like a mouse with a hoot owl in pursuit. Before he had major dental work done, he had unfortunate gaps between his upper front teeth, a big turn-off for me."

His most serious crush on a woman was rumored to have been with Elizabeth McPherson, who was eleven years his senior. She was a reasonably attractive art teacher who also taught physical education.

He called her "Bette," spelling it in a way inspired by the name of screen actress Bette Davis. "One night, he took her to dine at DeWeerd's house, and they sat at an elegantly decorated table laden with fine china, silver, and candles. She later claimed that "the pastor fluttered around like a butterfly. When he entered the kitchen, Jimmy, a clever mimic, made fun of his movements and whispered to me that he was 'DeQueer.'"

McPherson lived in Marion and drove to Fairmount High School every day. Since she passed the Winslow farmhouse, she made it a point to pick up Jimmy as part of her morning routine and drop him off at school. Ortense didn't like Jimmy being seen with this older woman, but apparently expressed no objection. McPherson's husband was disabled, requiring the use of crutches to move around in the debilitating aftermath of polio.

Sometimes, Jimmy shared his sketches with McPherson. She always remembered one in particular. "He was a victim being crushed by eyeballs, no doubt a representation of the probing eyes in Fairmount who disapproved of him."

McPherson had once been designated as the local high school's chaperone for a group of graduating seniors on a field trip to Washington, D.C., where there were rumors that she sponsored a beerfest where all the teenagers, male and female, got drunk. She later denied that.

Apparently, according to Jimmy, they became intimate during the trip. After his first night with her, he asked her to marry him. She turned him down for two reasons: She could not divorce her disabled husband, and there was a wide difference in their ages.

As Jimmy later told Brackett, "I was still a teenager, but I came to realize that I was capable of performing sex with both men and women. I didn't feel I had to make a choice, but could go back and forth between the sexes. Of course, because of the way men are built, they can provide that extra pleasure."

Although she later saw Jimmy in Los Angeles after her dismissal from the high school in Fairmount, "It was more of a fun thing. I got together with his beatnik friends, and he hung out with two or three friends of mine. We had beer parties on the beach, and weekend drives to Lake Arrowhead. I think he brought up marriage once or twice, but we drifted apart, although I continued to write him letters, even on the set of *Giant*."

"I did a sentimental thing," she recalled. "During that bus ride back to Indiana from Washington, I clipped off a lock of his hair while he was sleeping. I always carried it around with me."

A lock of hair was found in her handbag after she died in a car crash in 1990.

***

In a journal kept during his final months in Fairmount, Jimmy wrote: "Ath-

129

letics may be the heartbeat of every American boy, but I think my life will be dedicated to art and drama."

Jimmy's speech and drama teacher, Adeline Brookshire (also known for a while as Adeline Nall), also had an enormous impact on Jimmy's future career as an actor. In his sophomore year, he enrolled in her speech class.

Jimmy found her diminutive, articulate, and energetic, and he later credited her with exposing him to the beauty of the English language. She was the first to interest him in acting, casting him in key roles in school plays.

Teacher Adeline Nall..."Jimmy could work me around his little finger."

"Jimmy was both difficult and a gift," she recalled years later to a reporter. "He could be moody and unpredictable. He liked to keep people off guard, and he was often rude to attract attention. One day, in the middle of class, he offered me a cigarette. I almost popped him one for that."

"If he didn't win some competition, he would pant and rant for days at a time. I recognized a natural talent in the boy. He had it. He knew he did, and I knew it, too."

High school drama student James Dean as Frankenstein in *Goon With the Wind*

"But he could not take criticism, which is bad for an actor. All actors face a lot of criticism, both from the press and from the public. He didn't like to take direction from anyone. That was also bad for an actor who had to work under a director. There was another quality he had. He knew how to play people. He could work me around his little finger."

In his sophomore year, Adeline revived that old chestnut, *The Monkey's Paw*. Since 1902, it had been performed in high schools and colleges, a play with a moral that there's nothing you might wish for that doesn't carry bad luck with it. In this play, appealing to those with a penchant for the macabre, Jimmy was cast as

An Unlikely Movie Star...Jimmy at Fairmount High School, watching from the bleachers.

130

Herbert White, a boy who was killed because of his mother's foolish wish.

The following year (1947), Jimmy appeared as John Mugford—a mad old man who had visions—in the weirdly named *Mooncalf Mugford.* Adeline later recalled that she had to restrain Jimmy in one scene in which he practically throttled a girl cast as his wife.

That autumn, also in 1947, he appeared in the (autobiographical) play by Cornelia Otis Skinner, *Our Hearts Were Young and Gay,* set in Paris of the 1920s. In it, Jimmy interpreted the role of the playwright's father, the influential dramatic actor, Otis Skinner (1858-1942).

There's a famous photograph out there of Jimmy disguised as a Frankenstein monster in a Halloween production of *Goon with the Wind.* Jimmy was proud that, for his character as a monster, he had designed and applied his own makeup.

That play was followed by *You Can't Take It With You,* the famous Broadway hit written by Moss Hart and George S. Kaufman. *[Opening on Broadway in 1936, it ran for 838 performances. In 1938 it was released as a film starring Lionel Barrymore, Jean Arthur, and James Stewart.]*

In his high school's local production, Jimmy was cast as Boris Kalenkhov, a former ballet master. As a reviewer noted, he was seen "booming about, exuberant, pirouetting."

Jimmy's final performance in high school play, presented in April of 1949, was *The Madman's Manuscript.* It had been adapted from *The Pickwick Papers,* written by the then-25-year-old Charles Dickens. It was the purported memoirs of a raving lunatic, with Jimmy portraying the madman, in a *grand guignol* style. His most dramatic line was, "the blood hissing and tingling through my veins till the cold dew of fear stood in large drops under my skin, and my knees knocked together with fright!"

Presented before the National Forensic League *[an organization whose name was later changed to The National Speech and Debate Association],* he won first prize at the state level and placed sixth at the national level. He was very upset he'd lost at the national level, and blamed it on Adeline.

After his high school graduation with the class of '49, Jimmy ranked 20th in a class of some fifty students. DeWeerd delivered the commencement address.

Jimmy told his friends and fellow seniors that he was heading for California for a reunion with his father, and that after that, he would enroll in some college on the West Coast.

His fellow seniors threw him a farewell party, at which they sang "California, Here I Come," followed by "Back Home Again in Indiana."

Early the next morning, with Jimmy aboard, a Greyhound bus pulled out of Fairmount. It would cross the plains of America until it reached Los Angeles. It was June of 1949. The war had ended—victoriously for the U.S. and its allies—only four years before, and young men by the thousands had flooded out of the military and into California seeking fame and fortune. Jimmy was included among those hopeful hordes.

His Indiana years had come to an end.

***

In July of 1955, Jimmy spoke flippantly about Adeline, his former teacher: "One of my teachers was a frustrated actor," he told a reporter from *Photoplay.* "Of course, this chick only provided the incident. A neurotic person has the necessity to express himself, and my neuroticism manifests itself in the dramatic."

As for Adeline, in the aftermath of Jimmy's death, she went on to become the most celebrated high school teacher of a movie star in recent memory. She made a string of media appearances, and was featured in documentaries which included *The First American Teenager* (1976). She has also toured the country, lecturing and meeting fans of her former pupil and sharing stories of his first acting roles in high school dramas.

***

During his return visit to Fairmount, with his benefactor, Rogers Brackett, still conveniently far away in Chicago, Jimmy shared a reunion with Adeline Nall, his former drama coach.

As part of that venue, he addressed Fairmount High School's small student body, talking about the Pepsi Cola commercial that had launched his career, as well as the films he'd been in, including *Fixed Bayonets!* and *Sailor Beware.* He also named and described the famous people he'd met, including Lana Turner and Joan Crawford.

He followed his short speech about breaking into the movies with the impersonation of a matador in a bullfighting ring. Donning Sidney Franklin's blood-soaked cape, he delivered a performance that included the participation of a volunteer (a graduating senior) from the audience, who acted out the role of the bull. The show included some flashy pre-choreographed moves with Franklin's cape which delighted the young audience.

After his speech, Jimmy played basketball with the school athletics team before heading for the showers.

After a family dinner with his aunt (Ortense Winslow) and uncle (Marcus Winslow), he headed for a reunion with the Reverend DeWeerd, which evolved into a night of sex.

The following day, at Adeline's request, he directed the school's drama students in a play, *Men Are Like Streetcars,* repeating, sometimes verbatim, the acting tips taught to him in Los Angeles by James Whitmore.

A senior drama student, Jill Corn, interpreted the role of a girl who had to be spanked. Jimmy didn't like the way a young actor was spanking her, so he showed the class how it "was done." He spanked Jill so hard he made her cry, and Adeline had to pull him off her.

Although Jimmy's visit to Fairmount was short, a notification about his departure appeared in *The Fairmount News:* "James Dean and the Rev. James DeWeerd left Saturday morning (October 20) for Chicago, where they will transact business for a few days. Mr. Dean spent five days with his Fairmount relatives, Marcus and Ortense Winslow."

Jimmy stayed four nights in Chicago in a B&B where he slept in a double bed with DeWeerd. He didn't call Brackett at the Ambassador East until De-Weerd was out of town. Before the pastor left, he gave Jimmy two one-hundred dollar bills to help defray his upcoming expenses in New York.

Once back with Brackett in Chicago, Jimmy remained only four days with him before he grew restless and bored. Reacting to this, Brackett gave him a hundred dollars and a ticket to Manhattan aboard the *Twentieth Century Limited.*

Brackett also telephoned his composer friend, Alec Wilder, telling him to "look after Jimmy—and I don't mean in that way!"

Wilder was a closeted homosexual, who liked young men as much as Brackett, but rarely did anything about it.

Before leaving Chicago, Jimmy, in the arms of Brackett, told him, "I feel I'll meet my destiny in New York."

***

In Chicago, Brackett escorted Jimmy to the La Salle Street Station, where he caught the 5PM train to New York, scheduled to arrive there sixteen hours later. Wilder had agreed to "take your boy under my wing and look out for him until you move here yourself."

He had been a longtime resident of the Algonquin Hotel on West 44th Street. This had been the gathering place of the celebrated Algonquin Round

Stern, but urbane and kindly. Two views of composer Alec Wilder.

Table that attracted writers, critics, and actors including Tallulah Bankhead, Edna Ferber (Jimmy would star in the adaptation of her novel, *Giant),* Harpo Marx, Robert Benchley, George S. Kaufman, Dorothy Parker, Harold Ross (editor of *The New Yorker),* and the acerbic critic and journalist, Alexander Woollcott.

Wilder was working on a musical composition when the call from Jimmy came in from Grand Central Station. "Hi," he said. "The Little Prince has arrived in Manhattan!"

Fortunately, Wilder was a well-read man, and he understood the literary reference. "Take a taxi to the Algonquin. You're welcome to live with me here until you settle in."

Jimmy didn't really know who Wilder was, but he had agreed to live with this stranger based on Brackett's recommendation.

Born in Rochester, New York, Wilder—as a composer—was mostly self-taught. Some of America's favorite singers, including Tony Bennett, had recorded his songs. His "While We're Young," had been recorded by Peggy Lee; "Where Do You Go?" had been recorded by Frank Sinatra; and "I'll be Around" had been recorded by the Mills Brothers. Other popular songs written by Wilder eventually included "Blackberry Winter" and "It's Peaceful in the Country."

Over dinner in The Algonquin's restaurant, Jimmy was blunt in questioning Wilder. "How did you meet Rogers? Were you guys lovers?"

"Friends, never lovers," Wilder answered. "He's a chicken hawk. I was born in 1907. One afternoon, as I was walking through the lobby here, I heard this bellowing laugh. It rang out true and honest. I felt I just had to introduce myself to this man who seemed so full of life."

"I soon discovered that Rogers had been born in Culver City (California) and that he knew half the people who had ever walked across Hollywood Boulevard. He also knew the darkest secrets of the stars—the exact size of Charlie Chaplin's dick; that Barbara Stanwyck was a dyke who had had affairs with Joan Crawford and Marlene Dietrich; that Cary Grant had fallen in love with his wife's son *[a reference to Barbara Hutton and Lance Reventlow];* and that the favorite erotic snack for Charles Laughton, Tyrone Power, and Monty Woolley usually included some variation of human feces."

Beginning with Wilder, his first-ever contact in New York City, Jimmy started to fabricate heroic stories about his past.

According to Wilder, "I was this stranger, and he revealed to me just what a wild young man he was. One story he told me was about how he rushed into a burning building in Chicago and saved two children from being burned alive. I decided he wasn't very bright. He wasn't really mentally developed for a twenty-one year old. Many of the people I introduced him to swallowed his tales hook, line, and sinker. I never did."

After his first day and night with Jimmy, Wilder wrote Brackett saying, "I'm happy to oblige your request, and I'll look after the boy. He's certainly not the shy type. He parades nude around my suite. I will tell you what you already know: This is a very neurotic boy, a really mixed-up kid. He tries to con everybody. There isn't an ounce of maturity in him. I suspect there never will be. He's also reckless, running out in front of moving traffic with this god damn matador cape, treating cars like they're oncoming bulls in the ring. Rogers, you can't be serious about this kid."

Wilder continued: "The spilled blood of the matador seems to hold endless fascination for him. One night, I found him sticking safety pins into himself. He told me he wanted to increase his tolerance for pain."

During the previous two days, Jimmy continuing an ongoing rant about bullfighting, making the claim to Wilder that in Mexico, "I actually danced with the most ferocious bulls in the arena.

He claimed that he was going to use the rhythmic movements of the matador as part of his stage work," Wilder said. "He then gave me what he called 'the look.' That was when he put his head down with his eyes looking up. He then stared at me like I was the bull about to die. I thought he was crazy."

When Jimmy wasn't with Wilder, he went to the movie theaters, alone, near Times Square. Once again, he sat through *A Streetcar Named Desire,* focusing on the performance of, among others, Marlon Brando. More than once, he entered one of the theaters at 1PM and left around nine hours later. For food and drink, he purchased three cokes and two bags of popcorn, which collectively comprised both his lunch and dinner.

In addition to Tennessee William's A *Streetcar Named Desire,* Jimmy became fascinated with another movie that would impact his acting style. It was the 1951 release of *A Place in the Sun,* directed by George Stevens and starring Montgomery Clift, Elizabeth Taylor, and Shelley Winters. All three actors would eventually play a role in Jimmy's life during the months to come.

A Place in the Sun was a cinematic adaptation of Theodore Dreiser's novel, published in 1925, *An American Tragedy.*

Jimmy was mesmerized by Clift's brilliant performance alongside the luminous beauty of Taylor. He was also impressed with Winters' portrayal of a plain, ordinary-looking girl who gets pregnant and is subsequently drowned so that Clift can clear his road to marriage with the

Movies and players that deeply influenced Manhattan newbie, James Dean: Montgomery Clift & Elizabeth Taylor in *A Place in the Sun*

rich, beautiful, and socially connected girl played by Taylor. Ultimately, however, his murder of the girl played by Winters leads to his execution in the electric chair.

The day after watching the movie, Jimmy visited a library and checked out a copy of the original novel by Theodore Dreiser, reading it cover to cover in three days.

His deep regret was that he had not been awarded the role of the doomed lover played by Clift. He poured out his frustrations to Wilder. "I think you could have done it," Wilder said. "After all, the role calls for a man who is both masculine and sensitive, in need of a lot of mothering."

"The part would have fitted me like a second skin," he responded. "I'm jealous of Clift. *A Place in the Sun* has made him a major star."

Months later, Jimmy watched in dismay as both Brando and Clift lost their bids for an Academy Award, the Oscar going instead to Humphrey Bogart for his role in *The African Queen*.

At the time, Jimmy didn't realize that eventually, he would become intimately involved with both Brando and Clift.

Making "Snaketime" with Moondog the Viking
PANHANDLING AND PERFORMING ON THE SIDEWALKS OF MANHATTAN

Alec Wilder wasn't the only composer Jimmy met during his early days in New York City.

One day, Jimmy—jobless, hungry, completely broke, and strolling along Bleeker Street—wanted to stop at one of the cafés for a sandwich.

Suddenly, as if in a mirage, he heard the sound of a drumbeat coming from a strange-looking sidewalk musician. He wore a dirty, tattered cloak and a Viking helmet with horns. He had a long, scruffy beard and was obviously blind.

Jimmy introduced himself to Louis Thomas Hardin, learning that his nicknames included "Moondog" and "The Viking of Sixth Avenue." Moondog's usual turf stretched along three blocks of Sixth Avenue between 52nd and 55th Streets, where he spent his time selling sheet music and panhandling. Often, he just stood still, silently accepting the dimes and quarters that passers-by dropped into his basket.

Drawn to the outcasts of the world, the more bizarre the more intriguing. Jimmy, with Moondog, soon developed an "odd couple" friendship. Jimmy learned that he'd been born in Kansas and had started playing the drums at

136

the age of five. He'd made his first drum from a card-board box. When his family moved to Wyoming, he had a tom-tom made from buffalo skin. At the age of sixteen, he'd lost his eyesight in a farm accident that involved an exploding dynamite cap. He later learned some music theory from books printed in Braille.

During World War II, he moved to New York, where, in time, he met jazz performers who included Benny Goodman and Charlie Parker. Even Arturo Toscanini and Leonard Bernstein befriended him.

He made a living by selling copies of his poetry and (heavily edited) articles about musical philosophy and by performing in street concerts.

In time, Jimmy got to know him better and would soon seek him out. At first, he thought he was home-less, but found out that he occupied an apartment on the Upper West Side. Once, Jimmy visited him there. Moondog told him that his music was usually inspired by the traditions of the Native Americans he'd met in Wyoming, with input from classical music and con-temporary jazz. "I mix all that with sounds I hear on the street—the noise of traffic, the sound of a baby crying."

"Moondog," depicted above, was a blind musician whose performance art was often accompanied by rhythms from Jimmy as a street musician playing his bongo drums.

"The chatter of wives at an open market, the melody of ocean waves, the rumbling of trains on the subway, the eerie lament of a foghorn in the harbor. When I put it all together, I call it 'Snaketime.'"

He showed Jimmy instruments he'd created, one of which was the "Trimba," a triangular percussion instrument.

On a few occasions, Moondog allowed Jimmy to participate, for tips, in street concerts. Jimmy would play his bongo drums.

"I remember one cold winter day, we'd been making music out on the street for hours—me on guitar, Jimmy on bongos," Moondog said. "We'd made about two dollars each. I said, 'Let's split and get some food.' I spent my money in a coffee shop, but he decided to go hungry and see a movie instead."

***

One afternoon, as Jimmy and Alec Wilder were returning from lunch, they were walking through the lobby of the Algonquin. Coming toward them was the formidable Tallulah Bankhead, one of Broadway's great leading ladies, an actress known for her husky (and much-satirized) voice, her outrageous personality, and her devastating wit. She was also notorious for her private life, having nurtured a string of affairs with some of the leading men and ladies of the screen and stage. Her conquests had included Sir Winston Churchill, Marlon Brando, Johnny Weissmuller *("Me, Tarzan!),* and Hattie McDaniel, who had played Mammy in *Gone With the Wind.*

Unknown to Wilder, Jimmy already knew Bankhead, having met her at the home of Joan Davis when he was dating her daughter, Beverly Wills. Davis had become a regular on Bankhead's talk radio show.

There in the lobby, to Wilder's surprise, Jimmy made a running leap toward Bankhead, jumping up into her arms and wrapping his own arms around her. Wilder was stunned by this, and surprised that his trajectory hadn't knocked her down.

Then he kissed her passionately. "When they became unglued, I didn't ask how they knew each other," Wilder said. "But we did accept her invitation to a small private party later that night in her suite."

At 9PM Jimmy, with Wilder, knocked on the door of Tallulah's suite at the Algonquin. The sounds of a raucous party could be heard. To the surprise of both men, when she opened the door, Bankhead was completely nude. "Come in, *Dah-lings,*" she said. "The party is well underway, although so far, no one's fucked me yet."

Then she looked Jimmy up and down. "Perhaps my luck has changed."

Jimmy was flabbergasted that she'd be the hostess of a party in the nude, but Wilder was well aware of her antics.

When Bankhead darted off, Wilder engaged in a dialogue with Mabel Mercer, the cabaret singer. Jimmy wandered off among the thirty or so guests.

At one point, he encountered Helen Hayes. Although he hadn't seen any or her movies or stage performances, he recognized her face from the newspapers. She was the great *doyenne* of the Broadway stage, a distinguished actress short of stature and big on talent.

In a soft voice, Hayes said to Jimmy, "I told Tallulah that nudity was all right within the privacy of her suite. But I warned her to stay in her room and not run up and down the corridors in an undressed state."

"Good advice," Jimmy said, before moving on.

AT one point, Tallulah sought Jimmy out. Taking him by his arm, she led him across the room, where an actor who looked like John Barrymore stood by himself nursing a drink. "Mr. Dean, this is John Emery, my former husband. I divorced him in Reno in 1941."

After shaking Emery's hand, Bankhead made an impressive move. She unzipped her former husband's pants and pulled out a large, uncut penis. "Look at this whopper, darling." She said. "A two-hander, even though it's still soft. You don't encounter one of these monsters that often."

Smiling politely, Emery replaced his penis and zipped up again. "Oh, Tallulah, you must control yourself." He didn't seem all that embarrassed.

Jimmy suspected that that outrageous bit of *schtick* had been repeated many times during the course of their marriage.

The party wound down at around midnight. Before he exited, Wilder asked Jimmy, "Are you coming?"

"I'll be back soon," he said. "Tallulah has invited me to her bedroom. I'll catch you later."

At around 5AM, Wilder was awakened. Switching on the light, he saw a battered Jimmy. He didn't have much to say. But later that morning, over breakfast, he was more talkative about what had transpired.

"Ever since I first met Tallulah, I had this fantasy about my sticking my dick into that luscious mouth of hers." Jimmy confessed. "It has something to do with the way she moves her lips. Well, last night, my fantasy came true, plus a lot of other nightmare I didn't contemplate. She complained that I almost choked her to death with an explosion of cream. She said it was at least as thick as the cream her old Alabama cow, Deliah, used to give when she was a girl growing up in the South."

Three nights later, Bankhead called, inviting Jimmy and Wilder to join her at Norma's Room, a nightclub in Harlem, a cabaret that attracted black entertainers, including Lena Horne, Louis Armstrong, and Nat King Cole.

Before the night was over, Bankhead herself rose to perform on the small stage at Norma's. She danced the Black Bottom and sang her theme song, "Bye Bye Blackbird," followed by hilarious impersonations of Ethel Barrymore, Eleanor Roosevelt, and Bette Davis.

As a spontaneous climax to her equally spontaneous act, she turned three cartwheels, demonstrating to the audience that she'd forgotten to wear panties.

After that night in Harlem, Bankhead faded from Jimmy's life as fast and as impulsively as she'd entered it.

***

[In the early 1960s in Key West, Bankhead was escorted to a party at the home of a local designer, Danny Stirrup. Her escort was the novelist James Leo Herlihy, who had just directed her in the touring play, Crazy October.

At one point during the drunken evening, Darwin Porter asked her, "Is it true that you actually knew James Dean? Or is it only a rumor?"

"No, Dah-ling, it's the deadly truth. I got to play with his bongos and other things. He returned the favor. But he had to go and ruin it by telling me, at the end of the evening, that my mouth reminded him of Edith Piaf's."

Weeks after Jimmy's death, Porter was with another novelist, James Kirkwood, during a visit to Bankhead's apartment in Manhattan. During their visit, she claimed that she was heartbroken when news came over the TV that Jimmy had died in a car crash. "God has taken away one of his most talented and most beautiful children."

***

One night, Wilder invited Jimmy to go with him to hear his dear friend, Peggy Lee, perform at a nightclub. Jimmy was thrilled with the invitation, since Lee was one of his favorite singers.

Seated at a front row table, Wilder was delighted when she chose to sing something he himself had written and composed, "That's the Way It Goes," followed by his big hit, "While We're Young." Jimmy, as he later described them to Wilder, found the lyrics "laden with longing."

For years, he'd read about Lee, who had been dubbed "The Queen" by Duke Ellington. She numbered Bing Crosby and Frank Sinatra among her friends. Even Albert Einstein adored her. The press often documented her love affairs, including her on-again, off-again liaison with Sinatra.

To Jimmy, she seemed to sing and speak at the same time. He found her oval face beautiful, with a glittering, seductive aspect. She'd once been described as "perky, pretty, and bouncy, but genuinely soulful, world-weary, and resigned."

Before she joined them at table after the show, Wilder told him, "Peggy lives on the dark, moody side of the boulevard of broken dreams."

Shortly before midnight, Wilder and Jimmy welcomed her to their table. She and Wilder embraced like old friends, and Jimmy impulsively kissed her on both cheeks. "You are my dream lady," he said.

He listened as both Wilder and Lee discussed Sinatra. "We have this mutual admiration society," she said. "That is, when we're not fighting. Frankie's got a temper, as you well know."

"The Primal Male meets the Primal Female," Wilder said. "Your personalities just had to mesh. That is, until you guys have one of those knock-out, drag-out fights."

"No human being can live with either of us for long," she said.

When Wilder departed for the men's room, she turned all her attention to Jimmy. "Could I come by your suite tomorrow night and be your escort to your show?" he asked.

Jazz singer Peggy Lee gave Jimmy "fever."

"If it wouldn't make Alec jealous, I'd be honored," she said. "Is he in love with you?"

"It didn't work out," he said. "I'm staying with him at the Algonquin. Our relationship is totally one-sided."

"You mean he gives you a blow-job and then calls it a night?" she asked. "I know Alec very well. I even know about his tragedy. Why he'll never be a lover."

"You mean...?"

"Exactly," she said. "He admits he has the world's smallest penis. He gets his satisfaction getting oral with some young stud like you."

"A terrible affliction," he said. "But he has to live with that. Fortunately, I don't have that problem."

"You'd better not," she answered. "Life is too short for me to waste my time on trivia. Tomorrow night is fine. Come by at seven."

The following night, Wilder was scheduled to attend a private dinner with the distinguished cabaret artist Mabel Mercer, whose loyal following included everyone from Sinatra to a coven of gay devotees. Wilder had written her signature song, "Did You Ever Cross Over to Sneden's"

Jimmy told him he'd go to the movies, but at seven, he arrived at Lee's suite at the Sherry Netherland and was shown in by a maid. When Lee appeared, he kissed her on both cheeks. For the first time, he saw her without makeup. To him, she looked like a homespun girl from the plains of North Dakota, where she'd been abused by a wicked stepmother, or so he'd heard.

In anticipation of her act, within her hotel suite, Jimmy watched her as she transformed herself into a glamorous figure, carefully coiffed and made up. She said that earlier, without makeup, on an elevator, a woman had asked her, "Are you Peggy Lee?"

"'Not yet,' I told her," Lee said. "'Catch me later, darling.'"

Satisfied with her makeup, she told Jimmy to "Pour me a cognac, and don't be stingy, baby. That's a line I learned from a Greta Garbo movie."

She informed him that before going on-stage, she belted down a few cognacs to lubricate her throat.

He hailed a taxi to take her to the theater. Backstage, he accompanied her to her dressing room where she went through another elaborate check of her makeup and costume. He then accompanied her to the edge of the

Miss Peggy Lee. "Until we meet again," she told Jimmy.

sightlines of the stage. Along the way, she hugged each of her musicians.

Standing in the wings, ready to go on, she breathed heavily in and out, and that seemed to give her a burst of energy. Then she muttered a soft, intimate prayer.

He heard the announcer: "Ladies and gentlemen, it is my great pleasure to welcome the lady and the legend, Miss Peggy Lee!"

There was an enthusiastic reception as she walked onto the stage, illuminated by spotlights. She let out what sounded like a small scream and stamped her high heels on the floor as she burst into song.

She opened her act with her big hit from 1942, "Somebody Else is Taking My Place," followed by her 1943 hit, "Why Don't You Do Right?" That song had sold more than a million copies and had made her famous.

Later that night, he accompanied her back to her suite.

When William Bast came to live with him in New York, in reference to his sexual interlude with Lee, Jimmy told him, "I was nervous at first. After all, I was told that Frank Sinatra was a tough act to follow."

"In front of me, she defined her post-performance sexual workout as 'a coolout.' She was winding down. Actually, she was quite funny, doing an impression of what chickens do in North Dakota when it rains. 'They stand in the downpour and drown,' she told me."

"Our evening was great, some moments sublime," Jimmy claimed.

At one point, she admitted that her taste in men hadn't been very good except for her first husband, Dave Barbour, the guitarist and composer whom she claimed she still loved. "Finally, by one o'clock that morning, we did the dirty deed, and she made me feel like a real man. She's not devouring like Tallulah Bankhead. Yet she is demanding in a soft way. She aims to get her satisfaction, and with me, she did. In fact, before I left her suite, I proposed marriage to her," he told Bast.

"She didn't outright reject me, but was very kind. She said, "Jimmy...oh, Jimmy. You sweet, vulnerable, dear boy. I adore you. But marriage would ruin everything for us. Let's be really close friends who get together every now and then for a good fuck."

"Okay!" he said, before passionately kissing her goodbye.

Before he left, she said, "I have this very strong feeling about you. That you're going to make it big in the movies. I sense a great deal of hidden talent in you. You're going to become Mr. James Dean, not Mr. Peggy Lee."

***

The singer published her memoirs, *Miss Peggy Lee,* in 1989. She remembered Jimmy, relaying a rather vanilla description of their relationship. *[She* was not a "kiss-and-tell" kind of author.]

During his filming of *East of Eden* for Warners, he visited her several times on the set of *Pete Kelly's Blues* (released in 1955). She played an alcoholic singer, a role that would lead to an Oscar nomination as Best Supporting Actress.

One afternoon, Jimmy watched her perform in a scene where she had to sing off-key and out of tempo. "That must have been hard for you to pull off," he said. "You're always on key."

She introduced Jimmy to the stars of the film, including Edmond O'Brien, Lee Marvin, and a very flirtatious Janet Leigh. Martin Milner, another star in the film, was already known to Jimmy. In October of 1951, each of them had appeared in two separate teleplays. But whereas Milner had star roles, Jimmy was assigned small, uncredited parts. Milner eventually got together with Jimmy and recalled how they'd first met:

[In midtown Manhattan, at Cromwell's Pharmacy, hanging out with other actors, Jimmy's first TV role came from a pickup one afternoon when he was nursing a coke. It wasn't from a gay producer or director, but from a fellow actor, Martin Milner.

Four years older than Jimmy, Milner still had a boyish quality to him that Jimmy found appealing. Jimmy knew who he was, having seen him in the 1947 film, Life With Father, where he'd played John Day, the red-haired son of William Powell, with Irene Dunne cast as his mother.

The film also starred a very young Elizabeth Taylor. Perhaps as a means of asserting his macho credentials, Jimmy boasted to Milner, "One day, I'm gonna fuck that gal."

"Well, until she comes along, why not fuck me?" Milner asked.

"You sure get to the point, man," Jimmy said.

"I'm from Detroit, but I was raised in California," Milner said, as a sort of justification. "We move in fast when we're horny."

"Your timing is perfect," Jimmy said. "I have the hots, too."

"Let's go back to my hotel," Milner said. Jimmy followed along.

After the sex, the two young actors discovered that they genuinely liked each other, and that they wanted to be friends. They retreated to a movie together and later shared dinner together.

Milner told him that Frank Woodruff, who functioned at the time as both producer and director of the teleplay T.K.O. (Technical Knock-Out), was going to film a teleplay for the Bigelow Theater. "I think I can get Frank to cast you in a part. It's just a small role, but at least it's work."

The next day, he introduced Jimmy to Woodruff, who had been cast into one of the teleplay's minor parts. In it, Milner played a teenager who becomes a boxer to raise money for his father's expensive operation.

Jimmy's role was so small, he later told friends, "It's hardly worth mentioning."

He and Milner continued to see each other "for sessions in anatomy." Although they each asserted to the other that he wasn't gay, neither seemed to see anything wrong with two heterosexual actors "having a little gay sex on the side."

Milner liked Jimmy so much, he even got him another small role in a TV series that has virtually disappeared from Jimmy's radar screen. No biography seems to mention it, although his film clip with Milner is sometimes included in latter-day anthologies of Dean's early TV work.

Milner had signed to appear in two episodes of a popular TV series, The Trouble With Father, *starring Stu Erwin as a bumbling dad. Jimmy was hired for a role. He appears with Milner, who played Drexel Potter, the boyfriend of Joyce, a high school student whose father is Erwin. In their respective roles, Milner speaks of his love for Joyce, and Jimmy worries that he'll never find anyone to love him.]*

In her autobiography, Peggy Lee wrote: "Jimmy used to come over to visit me in my trailer while I was filming *Pete Kelly's Blues.* He'd arrive like a friendly cat. We were two shy people in a little room being comfortable with each other. Jimmy was always speeding around in his car, and it worried me. He was to die in a crash in Paso Robles before he completed *Giant,* his last film. He was unusually quiet, an intense person, and he wanted to be friends with me. He was one of those people you could not forget. You could feel things simmering and sizzling inside him, and his silence was very loud."

***

During his first days in Manhattan, Jimmy admitted, "I was overwhelmed by the city. It's a frightening place. I rarely left the area around Times Square."

Eventually, he began to branch out, getting up early one morning and walking all the way to the Battery *[Manhattan's southernmost tip]* where he rode the ferry to Staten Island. Once he rode the

Martin Milner, later best known for his steady roles as a staple in *Route 66 (1960-64)* and *Adam-12* (1968-75). Jimmy found him "boyishly comforting with an adorable innocence."

144

subway to Brooklyn, continuing all the way to Coney Island, where he ordered a hot dog.

He had arrived in New York with about five hundred dollars in his pocket. He later said, perhaps in exaggeration, that "I spent at least three-fourths of that watching movies to escape from my isolation, loneliness, and depression."

He knew the time had come for him to move out of Alec Wilder's suite and into cheaper lodgings. As he later claimed, "Alec was falling in love with me, and I could not reciprocate. I no longer paraded nude in front of him. I didn't want to throw temptation at him. The last couple of times he tried to make love to me, I was as limp as a dishrag. It was all so embarrassing."

When he informed Wilder that he planned to move out, the composer recommended the Iroquois Hotel, almost immediately next door, also on East 44th Street. It was clean and decent, but much cheaper. Dating from 1899, the Iroquois was one of the most historic in New York City.

During his first night there, he met the actress Barbara Baxley in the lobby. Born in California, Baxley, a life member of Actors Studio, was one of Tennessee Williams' favorite actresses. She appeared in the Broadway production of his comedy, *Period of Adjustment.*

In Key West during the filming of a movie based on Darwin Porter's best-selling novel, *Butterflies in Heat,* Porter invited both Baxley and another star of the movie, Eartha Kitt, for dinner at a popular local restaurant, The Pier House. Over drinks, both women discussed their emotional and sexual involvements with Jimmy. But whereas Kitt had developed a deep friendship with the actor, Baxley said that she never really got to know him. Ironically, she would eventually be cast as the malevolent nursemaid in *East of Eden.*

"When we first met at the Iroquois, I didn't know who he was, and he sure as hell didn't know who I was either," Baxley said. "We spent a weekend together. He was very frank, telling me he needed to reassert his manhood 'after having to service so many faggots.' Those were his words—not mine."

Baxley found him amazingly candid when speaking about himself. He told her, "I'm serious minded, an intense little devil, terribly *gauche* and so tense I don't see how people stay in the same room with me. I know I wouldn't tolerate myself, if I had a choice."

He also told her, "I know the best is yet to come for me in my career. But I also know that when stardom arrives, it will be one hell

Barbara Baxley...An affinity for gay men

of a disappointment."

Baxley also confessed that she wanted the relationship to last "at least through a season," but I knew I could never hold onto him. He wanted to wander, and there was no way in hell I could change his mind."

"I didn't find out about all the gay stuff until later. I was used to homosexuals, having been surrounded by them all my life. I never criticized a gay person."

Sleepless, Jimmy Wanders the Lonely Streets of the City That Never Sleeps

Installed at last in his new, and private, lodgings, Jimmy seemed to adopt as his own the rhythms of New York—a city that never sleeps. He became an insomniac, roaming the streets after dark, stopping in at late-night cafés and taverns, nursing a drink in one dive after another for many hours at a time. In California, he'd been tanned and healthy-looking, but he soon took on that New York pallor, and even developed bags under his eyes based on the cigarettes, coffee, and liquor he consumed late at night.

Even though he lived only a few doors away, Jimmy could be seen on most days sitting on the bellhops' bench at the Algonquin, watching well-heeled guests come and go.

Sometimes, Wilder joined him there, later recalling that he was brilliant at impressions. "He could imitate everybody from Cary Grant to Jerry Lewis. But his best were Laurence Olivier as Heathcliff and Vivien Leigh as Scarlett O'Hara."

As Wilder remembered it, Jimmy constantly bragged about himself.

"I have always lived the life of an artist," he told Wilder. "I studied the violin. I learned to tap dance better than Eleanor Powell. I gave standing room only concerts. In a play, I won first prize in Indiana. Most of all, I like to create art such as sculpture and paintings. If I fail as an actor, and I don't expect to, I'm sure I could become one of the world's greatest matadors."

To the folks back home in Indiana, he wrote: "I've discovered a whole new world in New York. A new way of thinking. This town is the end. It's talent that counts here. You've got to stay with it or get lost. I like it. New York's a fertile, generous city if you can accept the violence and the decadence."

As he grew more confident, he took longer and longer walks, at one time claiming that he strolled the entire north-to-south length (approximately 13 miles) of Manhattan's Broadway. Once, he walked to the Battery and rode the ferryboat over to Staten Island, where he walked along the decaying waterfront, a reminder of the borough's rich maritime heyday in the 19th Century.

Back in the Times Square neighborhood, he looked at all the big names appearing on the marquees of Broadway theaters, wondering if his own name would ever be up in lights like Marlon Brando's was when he starred as Stanley Kowalski in *A Streetcar Named Desire.*

In Greenwich Village, he adopted the Minetta Tavern *[113 MacDougal Street],* in existence since 1937, his favorite hangout. One night, or so it was reported, Jimmy was seen there in an intimate dialogue with Jack Kerouac. The wannabe actor and the future author of *On the Road* were seen leaving the tavern together.

Later, after Jimmy became famous, the Chelsea Hotel's night manager claimed that Jimmy had spent the night in Kerouac's bedroom.

He wrote to Rogers Brackett, who was still in Chicago, that the money he'd brought to New York soon dwindled to $44.16. "I counted every penny," he wrote. "That's all I've got left. I'm leaving the Iroquois today and checking into the YMCA on West 63rd Street. That's right near Central Park, where I can sit on a park bench and dream about my glorious future on Broadway. Please send $1,200 to Alec at the Algonquin. I'll go by every day to see if you've sent the big bucks."

Brackett did not send any money. Nor did he answer the letter. Jimmy was forced to accept a job washing dishes in a seedy tavern on West 45th Street, patronized by drug addicts, hustlers dressed as midnight cowboys, female hookers past their prime, and pimps peddling "drugs and pussy," as Jimmy put it. "I didn't last long. The manager said that the dishes looked even dirtier after I washed them."

He was frequently seen at Cromwell's Pharmacy at Rockefeller Plaza. In those days, it was known as "The Poor Man's Sardi's."

"It reminded me of Schwab's on Sunset Boulevard in Hollywood," Jimmy said. Management let actors spend hours sitting there, waiting for job offers or making calls to their agents. There was a bank of pay phones for that purpose.

Jerry's Bar on 53rd Street at Sixth Avenue became one of Jimmy's favorite hangouts. He was frequently seen there, often in the company of struggling out-of-work actors, each trying to get by, wondering where their next meal would come from. Jerry Lucci, who owned the tavern, would occasionally feed Jimmy when he had no money—a bowl of soup, a hamburger with French fries.   Sometimes, Jimmy stole the packets of catsup placed on every table. Later, back at the YMCA, he'd squeeze the catsup from its foil containers into cupful of hot water, thereby creating an *ersatz* form of tomato soup. Sometimes, he'd wander into a cafeteria, where he could usually make off with some rolls from the baskets of bread and crackers left there for paying customers.

Once, Lucci invited Jimmy into the kitchen and taught him how to make a spaghetti dinner. "It's cheap and it's good!" he told Jimmy.

"For months, Jimmy wore the same jacket and slacks he'd brought with him from Hollywood," Wilder said. "His clothes always looked like they needed a date with a dry cleaner. I didn't want to start lending him money, but I took pity on him and often gave him a few dollars for food. He also ran up a bill at the barbershop in the Iroquois. I paid the tab there because he needed to look well-groomed for auditions."

Bryan Lewis, an out-of-work actor who never seemed to find a job, met Jimmy at Jerry's Bar. "A lot of actors—at least the better-looking ones, hustled, often having sex with middle aged married men who wanted a quickie before heading back home to the wifey and kids. I made extra bucks that way, too."

"At first, I didn't think Jimmy was a hustler. But one day, when he was desperate for money, he showed up in a transparent fishnet shirt that was sort of mauve."

"He wore the tightest jeans ever seen on a human body. He'd bleached the crotch, and his genitals were clearly visible, completely outlined. He might as well have been nude. I saw him walk out with two older queens who always came in looking for fresh meat."

Jimmy did make some friends his own age. A native of the Boston area, Richard Gearin had served as a soldier in Korea. His post-war job was at the Greyhound Bus Station near Times Square on 50th Street. He remembered meeting Jimmy, who was carrying a copy of F. Scott Fitzgerald's *The Great Gatsby.*

"When Jimmy ran out of money and couldn't pay for a room at the YMCA, he crashed at my pad." Gearin lived way up at 110th Street at Amsterdam Avenue.

Gearin also said that Jimmy developed a pastime. He liked to go ice skating at Rockefeller Center. "He was no Sonja Henie, the Norwegian champ, but he became quite an expert. Once, he discussed the possibility that he might become a professional ice skater."

His new friend also went with Jimmy to the opening of two movies in which he'd briefly appeared: *Fixed Bayonets!* at the Rivoli Theatre and *Sailor Beware* at the Mayfair. *[These films opened, respectively, in November of 1951 and in January of 1952.]*

Around 1985, Gearin still retained the fondest memories of Jimmy. For a while, in 1985, he actually lived for a while on the Winslow farm in Fairmount as the guest of Marcus Winslow, Jr. and Mary Lou Winslow, Jimmy's relatives.

***

The time had come for Jimmy to move ahead with his career in the theater or on television. After all, that's why he had come to New York. Before leaving Hollywood, he'd been provided with the contact number of James Sheldon, who at the time was working for Young & Rubicam, the Manhattan-based advertising agency.

Back in Hollywood, the director for CBS, Ralph Levy, had told him that Sheldon was well connected and that he might send him out for some tryouts for acting gigs. Subsequently, Levy had called Sheldon with news that Jimmy was on his way to New York, asking if he could do something to help him get launched.

"Ralph was directing and sometimes producing shows for Jack Benny, Gracie Allen, and George Burns, and was a good friend of mine," Sheldon said. "I promised to do what I could, and said I'd give Jimmy a helping hand in Manhattan. Actually, I soon forgot about my promise until one afternoon quite a bit later. Jimmy called my office. I wasn't too interested, but I didn't want to go back on my promise to Ralph, so I invited him to my office the following afternoon. I was yet to become a director, so I didn't know if I'd be able to help him."

"Right on time, at three o'clock in the afternoon, Jimmy walked into my office," Sheldon said. "He was poorly dressed, a little shy, and wore glasses. I didn't immediately see that he was going to set Broadway on fire like Brando did. Reviewers referred to Brando as 'a walking streak of sex.' Jimmy was more like an Indiana farmboy, but there was something there. If he took off the glasses, dressed more provocatively, he might look sexy. He had a pretty face."

"I asked him to do a reading for me from the comedy-drama series *Mama*. He was very good. I smelled a whiff of Brando, and a whole spray of Monty Clift, yet he was different from those guys. There was something unique about him. It wouldn't have hurt if he'd grown a few inches taller back in Indiana."

"I had friends who were producing a TV show, *Mama*. The role of Nels had been played by Dick Van Patten, but he'd gotten an induction notice from the Army. I called over there and got Jimmy an audition."

He confessed that he hated auditions. "It's like having to strip down jaybird naked while an asshole appraises your stuff. But I'm game."

Mama, the TV drama/comedy, had been inspired by the Broadway hit, *I Remember Mama,* a 1944 play written by John Van Druten based on a Norwegian immigrant family in San Francisco during the early 20th Century. Marlon Brando had made his Broadway debut in the key role of Nels, the part now up for grabs within the play's adaptation into a TV series.

Jimmy met with Doris Quinlain, the assistant producer, and she was impressed with his audition. She arranged for another audition with the director,

Ralph Nelson, the following afternoon.

Nelson, too, was impressed. He later recalled, "Jimmy was with us for about two weeks. He got along at first. He'd learned that I, too, had been an actor before going off to war."

Born to a Swedish American family in Long Island, Nelson had worked with the Lunts, Katherine Cornell, and Leslie Howard. After the war, he returned to Broadway and, in the years to come, he would direct Cliff Robertson in *Charly* in 1968, which brought him a Best Actor Oscar. Nelson also directed such pictures as the comedy, *Father Goose,* with Cary Grant.

Depicted above is the original cast of the 1950s TV series *Mama*. Dick Van Patten, seated on the lower left, played Nels. Jimmy almost got the role. Irene Dunne starred in the screen version.

"Jimmy turned a bit hostile the day he learned that Brando had made his Broadway debut as Nels," Nelson said. "Perhaps he feared that some critics would remember Brando in the role and how great he'd been. Jimmy sensed that the Nels character on TV had been watered down to a more vanilla version. The part of the obedient son didn't really appeal to Jimmy that much. He would have preferred to play a more rebellious character."

As it happened, Van Patten returned to the role. At his induction, and after a physical examination, he was classified as 4-F. Returning to the studio, he said, "I guess the Army doctor didn't get turned on juggling my balls. I'm back."

Even though he didn't really like the role, Jimmy was terribly disappointed. Yet he was proud to have been cast. He told Sheldon, "Even though I lost the part, I did get cast on talent alone. That's a big difference between New York and Hollywood. In Tinseltown, I would have had to sleep with some jerk on the chance I might just get the role."

Had Jimmy stayed with the part of Nels, he might never have been the movie star James Dean. *Mama* as a TV series ran until 1957, and Van Patten went on to more acclaim when he appeared in an even more popular TV series, *Eight is Enough* (1977-1981).

When Jimmy became famous, cast members of *Mama* remembered him. Rosemary Rice, cast at Katrin, the teenage daughter, recalled, "Dean was just too serious for the role. Dick, in contrast, played Nels with more humor, the way the part was written, He was much better than Dean, who was often dark and moody. I felt uncomfortable around him."

Even though Van Patten reclaimed his role, he and Jimmy became friends. "We hung out together. There were no hard feelings. I took him to poker games that actors played after the Broadway shows shut down for the night. They were held at the old Forrest Hotel on 49th Street. Jimmy never played, but just sat and watched. We'd send him out for beer and cigarettes."

"We'd often meet at the stage door of the Alvin Theater after I finished a performance. Sometimes, we'd go over to Jerry's, where he was quite popular. One night, he shared the secret of his acting technique with me."

"Never learn your lines too well," Jimmy said. "That way you can appear to be searching for what to say next. It's more realistic that way. True to real life."

***

Jimmy didn't have just a business relationship with Sheldon. It developed into an intimate friendship. Some biographers have suggested that they were once roommates and that they may have been involved with each other on a sexual level. But Sheldon told reporters over the years that their relationship was close but platonic. They did not live together. At the time that Jimmy met Sheldon, he was married and living with his wife at Gramercy Park South. Jimmy often came over for dinner.

"I was a few years older than Jimmy, and he was still a bit green when I met him," Sheldon said. "I certainly was better connected, and he seemed to take advantage of that. He took more than he gave, but was a good friend nevertheless. Whenever he was broke, he turned on that little boy lost charm, and I gave him a few bucks. In all, he was a very lovable guy."

Sheldon became a TV director, and even helmed Jimmy in two made-for-television movies, *The Bells of Cockaigne* and *Harvest*. Sheldon also would direct several episodes of *McMillan & Wife*, starring Rock Hudson, who by then had only bad memories of Jimmy.

In time, Sheldon became a major TV director. One reporter claimed, "He practically wrote the book on how to direct a TV drama." He would helm some 1,000 TV dramas or comedies, including everything from *The Man from U.N.C.L.E.* to *Batman;* from *M*A*S*H** to *The Dukes of Hazard.*

He is often credited with discovering James Dean, though others have cited that honor for themselves.

"Jimmy was a very moody person who had a great smile and charm and loved to work," Sheldon said. "That was his whole life. And he really cared about what he did. And he did it in his own way, which didn't always conform to other people's way of doing things. And that kind of quality was an original quality. It was his. Sometimes, he would sit there. Wouldn't say a thing. And one moment, he'd be smiling and sparkling. And then he'd be aloof. I don't think he was being rude. I think he was wrapped up in what he was doing."

***

The most important thing Sheldon did for Jimmy involved introducing him to a theatrical booking agent, Jane Deacy. Ironically, although her name and contact information had already been supplied to Jimmy in Hollywood by Dick Clayton (who would become his future agent), he didn't initiate any contact with her until Sheldon arranged it.

At the time, Deacy worked for the Louis Shurr Agency, where she'd begun her career as a switchboard operator.

Deacy would play a major role in Jimmy's career. The moment he entered her office, she intuitively sensed that she'd encountered an actor of unique talent.

"Jane and Jimmy really hit it off from the first," Sheldon said. "Of course, like all of Jimmy's friendships, it was a love-hate relationship depending on his mood *du jour.*"

In time, he was calling her "Mom," and indeed she did mother him. "More than anyone else, Deacy helped make Jimmy a star," claimed Alec Wilder. "She was more than his agent. Actually, a friend and unofficially, a parent."

When she moved out of the Louis Shurr Agency and established her own agency at 60 East 42nd Street, he went with her. In time, she built an impressive list of other clients, including Marge and Gower Champion, Martin Landau (who became a friend of Jimmy's), Larry Hagman, Pat Hingle, and George C. Scott.

Deacy's first job for Dean was on the Saturday night CBS TV show, *Beat the Clock,* produced by Mark Goodson and Bill Todman and hosted by Bud Collyer. Jimmy's first gig was not on camera; rather, he was hired to teach contestants how to act out, spontaneously, various sight-and-situation gags.

BEFORE I FORGET
Directing Television: 1948-1988

James Sheldon

He was told to rehearse the contestants for their funny tidbits, and he turned out to be an expert coach. "His sense of the absurd, not to say the silly, was highly developed," said Venable Herndon, a playwright. "He could open himself up to the zaniest nonsense and act it into reality without the slightest embarrassment."

For this coaching, Jimmy was paid five dollars a day. A TV producer at CBS later claimed that "Jimmy got the sack because he was just too good and showed up the contestants. Any stunt you came up

Cover art for James Sheldon's memoir, several pages of which were devoted to his memories of directing James Dean in TV dramas.

with, he could pull off. He performed like a professional and the premise of the show was that contestants needed to be awkward amateurs."

[The producers of Beat The Clock, *Goodson and Todman, would go on to produce some of the longest-running game shows in TV history, including* The Price is Right, Family Feud, To Tell The Truth, I've Got a Secret, *and* What's My Line?]

"Jimmy really needed someone—a mother-like figure—and that was Jane," Sheldon said. "She got behind him and pushed and shoved him into greatness. From the beginning, she knew she had something hot to handle, and she set out to get him work. Boy, did she come through. He did an amazing number of TV shows, some with big names like Ronald Reagan, Anne Jackson, Jessica Tandy, John Forsythe, John Carradine, Rod Steiger, and Betsy Palmer."

Sometimes, Jimmy would disappear for hours at a time, and Deacy could not reach him. When asked where he'd been, he told her he'd been sitting on a park bench in Central Park. "The greenery reminds me of my boyhood growing up in Indiana."

TV Director and "Unstable Homosexual," Robert Stevens

Jimmy Hooks Up With "The Dracula of Manhattan"

After Jimmy failed in his attempt to join the TV cast of *I Remember Mama*, his friend, James Sheldon, continued to solicit roles for him in teleplays. One friend he sent him to was Robert Stevens, a producer/director who from 1948 to 1952 helmed 102 episodes of *Suspense Theater* for TV.

Born in New York, Stevens was eleven years older than Jimmy, but the two men, with completely different backgrounds, bonded almost immediately. Each of them seemed to have met a kindred spirit.

When the set and stage designer Stanley Haggart once asked Jimmy about his relationship with Stevens—he'd heard rumors at his TV studio—Jimmy was not forthcoming. He merely called Stevens "My Dracula of the Underground."

In a candid moment years later in Hollywood, Stevens discussed Jimmy with director Alfred Hitchcock and some of his associates. "Both Jimmy and I had a fire raging within us that mere missionary position type sex could not put out the flames."

Stevens immediately cast Jimmy in one of the TV episodes of his long-running series, *Suspense Theater*, appearing opposite actor William Redfield. In 1959, Stevens would recall that casting decision to a reporter. "Dean seemed to me to be very intense and ambitious, and he didn't strike me as being a very good actor. That proves how wrong I was."

Stevens might not have been that impressed with Jimmy as an actor, but he was powerfully attracted to him both as a dark lover between the sheets and as an ideal companion to accompany him on his nightly prowls through underground New York in the wee dark hours of the night.

In spite of drawing mixed reviews from his co-workers, Stevens had a long career spanning four decades as both a film director and producer. Hitchcock hired him for some episodes of *Alfred Hitchcock Presents,* and even Bob Hope used him to helm *Bob Hope Presents Chrysler Theater.* Stevens also worked with Ronald Reagan, the host of *General Electric Theater,* and he also directed the pilot film for Rod Serling's *The Twilight Zone.* He also directed dozens of plays for *The United States Steel Hour, Playhouse 90,* and *The Armstrong Circle Theater,* plus various individual episodes of many other TV series.

Partly because of his erratic personality, his work fell off in the 1970s, but before that, he also directed some big screen features, including *Never Love a Stranger* (1958), featuring a relatively unknown Steve McQueen along with John Drew Barrymore. Based on a Harold Robbins novel, *Never Love a Stranger* featured a miscast McQueen in the role of a Jewish lawyer.

Stevens later told his gay friends, "I once visited McQueen and Barrymore when they shared a hotel room. I found both of them buck naked wandering about and stoned. I patted both of their asses and gave each of them a blowjob."

He also directed a young Jane Fonda in *In the Cool of the Day* (1963), which was nothing more than a glorified soap opera set against the lush backdrop of Greece.

Producer Franklin Heller learned of Stevens' link to Jimmy. He had hired Jimmy before, having offered him a starring role in his teleplay, *Death Is My Neighbor.* "Stevens was definitely from *The Twilight Zone,* for which he'd created the pilot. Yet he was exceptionally talented in the days when TV was in its infancy and anything could go wrong, especially during live broadcasts. He brought imagination to the medium and his own kind of brilliance. Management tolerated his erratic behavior in spite of all the rumors circulating about his personal life. He held onto his job mainly because he was so god damn good at it."

John Peyser, another director at CBS, had helmed Jimmy in *Death Is My Neighbor*. He was called to fill in for Stevens when he didn't show up for work. "The guy would often blow his cork," Peyser said. "I'd be called in at the last minute to direct a script I hadn't even read. Rumors were circulating that Dean and Stevens were up to no good. Stevens was known at the studio as an unstable homosexual."

Any good-looking actor in New York at the time soon became aware that starring in a teleplay by Stevens usually involved a workout on his casting couch. By the dozens, actors—even those who were ostensibly straight—surrendered to his demands. The doorman at Stevens' apartment house once reported that on a Saturday afternoon and night, at least nine actors came and went from his apartment, usually spending less than an hour per visit.

Sheldon did not mention Stevens in his memoirs, but did tell a reporter than on a chance encounter in 1987, two years before Stevens' death, he saw him on the street. Stevens, living in retirement, invited him to lunch, during which time he revealed that he and Jimmy had been sexually intimate.

A sophisticated man, Sheldon was aware of Jimmy's penchant for associations with strange bedfellows. "He hooks up with the castigated, those whose lives are on the fringe. Point out someone as a mainstream reject, and Jimmy immediately gravitates to them. He was especially attracted to those who had been badly wounded and had a very negative attitude toward life—a creep, really. Jimmy would go out of his way to get close to such a person. You never knew who he would show up with next."

Hired by Stevens, actor William Redfield appeared with Jimmy in an episode of *Suspense,* and would always remember what a horrendous experience it had been. This New Yorker, born in 1927, was close to Jimmy in age, but what he'd experienced was wider and more varied in its range. As a boy, he had appeared on Broadway in the 1938 production of *Our Town.* Later, he would star in such prestigious Broadway plays as *A Man for All Seasons, Hamlet,* and *Barefoot Boy with Cheek.*

[Redfield's best known film role involved an appearance in One Flew Over the Cuckoo's Nest *(1975), starring Jack Nicholson. It was during its filming that his doctors diagnosed him with leukemia, which caused his early death at the age of 49 on August 17, 1976.]*

Stanley Haggart met Redfield on the opening night of *Midgie Purvis* (1961), a Mary Chase play starring Tallulah Bankhead. She had dedicated the play to Haggart. Over a late-night dinner at Sardi's, Haggart, Tallulah, and Redfield talked about Jimmy. Tallulah and Redfield, of course, had had very different experiences with him.

"In our teleplay for *Suspense,* I was to throw Dean a knock-out punch," Redfield said. "I had done a bit of boxing at the YMCA, but I was no Rocky Graciano. I was going to give him a theatrical punch, however, during rehearsal, I missed his face by at least two inches."

Jimmy looked at him with disappointment. "Come on, Billy boy," he said. "You can do better than that. Hit me like you mean it, mother-fucker!"

"Are you kidding?" Redfield asked. "I'd bloody your nose."

"That's what I want you to do," Jimmy said. "When we go on the air, I want you to leave me a bloody mess." Then he asked a bizarre question. "Would you make lemonade without any lemons? On the show, strike me like you're Jack Dempsey and some whore had cut off your dick in the middle of the night when you were asleep. Didn't the Actors Studio teach you about realism?"

"Against my instincts, I did hit Dean during the telecast," Redfield claimed. "A really powerful punch. Like he requested, he was a bloody mess when he hit the floor. It was not stage blood, but the real thing. At least, the critics praised our realistic acting."

After the broadcast, Redfield went to Jimmy's dressing room, where he found him trying to stop his nosebleed. "I apologized profusely. I saw that his jaw had started to swell. 'I'll never forgive myself,' I told him. He finally stopped bleeding and looked up at me—not with hatred, but with love in his expressive eyes."

"If there's anything I can do for you, name it," Redfield continued. "Anything to make it up to you."

"You *can* do something, as a matter of fact," Jimmy said. "That K.O. from you really turned me on."

"Then he grabbed me and kissed me passionately, feeding me his tongue."

"The boy had fed me his tongue as well," Tallulah chimed in that night at Sardi's. "In fact, he stuck more than his tongue in my mouth, *Dah-ling.*"

Jimmy Gets Kinky
AT LATE, LATE SHOWS IN NEW YORK'S SEXUAL UNDERGROUND

Jimmy's nocturnal prowls with Robert Stevens are mired in mystery. The main source of information about them come from two very different sources, one of whom was Bill Gunn, Jimmy's African American friend, a playwright, novelist, actor, and film director, a virtual Renaissance man.

Their descriptive details originated from Mark Ducus, a close friend of Stevens. Ducus tried to peddle salacious details about Jimmy's nocturnal adventures to Robert Harrison, publisher of *Confidential Magazine,* but Stevens threatened to retaliate with a multi-million dollar lawsuit for libel. Likewise, also under threats of a lawsuit, Stevens discouraged many other Dean biographers from writing about his relationship with Jimmy.

On several occasions, Ducus accompanied Jimmy and Stevens during their explorations of New York's sexual underground. Ducas told Jimmy that he and Stevens "used to be lovers, but now we're just sisters on the prowl for male flesh."

"Most of the places we visited would have been shut down by the cops if they knew of their existence," Ducus claimed. "Maybe they'd been bribed. When Dean ventured into these scenes from the sexual fringe, he seemed fascinated by how New York's denizens of the deep lived out their fantasies."

"Homosexuality in the early 1950s was known as 'the love that dared not speak its name,'" Ducas said. "The world that Stevens presented to Dean had nothing to do with love, and everything to do with sex. At the time, millions of New Yorkers were unaware of this bizarre twilight world, at least some of it happening within buildings in their immediate neighborhoods."

"One secret club back in the 50s was the Bull Pit, and it operated in Queens in what looked like a ballroom, perhaps from the Gay 1890s, so to speak," Ducus claimed. "It was still gay, but with a different meaning. Entrance cost $25—if the bouncer approved of you. Maybe a lot more if the entertainment was special that night."

"The owners hired as many as twenty well-built hustlers, each of whom performed really dirty strip acts. When they'd finished, they assembled and lay down in the center of the room. They were on their backs and spread-eagled, positioned into what the promoters called "a wheel of lust."

"The patrons were then invited to perform fellatio, or whatever, on the men, moving from one hustler—each with an erection—to the next every time a bell went off. Sometimes, when someone was fellating an especially delectable man, he had to be urged to move on to the next recipient."

"That went on for a bit, but erections are only temporary," Ducus said. "At the sound of a drumbeat, a patron was supposed to stay down on whichever hustler he had reached up until that point until he climaxed. When that *came,* so to speak, the show was over."

"It was all such fun," Ducus said. "Jimmy seemed to enjoy it very much— in fact, Stevens urged that he configure himself as one of the performers some night, forming part of the wheel. He didn't say no, but told us he'd have to give it serious thought. I didn't go out with the guys every night, so I never learned whether he got involved or not."

The trio of nightcrawlers often patronized an illegal bar in an old warehouse in the West Twenties, right off Manhattan's West Side Highway. Its cover charge was $40 a night. For that, the patrons would be allowed to drink all the beer they wanted.

In the backroom were seven claw-footed bathtubs, in which naked men— some of them drunk, some of them drugged—had passively positioned themselves.

Tanked up on beer, patrons of the bar were invited to urinate on the men in the tubs, in many instances aiming their streams of urine directly into the recipients' faces. "Victims" within the tubs rotated frequently throughout the course of the night, some of them, soaked with piss, returned to unleash warm streams of urine on whomever had replaced them within the tubs. As the evening wore on, the stench of urine was perceived by many as desirable, and in some cases, erotic.

"Jimmy was a real 'golden shower queen' and loved all the action," Ducus said. "In one night, he must have gone to the backroom a half-dozen times to relieve himself of all

that beer. Later, I heard that in Hollywood he got involved with some pissing scandals on the sets of *Rebel Without a Cause* and *Giant.*"

Both Stevens and Jimmy, according to Ducas, were especially turned on by bondage, "real S&M stuff." Sometimes accompanied by Ducas, but usually as a pair, Stevens and Jimmy visited a large, old-fashioned apartment on Manhattan's Upper West Side.

"I went with them only once, but I heard that the owner featured a variety of different exhibitions. The night I was there, he'd hired five Mandingo types. We were told that all of them had performed previously as 'Superman' in porn shows in Havana, venues for the most part attended by voyeuristic American tourists. Each of the performers had a monstrous dick."

"A lilywhite boy, no more that fourteen, was brought out. He'd been blindfolded. He was tied up and positioned on his stomach, his legs spread-eagled, and his rosebud was exposed to a full view of the audience, poor little thing. Then the Cubanos went to work on him. The kid screamed and pleaded with them to stop, but he was brutally sodomized by one after the other. His screams eventually died down to a long-suffering whimper. He was finally carried off from center stage, a bloody mess in need of stiches. I don't know what eventually happed to the kid. He probably ended up dead in some seedy alley."

The most bizarre of the stories that circulated about the nocturnal trawls of Stevens and Jimmy through Manhattan's sexual underground might have been apocryphal, but Ducas swore that the story was true. Later in life, Bill Gunn, Jimmy's closest African-American friend, claimed that Jimmy had relayed a similar story to him as well.

It is possible that it was Stevens who (formally) introduced Jimmy to the phenomenon of necrophilia—that is, an obsession, sometimes erotic, with corpses. As Jimmy told Gunn, "Back at Fairmount High, teachers didn't go into the subject all that much."

[Of course, necrophilia has existed for centuries, with covert references to it in the underground gothic or vampire literature of England's Victorians. More

recently, its adherents have encountered like-minded cohorts in large cities like L.A., London, and New York.

It has happened that a necrophiliac will make a deal with a seedy funeral parlor, whose staff might alert them when a young man or woman, perhaps dead in an accident at the peak of their beauty, is brought in for embalming or cremation. Covens of necrophiliacs have, in some cases, convened for some kind of communal encounter with the corpse. In less extreme cases, aficionados assemble for ghoulish sessions that are simulated without the actual presence of a corpse.

Allegedly, Stevens informed Jimmy that he was a necrophiliac voyeur.]

According to Ducus, Stevens once arranged for Jimmy to pose as a recently deceased fetish object for an assemblage of necrophiliacs. In preparation for his role, after submitting to a heavy application of body make-up, applied with the intent of producing a deathly pallor, he climbed into a coffin in a darkened room and closed his eyes, pretending to be dead.

One by one, the necrophiliacs fellated the "corpse."

"Dean was a crazy loon, and he would do anything," Ducas said. "He accepted the role on a dare from Stevens. Everything happened in silence. Dean never opened his eyes during the ceremony. I found the whole thing disgusting. Later, Jimmy told me it was one of the most exciting sexual thrills of his life. Sometimes, I suspected his elevator didn't go to the top floor.:"

"Later, Stevens and I got into a fight over this cute but very fucked-up Puerto Rican kid, and we never spoke again," Ducas said. "I'm sure that he and Dean drifted away from each other after Jimmy returned to Hollywood for other dreams and other adventures. I heard he took up car racing."]

[Before the end of his life, Stevens had retired to Westport, Connecticut. The police rushed him to the hospital after they discovered him—robbed, bludgeoned, and bloodied by some unknown assailant—within his home. He died shortly thereafter, on August 7, 1989, at the age of 68, of cardiac arrest.

Stevens was known to solicit strange men, some of them hitchhikers from beside the highways, and bring them back to his residence. There was speculation that he had encountered a psychotic hustler. No arrest was ever made.]

A Fascination for Coffins

IN INDIANA, JAMES DEAN REHEARSES HIMSELF FOR HIS EARLY DEATH

Jimmy would once again retreat to the interior of a coffin, but under completely different circumstances. This time, his ghoulish act would be photographed and displayed around the world.

The story began in Hollywood with his chance encounter with photographer Dennis Stock during the weeks preceding the release of his first major film, *East of Eden.*

Every Sunday afternoon, Nicholas Ray held a *soirée* within his suite at the Château Marmont on the Sunset Strip. Ray was considering casting Jimmy, whom he'd invited as one of his guests, in his upcoming movie, *Rebel Without a Cause.*

To the party, he had also invited Stock, whom he knew on a casual basis.

Ray had met Stock when he was on assignment to photograph Humphrey Bogart. Stock had joined Magnum, the famous photographer's cooperative. At the age of twenty-seven, he was the organization's youngest member.

At the party, at around three o'clock that afternoon, Ray led Stock over to introduce him to Jimmy.

"Nick guided me to a corner of the room where a young man reclined," Stock recalled. "His moody mood was similar to mine that day, as I wasn't comfortable at parties. After Nick introduced us, he left Jimmy Dean and I alone together to talk."

"There was nothing terribly imposing about this bespectacled young man at first," Stock said. "His responses were monosyllabic. But as we chatted, and drank wine, his tongue loosened a bit. He told me that he'd made a feature film, *East of Eden,* based on a John Steinbeck novel. I had not heard of him or the novelist. He insisted that I see the movie, which was going to be shown as a sneak preview in Santa Monica. I agreed. And so it all began."

"I saw the film, and I was stunned," Stock said. "So was the audience, who applauded the vitality of Dean's performance. It was mesmerizing. From that night on, I decided that a star was born, and I wanted to get in on witnessing the birth. Within days, I had an assignment for *Life* magazine to do a photo essay on just who this much-talked-about young actor really was. A possible cover shot was suggested."

Photographer Dennis Stock in the mid-1980s

"My assignment from *Life* involved photographing Dean's environment, the setting that reflected both his background and his personality, the setting that had produced this unique character. Of course, I knew at some point that meant going to Indiana farm country. But first, New York."

The following morning at Googie's, Stock and Jimmy reconvened for breakfast, and the photo shoot—one that would lead them together first to New York City and then to Indiana, was plotted.

Outside Googie's, Jimmy asked Stock if he wanted to get on his back.

"Do you mean, 'as a means of fucking me?'"

"That would be okay, too, but my invitation was to ride behind my back on my motorcycle as we explore the Hollywood Hills," Jimmy said.

As Stock later recalled, "For me, it was the 'white knuckle' ride of a lifetime through Laurel Canyon and beyond, zooming along winding roads. Piloting his motorcycle, Dean was a crazed motorcyclist." Having survived that ride, Stock snapped took some portraits of Jimmy within some of his usual Hollywood hangouts before they flew to Manhattan together in January of 1955.

"Dean seemed to come alive in New York," Stock said. "He told me he was a Manhattan baby, and that it was his kind of town, without the phoniness of Tinseltown."

During the first morning they spent together in New York City, Jimmy invited him to his favorite barber shop in the Times Square neighborhood. He needed a trim and a shave of his three-day beard with a freshly stropped razor.

Stock followed Jimmy as he made his rounds of the city. He invited Stock into his *pied à terre,* which had two porthole windows evocative of a cabin on an oceangoing yacht. Sidney Franklin's matador cape hung nearby. In reference to the pairs of bulls' horns affixed to the walls, Jimmy told Stock that they belonged to bulls that he had killed in a Mexican bullfighting ring.

"The sink was full of dirty dishes and an overflowing garbage bin. There was an impressive collection of literature on his shelf, with works by everyone from Shakespeare to Kafka. Scattered around the room was an array of empty beer cans. The man lived like a stray animal—in fact, he *was* a stray animal."

"Perhaps I wasn't reading his signals right, but Jimmy seemed to be flirting with me. I felt sex was on his agenda if I didn't make my exit from this fifth floor walkup on West 68th Street."

For lunch, Jimmy escorted Stock to one of his regular watering holes, Cromwell's Drugstore, where everyone seemed to know him. That afternoon, Stock followed him to one of Katherine Dunham's dance classes, where Jimmy introduced him to one of his closest friends, Eartha Kitt.

Dinner that night was at Jerry's Tavern, another hangout where half the patrons seemed to know Jimmy and wished him "Happy box office!" for his upcoming movie.

That night, Jimmy took him to Geraldine Page's dressing room, within the Broadway theater where she was getting ready to go on in *The Rainmaker,* a hit play that was later made into a movie with Katharine Hepburn. That play was written by N. Richard Nash, author of *See the Jaguar,* in which Jimmy would later perform in a crucial role.

The following day, Stock photographed Jimmy sitting among his peers at the Actors Studio listening to a lecture from Lee Strasberg. Later that day, he visited Jimmy at a rental studio on Times Square, where Cyril Jackson gave him lessons on the bongo.

During their stay in New York, Jimmy frequently failed to show up at appointments he'd made with Stock. "He was a little bastard, but I could relate to him. We were developing a friendship. In some ways, I felt he expressed different parts of my own character."

Even before they flew out of New York, Jimmy told Stock, "You are becoming my Boswell," a reference, of course, to Samuel Johnson's faithful personal historian, archivist, and companion.

The most iconic photograph that Stock ever snapped of Jimmy was taken one cold, rainy February day near Times Square. In fact, it became one of the most famous post-war photos in America, widely reproduced on T-shirts, coffee mugs, and postcards. In it, Jimmy is attired in an overcoat he'd bought at an Army surplus store. A soggy cigarette dangles from his mouth. His shoulders are hunched, his hands buried in the pockets of his coat.

After their time in New York, Stock and Jimmy flew together to Indiana, where his uncle, Marcus Winslow, met them at the airport and drove them to his farmstead. There, Jimmy was greeted by his aunt, Ortense Winslow, who treated him like a loving mother.

"Jimmy was a cute little boy," Ortense told Stock. "He wasn't afraid of anybody or anything. He was a pretty boy. I've heard people say he was too pretty to be a boy. He was fair skinned, with rosy cheeks and lips, and his mother dressed him real cute."

"His aunt and uncle were warm, generous people, and they seemed to shower love upon Jimmy," His nephew, Marcus Winslow, Jr., clearly adored Jimmy, treating him like an older brother."

As Jimmy navigated his way with Stock through Fairmount, he was treated like a local celebrity, even though *East of Eden* hadn't yet been released. He was often stopped and asked for his autograph.

"I roamed the town and the surrounding farmland with Jimmy, and I came to know him. We formed a friendship, but it would be a fleeting one. At times, I think Jimmy had seduction on his mind, but it never came to that. The closest it came was when he invited me into the bathroom we shared. He was in the tub, bathing, and he asked me to soap his genitals because he said that if he did so, it would turn him on too much. I politely refused."

At one point, Jimmy was photographed next to the tombstone of Cal Dean, his great-grandfather. He pointed out that the name Cal was also the name of the character he played in *East of Eden*.

Jimmy's nephew, "Little Markie," was only seven years old at the time, and Stock took pictures of him with his uncle as they fixed Markie's bicycle and as Jimmy pushed him around the snow-covered yard in his soapbox derby racer.

In the Winslow's barnyard, Jimmy posed with a 700-pound sow.

At one point, he entertained the barnyard animals with a performance on his bongos. "They need entertainment, too," he told Stock.

On another day, Jimmy appeared to be acting out lines from the title role of *Hamlet,* "exposing the Herefords and Poland China hogs to some of Shakespeare's most elegant soliloquies," Stock said.

That night at a school dance, an attractive young girl came up to Stock and told him that Jimmy used to date her. He failed to get her name.

"You know when you see a bird in a cage, how you want to open the cage door and say, 'fly, bird!' Well, that is the way I always felt when I was with Jimmy."

That night, back in Stock's bedroom, Jimmy got philosophical. "There really isn't an opportunity for greatness in this world. We are impaled in a crock of conditioning. A fish that in water has no choice. Genius would have it that we swim instead. We are fish, and we drown."

Stock didn't want to admit it, but he really didn't know what Jimmy was talking about.

The afternoon before they flew back to New York, Jimmy took Stock for a stroll along Main Street, leading him into Hunt's General Store, where he knew the owners. He then directed him to a room in the back where the Hunts displayed and sold coffins.

Jimmy headed toward one of them and climbed inside, asking Stock to snap pictures of him.

At first, Stock refused, considering it tasteless, but he acquiesced after Jimmy told him that the great *tragedienne* of the early 20th Century stage, Sarah Bernhardt, had posed for a picture from inside a coffin. "If Sarah can pull that stunt, so can I." After that, Stock shot him in various poses inside the coffin.

At one point, Jimmy closed its lid. He emerged, giggling, and said, "The trouble with the lid being closed it that it squashes my nose."

"He sat up for one picture and looked so very gloomy," Stock said. "It was the saddest picture I ever shot, and it made me even sadder seven months later when Jimmy, in a coffin, was shipped back to Fairmount for burial."

"When I developed the picture later, I realized that Jimmy was not pulling a prank of indulging in black humor. He was expressing the loneliness of a little boy lost. All his showmanship had gone out of the picture. Exposed was a young man who really didn't understand what he was doing and why he was doing it."

***

During their transit back to the Winslow farm, as an explanation for what had happened in the coffin, Jimmy told Stock, "I was mocking Death, telling the bitch I wasn't afraid of her. I wanted to get into that coffin to tell the world that James Dean is not afraid to die. I'm laughing in the bloody face of Death. I'm taunting the cunt."

The next day, aboard a plane heading to New York, Jimmy turned to Stock. "I have a funny feeling I'll never go home again. I'm saying goodbye to my past."

Stock's photo essay on James Dean was published in the March 7, 1955 issue of *Life* magazine. Later, his photos were released again within a book entitled *James Dean Revisited.*

Although the friendship between Stock and Jimmy was fleeting, producers deemed it significant enough to make a 2015 movie of the relationship. Entitled *Life,* it was directed by Anton Cordijin, starring Dane DeHaan as Jimmy, Robert Pattison (otherwise known for his Vampire roles) played Stock, giving a murmurous impersonation.

The New York Times described Pattison's performance as "perversely listed. He has been compared to Dean but in *Life,* he dials down his glow to nearly nothing to become a wan."

DeHaan delivered an unconvincing impersonation, which would make first-time viewers wondering what merited all the fuss about James Dean. The most convincing portrayal came from Ben Kingsley, cast as Jack Warner.

Jimmy to Dizzy Sheridan:
"Shall We Invite Queen Elizabeth to Our Wedding?"

One afternoon at a "cattle call" for CBS, Jimmy met a pretty young 22-year-old wannabe actress, Jane Wright. Based on the audition, neither of them got any job offers. When it was over, he walked with her to the Rehearsal Club, at West 53rd Street between Sixth and Seventh Avenues. Adapted from the architectural interconnection of two brownstones, it functioned as a residence for women. Living there were actresses, singers, and dancers staying for room and board at modest prices. Jimmy was invited in for a meal after telling Wright that he hadn't eaten in two days.

He never saw her again, as she checked out two days later to return to her home in Greensboro, North Carolina. She told Jimmy that she'd been turned down at least fifty times for show-biz jobs and that she had run out of money.

He felt comfortable in the public rooms of this women's residence, where young men sometimes waited for their dates. No men were allowed upstairs. Sometimes, one of the performers would give him half of her sandwich or perhaps a coke. He would sit there for hours.

One day, he was caught in a rainstorm and entered the lobby dripping wet. He sat down and put his wet boots on top of a coffee table. Had the supervisor been around she probably would have evicted him from the building. He sat there wearing a wet and undersized camel's hair coat that a young woman had given him. She'd worn it in college.

At that time of day (late afternoon,) the lobby was empty except for an attractive, rather tall woman who sat across from him. She struck him as a sensuous brunette, and he found her most appealing.

They talked casually. He learned that her name was Elizabeth Sheridan, but that most people used her nickname, "Dizzy." She told him she was a dancer, and the namesake within "The Sheridan Trio" which included her two partners: Fabio Diaz, who evoked a Mexican bandit, and Tony Marcello, son of an Italian butcher. Muscular, and perhaps with a nod to his father's profession, he was usually described as "beefy."

Dizzy would wait until 2000 to publish a memoir of her affair with Jimmy, entitling it *Dizzy and Jimmy.* In it, she recalled their first meeting early in 1952. "He was wet, and he was blonde. And his glasses were all wet. And he was a bit shorter than I was. He looked small and blonde and wet. And lovely. I just remember that he was terribly intense. And we intensely spoke about intense things."

The theme of their dialogue included the struggle of an artist trying to break into the performing arts in New York City. As they continued talking, it turned out that they each shared an interest in bullfighting. He hadn't expected that from her.

To eke out a living, she worked as an usher at the Paris Cinema on 58th Street at Fifth Avenue, near the deluxe Plaza Hotel. In time, he would visit her there. She slipped him in and fed him free popcorn and candy bars.

In the lobby of her residence, he told her that he needed to walk somewhere, but that the rain didn't seem to be letting up any time soon. "If you'll let me borrow your umbrella, I'll return it tomorrow afternoon." Somehow, she believed him, and went upstairs to fetch it.

At the exit, he smiled shyly at her and looked into her eyes. "You are the most interesting girl," he said, before opening the umbrella and heading off into the storm.

She didn't really expect to see him again, but nevertheless, she sat for three subsequent hours in the lobby of her building, waiting for him to return. The next day, just as she was about retire to her room, he entered the lobby with her umbrella.

He invited her over to Jerry's telling her it was his favorite hangout. Since both of them were on a tight budget, they agreed to share a hamburger. He ordered a beer and she asked for a Champale. "Can I have a taste of your drink?" he asked. She agreed, and then excused herself. When she returned, she noticed two white objects floating on the bottom of her glass. "What's that?"

"Do you mind fishing out my two front teeth?" he asked.

He had dropped his removable caps into her glass. Actually, she found him rather cute "with his toothless idiot grin."

"My father works with teeth. You found a sample of his work floating in your Champale. My mother, dead now, was an Indian squaw."

They soon began to date, and he learned that her father, Frank Sheridan, now divorced from her mother, a singer, was a distinguished classical pianist.

That Saturday night, she invited him to a big nightclub in Harlem, where The Sheridan Trio was appearing as one of the acts. Flanked by two part-ners, Dizzy performed the Apache dance, "Slaugh-ter on Tenth Avenue."

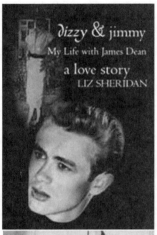

Jimmy later admitted, "I fell in love with Dizzy watching her get thrown around the stage by those guys. Of course, love is such a fleeting emotion. After the show, I took her to Jerry's, where she fell in love with me because of my clever napkin doo-dles."

That night, she remembered their first kiss, comparing it to two puppies cleaning each other.

***

After some time had passed, the loving couple were ready to mate, and each seemed willing to embark on a sexual encounter with the other. Nei-ther, alas, had any place to go for privacy. An op-portunity arose when Mrs. Sheridan, her mother, invited them for Sunday dinner at her home in Larchmont. Their house opened onto a view of Long Island Sound.

Between them, they'd saved about a hundred dollars. Dizzy suggested that on the day before they were expected at her mother's house for dinner, they travel together by train to Larchmont, and on that Saturday night, they register at a local hotel together as newlyweds. Consequently, defining

Dizzy Sheridan...a show-biz future as Jerry Seinfeld's mother.

themselves as "Mr. and Mrs. James Dean," they checked into the Bevan Inn, adjacent to the Horseshoe Harbor Yacht Club.

Locked away together for the first time, Dizzy said in her memoirs that they made love, both of them "exploding too quickly" while still clad in their underwear.

After a joint bubblebath, they indulged in another round. She later defined his entering her as "thrilling. I rose up and then cried out. He was moving deep within me, touching places I had never known before, secret even from myself."

Playfully, the next morning over breakfast, they smeared jam on each other's faces, then licked it off.

Arriving a few hours later for Sunday dinner at her mother's house, Jimmy was treated to his favorite dish, pot roast. He told Mrs. Sheridan that it was even better than the pot roast his aunt, Ortense Winslow, made for him every Sunday back in Indiana. Mrs. Sheridan was charmed by his politeness and good manners.

Back in New York, Jimmy saw Dizzy almost every day; if not, they talked on the phone four or five times a day. "Ours was a very private relationship. During the time we were together, we saw very few people. It was the way both of us wanted it."

She claimed that there was talk of marriage. They even went so far as to compose a guest list for their possible upcoming marriage. The guest of honor would be Queen Elizabeth. The others would include Noël Coward, Albert Einstein, Katharine Hepburn, and Spencer Tracy. Of course, Dizzy was completely unaware that Jimmy had already "tricked" with Tracy in Hollywood.

Ultimately, he resisted marriage. "I won't marry unless I can take care of a gal in a way she should be cared for, and I'm in no position to do that. Hell, I can't even look after myself."

According to Dizzy, "Most of the time he was quiet, sensitive, and intelligent. Sometimes, he would, after a long silence, look up at me and grin. That smile could warm a girl's heart."

"What nice girls didn't do, I did," Dizzy said. "We developed an intimate sexual relationship. For more than a year, we lived in a sheltered dream created out of our hopes for the future and our passion for each other."

On February 8, 1952, Jimmy turned twenty-one, and celebrated, with Dizzy, his official transition into adulthood.

Alec Wilder later revealed that Jimmy didn't like turning twenty-one, evaluating the event with, "I should have made it by now. I would have if the fucking directors and producers weren't so stupid. They're nothing but jerks."

"Jimmy came to see me only when he was depressed," Wilder said. "That was most of the time when he didn't get an acting job. He grew increasingly bitter after his birthday."

"One night he called me at two o'clock in the morning, telling me he was about to die. He said he wanted to bid me a final farewell. I told him to come over right away so we could talk. But he wouldn't do that. He wouldn't even tell me where he was staying. When I insisted, he hung up. An hour later, he called to tell me he was all right."

"I merely dreamed I was dying," he told Wilder. "I'm not really dying."

When he put down the phone, Wilder later wrote in his journal. "There is one thing I have noticed about Mr. James Dean, boy actor. He can run through an entire gamut of emotions in just twenty-four hours, or even less."

When Dizzy and Jimmy saved up enough money, they decided to rent a studio at the Hargrave Hotel. It had two large windows overlooking Columbus Avenue at 71st Street. Jimmy compared it to the size of a broom closet, containing a double bed and an old-fashioned bathtub with "lion's claws" for feet.

Dizzy recalled that both of them stood nude in front of a full-length mirror, admiring the contours of their bodies. "We retired to the bed, where we stroked each other's bodies. By the time he entered me, we were ready to explode together."

She recalled candlelit dinners where they often shared a bowl of shredded wheat while he dreamed of eating a big, juicy steak. They sometimes strolled through Central Park, holding hands and avoiding the muggers. "Mostly, we sat and talked for hours about our lives and what we wanted to do with them. He just hung on to me, knowing I was lonely at the time, too. We became inseparable."

***

Although he'd been fired from his job at CBS's *Beat the Clock,* Jimmy returned to the studio to play a key role in the CBS Television Workshop Series, a segment entitled *Into the Valley*. Directed by Curt Conway, it was a jungle warfare drama. Jimmy was cast as one of the "dogfaces," the role similar to his brief part in Hollywood when he appeared in the movie *Fixed Bayonets!*.

The scenario for *Into the Valley* was based on an account of the brutal battle between the Japanese and American soldiers on Guadalcanal, as written by the novelist and war correspondent, John Hersey.

Jimmy became intrigued after reading Hersey's story and wanted to learn more about his work. He went to the New York Public Library, where in one sitting, he read a sort of masterpiece by him, a story about survivors from the ruins of Hiroshima, which had been destroyed by an atomic bomb in 1945. These characters included everyone from a widowed seamstress to "a man of God."

He was even more fascinated by Hersey's novel, *A Bell for Adano,* the tale of the Allied occupation of a Sicilian village during the closing months of World War II. Later, it won a Pulitzer Prize for Hersey and was adapted into a movie starring Gene Tierney and John Hodiak.

Jimmy's next assignment—also for CBS— was a part within *The Web,* a series whose episodes focused on ordinary people caught up in extraordinary situations rife with danger and intrigues.

"Dean was a young man seeking to solve the murder of his brother," said Franklin Heller, its producer. "We needed a strange, eccentric character, and Dean sure fitted that bill." Heller cast two major stars, E.G. Marshall and Anne Jackson, into the lead roles. At the time, she was married to another distinguished actor, Eli Wallach.

Jimmy was cast as a "dogface" in a teleplay based on a drama inspired by the writing of the Pulitzer Prize-winning American writer and journalist, John Hersey *(above).* His account of the aftermath of the atomic bomb dropped on Hiroshima was judged as the finest piece of American journalism of the 20th Century by a 36-member panel associated with New York University's Journalism Department.

Heller would go on to direct *What's My Line?,* the longest-running TV quiz show in that medium's history. "Before I could do that, I had to survive James Dean," he recalled. "He was the most difficult actor I ever worked with, rude and hostile. I wanted to fire him, but Marshall and Anne insisted I keep him on."

"Dean was an absolute horror until we went on the air, and then he performed with perfection," Heller said. "But he was very moody during rehearsals, always wanting to know what his god damn motivation was. I found him a pain in the ass. Finally, I told him his fucking motivation was to earn a paycheck."

Most actors merely walked through rehearsals, saving their real stuff to strut before the camera," Heller said. "Dean wanted all his rehearsals to be blood, sweat, and gore. In one scene, an actor was supposed to strike him. Dean ordered the actor to hit him hard. He did. Dean ended up bloody on the floor, but he took it like a man and didn't complain at all. We suspected he might be a masochist and that he got a sexual thrill by having the stud beat him up."

Jackson claimed she liked Jimmy, even though he monopolized Heller so much he didn't have time to direct any other members of the cast. "I thought that with the right training and direction, he might become another Brando.

Incidentally, in case you weren't around in 1952 to see the drama, I was revealed as the person who murdered Jimmy's brother."

Jimmy had several long talks with Marshall, who, along with Marlon Brando and Montgomery Clift, as well as Julie Harris and Kim Stanley, made up the original coven who founded Actors Studio. Jimmy had great respect for Marshall, who had starred on Broadway in such plays as *The Skin of Our Teeth* and *The Iceman Cometh*.

Jackson would later appear with Jimmy in the Off-Broadway play, *The Scarecrow.* Even though Heller had feuded with Jimmy, he later hired him again for the 1953 TV drama, *Death Is My Neighbor.*

Some producers at NBC saw Jimmy perform and were impressed. In those days, one studio was always trying to steal the best actors from their rivals. Jimmy was called over to NBC where he was offered a role in the production of *Martin Kane, Private Eye.*

Agent Archer King said the director at NBC, "found Jimmy impossible to work with, and unlike Heller, simply wasn't patient enough to continue nurturing Jimmy. After three days, he was fired."

His agent, Jane Deacy, reassured Jimmy. "You're every bit as good as you think you are. But it's going to take a long time and a lot of patience on your part to convince others of that."

"Time is something I don't have," he told her.

***

Still at CBS, Jimmy complained that his next role was too small, defining it as one of those "if you blink you'll miss me" parts. For Westinghouse Studio One, he signed on to appear as a bellhop in the drama *Ten Thousand Horses Singing.* It

One of the most distinguished of American actresses, Anne Jackson, born in 1926, was still working in 2016 in cameo roles. She married actor Eli Wallach in 1948 and was still married to him upon his death in 2014. She was one of the first of the big stars in New York to see the potential of James Dean, predicting a great future for him.

After the first two days, the directed wanted to fire James Dean from the teleplay in which he was performing with its star, E.G. Marshall. But the veteran actor took up for him and demanded that he stay.

Marshall recognized talent when he saw it. As a founding member of the Actors Studio, he knew Marlon Brando and Monty Clift. He told Jimmy, "Maybe not today, but at least by tomorrow, you're going to be every bit as good as those two...maybe even better!"

aired on March 3, 1952.

Directed by John Paul Nickell, the teleplay starred John Forsythe, Catherine McLeod, and Vaughn Taylor. Worthington Manor, who both wrote and produced the episode, eventually evolved into one of the most prolific and creative voices of the Golden Age of television in the 1950s. Jimmy spoke to him only briefly. The producer told him, "My aim is to develop a national audience for TV drama without lowering artistic standards."

"Good luck, sir," Jimmy said. "I'm with you."

Nickell helmed Jimmy in his scene. A Kentuckian, he would go on to direct such hit series as *Ben Casey, Bonanza, Lassie,* and *The Virginian.* Years later, he didn't remember directing Jimmy in this little drama.

In it, as a bellhop, Jimmy rides the elevator to the tenth floor, carrying the baggage for a quarreling couple. At their destination, a woman (McLeod) is abused by her companion (Taylor). Forsythe comes to her rescue. Taylor takes off his glasses and punches Forsythe in the jaw. Jimmy is seen reacting to the violence. During the course of the scene, he uttered only one line, "Ten, please," delivered when he first stepped onto the elevator.

"I guess I was in the minority in that I just didn't see what James Dean had," said actor John Forsythe, depicted above in 1958. "I was in the first class of students when Actors Studio was founded, and I thought I recognized talent when I saw it, but in his case, I guess I was wrong."

Forsythe went on to star in a trio of TV series, spanning four decades: *Bachelor Father, Charlie's Angels,* and *Dynasty,* the latter running for most of the 1980s.

Born in 1910, Taylor would star with Jimmy in two other teleplays, *Harvest* and *The Bells of Cockaigne.* Later, Taylor would appear with Elvis Presley in *Jailhouse Rock* (1957); Paul Newman and Elizabeth Taylor in *Cat on a Hot Tin Roof* (1958)*,* and in Alfred Hitchcock's *Psycho* (1960).

***

Later that March in 1952, Jimmy was assigned his first starring role. It was within the 30-minute drama *The Foggy, Foggy Dew,* produced for CBS's Lux Video Theater. An actor and director, Richard Goode, cast Jimmy in the role of a happy teenager, an unusual part for him.

In the plot, he is seen leading a well-adjusted life with his foster parents, played by Richard Bishop and Muriel Kirkland. The young boy thinks those are his real parents.

One day, he meets his biological father, James Barton, who is a drifter roaming the countryside with his guitar. When he learns that Jimmy is happy with his foster parents, he decides not to reveal his true identity.

At the time, Barton was also appearing on Broadway in *Paint Your Wagon.* One day, he gave Jimmy some complimentary tickets to his show.

The title, *Foggy, Foggy Dew,* derived from an 1815 English folk song. In the 1940s, Burl Ives popularized it in America, but was arrested in Utah by a local sheriff who interpreted it as too bawdy to be performed in public, in Utah, at the time.

***

One Friday afternoon, Alec Wilder invited Jimmy and Dizzy Sheridan to the Algonquin for tea. He recalled that "she was a fine young woman."

Later, he told Jimmy, "She seems to have a good influence on you. You seem calm around her, less neurotic. She'll keep you from wandering down too many dark alleys."

Two days later, on a Sunday afternoon, Wilder phoned Jimmy and invited him to drop by his suite late that afternoon at 6PM. "I have a surprise for you."

At the appointed time, Jimmy arrived and knocked on the door. It was not Wilder who answered, but Rogers Brackett.

"Guess who has moved to New York?" he asked Jimmy, pulling him inside the apartment and pressing his mouth down on his.

Chapter Five

SEE THE JAGUAR

The Play's a Dud, but Jimmy Opens on Broadway to Rave Reviews

James Dean Blazes a Celebrity-Studded, Pants-Dropping Trail Through Manhattan in a Saga Starring Grace Kelly

His Feud With The Actors Studio
After Auditioning as "The Matador," Lee Strasberg "Gores Him in the Gut."

After Rogers Brackett wrapped up his advertising work in Chicago, he rode the *Twentieth Century Limited* to New York and his new Life. From afar, stating his intentions to Alec Wilder, he planned to "reclaim Jimmy."

The composer told Brackett that "Jimmy thinks he's in love with this dancer, Dizzy Sheridan. There's some vague talk of marriage. If anything will break them up, it's their mutual poverty."

Since dancing gigs for The Sheridan Trio were few and infrequent, Dizzy had been forced to accept a low-paying, part time job as a photo researcher.

After his reunion with Brackett in Wilder's suite at the Algonquin, Jimmy's "moment of truth," to use Jimmy's bullfight terminology, had arrived. He had to confess to Dizzy the details of his relationship to his mysterious mentor, Brackett.

In lieu of full disclosure, he opted to present her with a limited, highly edited version, with the excuse that "when I was down and out in Hollywood, Brackett got me film and radio work." He did not let her know that he'd lived more or less openly with Brackett as his male lover.

"He's now arrived in New York to find an apartment and establish himself," Jimmy said. "I have to tell you the truth. Rogers is a little bit queer. He even came on to me, and you, of all people, know what a *toro* I am in bed. He wanted to suck my cock. I was broke and really desperate, so I gave in to him. Many out-of-work actors have to do that, as you know, 'cause you're in show business yourself. It's all about the casting couch. In Hollywood, or so it seems to me, about as many guys as gals are forced to lie on that couch."

"When it was over, I felt really, really bad, like a male whore. I had done something distasteful, completely repugnant to my true nature. And I still haven't come to terms with myself for doing it."

"As you know, both of us will soon be on the street unless we can raise more money. Brackett has volunteered to help me find work in New York. That guy knows fucking everybody in the industry."

"But what will you have to do for him?" she asked.

"I gave into him just that one time," he said. "I can hold him off."

"I'm not so sure about that."

"And of course, I'll need to spend time with the queer."

"Some time?" she asked. "Exactly what does that mean?"

She later wrote of her shock at hearing about his involvement with Brackett. "I felt physically ill. After all, we'd promised to be together forever. My stomach was churning. I was a wreck." She finally told him, "I want to meet this Brackett creep. Perhaps when he sees that we're a loving couple in a committed relationship, he'll back off."

"That can be set up," he said. "I want him to know that, too, so he'll stop pursuing me."

Later that morning he left the apartment without telling her where he was going. He didn't come back until well after midnight when he staggered in drunk, collapsing onto the bed.

Another blow, this one to both of them, occurred at around 10AM the following morning. The building manager pounded on their door. Groggy, Jimmy buried his head under the pillow as Dizzy answered the knock. Bluntly, the manager informed her that because of their mounting and unpaid back rent, the owner of the building had ordered them out no later than the following morning.

After she left, Dizzy turned her anger onto Jimmy, accusing him of spending the previous day with Brackett. "I think he's a queer. *So are you!*" She screamed the words at him at peak lung capacity.

"I thought you'd understand," he said. "I thought you were different. But you're just another stupid cunt!"

"How dare you call me a cunt, you little prick," she yelled at him.

He rushed about the apartment, ripping Sidney Franklin's matador cape from the wall and stuffing his meager clothing into a battered suitcase.

As he stormed out, heading down the steps, she yelled down at him, "*Olé!*, you bastard!"

After searching throughout most of the day, hoping to find a cheap place to live, Dizzy, through a contact, located a little basement apartment in Hell's Kitchen between the Hudson Piers and 9th Avenue. The rent was only eight dollars a week. She took it.

Having no way of getting in touch with Jimmy, she went to Jerry's Tavern that night, hoping he'd show up. She found him there looking desolate. He apologized for his outburst that morning, and she did the same. They reconciled, and he followed her back to her tiny (new) rental, which looked so small he labeled it "the bird's nest."

The following evening, he agreed to escort her to Brackett's new apartment, explaining that, "This old queer can help me a lot if he'll just stop hitting on me."

She later wrote that she interpreted Brackett as "a sexual predator, a well-connected old queen who took advantage of a star-struck impressionable kid."

Upon entering Brackett's building, Jimmy paused in the lobby, assuring her, "You're worth a hundred Bracketts."

Introduced to the producer, she found him "a vision in beige—beige hair, beige clothing, beige shoes, beige carpeting, and beige furnishings." A flickering fireplace provided a welcome touch of flame.

As she sat with Jimmy on Brackett's beige sofa, he possessively held her hand as if to signal to Brackett, "I'm not queer. I'm in love with a female."

An hour progressed awkwardly, punctuated with a bit of name dropping and an unspoken one-upmanship as to who was more familiar with Jimmy's taste in food, drink, and interests.

Brackett had heard of Dizzy's father, the classical pianist, who was, coincidentally, acquainted with Alec Wilder.

She didn't like Brackett, and he didn't like her, although both of them tried to conceal their resentment of each other. She finally made an excuse to leave, hoping that Jimmy would go with her. In the hallway, he promised that he'd catch up with her later at Jerry's. He claimed he had some urgent matter to discuss with his producer friend. "It's work related," he assured her. "No funny business."

As Brackett later revealed, the business that then ensued wasn't funny at all. After Dizzy departed, he demanded that Jimmy take him to bed—"and fuck me real hard, like you really mean it. It'll be your atonement for bringing that possessive little creature here."

The next day, he didn't return to her cramped little apartment, but went instead to live with Brackett in his elegant apartment on 38th Street, just off Fifth Avenue near the site where a young Jacqueline Kennedy, married at the time to a senator from Massachusetts, shopped when she was in New York, Lord & Taylor.

During their first week together, Brackett tried to reassert his dominance over Jimmy. "I plan to keep you drained of all your honey so you won't have anything left for that silly bitch."

In the days ahead, Jimmy saw Dizzy whenever he could. Their relationship continued, but certainly not with the same intensity it had in the beginning. For a time, she left Manhattan for a gig in New Jersey.

On most evenings, he was seen out on the town with Brackett "and his queer friends," as Jimmy called them. Mostly, they were gay men who worked in advertising or in television. Jimmy went with Brackett to concerts, the ballet, Broadway opening nights, and to such restaurants as "21" or Sardi's, where they often sat at tables with celebrated stars such as Bette Davis or Joan Fontaine. Late one afternoon, as Wilder was moving through the lobby of the Algonquin Hotel, he spotted Jimmy and Brackett talking with a drunken novelist, William Faulkner.

On evenings when he was free, and Dizzy was in town, Jimmy often ate a plate of food with her at Jerry's, which was still a favorite hangout. They seemed to hold out some vision of their future together, although those hopes grew less intense and less realistic as time went by.

Other romantic involvements, both male and female, would loom in Jimmy's future, especially after he became involved in the Actors Studio.

***

April of 1952 had been a month without work for Jimmy, but after Brackett's return to New York, and because of his intervention, small roles emerged for him in a trio of teleplays scheduled to be aired in May or, in one instance, on June 2. The first was a teleplay about young Abraham Lincoln; the second was an episode set at the end of the Civil War featuring then-President Lincoln.

Instead of working at CBS, Jimmy found himself at NBC, playing the role of young Lincoln's friend, "Denny," in a telecast entitled *Prologue to Glory,* a presentation of Kraft Television Theater.

The play from which it had been adapted had been written by E.F. Conkle and had opened on Broadway in 1938. In the TV version sponsored by Kraft, Conkle was also the producer and director.

The teleplay focused on Lincoln's romance with Ann Rutledge and his grief over her untimely death. Cast as Lincoln was Thomas Coley, who had previously starred on Broadway in such plays as *The Taming of the Shrew* and *Harvey.* Pat Breslin, a New Yorker and the daughter of a judge, played Rutledge.

Up until then, the young actresses Jimmy met tended to aspire to stardom in Hollywood films. Breslin, however, was part of a new breed of actress that emerged in the 1950s. Her ambition involved starring in dramas and comedies configured specifically for television. She'd later achieve success with Jackie Cooper, appearing as his girlfriend (later, his wife) in the NBC sitcom, *The People's Choice* (1955-1958). She would also co-star with Nick Adams, Jimmy's former Hollywood lover, in TV's *The Rebel.*

After finishing *Prologue to Glory,* Jimmy returned to CBS to appear in another teleplay, *Abraham Lincoln,* as produced for *Westinghouse Studio One.* Its director, John Paul Nickell, cast him as a tragic young soldier, William Scott. *[In a previous teleplay, Nickell had hired him as a bellhop in* Ten Thousand Horses Singing.*]*

Following a script written by the British playwright, John Drinkwater, *Abraham Lincoln* had first been performed in London in 1918 and later in New York. It followed the life of Lincoln beginning with his presidential nomination in May of 1860 and ending with his assassination in 1865. Lincoln's assassination at Ford's Theater was not depicted in the telecast. "I want the viewer to imagine it," Nickell said

The role of the soldier, a Vermont farm boy who had lived and worked with his mother before being drafted into the Union Army, was Jimmy's most memorable and sympathetic to date. In the drama, he has been court-martialed and sentenced to be executed by a firing squad at daybreak. The action takes place on the eve of the battle that ended the Civil War.

The President learns of the youth's impending death, and orders that the soldier be brought before him. He also learns that the young man had just completed a 23-mile march and had volunteered for double guard duty as a favor to a sick friend and fellow soldier. Based on his portrayal of the wide-eyed and frightened soldier facing death in the morning, Jimmy wins the empathy of the President, who drafts a letter, pardoning him from the firing squad and ordering him to return to his regiment. In gratitude, Jimmy salutes Lincoln for sparing his life.

Lincoln was portrayed by Robert Pastene, who later said, "Young James Dean was perfect for the role. He looked like one of the soldiers in a photograph by Matthew Brady, who captured on his early camera all those marvelous pictures of soldiers during the Civil War."

Born in 1918 in Massachusetts, Pastene was a successful character actor, who predicted "great things for Jimmy's future as an actor. He had an exceptional talent, and I liked it off camera when he called me Abe. I found him most endearing."

Judith Evelyn, cast as Mary Lincoln, originally arrived in New York from South Dakota with the intention of working on Broadway. She is remembered today, if at all, as the lonely alcoholic spied on by James Stewart from across the courtyard in Alfred Hitchcock's *Rear Window* (1954). Jimmy would later have a reunion with her when she played Nancy Lynnton in *Giant*.

In a conversation with her, he learned that she and her boyfriend, the Canadian radio producer Andrews Allan, had miraculously survived the sinking of the British transatlantic liner, the *SS Athenia*, at the outbreak of World War II.

[Built in Glasgow in 1923, the SS Athenia *was a British steam turbine passenger liner that was torpedoed by a Nazi submarine in September of 1939 off the Atlantic coast of Canada. It was the first U.K. ship to be sunk by Germany during World War II, killing 128 civilian passengers (28 of them U.S. citizens) and crew members.*

The act was immediately condemned as a war crime, yet did not immediately provoke the entry of the U.S. into the then mostly European conflict. At the time, Nazi authorities denied that one of their vessels had sunk the ship, delaying admission of any connection to the act until January of 1946.]

Jimmy's final teleplay that spring season, introduced by Sarah Churchill, was *The Forgotten Children*, an episode within the Hallmark Hall of Fame series.

It starred the very talented Cloris Leachman portraying Martha Berry (1866-1942), the American philanthropist who advocated teaching reading and writing to impoverished children in the remote hill regions of the Deep South.

In an unusual departure from his norm, Jimmy had been cast as a Southern dandy in frilly formalwear, sitting on the white-pillared porch of the Berry mansion in 1887. His role was that of "Bradford," an insensitive Southern aristocrat who does not think women, specifically Martha, should enter the workplace.

When Martha assures him that she is an emancipated woman, Jimmy sneers, "The only emancipated woman I ever knew lived in a side street of Memphis." The character he's portraying is then chastised for his reference to a prostitute in the presence of genteel southern ladies.

Later, Jimmy (as Bradford) again shows how insensitive he is in a confrontation with a trespassing hillbilly girl whom he calls "a little savage" and "trash."

Iowa-born Leachman was one of the most talented actresses Jimmy had ever met. He was surprised she had gotten her start through a beauty pageant in Chicago. "You're one good-looking woman," he told her, "but you don't look like the kind of gal who enters beauty contests."

"All of us have to start somewhere," she assured him. She would go on to win eight Emmys and a Best Supporting Actress Oscar for her memorable role in *The Last Picture Show* (1971).

The director and producer of *The Forgotten Children,* William Corrigan of North Dakota, became one of the leading directors of television's Golden Age. Among his many achievements, he would helm a total of 91 episodes for *The Armstrong Circle Theater*, and would also make adaptations for television of such big screen staples as *The Strawberry Blonde* and *The Miracle on 34th Street.*

Over lunch he talked to Jimmy about his future, advising him against a return to Hollywood with the hopes of becoming a movie star.

"Television drama is the coming thing," he claimed, "especially for a lot of young actors in their twenties. The big studios like Fox and MGM won't let their stars under contract perform on television, Also, top talent on Broadway has utter disdain for television. Yet TV will provide a means to learn and to make a name for young actors like you in their twenties."

[After Jimmy's death, Corrigan said, "If he had taken my advice, and obviously, if he had lived, I would have cast him as the star in many of the teleplays I directed. Alas, it wasn't meant to be."]

Jimmy's Sexual Liaison with Sarah Churchill,
THE REBELLIOUS DAUGHTER OF SIR WINSTON

As Jimmy confided to Alec Wilder, "I've had this incredible luck of hooking up, however temporarily, with some famous people—first Joan Crawford, Judy Garland, Walt Disney, and Cole Porter on the West Coast; and Tallulah Bankhead and Peggy Lee in New York City. But about the last person on the planet I expected to ever become intimate with was Sarah Churchill."

Their introduction came through Brackett, who, as an employee of Foote, Cone, & Belding, was the advertising agent linked to promoting the hit TV series, *The Hallmark Hall of Fame.*

Through a connection, he arranged a (minor) job for Jimmy on the show. Only his hand was shown on camera, appearing at the end of the teleplay, writing the credits on a blackboard. Sarah had been hired as the series' well-spoken, upper-crust hostess—in effect, the figurehead and very posh symbol of the entire *Hallmark* series.

Brackett had known Sarah ever since she signed on for an appearance with his summer stock company in Marblehead, Massachusetts. When Jimmy met her, she was living in a luxurious penthouse on Manhattan's Central Park South. She became so close to Brackett that she entrusted him with the keys to her apartment, with the request that he look after it whenever she was out of town.

After every Saturday night show, she invited its cast and crew to her apartment for what she defined as a "post-broadcast *soirée."* There, the liquor flowed, often into Sarah herself.

From the beginning, Jimmy launched a flirtatious relationship with her, jokingly referring to her as "the daughter of a bulldog." Although she'd been born in London in 1914 at the outbreak of World War I, she looked much younger and was quite attractive, with her Titian red hair and her emerald green eyes.

Two views of Sarah Churchill. *Lower photo,* with her celebrated father, Sir Winston. She was the "black sheep" of the Churchill family.

"I'm the lamb who strayed from the fold," she confessed to Jimmy at one of her parties. "At seventeen, I broke free from the flock and set out to discover the world, finding it one cruel place. I had dreams of becoming a film star. Still do. But that isn't easy, even with a famous name like mine."

She enthralled him with tales of her fabled life, including details about the time she accompanied her father to the 1943 Teheran Conference, where she was introduced to Franklin D. Roosevelt and Josef Stalin. "The bloody Stalin came on to me," she claimed. "I think it would have been a feather in his cap to have seduced the daughter of Sir Winston."

She also told him that "After all the good men left Britain to fight in World War II, thank God the Yanks arrived in time to take care of the sexual desires of the deserted sweethearts, wives, and recently bereaved widows."

She was married to Anthony Beauchamp, but admitted, "I never know where he is. Despite my status as a married woman, I'm pretty much a free agent. My father does not approve of my marriage and is very cold, even hostile, to my husband."

One Saturday afternoon, when Sarah had not arrived on time for the filming of her hostess duties for the Hallmark series, Brackett placed some frantic calls, without success, to her penthouse. Finally, in desperation, he gave Jimmy the keys to her penthouse and instructed him to go immediately to see what was wrong and, if possible, to fetch her. "She drinks, as you well know, a lot."

At the door to her penthouse, Jimmy rang her bell at least ten times before using her key to let himself in. He found Sarah sprawled nude and drunk on her bed. He later told his friends at Jerry's, "I was such a devil. Such an opportunist."

In a call to Brackett, he claimed that he found Sarah "drunk and threatening suicide. I'd better stay with her. Who knows what might happen. Tonight, you can get someone else to write the damn credits on that blackboard."

Brackett agreed, promising he'd be right over as soon as the show went off the air.

If Jimmy is to be believed, he seduced Sarah after that phone conversation with Brackett. Bragging about it later to his friends at Jerry's, and later to William Bast, he was said to have stripped down before piling on top of the drunken aristocrat. "In midfuck, she woke up and and we checked each other out, eyeball to eyeball. She seemed pleased, and told me, 'Go to it, kid.'"

Three hours later, Brackett rushed into Sarah's penthouse. He found Sarah fully clothed and sitting on her sofa with Jimmy, having yet another drink.

When she left the room for a moment, Jimmy falsely claimed, "I talked her out of her suicide threat. She's okay now."

***

[In November of 1955, Jimmy was scheduled to return to the set of the Hallmark Hall of Fame TV series. This time for an appearance not as a disembodied hand writing anonymously on a blackboard, but as the star of a TV adaptation of The Corn is Green, *that play by the gay Welsh playwright, Emlyn Williams.*

As a teenager, Jimmy had seen the film adaptation (1945), starring Bette Davis, of the play, which had first been produced in 1940. In this autobiographical tale, a 50-year-old spinster, Miss Moffat, inspires her young male student to greatness.

Two months before filming was scheduled to begin, Jimmy was dead.]

***

Rogers Brackett's other best friend in New York was the designer and art director, Stanley Mills Haggart. For many of Brackett's TV advertisements or shows, Haggart provided the art direction. Arguably, he had more Hollywood connections than Brackett, having arrived in 1917 in what was then a fledgling "frontier town" with his (formidable) mother.

Over the years, he developed friendships with some of the luminaries of the silent screen, including a very young Greta Garbo, Gloria Swanson, Mary Pickford, Joan Crawford, William Haines, Ginger Rogers, and Lucille Ball. He became emotionally and sexually involved with the emerging star, Randolph Scott, and later, lived with Scott and Cary Grant, running their household while they were away at work at the studios. Through Grant, he met Katharine Hepburn and Tallulah Bankhead. He was also a close friend of several American playwrights, including Tennessee Williams, Arthur Miller, and William Inge. He was also the former lover of Harry Hay, founder of the Mattachine Society. Years later, the diarist, Anaïs Nin, introduced Haggart to Gore Vidal, with whom he enjoyed a long friendship.

Stanley Haggart (seated) in the 1930s, with his celebrated companion, British director Peter Glenville, relaxing in the garden of the house they shared in Saffron Walden, U.K.

Haggart became friendly with the *Who's Who* of Hollywood when he hooked up with William Hopper, son of the popular Hollywood columnist, Hedda Hopper. For many months, he became her

182

"leg man," prowling through the nightspots of Hollywood with her gay son, William, gathering information that Hedda might either use or bury, depending on studio politics and censorship standards of the time.

Although Hedda adopted many anti-homosexual platforms, and endorsed or reinforced them in her columns, Haggart maintained that in private, she was relatively tolerant. She was obviously aware of her son's sexual proclivities, but never confronted him with it.

Stanley Haggart, privy to most of the secrets of *le tout* Hollywood and Broadway, including many associated with Rogers Brackett and James Dean.

She was always warm and welcoming to Haggart, although telling him, "I'm glad to know a lot of the secrets you guys pick up at night but, as you well know, I can't print much of the crap. But I still want to know. *Hedda always wants to know.* I think I can use some of this information to my advantage when I face a recalcitrant star who won't cooperate with me. I can always threaten them. If they don't give me the personal data I want, I can destroy them by publishing their secrets."

As his Manhattan residence, Haggart had rented all four of the apartments (the entire allotment on that floor) on the top floor of a midtown apartment building. Although he was legally obligated to retain the floor's communal hallway and the original entryways to each of the individual apartments, he interconnected their interiors by knocking down some of the interior walls, eventually reconfiguring the top floor's layout into a huge, mostly interconnected spaces. Its inner doors could be opened or close, and its individual interior spaces flexibly configured for the housing of friends who frequently flew in from Hollywood. The result was an articulate, warm, artistically stimulating, and comfortable environment interspersed with both private and communal spaces. Its appeal became widely appreciated within Haggart's vast circle of friends and business acquaintances.

A *raconteur,* Haggart often invited between ten and twelve guests for dinner. They enjoyed the cuisine produced by a huge black cook from Harlem who set a lavish table. Her cuisine nourished luminaries from Hollywood as well as the theatrical elite of New York, including figures from the dance world such as Martha Graham.

Based on Brackett's bringing him to his home for dinner, Haggart later recalled his first impressions of Jimmy.

"At first, he was shy and awkward around me," Haggart said. "I think he didn't want me to assume that he was just another of Rogers' toy boys. Peering at the world through his horn-rimmed glasses, he seemed to find the place baffling, especially New York. He didn't care much for small talk, but I saw him closely observing me. I feared at first that he was thinking, 'How can I use this man?'"

"In those days, I fancied myself a handwriting analyst, and Rogers insisted I give a reading on Jimmy's. I asked him to write out some lines (he selected something from *Hamlet),* and I interpreted his handwriting. But I didn't give him an honest verdict. I thought he was suicidal, but it wasn't a conscious thing with him. Of course, I could be wrong, as I so often was."

"It became obvious from his handwriting that he must have suffered a lot in childhood. As an adult, that affected his judgment of people, if indeed he could be called an adult. He'd turned his insecurities inward, and it had taken hold of his personality."

"Actually, I thought he didn't like me, but at the door, he hugged and kissed me goodbye, like Rogers always did. He whispered to me, 'I want to see you.' I thought it was a sexual come-on, but I was wrong."

Late the next afternoon, when Haggart returned to his home from a day's work, it was raining heavily. "To my surprise, Jimmy was standing in the doorway, waiting for me. He was soaking wet. I, of course, invited him upstairs. Once I got him there, I offered him a bathrobe and suggested that he remove his clothes so that I could dry them. He rejected the robe, but stripped off his clothes, all except for his underwear, and handed them to me.

Emerging from the kitchen, I offered him freshly brewed coffee and a pastrami sandwich. He drank the coffee and devoured the sandwich and asked for some ice cream. He still hadn't put on his clothes, and I thought he was trying to entice me. I had assumed he was a hustler."

"But it wasn't that," Haggart continued. "He told me that he'd particularly loved my rear apartment. It enjoyed direct access to a rooftop terrace I'd 'decorated' with potted plants and shrubs. He called it 'a retreat from the world.' He said he sometimes needed a place for privacy with someone else, perhaps a stranger. At times, he found that being with Rogers was overwhelming, and he wanted to ask me a huge favor. He wondered if he could use that back apartment any time he wanted as a means to escape from the world."

"I told him he could. I didn't think I was being disrespectful of my friendship with Rogers. As Jimmy and I were talking, I knew that Rogers was entertaining an extraordinarily handsome young actor he'd cast in a commercial. So he was cheating on Jimmy, anyway."

"At any rate, I never assumed that those two had promised fidelity to each other. I not only agreed to let him use the apartment, but I told him that it could become his secret love nest if he so desired."

"He jumped up and kissed me, and told me he wanted to repay me for my generosity. He took my hand and placed it on his crotch. 'It's yours if you want it,' he said. But I withdrew my hand. 'That's not necessary,' I told him. 'Believe it or not, there are people in the world who can be generous without you having to put out to show your gratitude.'"

"My aunt, Ortense Winslow, in Fairmount, Indiana, told me there would be people like you in the world, but I never believed her."

"At the door, he hugged and kissed me passionately, promising we'd meet again real soon."

"That might just have been something to say," Haggart said, 'but in his case he meant 'real soon.'"

"Let's be friends for always," he said. "I like you."

"Until death do us part," Haggart responded.

He later recalled, "That was a strange thing for me to say. I meant it in a sort of flippant, irreverent way. The rest of Jimmy's life passed so quickly, both in New York and when he visited my home in Hollywood. I felt I was just getting to know and understand him, and then he was gone in a flash. It was like someone riding on an airplane, sitting back and having a drink, and the next minute that plane is plunging to earth in flames."

***

During the days to come, Jimmy sometimes made use of Haggart's rear apartment at least once, and sometimes three times a week. Often he didn't introduce his guests to his host.

One night, Jimmy dropped by and, after a meal, asked Haggart to accompany him to the Astor Bar for a drink. This was the first time Haggart saw Jimmy actively cruising in a public setting.

Gay bars (and gay activity in general) were illegal in those days, but the Astor Bar on Times Square was the discreet pickup joint for homosexuals, often middle-aged, often married, out to snare a young man who was usually broke and often an unemployed actor. Within inner circles, *habitués* of the Astor Bar were sometimes defined as "The "Closet Brigade." It was also a dangerous hunting ground, because the person a gay man picked up might be a vice cop, which led to arrest, imprisonment and/or heavy fines, public exposure, and its subsequent humiliation and/or job loss.

As Haggart closely observed, Jimmy seemed to be viewed as fresh meat by the largely middle-aged clientele, and he received several propositions. One man was quite attractive, perhaps thirty-five in age, and well dressed in what was known as the Brooks Brothers style. Haggart noticed that he wore a gold wedding band.

When Jimmy went to the Astor's oval-shaped bar for another round of drinks, it became obvious to Haggart that he was being propositioned by the man.

When he returned to Haggart's table, Jimmy asked if he could bring the man back to his apartment, and Haggart agreed. Jimmy told him that the man was an advertising executive connected to *The Kate Smith Show,* which aired on NBC.

Jimmy's pickup of the man occurred in the late spring of 1952.

[Fast forward to January of 1953. Jimmy came by and asked Haggart to make a big bowl of popcorn. He then turned on the television. As they sat eating popcorn and watching The Hound of Heaven, *an episode of* The Kate Smith Show, *it became clear that Jimmy had been cast as an angel.]*

He didn't always use Haggart's apartment just for sexual liaisons. Often, he would arrive unannounced for access to the lavish meals cooked every night by Haggart's cook from Harlem. He'd tell Haggart that he was tired of hanging out with Brackett's coterie of "queer friends."

"I get tired of them ogling me or following me to the toilet at a restaurant," Jimmy said.

On most of the nights he appeared, Jimmy rarely got caught up in the conversations whirling around among Haggart and his guests. Often, after eating, he would sit in a remote corner of the living room, not saying a word, but looking sullen, even hostile. Sometimes, he'd just stand up, leave the table, and exit from the apartment, not even thanking his host for dinner.

Haggart indulged Jimmy's rude behavior, although many guests expressed dismay at why Haggart tolerated him.

One night was different from the others. Haggart had invited a friend over for dinner, Lemuel Ayers, who was also of friend of Brackett's. Both Haggart and Ayers were members of the same labor union, United Scenic Artists.

"He was a scenic designer but a much bigger deal than me," Haggart admitted. "He'd had a brilliant career on Broadway, having designed or contributed to the 'look' of productions that included *Oklahoma!; High Button Shoes; Kiss Me, Kate;* and *Cyrano de Bergerac.*"

Jimmy didn't seem much interested in Ayers until it was revealed that he'd invested in an option on a play entitled *See the Jaguar,* which contained a key role for a young male actor. Ayers said he was considering offering the part to Anthony Perkins, the son of the famous actor, Osgood Perkins.

"Tony's name was already familiar to Jimmy, and not in a good way. He still suffered from memories associated with how, back in Hollywood, George Cukor had dangled in front of him a role in the Spencer Tracy movie, *The Actress,* before eventually awarding it to Perkins.

Although Jimmy at that point did not reveal to Ayers that he, too, was an actor, Haggart watched as he began to "turn his charm and powers of articulation onto Lem," as Haggart nicknamed his friend.

Although he was married with children to Shirley Ayers, a wealthy woman, Lem was a well-known homosexual. He lived with Shirley in a lavish apartment in Manhattan, but they were better known for their estate at Stony Point in Rockland County, north of the city. Here, they regally entertained the theatrical elite within a mansard-roofed mansion, that had been built in 1849 on a dozen heavily wooded acres a mile or so from the Hudson River.

Alec Wilder, Brackett, and Haggart were frequent visitors there, along with an artistic elite of artists, producers, and show-biz personalities.

[One member of their entourage was novelist John Steinbeck, who, coincidentally, would create the story of Jimmy's first feature film, East of Eden. *Other guests on occasion included theatrical producers David Merrick and Lucille Lortel, actor Mel Ferrer, and an array of actresses who included Mary Martin, Ethel Merman, and Agnes Moorehead. Orson Welles visited on two separate occasions.]*

"Jimmy was never hostile around Lem," Haggart said. "Shirley wasn't there that night, and it was just as well, although she was aware of her husband's adventures. Before the night was over, Jimmy was practically crawling over Lem. It was on one of those occasions that an embarrassed host should tell his guests, 'get a room,' but I didn't have to do that, because before midnight, Jimmy made an offer inviting Lem onto the garden terrace for a view of the city."

"I didn't see Lem until two days later, when he had nothing but praise for Jimmy, practically wanting to adopt him."

"However, I did encounter Jimmy the next morning in my kitchen. He was wandering about naked with a semi-erection, which he called a 'piss hard-on,' trying to make a pot of coffee. I agreed to cook breakfast for him. He wanted bacon and eggs. My cook wasn't scheduled to arrive until noon, which was just as well, considering how Jimmy was dressed. 'Dressed,' of course, is not the right word."

During the weeks to come, Jimmy and Ayers made frequent use of Haggart's love nest. Once, when Haggart peered out onto his garden terrace, he found both of them enjoying the summer sun in the nude.

At one point, Jimmy told Haggart that he'd been invited to go yachting that August with Ayers and his wife, Shirley. "We'll be cruising around Cape Cod."

Haggart asked him about the status of *See the Jaguar* and whether Ayers had decided to cast him as the young male lead in lieu of giving the role to Perkins.

"Not yet," Jimmy answered. "But it's just a matter of time."

Brackett seemed unaware of the sexual and emotional link that had developed between Jimmy and Ayers. In fact, based on their perceived status as "a couple," Brackett and Jimmy received two separate invitations to the Ayers family's country house in Stony Point. Sometimes, both of them were included in evenings at The Algonquin, along with Alec Wilder, Haggart, and David Swift with his wife, Maggie McNamara. Sarah Churchill sometimes joined the coven. Behind her back, Jimmy referred to his former conquest as a "dipso." *[A dipsomaniac is someone with an uncontrollable craving for alcoholic liquors.]*

This confusion, or lack of communication, about the status of the relationship between Jimmy and Brackett was a precursor of the changes that were about to take place. Both Haggart and Wilder shared front-row seats to watch as they unfolded.

***

The changes became obvious late one Saturday afternoon when Jimmy arrived alone at Haggart's apartment, wanting to talk privately. He looked agitated and troubled.

"He seemed filled with indecision," Haggart said. "He admitted quite frankly that at this point in his career, he did not want to sleep with older men as a means of getting ahead in the theater, and that he wanted to have sex with men or women his own age."

"More than a sleeping arrangement, I want to forge ahead on my own talent, not having someone offering me roles because of my performance on a casting couch."

Unknown to Haggart, Jimmy had expressed the same sentiments to others, too.

"Besides, except for you and Lem, none of Rogers' friends like me," Jimmy said.

"I've seen you around Rogers' friends," Haggart said. "You become surly and withdrawn."

"That's because I don't like to be fawned over by a pack of queers," Jimmy protested.

"If you're going to stay in show business, you'd better get used to being surrounded by 'a pack of queers' as you call them. Half the guys you meet will be gay. And they won't like you calling them queer. Let's face it: Being a star involves getting people to like you—those who will cast you in roles and, of utmost importance, the public. That's the price of stardom. Get used to it or get out."

"I hate being used by Rogers like some Saturday night whore," he said. "He makes me feel cheap. I'm more than some floozie."

"I can't advise you about what to do," Haggart said. "And in addition, I'm a friend of Rogers. He gets jobs for me, he sometimes hires me as an art director, and I have to maintain some loyalty to him. So if you're expecting me to urge you to leave the comfortable life he's providing for you, I won't do it. My point is that if you feel compromised because you're living a comfortable life, then go live on the hard, cold streets. "

"What you're telling me is that I have to make up my own mind and suffer the consequences," Jimmy said.

"Suffer, perhaps, or else triumph on your own. I think you have the talent for it. But it'll be a rough ride."

"What if, after staging a dramatic walkout from Rogers, I fail to become a big star?" Jimmy said.

"Do what I did," Haggart said. "In the 1930s, I had dreams of becoming a leading man in Hollywood, a romantic leading man, that is. But it didn't happen for me. So I came to New York, reinvented myself as an art director, and here I am, leading the good life."

"I can't imagine myself being anything but an actor."

"Then you must go out there and succeed at any price," Haggart advised.

When Jimmy left the apartment, Haggart didn't know whether he'd move out of Brackett's apartment or not.

He would soon find out.

***

Unexpectedly, Jimmy received a call a few days later from William Bast, his former roommate from Santa Monica. Bast told him he'd just arrived in New York and that he'd checked into the YMCA, where Jimmy had once stayed during leaner times. Bast had been graduated from UCLA in late May.

Over a "get re-acquainted" breakfast, Jimmy told Bast that he was back living with Brackett, who was procuring small roles for him in teleplays.

Jimmy was not forthcoming with a lot of additional information, but Bast assumed that he also had another involvement. He spoke of a dancer named Dizzy Sheridan. "She'll be joining us for breakfast."

Almost as soon as he'd said that, she appeared. Bast later remembered her as being a "long. lithe, supple beauty with pixie humor. She was warm and friendly, and very broke. She wasn't pretty in the conventional sense, but she was right there where you could touch her and know that she was real."

Over breakfast, Bast spoke of his dilemma in finding a place to live. "I don't want to spend every night running from the homos at the Y."

Dizzy suggested that he and Jimmy pool their resources and look for a place together. She was not aware that Jimmy and Bast had once shared a lodging in Santa Monica as part of a union that had ended violently.

After breakfast, all three of them strolled along the sidewalk, spotting the Royalton across the street. "I know someone there," Jimmy said.

Dizzy had to leave them. After her departure, Jimmy, with Bast, walked across the street and into the lobby of the Royalton. After riding the elevator to one of the upper floors, they arrived at the door to one of the apartments and rang its bell.

After a while, Jimmy rang again. Finally, the door was opened a crack. Recognizing who had rung, Roddy McDowall opened the door more fully, standing there sleepily, wearing only a pair of briefs. "Oh, it's you, Jimmy. Come in. Who's your friend?"

"William Bast, a writer from Hollywood."

When McDowall disappeared into the bathroom, Bast turned to Jimmy. It was obvious to him that Jimmy was having a fling with this former child star. Bast remembered him from playing opposite an 11-year-old Elizabeth Taylor in *Lassie Come Home* (1943).

Bast later recalled, "Count on Jimmy. Although Brackett's boy, he was slipping off banging Dizzy Sheridan, Roddy McDowall, and God knows who else."

Fully dressed, McDowall emerged from the bathroom and listened to their plight about finding a place to live. He suggested that they check at the desk in the Royalton's lobby.

Half an hour later, at the door, McDowall kissed Jimmy on the lips. "See you at five this afternoon," he said before turning to shake Bast's hand.

At the desk, Jimmy and Bast learned that the only accommodation available in their price range was the size of a broom closet.

Jimmy remembered his stay at the Iroquois and asked Bast to walk over with him. There, their luck improved. For ninety dollars a month, they rented a room with twin beds and a bath. It was more expensive than what they'd paid in Santa Monica, but this was Manhattan.

As the day drifted into night, Bast came to know a different Jimmy. "Whatever the price he'd paid, he owed Brackett an enormous debt for opening up his narrow world to greater resources of knowledge, experience, and awareness, as well as valuable social contacts. Sadly for Brackett, he failed to recognize his *protégé's* almost pathological abhorrence of indebtedness, and that Jimmy could not merely bite, but eventually devour the hand that fed him."

"Jimmy was stronger than he'd been in Hollywood, more independent. He had greater confidence in himself. After all, he was now hanging out with Sarah Churchill. He had an aura of contained excitement about him."

Bast did not know if he'd phoned Bracket or not, but he spent the night with Jimmy in their drab new lodgings at the Iroquois. Bast later wrote: "It felt good to be reunited with my teammate. Or was 'teammate' the right word for it? Maybe it was something more. Our new relationship had not been defined. Surely anything was possible."

The next morning, Jimmy escorted Bast to Brackett's apartment after he'd departed for a day's work at his ad agency. Hurriedly, Jimmy packed his belongings, including some new clothes Brackett had recently purchased for him. He also took Sidney Franklin's blood-soaked matador cape, which he would use to decorate the bare wall of his new lodging. He left a note for Brackett to read when he returned from work.

In a taxi, Jimmy turned to Bast. "I'll never live with him again."

From their new lodgings, Jimmy set out to show Bast the world he'd discovered. Sometimes, Dizzy joined them; at other times, she was busy.

Jimmy never specifically informed Bast whether he'd called Brackett for a concluding dialogue, but Bast suspected that such a talk took place. Even though he'd moved out without notice, he obviously didn't want to lose a valuable contact like the producer.

Within two weeks, Bast had found a job at the New York headquarters of CBS, based at least to some extent on his successful stint as an usher at a CBS theater in Los Angeles. At the company's New York location, he started out in the mail room with the assurance, "You can work your way from here to the top."

Announcing "Christine White," an Ambitious Newcomer

But Is It Love?

Even though Jimmy was still romantically involved with Dizzy Sheridan, another pretty young woman was about to enter his life. Their meeting began unexpectedly.

Late one morning, he visited the office of his agent, Jane Deacy, hoping to "goose her into stirring up some more gigs for me. Summer was coming, and reruns were dominating the TV set."

In her reception area, he encountered a thin, blonde-haired, and rather pretty young girl in a red polka dot dress typing away. He assumed that she was Deacy's new secretary.

He approached her and stood looking down at her, perhaps surveying her bosom, or perhaps checking out what she was typing. "Get lost!" were her first words to him. "I'm busy."

Although he moved away, retreating to sit on a couch, he continued staring at her. Every now and then, she looked up from her typing. "You're spoiling my concentration. If you don't stop staring, I'll charge admission."

He picked up the latest copy of *Photoplay* and pretended to read it, but he kept staring at her until it was time for a 12:30PM luncheon break. So far, Deacy had been tied up with other actors trying to cement deals.

Picking up her purse, the young woman walked past Jimmy. Perhaps she felt guilty for treating him so rudely. She glanced back at him. "What's your name?"

"James Dean...but you can call me Jimmy."

I'm Christine White. My friends call me Chris. But you can call me Miss White."

"I could be your friend if you'd go with me for a cup of coffee. We could split a hamburger. I'm low on bread."

"So am I," she said. "But OK. Let's walk over to the Blue Ribbon Café."

Over a shared burger, her wall of indifference began to crumble. She genuinely liked Jimmy, although she thought he was much too short for an actor— and those horn-rimmed glasses had to go. Under questioning, he gave a highly edited version of his life.

She was more forthcoming. Born in Washington State, she had come to New York to try to break into the theater. She'd developed a desire to be an actress since appearing in college plays at the University of North Carolina at Chapel Hill. She later graduated from Catholic University, where she majored in speech and drama. Along with three other underfinanced and wannabe actresses, she was living in a studio apartment on Madison Avenue at 92nd Street.

She told him that she wasn't a secretary, but a new client of Deacy's, and that instead of typing anything associated with her new agent, she'd been typing a scene she'd written for presentation at Actors Studio as part of an audition.

"I've been wanting to get into the Actors Studio ever since I came to New York," he told her. "I have a letter of recommendation from James Whitmore to Elia Kazan. I figured they did all right for Monty Clift and Marlon Brando, so why not me?"

"Why not?" she asked. "My scene takes place on a beach with another actor playing a bum who's at least twelve years older than me. Perhaps you'll do."

"I'll help you with your script. We'll work together, rehearsing and polishing it. How about it?"

"I've been looking for an actor," she said. "Perhaps you're it."

"I'm not only it, I'm more than it. I'll become Laurence Olivier to your Vivien Leigh."

"Let's go for it," she said. "You can call me Chris."

Christine White

192

***

Three nights later, Jimmy escorted White to Haggart's apartment. "We're working on this skit together to rehearse for an audition at Actors Studio. Do you mind if we use the little apartment in back?"

Haggart was most gracious, but first he introduced them to his dinner guests. They included the actress Kim Stanley and her lover, Brooks Clift, an advertising executive who was the brother of Monty Clift.

Both White and Jimmy were delighted to meet and talk with Kim because they knew she had been a student of the Actors Studio, and famously trained by both Elia Kazan and Lee Strasberg.

Kim had made her Broadway debut in 1949 and was considered by some at the time as the most promising young actress on Broadway. Haggart invited Jimmy and White to join their dinner party, and it was at around midnight that his quartet of guests broke up.

Brooks and Kim left for her apartment, and Jimmy and Chris retreated to Haggart's rear studio. Before bidding good night to Haggart, Jimmy said, "Chris and I are virgins. This will be the first time we've ever done it. We're just going to let nature take its course, and see what happens. It's all learned as you go."

Haggart was amazed that Jimmy could say that with a straight face, but—in front of White—he remained dis-

Kim Stanley...in love with Monty Clift's older brother, Brooks Clift.

creetly silent, and otherwise wished them luck.

Over the course of the next few weeks, Chris and Jimmy came and went from Haggart's rear apartment. Their host was aware that Jimmy had reconciled to some degree with Brackett, and that their friendship was now being conducted on radically different terms from what it had been in the

Brooks Clift (*left*) shown with his more famous, and more screwed-up brother, Monty.

past. Jimmy, who confided to Haggart that he planned to seduce his room-mate, William Bast, was still carrying on his affair with Dizzy.

"I'm working up to it, like giving him gentle little kisses on the mouth and indulging in teenage talk like 'Have you ever tasted semen?'"

When White was alone with Haggart, she told him, "Jimmy is still a very young boy. Rather impish, but with a certain kind of charm. Wouldn't you agree?"

"My sentiments completely," Haggart assured her.

She then made an odd comparison. "Jimmy and I are like two mudlarks splashing around on the street."

Throughout most of the summer, Jimmy spent whatever time he could with White, writing and rewriting her script and rehearsing it endlessly. Haggart witnessed the first tryout, and he made several helpful suggestions which they incorporated. In the script, White, a very nervous girl, meets a beach bum. The setting is Cape Hatteras in North Carolina. A hurricane is looming.

Roots was the title of the skit. It had been inspired by a dialogue between Jimmy and White, after she asked him, "What have you done for most of your life?"

He answered: "Ripping off the layers to find my roots."

After they rehearsed their audition skit in front of Haggart, Jimmy told him, "Chris and I are partners in crime. We are soulmates."

Late one night before closing, the manager of Jerry's Tavern allowed Jimmy and Chris to perform their skit in front of his diners, who applauded loudly. They also rehearsed in Central Park, often in front of otherwise idle curiosity seekers.

An interlude in their respective commitments fell upon them in August. Taking advantage of it, Jimmy accepted an invitation to sail with Lemuel and Shirley Ayers aboard their yacht around Cape Cod.

[Years later, White wrote about her first meeting with Jimmy for International Press Bulletin. *For some reason, she chose to express herself in the third person: "He walked slowly back to the doorway. She looked at his hunched shoulders, the pockets with hands in them. If he were an actor, she might have talked to him, but ambition was too precious a power to waste on a funny-looking guy with glasses who couldn't possibly be an actor. She watched him hesitate in the doorway, then careen around the frame and dis-*

Christine White *(left)* about a decade after her first introduction to James Dean, in an episode of *The Twilight Zone* entitled *Nightmare at 20,000 Feet* (1963).

appear into the waiting room."

In the 1960s in Hollywood, years after Jimmy's death, Haggart by chance encountered White. She was appearing in roles on television in shows that included Bonanza, Perry Mason, The Rifleman, *and* The Untouchables. *Her most famous TV role had been* Nightmare at 20,000 Feet, *aired in 1963 for the TV series,* The Twilight Zone.

She spoke with sadness about Jimmy. "In that summer of 1952, we believed the world was ours, and that everything was possible. He seemed like such an all-American boy to me. At first, I didn't see this moody, promiscuous, even dangerously suicidal young man. At least not at first. I thought about marrying him and settling down and having joint stage careers. How foolish dreams can be."

Haggart never saw her again.]

***

For their annual yachting vacation aboard *The Typhoon,* Lemuel and Shirley Ayers invited Jimmy to accompany them as their cabin boy, although he'd had absolutely no prior experience sailing.

The trip began near their estate on the Hudson River. They sailed down the river, then continued on into the open sea to Martha's Vineyard. From there, they embarked on a casual ten-day exploration of the coast of Cape Cod. During the first two days of their trip, the weather was so rough that Lemuel said, "Only a member of the Kennedy clan could sail through waters like this."

When he returned to New York, Jimmy gave Bast a highly edited version of that sea adventure.

"You mean. Lemuel took his wife along when both of us knew that one of the purposes of the trip involved seducing *you?*"

"I made a few visits to Lem's stateroom for a blow-job while Shirley was on deck. "She's a very understanding wife and has a really masculine voice."

"It was a wild trip on the seas," Jimmy recalled. "At one point at this party where Lem's friends came aboard in Provincetown, Lem stripped me completely naked and had me appear as Neptune on a throne he'd made. After all, he's a scenic designer. I went over big with his gay pals that night, and I got a lot of sleepover offers. Fortunately, Shirley was away that night visiting these two dyke friends of hers."

While aboard, Jimmy heard Lem discussing his play, *See the Jaguar,* scheduled for an opening that autumn. He had already signed Arthur Kennedy as the lead, with Michael Gordon directing it and Alec Wilder composing the music. To Jimmy's great delight, it included an important role for a teenage boy.

By the fourth day of the cruise, Jimmy was actively campaigning for inclusion in the cast, but without directly asking for that key role.

"At least Lem is assured of access to your dick—at least until he's signed someone else to the part," Bast commented, sarcastically.

Before the end of the cruise, the only assurance Jimmy had received from Lem was his promise that he'd arrange for a reading in front of Gordon, *See the Jaguar's* director. "If you're good at the reading, the part is yours."

Jimmy eagerly read the play, learning that the character of Wally Wilkins is seventeen-year-old boy who has been locked up since childhood by his paranoid mother, who wants to shield him "from the terror of the world."

To lure potential "angels" who might invest in the production of the play, Lem staged a series of theatrical sales presentations. The first of them was a run-through that unfolded within the luxurious Fifth Avenue apartment of Shirley's wealthy aunt. There, actor James O'Rear read the part of the teenage boy, even though he was in his thirties at the time and wrong for the role. Accompanied by Brackett, Jimmy attended, although he was severely disappointed that Lem had not asked him to deliver the reading.

Boris Karloff, best known to movie audiences as Frankenstein, attended the reading. Later, within earshot of Jimmy, the aging actor lavished praise on O'Rear's talent to Lemuel. That made Jimmy jealous to the point of overt anger.

By the end of summer, Lem still had not raised enough money to mount the play, so he staged a more lavish presentation at the Warwick Hotel. Once again, O'Rear was summoned to portray the teenaged boy.

Later, Jimmy complained to Brackett that, "The guy is reading my part. After all, I paid my god damn dues on that fucking wind-tossed yachting trip."

In September of 1952, Lem's fundraiser at the Warwick drew the attention of writers at the *New York Herald-Tribune,* who noted: "Producer Lemuel Ayers doesn't seem to be worried about being able to raise the rest of the cash needed for *See the Jaguar.* Mr. Ayers, the noted scenic designer, has gone ahead and arranged for tryouts in both Boston and Hartford."

Jimmy called Lem at his Manhattan apartment, learning that Shirley was out. He asked if could come by.

Two hours later, as he sat on the Ayers' sofa, Lem's fingers moved toward his zipper, as they had so many times before.

"Before I let you suck it, what about my audition?"

"I'll arrange it," Lem vowed.

"You'd better mean that," Jimmy said. "OK, go ahead, have your fun, but swallow every drop so I won't have to shower."

***

196

At long last, the day had come for Chris White and Jimmy to audition for admission to the prestigious Actors Studio, home turf of Brando, Monty Clift, Julie Harris, and so many others. A lot depended on his getting accepted. After all, his stated reason for coming to New York involved learning Method acting as promulgated by the Actors Studio.

Both White and Jimmy faced stiff opposition. Some 150 other young men and women were also auditioning for admission, and fewer than a dozen, maybe less, would be accepted.

The father of the Method was the Russian director and co-founder of the Moscow Art Theater, Konstantin Stanislavsky (1863-1938). As taught by Lee Strasberg, aping the master, the actor "learns to use his senses, his mind, and especially his feelings as effectively as he employs his voice and body to project his character."

The day was cold and windy as Jimmy and White headed out. He was not adequately dressed for the bitter weather. They took the elevator to the tenth floor of 1697 Broadway, near 54th Street. Getting off, he was freezing, and he went and sat on the hall radiator. "My balls are frozen. I'm defrosting them."

When he was warmer, he shocked White by telling her, "I can't go through with it. I'm too nervous."

"Listen to me, you little prick," she said, confronting him. "This was my audition all along. You horned in. Now you're trying to fuck it up for me." She reached into her handbag and took out two cans of Budweiser that had been intended as props for their upcoming presentation. "Here, drink this," she said. "Maybe you won't be so nervous."

He gulped it down.

Within a few minutes, the secretary came out and called for Dean, a name near the top of the list of candidates whose auditions had been scheduled for that day.

White was stunned when he bolted from the room, heading for the stairwell, not the elevator. She quickly recovered and asked the secretary to put their names under "W" for White, which meant that they'd be called near the end.

Within half an hour, Jimmy reappeared with two cans of unopened Budweiser. "I just couldn't do the audition pretending to drink beer from an empty can," he explained to her. "Also, running up and down ten flights of stairs has made me less nervous."

When their names were recalled, Jimmy removed his glasses and raced out onto the stage. Since he was so nearsighted, he missed his mark by almost ten feet, hitting the hard floor with a bang. It was supposed to represent sand on a beach before the debut of a hurricane.

Nervously, White followed his dramatic entrance. He could hardly make her out, so he squinted at her. He flipped open the can of beer and said, "Hi," which was not in the script.

Their scene about loneliness and alienation began. They'd rehearsed it many times, but he threw her off by inserting impromptu phrases. Although she masked her feelings, she was furious.

The scene's ending called for him to invite her into his ramshackle beach shack, but she runs away. The skit was suddenly over.

From the front row, there was a long silence. Elia Kazan asked, "Who wrote this skit?"

Nervously, White stepped forward. "I'm the culprit."

"It was okay," Kazan responded.

"Rather sensitive," Cheryl Crawford chimed in. *[Producer Cheryl Crawford was one of the founding members of the Actors Studio. She had produced such plays as* Porgy and Bess *in 1941, as well as Tennessee Williams'* The Rose Tattoo *(1951). Later, she expressed a dim view of Jimmy. "As a human being, he was just too sick."]*

Finally, Lee Strasberg spoke. "I found the scene quite natural. That's why I let you guys run three minutes' overtime."

Days would go by before they were notified that they had both been accepted into the Actors Studio. Of the dozens who had applied, fewer than ten had been accepted.

To celebrate, Jimmy asked White out to a dinner at Jerry's Tavern. "Maybe he'll let us dine for free, since he's been rooting for us."

On the way there, and quite by coincidence, Jimmy and White ran into Dizzy, who was returning from her summer dance gig along the Jersey Shore. Embarrassed to be caught with an attractive young woman, Jimmy explained to Dizzy that White had been his partner in his successful audition before the admissions committee at the Actors Studio.

Dizzy seemed satisfied with that explanation and set up a time to meet him the following evening after she'd settled back into her Manhattan routine.

The two female rivals for Jimmy's love would never meet again.

***

As the autumn winds blew into New York, and the multi-colored leaves began to fall in Central Park, it was time for Jimmy to find a place to hole in for the winter. Dizzy and Jimmy decided once again to set up residence together, this time in a large but bleak apartment at 13 West 89th Street, just off Central Park West. There was a big difference from their previous arrangement. This time, they would have two roommates, William Bast and a woman identified only as "Tina." Both Jimmy and Bast had attended UCLA with Tina.

The only decoration on the walls was Jimmy's battered and ragged matador cape. The furnishings consisted mainly of bare mattresses with no linens.

Dizzy and Jimmy shared the sole bedroom with twin beds, and Tina and Bast agreed to sleep on day beds in the living room. The kitchen had virtually no utensils. Jimmy suggested they could eat with their hands—that is, if there were something to eat in the bare cupboards. Bast remembered their first night in the apartment. They each shared a bowl of boiled vermicelli, the only food left. "We picked off the bugs floating on top."

Two weeks later, Jimmy arrived at the apartment with a large box, which his three roommates assumed contained foodstuff. When he opened it in front of them, it turned out to be an expensive set of luxurious pillows and bedsheets from Bloomingdales.

The objects were a gift from Rogers Brackett, with whom Jimmy still maintained an uneasy truce, not having submitted to the producer's never-ending requests to move back into his apartment with the luxuries associated with it.

In an act of showy ostentation, Jimmy spread the chocolate-colored sheets over his bare mattress, arranged the pillows, stripped down to his briefs, and crawled inside after wishing his roommates a good night.

Angered and envious, all three of them moved toward his bed, overturning his mattress and sending him sprawling onto the cold floor.

"There was little privacy," Bast said. "I got a preview of the breasts and vaginas of Tina and Dizzy, and each girl learned how we were hung. Of course, Dizzy and I had seen Jimmy in the nude many times before. Tina hadn't. She grew accustomed to his parading around the apartment with his balls dangling."

Bast also remembered the maze of bras, panties, and stockings hanging out to dry in the bathroom; the complaints about toilet seats being left up; the bathtub rings; and the snoring from both Jimmy and himself. There were also conflicts about dishes. "We had a few dishes by then being left unwashed in the sink. There were fights over which radio programs to listen. We were not a compatible quartet."

As each day went by, Jimmy grew more irritable and difficult to live with, as he faced increasing anxiety about why he had not been called for an audition of *See the Jaguar.*

A surprise invitation came in for Jimmy to visit his aunt and uncle, Ortense and Marcus Winslow, in Fairmount, Indiana. He was told that his father, Winton, would return to Indiana for a short visit. If Jimmy could make the trip, the dentist technician would arrive with two new front teeth for his son.

Jimmy invited Dizzy and Bast to join him on the trip. They immediately complained that they did not have the plane fare. "That's no problem," Jimmy said. "We'll hitchhike. It's only 800 miles." He told them that he'd seen that 1934 movie, *It Happened One Night*, starring Clark Gable and Claudette Colbert. Colbert had shown Gable how to hitchhike by lifting her skirt and revealing one leg. "What I'll do is unbutton my shirt and reveal my chest. If not that, I'll pull up my pants' leg and show off one of my shapely gams."

"Then you'll be queer bait," Dizzy said. "But we'll go with you since you've promised comfortable beds and all the food we can eat. I also want to go horseback riding."

It was an unseasonably cold morning on October 9, 1952, as this trio rode a bus from midtown Manhattan to the New Jersey side of the Lincoln Tunnel. Rejecting Jimmy's suggested technique, they each stuck out their thumbs and, within an hour, they'd procured a ride to the (far western) end of the Pennsylvania Turnpike.

They still had to cross the width of Ohio. Bast said they were picked up by a "weasel-like man, real creepy, and an obvious sexual pervert. Everything he said to us was sexually suggestive. Finally, it all came out when Jimmy and I went to take a leak with him in a gas station. He said he liked to lick the balls of young men and eat pussy. He wanted the four of us to check into a sleazy motel for the night. We didn't get back into his car, heading instead for the open highway with our thumbs out."

Luck was on their side. A Nash Rambler slowed down and offered them a ride, the motorist claiming that he'd be driving throughout the night *en route* to Dubuque, Iowa, for an exhibition baseball game. It turned out that he was Clyde McCullough, at the time a famous player for the Pittsburgh Pirates.

When they stopped for dinner, he invited them to join him, but they told him they were on a limited budget. "Forget it," he said. "I'm loaded. Order anything you want."

Jimmy ordered "the biggest steak you've got." After devouring it, he asked the waitress, "Can I have seconds?"

"As long as you're paying, or your friend here, you can have the whole cow," the brassy waitress snapped.

COLLECTIBLES: Clyde McCullough, depicted on a baseball card as he appeared in 1951, around the time he picked up Jimmy and his entourage as they were hitchhiking to Indiana.

The sports figure drove them to a point where Marcus could motor up from Fairmount and haul them back to his farm. All three of them thanked McCullough profusely for his hospitality.

[It was twenty years later, while watching Giant, *that McCullough turned to friends and said, "God Almighty! I once picked up a hitchhiker who turned out to be a big-time cow eater in this little dive. My passenger was James Dean, and I'm not making this up."]*

At the Winslow Farm, Jimmy introduced his aunt and uncle, whom he referred to as "Mom" and "Dad" to his best friends, Bast and Dizzy. Bast recalled, "They were wonderful to us. We've never eaten so much—fried chicken, thick steaks, cream gravy and mashed potatoes, cornbread with rich butter, and endless ears of corn on the cob and green beans cooked in bacon fat."

In the barn, Jimmy rescued his motorcycle, a CZ, from mothballs and went roaring through the countryside with Dizzy hanging onto his back for dear life.

After a reunion with his former drama coach, Adeline Nall, the teacher asked Jimmy to address her drama class about insights into the New York theater and how to break into it. Bast was asked to talk about writing for films, and Dizzy performed some of her best modern dance movements. "All three of us were very green in our so-called professions, but the students were impressed," Bast said. "Of course, Jimmy gave a very limited impression of how to break into show business. He left out that he had been on many a casting couch."

In front of Nall's class, he demonstrated an actor's changing faces by saying, "My name is James Dean" in several different ways, beginning with a melancholy sadness and ending tearfully. Along the way he said the line with aggression, with reluctance, with manic energy, and also hysterically, as if he were shouting, "FIRE!"

On the third day, Winton Dean arrived with Jimmy's new front teeth. Painfully, both Bast and Dizzy observed Jimmy's attempt to embrace his cold, distant father.

"At least we got to see what Jimmy would look like in twenty-five years," Bast said. "Winton was very reserved and self-conscious around his son. He didn't laugh or smile once during his short visit. Watching father and son left me with nothing but a deep sadness. At least Jimmy made off with two new front teeth. He knew that Jimmy didn't have money and would have to hitchhike back to New York. He could have lent him at least a hundred dollars, but he chose not to."

Fortunately for Jimmy during that return visit to Fairmount, his child-molesting pastor, James DeWeerd, was in Chicago, so some potential embarrassments were avoided.

Shortly after Winton's return to California, a call came in for Jimmy from his agent, Jane Deacy, in New York. Lemuel Ayres wanted him right away to audition for *See the Jaguar*. He had raised enough money to bring the play to

Broadway for an opening on December 2 at the Cort Theatre.

Before leaving Indiana, Jimmy paid a visit to his mother's grave. In front of Bast, he broke down and cried. "The pain of desertion is still there," he said.

Marcus drove the trio from his farm to the main highway for the beginning of their long hitchhike east.

Their most memorable ride *en route* to the outskirts of New York was with a drunken Texan driving a big cream-colored Cadillac. He came to a screeching halt and called out to them, "Y'all jump in!" As he drove along, he kept a bottle of whiskey between his legs, every now and then taking a gulp.

He seemed rather rich and invited all of them to dine with him at a steak house. Everyone ordered a T-bone, but the Texan claimed, "These tough pieces of leather must have come from Kansas. You guys will have to come down to my ranch in Texas to get the steak of a lifetime."

At a gas station, when Dizzy was in the toilet, the Texan told Jimmy and Bast, "I drive up once or twice a year to New York. You see, I'm into black poontang, and there's this place in Harlem I should give you guys the address to. In my home state, it's frowned upon for a white man to like black pussy."

En route to New York, he stopped the car, opened the door, and "vomited the Rio Grande" (Bast's words). He explained to his passengers that he had an ulcer but liked to drink and eat a lot. "I enjoy the taste, but then I have to throw it all up. My ulcers can't handle it."

After that, he seemed too drunk to drive, so Jimmy took the wheel. When they'd reached one of the outer boroughs of New York, he stopped at a subway station, where they got out and caught a train into Manhattan. Bast and Jimmy moved the Texan to the back seat, left the keys with him, but locked his car doors so he could sleep off his drunk before heading to Harlem.

Arriving exhausted with Bast and Dizzy in Midtown, Jimmy learned that his audition reading of *See the Jaguar* had been scheduled for ten o'clock the following morning. He desperately wanted the role and was filled with anxiety. Yet at other times, he was very optimistic because of his intimate connection with Lem Ayers.

Jimmy told Dizzy, "I want to be a big Broadway star."

She later wrote, "I hope Jimmy has a big career as an actor, but I also wanted him to want nothing more in his life than me."

James Dean, Tom Tryon, and Jack Cassidy
SOMETIMES, IN SHOW-BIZ, THREE'S NOT A CROWD

Dizzy Sheridan's wish to have Jimmy want her did not come true, although her hope for his big career was on the horizon. If she wanted to keep Jimmy in her life, she would have to learn to share him with others, both men and women.

Less than a week after returning to New York, he was pursuing Chris White again. Not only that, but her new boyfriend as well.

Perhaps with a touch of malice, Rogers Brackett showed Jimmy an item in Walter Winchell's gossip column. It claimed that the handsome young actor, Tom Tryon, had been seen dating starlet Chris White. "Rumors are that the nuptials are to be in Hartford, Tryon's hometown."

Consumed with jealousy, Jimmy demanded, "Who is this Tyrone Power?" deliberately misstating his name.

He later told Bast, "I feel a sense of betrayal. But I'm not going to confront her. I have another, much better, scheme."

Hot, talented, artistically versatile, and movie-star handsome: Tom Tryon.

Tryon, who was five years older than Jimmy, had served for three years in the U.S. Navy beginning in 1943. Upon his return from the war in the Pacific, he entered and later graduated from Yale.

Back in New York, he had studied acting under the tutelage of the acting coach Sanford Meisner, who at the time was as well-known as Lee Strasberg.

Currently, Tryon was one of the players in the long-running Broadway musical *Wish You Were Here*, starring alongside Jack Cassidy, Patricia Marand, and Sheila Bond. [Studded with musical numbers, many of which went on to successful lives as hit singles, it had opened in June of 1952 on Broadway at the Imperial Theatre, running for almost eighteen months and 600 performances.]

Jimmy was aware that Brackett knew the director of the play, and he asked him if he would obtain seats to see a Saturday night show.

Brackett was willing and seemed delighted that Jimmy wanted to go on a very public date with him again, since he'd been slipping around and seeing him privately instead of dining out or going to the theater with him, as he had done months before.

After the show, Brackett and Jimmy went backstage to greet the director and to congratulate the stars. Jimmy left Brackett as he was talking to Cassidy and the director. He wandered over to introduce himself to Tryon.

Years later, Tryon, at his home in Key West, told Darwin Porter, co-author of this biography, what then transpired between Jimmy and himself:

"I didn't know who Dean was at the time. He had yet to open on Broadway in *See the Jaguar*. He really turned on the male charm. I had never been so lavishly congratulated on my acting in my life. He also told me I was a good-looking guy. He must have learned that I was gay, because he claimed that the moment I walked onstage, he got an immediate erection."

"I considered him very sexy and handsome, too, though a little bit short for me. Mostly, I go for guys who are tall in the saddle. He was doing more than talk to me. He was standing so close, we could have had sex."

"He told me that he wanted to let me in on a secret, but swore me to keep it to myself. He said that he was about to be cast as the second male lead in a play called *See the Jaguar* produced by Lemuel Ayers. I'd heard of him. Dean revealed that Ayers was in the process of deciding whether he wanted to cast Arthur Kennedy as the primary lead. Dean went on to say that Ayers was not satisfied with Kennedy, and that he was discreetly searching for another actor to play the male lead instead."

"Dean suggested that secretly, he could arrange an invitation for me to the Ayers estate up on the Hudson, and that after Ayers met me, he'd be sure to favor me as *See the Jaguar*'s leading actor. He also claimed that even though Ayers was married, he was as gay as a feather boa."

"My dream," Tryon continued, "involved appearing as a star in a Broadway play. Stupid schemer that I was, I fell for Dean's line. Later, of course, I realized what a bullshitter he was, and the real reason he came on to me."

"No doubt he was turned on. I was at the peak of my male beauty back then. But, as I was to learn later, he had vengeance on his mind. Specifically, he wanted to punish his girlfriend, Chris White."

"The main reason that had motivated my decision to go out with Chris involved press and public perceptions. I was an actor on the rise, with hopes of becoming a movie star, and I wanted to dispel rumors that I was gay. There was nothing very serious between Chris and me."

"Arriving at the Ayers estate on Sunday, I found Lemuel and Shirley marvelous hosts. I think he had the hots for me, but I belonged to Dean that weekend. Frankly the sex was great. Jimmy and I performed every known act, and a few he invented. I discovered a streak of masochism in him. At times, he wanted me to hurt him, and I obliged, but I'm not much into that. Otherwise, he did everything I wanted him to do—and then some."

"By Monday night, when we returned to New York, I was fairly certain that Lem would consider me as the lead actor in his upcoming play. As for Dean, he was talking seriously about the two of us living together. I mean as a sort of unofficial husband and husband, with me as the top."

***

A few days after their return to Manhattan, Jimmy received a call from Tryon. "You want some more of this hot young actor?" Jimmy asked him.

"I can't get enough," Tryon said. "But I'm calling with a slightly different invitation. Jack Cassidy wants to have us up to his suite for a late night supper tonight after the show."

"He's gay, right?" Jimmy asked.

"Let's call him bisexual. After all, he's married to the actress Evelyn Ward."

"I'm game for anything," Jimmy said. "I'll meet you at the theater's rear entrance after the performance. I'll be your Stage Door Johnny."

After sitting through another performance of *Let's Do It Again*, Jimmy was waiting outside when Cassidy and Tryon emerged that night from the theater. As a trio, they headed out into the street, looking for a taxi. Along the way, Cassidy encountered a bevy of young women or late teenaged girls clamoring for his autograph.

[Jack Cassidy, five years older than Jimmy, was the handsome star of the musical, Wish You Were Here, in which Tryon had a secondary role. Jimmy knew very little about him, other than that he was a singer and actor.

A lot of his success derived from his talent as a musical performer on Broadway. His persona was often that of a vain, shallow, urbane, super-confident egotist with a dramatic flair.

His son, David Cassidy, born in 1950, later became a teen idol and pop star, best known for his key role in the 1970s musical TV sitcom The Partridge Family.

After divorcing Ward in 1956, Jack married actress and singer Shirley Jones, with whom he had three more sons, including Shaun Cassidy. In his 1994 autobiography, C'Mon, Get Happy, *David claimed that his father was bisexual, as did Jones. He suffered from bipolar disorder, and could be seen watering*

Partial Portrait of a Dysfunctional Family: Jack Cassidy *(left)*; his second wife, Shirley Jones *(center)*; and Jack's son by his first wife, pop singer and teen idol, David Cassidy.

his lawn in the nude.

Jack Cassidy died in 1976, alone in his apartment when he fell asleep drunk and ignited his Naugahyde couch. His body was identified by his dental records and a signet ring.]

Over dinner in his suite that night in 1952, Cassidy amused Jimmy and Tryon with stories of his life.

Jimmy found Cassidy dashing and debonair, admiring his devil-may-care attitude. He was refined, suave, and charming, but Jimmy sensed a dark streak in him.

Privately that night, surrounded by like-minded companions, he indulged in gay chatter.

Jimmy learned that he and Cassidy had shared something in common: Both of them had been seduced as part of casting auditions by Cole Porter.

Cassidy had continued his sexually charged visits to Porter's bedroom. "I made him work for it," he said. "I'd strip naked and sit in a corner with my big cock dangling over the side of the chair. Cole, that old sod, had to get out of his wheelchair and crawl across the carpet for access to what I have."

Jimmy found the story insensitive and sadistic, but strangely erotic. "I'll have to try that someday. All I need is a cripple."

"When I was a teenager," Cassidy continued, "I cultivated my voice and my speech

"TUBSTRIP IS GREAT CAMP... SOMETHING FOR EVERYONE!"
- *Variety*

CALVIN CULVER in

TUBSTRIP

NOW PLAYING!   LIMITED ENGAGEMENT!
ENTERPRISE THEATRE
430 MASON STREET (OFF GEARY)
Call for Reservations and Information 982-2277

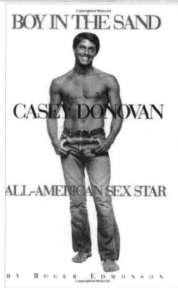

BOY IN THE SAND

CASEY DONOVAN

ALL-AMERICAN SEX STAR

B Y   R O G E R   E D M O N S O N

Midway through his career as a porn star, Cal Culver *(aka. Casey Donovan)* wanted to break into screen acting. In pursuit of that goal, he made overtures for a role in a possible film production of Patricia Nell Warren's *The Front Runner;* and Darwin Porter's *Butterflies in Heat,* later filmed in Key West as *The Last Resort.*

Despite Culver's considerable talent as an actor, film producers refused to hire him, based on his notoriety in porn. He billed himself as "The New James Dean," and for a while, he thought he'd be awarded the lead role in a film, *The James Dean Story,* but the deal fell through.

patterns by seeing about ten movies a week, preferring double features," Cassidy said. "John Barrymore was my idol. I modeled a lot of my style after him."

[By 1976, Cassidy had perfected his Barrymore persona to such an extent that he was hired to portray "The Great Profile", Barrymore himself, in the feature film W.C. Fields and Me.*]*

Two nights later, Jimmy dropped in for a visit with Stanley Haggart, this time without a companion. Running low on cash, he wanted to see if Haggart could get him cast in one of his television commercials. He didn't want to go back to Brackett and ask him.

Haggart knew Cassidy. After learning that Jimmy had spent the night in his hotel suite, along with Tom Tryon—who would later become a friend of Haggart's in Key West—he asked about him.

"We had a three-way," Jimmy admitted. "I don't want to go into a blow-by-blow account of what happened. But Tom screwed me as Cassidy and I blew one another."

"Then, after the sex was over, Cassidy got drunk with us and broke down and cried. He told us that his mother had borne him late in her life, and that she had never loved him. 'She rejected me,' Cassidy said, 'and hired a woman two doors away who had just had a child to nurse me. I can never remember my mother ever having kissed me.' In response to that, I said 'The same could be said for my father.'"

***

Tryon's dream of appearing as the male lead in *See the Jaguar* never materialized. The actor learned later that Ayers had never deviated from his desire that Arthur Kennedy be designated as the play's male lead, even though Jimmy had dangled it in front of Tryon as a trophy that was up for grabs.

Years later, according to Tryon, "Basically, the role had been assigned to Kennedy even before I got involved with jimmy. It was never really available at all. After that night with Jimmy and Cassidy, I never saw the boy again. If there's one thing I hate, it's a liar."

[Although bigtime stardom eluded him, Tryon went on to greater things. His greatest role came in 1963, when Otto Preminger cast him as an ambitious Catholic priest in The Cardinal, *for which he received a Golden Globe Award for Best Actor in a Motion Picture Drama. "Preminger practically killed me. Never before and never again would I suffer such abuse."*

"I almost got to work with Marilyn Monroe on her last unfinished picture, Something's Got to Give, *directed by George Cukor. But when Marilyn was fired, I was, too."*

By the late 1960s, Tryon was disillusioned with acting, and he went on to become a famous writer, specializing in horror and mystery books. His best known work was The Other *(1971), about a boy whose evil twin brother may or may not be responsible for a series of deaths in a small rural community in the 1930s.*

When Darwin Porter became Tryon's friend in Key West, Tryon had taken as his live-in lover Cal Culver (also billed as Casey Donovan), the leading gay male porn star in America.]

***

Awakening early for his first audition for the role of Wally Wilkins in *See the Jaguar,* Jimmy borrowed William Bast's only clean white shirt and his charcoal-gray slacks that had just come back from the cleaners. After endless preening, he asked Bast and Dizzy, "How do I look?"

After winning their approval, he headed toward the Royalton Hotel, where his sometimes lover, Roddy McDowall lived. N. Richard Nash, the author of *Meet the Jaguar,* was conducting the reading in McDowall's room, for reasons known only to him.

Jimmy knew very little about Nash. Born in Philadelphia, he'd been a ten-dollar per match boxer before going on to study English literature and philosophy in college. He had written for Broadway before, having authored works that included the Shakespearian-themed comedy, *The Second Best Bed,* produced in 1946, and the highly acclaimed drama, *The Young and the Fair* (1948). His greatest success would come later, when he wrote the original Broadway version of *The Rainmaker* (1954), which was adapted into a movie two years later starring Burt Lancaster and Katharine Hepburn.

Nash recalled Jimmy's reading. "He wasn't really trying to sell himself to me, and I respected that quality in him. As he began to read for the role of Wally, I sensed he had something that other actors didn't. We'd auditioned at least a hundred of them before Jimmy read for me. At the end of his reading, I told him, 'If it were up to me, I'd give you the role this morning. But you'll have to read tomorrow afternoon before our director, Michael Gordon. You have that special quality the role of Wally calls for."

"You mean, I can play retarded?" Jimmy asked, jokingly.

Before it opened, Nash had billed *See the Jaguar* as "an allegorical Western without the horses." Set in the "backwash of civilization," the rural South, it was loaded with symbolism, much of it difficult to understand. One early reader of the play had dismissed it, accusing Nash of having "earthy characters break from their role to spout philosophical pronouncements."

[In the play, Wally Wilkins is a seventeen-year-old boy, who has been locked up since he was a child in an ice house by his neurotic mother, ostensi-

bly to protect him from the cruelty of the world. Shortly before her death, she releases him. As an innocent naïf, he discovers the cruelty and horror of the world, encountering both brutality and beauty.

A kindly schoolteacher, Arthur Kennedy, aided by his pregnant partner, takes him in and shelters him to the degree he can. Kennedy's partner was portrayed by Constance Ford, who had been awarded the role after Maureen Stapleton turned it down.

After his release from his prison, Wally had set out with a rifle, and at one point, he kills a mountain jaguar about to attack him. That angers the local sheriff (played by Cameron Prud'Homme), who, previously, had built a cage with the intention of exhibiting the animal as a sideshow at his gas station. He'd even painted a sign—SEE THE JAGUAR—with the intention of displaying it, along with a menagerie of other abused and caged wild animals, as a tourist attraction.

When the sheriff's hopes about capturing the jaguar alive are thwarted, he captures Wally and displays him in the cage in lieu of the jaguar. The teacher (as played by Kennedy) later frees him, an act of defiance that so enrages the sheriff that he shoots him as "retribution" for his kindness.]

During his second audition, this time in front of the director, Michael Gordon, a very different-looking Jimmy showed up for his reading.

Born a Jew in Baltimore, and later a member of the left-wing Group Theatre, Gordon was, at the time of Jimmy's audition for *See the Jaguar,* under scrutiny from Congressional witch-hunting committees, as spearheaded by the dreaded Joseph McCarthy. Gordon was a friend of director Elia Kazan and John Garfield, one of the few Hollywood actors that Jimmy admired.

Shortly before he met Jimmy, Gordon had directed the 1950 production of *Cyrano de Bergerac,* which had won a Best Actor Oscar for José Ferrer.

[Amazingly, after Gordon survived the blacklist, film producer Ross Hunter hired him to direct a comedy for a 1959 release. It was Pillow Talk, *starring Rock Hudson and Doris Day. It became one of the biggest-grossing box offices successes of that year.]*

"I couldn't believe it," Nash said. "The day before, Jimmy had been so neat and well-dressed. But when he showed up to meet Gordon, he looked like he was recovering from a two-night drunk. He was disheveled, his hair uncombed, and one of the lenses in his spectacles had been cracked. His reading was very bad. Gordon met with me and rejected Jimmy, even those he was close to Ayers, the producer."

"Finally, I persuaded Gordon to give Jimmy a final chance the following day. I went to Jimmy and angrily asked him, 'What in hell happened to you?'"

Jimmy told the playwright that he'd had a sleepless night owing to a personal problem. He hadn't repaired his glasses, since he had no money.

Nash agreed to lend him ten dollars. But when he showed up the following afternoon, although he was neatly dressed, he wore no glasses. "You don't need glasses anymore?" Nash asked.

"I went to buy a new pair with your ten dollars, but I saw this vicious-looking knife in a store window. So I went inside and bought it. I'm carrying it now."

Then he claimed that two friends had rehearsed with him throughout most of the night, and that he knew all the lines by heart, so he wouldn't have to read from the script.

The difference in the quality of his third reading from that of the reading he had flubbed was amazing. Even Gordon admitted that Jimmy read the lines this time with deep understanding and perception. When it was over, Gordon told him, "the part is yours."

Rehearsals were scheduled to begin on October 20th, 1952. Back at his apartment, he told Bast, "I've got it! I'll dazzle Broadway! I'll be a star at the age of twenty-one."

Bast later confessed that he was jealous of Jimmy, since he, too, had wanted to be a bigtime actor until deciding that he had a better chance at writing scripts than performing in them.

Alec Wilder had been commissioned to compose *See the Jaguar's* musical score, and he met with Jimmy to teach him the lyrics of his big musical number, "Green Briar, Blue Fire."

"The kid was tone deaf. Imagine Jimmy auditioning for the role of Curly in *Oklahoma!* We rehearsed and rehearsed. He finally got it half right. But Frank Sinatra need not fear any competition."

Wilder also wasn't impressed when he saw Jimmy coming under the spell of Arthur Kennedy. *[Arthur Kennedy had originally billed himself as "John Kennedy," changing it after perceiving too many comparisons to the then-on-the-rise politician with the same name.]*

A competent but average-looking actor, Kennedy's career had been built on a widely diverse cluster of roles, some of them trivial and forgettable, that had included villainous portrayals in both Westerns and police dramas. Like Jimmy, he studied at Actors Studio.

His big film break had occurred when James Cagney discovered him and cast him as his younger brother in City for Conquest *(1940). What especially impressed Jimmy was that he'd been in the original casts of some of Arthur Miller's great Broadway dramas, most visibly as Biff Lomon in* Death of a Salesman *(1949). He'd gone on to play Chris Keller in Miller's* All My Sons *(1947), and there was talk that Miller wanted him as a key player in his upcoming drama,* The Crucible *(1953).*

The New York Film Critics had designated him as Best Actor for his role in Bright Victory *(1951), in which he played a soldier facing an uncertain future after being blinded. That year, he was also nominated for a Best Actor Oscar, but lost to Humphrey Bogart's performance in* The African Queen.*]*

"I stood by and watched Jimmy hero-worship Kennedy and all that Method crap," Wilder said. "Kennedy brainwashed Jimmy into believing that no one in the production was of any consequence except the actor. That simply is not true. What about the director and the playwright, not to mention the composer? I've always felt that this attitude instilled in Jimmy accounted to a great extent for his shocking behavior when he hit the big time in Hollywood."

Kennedy had a very different impression of Jimmy. "I liked the kid a lot. He was uniquely talented. He didn't suffer all the posturing, mannerisms, and mumbling of Brando. He delivered his lines pure and clear, and had one of the most sensitive faces of

Arthur Kennedy, cast as a school teacher in *See the Jaguar,* talks with his pregnant partner (Constance Ford) about seventeen-year-old Willy Wilkins (James Dean), who has been locked up by his paranoid mother since childhood.

any young man in the theater. But I must add a *caveat*. He was the most peculiar actor I've ever worked with, and he tried to murder the director."

For the most part, Jimmy took Gordon's direction without protests. However, there was major disagreement over the interpretation of one scene that Jimmy was to perform with Kennedy. "Gordon insisted that Jimmy play the scene one way, but he protested that such an act would ruin his own interpretation of the role," Kennedy said. "Things got out of hand. Finally, in disgust, Gordon called Jimmy 'a little punk.' That set Jimmy on fire."

"He pulled out this knife he'd recently bought and lunged toward Gordon. I did something either dumb or smart. I positioned myself between them, thereby preventing Jimmy's execution on the electric chair for murder. That was the smart thing I did. The stupid thing I did was that I might have had the knife plunged into my gut."

Cast as Kennedy's pregnant girlfriend, Bronx-born Constance Ford had little personal contact with Jimmy in *See the Jaguar*. Later, they'd co-star together in a teleplay with Ronald (then an actor) Reagan.

She was friendly with Kennedy, however, having previously appeared with him in Arthur Miller's *Death of a Salesman*. Later, she became known for her portrayal of Ada Hobson on the long-running daytime soap opera, *Another World*.

[As a fashion model during World War II, Ford's image had been closely associated with a massive ad campaign by Elizabeth Arden hawking lipstick in a shade of scarlet marketed as "Victory Red." All of the big-name female stars of World War II—Betty Grable, Lana Turner, and Veronica Lake—wore it. Even Tallulah Bankhead added to public perceptions of its desirability with public statements that included: "I wouldn't walk out the door without a coat of it on, Dah-lings."]

Jimmy shared a dressing room with Philip Pine, an actor who played "Hilltop," a character with an obsessive lust for Kennedy's pregnant girlfriend, as played by Ford. "Jimmy plastered the wall with bullfight posters," Pine recalled. "I think he wanted to be a matador more than an actor."

Eleven years older than Jimmy, the California-born Pine would develop a career that spanned seven decades in television and film. He was also a writer, director, and producer. He often appeared in TV Westerns, portraying legends who included Kit Carson.

He would forever remember Jimmy: "He was a real pain in the ass, a sentiment echoed by many other actors, including Rock Hudson, although Hudson may have meant that literally."

"His lack of discipline created tension. Once, he thought the director was treating me like an adult and him like a kid. He believes only in himself and to hell with everybody else."

"In spite of my resentment, we became friends and often would go out drinking together and chat for hours— real personal stuff—about our hopes and dreams."

"He didn't have a good pair of shoes, so I arranged through Actors Equity to get him a new pair. We would rehearse a scene, and without any warning, he would play it completely different from the way we'd rehearsed. Even though he pissed me off, I had a soft spot for him. He was undisciplined. He didn't have an understanding that a theater company needs to work together like a harmonious family. But I knew he was deeply insecure. Without saying a word—his face said it all—he seemed to be crying out, 'Love me. Why won't someone love

In a sensitive scene with Arthur Kennedy *(left)*, a barefoot James Dean, looking years younger than his actual age, gives a brilliant performance as a bewildered lad who, after years of being locked away, is coming upon both the beauty and brutality of the real world.

me?'"

"Jimmy and I both knew hurt," Pine said. "We grew up without fathers. We bonded over that. I wanted to let him know that an actor can use pain and hurt he'd suffered to enhance a performance."

"I knew Jimmy before he became a legend. I even replaced him in a role on Broadway. Yes, there was some envy and jealousy on my part, not uncommon among actors. God damn it, why didn't Elia Kazan discover *me* instead of Jimmy?"

Released at last from his confinement, and on his own, coping with new realizations about the world and its inhabitants, the character interpreted by James Dean in *See the Jaguar* fights back.

Tryouts had originally been slated for Boston, but blue nose city fathers, who were still censoring the art and entertainment industries back then *[BANNED IN BOSTON! eventually became an activist slogan in the battle for weakening the grip of censorship in America.]* read the script and rejected it as "indecent." In reaction, Lemuel Ayers selected Hartford and Philadelphia as the sites for trial runs instead.

During its first performance in Hartford, because of technical difficulties, the curtain rose half an hour late. Jimmy upstaged Pine. He was supposed to be submissive when he is dragged offstage by Pine, but instead, he put up a fight and fiercely resisted. Furious, Pine managed to subdue him and somehow managed to drag him into the wings.

Each of the local papers criticized Nash's play, but gave special accolades to Jimmy. *The Hartford Courant* described his performance as "tender and touching."

The trial run then moved on to Philadelphia, where it opened on November 8 at the Forrest Theatre. Pine recalled that Nash was up every night, hysterically rewriting the script, desperate to plug the "loopholes in my play."

As in Hartford, the Philadelphia papers, despite his rewrites, were not kind to Nash. Once again, however, Jimmy was hailed for his stage debut. *The Philadelphia Bulletin* praised his "excellent character portrait" of the innocent kid, and his acting was also lauded by *The Philadelphia Inquirer,* its review suggesting that the theater had a new star shining.

Lem Ayers was a friend of Tennessee Williams, and he invited the playwright to Philadelphia to see his bound-for-Broadway discovery.

Later, Ayers threw a party for the cast and crew at Philadelphia's Variety Club. A slightly drunken Tennessee arrived. The actor and the playwright would later develop a relationship, but, as Jimmy later reported, "On that night in Philly, Tennessee only flirted with me. Outrageously so."

"Not since I first saw Brando as Stanley Kowalski in *A Streetcar Named Desire* have I had such a thrilling night at the theater. I found your acting and male beauty startling," Tennessee claimed.

Jimmy knew he was exaggerating, but he appreciated the flattery.

Tennessee gave him a card with his name and New York City address on it. He also threw out a tantalizing tidbit. "We have a mutual friend, David Swift. He's invited both of us to his Christmas party."

"I'm looking forward to it," Jimmy said.

"As soon as I get to New York, I'll start working on a play that includes you as its star."

"I'm sure you will," Jimmy said. "You wouldn't be trying to hoodwink a farm boy from Indiana, would you?"

"Me? Never!" Tennessee answered "Unlike a character I'm creating, Big Daddy, I have never believed in mendacity."

"Until Christmas," Jimmy said, kissing Tennessee on the lips.

"I hope you're my present under the tree."

***

See the Jaguar opened in December at the Cort Theater. Lemuel Ayers invited several friends, including Mildred Dunnock, the distinguished actress who was part of the Actors Studio. "I want you to get a look at James Dean," he told her. "My new discovery. I think he'll be sensational."

[Dunnock, in the autumn of 1954, would be co-starring with Jimmy in a teleplay for CBS.]

Later, after sitting through *See the Jaguar*, she delivered her own review: "Poor Dean. He was trying to breathe reality into a heavy plot that was far too loaded with portentious symbolic references. It was an uphill struggle for him, but he tried valiantly to cope with the impossible lines. Nash should have been kicked in the pants. Dean could tell his lines weren't real. They rang a false note. Something an *enfant sauvage* wouldn't say. Even so, he brought some *faux* Method magic to this clunker."

Nash, of course, had a very different view from that expressed by Dunnock: "Jimmy was the only one in the cast who truly caught the spirit of what I was trying to convey. He had from the beginning."

After its opening on Broadway, the cast convened at Sardi's to await the reviews in the morning papers. Jimmy invited Bast and Dizzy to the dinner party, assigning them to a table in a far corner. He didn't spend much time with them.

To the jealous Bast, "Jimmy's feet were never on the ground. Like Peter Pan, he flew from table to table, accepting congratulations from his adoring public. I truly felt he was on the road to stardom, even before the newspaper reviews arrived. There was adulation in the restaurant. Broadway had a new prince, or at least that was what Jimmy thought. Personally, I had my doubts. I thought the play stunk."

At long last, the morning papers arrived, and Jimmy devoured the reviews. His acting received raves, but Nash's playwrighting skills were attacked as "murky and at times, silly," One described the play as pretentious, claiming that it "was a contrivance of *jejune* symbolism."

Richard Watts, Jr., in *The New York Post,* claimed, "James Dean achieves the feat of making the childish young fugitive believable and not embarrassing." Although praising Jimmy, the critic went on to define the play itself as "full of sound and fury, signifying nothing."

In *The New York Herald Tribune,* Walter Kerr wrote: "James Dean adds to an extraordinary performance in an almost impossible role." One of the most sensitive comments was made by George Freedley in *The Morning Telegraph:* "James Dean acted the mentally retarded boy with sweetness and *naïveté* that made his torture singularly poignant."

Actress Margaret Baker, who played Jimmy's deranged mother, was also at Sardi's that night. As regards the opening night of *See the Jaguar,* she pronounced it, "the nicest funeral I have ever attended."

After those bad reviews, except for Jimmy's performance, *See the Jaguar* played to dwindling audiences. Lemuel closed it after four more performances.

***

After Sardi's, Jimmy invited Dizzy to the Royalton Hotel, where Lem had, as an opening night gift, offered him a single night's lodging in a suite, complete with room service. Jimmy ordered dinner for the two of them, choosing a juicy big steak for himself.

Midway through the meal, the manager telephoned, suggesting that "the young lady will have to leave after her dinner. It is hotel policy. We have a house detective."

When their meal had ended, he accompanied her out onto the sidewalk and hailed her a taxi. Then he kissed her goodbye.

She later claimed, "I knew our love affair was over."

[Billing herself years later as "Elizabeth Sheridan," she would go on greater glory, her face becoming known in thousands of homes across America when

she played Jerry Seinfeld's mother in the hit TV sitcom, Seinfeld, *whose much-awarded 180 episodes were originally released between 1989 and 1998.]*

The next morning, Jimmy returned to his shared apartment uptown to find Dizzy gone, but Bast was there. He packed his meager belongings and announced that he was moving out. He made a point of noting that he was going back to the Iroquois, where both of them had lived. "But this time, I'm renting only a single room. Like Greta Garbo, I want to be alone."

Later, when Dizzy was apprised of the news, she wrote: "I knew that our romance no longer burned with the intensity we once felt. Our love had already moved into the comfortable stage, its brilliant colors gently diminishing like a rainbow too long in the sky."

With Jimmy gone, Tina, Bast, and Dizzy could no longer afford their apartment, and each of them moved out to go their separate ways.

From the Iroquois, Jimmy called his agent, Jane Deacy, who was lining up teleplays for him. "Being an actor is the loneliest thing in the world," he said. "You're all alone with your imagination, and that's all you have."

During the week that followed, he visited the apartment of Stanley Haggart, this time, alone. He told his older friend that he had been going through affairs with both men and women at an unprecedented rate. "I run a bed-and-breakfast," he claimed. "In my bed at night, breakfast the next morning, and then *adieu.* In the last week, I've had at least ten conquests, six women and four men. All were my own age, often much younger. No more god damn aging producers and directors for me...*unless.*"

He didn't complete his sentence.

When Haggart asked why he felt compelled to take on so many different sexual partners, Jimmy answered, "I'm a tumbling tumbleweed. My favorite song—in spite of the fact that that shithead, Roy Rogers, sings it—is 'Don't Fence Me In.'"

He also revealed that Deacy was getting lots of job offers for him. "MGM wants me to fly to Hollywood for a screen test. She turned them down. She wants me to become more seasoned, and she's lining up more TV dramas for me. Frankly, I'm impatient to become a movie star, but before that, I want to study with the Actors Studio," he said.

Although many new lovers loomed on his horizon, Jimmy rarely, if ever, lived with anyone again. "I want my lovers to pass through my

Frank Corsaro, as depicted in an National Endowment for the Arts interview documenting his contributions to the New York City Opera; to operatic stagecrafting; and to the interconnectedness of an opera's music with a sense of dramatic technique.

life like ships in the night. Pardon the fucking *cliché*."

***

To his aunt and uncle in Fairmount, Jimmy wrote about how proud he was to be a part of the Actors Studio—"and it's free. Very few get in. It's the best thing that can happen to an actor. I'm one of the youngest to belong. If I can keep up and nothing interferes with my progress, one of these days I might be able to contribute something to the world."

On his first day at the studio, Jimmy met Frank Corsaro, who was to have an important impact on his life.

[A native New Yorker, born in the Bronx, Corsaro eventually became known as one of the country's foremost stage directors of opera and television. One of his best-received and most famous productions was the original Broadway version of Tennessee Williams' The Night of the Iguana (1961), starring Miss Bette Davis. In 1988, after a hugely successful career with the New York City Opera, and New York's Metropolitan Opera, he was designated as Artistic Director of the Actors Studio.]

When Jimmy first became friends with Corsaro, he was known for his cultural background, his wit, and his keen intelligence. Jimmy found him intellectually stimulating, and Corsaro expanded his knowledge, introducing him to literature (especially the novels of Aldous Huxley) and the music of Arnold Schönberg and Johann Sebastian Bach.

According to Bast, "Jimmy fell completely under Corsaro's influence. He was a slight little man, a bundle of nervous energy that kept him plugged into some electric current both night and day."

***

Before auditioning for Lee Strasberg, Jimmy learned what he could from his peers about the director and acting teacher. He'd been born in Ukraine during the final days of the Austro-Hungarian Empire.

Along with director Harold Clurman, he'd co-founded the Group Theater in 1931, America's first true theatrical collective. When Jimmy met Strasberg, he had just become the director of Actors Studio.

Although others may lay claim to the title, Strasberg was recognized as the father of Method

Grand Dragon and Grand Master of Method Acting: Lee Strasberg in 1978.

217

acting in America. In time, he'd train such illustrious actors as Anne Bancroft, Dustin Hoffman, Monty Clift, Jane Fonda, Paul Newman, Marlon Brando, Al Pacino, Robert De Niro, and Julie Harris.

DELL BOOK 714

The novel of a bullfighter and his destiny   25¢

MATADOR

A Book-of-the-Month Club Selection
BARNABY CONRAD

Strasberg told Jimmy that each new member had to perform a theatrical piece to an audience comprised of his or her fellow students. After reviewing and rejecting many scripts, Jimmy settled on a piece adapted from *Matador,* a novel by Barnaby Conrad, that had sold three million copies.

Unlike Jimmy, Conrad had actually faced a bull in a ring, and as a result, he had been badly injured, afflicted with a wound so damaging that he was rejected for admission into the U.S. Navy in 1943.

Jimmy envied the life Conrad had led, hanging out in Seville, Madrid, and Barcelona with such bullfighters as Manolete, Carlos Arruza, and Juan Belmonte. *Matador,* Conrad's second novel, had been a gift to him from his pastor lover back in Fairmount, James DeWeerd.

The scene inspired by Conrad was actually very dramatic, that of an aging matador who accepts a challenge from a young bullfighter to enter the ring for a final time, knowing that it might well lead to his "death in the afternoon." Without saying a word of dialogue, Jimmy wanted to act out the bullfighter's emotion before he comes face to face with death itself.

For props, he used Sidney Franklin's blood-soaked cape, a candle, and a statue of the Virgin Mary.

Halfway through his solo performance, he seemed to realize that the skit wasn't working. He cut it short and, in an attempt to gracefully conclude his time on stage, with his back to the audience, he performed a set of *muleta* passes.

Geraldine Page, also a student at Actors Studio, was in the audience that day. Within months, she would be co-starring on Broadway with Jimmy in *The Immoralist.*

"I didn't hear all of Lee's attack on the *Matador,* because I had to leave for an appointment," Page claimed. "But other members of the studio told me it was not only a devastating critique, but that Jimmy was devastated by it. Lee had done the same thing for me when I performed my own introductory skit at Actors Studio. He asked me, 'Who are you trying to impersonate, Joan Fontaine?'"

After a performance, Strasberg always asked an actor, "Just what are you trying to accomplish?"

At that time, Jimmy lacked the understanding of exactly what he wanted to do as an actor, and he couldn't come up with an answer. He wanted to become the first post-modern actor, but wasn't exactly sure what that meant.

Strasberg continued. "In the *Matador* skit, you were acting, not being. You must learn the difference if you ever want to succeed in the theater. There is a mammoth difference between the actor who thinks that acting is an imitation of life, and the actor who feels that acting is living." From there, Strasberg went on to caustically rebuke Jimmy's performance.

Strasberg was accurate in his attack on Jimmy's motivation and his characterization, even though he had performed many of the matador's movements to perfection.

As Strasberg lashed out at Jimmy's acting, he sat slumped down in his seat, scowling in a sort of poutish mess. An original member of the studio, David Stewart, phrased it vividly: "Dean sat there like his skin was being ripped off."

From the start, Jimmy showed that he lacked an actor's ability to take criticism.

David Garfield in *A Player's Place* explained it: "Dean's *Matador* provoked a long and penetrating critique from Strasberg. Dean listened impassively, but the color drained from his face. When Strasberg had concluded his remarks, the young actor slung his matador's cape over his shoulder and silently walked out of the room."

It would take many weeks and much urging before he returned.

The next day, he bitterly complained to Bast, "I can't let Strasberg attack me. He doesn't understand what I'm trying to do. I don't understand it myself. I need more experience. I don't know what's inside me yet. If I let him dissect me like a rabbit in some laboratory, it might destroy the creativity bubbling up in me. Strasberg doesn't have the right to tear away at my very soul. He's trying to sterilize me. If you attack a guy enough, you destroy his guts. What's an actor without guts?"

Bast claimed, "Jimmy simply didn't have the stomach to survive the soul-searing, psychologically destructive criticism Strasberg seemed to take pleasure in dishing out."

To his friends, Jimmy was very critical of Strasberg, calling him "a mess of hot air. He also has a personal vindictiveness against me."

John Stix, who chaired the studio's board of directors, claimed, "Jimmy's self-indulgence was not tolerated by Strasberg. Nor did he allow him to use it as a defense against criticism. He disliked everybody there except for Geraldine Page and Kim Stanley, who allowed him his indulgences. By the time Jimmy arrived, Clift and Brando were already stars."

Months later, when Page actually co-starred on stage with Jimmy, she claimed, "He learned a lot more about acting from Monty Clift and Brando than he did from Strasberg."

"It wasn't my criticism that kept Dean away," Strasberg later claimed. "He was sensitive about letting other people get too close unless they were very special. Marlon Brando and Paul Newman were special. So was Marilyn Monroe and even my daughter, Susan. He seemed to shy away from people, even those who wanted to be his friend. He was afraid they would get to know him and judge him. He didn't want to be judged, yet every actor has to face the critics."

Elia Kazan shared similar memories. "I didn't see Dean very much at the Actors Studio. He went there only a few times. I remember him sitting out in front, a surly mess. He didn't want to participate in anything, seemingly there only as a venue for judging his fellow actors."

After Jimmy's death, Strasberg told a reporter, "I sensed a doomed quality in the boy. There was something destructive about him. Frankly, he didn't learn anything at my studio, because he never wanted to give of himself. Acting is nothing but giving."

During one of his rare interviews, Jimmy spoke to Erskine Johnson, the well-known Hollywood columnist. "The most important lesson I took away from the Actors Studio was how an actor should take care of himself. How an actor need to protect himself from the glitz of Hollywood and from the hazards of the stage and this new medium of television."

"There are tricks to every trade, as there are in acting, and I learned some of them. Some of these tricks can help you survive bad scripts and bad directors, even bad actors with whom you have to work. However, so far, I haven't had the need to unleash my bag of tricks."

***

Tennessee Williams had accurately described the forthcoming invitation from their mutual friends, David Swift and Maggie McNamara. However, it was not for a Christmas Party but for a New Year's Eve celebration.

Assuming that Rogers Brackett and Jimmy were still an interconnected couple, the Swifts extended an invitation to both of them. Jimmy was seeing Brackett only infrequently, yet agreed to escort him to the party anyway, knowing that Tennessee would be there. He kept telling friends, including Stanley Haggart and William Bast, "Look at what Tennessee did for Marlon Brando. Imagine what he could do for me, an actor with real talent."

Arriving at the door to the Swift apartment, Brackett and Jimmy were greeted by McNamara, who kissed both of them on the cheeks. She gave no indication that she'd ever been intimate with Jimmy in Chicago.

As he'd later relate to Bast, "The guest list was short but choice. I was the only one there who had not won any theatrical awards or produced any hit shows.

"Tennessee was already drunk, and he introduced me to his chief rival, playwright William Inge, who practically creamed in his pants when he shook my hand. I didn't think I was going to get my paw back. I heard that in the 1940s, these two guys used to be lovers."

At the party, McNamara introduced Brackett and Jimmy to Grace Kelly and her lover, Gene Lyons, a television actor from Pittsburgh. To Jimmy, Grace evoked a goddess—blonde, prim, proper, and ladylike—but he sensed a strong undercurrent of sexuality within her. "She put the 'grace' in graceful," he later said. "She was both serene and serenely beautiful. Probably born a rich girl, she acted like one. I dig her…I mean, I *really* dig her. Up to now, when stacked up against Grace, the girls I've screwed were Saturday night whores in comparison to this stunning young beauty."

Like Jimmy, Grace had appeared in commercials and teleplays. Her biggest break had come when she'd been cast opposite Gary Cooper in the Western, *High Noon* (1952).

[Gary Cooper, in an irreverent and disrespectful reference to Grace Kelly, once said, "She looks like a cold dish with a man until you get her pants off, and then she explodes."]

Grace Kelly, in an MGM publicity photo that managed to hint at her upcoming status as Her Serene Highness, Princess of Monaco.

Both New York and Hollywood were buzzing with rumors that during the making of *High Noon,* she and Cooper had become lovers, in spite of the difference in their ages. *[He was born in 1901, Grace in 1929.]*

In time, of course, Cooper became just one of many big-name stars headed for her bed: Marlon Brando, Cary Grant, Clark Gable, Bing Crosby, William Holden, Ray Milland, Frank Sinatra, and James Stewart, as well as designer Oleg Cassini and the Shah of Iran (Mohammed Reza Pahlavi) thrown in for extra seasoning.

One of her lovers, actor Don Richardson, expressed his disappointment in her when she ran off with Jean-Pierre Aumont, the handsome French actor. "She fucked everybody she came into contact with who was

The future prospects of Gene Lyons (above), her date the evening Jimmy met her, were not as glamorous.

221

able to advance her career. She screwed agents, producers, directors, bigtime stars, whomever."

At the party, in response to Brackett and Jimmy's applause for her performance in *High Noon,* she expressed disappointment with her part: "It was Gary's picture. You look into his face and you know everything he's thinking. You look into my face and you see nothing but a blank stare. I thought I was going to be a big movie star. I'm not so sure. Frankly, now that I'm back in New York, I think I should take acting lessons."

Lyons, her escort, seemed to suffer through the party from his seated position on a sofa, sometimes holding her hand. The red-haired Irishman was tall and good-looking, but it was obvious he'd had too much to drink.

Grace told them that she was taking him home to Philadelphia to meet her father, Jack Kelly. "I want him to see if Gene is marriage material."

"If he has me investigated, he'll learn that I'm already married," Lyons said, "but seeking an annulment."

"Everybody in the theater claims that Gene looks like Marlon Brando, but I think he's so much more handsome than Brando," Kelly said. "Don't you think so, James?"

"I couldn't agree more," Jimmy answered, diplomatically, though perceiving that Gene wasn't all that handsome, or all that charming, either.

"The reason I asked you is that you seem to know what the standard of male beauty is, to judge by your looks," she said. "The question is, do you take advantage of your good looks, using that as a weapon on those who fall under your spell?"

He couldn't believe she was flirting with him. He removed his glasses, so she could get a better look at his face.

Jimmy talked briefly with Lyons when Grace went to powder her nose. He was surprised to learn that he was a lifetime member of the Actors Studio. Quite by coincidence, Jimmy would soon be starring in a teleplay opposite him. In most cases, most of their off-screen talk would center around Grace.

At some point, Swift broke away from his other guests and chatted with Brackett and Jimmy. He had achieved great success in July of 1952 when NBC went on the air with his TV sitcom, *Mister Peepers,* starring Wally Cox as a junior high school science teacher.

"It's been a long journey," Swift claimed. "I dropped out of school when I was seventeen and

"I cannot write any sort of story unless there is at least one character in it for whom I have physical desire," Tennessee Williams (depicted above) told James Dean.

rode the rails to Hollywood. I began as an office boy for Walt Disney, but by 1938, I was his assistant animator. He told people I was like the son he never had."

"I bet," Jimmy said sarcastically.

Swift was visibly taken aback by Jimmy's sarcasm.

"Do you know something I don't?" he asked, rather sharply. Both Swift and Brackett stared at Jimmy, waiting for some revelation.

Feeling trapped, Jimmy extricated himself with: "Sorry—It was a stupid thing to say. I don't know Disney myself. I think one night I shook his hand at a party at George Cukor's house. I'm not the type of actor for a Walt Disney movie—unless maybe if a Minnie Mouse role comes up."

Maureen Stapleton, one of Tennessee's favorite actresses, arrived at the party with her husband, Max Allentuck, the general manager to producer Kermit Bloomgarden.

Jimmy knew of her long association with the Actors Studio and was impressed with her talent, especially her star involvement in Tennessee's Broadway version of *The Rose Tattoo,* which would earn her a Tony Award for Best Featured Actress in a play.

Like others at the party, she was an alcoholic. "Marilyn Monroe gets the ditzy blonde roles, although I suspect the girl has real talent. As for me, when I come out on the stage, people take one look at me and say, 'Jesus, that broad better know how to act—or else, what in hell is she doing up there?'"

During the course of the evening, Tennessee, also drunk, kept making passes at Jimmy, which he planned to intercept within a different setting at some future date.

Inge also seemed sexually attracted to Jimmy, but shy and introverted, living deep in the closet. He implied to Jimmy that he'd like to get together to discuss starring him in one of his upcoming plays. Jimmy hoped it would be the previously announced Broadway opening of *Picnic. [Inge's much-awarded, much-celebrated* Picnic, *opened on Broadway in 1953 and ran for almost 500 performances. Its original version featured Ralph Meeker as the male lead, with Paul Newman in a secondary role.]*

Jimmy was understandably impressed with Inge as a playwright. Brackett had taken him to see *Come Back, Little Sheba* on Broadway, which

As an actor, Maureen Stapleton gave Jimmy some advice: "Sometimes the acceptance of a lesser role, or even a rotten part, regardless of how humiliating, is the result of needing a paycheck."

had won a Tony for its star, Shirley Booth.

Like most of the other guests, Inge, too, was a heavy drinker.

Jimmy would later tell Stanley Haggart, "In spite of what I told you, I know that at some point, I'll have to shack up with both Bill Inge and Tennessee—call it 'singing for my supper.' They're the hottest playwrights in town, and I know they want to get into my drawers. So I've changed my mind about sleeping with old queers. Girls are always changing their minds. So why not guys?"

On New Year's Day, Jimmy telephoned Bast to report on the party. "Both Tennessee and Bill Inge are hot for me as an actor. Each of them wants to star me in a play. Which ones, I don't know yet.

"What do they know of you as an actor?" Bast asked, skeptically.

"Tennessee saw me in the Philadelphia preview of *See the Jaguar.*"

"Aren't you jumping to conclusions?" Bast asked. "Why not face up to the truth? Those two queens just want you to fuck them! They're using that casting shit as bait."

"You're god damn jealous!" Jimmy shouted, enraged, into the phone. "I'll think I'll go for a week without speaking to you. After that, we'll see about our so-called friendship."

Then he slammed down the phone.

***

Two weeks after meeting Grace Kelly, she called Jimmy at the Iroquois, having been provided with his phone number by David Swift. "So sorry to bother you, dear, but I have a problem. You were so charming at the New Year's Eve party given by David and Maggie. I just knew you'd help a damsel in distress. David thought you would."

"For you, I would climb the highest mountain, swim to the bottom of the deepest ocean," he said.

"That's a bit dramatic, but I love it," she said. "Sarah Churchill is throwing this elegant dinner at her penthouse. David told me you were a good friend of hers. Normally, I would invite Gene (Lyons), but he's a bit incapacitated."

Jimmy knew that meant he was too drunk to escort her. Without her having to ask, he immediately chimed in, "I'd love to be your escort."

"Oh, that would be delightful," she said. "The answer to a girl's dream."

After negotiating his way through the details with her, he put down the phone, later telling Bast about the invitation. "I am thrilled. Tennessee and Bill Inge have the hots for me, and now the ice queen herself. *High Noon* Grace Kelly wants to see what I'm hauling around in my jockey shorts."

"It sounds to me like she merely wants you to escort her to Lady Sarah's bash. What are you going to do? You don't have a tux."

"Leave it to Jimmy," he said, speaking in the third person. "I'll turn on the James Dean charm and have that tux by five o'clock this afternoon."

An hour later, he was inside Swift's apartment. "You started this thing about me being in the escort business. I need some fancy duds."

"I have three tuxedos," Swift said. "If you can't fit into one of mine, I'll rent you one from a place nearby."

At exactly five o'clock, Jimmy called Bast "I have the tux. I've tried it on. I look like a million dollars."

"I knew you in Hollywood when you had only one pair of jeans."

"Jimmy is coming up in the world," he said.

"I hear Gary Cooper (they call him 'the Montana Mule') is a tough act to follow," Bast said.

"Whatever I lack, I'll make up for with youth, beauty, and stamina. I hear Grace is going to become the Queen of Hollywood. Guess who'll be her Prince Consort?"'

***

Inside her penthouse, as hostess at her dinner party, Lady Sarah welcomed Grace and Jimmy warmly. "Come in, dear hearts," she said, "and let the butler get you a drink. I've had a few libations already."

To Jimmy, that was obvious.

As he would later tell Stanley Haggart, "I was the only nobody there."

Sarah introduced him around. First, he met the French star, Louis Jourdan, who had been recently voted the most handsome man in the world. Shortly thereafter (in 1956), he'd be making a movie with Grace (*The Swan),* in which he'd be cast as a tutor in love with a princess-to-be, a bit of real life casting. Ironically, Jimmy, too, would soon be co-starring with Jourdan in the Broadway play, *The Immoralist.*

To Jimmy's surprise, Jourdan's escort for the evening was a most unlikely choice—Danny Kaye, the red-haired, highly excitable comedian who always seemed to be cavorting hilariously on screen.

Later, the tipsy Sarah whispered into Jimmy's ear: "Louis and Danny are lovers—that is, when Danny isn't having to fuck Larry Olivier."

Looking as elegant and serene as Grace herself, another (slightly older) blonde goddess, Joan Fontaine, arrived at the party with an obviously gay escort. Jimmy had previously met her at Sardi's.

Cecil Beaton arrived with Roddy McDowall, but whereas Roddy hugged and kissed Jimmy like an old friend, Beaton pretended to be meeting him for the first time. Memories of staging that sexual exhibition for Beaton and his British friends came rushing through Jimmy's brain. He was tempted to say to him in front of the other guests, "Cecil, I haven't seen you since you last sucked my dick," but discretion won out.

Douglas Fairbanks, Jr. was another guest. He was the most elegantly dressed of all the male guests. His date was the formidable Marlene Dietrich, his old flame from the 1930s. After Sarah introduced her to Jimmy, she eyed him skeptically.

Months later, columnist Hedda Hopper asked Jimmy if he'd like to meet Dietrich. He didn't tell her he already had. "I don't know if I would," he said. "She's such a figment of my imagination. I go *whoop* in the stomach when you ask me if I'd like to meet her. Too much *woman.* You look at her and you think, 'I'd like to have that.'" *[Jimmy's quote about Dietrich appeared in Hopper's book,* The Whole Truth and Nothing But.*]*

After his death, Dietrich shared her opinion of Jimmy to Hopper. "He was small, ugly, hunchbacked with a potbelly, and bow-legged. If he'd lived, he'd have a larger potbelly, wear a wig, and have died of AIDS."

Fairbanks was more charming than Dietrich, announcing to anyone within earshot, "I saw Bette Davis the other night," he said. "She recalled our first meeting at a party. I was married to Joan Crawford at the time. We chatted politely until I suddenly thrust my hand into her bra. I felt her tits—rather large. I recommended that she use ice on her nipples like my wife did. Bette later said she found my behavior appalling. Imagine saying such a thing about a gentleman like me."

"Sarah told me that Noël Coward will be arriving soon," Fairbanks said to Jimmy. "Watch out for that one. He had such a crush on me back in the 1930s. Did you know that he wrote that hit song about me, 'Mad About the Boy?'"

Fairbanks had no sooner uttered that revelation than in walked Noël Coward himself, with Judy Garland on his arm.

Garland hugged and kissed Jimmy like a long-lost lover. "Darling," she said, in reference to their drunken three-way long ago back in Los Angeles. "You took French leave. You didn't even stick around for breakfast with John *[Carlyle]* and me."

"Catch me next time."

"I didn't realize you knew this divine boy, Judy," Coward said.

"He was my lover," she said. "As you well know, I can't rely on the unreliable dicks of the jerks I've married."

Throughout the remainder of the evening, Coward and Sarah—although giving the impression that they were the best of friends—shared some long sequences of rather cutting banter.

"Noël, darling," Sarah said. "Opinions about you vary so. Lord Louis Mountbatten once told me that no one could prick the bloom of pomposity quite like you. On the other hand, Rex Harrison claims that in so many ways, you're a terrible cunt."

"I admit to both charges," Coward responded.

At one point, Coward joined Jimmy on the sofa during a moment when Grace was away. Then he very bluntly asked him, "Are you gay, dear boy?"

"I can take it or leave it," Jimmy said.

"I can take it, but not with a woman," Coward said. "All that open plumbing revolts me. I imagine doing it with a woman is like feeling the skin of a rattlesnake. Perhaps you and I will get together during my time in New York. As Mae West might say, 'Come up and see me sometime.' The sooner the better. How about tomorrow night in my suite at the Waldorf Astoria? I'll leave clearance for you at the desk."

"I'll count the hours," Jimmy promised.

Based on Coward's influence in the theater and his "celebrity quotient," Jimmy had every intention of keeping that date. But the following morning, something came up.

After the party at Lady Sarah's, Jimmy had escorted Grace back to the Plaza. She had kissed him good night in the lobby, but had not invited him upstairs.

She telephoned him at eleven the next morning. It seemed that Gene Lyons had still not recovered, and that he had accused her of cheating on him. In the aftermath of the fight that ensued, they had canceled their plans for a rendezvous that night.

Into her end of the phone, Grace said to Jimmy, "I had planned this lovely dinner for him in my suite," she said. "And I hate to dine alone. I even purchased a lovely new gown from Oleg Cassini, and I'm dying to show it off. Would you be a doll and fill in for Gene one more time? At eight o'clock tonight?"

"Would I ever!"

Bubbling over with excitement, Jimmy phoned Stanley Haggart. "Can you believe it? Two dazzling invitations at the same time tonight—one to Noël Coward's suite, another to Grace Kelly's. What to do? I'm not really suited to Coward's comedies or musicals. I'd do better as Grace's co-star in her future movies. She's going to be big. She told me she's returning to Hollywood. MGM wants to cast her in a jungle movie with Clark Gable and Ava Gardner."

"Well, it looks like Coward's loss will be Grace's good fortune," Haggart responded.

***

The question remains unanswered. Did Jimmy seduce Grace Kelly that night in her suite at the Plaza? Or, phrased another way, did she seduce him?

When Haggart was asked about this, he said, "Frankly, I don't know. He never described to me how the evening went."

"A guy has to keep some secrets," Jimmy had said.

"And I was too polite to ask," Haggart said. "But based on their reputation—and I mean, both of their reputations—I can be almost 90% certain that they did the dirty deed. And why not?"

***

As preposterous as it sounded at the time, Jimmy's dream of co-starring with Grace Kelly almost came to be. After she left New York for Hollywood, she did not disappear from his life completely. They would meet again when George Stevens wanted to cast them together as co-stars in *Giant* with Rock Hudson.

In the meantime, his agent, Jane Deacy, called, saying, "My phone's been ringing off the wall. NBC, CBS, and ABC each want you to star in teleplays. You're hot, kid. You're going bigtime."

Chapter Six

Jimmy's Affair with
STEVE McQUEEN

Competition Onscreen and After Dark

How McQueen's Idol Worship of Jimmy Was Later Transferred to Paul Newman

In the early 1950s, three young actors in New York—James Dean, Paul Newman, and Steve McQueen—frequently arrived for the same casting calls. Mostly, the auditions involved teleplays, but in some cases they were for an aggressively sought-after role on Broadway.

Jimmy's agent, Jane Deacy, was quoted as saying: "That trio of good-looking men came to be viewed by directors as the same "type." If Jimmy were right for a role, it was also deemed suitable for either Newman or McQueen. Later, film directors in Hollywood more or less had the same view, too. Jimmy was set to star in *Somebody Up There Likes Me,* in which McQueen would play a small role. After Jimmy died, Newman was cast as the lead. McQueen also thought he'd be a more ideal choice to have played Jimmy's role in his three big feature films, especially *Giant."*

Deacy's remarks were later confirmed by Shelley Winters. "Steve told me he'd have been better than Dean in *East of Eden, Rebel Without a Cause,* and in *Giant,* too.

She quoted McQueen as saying, "The role of Jett Rink in *Giant* had my name written all over it. The scene where Dean got drenched from the oil gushing out of the well seemed ripped from a page of my own life. When I was a kid in Corpus Christi, I was hired as a roughneck, a job that used to be called a roustabout. I worked at drilling sites and, on many an occasion, I was bathed in oil."

"At night, I hung out in seedy taverns with wildcatters. That trade is full of men with empty pockets and big dreams."

"If I'd been in *Giant,* I would have fucked Elizabeth Taylor, Rock Hudson, and Sal Mineo."

Author David Dalton collectively referred to Newman, McQueen, and

MANFLESH AND GRIST FOR THE HOLLYWOOD MILLS
Three ferociously competitive young actors emerged during the 1950s, each auditioning for the same types of roles. Each of them studied, and in some cases, mimicked the others' styles. *Above, left to right*: Steve McQueen, James Dean, and Paul Newman.

Dean as "a cluster of types. A new kind of hero was coming into being, and it was inevitable that a lot of people shared the same idea. In the beginning of their careers, their *personas* were just drawing boundaries, and they were sensitive about being compared to each other."

In the beginning, Jimmy bonded with his fellow actors, even becoming intimate with them. A bisexual streak prevailed among all three men. Specifics about the bonding between Jimmy and McQueen has never been fully explored, because many of the details are missing. But in the wake of Jimmy's death, some eyewitness accounts surfaced, although still remaining sketchy.

In *The Mutant King,* a biography of James Dean, Dalton wrote that McQueen one night at a Hollywood party encountered Martin Landau, a good friend of Jimmy's. McQueen told Landau, "We've met before." He reminded him that he had first seen him when he'd driven his car into a garage on West 69th Street in Manhattan. A few minutes later, Jimmy roared in on his motorcycle. "Work had to be done on both vehicles, and I was the mechanic on duty," McQueen said.

What eventually evolved from that happenstance meeting in the garage was provided by Rogers Brackett, who was supporting Jimmy at the time and living with him in his apartment. "Perhaps to make me jealous, Jimmy confessed to me how he'd initially met McQueen and how he hooked up with him later. At the time, I had never heard of him. That day at the garage, after Landau went away, Jimmy slipped McQueen a slip of paper that said 'CALL ME.' The number he gave him happened to be my number, because Jimmy was living with me at the time."

As was so often the case with Jimmy, he provided an entirely different account of what happened that afternoon in the garage to author Michael Munn. At the time, McQueen had not been able to snag an acting gig, so he took a job as a mechanic instead. "I figured my acting career was over," he told Munn. "No offers. But then one day in comes James Dean, and I serviced his car." *[Actually, it was a motorcycle.]* "I felt humiliated because I knew I should have been making money acting, and now I was servicing Dean's fucking car."

Young Steve, as a Marine (both photos above). Like Jimmy, it took some conscious effort for him to develop and evolve his style as an actor.

Brackett claimed that Jimmy's seduction of McQueen first took place in his apartment during a time when he was away in Chicago shooting a commercial. "Those guys used my bed. Jimmy later told me all about it. He claimed that McQueen was not a great lay and just lay there with him doing all the work. And from the things I heard among show-biz pros, McQueen was and continued to be willing to drop his shorts for career advances. So was Jimmy, for that matter."

Jimmy presented yet a different version of his sexual link to McQueen to Stanley Haggart. "I know why girls and some men grow crazy over Steve as a lover. He has great technique: He tongues you all over and gets you so worked up you're hot as a firecracker. Then he comes on like gangbusters. We're equally matched in sexual equipment. We could be brothers. That is, if brothers commit incest."

"I always thought that Jimmy was more gay than straight," Brackett said. "But from what I later heard, McQueen was more the ladies' man. That didn't mean he hadn't done a lot of hustling like Jimmy himself. He had had some affairs with men on the side. It was later revealed that he'd played in some porn movies in Cuba. Let's write him up as bisexual. When stars like Monty Clift or Brando rang up McQueen, he always seemed ready, willing, and able to show up at their doorstep."

"Jimmy, indeed, had an affair with McQueen," Brackett claimed, "But at the same time, he was carrying on with other actors and had a girl or two on the side. And he took care of me. Boy, did he have stamina. He was one busy boy."

Paul Darlow, a friend of Jimmy's, told author Christopher Sandford about an encounter he'd witnessed between Jimmy and McQueen at Jerry's Tavern. Darlow was sitting with them.

Jimmy suddenly ordered McQueen, "Do my hair."

"McQueen rose from the table and obliged," Darlow said. "He patiently back-combed Dean's soon-to-be famous hair, making it thick and shiny as a mink's. McQueen was breathing and lightly chuckling down the back of Jimmy's neck."

By this point in his career, Jimmy had started to carry around a hairbrush. His agent and a few directors had complained about his unruly hair. Darlow later speculated, "Perhaps Jimmy was getting made up for his next casting call, with the understanding that he'd be competing with well-groomed actors."

After he'd applied the finishing touches to Jimmy's hair, McQueen asked him, "Would you do mine?"

"Drop dead," said Jimmy.

"Come on, JD, don't you dig my fur?"

"No," Jimmy said. "It always looks so Dago to me."

Despite the putdowns, Jimmy was still seen coming and going from McQueen's shabby little apartment on the fifth floor of a tenement building on

East 10th Street, where the rent was twenty-five dollars a month. Its bathtub was in the kitchen, directly adjacent to his gas-burning stove. When the bathtub wasn't being used, McQueen covered it with a lid and used its surface as a countertop.

The veteran actress, Uta Hagen, once invited McQueen and Jimmy to a student performance at the HB Studio. It was understood that when it was over, members of the audience would deliver their critiques. Karl Malden was also invited. Jimmy had met him at the Actors Studio and had also seen his performance in the film version of *A Streetcar Named Desire* (1951) with Brando and Vivien Leigh.

"Critics accused me of imitating the acting style of James Dean in that stinker, *The Blob,*" McQueen said. "Maybe I did. But from now on, I'm going to be Steve McQueen, an original."

"I arrived late and sat in the back row," Malden later said. "McQueen and Dean were about twelve feet away. They weren't watching the play—Ibsen, I believe—but were into each other. They engaged in what we used to call a necking session. Dean giggled, but McQueen was more the silent type. A lot of actors back then, if you could imagine such a thing, called those two 'swishes,' but in my view, both young men were too macho for that label. I didn't condemn their sexual behavior, but there was a time and place for everything. They had been invited to watch the play and to take it seriously. Their commando act could wait for later."

"At the end of the play, I stood up and advised those two lovebirds to get a room."

The bonding between Jimmy and McQueen flourished, but only for a while. According to claims from other actors, "McQueen came to idolize Jimmy. In his auditions, he began to sound like Dean." Those words came from James Sheldon, one of Jimmy's mentors.

McQueen told Sheldon, "Jimmy is the greatest actor in New York, much better than Clift and Brando. If he's influenced me, so what? I don't want to sound like a mushmouth like Brando."

Five years after Jimmy's death, in reference to McQueen's performance in *The Blob* (1958), critics claimed that in it, "He stole the *persona* of James Dean, adapting it for his own acting style. *James Dean is not dead!* He lives on in Steve McQueen."

Biographer Penina Spiegel explained why McQueen was called "The Shadow" by certain actors who knew both Jimmy and him. "He seemed to stalk Dean," she wrote. "They shared a certain sulky arrogance, a self-absorbed moodiness, and an intense sexual appeal. Yet while Dean went on to collect film roles, McQueen was still struggling, still going nowhere."

Not just Spiegel, but others, noted how McQueen followed Jimmy around "like a puppy dog trailing its master." Ironically, the same charge was being made about Jimmy stalking Brando.

McQueen tried to emulate Jimmy in almost any action or bit of stage business he made. At the Blue Ribbon Café, he would order what Jimmy ordered. McQueen used to drink his coffee with cream, but when he saw Jimmy drinking his black, he gave up on the cream.

"Steve would even imitate Dean's reading of a newspaper, how he held the paper, how he turned the pages," Spiegel wrote.

Mildred Sacher, at the Blue Ribbon Café, frequently saw McQueen and Jimmy sharing a table. She came there daily to catch up on the latest gossip and to learn of any auditions for Broadway plays. "I remember James Dean and the guy who later became Steve McQueen. He was calling himself 'Steven' in those days. They came in together almost every afternoon. They never paid attention to anybody else, just talked to each other. McQueen seemed to hang on Dean's every pronouncement as if it were God's word. It was clear to me that McQueen idolized Dean, perhaps wanted to be him. All the girls back then—mostly out-of-work actresses—thought Dean and McQueen were gorgeous, at least in a slightly offbeat way. I never flirted with them. I assumed they were satisfied with each other and didn't need a woman interfering."

Many men who lived in Greenwich Village [i.e., the West Village] in the early 1950s recalled McQueen and Jimmy riding shirtless on their motorcycles through the district. "They wove dangerously in and out of traffic," claimed Samuel Miller, a florist, who lived in an apartment building near McQueen when he moved there from the East Village.

"They were always speeding. I don't know how fast they were going, but enough so to be a menace. If you heard them coming, you got out of their way. They seemed to be daring Fate, tempting Her to cause an accident."

"They sure liked to take their chances. They also showed off their bodies, often in shorty-short shorts. They weren't exactly Steve Reeves, but they were sexy nonetheless. Such scrumptious testosterone. A guy can dream, can't he?"

Arthur Kennedy, who had co-starred with Jimmy in *See the Jaguar,* recalled Mc-

Arthur Kennedy had the rare privilege of working with both James Dean and Steve McQueen on the stage and on the screen. He starred with Jimmy on the stage in *See the Jaguar* and with McQueen in the Paramount movie, *Nevada Smith* (1966), based on a character in the Harold Robbins novel, *The Carpetbaggers.*

Queen attending all five performances of the short-lived play, and coming backstage to rave about Jimmy's acting. "He didn't mention my acting," Kennedy said. "I didn't learn until later that they had a reputation for seducing girls, especially McQueen. When I saw them, they had eyes only for each other."

"I went out with them on two different occasions for some serious boozing," Kennedy said. "They were real hotheads. If someone looked at one of them, especially the wrong way, they were ready for a fist fight. In Dean's case, perhaps a knife fight. He still carried around that lethal weapon with which he'd threatened Michael Gordon, the director of *See the Jaguar.* I felt that Dean would one day completely lose it and stab someone."

McQueen was aware of the anger bubbling inside Jimmy, as well as his own anger management problem. "Jimmy seemed all too eager to stab someone, but he can thank Jupiter, or whatever god he worships, that he never did. Prison rapists would have had a field day with him."

"When I was much younger, I would go to war if someone looked at me the wrong way," McQueen said. "Hell, one afternoon, I stole a knife from a butcher's shop and went home to kill my mother and shithead stepfather who had been sexually molesting me. Fortunately, they weren't at home, and I got a grip on myself."

"In spite of his violent streak, Dean had a sensitive side," Kennedy claimed. "But I found McQueen hostile on most occasions. To me, he remained the eternal juvenile delinquent. I'd heard awful stories about him—reform school, rolling drunks, breaking into houses. I thought he was a very unsavory character and could only harm Dean. I once advised Dean to drop McQueen. 'Nothing good will come out of your relationship with him,' I said."

Jimmy was defiant at the suggestion. "I don't drop an acolyte until I'm finished with him. When I accomplish what I want with him, then he's toast."

Kennedy asked, "What could you possibly want with McQueen other than the obvious? He's rough around the edges. He must have barely made it through the eighth grade."

"Don't put him down," Jimmy said. "He's got some good points. He's like a wild stallion. He needs to be broken in. I'm the cowpoke in the saddle who can do that."

"At the time, I didn't know what made McQueen tick, but I got to know Dean rather well," Kennedy said. "For a brief time, I was like an older brother he admired and looked up to, especially as an actor. There was talk

Dennis Hopper: "As an actor, I was confused. Should I be a new James Dean, or a new Steve McQueen?"

that we were lovers. That's ridiculous, of course. I wasn't screwing him, but he did discuss his homosexuality with me. He lived in fear of exposure and what it might do to his career if he became a movie star. Broadway was a more tolerant place than Hollywood."

"He also told me he was frustrated in his relationship with McQueen, because McQueen wouldn't let him fuck him," Kennedy claimed.

"He's driving me up the wall, but he won't give in to me," Jimmy told Kennedy. "I'm going to get him high one night, tie him up, and rape him."

"Dean never explained what 'broken in' meant, but I got his drift," Kennedy said.

"Amazingly, I got to know McQueen years later, when we both starred in the movie *Nevada Smith*," Kennedy recalled. "He was the biggest star in the world then. At the peak of his career. I had totally misjudged this juvenile delinquent. It's incredible how far you can climb in America if you get the breaks. I ended up with the greatest respect for him as an actor. Of course, he had the morals of an alleycat, but that was part of his macho charm."

Journalist John Parker noted, "In between selling ballpoint pens, McQueen was slowly emerging into the spotlight. He and Dean led parallel lives—penniless and often at low ebb."

Dennis Hopper, on the set of *Rebel Without a Cause*, claimed that Jimmy was having an image problem. He quoted him as saying: "You know, I've got to make it as James Dean. In this hand, I'm holding Marlon Brando, saying, 'Fuck you!'. And in this hand, I'm holding Monty Clift, saying, 'Please forgive me'. And so it goes. 'Fuck you. Please forgive me.' Somewhere in the middle, you'll find James Dean."

"After *The Blob* (1958) was released, many people in Hollywood told me to stop acting like Dean," McQueen said. "They assured me I had my own unique talent and that I should let Dean die in the Porsche graveyard. That I should go on and be myself. And so, I followed that advice. Fuck Dean's sensitivity on screen."

During the making of *Never So Few* (1959), co-starring Frank Sinatra and Peter Lawford, McQueen told Lawford, "I intend to become the screen's most idolized tough guy. I'm abandoning Dean's sensitivity on camera. After all, considering my background, the tough guy image is for me. I've tried many things—porn star, hustler, gigolo escort, merchant seaman, lumberjack, roughneck in the Texas oil fields, and a kick-ass Marine. Who better to star in TV's *Wanted—Dead or Alive,* than me? If Dean could rise from his grave, he'd be imitating me today."

Author Christopher Sandford wrote that "the nagging threat of homosexuality" hung over McQueen's head. He was legendarily touchy on the subject. However, he took Bill Claxton, the photographer, on a tour of his former haunts in Manhattan, including some of the places where he'd hung out with Jimmy. "He would show me where he'd lived, places he'd worked as a hustler," Claxton claimed. "He had some pretty wild stories."

Sandford noted that, "A persistent rumor that McQueen dabbled in cross-dressing was a vile slur, but expressed a view that some people had of him. Those were McQueen's omnisexual days, when he soul-kissed James Dean and hustled around New York," Sandford said.

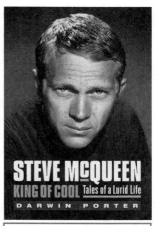

McQueen himself later admitted, "I lived on the brew and cocaine, along with acid, pot, and fuck-flings. Yes, I attended bisexual orgies, one of them taped by the FBI at the Gramercy Park Hotel in Manhattan. Dean was invited, but didn't attend. I bet that ugly old queer, J. Edgar Hoover, got an eyeful watching the tapes of me in action. I bet his fat butt was twitching and his cocksucking mouth was slobbering when he saw me in all my glory."

The most definitive portrait of McQueen's private life appears in Blood Moon's own biography—*Steve McQueen—Tales of a Lurid Life,* by Darwin Porter.

According to its author, Darwin Porter, as quoted in *London's Express*: "Steve McQueen has become an iconic hero, forever cool, but it's ironic because he was never really cool; he was a Molotov cocktail that could explode at any time. His fans never knew the real Steve McQueen."

Addressing McQueen's allure, author Penna Speigel wrote: "He was catnip for women. Women who from others would require courtship—dinners, roses, compliments—fell instantly into his bed like ripe fruit dropping from a vine. He had a wonderful vitality, a soaring, wild energy, combined with his striking blue eyes. Hard-muscled body, and his little boy vulnerability, this was a powerful appeal to women. Some of them were as surprised to find themselves in Steve's bed as Lady Chatterley was to be in her gamekeeper's."

Rod Steiger, who had met McQueen at the Actors Studio and who had co-starred with Jimmy in a teleplay, weighed in with his opinion. "I knew Brando. I knew Paul Newman. I knew James Dean. I understand why they made women—or men in some cases—turn hot under the collar. To me, McQueen looked like a grease monkey. From working on those cars and motorcycles all day, he seemed covered in grease, with dirty fingernails."

"He was also illiterate. He couldn't converse on any topic except cars. Dean knew a little about a lot of things. Brando could converse on such subjects as civil rights for blacks. How Indians had been defamed in the movies, left-wing politics, turncoat commie-outing Elia Kazan, and James Dean, one of his favorite topics."

"McQueen was a narcissist," Steiger continued, "although I don't think he knew what it meant. He shared that quality with Brando and Dean. But when McQueen told a gal, 'Come here, baby,' the bitch came running."

Jimmy left McQueen, among others, behind when he went to Hollywood to star in *East of Eden*. But he still called McQueen on infrequent occasions. "I haven't forgotten you, kid," he said. "Why don't you come out to the coast? I'm sure I can find a job for you out here somewhere."

As tempting as that offer was, McQueen turned him down, preferring to remain dejected and broke in Manhattan. He felt he had a better chance there, either in finding roles in teleplays or perhaps on Broadway.

Not wanting to make his plight appear too dire, McQueen bragged about his conquests with women, including his on-again, off-again affair with Shelley Winters. "I've picked up with her just where you left off." He also bragged to Jimmy that he was sleeping with many wannabe actresses, claiming, "I find the pickings great at coffeehouses on Bleeker Street."

Not to be outdone, Jimmy boasted, "Since arriving in Hollywood, I've been getting so many propositions from both men and women that I'm going to have to hire a social secretary. Some of the biggest names in Hollywood are after me. But that was true even before I became famous. You either have it or you ain't got it, the way I figure it."

Late one night in New York in 1954, McQueen picked up his phone after its fifth ring. "Hi," came a voice over the wire. "I'm in town and ready to fuck."

"Who in hell is this?" McQueen asked sleepily."

"It's Jimmy," came the voice. "The toast of Hollywood. Your rebel without a cause. I'm calling you because you're the only guy in New York who knows how to use your pecker."

"Well, I'll be a rat's ass," McQueen said. "The bigtime movie idol himself. Get that much-used ass of yours over here."

According to reports, Jimmy and McQueen were up all night, rising at around two o'clock the next afternoon for a very late breakfast at their once-regular turf, the Blue Ribbon Café.

Jimmy tantalized McQueen with his adventures in Hollywood. He seemed amused by his growing reputation and the scandalous stories already being spread about him. "The word is I'd fuck a snake—and have—to get ahead. Whoever said that was right on the mark."

Jimmy told McQueen about the wild affair he'd had with a very young Sal Mineo, who had portrayed Plato in *Rebel Without a Cause*. "Sal plays the first gay teenager in movies. Nicholas Ray filmed a scene in which we kiss, but I'm sure that will end up on the cutting room floor."

"Some people in the press are writing that my personality is androgynous," Jimmy told him.

"I don't know what that means," McQueen said.

"Neither do I."

During the course of their day together, McQueen began to realize how Jimmy had changed after two movies in Hollywood. He filled him in on stories of his visits to The Club in Hollywood, an S&M bar and hangout for the leather set. He claimed he'd discovered the pleasure of having guys stub out their cigarettes on his ass, and even showed McQueen some of the burns.

"Don't try to pull any of that shit with me," McQueen warned.

"I won't," Jimmy said. "You're not the type to enjoy the pleasure of pain, only the infliction of pain on others."

"You got that right!" McQueen answered.

Before mid-afternoon, Jimmy revealed his secret career moves. "Offers are pouring in even from fuckers who haven't seen my films. I may be offered a part in Edna Ferber's *Giant*, which is set in Texas. There's talk that I'll star opposite William Holden. "

"I'm also after another role," Jimmy said. "Robert Wise is talking to me about playing Rocky Graziano in a movie called *Somebody Up There Likes Me* (eventually released in 1956). That's my lead-in for us to go to the gym today. I want to practice my boxing."

"That's not for me," McQueen said. "I tried boxing. I'm no good at it."

Jimmy could be very persuasive, and soon McQueen found himself in a Brooklyn gym boxing with the actor.

Unknown to either of them that day, there would in the near future appear two additional contenders for the role of Rocky Graziano in that film, such formidable talents as Marlon Brando and the ultimately successful actor who got the role, Paul Newman.

***

After that, Jimmy disappeared to do whatever he was doing in the precious few months that remained for him on this Earth. To his surprise, McQueen, still in New York, received another call from a Hollywood star, Rock Hudson himself, who reminded McQueen that they had met while he was bartending at Monty Clift's party.

"I know who you are," McQueen told him, "and I don't need to be reminded of where I met you. How can a guy forget meeting Rock Hudson?"

"I'll take that as flattery," Hudson answered. He invited McQueen for dinner that night at his hotel, holding out a tantalizing proposal. "I think I've found the ideal role for your movie debut."

That night, in his hotel suite over a steak dinner ordered from room service, Hudson was gracious and charming and filled with anecdotes about Hollywood. He also had a sense of self-deprecation delivered with good humor. "A friend working with John Wayne told me the Duke, referring to me, said, 'What a waste of a face on a queer. You know what I could have done with that face?'"

"I have this great friend, Mark Miller," Hudson said. "Before coming to New York, he warned me, 'Just because it wiggles, you don't have to fuck it.'"

Eventually, Hudson got down to business. He told McQueen that all of Hollywood was talking about the casting of *Giant* (released in 1956), based on the Edna Ferber novel and set in Texas. "William Holden wants it. Alan Ladd wants it. Gary Cooper wants it. Clark Gable wants it. But right before flying to New York, George Stevens, its director, called me to say that the role of Jordan Benedict belongs to me. Those

Rock Hudson to Steve McQueen: "I don't want to co-star with James Dean in *Giant*. I want you to play Jett Rink."

other golden oldies can sit around their dens looking at old movie stills of themselves. The Hollywood of the late 50s will belong to guys like us. Incidentally, I'll be appearing opposite Elizabeth Taylor. I know you know her. I saw her talking to you when you were tending bar at Monty's party."

"Miss Taylor doesn't have a clue as to who Steve McQueen is," he answered. "But she'll get the idea one night when I'm fucking her."

Hudson appeared only mildly startled by that statement. "Here's how you fit in. Stevens is considering Jimmy for the role of Jett Rink, but I don't want him anywhere near that movie. The bastard will upstage me. I'm trying to persuade Stevens to cast you instead."

"Hey, pal, that sounds great, but I don't know if I'm up to such a big break," McQueen said.

"Do you think I was up for my big breaks when they happened?" Hudson asked. "I was thrown into a part and ran with it. There I was appearing opposite Oscar winner Jane Wyman, and I didn't have the experience. Sometimes Hollywood throws you into the big time whether you're ready for it or not."

"Let's go for it," McQueen said. "I'm a fast learner."

"It's not definite, and Stevens is a hard man to convince, but I wanted your permission before I begin my big push of you," Hudson said. "There's no way I want to work with Dean."

Years later it was revealed that McQueen was just one of many young actors that Hudson promoted for the role of Jett Rink. The speculation was that he feared that Jimmy, based on the favorable reviews of his previous films, would steal the movie from him.

Ever the opportunist, Hudson also used the role of Jett Rink as an alluring tool for seduction, even though he made it clear that he had only the power to recommend a candidate, and that he wasn't responsible for the final casting decisions.

A room service waiter reported that he found both men in bed together and presumably nude when he delivered their breakfast the subsequent morning in New York.

Before leaving New York, Hudson promised that he'd hang out with McQueen when he made it to the coast, regardless of the outcome of the casting of *Giant.*

"I have this gut instinct that we're going to work together one day, and that each of us, in our own separate ways, is going to become the biggest box office attraction in the country."

*   *   *

When Jimmy left New York to fly back to Los Angeles, both he and McQueen were filled with rosy visions of their future. When they kissed and embraced, it was for the last time.

In *The Thomas Crown Affair* (1968), Steve McQueen and Faye Dunaway performed what some critics called "The sexiest kiss in the history of cinema."

The next news McQueen heard about Jimmy came a few months later via television. His friend was dead in a car crash in California.

"I'll probably die in a machine, just like Jimmy," McQueen told the actor, George Peppard. "I can see it now. Some lonely stretch of highway along some back road somewhere. Death will be instant. I'm sure my head will be severed like Jimmy's. But what a way to go. Floorboarding it and rushing head-on to meet death. If cars weren't meant to go fast, they wouldn't have been made to do so. Man craves speed. The only time I feel really alive is when I'm speeding and defying death. I understand Jimmy's need."

McQueen rather callously told Hudson and others one drunken night, "I'm glad Dean is dead. That eliminates my main competition."

When Jimmy passed on from this world in 1955, McQueen transferred his idolatry of the late star to another emerging star, Paul Newman. He also redirected the jealousy he'd felt about

Steve McQueen told a reporter that he and James Dean shared the same philosophy of life. "I live for myself and I answer to nobody. The last thing I want to do is to fall in love with some broad."

Jimmy onto Newman, who was getting starring roles before he did.

Comparisons between the two stars became a part of the national consciousness, and widely publicized. In a discussion by feminist icon Erica Jong about the difficulties of achieving the "ultimate orgasm," she wrote in *Esquire:* "Who has the bluest eyes, Newman or McQueen? It is difficult to say, but McQueen's twinkle more. He makes me think of all those leathery-necked cowboys at remote truck stops in Nevada. Does he wear pointy boots? And does he take them off when he screws?"

In the wake of Jimmy's death, a writer cited McQueen as "The Next James Dean," and a reporter for *Movie World* wrote: "Steve McQueen is the logical successor to James Dean. The clique that worships Dean has a new Messiah in McQueen. Luckily, he is living longer than Dean did, so the cult will have a long, long time to thrive."

When McQueen read that, he said, "Fuck it! I want to be the next Bogie."

Despite the forecast of *Movie World's* columnist, Steve did not have that much longer to live. He died of a heart attack at the age of fifty in 1980.

But before that, he evolved into a top-tier movie star, luring audiences to the box office throughout the 1960s and 70s with such hits as *The Great Escape* (1963), *The Cincinnati Kid* (1963), *The Sand Pebbles* (1966; it led to Steve's nomination as Best Actor that year); *Bullit* (1968); *The Magnificent Seven* (1970), *Papillon* (1973), and *The Towering Inferno* (1974), within which he competed with Paul Newman for top billing.

McQueen, Faye Dunaway, & Paul Newman in *The Towering Inferno* (1974)

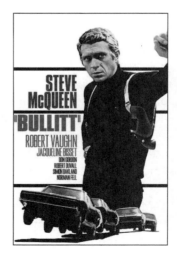

Chapter Seven

Jimmy's Jailbait. His Affair & Correspondence With

BARBARA GLENN

A Jewish Sweet Sixteen Wannabe Actress from Queens

He Takes Her Virginity, Slaps Her Around, Accepts Money from Her, Sends Her Psychotic Love Letters, and Talks of Marriage

Reckless Motorcycle Rides Through the Canyons of Manhattan

The setting was Cromwell's Pharmacy, within the NBC Building in Manhattan, as 1952 was drawing to a close. A just-turned sixteen-year-old wannabe actress, Barbara Glenn, who descended from a Jewish family in Queens, was sitting at a table sipping soda with her actor friends, Martin Landau, Rusty Slocum, and Carol Sinclair.

Barbara Glenn with James Dean at the beach. He later described her as "my neurotic little shit."

At this time in his life, James Dean made almost daily visits to this actors' hangout, with its bank of pay phones where hopefuls were always phoning their agents to see if any acting gigs had come through.

"Who's that attractive man?" Glenn asked, as she stared at Jimmy, who stood about twelve feet away. He had already signaled a greeting to his friend Landau.

"I know him," Landau said. "I'll bring him over and introduce you to him." Then he walked over to alert Jimmy that he had an admirer.

From a distance, Jimmy appraised her. "Looks like jailbait to me." Nonetheless, he came over and greeted her, although he didn't have much to say.

At least she learned that he was set to open that night on Broadway in *See the Jaguar,* a play starring Arthur Kennedy.

Glenn later shared her impressions of that afternoon. "Martin told me that Jimmy thought I was 'magnificently gorgeous.' Jimmy seemed rather shy, and didn't talk much, but I found him appealing, but not devastatingly so. He was different from the people I knew, not that I knew many. He was so very young. Actually, I thought he was my age until I learned otherwise. I felt he might be boyfriend material. He was good looking enough, but I sensed something beneath his surface. There was an aura of danger about him, but not enough to scare me off. I wished him luck on his opening night and agreed to meet him at Cromwell's the following afternoon to hear about it."

At table with Glenn, Slocum, a late teenager wannabe actor, observed her flirtation with Jimmy. "I didn't think much would come of it, just another of Jimmy's passing fancies. He'd hook up with some girl in the afternoon. When you'd see him later that night at Jerry's, that girl would be someone else. The afternoon brunette had been replaced by the night's blonde or redhead."

"Jimmy had this technique when talking to you of making you feel you were uttering words of wisdom and you were the most fabulous person he'd ever met," Slocum said. "I saw him pull that stunt on the very young and impressionable Barbara Glenn. All of us at the time were just the little girlfriends or little boyfriends of Jimmy's. We came and we went, like the hamburgers served at Cromwell's."

The next day, Jimmy met Glenn at Cromwell's for a soda, telling her that *See the Jaguar* had won raves for his performance, but that the play itself had been critically denounced. "I'll probably be back knocking on the doors of casting agents in a few days."

She remembered he brought her a short story to read, "A Tree of Night" by Truman Capote. It was the tale of a college girl traveling on a crowded train. On board, she encounters two grotesques, a zombie-like man and a mysterious woman with an oversized head. He told her it was an allegory about a sane person who can succumb to the terror hidden within one's darkest soul.

Then he leaned over the table and told her, "You remind me of my mother, Mildred. She deserted me long ago. I mean, she up and died on me. She wasn't even thirty."

As Glenn later recalled, "No sixteen-year-old girl wants to hear a prospective boyfriend tell her she reminds him of his mother, but our relationship survived that disaster."

"I felt sorry for him. His mother died even before America entered World War II, but he still hadn't recovered from her loss. He also told me that his father, Winton, had also abandoned him when he was just a boy. When he discussed his parents, he reminded me of a nine-year-old, a little boy lost."

"Soon, we were dating," she recalled. The two of them could be seen speeding through the canyons of Manhattan on his motorcycle, with Glenn holding onto Jimmy for dear life. "He was a terrible cyclist, weaving dangerously in and out of traffic."

"When I survived yet another ride on that motorcycle, we used to sit and talk quietly on a bench in Central Park," she said. "I had to walk on eggshells when chatting with him. The slightest remark could make him furious."

"I was always fearful of his motorcycle riding," Glenn claimed. "I consider his machine an instrument of death. I remember half of my time with Jimmy involved waiting for him to show up, because he was always late, and I was always wondering if he was going to make it. I always had the feeling that somehow, some way, some day, he was not going to show up. He did crash his motorcycle on one occasion. Fortunately, he wasn't badly hurt. But what about the next crash, or even the crash after that?"

"I can never get along without my little cycle," he claimed. "I guess I'll never sell it. It's like a brother to me. Of course, there is danger. I'm reminded that an actor with only half a face is no actor at all."

Their motorcycle rides often came to a stop in front of Figaro's, their hang-out in Greenwich Village at the corner of MacDougal and Bleeker Streets.

When he introduced her one night to Arthur Kennedy, backstage at one of *See the Jaguar*'s few performances, he warned the older actor, "Barbara's neuroticism is the equal of my own, and that's saying a lot. But her eighteen-inch waist and thirty-six inch bust go a long way."

As one of Glenn's girlfriends later reported, "Every sixteen-year-old girl supposedly has to lose her virginity. Although I wasn't there, I just assumed that Barbara eventually lost hers to this Jimmy Dean, who apparently liked to deflower virgins."

William Bast wanted to know who this new woman—or girl—was in Jimmy's life. During a telephone call, he described her as, "She's good looking, as busty as Marilyn Monroe, tall, very, very young, rather thin, as hyperactive and combustible as I am. We have lots of fights, tons of makeup sessions. We both have the temperament of Mount Vesuvius."

During the spring of 1953, the two of them often engaged in epic battles, but would eventually come together and be seen on his motorcycle again.

"Sometimes, I would scream at him and pound his chest," she said. "People who knew us compared us to a fighting cat and dog."

At times, he was worried that he might accidentally get her pregnant. "I hate using a rubber," he told his friend, Stanley Haggart. "It dulls the sensation for me. I like skin meeting skin, like rubber hitting the road in a car."

With summer approaching, Barbara managed to get a gig at the Cragsmoor Playhouse in the Catskills. When Jimmy heard the news, he exploded in anger.

Friends of her were giving her a farewell party, to which she invited him. "He showed up in a real foul mood, ignoring everybody, even me," Glenn said. "It was a horrible night. He finally stormed out the door without even a good-bye."

Devastated, she left her own party to find him, figuring he might have gone over to Jerry's Tavern, where he often spent his evenings. He wasn't there. She sat alone at a table, not managing to hold back her tears. About an hour later, he showed up.

"He didn't apologize for his outrageous behavior," she said. "That was not his style. He just held my hand and looked deeply into my teary eyes. Without saying a word, we made up and later spent the night together."

He wrote to her in the Catskills, complaining that except for some tele-plays that spring, "the pickings are slim here. Television has gone into the summer doldrums. Jane Deacy has lined up only two or three teleplays for me, each of which pays starvation wages."

He told her he was going to perform two dramatic readings, one of which was from *Metamorphosis,* a stage play adapted from the novel by Franz Kafka. "It was really Kafka's nightmare," he wrote. "I play a man who wakes up one morning to discover that overnight, he's been transformed into this hideous giant insect. My reading is set for August at the Village Theatre. Definitely off-Broadway."

The second reading was of Jonathan Bates' play, *The Fell Swoop,* presented on June 23 at the Palm Gardens in the New Dramatists' headquarters on West 52nd Street.

During the summer of 1953, Jimmy lived in Bates' apartment during periods when he was out of town. Rather cherubic looking, Bates was Irish and worked as a purser for Trans World Airlines. He had three dogs, and, in exchange for free lodging, Jimmy agreed to feed and walk his animals whenever Bates was away tending to business abroad.

"Jimmy was an animal lover," Glenn said. "But he complained about having to walk them, and he also said that the dogs kept him up at night."

Glenn often visited him in Bates' apartment, which was above the Brown Derby Restaurant at 40 West 52nd Street. "I remember its cabaret sign flashing all night, lighting up the living room with its neon glow."

Jimmy told Glenn that he'd lost a few pounds. "Meals are few and far between unless I bum a few."

"That drew a response from her, and she sent him a check for a hundred dollars, with a note: "For seventy-five cents, you can get a huge plate of spaghetti and meatballs on Thompson Street in The Village.

During her months with him, Glenn would often supply Jimmy with enough cash to tide him over between work assignments in teleplays.

For some reason, he eventually wrote to Glenn in the Catskills, describing the nighttime scene in Manhattan, a venue with which she was already familiar.

"In the pensiveness of night, the cheap, monotonous, shrill, symbolic sensual beat of suggestive drums tattoos orgyistic images on my brain. The smell of gin and 90% beer, entwine with the sometimes suspenseful, slow, sometimes labored static, sometimes motionless, sometimes painfully rigid, till finally, the long-waited for jerks and convulsions that fill the now thick chewing gum haze with a mist of sweat, fling the patrons into a fit of suppressed joy. The fated 7 days a week bestial virgin bows with the poise of a drunken pavlova. Rivulets of stale perspiration glide from and between her once well-formed anatomy to the anxious, welcoming front-row celebrities who lap it up with infamous glee. The Aura of Horror. I live above it and below it...It is my Divine Comedy. The Dante of 52nd Street. There is no peace in our world. I love you. I would like to write about nice things, or fiction, but we shouldn't avoid reality should we? The things I have just written are the truth. They are very hard to write about. I am lonely. Forgive me. I am lonely. Love, Jim."

In a letter he wrote to her in August, shortly before her return to New

York, he said:

> *"I am very lonely for you. I am alone. Thoughts are sweet, then wicked, then perverse, then penitent, then sweet. The moon is not blue. It hangs there in the sky no more. Forgive me for such a sloppy letter. I'm a little drunk. I drink a bit lately. You see, I don't know what's going on. Remarkable lot, human beings. In an antiphonal azure swing, souls drone their unfinished melody. When did we live and when did we not? In my drunken stupor, I said a gem. Great actors are often time pretentious livers. The pretentious actor, a great liver. God Damnit! I miss you!"*

When Glenn returned to New York, she resumed her relationship with him. She didn't ask him if he'd dated other girls while she was away. But he did say, "You must have met a lot of handsome guys this summer, chasing you up and down those Catskill mountains."

"He was physically as gorgeous as ever," she said. "Still, with that lost boy quality. He obviously hadn't found himself since I left him. When I did ask him a direct question, he mumbled an answer. I came to suspect he was leading a double or triple life, one with me, and two or three with other lovers. He seemed to have a lot of needs to satisfy, and I suspected I couldn't fulfill all of them. Yet he talked of marriage, but didn't give me a direct proposal, much less an engagement ring, not that he could afford one."

As 1953 progressed through autumn and winter, he would disappear from her life for two or three days at a time without calling. Once, he was gone for two weeks and returned without apologies or explanations.

His friend, Stanley Haggart, was aware of at least two affairs he was having, one with the actor John Kerr, and another with Betsy Palmer. He'd appeared in teleplays with each of them.

"There were a few others along the way," Haggart recalled. "I vaguely remember a woman named Arlene Sachs. Jimmy told me some wild stories. All this was going on before he left for Hollywood to work with Elia Kazan. I don't think Barbara Glenn knew half of what Jimmy was up to. Perhaps I'm wrong."

His love affair with his old motorcycle ended when he saved up enough money to purchase a better one. Even though it was deep in winter, he told Glenn that he planned to ride his motorcycle back to Fairmount.

"Please, if you're going to die, why not stay in New York?" she asked him.

"No," he said. "I'm heading home to Indiana, all eight hundred miles, and on my new motorcycle. I've got to try it. It's great...don't worry."

"It's your life," she said, almost wanting to give up on him and stop worrying about his safety.

"Soon, he was presumably in Indiana," she said, "or else dead on the highway somewhere. I didn't hear from him for a couple of weeks. When he came back to Manhattan, he told me horrendous stories of snow and ice that would make Greenland look like a tropic zone."

"There were times I practically froze to death," he claimed, "but I drove all the way there and all the way back without one accident, except that time on an icy road when I crashed into a snowbank. But I emerged without a scratch, except I hurt my balls. But they're in working order once again."

At long last, Jane Deacy got him another role on Broadway, this time for an appearance as a blackmailing homosexual Arab boy, tangling with French actor Louis Jourdan and co-starring Geraldine Page, in the stage adaptation of André Gide's autobiographical novel, *The Immoralist.*

After weeks of traumatic rehearsals and endless conflicts with his fellow actors *[for more on this, refer to chapter 14 of this biography]*, tryouts were in Philadelphia. From there, he wrote to her from his lodgings in the St. James Hotel, illustrating his letter with whimsical illustrations and doodles.

> *"I hate the god damn brown makeup I'm forced to wear. The play is full of shit. Stereo-phonic staging and 3-D actors. I's so bad it will probably be a monstrous success since the theater-going public on Broadway is stupid, filled with bored housewives and insurance salesmen guaranteed to sleep through most of the play after a hard day's work."*

"I bought a new magenta-colored gown for the opening night of *The Immoralist,* and thought I looked dazzling," Glenn recalled. "I thought it was going to be a glorious night for Jimmy. His aunt, Ortense, and his uncle, Marcus Winslow, flew in from Indiana. I was not introduced to them, and I got the idea that Jimmy had told them I was going to be his bride."

"I met Jimmy backstage in his dressing room, and he invited me to Sardi's, where the cast would be headed after the show. But instead of dressing up, he put on a smelly T-shirt and a pair of ripped blue jeans."

Of course, once at Sardi's the doorman turned him away, and he had to go back to his apartment and put on a suit.

"When he did arrive, the tension was awful," she said. "He immediately insulted Louis Jourdan, and also the director, Daniel Mann. He told them he didn't want to be in their stupid play 'written by that French faggot, André Gide.' I couldn't take his bitching any more, and I left quickly. He followed me onto the street, and we had this big blow-up fight there on the sidewalk."

"Orson Welles was coming in the door with Janet Leigh, of all people. They stopped and witnessed our domestic violence. At one point, Jimmy slapped me, and I ran screaming down the street. We didn't speak for days, but once again, we made up. I knew, though, that our relationship was doomed."

***

When Jimmy went to Hollywood to film *East of Eden,* he wrote letters to

Glenn in New York, telling her how miserable he was. *[One of them is repli-cated, with its errors in spelling and grammar, immediately below.]*

> *"I don't know why people reject me. I don't want to write this letter. It would be better to remain silent. Wow! Am I fucked up.*
>
> *Got here on a Thursday went to the desert on Sat, week later to San Francisco. I DON'T KNOW WHERE I AM. Rented a car for two weeks. It cost me $138.00. I WANT TO DIE. I have told the girls here to kiss my ass and what sterile, spineless, stupid prostitutes they were. I HAVEN'T BEEN TO BED WITH NO BODY. And won't until after the picture and I am home safe in N.Y.C. (snuggly little town that it is) sounds unbelievable, but it's the truth I swear. So hold everything stop breathing. Stop the town all of N.Y.C., untill (should have trum-pets here) James Dean returns.*
>
> *I got no motorcycle I got no girl HONEY, shit writing in capitals doesn't seem to help ei-ther. Haven't found a place to live yet HONEY. Kazan sent me out here to get a tan. Haven't seen the sun yet (fog and smog). Wanted me healthy looking. I look like a prune. Don't run away from home at too early an age or you'll have to take vitamens the rest of your life. Write me please. I'm sad most of the time. Awful lonely too. (I hope you're dying) BECAUSE I AM.*
>
> *Love,*
> *Jim (Brando Clift) Dean*

While he was in Hollywood, she wrote him with news that she'd gotten a job posing for a swimsuit photo layout. He wrote back, "Boy, that's selling out cheap."

Years later, she remembered her feelings at the time: "He accused me of selling out cheap. A boy who had allegedly posed for nude pictures, perhaps even porno."

Before the filming of *East of Eden* began, director Elia Kazan summoned all the principal actors, including Raymond Massey and Julie Harris, to re-hearsals. Jimmy wrote to Glenn in New York with a description of how they were progressing. His reference to "Lennie" in his letter was about Jimmy's good friend, Leonard Rosenman, who had been commissioned to compose music for the film.

> *"Have been very dejected and extremely moody last two weeks. Have been telling every-body to fuck off and that's no good. I could never make them believe I was working on my part. Poor Julie Harris doesn't know what to do. Everyone turns into an idiot out here. I have only one friend, one guy that I can talk to and be understood. I hope Lennie comes out here. I need someone from New York. Cause I'm mean and I'm really kind and gentle. Things get mixed up all the time. I see a person I would like to be very close to (everybody), then I think it would just be the same as before and they don't give a shit for me. Then I say some-thing nasty or nothing at all and walk away. The poor person doesn't know what happened. He doesn't realize that I have decided I don't like him. What's wrong with people. Idiots. (I won't fail please.)"*

In May of 1954, from Hollywood, he wrote this to Glenn:

"Pleased to hear from you. That's putting it mildly. Gadge [Elia Kazan] *and Tenn* [Tennessee Williams] *are nice but I wouldn't trust the sons-a-bitches far's I could throw them. They can take advantage of you like nobody else.*

"HONEY!!! I'm still a Calif, virgin, remarkable no. I'm saving it—H-bomb Dean.

"A new addition has been added to the Dean family. I got a red '53 MG (milled head, etc. hot engine). My sex pours itself into fat curves, broadslides, and broodings, drags, etc. You have plenty of competition. My motorcycle, my MG, and my girl. I have been sleeping with my MG. We make it together, honey."

In yet another letter to Glenn, he wrote:

"I haven't written because I've fallen in love. It had to happen sooner or later. Enclosed is not a very good picture of him. That's Cisco the Kid, the new member of the family. He gives me confidence. He makes my hands strong. May use him in a movie." [Jimmy was referring to his latest acquisition, a thoroughbred palomino horse.]

It was during his filming of *East of Eden* that Glenn wrote Jimmy a "Dear John" letter, informing him that she'd met someone new, the love of her life, and that she had agreed to marry him.

Jimmy accepted the news good-naturedly Actually, it wasn't that painful to him, because he was dating Pier Angeli, the Italian actress.

After mailing her "Dear John" letter, Glenn's affair with her new love came to an abrupt end when she discovered that her husband-to-be was simultaneously engaged to another young actress. She broke up with him, but a few weeks later, fell madly in love once again—this time with the man she would eventually marry.

When he returned to New York, she confronted Jimmy with news about the changes in her life, telling him she could no longer be his girlfriend. "This time I mean it," she told him. "This man really loves me and doesn't have a cheating heart like some men I've known."

Jimmy realized that that reference included him.

To her surprise, he asked to meet her husband-to-be. She reluctantly agreed, fearing he would make a scene. However, their dinner went pleasantly enough, although the two rivals in love had little to say to each other.

Jimmy later told William Bast, "When he got up to go to the men's room—men don't call it powdering their noses, do they?—I followed him. There were three urinals. I stood beside him and looked down. His piss was white, not yellow. If she didn't already know it, I should have warned Barbara that she wouldn't be getting 'Long John.'"

After dinner, Jimmy insisted on seeing her alone for a final farewell and, to the surprise and dismay of her new lover, she returned with Jimmy, alone, to his apartment on West 68ᵗʰ Street.

There, he shocked her by pleading with her to marry him, not her intended *fiancé*.

She noticed a small suitcase on his bed. It was filled with cash. "This looks like a lot of money," she said.

"Now that you have money yourself, are you trying to pay me back? From the looks of things, I never lent you all this much."

"You can't leave me, Barbara, *please!*." He was pleading, beseeching her. "If you leave me, I'll kill myself. My death will be on your hands. Do you want that?"

"Of course I don't, and you're not going to kill yourself," she said. "You and I wouldn't last in a marriage for more than two weeks, and in your heart, you know that I'm getting married to the man you met tonight. And that's final. I'm leaving. Goodbye forever, Jimmy. Don't ever call or write to me again."

As she headed out the door to the stairwell, he ran after her, carrying the suitcase of money. Impulsively, he threw some of the cash after her, the bills cascading down upon her.

She did not look back. All she remembered was his calling out to her. But instead of "Barbara," it was "STELLA! STELLA! STELLA!" He had lapsed into a re-enactment of the famous scene where Brando screams with primal anguish for his wife in *A Streetcar Named Desire*.

***

After hearing about Jimmy's death in 1955, Glenn told a reporter: "He was a terribly destructive person. Our relationship was destructive. I knew he would destroy himself in the end, and that's why his death did not come as a surprise. It was as if my reaction to it happened so long ago."

Chapter Eight

JIMMY EMERGES AS A STAR IN THE EARLY DAYS OF
TELEVISION

Projected across America Through "Little Black Boxes,"
He Emotes Onscreen with Blanche DuBois, Scarlett
O'Hara's Mother, & Sweet Sixteen-er, Natalie Wood

HE MAKES LOVE TO THE ACTOR PLAYING JESSE JAMES,
THEN PLAYS A PUNK WHO THREATENS TO ASSASSINATE RONALD REAGAN

Splendor, Not In the Grass,
But on the Casting Couch of Playwright Bill Inge

JIMMY SIZES UP HIS RIVALS:
BEN ("JOCKO") GAZZARA AND JOHN ("*TEA & SYMPATHY*") KERR

James Dean's debut appearance on television was in a Pepsi Cola commercial. From there, he went on to a somewhat amazing career starring in teleplays during the early 1950s' Golden Age of television. The general public today know him for only three movies, *East of Eden, Rebel Without a Cause,* and *Giant*. But his diehard fans are aware of his many star turns on television, sometimes as part of live tele-dramas.

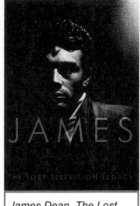

James Dean, The Lost Television Legacy

Often, he appeared in a single episode of a prolonged series whose names—once household words—included *Kraft Television Theater, Robert Montgomery Presents, Danger,* and *General Electric Theater*. Many of these episodes have disappeared forever; others believed to have been lost have been recovered during the 21st Century, based to some degree on the legend of James Dean as it gains new aficionados.

On the 60th anniversary of his death in 1955, many of Dean's teleplays were digitalized and rediscovered, including several premieres which were broadcast on Turner Movie Classics. Fans can also buy a boxed set: *James Dean: The Lost Television Legacy,* featuring nineteen full episodes, each meticulously remastered.

Most of these teleplays were filmed in his "black box" banner year of 1953, just before he migrated to Hollywood for a starring role in *East of Eden.* Two of his best-known television roles include his appearance in the *You Are There* series in which, as "the coward," Bob Ford, he shoots Jesse James. Later, in an episode of *General Electric Theater*, Jimmy points a revolver at the head of Ronald Reagan, cast as a doctor, threatening to shoot him if he doesn't remove a bullet from his (wounded) pal.

Many of his co-stars in these teleplays have faded into the dusty archives of early television, but Jimmy also appeared with some names that endure, including Dorothy Gish, the legendary star of the silent screen. Other first-rate actors included John Carradine, Cloris Leachman, Rod Steiger, Walter Hampden, Jessica Tandy, Hume Cronyn, James Kerr, Ed Begley, Betsy Palmer, Natalie Wood, Mary Astor, and Paul Lukas. In real life, he would seduce three of these co-stars, one male and two females.

During the course of his brief glory days in television, he would appear in a wide range of roles. Characters he'd portray on the "small screen" included a wrongly accused victim being sent to the electric chair; an ex-convict struggling to start a new life; the restless son of a farming couple; a lovestruck stable boy with dreams of glory; a "hepcat killer, and a young French aristocrat accused of stealing his stepfather's money.

The chapter that follows describes many of the television roles he portrayed, along with his interactions (successful, unsuccessful, and sometimes abysmal) with directors, producers, other actors, and his romantic peers.

The Hound of Heaven

AT THE GATES OF HELL

Early in 1953, Jimmy was cast in *The Hound of Heaven,* an episode on *The Kate Smith Hour* that was aired on NBC on January 15.

During rehearsals, he met the star of the show, John Carradine, who was known mostly for his Western and horror films, despite his status as a famous Shakespearean actor and a former member of the stock companies of both Cecil B. DeMille and John Ford. He told Jimmy that he'd tested for the title roles in both *Dracula* and *Frankenstein,* "but Bela Lugosi and Boris Karloff beat my ass."

Jimmy had seen only one of his films, *The Grapes of Wrath* (1940) starring Henry Fonda, in which Carradine had played the doomed preacher, Casey. His deep, resonant voice had earned him the nickname "The Voice." During the course of his career, Carradine claimed that he had appeared in some 450 movies, the earliest ones uncredited. During rehearsals of *The Hound of Heaven*, Carradine walked around the set reciting Shakespeare soliloquies.

He confided in Jimmy that his dream had involved being the partriarch of an extended Carradine family. He'd married Ardanelle Cosner, who gave him two sons (Bruce and David), but she'd thwarted his plan for having more children by self-inflicting "coat hanger abortions" without his knowledge.

James Dean as a goofy hillbilly angel in *The Hound of Heaven.*

255

He asked Jimmy if he'd like to settle down and have "a brood of little Jimmy Deans."

"Like hell I would," Jimmy responded, sarcastically. "Anything but that. I want to be the one and only James Dean."

The script for *The Hound of Heaven* had been written by Earl Hammer, Jr., who later became known for the hit TV series, *The Waltons,* and for *Falcon Crest.* He created the famous line, "Good night, John Boy."

In Hammer's plot for *The Hound of Heaven,* Carradine was cast as Hyder Simpson, a roughneck Appalachian man whose faithful companion is a dog named Rip. He and his hound die and go to what Hyder thinks is the gate to Heaven. The gatekeeper there informs him that he can enter, but no dogs are allowed.

Suddenly, "Angel" (Jimmy) appears, warning him that he is not at the pearly gates of Heaven, but at the gates to Hell, where fire and brimstone await him. Whereas the man was willing to walk into a horrible fate, Rip was too smart for that and knew, instinctively, that they were facing not salvation, but doom.

The Case of the Watchful Dog

MOONSHINE & SOUPED-UP HOTRODS

Jimmy's next teleplay was with minor actors (they included Graham Denton and Dorothy Elder) in *The Case of the Watchful Dog,* broadcast on NBC on January 29. Director Daniel Petrie cast Jimmy in the role of a gun-toting juvenile delinquent, the son of a moonshiner, who drives a souped-up hotrod that hauls illegal booze to an undercover distribution center.

The drama was part of a TV series, *Treasury Men in Action,* whose episodes focused on real crime dramas inspired by the case files of the U.S. Customs and Treasury Departments. Federal agents in the series battle tax evaders, moonshiners, gun-runners, smugglers, and counterfeiters.

Jimmy starred as Randy Meeker, who breaks with his father, Clay, after he shoots Randy's beloved hound because his barking might draw revenue agents to his illicit still. As it happens, the revenue agents are able to trace the location of the still through the license plate on Jimmy's hotrod. After it aired, the show was soon forgotten.

Although Jimmy would become known as "the terror of directors," he worked smoothly with Petrie, who would later make such signature films as

A Raisin in the Sun (1961). He would also direct Laurence Olivier in *The Betsy* (1978) and would go on to win many Emmy and Directors Guild awards.

Jimmy Kills the Character Known as Jesse James on Screen

BUT OFF SCREEN, MAKES LOVE TO THE ACTOR WHO PORTRAYED HIM

Very different scenarios played out—both on the TV screen and behind the camera—in Jimmy's next teleplay. At CBS, he was cast in *The Killing of Jesse James* as part of the *You Are There* series, an anthology of major historical events hosted by Walter Cronkite. Although the series had originated on radio, it made a smooth transition to television. The show that immediately preceded Jimmy's debut in the series had been a re-enactment of the Hindenburg disaster in New Jersey—a fiery inferno of a hydrogen-filled blimp that was played out before the world.

Its director was Sidney Lumet, a native of Philadelphia, who would segue from helming TV programmers to being nominated for Best Director by the Academy Awards for such feature films as *Twelve Angry Men* (1957); *Dog Day Afternoon* (1975); and *Network* (1976).

In time, Lumet would direct Ralph Richardson, Richard Burton, Katharine Hepburn, James Mason, Henry Fonda, Dustin Hoffman, Anne Bancroft, and Albert Finney, among many others. He won praise from all of these stars, including from Jimmy himself, who called him, "an actor's dream."

"If I had any problem with him," Jimmy said, "it was his praise of the acting of Marlon Brando. Although he was straight, he seemed to have the hots for Stanley Kowalski."

[In 1959, Lumet would direct Brando with Anna Magnani in Tennessee Williams' The Fugitive Kind.*]*

"Lumet was electric, bubbling over with energy, a hard-boiled straight shooter," Jimmy said. "He taught me a lot."

At the time Jimmy met Lumet, he was married to the actress Rita Gam, a close friend of Grace Kelly's. He would later marry the heiress Gloria Vanderbilt and, after that, Gail Jones, the daughter of singer Lena Horne.

He told Jimmy that he had selected Cronkite as the anchor man "because the premise of many of our shows is so silly, and so outrageous, that we need somebody who is very believable, very homespun, very American."

Into the role of Jesse James, Lumet cast the handsome and rising young actor, John Kerr, with Jimmy playing his assassin, Bob Ford. Until Kerr arrived on the set, Jimmy was eager to learn as much as he could from Lumet, perhaps hoping he would cast him in future productions, either on TV or on the big screen.

In the teleplay by Leslie Slate, Jimmy and Kerr each appear near the end. The beginning of the script focuses on events leading up to the fatal shooting of Jesse James. The notorious outlaw enters a saloon for a drink, during which time, he stands on a chair to straighten a picture. Ford, as played by Jimmy, shoots him in the back, opting to collect a reward of $10,000, although the governor later gives him only $500.

[Brad Pitt and Casey Affleck would deliver a far more detailed version of the shooting in a 2007 movie, The Assassination of Jessie James by the Coward Robert Ford.*]*

It was a memorable day for Jimmy when Kerr walked into his life. A New Yorker born to a British father, he was a graduate of Harvard and had worked in summer stock in New England. While taking a class in Serbo-Croatian language and literature at Harvard, he had met a fellow student, Priscilla Smith, and had married her in 1952. The union would last for twenty years and produce three children before they divorced.

Jimmy was fascinated by Kerr. "I figured that by then, the honeymoon was over and John Boy might want some other kind of action," Jimmy confided to Lumet. The director had a front-row seat to watch Jimmy's seduction of Kerr, a tale he'd later relate to other actors such as Marlon Brando, Rod Steiger, Anthony Perkins, and Anne Bancroft.

"I think Jimmy realized that Kerr was a closeted bisexual before the actor admitted it to himself," Lumet later said. "From the day they met, Jimmy had his radar out. He moved in on Kerr. When he talked to him—and he chatted a lot—he stood only inches from him, their lips almost touching. It was as if Jimmy were breathing down Kerr's neck. When he wanted to, Jimmy's voice sounded like soft music to the ear."

"How far was Kerr willing to go when confronted with this charming young

John Kerr...Jimmy opens the door to his closet. *Lower photo:* Kerr with France Nuyen in *South Pacific* (1958).

conquistador?" Lumet was asked.

"All the way, I was certain. Once, Kerr had limbered up with some exercises. He sat down in a chair and was sweating. Jimmy came over with a tissue to mop his brow. When Kerr looked up at Jimmy, his throat seemed to tighten with tangled emotions. Jimmy looked into his watery eyes with a face of angelic purity and innocence that was actually a mask of the devil in disguise out to snare this tender boy."

Jimmy could have been mouthing Deborah Kerr's famous line when she ap-

John Kerr (playing a sexually ambivalent student) with Deborah Kerr (the empathetic wife of the director of his prep school) in *Tea and Sympathy* (1956).

peared in the film version of *Tea and Sympathy,* in which she starred with Kerr *[to whom she was not related, despite the similarity of their family names].* "Years from now, when you talk of this, please be kind."

"I think the prelude to the actual seduction began with a ham sandwich on rye," Lumet said. "Both boys were having lunch on the set. At one point, Jimmy reached over and just took Kerr's sandwich from him, had a big bite of it, then handed it back. It was a very symbolic gesture, as Jimmy obviously wanted to take a bite out of Kerr. After work, the two wandered off together, and I was certain about what those two boys would be doing within an hour or so."

"But by the next morning, a new scenario played out before my eyes," Lumet said. "Jimmy was no longer catering to Kerr. Instead, Kerr was catering to Jimmy, who seemed in complete control of the relationship. He even brought Jimmy a cup of coffee at around ten o'clock and then later, went out and got him a package of cigarettes when he ran out. He also brought Jimmy his lunch that day. Something inside Kerr had been liberated, perhaps his darkest secret, which he had concealed since he was a boy."

"Jimmy had this amazing power to bind another human being, male or female, to him," Lumet said. "Kerr became his willing victim. Sexual drive, creative drive. Perhaps it's a wild thing to speculate, but I felt than in time, Jimmy's liberation of Kerr made him a better actor, especially in *Tea and Sympathy.* Kerr fell in love with Jimmy, but I don't think Jimmy ever loved anyone but himself."

"I remembered the last afternoon, when I saw them walking off together," Lumet said. "Both of them looked so handsome, so full of life, so in love. They were perfectly matched. But I knew storm clouds were on the way. After all, Kerr was married. He was also in love with a man. How was he going to solve that dilemma? It would take Hamlet himself to ponder it."

"I learned that both of them would be co-starring in another teleplay at the end of the summer," Lumet said. "I was certain their romance would last the summer. Of course, Frank Sinatra sang about how romances go with the summer winds."

No Room

SAFECRACKER JIMMY IS SAVED FROM A LIFE OF CRIME

Jimmy's next teleplay was not memorable at all. Weeks after finishing it, he had almost forgotten it. CBS cast him in *No Room,* an episode within its popular *Danger* series that focused on tales of suspense, murder mysteries, and psychological dramas.

The script had been written by Mary Stern, who created a role for Jimmy of a would-be safecracker, who is saved from committing a burglary that might have landed him in prison. He wasn't impressed with his part, but the producers of *Danger* were, and as the series progressed, they'd hire him to perform in three more episodes.

If he had a regret at all, it involved the fact that this particular episode would not be broadcast in Fairmount, Indiana, thereby ensuring that his relatives, Ortense and Marcus Winslow, would not get to see it.

During the shoot, he related to the female co-star, Irene Vernon, since she was a fellow Hoosier born in Mishawaka, Indiana. Her movie career in Hollywood had gone nowhere, and she was trying to establish herself as a television actress. About a decade later, her most memorable role became that of Louise Tate on the hit TV series, *Bewitched* (1964-1972).

Born and reared in Brooklyn, one of Jimmy's colleagues, Martin Kingsley, had worked in radio, TV, and on the stage. A Hungarian, he once brought a container of goulash to Jimmy for his lunch "so you can taste the real thing. It was from Mama Gabor's own kitchen." He was referring to Jolie Gabor, the mother of three famous and glamorous daughters, Zsa Zsa, Eva, and Magda.

"There was a saying at the time that Brando changed the way actors acted," Kingsley later said. "That may be so, but James Dean changed the way actors lived. No one like him had come before, and no one like him has emerged since."

The Case of the Sawed-Off Shotgun

DEFYING JOSEPH MCCARTHY'S COMMUNIST BLACKLIST

In April of 1953, Jimmy returned to NBC to film another episode for the hit series, *Treasury Men in Action,* based on a true story from the files of the U.S. Customs and Treasury Departments. Ironically, he'd be working with a blacklisted director, Donald Pressman, and he'd make a friend, Ben Gazzara, who would later emerge as a rival for procurement of the same roles.

Jimmy's rival: young Ben Gazzara

Jimmy was cast in the teleplay as a hoodlum, Arbie Feris, a name he hated. "It sounds like a fag," he told its writer, Albert Aley. Arbie, recently released from reform school, is plotting a career as a gangster.

Gazzara was cast as "the good boy" trying to persuade Jimmy to be a "clean-cutter," and urging him to attend meetings of the local Boys' Club to learn about decent living and honor.

A native of Tiblisi, Georgia, then part of the Soviet Union, Pressman had arrived in the United States with his family when he was nine years old. His parents were musicians formerly associated with the Russian Grand Opera Company.

Pressman's left-wing politics fascinated Jimmy. Pressman told him that he'd joined the communist Party in the 1930s, based on its alleged support of integration, civil rights, and socialized medicine. During World War II, he served as a solider in the U.S. Army, during which time he'd won two Purple Hearts.

After the war, he'd studied acting in Manhattan with Sanford Meisner, and later became an acting coach himself, teaching such students as Gregory Peck, Tony Randall, and Eli Wallach.

Pressman became one of the first major directors associated with the emerging medium of television. At Studio One in Hollywood, he'd directed Grace Kelly in Molnar's *The Swan* for television. She would later appear in the same role on the big screen, opposite Louis Jourdan, Jimmy's upcoming co-star in the Broadway play, *The Immoralist.*

Right after helming Gazzara and Jimmy, based on his having been black-listed, Pressman would be banned from television. He would return later to direct such "unknowns" as Al Pacino.

Based on the script of *Sawed-Off Shotgun,* Jimmy, cast as Arbie, steals a gun from a bootlegger, Blackie Bowman (Joseph Downing). In a failed robbery attempt at a filling station, he leaves the gun behind, giving Federal agents the clue they needed to track him down. Blackie plans to kill Jimmy, but he's arrested and sent to prison. Arbie gets off with probation.

Jimmy enjoyed working with Downing, a New Yorker who had appeared in major Hollywood gangster movies that included *Angels with Dirty Faces* (1938), a James Cagney film, and *Johnny Eager* (1941), starring Robert Taylor and Lana Turner.

"I never got around to fucking Lana," Jimmy claimed, "but I met her in Hollywood."

"I didn't screw her either," Downing said. "But Taylor sure did, although I heard he preferred men."

At the time Jimmy started hanging out with Gazzara, he was working as an elevator operator in *The New York Times* building.

Jimmy was intrigued with Gazzara, rightly assuming he might emerge as future competition for acting roles. The Italian American had grown up in the Kips Bay neighborhood of Manhattan. "I was a street kid," he told Jimmy. "My love of acting saved me from a life of crime."

Jimmy never really became Gazzara's friend, but he tricked him into thinking he was. He would later tell Shelley Winters, "What was really going on in our relationship—strictly non-sexual—was my sizing up tomorrow's competition. The word is out that Gazzara is 'the next Marlon Brando.'"

"To hell with that," Winters said. "This year alone, I've met at least a dozen actors who have been called 'the next Marlon Brando.' I'm tired of hearing that. I know Marlon. He's fucked me. You had better develop your own style, your own technique. There's only one Stanley Kowalski. When Tennessee wrote *A Streetcar Named Desire,* he pictured Stanley as having a big dick. Marlon doesn't. But on stage, he acted like he had a big dick, and for an actor, it's illusion that counts."

End as a Man

JIMMY VS. BEN GAZZARA (AKA "JOCKO")

Within a month of working in a teleplay with Ben Gazzara, Jimmy would end up on the stage with him in May at an Actors Studio production that was staged at the Theater de Lys on Christopher Street in Greenwich Village.

End as a Man, with its homosexual undertones, was a play based on Calder Willingham's shocking novel about the brutality of life in a Southern military academy. The lead role of "Jocko de Paris" would be brilliantly portrayed by Gazarra. Its director was Jack Garfein, who would marry Carroll Baker, later to co-star with Jimmy in *Giant.*

In its search for "angels" (financial backers), three in-house performances were staged during May and June of 1953.

In addition to Gazzara, three actors in the play would go on to become famous: Pat Hingle, Anthony Franciosa, and Albert Salmi.

Ben Gazzara playing a sadistic military cadet (Jocko) in a homoerotic scene from Calder Willingham's *End as a Man (aka The Strange One)*

Jimmy had wanted to play Jocko, but Garfein thought that Gazzara would be better-suited for the role. In the play, Jimmy's part "practically amounted to shit" *[his words].* He appeared in the third act as a cadet officer at a court trial, wearing a dress military uniform with gold braid and a red sash. "I was just window dressing," he said. "Gazzara ate up the scenery with his sadistic Jocko. I was just this prissy little cadet wearing a butt plug."

Born in what used to be Czechoslovakia in 1930, Garfein was a survivor of Auschwitz, the Nazi concentration camp, a horrifying venue liberated by the Allied armies in 1945.

"I loved Jimmy," Garfein later recalled, "and we were close for a while. But he didn't always have the best manners. One night in Hollywood, I was dining with him when Hedda Hopper walked in. He just got up and left our table and spent about an hour talking to this bitchy columnist, even though I knew he despised her. I just sat alone at our table nursing a drink and waiting for the wandering boy to return."

Willingham, originally linked to his birthplace in Atlanta, watched with trepidation as his play evolved upon the stage. He had spoken to Jimmy, expressing his insights and various interpretations of its lines, and describing his drama as an indictment of the macho culture of a military academy, which he deplored. With its hints of homosexuality, his writing would lead to a conflict with the New York Society for the Suppression of Vice, which unsuccessfully brought obscenity charges against the publisher, Vanguard Press, which had printed *End As a Man.*

After seeing the Actors Studio production of his play, Willingham hosted a party for the players at his apartment on West 28th Street. "Dean had an almost nothing role to play," the novelist recalled, "but at my party he—not

Gazzara—was the star. Dean dominated the gathering. He told jokes. He did this hilarious impression of Marlon Brando. He even performed a dance he'd learned from Eartha Kitt. He leaped across the living room like Anna Pavlova. He slobbered. He farted. He goosed the girls and pinched Tony Franciosa's butt and asked him if he'd like to get fucked. He bit Pat Hingle's tit and grabbed Salmi's crotch. After releasing Salmi's balls, he announced, 'Now I know why Paul Newman likes this guy so much.'"

"He not only was the life of the party, but at the end of the evening, he made off with a potential angel, Claire Heller," Willingham said. "She was the daughter of a rich San Francisco banker. Or is banker and rich redundant?"

The cast saw Heller and Jimmy wander off into the night together, and every actor hoped she'd back the show, or else get her father to put up the money.

Since Jimmy's regular girlfriend at the time, Barbara Glenn, was away in the Catskills, he started seeing Heller on a regular basis. "They became an item that summer," according to Terry Parks, a waiter at Jerry's tavern. "Jimmy was either with John Kerr or with Heller when he came in."

When *End as a Man* went to Broadway, Pat Hingle was one of the stars at the Vanderbilt Theater. Later, on Broadway, he would star in the role of Gooper in the original Broadway production of Tennessee Williams' *Cat on a Hot Tin Roof* (1955), which would cast Gazzara as Brick, the repressed homosexual married in the play to Barbara Bel Geddes, "Maggie the Cat."

Hingle said, "If Jimmy had been available, you know he would have convinced Tennessee to give him the role that went to Gazzara and later to Paul Newman in the movie with Elizabeth Taylor. She probably would have lobbied for Jimmy, too."

Carroll Baker remembered seeing Heller and Jimmy together on occasion during that summer, although they did not go out much. "From what I was told, they were happy to spend quiet evenings listening to classical music, often baroque. Claire told me that Jimmy liked the attention he got from girls, but pretended that it annoyed him. At parties, he preferred to sit in the corner with his bongo drums instead of mingling."

"Most of their affair seemed to have been conducted within her apartment at 45 Tudor City Place. He confided in her, and she was careful not to betray his trust. His attitude toward her was somewhat cavalier and at times almost rude. Claire, on the other hand, was refined, gentle, and understanding. More than anyone else, she understood the troubled rebel within him."

When they were seeing each other, as struggling actors, Gazzara had praise for Jimmy. "He was short but with presence." He later wrote, "He had movie star good looks, blonde hair, and blue eyes. What a combination! You didn't have to be an expert cameraman to know that Jimmy would photograph well."

When *End as a Man* finally made it to Broadway, Jimmy was not available to appear in his minor role. He had just landed a key role in William Inge's teleplay, *Glory in the Flower,* and had to bow out.

In February of 1954, when the stars of the Broadway production of *End as a Man* went on strike for more money, Jimmy met secretly with Garfein. Perceiving that Garfein and his team might opt to break the strike by firing the existing cast and hiring an all-new one, he offered to take over Gazzara's role of Jocko. Jimmy was unhappy with his role of the Arab boy in *The Immoralist* and wanted to move on. The strike, however, was quickly settled, so his offer was never accepted.

Still imagining Jimmy as a friend, Gazzara soon learned of Jimmy's "behind-my-back betrayal."

His alleged betrayal of Gazzara escalated. Later, after Hollywood's major-league producer Sam Spiegel expressed interest in adapting the Broadway version of *End As a Man* into a film, Jimmy phoned him, saying, "I'd be far better in the role of Jocko than Gazzara."

Gazzara later said, "Garfein, also the film's director, stood behind me even though Jimmy at the time was a hot commodity. By the time *End as a Man* was filmed—retitled *The Strange One* (1957)—Jimmy was no longer around."

Gazzara later lobbied for the role of Rocky Graziano in *Somebody Up There Likes Me* (1956), which had originally been intended for Jimmy. But he lost the role to Paul Newman. "Fuck Newman!" Gazzara responded in anger. "Too bad he wasn't in that Porsche with Dean."

Gazzara's dislike of Newman increased after he was awarded the film role of Brick in the film version of *Cat on a Hot Tin Roof* (1958), a role that Gazzara had developed and performed so long and so successfully on Broadway.

"Did you know that Newman and Dean were faggots?" Gazzara sometimes asked anyone willing to listen. He harbored a grudge against each of them throughout the rest of his life.

Despite his negative views, Lee Strasberg perhaps maintained a sympathetic place in his heart for Jimmy. In 1955, in the immediate aftermath of Jimmy's death, Gazzara encountered Strasberg at the Actors Studio, finding him crying.

Later, Gazzara reflected on his own failed friendship with Jimmy. "It was sad that his ambition and pride got in the way of our friendship. When I heard the news of his death, I could think only of the days we'd spent struggling to get any kind of job. James Dean had his fantastic moment in the sun."

The Evil Within

JIMMY AND THE MAD SCIENTIST

Only twice did Jimmy perform in teleplays for ABC. The first came when director Don Medford cast him in the hit TV series, *Tales of Tomorrow*, an anthology of science fiction dramas and tales of the supernatural.

Written by Manya Starr, *The Evil Within* starred Rod Steiger and Margaret Phillips. Ironically, Steiger had made his film debut in *Teresa* (1951), co-starring Pier Angeli, who would later become "the love of my life" *[Jimmy's words]*.

He had become friends with Steiger when—hoping for the lead role of Curly in *Oklahoma!*—he had auditioned with him. Whereas Steiger wound up in the cast, Jimmy did not.

Jimmy as an absent-minded, pencil-chewing lab assistant in *The Evil Within.*

When he was cast with Jimmy in the teleplay *The Evil Within,* Steiger was on the dawn of stardom. It came the following year (1954), when he was nominated for an Oscar as Best Supporting Actor for his performance in *On the Waterfront. [That same film would bring an Academy Award for Best Actor that year to Marlon Brando.]*

In *The Evil Within,* Steiger played an eccentric research scientist, who produces a serum that releases the evil that innately lies within the heart of a person. When the refrigerator in his laboratory breaks down, he brings his serum home and puts It in his own refrigerator, alongside his foodstuff.

His wife (Phillips) accidentally spills the serum onto her apple pie, and the evil side of her personality emerges. Inevitably, ferocious conflicts soon emerge with her husband, as played by Steiger.

Portraying Ralph, a laboratory assistant, Jimmy appears on screen for the first time wearing his glasses. He doesn't have much to do in the role, except push back his spectacles or suck on his pencil.

At the wrap, Jimmy told Medford, "That Steiger can play any role, except maybe that of a female burlesque dancer."

He didn't live long enough to see how right his appraisal was. Versatile and volatile, Steiger was the centerpiece of a career that eventually encompassed portrayals of gangsters, police chiefs, a disturbed priest, a perhaps psychotic Army sergeant, a Mexican *bandito,* an embittered Jewish Holocaust

survivor working as a pawnbroker, a ruthless Russian politician; and impersonations of Al Capone, Mussolini, and Napoléon.

Something for an Empty Briefcase
"A Sexually Ambiguous Jimmy"

Director Don Medford once again cast Jimmy as the lead in a teleplay, this one for a *Campbell Soundstage Production. Something for an Empty Briefcase* was aired on July 17, 1953.

Jimmy signed to play the young and foolish Joe Adams, a 22-year-old who has been released from prison on a charge of petty larceny. He asked Medford, "in a nutshell, what is this play about?"

"A dancer tries to save a two-bit crook from a life of crime," the director said. "She falls for a young punk, who is full of rage and passion."

Campbell's Soundstage Productions Presents...

"That's me, all right," Jimmy said, "but I don't like the title. Why not *Rage and Passion?*"

"Forget it!" Medford said.

He called all his actors to a rehearsal. They included Don Hanmer, Robert Middleton, and a Viennese, Susan Douglas, whose original name was "Zuzka." Together, they read through the script by S. Lee Pegostin.

"Even on the first read-through, Dean was brilliant," Medford said. "I kept him behind after letting everyone else go. I told him, 'I want you to think what stimulated such a great performance from you so you'll be able to do it again when it really counts.'

James Dean, playing an ex-con, with Susan Douglas, who falls in love with him after his failed attempt to mug her, in *Something for an Empty Briefcase*.

For him, every moment was for the first time. He didn't retain anything from one rehearsal to the next. I tried, but failed to improve his retention."

Interpreting the role of the ex-con, Jimmy carries an empty briefcase, which seems to him to be a symbol of the white collar job he'd like to find. He desperately needs money, but has only $1.37 to his name.

An old pal, Mickey (Hanmer) wants him to pull the proverbial "one last job" for the mob boss, Mr. Sloane (Middleton).

Joe (Jimmy) decides to rob Noli (Douglas), who has arrived in New York to study dancing, but after their first encounter, they develop a relationship "all gooey and romantic." At times, Jimmy speaks in his normal voice, but on occasion, he reverts to a Brando-esque mumble.

One reviewer noted that Jimmy portrayed his character as "sexually ambiguous in a black pullover and tight-fitting trousers, looking as if he would have a better chance of becoming a chorus boy."

Ohio-born Middleton, known for his booming voice, large size, and beetle-brow, was virtually type cast as the mob boss. Middleton told Jimmy, "If a director wants a mountain bully, a corrupt mob boss, or the leader of a lynch mob, he sends for cigar-chomping me."

After his appearance with Jimmy, Middleton would star opposite Humphrey Bogart in *The Desperate Hours* (1955), one of Bogie's last films. He would also co-star with Gary Cooper in *Friendly Persuasion* (1956), and with Elvis Presley in *Love Me Tender* (also 1956).

Variety found the plot "something that belonged to the Dead End Kids' school of literature. James Dean's mugger and repetitive hand gesturing were on the ludicrous side, if their intent was to show the sensitivity and groping of the suddenly awakened thief."

Jimmy was devastated by the negative appraisal of his acting techniques.

Sentence of Death

Betsy Palmer's "Asexual Lover"

As the summer of 1953 moved inexorably toward autumn, Jimmy was given a key role in *Sentence of Death,* an episode on CBS's *Westinghouse Studio One* summer theater series, to be aired on August 17. The director, Matt Harlib, cast Betsy Palmer and Gene Lyons as the other leads. Jimmy had met Lyons during that actor's torrid affair with Grace Kelly.

Lyons was in mourning over the loss of Grace. He told Jimmy that he'd fallen in love with her when they had co-starred together in a teleplay, *The Rich Boy,* based on a short story by F. Scott Fitzgerald.

"My real life mirrored what the narrator of the teleplay said," he told Jimmy. "'From the beginning, they were in love with each other,' the narrator had said in its opening scene. "Just like Grace and me."

"In the play, our love turns sour, just as it did with Grace and me," Lyons said. "As the rich boy, I had a drinking problem. Talk about type casting. At the end of the play, the boy and girl go their separate ways, as Grace and I did. Fiction repeats itself in real life."

At least during the teleplay, Lyons managed to control his drinking to get through the shoot. In Hollywood, Grace was beginning the most promiscuous period of her life, often in relations with big name movie stars.

"I didn't think Gene would ever recover from the loss of his blonde goddess," Jimmy said.

"I met her father," Lyons told Jimmy. "He's rich and thought I was shanty Irish. It's true that I was born

The cinematic pairing of these two Hoosiers, James Dean and Betsy Palmer, in the 1953 television drama *Sentence of Death*, was noted in newspapers and entertainment columnists throughout Indiana.

into poverty in Pittsburgh. Somewhere along the way, my goal and Grace's goal changed. When we first met, both of us wanted to make it on the stage. But now, she's gone Hollywood. Her aim is to become a movie star, bigger than Elizabeth Taylor. Not only did the father not like me, but neither did Grace's mother, warning her never to marry an actor."

Actress Lee Grant had been Lyons' former lover. She voiced her opinion of what had gone wrong between Grace and Lyons: "He loves Old Bushmills. He was a really great, attractive Irishman, very complex and poetic. He loved saloons and his foot on the bar. He was wonderful company, and had an enormous talent. But it was the Irish whiskey that ruined his affair. He had a very quick slide down after Grace left him for the green, green pastures of Hollywood."

Jimmy told his co-star, Betsy Palmer, "I would like to have appeared in that teleplay with Grace. It could have been called *Fire and Ice.* By the end, I as Fire would have melted Ice."

"Stop it" Palmer said. "You're making me jealous. As a blonde, I can't compete with Grace Kelly, much less with Marilyn Monroe. And I want you for myself."

"If you mean that, you're on," he said. As they rehearsed *A Sentence of Death,* Jimmy began to date Palmer. His regular girlfriend, Barbara Glenn, was out of town.

Matt Harlib was a New Yorker, who had originally joined CBS as the first director of Arthur Godfrey's live radio show before switching to helming teleplays. He'd been told that Jimmy was a difficult actor to direct. "Bring him on," Harlib told the teleplay's producer, John Haggott.

Adrian Spies had written a script about a young man, Joe Palica, wrongly accused of murder, and then tried and sentenced to death. Harlib had nothing but praise for Jimmy's performance as the doomed young man headed for the electric chair. "Dean could combine both grief and fear on his face. He would utter a sob, take a quick intake of air to express his desperation, and stifle back tears. His fate was reflected in his eyes."

Palmer was cast as Ellen Morrison, the mink-clad "Dizzy Darling of the Tabloids," and noted for her promiscuity. As an outrageous flirt, she stumbles into a mom-and-pop drugstore to make a phone call and order a turkey sandwich. There, she witnesses the owner of the store (Fred Scollay) being shot. Mrs. Sawyer (Virginia Vincent) also witnesses the slaying of her husband, and Morrison gets a good look at the killer.

In a police lineup, the widow singles out Jimmy as the killer, but Palmer's character does not agree, claiming that the murderer was tall and dark.

Later, after Jimmy is sentenced to death, Palmer is sitting in a bar when she spots the real killer. Lyons was cast as the sympathetic policeman, Paul Cochran, who believes Palmer and works to free Jimmy from the electric chair. Eventually, the killer is apprehended. He turns out to be the lover of the widow, who wanted her husband killed. In the aftermath, the innocent man is set free.

During and after the teleplay's filming, Jimmy began spending his nights in Palmer's apartment, where he got to know her. A fellow Hoosier, she was five years older, the daughter of a chemist who had emigrated from Czechoslovakia. She had gotten her first acting job in New York in 1951 and had become a lifetime member of Actors Studio.

By 1958, she'd become a household name when she replaced Faye Emerson as a panelist on the quiz show, *I've Got a Secret,* remaining as a player with the show until its finale in 1967.

"In my little kitchen, I cooked budget meals for James," she said. "I used his real name, as I didn't like nicknames. We didn't have much money, so we had a lot of meatless pasta that summer. Our dating consisted mostly of strolling the streets and occasionally taking in a movie. We had sex but often, we didn't. On most nights, we sat and talked or else listened to music, perhaps both. I began to think James was asexual."

"Walking down the street with him was an adventure in itself," she said. "Suddenly, he might defy death by jumping in front of a car, causing the driver to panic and slam on the brakes."

"He told me he had once been a bullfighter in Mexico and that he was used to defying death," she said. "I was horrified at such reckless behavior. Even if he weren't killed, he might have been crippled for life."

"To me, James was the little boy lost," she said. "The lamb who strayed from the flock. He didn't really know where he was going, but wanted to get there fast. He was like a comet shooting across the sky. I wanted to tell him to slow down, because at the pace he was going, he would drop before he reached the finish line."

Death Is My Neighbor

The Psycho Janitor and the Beautiful Cover Girl

For an August 25 telecast, Jimmy once again returned to *The Hangar* TV series on CBS, this time to star in a script by Frank Gregory, *Death is My Neighbor.* Director John Preyser reunited with his girlfriend, Betsy Palmer.

The star of the drama was one of America's most distinguished actors, Walter Hampden. Born in Brooklyn in 1879, he was especially well-noted for his portrayals of famous Shakespearean characters such as Richard III, Shylock, or Macbeth. He was even more famously associated with his starring role as Cyrano de Bergerac.

Jimmy paired once again, this time as a psychotic janitor, with his friend, Betsy Palmer, a fashion model, in the CBS telecast of *Death is My Neighbor.*

Jimmy had seen him in only one movie, *The Hunchback of Notre Dame* (1939), in which he'd been cast as the good Archbishop of Paris, with hideously grotesque Charles Laughton as the deformed Quasimodo.

When Jimmy met Hampden, he was preparing to fly to Hollywood for the filming of *Sabrina* (1954), with Humphrey Bogart, William Holden, and Audrey Hepburn.

Had Jimmy gone to Hollywood to star in *The Silver Chalice* (1954), he would have worked with Hampden in his role as Joseph of Arimathea. When he turned down that role in the film, it went to Paul Newman.

Producer Franklin Heller recalled how, at the first read-through, Jimmy had thrown the script on the floor, denouncing it as "a piece of shit."

"I threatened to fire him," Heller said, "and would have had not Hampden intervened and pleaded with me to keep the little punk on."

"I've seen this young man on television before, and he's very talented," Hampden had said. "As a matter of fact, I think he's going to be a big star. Let him play the part, I beg you. I'll work with him."

Heller complied with Hampden's request.

"I'd been told that Jimmy treated his directors like real assholes," Peyser said. "But I hadn't met an actor I couldn't handle, and that includes Rod Steiger. I took Jimmy on. He challenged me time and time again, but I showed him I was boss. The result was terrific."

Peyser said that Hampden was getting old, and he would either flub his lines, or forget them completely. "I asked Jimmy to be kind and to help him out. He heard my appeal and quit mumbling and spoke lines clearly enough for Hampden to hear them."

In Hampden's big scene, he summoned all his juices, including tears coming down his cheeks—and this was only a rehearsal," Peyser said. "But the old guy impressed Dean because he was giving so much. After that, Dean was most courteous to Hampden, bringing him coffee, even finding a chair for him to sit on and rest between takes."

"At the end of the shoot, Hampden even invited Dean and his girlfriend, Betsy, to the Players Club, of which he had been president for twenty-seven years."

"When I saw the final show, I was impressed with Dean's work in this routine meller [melodrama]," Peyser said. "Dean was magnetic."

"A lot of viewers thought Dean was inspired by Brando's performance as Stanley Kowalski," Peyser said. "To some extent, that was true. But Dean made the role his own."

"To be a fine actor," Peyser had told Jimmy, "you must remember two things: Concentration and unlimited imagination. With those, there is no limit as to what you can do."

Palmer weighed in with her opinion. "I think Jimmy has intense concentration, but that's because he's nearsighted."

In *Death Is My Neighbor*, Jimmy was cast as "JB," a psychotic young janitor who is replacing an aging caretaker (Hampden), who is about to be fired.

A glamorous model and cover girl, Netta (as portrayed by Jimmy's on-again, off-again girlfriend Betsy Palmer) moves in, attracting Jimmy's lustful eye. She rejects his advances. Thwarted and vengeful, he plots her murder, with the intention of blaming it on Hampden.

In jeans and bare-armed, in a form-fitting polo shirt, Jimmy made one sexy janitor. In one scene, he dances "crotch-to-crotch" with Palmer. He later told Peyser, "Betsy gave me a hard-on."

"Save it until you get back to her apartment," Peyser said. "It's television, for god's sake."

Eventually, the police learn of JB's plot. They arrest him and he's entrapped into a confession before he is sent blubbering off to prison.

A player in television during its infancy, Peyser would go on to become one of the medium's greatest directors, helming such series as *The Untouchables, Bonanza, Perry Mason,* and *Hawaii-5-0.*

"Although James could pull himself together, he was basically a slob," Palmer claimed. "I don't mean he was dirty, but he often wore dirty clothes. He would take a bath before going on camera, however. Mostly, his hair was unkempt, his scalp flaked with dandruff. "

"He cut his own hair," she said, "calling it 'The Jim Trim.' Young actors would spend their last dollar going to the barber, ever ready for a casting call. James preferred to be his own hairdresser. That meant short on the sides, a full head of top hair combed back. Of course, it was mandatory to wear his jacket, a white T-shirt, jeans, and lots of attitude."

On movie dates, Palmer noted that Jimmy had a unique way of giving a review. Such was the case when they went to see *Lone Star,* starring Clark Gable and Ava Gardner. Later, at Jerry's Tavern, Jimmy gave his review of Gable's performance. "He's a real hot shoe. When you ride, you wear a steel shoe that goes over the bottom of your boot. When you round a corner, you put that foot out on the ground. When you can really ride, you're called a hot shoe. Gable rides like crazy."

"I was too polite to ask him what in hell he was talking about," Palmer said.

"By the autumn after our last teleplay, we sort of drifted apart," Palmer said. "A man entered my life, Dr. Vincent Merendino, and I fell in love with him and got married. We had a daughter. Once or twice, I tried to get in touch with James, but could never contact him. I never saw him again, but had relatively fond memories of our brief summer romance."

Jimmy vs. John ("I Don't Want to Be Gay") Kerr

THEIR CASTING TOGETHER IN "TRUE CRIME: REX NEWMAN"

Once again, those two lovers, John Kerr and James Dean, were cast together in *Rex Newman,* an episode that aired on September 11, 1953 within NBC's *The Big Story* TV series. Once a week, it dramatized true crime adventures that had been solved by dogged newspaper reporters. In this case the real-life drama described in the teleplay had been exposed by *The Globe and the News,* published in Joplin, Missouri.

Jimmy was more convincing that Kerr in *Rex Newman.* It was hard to believe that Kerr, with his clean-cut all-American look, was a cold-blooded killer.

In this episode, Jimmy and Kerry were exposed as part of a bungled robbery and murder, with Wendy Drew playing Jimmy's love interest. It was written by Alvin Boretz and directed by Stuart Rosenberg, with

NBC Television presents

narration by Bob Sloane. Although Jimmy tangled with Rosenberg on at least three occasions, the director ended up with great respect for his talent.

A still shot from NBC-TV's *Rex Newman*, starring doomed lovers, James Dean and Wendy Drew.

"If Jimmy had lived and continued to mature as an actor, I would have cast in in a future film I directed," Rosenberg claimed.

No doubt, he was referring to the 1967 release of *Cool Hand Luke*, which starred Paul Newman in the tale of an incorrigible Southern bad boy who is arrested for a dumb crime and sent to a brutal prison work camp where he defies authority from his sadistic redneck jailers. "Paul did a great job, and the public for the most part agreed, but Jimmy might have brought even greater depth to it, enough to at least be nominated for an Oscar," Rosenberg said.

After he'd completed its filming, Jimmy in the months ahead hardly remembered what was going on before the cameras. To him, the drama he and Kerr engaged in was more daunting.

"Perhaps sensing what a rival Kerr would be in the future, Jimmy tried to dominate the boy," said his friend, Stanley Haggart. "Those two lovers used my rear garden apartment frequently during the summer of 1953. As their affair played out. I sensed that Kerr liked the gay sex, but didn't want to be inducted into a world of homosexuals. After all, he had recently married. I think he saw himself as a family man with children. At least that is what I surmised when I read his handwriting, of which I'm supposed to be an expert. Actually, I'm not."

Jimmy later revealed to Haggart what happened during the weekend in September when Kerr's sexual involvement with Jimmy came to an abrupt end.

Haggart had arranged for them to make use of a small cottage owned by a friend of his, William Hunt, who often used it for gay beach parties. The summer crowds had already departed when Kerr and Jimmy arrived for their weekend on Long Island at Montauk Point.

As Jimmy remembered it, "It rained Friday night, all day Saturday and into Sunday morning."

Jimmy had hoped that the weekend would provide him with more time to get to know Kerr better. So far, most of their encounters had been brief, with little time to talk after the sex act was completed. The disruption began when Kerr was performing fellatio on Jimmy, as he had done several times before. But that time on Long Island was different, as Jimmy would later relay to Haggart.

Up to that point, Kerr would let Jimmy climax in his mouth, and would then spit out his semen. Jimmy had protested Kerr's refusal to swallow "my love offering. I want my seed in your belly as a token of your love for me."

"But I don't like the sticky god damn stuff in my mouth, much less in my stomach," Kerr always complained. "I don't like the taste of it."

Out in that summer cottage, after he exploded in a climax, Jimmy took charge. He kept his penis in Kerr's mouth, virtually choking him until he swallowed.

"God damn you!" Kerr said when Jimmy finally withdrew from his mouth. "You forced me to swallow."

"If you loved me, you'd take it like a man," Jimmy said.

Kerr disappeared into the bathroom, where Jimmy heard him trying to vomit. He reappeared after a shower, and retreated into the bedroom. Then he emerged fully dressed with his suitcase packed.

"You going somewhere?" Jimmy asked.

"This is our last time together," Kerr said.

"But the fun's only begun," Jimmy protested.

"For me, it's over," Kerr answered. "I admit that most actors, including myself, are a little bit homosexual, some a whole lot. I welcomed the experience with you, my 'induction,' so to speak. I think it'll make me a better actor."

"So what's your damn problem?" Jimmy asked.

"I've decided that the homosexual lifestyle is not for me," Kerr said. "I want to return to the straight world, where I fit in better."

"But there's a side of you that's gay," Jimmy said.

[By the time of this encounter, the word "gay," as a synonym for homosexual had already come into general usage.]

"I admit that, and I enjoyed our sex, especially when you let me fuck you. It's so different being with a man from being with a woman. But my times with you make me suffer guilt and question my manhood. I don't like what I'm doing with you. It's not fair to the woman I married."

"Okay, babe, if that's your wish," Jimmy said. "I won't force you. But it's too late to return to the city tonight. I'll drive you back in the morning. There's only one bedroom. It's mine. You can sleep on the sofa."

Jimmy then put on his jacket. "There's a bar about three miles from here where I understand the pickings are real good. I'm sure I'll be returning later tonight with someone. I hope we don't keep you awake."

"Do as you please," Kerr said, heading for the kitchen. "I need a drink."

Three hours later, as Jimmy had predicted, he returned with a young man. They retreated together to the bedroom, as Kerr lay awake, alone on the sofa, listening to the sounds of their love-making.

Jimmy kept his promise to return with Kerr to the city the next morning. Both men were in a bad mood. The trip back to Manhattan was in silence.

Kerr got out of Jimmy's car in front of his apartment building and disappeared inside.

There was no goodbye.

***

During the months to come, Kerr became one of Jimmy's main rivals for choice roles that eluded Jimmy and went to his discarded lover. Originally, Jimmy had tried to get in touch with Mary Chase, author of *Harvey,* a play that had been adapted into popular movie, released in 1950, starring James Stewart, whose companion was a six-foot invisible rabbit. Her latest play, *Bernardine* (1952), had a role that Jimmy thought would be ideal for him, even though he had only heard about the play and not actually read its script.

At the time, he was seeing a great deal of the lyricist, Marshall Barer, who had been a visitor to Rogers Brackett's Manhattan apartment during the period when Jimmy lived there. Barer would later end up on the list of Dean's "Lovers, Flings, or Just Friends?" in Mart Martin's book, published in 2000, *Did He or Didn't He?*

"I'm going to meet Chase and get her to cast me as the lead in *Bernardine*," Jimmy told Barer. "I'm sure I can convince her to change the title from *Bernardine* to *Jimmydine*." Regrettably, he was unable to reach her on the phone, since she'd left for a vacation in Colorado.

By the time Chase returned, the producers had assigned the lead in her play to John Kerr. That would mark that actor's debut on Broadway, his appearance winning him a Theater World award.

Around the same time, Jimmy had also wanted to appear on Broadway in Robert Anderson's *Tea and Sympathy,* a 1953 drama about a sensitive student accused of being gay. But it was decided that Jimmy was too strong for the role, which went to Kerr instead.

Kerr's stage performance won him a Tony as Best Supporting Stage Actor of the year. *[Jimmy had been in the running for that award, too, but failed to receive a nomination for his performance as an Arab boy in* The Immoralist.*]*

When *Tea and Sympathy* was adapted into a film in 1956, Kerr played the same character he had interpreted in the play, this time opposite Deborah Kerr (no relation). Of course, Jimmy was already dead by then.

Jimmy's competition with Kerr continued in Hollywood, when Vincente Minnelli wanted him for the 1955 film, *The Cobweb.* That role, too, went to Kerr.

Some executives thought Kerr might play the lead in *Rebel Without a*

Cause, but Jimmy was the favorite. For a while, Kerr was considered for the role of Jet Rink's adversary in *Giant,* but that role went to Dennis Hopper.

Ironically, at the time of his death, Jimmy had agreed to star in a theatrical revival of Emlyn Williams' play, *The Corn Is Green,* which had been a successful movie starring Bette Davis in 1945, based on an original Broadway play that had first been presented in 1940. The role went to Kerr instead.

Kerr did appear in the 1958 film adaptation of the Rodgers and Hammerstein production of *South Pacific.* His singing voice was unconvincingly dubbed, and his career waned after that.

In 1970, he passed the California Bar and became a full-time Beverly Hills lawyer, drawing heavily upon his history as a handsome film star to attract business.

Glory in the Flower

DOWN AND DIRTY ON THE CASTING COUCH WITH WILLIAM INGE

Omnibus, sponsored and broadcast through CBS, became the longest running cultural series in the history of commercial television. It ran without advertising breaks and focused on the production of TV entertainment based on material from critically acclaimed writers, among them William Faulkner, Carson McCullers, James Thurber, John Steinbeck, Ernest Hemingway, and T.S. Eliot. To that august list could be added William Inge, then one of the hottest playwrights in the county.

Kansas-born, Inge was known as "the playwright of the Middle West," a region from which Jimmy himself had emerged.

He became noted for his portraits of smalltown life in the American heartland, with predicaments centered around solitary protagonists encumbered with strained sexual relationships.

Specifically written for television, *Glory in the Flower* was set in a seedy roadhouse in the Middle West, where rowdy teenagers hung out. Through some connection, Jimmy managed to obtain a copy of the script, with the understanding that television premier was scheduled for October 4, 1953. Most of the cast had already been selected by director Andrew McCullough, and a prestigious

William Inge, author of *Glory in the Flower.*

one it was, starlighted by Jessica Tandy, who had scored huge recent success as Blanche DuBois in the original Broadway version of Tennessee Williams' *A Streetcar Named Desire,* also starring Marlon Brando.

In *Glory to the Flower,* she was cast as Jackie, a school teacher in her 40s. During her own school days, she had "thrown herself" at Bus Riley, the best-looking guy in her class. Years later, when Bus (Ed Binns) returns to town, he's not the man he was. He has turned into a lewd, womanizing troublemaker, and her illusions about him are shattered.

Jessica Tandy...shattered illusions.

Tandy's real-life husband, the Canadian actor, Hume Cronyn, was cast as a philosophical bartender uttering such lines as, "Maybe we make it too tough for today's teens. Maybe they're afraid."

The role of Bronco Evans was still up for grabs, and Jimmy wanted it. He was seeing Tennessee Williams at the time, and he went to him for advice. Jimmy had already met Inge at a New Years' Party hosted by David Swift and his wife, the actress, Maggie McNamara. Inge had phoned him twice, but Jimmy hadn't returned the call until he heard about the new teleplay.

Actually, he admitted to Stanley Haggart, "I'm really pissed that Inge didn't use his influence to get me a role in his big hit, *Picnic.*"

Produced that same year, Picnic's lead role of a drifter had gone to Ralph Meeker who played a stud who sets women's hearts aflutter. Another role in *Picnic* that Jimmy might have played was that of Meeker's small-town friend. That role was awarded instead to Jimmy's rival, Paul Newman.

Meeting in Tennessee's New York apartment, the playwright assured Jimmy, "You are Inge's type. He goes for corn-fed farm boys from the Middle West, especially if they're as good-looking and well-built as you are. You can get the role if you don't mind taking off those jeans and dropping those jockey shorts, as you've already done on a number of occasions with yours truly, this slightly decadent Southern playwright who waited too late in life to start having sex and is desperately trying to make up for my oversight at this late date."

Tennessee telephoned Inge on Jimmy's behalf, and an appointment was set up for the following evening.

Unlike his usual lateness, Jimmy showed up on time for a drink with this former teacher of drama and English. Inge sensed a nervousness in him, and gave him a vodka and tried to bond with him through a discussion of their Midwestern roots.

"The town Kansas where I grew up, Independence, was a lovely old place with shade trees and large Victorian houses along Main Street. It had a river that ran through. There was an old wives' tale that the Indians had left a curse on the river when they were driven out. Many people were drowned in that river, the revenge of the Indians, or so legend has it."

The alcohol put Jimmy at ease, and he read some of Bronco's scenes for Inge, who was very impressed, feeling that the young actor had captured the spirit of a character who liked to jitterbug to the sound of Bill Hayley and the Comets singing "Crazy Man, Crazy" on the jukebox. Bronco was in trouble with the police, who had caught him with pot.

After his reading, Inge told him, "You have the sex appeal of Bronco, and you also captured his wild, rebellious nature. Forgive me, but I'm considering writing in a scene where Bronco appears shirtless. Do you mind removing your shirt so I can see how you'll look half-naked on stage?"

"Not at all," Jimmy replied. Tennessee had warned him that Inge would be a bit shy about requesting what he really wanted, and that Jimmy would have to be the aggressor.

"Bill will want to give you a blow-job—nothing else," Tennessee said.

Jimmy slowly removed his T-shirt in front of Inge's admiring gaze. But he did more than that. He also unzipped his jeans and took them off, reserving his jockey shorts for a finale. When he finally dropped his underwear onto the carpet, he moved toward Inge, who was on the sofa and "eager to worship at my shrine," as Jimmy described it to Tennessee later at a dinner party at Stanley Haggart's apartment.

As Jimmy boasted, "Inge's mouth was watering. By the time I'd finished with him, or rather, he finished me off, I knew I was Bronco."

He stayed on and talked to Inge until around midnight. Inge held out the possibility that he might write big screen roles that would have a character that Jimmy could play.

Warren Beatty would emerge in the playwright's future, and Inge's crush on Jimmy would eventually be transferred as a virtual obsession onto Beatty, who would star in his 1959 play, *A Loss of Roses,* as well as in film roles—*Splendor in the Grass* (1961) with Natalie Wood, and *All Fall Down* (1962) with Eva Marie Saint—that made Beatty a star.

Inge later revealed that he wished Jimmy had lived to play the male lead in the film version (1956) of *Bus Stop,* starring Marilyn Monroe. The key role of the redneck cowboy went to Don Murray instead.

Before Jimmy left the apartment, the playwright had gotten very drunk. He told

Warren Beatty, later the object of Bill Inge's obsessive affection, with Natalie Wood in Inge's *Splendor in the Grass.*

279

Jimmy, "People do not approve of the way I live my life, but they sometimes applaud my work. I'll keep writing for public exposure while keeping my private life very private. But commercial success does not bring happiness. The only thing that can do that is love, which has never come my way."

The next day, Inge lunched with the director of *Glory in the Flower,* Andrew McCullough, and almost demanded that he cast Jimmy in the role of Bronco.

"I knew what was up, and that Jimmy had put out," McCullough claimed. "The old casting couch routine. When I met with Dean, I found he had an awful attitude—very snotty, very arrogant. As he started to read his lines, he put his feet up on a table, pulled out this very dangerous looking knife, and stabbed it into the table. I guess he was trying to send a signal to me not to reject him for the role of Bronco—or else curtains for me."

On the first day of rehearsals, Jimmy met his fellow actors. The one he pursued most aggressively was Jessica Tandy. He had not seen any of her performances as Blanche DuBois on Broadway, but her interpretation of that role had become something of a legend, even though it was later overshadowed by Vivien Leigh's Oscar-winning portrayal of that character on the screen. Brando, of course, had starred as Stanley Kowalski in both the original stage version and in its later screen adaptation.

Jimmy knew little about Tandy before meeting her. The London born-and-bred actress had already appeared on various stages with such luminaries as Laurence Olivier and John Gielgud. She had been married to actor Jack Hawkins, but divorced him and later married Hume Cronyn, who was also in the cast of *Glory in the Flower.* In time, Tandy would go on to appear in some 100 stage productions and some 60 feature films.

What Jimmy really wanted to hear from her was a rundown of her experiences of working with Brando in *Streetcar.*

"Tennessee fell in love with Brando and sacrificed my role of Blanche from its original script," Tandy charged, "and beefed up Brando's part instead of mine—even though Brando said that he always detested the role of the brutish Stanley Kowalski. I came to hate Brando."

That was music to Jimmy's ears.

Tandy told him a story about the brutality of Elia Kazan as a director that he feared she had exaggerated beyond belief. He would remember it vividly when Kazan directed him in *East of Eden.*

"Kazan thought I was too strong to play a delicate moth like Blanche," Tandy said. "He decided to break my spirit, and he did it in the most humiliating way, the worst experience I've ever had in the theater. He had one of the stagehands tie me up. Then he called in other actors like Karl Malden to attack me as a woman. You know—my 'small tits, my pus-laden vagina, and even my cunty smell,' in their hideous words. Of course, I was reduced first to tears, and then to hysteria. Then, for Kazan's *coup de grâce,* he summoned Brando for my utter humiliation. He whipped out his penis and urinated on me."

Jimmy listened to this with stunned disbelief.

"Brando detested me, and the feeling was mutual," Tandy claimed. "In out-of-town tryouts, I never knew how he'd play Kowalski. One night, he acted the role like some campy homosexual queen. One night in the middle of a performance, he stormed off the stage, shouting, 'My God, how can I play opposite this bitch? She thinks she's Ophelia.' In all, I think Brando is a selfish, psychotic bastard. There was no sexual magnetism between us on stage the way there was between Vivien and Brando in the movie."

In their television performance together of *Glory in the Flower,* Jimmy's most memorable scene with Tandy began when he forced his attentions onto her. "Dance with a real cat!" he yells at her. "Hey, this is the atomic age, man!"

Grabbing her, he whirls her away and after a step or two, she trips and goes sprawling onto the floor. Jimmy is horrified, protesting, "It's not my fault. After all, I didn't do it on purpose. You don't have to blame me." Later, he moans at the door to the men's room, "Everybody blames me!"

Jimmy "pissed off" Cronyn, Tandy's husband, who was portraying the bartender. The antagonism began when Jimmy asked him, "What is it like being married to a woman with far more talent than yourself?"

"Those are fighting words," Cronyn said. "Need I remind you, punk, that I was a member of the 1932 Olympic boxing team?"

"Oh, yeah," Jimmy said. "Listen old man. I was shitting my diapers that year."

"Dean was completely unprofessional in every way," Cronyn said. "At one point, I was supposed to search his pants to remove a bottle of whiskey, since he was too young to drink on my premises. A bottle was supposed to be in his hip pocket. I searched, finding nothing, although I virtually had to feel him up. There was one place I hadn't touched, and that was his crotch. Of course, that's where the bottle of whiskey was resting, bulging out from his pants like some monstrous erection."

Hume Cronyn with Jessica Tandy. Did she really suffer through Marlon Brando's "golden shower?"

Ed Binns, an actor from Philadelphia, had been cast as Bus Riley, the male lead. He would be a star of film, stage, and television, his career spanning four decades. In his most famous production, *Twelve Angry Men* (1957), he'd been directed by

Sidney Lumet, who had previously helmed Jimmy in a teleplay. Binns would go on to star in such films as a police detective in Alfred Hitchcock's *North by Northwest* (1959), starring Cary Grant.

At one point in the drama, Bronco tangles with Bus (Binns), who grabs Jimmy by the shirt and threatens him, calling him "a little goon" and slapping Jimmy's face. Then, after Jimmy denounces Bus as phony, Bus knocks him down. From his position sprawled out on the floor, Jimmy cries out, defiantly, *"No one's gonna tell me what to do!"* The bartender then orders that Jimmy be forcibly removed from the tavern.

Cast as a visiting salesman, Frank McHugh didn't know what to make of Jimmy. The veteran actor represented Old Hollywood. "What was this Method acting shit?" he asked. "To me, acting was how to make a living. I came from a theatrical family in Pennsylvania. My folks never heard of acting technique. They just got out there before the headlights and strutted their stuff."

McHugh had gone to Hollywood as a contract player in 1930 at the dawn of the Talkies. He was used mostly for comic relief, and became the best friend of James Cagney, performing in nearly a dozen of his films.

"I worked with the biggies," McHugh told Jimmy. "Bing Crosby, Gene Kelly. Usually, I was a sidekick."

"I told Dean I was heading to Hollywood to appear with Marilyn Monroe in *There's No Business Like Show Business,* and he said 'I plan to fuck her.' I was surprised that he wanted to make it with a woman. Everybody in the cast told me that he was a homosexual."

The reviews of *Glory in the Flower* were bad and particularly devastating to Inge. *Variety* was fairly kind, however, claiming that the play "made for a high class, varied hour-and-half of entertainment, with just an occasional bit of pretentiousness or archness creeping in."

McCullough would survive directing Jimmy and would work with him again in the future. "He had a real talent, even holding his own against the formidable Miss Tandy. When not acting, he was often sullen and contemptuous of the young gals who buzzed around him, finding him sexy. I told him he'd be ideal for the movies since he did not have one single bad angle, unlike many film stars. I'd never worked with an actor who had such magnetism."

In many ways, the role of Bronco Evans in the teleplay was a rehearsal for Jimmy's part of the disaffected anti-hero, Jim Stark, in *Rebel Without a Cause.*

***

The telescript for *Glory in the Flower* was later rewritten considerably and turned into a screenplay for a feature film entitled *Bus Riley's Back in Town* (1965), starring Michael Parks and Ann-Margret. Inge was very unhappy with the final result. He asked that his name be removed, and that future writing credits be attributed to a pseudonym, "Walter Gage."

On June 10, 1973, a bulletin came over television sets that the celebrated playwright, Bill Inge, author of *Come Back, Little Sheba, Picnic,* and *Bus Stop* had committed suicide by carbon monoxide poisoning. He was sixty years old.

He last plays had attracted little notice or critical attention, and he'd fallen into a deep depression, convinced that he would never be able to write well again.

Years later, Inge's teleplay, *Glory in the Flower*, was revived and presented in Toronto, where it did not fare well in the view of critic Kelly Kleiman: "This work should have been left to its obscurity. The characters are familiar—beaten-down salesmen, fighters who were never contenders, small town folks with pipe dreams, fraudulent big shots, disillusioned lovers. The title comes from the same line of Wordsworth that provided the name of *Spendor in the Grass*—perhaps Inge never read another poem."

Keep Our Honor Bright

JIMMY HELPS SATIRIZE THE MCCARTHY HEARINGS

On October 14, 1953, NBC broadcast *Keep Our Honor Bright* for *The Kraft Television Theater*. Critics claimed that it was inspired by the communist witch hunt hearings led by Senator Joseph McCarthy of Wisconsin.

The comparison of a college student facing expulsion for cheating with the Senate hearings was a bit farfetched. At around the same time, Arthur Miller's *The Crucible,* produced on Broadway in 1953, put the exposé of the Senate hearings into better in focus.

Keep Your Honor Bright was written by George Roy Hill, a TV writer and actor before he became more famous as a director, helming Paul Newman and Robert Redford in *Butch Cassidy and the Sundance Kid* (1969) and again in *The Sting* (1973), for which he won a Best Director Oscar. Hill not only wrote *Keep Our Honor Bright,* but appeared in it as a news broadcaster.

Roy Cohn (*left*), with Joe McCarthy...on a communist witch hunt.

The teleplay was both produced and directed by Maury Holland, a regular who often labored in both of those functions on various episodes of *The Kraft Television Theater*. A native of Louisiana, Holland was a former vaudevillian and Broadway actor.

Hill liked Jimmy enough to take him flying in his private plane. He'd obtained his pilot's license at the age of sixteen. On Jimmy's first time up, Hill decided to play a practical joke on him, steering his plane into a simulated nose-dive, yelling and screaming that they were plunging to their deaths. How Jimmy handled this fake emergency is not known. Did he go into a panic or did he face death with bravery?

During World War II, Hill had been a cargo pilot in the South Pacific and was very skilled. During the filming of the *Butch Cassidy* film, Newman was also subjected to Hill's "nose dive."

"If you showed up late for a shot, he would teach you a lesson," Newman said. "He'd take you up in that not trustworthy plane of his and scare the bejesus out of you."

In the plot, Jimmy was cast as Jim Cooper, who, as a senior at the university, is caught cheating on his final exams. In retribution, he is summoned before a kangaroo court of fraternity brothers.

In the script, Jimmy readily admits his guilt, claiming, "I don't know why I did it. It just happened. I don't like to beg. I'm begging now. Please don't expel me!"

Despite his pleas, the brothers decide that he has brought them dishonor and that he should be expelled.

Later, he swallows an overdose of sleeping pills, but his suicide attempt fails.

To save his own skin, Jimmy's character is ready to expose forty other students who also cheated on their exams. This was an obvious reference to Hollywood actors and directors—one of whom was Elia Kazan—who had exposed ("ratted on") colleagues who had shown sympathy for claims and beliefs of the communist party.

In the teleplay, Jimmy appeared with a cast of some thirty players, but the only one he remembered was Bradford Dillman. A native of San Francisco, he was about Jimmy's age and equally good looking. Like Jimmy, he had studied at the Actors Studio and would later marry Suzy Parker, one of the most famous models in America at the time.

Jimmy sized up Dillman to Hill: "Tomorrow's competition."

Life Sentence

JIMMY PLAYS AN EX-CON CONFRONTING HIS MASTURBATORY FANTASY

Once again at NBC, Jimmy starred in *Life Sentence,* an episode in the series of *Campbell Soundstage Dramas* that was aired on October 16. It was written by S. Lee Progostin and directed by Garry Simpson.

Jimmy was cast as a convict, Hank Bradon, perhaps psychotic. The object of his fascination was a beautiful blonde, Jean Ryder (Georgann Johnson), who fights with her husband (Nicholas Saunders) and fatally shoots him. She later tries to blame the shooting on a convict from the prison that adjoins her property.

Johnson was a tall, statuesque blonde, born in Iowa, who would go on to appear in such films as *Midnight Cowboy* (1969), but is

Jimmy, playing a horny, just-released ex-con, manhandling the object of his suppressed desires, as played by Georgann Johnson.

better known as the mother of the title character in *Dr. Quinn, Medicine Woman,* a TV series that ran from 1993-1998.

Jimmy's character works in the prison garden, where he can spy from afar on Johnson on her front porch. When he finishes his time in prison, he arrives on her doorstep, begging her to go away with him. She threatens to call the police, but he warns her, "If you do, I'll bash your skull in."

He tells her he has had a masturbatory fantasy of her wearing a sunflower yellow bathing suit. "I dreamed of you on a surf board swimming across the white fluffy waves." He grabs for her and she protests, "You're hurting me."

Sexually excited by her, he says, "That's the first time I've touched a woman in five years."

In general, viewers found Jimmy's performance creditable, based on emotions which swung from sentimental to psychotic within minutes.

Critic Robert Tanitch wrote: "It was a pity that the director should have allowed Dean to go right over the top at the end of the threatened rape scene and rip open the top of his shirt in an unnecessary and embarrassing theatrical gesture in which he seemed to be reaching out for a Marlon Brando-like climax and missing it."

The Bells of Cockaigne:

IRISH BLARNEY ENHANCED WITH JIMMY'S TELEVISED "STRIPTEASE"

Jimmy followed *Life Sentence* with a return to NBC to film *The Bells of Cockaigne*, a teleplay for the series, *Armstrong's Circle Theater*. Aired on November 17, it was written by George Lowther and directed by Jimmy's close friend, James Sheldon. Its star was Gene Lockhart, cast as a janitor, who had worked with Jimmy before during his first major produc-

tion, the religious drama, *Hill Number One*.

A Canadian, Lockhart was strictly a professional who always showed up on time and was letter-perfect in his lines. He'd made his debut in the theater at the age of sixteen, appearing on stage in comedy sketches with Beatrice Lillie. From 1922 onward, he would be cast in some 300 films, including *Miracle on 34th Street* (1947), starring Maureen O'Hara.

Sheldon had learned how eccentric Jimmy could be as an actor, showing up late and spontaneously rewriting his lines without warning.

Jimmy (with his anonymous benefactor, Gene Lockhart), in *Bells of Cockaigne*. Impersonating a stevedore laboring on the docks, he remained shirtless throughout most of the teleplay.

Lockhart complained to Sheldon about him: "He's always late, always wrapped up in himself and not accommodating at all to his fellow actors."

Sheldon said, "I think Jimmy is unaware of other people's worlds. He was doing his thing his way, and it works well for him but it often leaves the other actors without anything to play off."

Also in the cast was veteran actor Vaughn Taylor, with whom Jimmy would soon work again.

As the stevedore, Joey, Jimmy appears as a heavy duty laborer, and is shirtless throughout most of the teleplay. As he told Sheldon, "I bet I turned on the homos and women, too, by showing off my lilywhite body and suckable tits."

He is struggling to support his wife and their asthmatic young son, who is in dire need of medical treatments that Jimmy can't afford. In this production,

Jimmy appears rather skinny and looks undernourished as he works with a corps of beefy, muscled stevedores.

To escape from poverty, and to aid his son, Jimmy as Joey joins a gambling ring of other stevedores and blows his entire paycheck.

In the meantime, Lockhart as the janitor tells Taylor that he wants to win a $500 lottery prize, which he plans to spend on a trip back to his native Ireland. His dream comes true, and he wins the lottery.

"When you get something which you've been waiting for a long time, you hear the Bells of Cockaigne," Lockhart remarks.

[Cockaigne is a reference to an imaginary fantasy island where one lives in luxurious comfort, freed of worldly problems.]

When Lockhart as the kindly janitor learns that Jimmy had lost his paycheck to the other stevedores, he pulls off a ruse. He claims that Jimmy had the winning $500 lottery ticket, and he relinquishes his prize money to him as a means of paying for his boy's medical expenses. Of course, the inevitable happens: Lockhart hears the bells of Cockaigne ringing as the play, dripping with sentimentality, ends.

A reviewer wrote, "The Bells of Cockaigne may have been true, but it plays like a bit of Irish blarney."

A Long Time Till Dawn

EMULATING DEATH IN THE STYLE OF JAMES CAGNEY

Jimmy was in such demand during November of 1953 that he was cast as the star of another teleplay, *A Long Time Till Dawn*, set to be aired on November 11 as an episode on the popular *Kraft Television Theater*.

The drama had been written by Rod Serling, perhaps the most brilliant writer of television's Golden Age in the 1950s. Serling was not only a screenwriter, but a playwright, producer, and narrator, best known for his science fiction anthology, *The Twilight Zone*. Called "the angry young man of television," he was at constant war with TV executives and sponsors about such issues as censorship, racism, and war.

The teleplay was both produced and directed by Dick Dunlap, one of the most prolific directors in the history of television, helming some 1,000 tele-

James Dean as a remorseful gangster in *A Long Time Till Dawn*.

287

plays before the end of his career.

"He was one of the few queer directors who didn't try to get into my pants," Jimmy alleged. "My God, the man was a pro. He got his start at the age of five working in silent pictures."

In addition to Jimmy, he would go on to direct such stars as Frank Sinatra, Robert Preston, Eva LaGallienne, Eva Marie Saint, Melvyn Douglas, Lee Remick, Peter Ustinov, Jason Robards, Helen Hayes, José Ferrer, John Gielgud, and Elvis Presley.

"I thought Jimmy might become a star, at least in some B pictures about juvenile delinquents with Mamie Van Doren or Jayne Mansfield. But a legend like Marilyn Monroe? Never!"

Once again, Jimmy was cast as a convict, this time named Joe Harris, who is both a poet and a gangster. Serling described the character as a young man with "violence and big blue eyes, a strange boy, a sensitive kid, but without remorse or conscience. He's got brains, but his logic is like a little boy's."

After serving his sentence, Joe heads for home, where his estranged parents live in a leafy suburb of New Jersey. Joe is in search of his wife, Barbie Harris (Naomi Riordan), who has deserted him.

The teleplay opens with a scene in a delicatessen, where Jimmy reverts to some Method acting techniques, even sucking on the collar of his shirt. The deli owner knowns where Barbie went, but refuses to tell. In a fit of anger, Jimmy attacks the man and beats him up. Without meaning to, he kills the owner of the store and flees to his father's home.

Actor Ted Osborn was cast as the stern, unforgiving father, Fred Harris.

Jimmy's character pleads with his father to forgive him. "I'm not going to make these mistakes anymore," Joe says.

The teleplay evolves into a father-son conflict that would be played out better in Jimmy's upcoming *Rebel Without a Cause.*

Soon, Joe learns that his wife, Barbie, is upstairs. He emotes well in his scene with her, as played by Riordan, a Michigan-born actress wo would star in many TV series, including *Armstrong Circle, Lux Video, and the Philco-Goodyear Television Playhouse.* Her most unusual role would not come until 1980, when she starred in *Jane Austen in Manhattan.*

In bed with her, his wife in the teleplay, Jimmy's character confesses to the killing, but claims, "He had no business hitting me. I didn't mean to kill him."

When she urges him to give himself up, he turns on her. "You're just like the rest of them. You're all against me, all of you." At this point, he retrieves a pistol from his suitcase.

The police are on Joe's trail, surrounding his father's home. Fearing that it's the end, Joe reverts to childhood, clutching his baseball to his chest and cuddling up in a fetal position on the bed. He looks as vulnerable as a helpless child.

From the yard below, in dialogue culled directly from the script for one of those 1930s gangster movies from Warner Brothers with George Raft or Edward G. Robinson, one of the cops yells, "Put down your gun and come down or we'll come up after you."

Joe calls down, "You're crazy, all of you, crazy," before appearing at the window with another *clichéd* line, "Come and get me!"

The police then launch a barrage of gunfire aimed at the window, hitting Joe in the chest. In death, he falls to the ground below.

Serling later said, "The kid did my teleplay brilliantly. I can't imagine anyone playing that particular role better. There was an excitement and intensity about him that he transmitted to the TV public out there."

The New York Times wrote, "James Dean's jittery performance demonstrates how annoying the mannerisms of Method acting can be." Another reviewer pointed out that Jimmy's performance "was unduly influenced by the acting of Marlon Brando, including some of his vocal intonations."

Another critic labeled Jimmy's performance as "wonderful, but somewhat spoiled by Serling's script, which makes us dislike the character from the beginning. Joe is vulnerable, but underneath, he's also quick tempered, abusive, and a liar. Yet he truly wants redemption. His monologue about nostalgia is beautiful."

Harvest

JIMMY CO-STARS WITH DOROTHY GISH AND ROBERT MONTGOMERY

Still in November, Jimmy's favorite director, also his mentor, James Sheldon, hired him once again to star in a teleplay, *Harvest,* for NBC's *The Johnson Wax Program.* A Thanksgiving parable scheduled for broadcast on November 23, it was part of *Robert Montgomery Presents* and set amid Quakers living on a farm.

Montgomery had made his film debut in 1929 at the dawn of the Talkies. In time, he would star with such luminaries as Greta Garbo in *Inspiration* (1930); with Norma Shearer in *The Divorcée* (also 1930); and in the psychological chiller, *Night Must Fall* (1937), for which he received an Oscar nomination. A staunch Republican, anti-communist and homophobe, he had been elected president of the Screen Actors Guild in 1935.

George Cukor, who had worked with Mont-

289

gomery early in his career, attributed his anti-gay distaste as a "cover-up for his own homosexual liaisons as a young man." When Cukor knew Montgomery, he claimed he was sexually involved with a handsome, well-muscled stagehand. "Robert was like J. Edgar Hoover," the director said. "He felt that by attacking gay people, he was throwing suspicion away from himself, and his own checkered past."

Privately, Montgomery referred to Jimmy as "that sawed-off little queer punk from Actors Studio where all the boys there, from Monty Clift to Paul Newman, are homos!"

Sheldon said that "Montgomery made it respectable for bigtime stars to appear on television, which in the beginning was seriously frowned upon by the studios. He introduced many high-class dramas on TV and acted in some of the episodes himself." Notable guest stars in his series included James Cagney, Claudette Colbert, Grace Kelly, Angela Lansbury, Jack Lemmon, Paul Lukas, Roger Moore, Raymond Massey, Burgess Meredith, Dorothy McGuire, and Constance Bennett.

Harvest starred the legendary Dorothy Gish, sister of the more famous actress, Lillian Gish. D.W. Griffith had made both of them household names in the early days of silent pictures. Ed Begley was also in the cast, as was Vaughn Taylor, with whom Jimmy had recently worked in *the Bells of Cockaigne.*

The story of *Harvest* revived Jimmy's memories of Fairmount, when he had lived with Ortense and Marcus Winslow on their farm. The dialogues, especially the running commentary by Sandra Michael, was a bit preachy, and the soundtrack contained a soulful rendition of a hymn whose lyrics included "Bless the folk who dwell within, Keep them pure and free from sin."

For Jimmy, his greatest thrill involved meeting and talking to Dorothy Gish. Mary Pickford, "America's Sweetheart," had introduced the Gish Sisters to D.W. Griffith, who had cast them in silent films for Biograph. In time, Dorothy would star in more than 100 short films and features, something with her sister, Lillian.

"The greatest compliment my sister ever gave me," Dorothy said to Jimmy, "was to tell me that my performance was almost as good as hers."

Washed up as a matinee idol, homophobe Robert Montgomery reconfigured his failing career into that of an (egomaniacal) Master of Ceremonies on TV.

Lower photo depicts him as a dashing, predatory rake in *Night Must Fall (1937).*

She also told him that she had married only once, and that was to James Rennie, a marriage that lasted from 1920 to 1935. "I'll never marry again. The institution is not for me."

"You're preaching to the choir," he said. "Imagine being tied down to just one person."

Ed Begley played Jimmy's father, Carl Zelenka; Gish his mother, Ellen. Jimmy was their son, Paul. Ed wanted Jimmy to follow in his footsteps as a farmer, but Paul has wanderlust in his eyes.

Unlike some actors, Begley worked smoothly with Jimmy. A New Englander, he had dropped out of school in the fifth grade and ran away to work in the circus. During World War I, he joined the Navy. He later became a veteran of Broadway shows and a star on radio. By the late 1940s, he was making feature films in Hollywood and, in time, starred in teleplays. By 1962, he would play a crooked southern politician in Tennessee Williams' *Sweet Bird of Youth,* star-ring Paul Newman as the hustler, Chance

Two views of Jimmy living among Quakers on a farm in *Harvest. Top photo* shows Dean with Nancy Sheridan and *(lower photo)* with Dorothy Gish.

Wayne, and Geraldine Page as a fading movie star. In its Broadway version, the Chance Wayne character had been castrated by the political boss.

"Jimmy Dean wasn't a seasoned actor when I worked with him," Begley said. "But I had high hopes for the boy, even though he was a bit reckless."

In the final part of the drama, Jimmy enlists in the Navy and appears in a sailor suit at a homecoming Thanksgiving dinner. "He looked real cute as a sailor," Gish claimed. His appearance brought several hundred fan letters from impressionable girls and from many gay men."

Taylor's character of Gramp doesn't join the family for its Thanksgiving dinner. In the play, he dies before attaining his 100th birthday. He looked the right age on camera, although he was still in his 40s, having been born in 1910. His "son," Begley, was born in 1901. Taylor could be made up to look decades older, and he was making a career of playing elderly characters.

One reviewer wrote, "Country boy James Dean broods, then broods some more, broods in the kitchen, broods at the mailbox, broods on the front porch, and experiences *angst*, often in silence."

The Little Woman

JIMMY SUCCESSFULLY INTERACTS WITH A SCENE-STEALING CHILD ACTRESS

Jimmy didn't make an appearance again in a teleplay until March of 1954 because he had other commitments, such as starring in *The Immoralist* on Broadway.

Once again, Andrew McCullough offered him a lead role in *The Little Woman,* an episode within the popular *Danger* series on CBS. His co-stars included child actress Lydia Reed and Lee Bergere, who played a cop on his beat.

In a script by Joe Scully, Jimmy was cast as a counterfeiter on the lam. He hides out with a poverty-stricken little girl (Reed) who lives in a world of her own, a playhouse in a seedy alleyway. Scully, a major writer for television at the time, said he created the character of Augie, the young delinquent, specifically for Jimmy to play.

McCullough expected trouble from Jimmy, but didn't find it. "Even though working with a child, he gave one of the most generous performances I've ever seen. Not one ounce of ego."

"I heard that Dean did not cooperate with other actors," Bergere said. "But I found him right on the mark, and we got along fine."

During World War II, Bergere had supervised the entertainment for American soldiers stationed in North Africa. Before that, He'd been an understudy on Broadway for Danny Kaye. Later, in the 1980s, he became known for his role of Joseph Anders in the hit TV series, *Dynasty.*

Reed, in the title role, would later become famous when she starred as Hassie McCoy in 145 episodes (aired between 1957 and 1963) of ABC's sitcom, *The Real McCoy,* with veteran actor Walter Brennan, who usually played a hayseed sidekick in westerns.

In 1956, Reed would be cast in *High Society,* with Bing Crosby, Frank Sinatra, and Grace Kelly, a remake of *The Philadelphia Story* (1940), that had starred Katharine Hepburn, Cary Grant, and James Stewart.

In a review of *The Little Woman,* one critic claimed that "Dean is a brooding, self-involved actor so many times, perhaps too many times, but with Lydia Reed, he shows us that he has a gift for interacting with a child."

In its review, *Variety* wrote: "Child actress Lydia Reed has built herself a dream world in a slum alley—

Child starlet Lydia Reed, as she appeared on *The Real McCoys* (1957-1963) a few years after her appearance with Jimmy.

a habitat with all the props and knickknacks—and her best friends are Lee Bergere and James Dean, who gets himself involved as a transmission belt for a couple of traveling burglars and safe-breakers, who were intending to steal plates used for counterfeiting. On the run from police, he is provided shelter by the eight-year-old girl. It wasn't much of a yarn, but the thesping is good, particularly that of Reed. A neat first try for McCullough, who is bringing the *Danger* series out of its rut."

Run Like a Thief

WITH KURT KAZNAR IN HOT PURSUIT, JIMMY HANGS OUT WITH SCARLETT O'HARA'S MOTHER

Involved in other pursuits during the summer of 1954, Jimmy did not appear in another teleplay until that September. Director Jeffrey Hayden cast him as the young *protégé* of gay actor Kurt Kasznar, a waiter in a hotel. Jimmy becomes disillusioned with Kasznar when he learns he is a thief.

With a script by Sam Hall, the NBC presentation was telecast on September 5 as part of the *Philco TV Playhouse* series.

It was one of Jimmy's less prestigious teleplays, although it got fairly good reviews. *Variety* wrote, "This was the first *Playhouse* under the Gordon Duff production, and it offered proof that prior high standards of the program would be preserved. It has good performers and created a good deal of suspense."

Director Jeffrey Hayden, a New Yorker, had married Eva Marie Saint in 1952, and he would make a career out of helming episodes within TV series. He would later direct a feature film, *The Vintage* (1957), which starred Jimmy's most serious romance, Pier Angeli. Of course, Jimmy wouldn't be around by the time that film was released.

As a hotel worker, Kasznar discovers a diamond necklace, which belongs to the owner (Barbara O'Neil) of the establishment. But instead of returning it to its rightful owner, he gives it to his wife (Gusti Huber). When Jimmy learns what he has done, he brands his mentor a thief.

The Hollywood Reporter claimed, "James Dean as the *protégé* emerged as a rather unclear figure, even

Kurt Kasznar, a profligate, unapologetic, amusing but predatory homosexual on the make for Jimmy.

though thesping was beyond reproach. He was the man the script by Sam Hall forgot to explain. The void made a difference."

Jimmy was thrilled to meet O'Neil, a fellow Midwesterner from Missouri. In 1939, she had starred in his favorite movie, *Gone With the Wind.* She had been cast as Ellen O'Hara, Scarlett O'Hara's prim and respectable mother, even though she was only three years older than her on-screen daughter, Vivien Leigh. Lillian Gish had rejected the role.

When Jimmy met O'Neil, he was hoping that it would lead to an introduction to the director, Josh Logan, whom O'Neil had divorced in 1942. He asked her to set up a meeting with Logan, but O'Neil said, "We're not speaking. Our ill-fated union ended long before our divorce. Frankly, my dear, as Rhett Butler might have said, Josh would have preferred a guy like you to a wife like me. I have never remarried, and I like it that way."

Barbara O'Neil as Ellen O'Hara *(right)*, with Vivien Leigh as Scarlett O'Hara, her rebellious daughter, in *Gone With the Wind* (1939).

Jimmy was intrigued by the Viennese actress, Gusit Huber, who had a bit part in the teleplay. Kasznar, a fellow Viennese, told Jimmy that she'd been a Nazi. Josef Goebbels had lured her into making propaganda films for the Nazis, at least in Kasznar's view. He detested her. In the 1930s, she had refused to work with Jewish actors or directors. "Not that there were many Jews still left in Berlin," Kasznar said. "Those that were were sent to the ovens."

However, at the end of World War II, Huber had married a U.S. Army officer and moved to the

A contrast in types: Kurt Kasznar with James Dean.

United States, where she had tried to conceal her National Socialist background.

In 1959, she would be cast as the mother of Anne Frank in *The Diary of Anne Frank.* Many Jews objected to her in the role of the mother of this anti-Nazi heroine, but the director, Garson Kanin, stood by his choice. It would be Huber's last movie role.

From the first day, Kasznar turned out to be a problem for Jimmy. "He had his tongue hanging out when I was introduced to him," Jimmy told Stanley Haggart.

The New York Times had called the actor "a big, glib, dapper man who spoke with an accent and was almost always cast as some sort of Continental gentleman." As a soldier, he had fought on the American side during World War II, and was among the first Army photographers to film the ruins of Hiroshima and Nagasaki, which had been laid to waste by atomic bombs.

In an attempt to impress Jimmy, Kasznar told him that he'd worked with the celebrated director, Max Reinhardt. "He taught me to act, write, built sets, even how to live."

"Kasznar was hot for my tail, and I couldn't shake him," Jimmy told Haggart. "He told me that his friend, Rock Hudson, let him give him blow-jobs. 'Why can't you, Jimmy?' he asked me. 'After all, Rock is a far bigger star than you.' I finally gave in to him. After about three blow-jobs, his curiosity was satisfied, and he let me alone for the duration, having shacked up with one of the cameramen. Kasznar's mouth is a suction pump. He told me he once blew twenty guys in one night in a bathhouse on 28th Street."

Padlock

MILDRED DUNNOCK FINDS JIMMY OBNOXIOUS

In November of 1954, Jimmy returned to CBS to appear in another episode of its *Danger* series in which he'd starred before, most recently in *The*  *Little Woman.* This time around, he was in distinguished company, co-starring with Mildred Dunnock and directed by John Frankenheimer. He was already acquainted with Dunnock from his time at the Actors Studio, and she had gone to see him in *See the Jaguar.*

A story of suspense, Jimmy was cast in *Padlock* as a gunman fleeing from the police, a role now familiar to him. He tries to rob an eccentric old lady (Dunnock).

She recalled working with him. "He came into rehearsal like something that might have been shot out of a cannon. He seemed to have energy enough to walk up a steep wall."

Frankenheimer and Jimmy were only a year apart in age. This native of New York City's Outer Borough of Queens became known for his social dramas and his action/suspense movies, including such future features as *The Manchurian Candidate* (1962) and *Seven Days in May* (1964).

He was one of the last remaining directors who insisted on having complete control of his productions, as he would assert in some thirty feature films and more than fifty plays.

He made it clear from the beginning that he was the director, and that

Jimmy should execute a scene according to his specifications. Jimmy would become just one in a long list of stars Frankenheimer would direct: Mickey Rooney, Frank Sinatra, Burt Lancaster, Warren Beatty, Kirk Douglas, Ava Gardner, Faye Dunaway, and David Niven.

[As a footnote to history, in June of 1968, Frankenheimer was the driver of the car that then-Senator Robert F. Kennedy used for transportation to his speaking engagement at what turned out to be the scene of his assassination, the Ambassador Hotel in Los Angeles. En route to the hotel, from behind the wheel, Frankenheimer found the presidential candidate "Jubilant. He was going to beat Eugene McCarthy for the nomination, and he predicted he'd clobber that asshole Nixon. Alas, it was not to be."]

James Dean as a punk, menacing Mildred Dunnock.

Months before their appearance together in the teleplay, Jimmy had deeply offended Dunnock during his audition for a role in a revival of George Bernard Shaw's *Candida*. Dunnock wanted the starring role that had once featured a *grande dame* of the American theater, Katherine Cornell, who had played alongside Marlon Brando. In the revival Jimmy sought Brando's former role.

As a test of his suitability, Dunnock alongside Eric Bentley, the playwright, critic, and author, agreed to meet with Jimmy.

"He came in like some unkempt street urchin," she claimed. "He wore some ragged clothing that appeared to have been purchased at some secondhand store on the Lower East Side. He was unshaven, and from the smell of him, he needed a long soak in the bathtub. He read for Eric and me. Unlike Brando, Dean was totally wrong for the part. I thought he was better-suited to playing a gas station attendant rather than a poet. His middle name might have been Byron, as he told us, but he was not Byronic."

I'm a Fool (for Jail Bait)

Jimmy Meets Natalie ("Sweet Sixteen") Wood

Don Medford had helmed Jimmy in the May (1953) teleplay, *The Evil Within* for the TV series, *Tales of Tomorrow*, in which he had co-starred with Rod Steiger. Medford wanted to work with him again, casting him in a very different role as a nineteen-year-old country boy who had left home to become a "swipe" (stable boy) at a race-track. *I'm a Fool* was an episode within *The General Electric Theater,* which aired on November 14, 1954, and was introduced by its host, Ronald Reagan.

Arnold Schulman had adapted it from a Sherwood Anderson short story. Anderson had become known for inspiring such other writers as John Steinbeck, William Faulkner, and Ernest Hemingway.

As Jimmy's co-stars, Medford had cast Eddie Albert and Natalie Wood, who was sixteen at the time. She played a rich girl who was Jimmy's love interest. She would become his much more famous love interest within a few months, when Nicholas Ray cast her in *Rebel Without a Cause.*

A blurred depiction of James Dean in *I'm a Fool.*

Medford recalled the first day of rehearsals when he was driving to its location in a remote section of East Los Angeles. "Suddenly, from out of nowhere, this motorcycle rider was zigzagging dangerously in and out of traffic and recklessly changing lanes on a whim. He practically hit my car. As he did, I looked into the face of this fool. My god, it was Jimmy Dean."

"At one point, he threw both hands up in the air and gunned the motor, racing ahead in some sort of no-hands balancing act. He could have been killed that morning, and by afternoon, I'd be looking for another actor. When he got to the rehearsal hall in one piece, I gave him a stern lecture. 'Do you want to die on the highway?' I asked him 'Keep driving like that, and you'll soon learn you have no tomorrow.'"

"He just gave me that soon-to-be-famous smile of his and walked away," Medford said. "He'd already filmed *East of Eden* at the time. Although it had not been released, the advance notices for him were terrific. He was already being hailed as the new Brando."

Wood recalled her first impression of him. "He crawled through an open window into the rehearsal hall instead of using the front door. He looked rather ragged with uncombed hair. His pants were held up by two large safety pins. He was very introspective and didn't mingle with us that first day."

She had heard about him. A few days before, along with a girlfriend, she had tried to meet him at his hangout at Googies in Hollywood. But her mother had come for her and put her in the car to haul her home to bed.

"On the second day of rehearsals, I was standing outside, coughing on my first attempt to smoke a cigarette, and up roared Jimmy on his motorcycle. I just assumed he was a junior version of Marlon Brando in *The Wild One.* Jimmy mumbled so you could hardly understand him. He was good looking, but eccentric. During the morning, his mood shifted suddenly, at one point charming, reverting to hostile, all within a period of a minute. It was amazing."

"I didn't think he liked me, but then, he invited me to lunch. I got on the back of his motorcycle for a hysterical and dangerous ride to a local greasy spoon that served god awful food," she said. "Over a bacon-and-cheese sandwich, he seemed to recognize me."

"You were that little girl in *Miracle on 34th Street,* a child actress." He looked into her face for confirmation.

"That was me all right," she said. "Better a child actress than acting like a child."

He laughed and that seemed to bring down the barrier he'd erected around himself. From that luncheon, a friendship blossomed that would turn into a love affair on the set of *Rebel Without a Cause.*

She explained that she was trying to make the transition from child actress to roles that called for a young woman. "Shirley Temple didn't pull it off, but Elizabeth Taylor seems to be managing," Wood said. "Most child actors, as you probably know, fade into obscurity."

He began to learn about her, finding that she was seven years younger than himself, the daughter of Russian immigrants.

"Even before the release of *East of Eden,* Jimmy had already achieved some sort of mythical status in Hollywood," Wood said. "I had never seen anything like it. Without any movie of his being released, he was viewed as a major Hollywood star, right up there with Brando and Monty Clift."

At the time that Wood worked with him and became his friend, she recalled that he was already recovering from his failed romance with Pier Angeli, who had unexpectedly wed the singer, Vic Damone. "He told me that Pier's mother was a control freak, and that she also detested him. She definitely did not want Pier dating him, much less marrying him."

"I was not Italian, and I was not Catholic," Jimmy said. "Both were no-nos in her god damn book of rules."

Wood said she had to babysit with Jimmy on many a moody night as he poured out his deep despair. "He was like a lovesick fool in awful shape. I think he really loved Pier—that is, if he ever really loved anyone. I always had my doubts about that."

"At any rate, he awakened in me the possibility that I might become a serious actress and not just a movie star," she said. "Up to that point, I thought being a movie star was what I wanted. I viewed acting like something you take for granted—you know, like being a girl."

Ironically, when Wood met Jimmy, she had just completed *The Silver Chalice* (1954), in which she'd been cast as Helena, a teenage slave girl who grows up to become the character played by Virginia Mayo. Paul Newman made his unhappy screen debut in this color film.

Jimmy told Wood that he'd been offered the Newman role, but had turned it down after reading the script.

Natalie Wood as a child actress in *Miracle on 34th Street*.

"Paul hated his role, even complaining about his costume," Wood said. "He said it was a cocktail dress in which he showed off his knobby knees and skinny legs."

"I would have looked terrific in that costume," Jimmy bragged. "My legs have been compared to the male equivalent of Betty Grable's."

Jimmy studied the script of *I'm a Fool*. Before he left home, his character, named only as "The Boy," had been told that "clothes make the man." According to his mother, "Put up a good front and the world is yours."

He sets out to prove that is true within a turn-of-the-20th-Century setting, the era of the horse and buggy. With his new suit and brown derby hat, he aspires to be a "swell," hanging out with an upper class crowd, pretending to be one of them.

Wood, cast as Lucy, is deceived by his deception that summer, and he falls in love with her. He deceives her with (false) information about owning a large Victorian house and a big stable of racehorses. The plot had cast him as a dreamer fabricating his background while smoking a twenty-five cent stogie.

Wood and Jimmy performed the dramatic highlight of the teleplay. It took place at a train depot from which she is departing, and he is bidding her farewell. She promises to write to him, but then he realizes that she doesn't know his real name or address. As the train fades into darkness, he cries out, "I'm not Walter," the fake name he'd given her, along with a false address. Then, as an actor, Jimmy followed the clue that Anderson had written into his original story: He "busted out and cried like a kid."

Wood's biographer, Gavin Lambert, wrote about the poignancy of their goodbye scene. "It was beautifully played by both of them. Dean was already the archetypal troubled outsider of this generation and the constantly inventive actor, and Natalie displayed an emotional depth that so many shallow teenage roles had denied her. The ache of loss and missed connections seemed personally resonant for both of them, as the youthful romantics at once eager and wary, as if they suspect that the world may never be theirs."

Biographer Donald Spoto wrote that "Jimmy's attack on the role was properly callow, his protestations of self-importance more sad than pompous, his affection for the girl rightly pathetic in its doomed, precipitous misjudgment."

Eddie Albert claimed that most of the cast, except for Wood, had Broadway experience. "Jimmy's Method acting was new to us, but he did it with a sense of humor. I liked him, and was pleased when *Variety* lauded his role as 'moving and excellent.'"

Jimmy was fascinated and horrified at the dilemma that Albert was facing in his career. At the time, he was married to the Mexican actress known as "Margo." She was shunned for her far-left views and for her friends in the American Communist Party. In the early 1950s, her name appeared on Senator Joseph McCarthy's Red Channels list, which purported to unveil camouflaged Communists in the entertainment industry. These names included Lucille Ball, who had once registered as a communist in the 1930s; playwrights Arthur Miller, Lillian Hellman, and Charlie Chaplin.

"All of us are living in fear," Albert told Jimmy. "Some of my friends have lost their jobs. Dalton Trumbo, probably the most brilliant scriptwriter in Hollywood, is having to submit scripts under a pen name. Some great talents have become waiters or garbage collectors."

"Just when my career was really starting to take off, I find that some of the major studios don't want to use me," Albert said. "I was saved from being completely blackballed as a commie because of my World War II time in Tarawal, where I was viewed as a hero. I was the pilot of a Coast Guard landing craft that rescued almost forty Marines and later saved some thirty other guys, all this while under heavy Jap artillery. My war record has kept me off the blacklist, but damage has been caused."

In the same year that Jimmy co-starred with Albert, he was nominated for an Oscar as a Best Supporting Oscar for his role in *Roman Holiday* (1953) with Gregory Peck and Audrey Hepburn. But it wasn't until his 1960s TV sitcom, *Green Acres,* with Eva Gabor, that Albert became a household word.

Producer Mort Abrahams said he never got to know Jimmy, "because he seemed very standoffish. So I let him be. However, I did introduce him to Ronald Reagan, our host. Reagan came onto the set to watch the final rehearsal so he could introduce it when *I'm a Fool* went on the air."

At that time, Reagan's movie career, more or less, was being assigned to mothballs with a few lackluster films left to him. He'd also married MGM starlet, Nancy Davis, whose MGM career would soon fade into the dustbin of Hollywood history.

Reagan recalled Jimmy as "being an intelligent young actor, with a tendency to brood. He seemed to live only for his work. He was completely dedicated to his craft. He was a shy person, yet could hold a good conversation on many wide-ranging topics."

[After Jimmy's death, I'm a Fool *was re-broadcast, with Reagan again introducing the teleplay, calling it one of the landmarks of Jimmy's short film career.*

"Those of us who worked with Jimmy Dean carry an image of his intense struggle for a goal beyond himself and curiously enough, that's the story of the boy he plays tonight."]

After *I'm a Fool,* Jimmy thought he would never work with Reagan again.

As a surprise to him, he learned that in his next teleplay, he would actually be co-starring with him.

The Dark, Dark Hour

ONSCREEN, JAMES DEAN THREATENS TO ASSASSINATE RONALD REAGAN

Producer Mort Abrahams was not too keen on starring Jimmy again in another episode of *General Electric Theater,* but its director, Don Medford, who had helmed him in *I'm a Fool,* wanted to employ him. Abrahams agreed, especially when Ronald Reagan, the host of the series, said he wanted to appear with the budding young actor. "I think he's going to the top, and you'll be glad you hired him," Reagan told his producer.

With a script by Arthur Steuer as dark as sinister as its title, *The Dark, Dark Hour* was scheduled to be aired on December 12, 1954. "It was hardly a Christmas show," Reagan said.

In fact, it ran into the censors at General Electric. The first version of the script was rejected. "The suits over there thought it portrayed hoodlums in a sympathetic light," Reagan said. "How wrong they were. What we did was remove some of the controversial dialogue and resubmitted it. This time, it was green-lighted."

Its actual filming took place at Republic Studios at 4024 Radford Avenue in North Hollywood. Jimmy was cast once again as a "hepcat hoodlum," in a familiar juvenile delinquent role that by now was almost a James Dean archetype. His partner in crime was Peewee (Jack Simmons). Reagan played a small-town doctor married to an unsympathetic wife, Constance Ford, who had appeared with Jimmy on Broadway in *See the Jaguar.*

Jimmy insisted that Medford cast

THEATER
RONALD REAGAN

Ronald Reagan's millionaire bosses at General Electric helped shift him from a liberal Democrat to an archly conservative Republican.

Simmons as Peewee, whose character had been wounded in a foiled robbery attempt. The hoodlums break into Reagan's house as he's asleep upstairs with Ford. As Jimmy aims a gun at Reagan's head, he demands that the doctor remove a bullet from Peewee.

Reagan replies that he has to call the police, and that he is not qualified to perform the surgery that's required. Jimmy responds that if he doesn't remove the bullet, he'll be killed. Before the teleplay's end, as could be predicted, the doctor overpowers Jimmy as part of an unconvincing climax.

Although this is a scene from a teleplay, not from real life, the hour was, indeed, dark for the future president's career as an actor.

Simmons became one of the most mysterious relationships in Jimmy's life. Perhaps his all time closest friend, Simmons would be with him during the upcoming filming of *Rebel Without a Cause.* Medford was not impressed: "By casting Simmons as Peewee, I think I gave him the wrong impression that he was an actor."

"Reagan was his usual wooden self," Medford said, "but Jimmy brought imagination to his role. When the doctor is out of the room, he turns on the radio and pretends to jitterbug with his dying friend. Not only that, but at one point, he taps on the lens of Simmons' glasses and asks, "Are you home, Peewee?"

Peewee ultimately dies on Reagan's makeshift operating table.

The future president of the United States was host of *The General Electric Theater* from 1954 to 1962. His acting gig with Jimmy occurred during his first year hosting the series, a job that paid him $125,000 a year.

Over dinner one night, Reagan told Jimmy that he almost didn't get the job, and that he was almost desperate, as his bank account was sinking toward zero. "I was the ninth choice. Other actors had already turned it down—Edward Arnold, Kirk Douglas, and Walter Pidgeon, as I recall."

Apparently, Jimmy didn't tell Reagan just how well he knew Pidgeon.

"I used Robert Montgomery as a role model, and I know you were on his series," Reagan said. "He was also president of the Screen Actors Guild before me. I was impressed with his own TV anthology series and wanted to follow in his footsteps. Even my former wife *[a reference to Jane Wyman]* is in negotiations to host her own TV series."

"Right from the beginning, *General Electric Theater* came in number three after *I Love Lucy* and *The Ed Sullivan Show.* My job offer came in the nick of time. I'd been reduced to performing as an emcee at a burlesque show in Vegas. At home, Nancy was manning the vacuum cleaner. But things have turned around for us."

"I think Jimmy was experimenting with his part," Reagan said. "At rehearsals, he would always vary his performance. You never know what he was going to do next. By the time the show was televised, he had arrived at the performance he wanted. As his co-star, I lived in amazement at what I was going to have to respond to. He sure kept me on my toes like a ballet dancer. I'll tell you one thing about Jimmy: I liked him, but he wasn't easy to know. I read in Sidney Skolsky's column that he was undisciplined and irresponsible, but that didn't reflect the dedication I saw in this young actor."

"One of my best friends was Robert Taylor," Reagan said. "Bob told me that Monty Clift, Brando, and now James Dean would soon be replacing us, a bunch of guys who broke into the movies in the 1930s as leading men. He cited not only ourselves, but added Ty Power, Errol Flynn, and an aging Clark Gable to the list of endangered species."

"I was struck by how much Jimmy off camera resembled Jimmy on camera," Reagan said. "He worked hard, even struggled, to perfect his role and his craft as an actor, and I admired him for that. He rehearsed with the same enthusiasm he brought to his actual performance. Most of us just glided through a rehearsal, saving our juice for the shoot. Not Jimmy. He didn't hold back his punches, but took every rehearsal like a boxer in the ring, trying to win every round. He seemed to have boundless energy."

According to his contract with General Electric, Reagan had the right to star in at least six episodes per season. He was allowed to make his own choice of roles he felt suitable for. At first, he'd expressed delight at playing the embattled doctor under siege from Jimmy. However, when General Electric executives watched *The Dark, Dark Hour* on their television sets, they hated it.

"Both Abrahams and I were fired, at least temporarily," Reagan said. "I was allowed to come back." In a press conference, Reagan falsely claimed that he was coerced into accepting the script and the role. "That was a damn lie," Medford claimed. "He asked to do it. The script didn't glorify delinquents. Jimmy was clearly a punk threatening to kill an innocent man. Simmons dies. What kind of glorification was that? If anything, the teleplay showed that crime didn't pay, and could even lead to death or imprisonment."

Reviewers didn't like the show. *Variety* claimed, "Reagan's part is negatively enacted, and Constance Ford as his wife is called upon for illogical action as she fails to understand why her husband, though covered by a gun, doesn't immediately attack the delinquents. This role is played by James Dean, but he has been called upon to overact."

Some viewers found *The Dark, Dark Hour* evocative of the soon-to-be-released *The Desperate Hours* (1955), starring Humphrey Bogart and Fredric March. It, too, depicted an escaped convict breaking into a household and terrorizing a family in ways that were remarkably similar.

Stephen Vaughn later wrote how important appearances on *General Electric Theater* were for Reagan as a politician. "He mastered performing before microphones, cameras, and audiences, as well as how to dramatize events. He gained training in propaganda and public relations."

Another biographer, Anne Edwards, claimed that Reagan also developed people skills while working for General Electric and making speeches around the country at various GE plants.

She noted Reagan's appearances before employees. "The women would come running up to him with mash notes and requests for an autograph. Standing aside, the men would look at Reagan skeptically, making derogatory remarks such as 'I bet he's a fag.' Then, Reagan would talk to the girls just so long before going over to the male employees. When he left, ten or fifteen minutes later, these same men would be slapping him on the back and saying, 'That's the way to go, Ronnie.'"

For decades, *The Dark, Dark Hour* languished in some dusty vault, but resurfaced in 2010. Many in the movie colony were surprised that President of the United States had appeared in a drama with the legendary James Dean, or that the script concerned a threatened assassination and its associations with John Hinckley, Jr.'s, attempt on the life of Reagan. One critic who watched it claimed, "*The Dark, Dark Hour,* starring James Dean and Ronald Reagan, has emerged from some archive of the Eisenhower era. For those of us who weren't around to watch Reagan movies in the late 1930s or 40s, our former president shows he made the right choice when he switched his career from the movies to politics. He was far better suited to the political arena."

***

In 1962, Darwin Porter *[co-author if this biography],* as a guest of novelist James Leo Herlihy, visited the movie set where an adaptation of his novel, *All Fall Down,* was being filmed. Its film

The Desperate Hours (1955). The movie version of this Broadway hit was, indeed, successful with Jimmy's nemesis, Humphrey Bogart, in the lead. Many viewers thought Bogart did it better than Jimmy in his interpretation of a teleplay with a roughly equivalent theme.

script was by William Inge, who was suffering through a powerful crush on Warren Beatty, the movie's lead. His co-stars included Angela Lansbury and Eva Marie Saint.

Inge had transferred his sexual attraction for Jimmy onto Beatty. He was also writing another script for Beatty, *Splendor in the Grass,* which would star Natalie Wood, Jimmy's co-star in *Rebel Without a Cause.*

Constance Ford had only a small role in *All Fall Down.* Over lunch, Ford told Herlihy and Porter that Inge had claimed that if Jimmy had lived, he would be starring in both of the Beatty movies. Not only that, Inge would have preferred for Jimmy—if he had lived—to appear opposite Marilyn Monroe in *Bus Stop* instead of Don Murray.

She also claimed that when she had appeared with Jimmy and Reagan in *The Dark, Dark Hour,* "I hated my role as the doctor's wife. I even got hate mail. I think this rather mean-spirited wife's role prepared me to play the heartless mother of Sandra Dee in *A Summer Place* (1959)."

She said that by the time she and Reagan appeared together on television, "We both realized that we were not going to be bigtime movie stars like Spencer Tracy and Bette Davis. Movie roles were drying up. It was TV or oblivion. But both of us, even back then, thought Jimmy was going to become one of the biggest stars in Hollywood. He had something. If only he'd been a little taller. Of course, a midget like Alan Ladd did okay."

"I never knew what Jimmy was going to do," Ford said. "Once he came to rehearsal wearing only a pair of white jockey shorts. Naturally, I checked out his basket, as his dick was clearly outlined. I saw Reagan doing the same. I'm not suggesting that Reagan has a gay streak in him. But I'm told that straight men, in a shower, like to size up other men to see how they measure up."

"Jimmy and I talked a bit, and he told me he got some real wild fan mail," she said. "Even from old ladies who asked him to wear tighter pants in his next drama."

"People were comparing me to Brando before I really knew who in the hell Brando was," Jimmy told Ford. "I am neither disturbed by the comparison or flattered by it. I don't want to be a good actor. I want to be the best actor there is. Hear that, Marlon Brando? Marlon, are you listening?"

"I liked Jimmy and flirted with him, but he didn't make a pass at me," she said. "Reagan had had a reputation at Warners of seducing many of the starlets, or even stars like Lana Turner before she went over to MGM. But he didn't proposition me. Of course, by the time I met him, he had settled down with Miss Nancy, who hovered over him like a guard dog. She came onto the set looking out for her interests. Perhaps she feared Jimmy would seduce her husband, as I'm sure she'd heard all the rumors that Jimmy worked both sides of the fence."

"I got the impression that Jimmy and that Jack Simmons guy, who played Peewee, were lovers. But I had no direct knowledge. Someone told me that Nancy was following Reagan around to protect him, and Simmons seemed to be watching over Jimmy. Alas, I left the General Electric set with my virginity intact."

The Thief

JIMMY PLAYS AN 18TH CENTURY FRENCH ARISTOCRAT

By January of 1955, Jimmy was already a movie star, but he signed to star in two more teleplays before oblivion. In a rare stint for ABC (he usually worked for NBC or CBS), he took the role of *The Thief* as an episode within *The United States Steel Hour*. It was telecast on January 4, 1955.

Directed by Vincent J. Donehue and produced by John Haggott, *The Thief* was adapted for the TV screen by Arthur Arent. It was the work of the once celebrated French dramatist, Henri Bernstein, and had opened in Paris in 1906, both shocking and delighting the audiences of that day. It would later become a stage hit in both London and New York. Jimmy said "I accepted the role because it was a challenge. I was tired of playing a juvenile delinquent. Why not a nineteen-year-old French aristocrat with me dressed as a stylish fop with an elegant coiffure? A gentle and polite teenager pining over the lost love of my Marie-Louise Voyson (Diana Lynn), who had married an older man. I liked my character's name. Monsieur Fernand Lagarde."

In the teleplay, Lynn was married to Phillipe Voyson (Patric Knowles). Jimmy's parents were Charles and Isabelle Lagarde (Paul Lukas and Mary Astor).

Lagarde *père* hires a house detective to mingle with his other guests, because 12,000 francs have been stolen from the purse in his wife's bedroom. The detective suspects the well-mannered son. He was known to have lost money at the racetrack and was also having an affair with a Parisian actress known for her luxurious tastes. He had only a small allowance.

Jimmy as Fernand admits he's made off with the francs to purchase expensive clothes for his former childhood sweetheart (Lynn).

"How long has this calf-love been going on with this boy?" Knowles asks.

Fernand is banished to Brazil for two years as punishment for being a wayward son.

Jimmy's character is reduced to tears. "I learned to shed a tear on cue," he said. "Maybe not as good as Margaret O'Brien."

Unlike some of Jimmy's other directors, Vincent Donehue survived Jimmy's performance and his direction of the volatile actor. Jimmy told Donehue, "I'm leaving Hollywood and heading back to New York. I don't need Tinseltown. Maybe they don't need me either. But I think they really do. I've got the upper hand. If they want me, the fuckers are going to pay."

James Dean as a member of the pre-revolutionary French aristocracy in *The Thief*

Donehue was known mainly for his theater work, with only an occasional TV credit. He had helmed a Broadway play, *A Trip to Bountiful* (1953), starring Lillian Gish, Jo Van Fleet, and Eva Marie Saint. Jimmy was anxious to hear his impression of Van Fleet, with whom he would later co-star in *East of Eden.* "A strange, mysterious woman," Donehue said. "I don't know her at all."

The same year he directed Jimmy, Donehue was also helming Kim Stanley in *The Traveling Lady* and would, in the year after Jimmy's death, direct Tennessee Williams' *27 Wagons Full of Cotton* (1956) with Maureen Stapleton, whom Jimmy knew.

Donehue recalled his first attempt at directing Jimmy. "We went through his opening scene, and he seemed a bit out of character. I suggested an alternative way of playing Fernand. He looked at me as if I had killed his mother, or at least murdered his father. Then I guess he wanted to shock me and the cast. He went over in front of all of us, took out his cock, and pissed all over the stage floor."

Each of the major stars—Diana Lynn, Mary Astor, Paul Lukas, and Patric Knowles—had very different reactions to Jimmy. Astor was not impressed, and expressed her feelings about him in a memoir, *A Life in Film*: "She wrote: "I found out how hard it was to work with a mumbler when I did *The Thief.* That was before his great success. He was six feet away from me in one scene, and I could barely hear what he was saying. What I could hear seemed to have nothing to do with the script."

"I wasn't up on Astor movies, because I wasn't a fan," Jimmy said. "I'd seen her in *The Maltese Falcon* (1941) when I was a kid, but that was because Bogie was the star. I was told that Astor worked in silent pictures and got screwed by John Barrymore. She was involved in some big scandal back in the 1930s when the contents of her diary were exposed. She had written of her steamy affairs with playwright George Kaufman and actors like Clark Gable and Ronald Colman."

"What people didn't know, other than she was a whore, was that she was an alcoholic. By noon she was drunk, but she concealed it well. I'd heard she had tried to commit suicide with sleeping pills. If I had been there, I would have given her an extra bottle to finish the job."

Lukas agreed with Astor about Jimmy's mumbling: "I didn't know what he was going to say, when he was going to say it, and, once said, what was it? I disliked him even more than Mary did. This son of a bitch is absolutely crazy."

A Budapester, Lukas had won an Oscar for his performance in *Watch on the Rhine* (1943). To take home that Oscar, Lukas had beat out Humphrey Bogart for *Casablanca* and Gary Cooper for *For Whom the Bell Tolls*. At the age of sixteen, Lukas had made his film debut in his native city and had begun a career often cast as a villain. He'd worked with Max Reinhardt before emigrating to the United States to appear in films.

Mary Astor called Jimmy "a mumbler," and he retaliated, claiming that she was "an alcoholic whore."

"I was supposed to be impressed with Lukas' credits," Jimmy said. "I guess he was an OK actor, no great excitement that I saw. How he made it as a leading man is a mystery for the ages. He was a Jew, but I was told he could play a Jew-burning Nazi or a Gestapo agent. He shouldn't have taken that Oscar away from Bogie, who was another son of a bitch like Lukas himself. I guess they're all sons of bitches in Hollywood. Not the females. They're all whores."

An actor from the West Riding district of Yorkshire, Patric Knowles had made his film debut in 1933. Some critics compared his good looks to that of matinee idol Errol Flynn, his rumored lover. The two actors appeared in several pictures together, including *The Charge of the Light Brigade* in 1936, where they formed a tight bond.

They went on to make other movies, including *The Adventures of Robin Hood* (1938). "I was often a straitlaced character stacked against Errol as the adventurer." Knowles later defended Flynn against charges that he had been a Fascist sympathizer and a Nazi spy.

Jimmy bonded with Diana Lynn, finding her "a pert little kitten with an impish quality and a great sense of humor." She had been a child prodigy and a celebrated pianist by the time she was twelve, later becoming a child actress, appearing in pictures such as *The Major and the Minor* (1942) with Ginger Rogers and in Preston Sturges' *The Miracle of Morgan's Creek* (1944). She had also starred in the 1949 *My Friend Irma* with Dean Martin and Jerry Lewis. Jimmy shared information with her about how he had inter-related with them on the set of *Sailor Beware!*

Lynn had also co-starred with Ronald Reagan in his much-ridiculed *Bedtime for Bonzo* (1951), in which both of them had babysat with a chimp who stole the picture from them.

"I flirted with Ronnie," she told Jimmy, "but he didn't stray my way, even though I heard he used to cheat on Jane Wyman during their ill-fated marriage. But with me, he was as clean as a hound's tooth."

"Diana had a dream, and that was to become another Grace Kelly," Jimmy said. "Like so many of us, our dreams don't come true."

When *The Thief* was released, one reviewer pointed out, "A comedy of manners rarely survives its original audience and era. That's why *The Thief* seems so dull, in spite of such stellar performers as that of Paul Lukas, Mary Astor, and James Dean."

In his review, Robert Tanitch wrote: "*The Thief* may have been mechanical, romantic rubbish, but Dean acted the role of 'hero and young imp' with total sincerity within the conventions of the genre and, contrary to what Mary Astor said, he was totally articulate."

In *The Independent,* Gilbert Adair claimed, "James Dean attempts to combine the boyish with the Charles Boyer-ish."

The Unlighted Road ~ JIMMY'S LAST TELEPLAY

Jimmy's career in teleplays came to an inglorious end in May of 1955 when he signed to star in *The Unlighted Road* for CBS's *Schlitz Playhouse of Stars.* It was a thirty-minute thriller in which he was cast as Jeff Latham, a veteran of the Korean War who had been discharged from the U.S. Army.

"I don't know why I signed on to appear in this turkey," he later said. "I didn't know the director (Justus Addiss); I didn't know the producer (William Self), and I didn't know any of my fellow actors."

[The cast included Murvyn Vye, Edgar Stehli, Pat Hardy as the love interest, Voltaire Perkins, and Charles Wagenheim.]

Before flying to the West Coast, he had seen his close friend, Bill Gunn, a young African American actor. Gunn was with Jimmy when he was packing for his trip.

"Jimmy had this foreboding, this fear of flying," Gunn said. "It was like he was anticipating his own death, which would come in September. He told me that planes sometimes 'just fall out of the sky.'"

Before heading to the airport, he went to his closet and gave Dunn his one blue suit. "I have a feeling I won't be needing this anymore."

"But if you're going to be in a plane crash, the undertaker will need to dress you up in this suit," Gunn said.

"Not needed. My body will be so far gone that it won't even make a good-looking corpse."

"God damn it, dude," Gunn said. "You're one morbid kid."

The script for the badly titled *The Unlighted Road* was by Walter C. Brown, with Jimmy cast in the star role.

"At least I got to wear a leather jacket and strike my by now familiar pose with a cigarette dangling from the corner of my mouth."

Drifting from odd job to odd job, Jimmy's character is hired to work in a seedy diner where he meets his love interest, Pat Hardy, cast as Ann Burnett.

James Dean played the unwilling, unlikely (and presumably, beer-drinking) hero of *The Unlighted Road*

In *The Unlighted Road,* Jimmy becomes a pawn in a racketeering scheme, where he discovers that his boss and benefactor is the director of a crime syndicate dealing in stolen goods. One night, having been coerced into transporting contraband alone on an unlit road, he's shot at by what he believes are cops racing after him in hot pursuit. Suddenly, the driver of the car that's chasing him loses control and fatally crashes his car into a tree.

His malevolent boss soon twists this to his advantage. Emphasizing that Jimmy has been associated with a cop killing, he blackmails his hapless victim into continuing a life of crime.

As it turns out, the driver who crashed was not a policeman, but a crook who had lost control of his car because he'd been shot by other gangsters.

Jimmy was paid $2,500 for his appearance in *The Unlighted Road*. "Schlitz didn't have to sell that much brew to pay my salary."

Variety wrote that "Dean provides an interesting, offbeat personality, but underplays so much that his performance loses some of its effectiveness."

Reviewer Robert Tantich claimed, "It was a pretty poor script. There was no suspense and no characterization, only a few good close-ups of Dean's face. Still, such was the demand for anything with him in it that *The Unlighted Road* was shown no less than five times after his death."

Alas, his role as a television star had come to an end. But within months, three of his films would be released "that will make him a star forever," in the words of columnist Louella Parsons.

There was an unexpected consequence from the completion of *The Unlighted Road*. Jimmy found Pat Hardy "sweet, coy, and rather sexy," and began dating her.

"Chalk that one up to one of the big mistakes of my life," he later claimed.

Chapter Nine

James Dean vs.
MARLON BRANDO

Rivals on Screen, Master & Slave After Midnight

Jimmy Threatens to Stab Anyone Who Calls Him
"The Mickey Mouse Marlon Brando"

Brando: "He Was Not a Contender"

James Dean's link to the life and legend of Marlon Brando, his rival and inspiration, began long before the two Method actors had even met.

Nicholas Ray had directed Humphrey Bogart in the 1949 *Knock on Any Door*, casting John Derek in the part that both Ray and Bogie had wanted for Brando. Brando rejected any involvement in *Knock on Any Door*, but Ray was not put off by that refusal. "I want to direct Marlon in his screen debut," he told Bogie and others in Hollywood.

Ray was not the first to envision Brando as Jim Stark, the alienated centerpiece of *Rebel Without a Cause*. William Orr, in charge of talent at Warner Brothers, had worked on the original script. In its first draft, Jim Stark is depicted as a psychopath who is driven to commit a senseless murder by horrendous memories from his childhood.

Later, Orr said, "In New York, I was told that the best actor for the role was one named 'Marlin Brandin,' or was it 'Marlo Binden?' When we looked him up, he was running an elevator at Macy's. He said his correct name was Marlon Brando and that he was from Nebraska. He didn't seem interested in the role at all, but I thought that was just an act."

"Despite his hostility, I lured him to my office," Orr said. "It took some persuasion, but I finally signed him for the role. We even made a screen test with him, but nothing came of it until Nicholas Ray came to Warners and got involved. He was really hot to direct *Rebel*."

A few months later, during the closing weeks of the Broadway version of *A Streetcar Named Desire*, with the understanding that Brando would soon be searching for another gig, Ray arrived with a vastly revised script for Brando's consideration. It was *Rebel Without a Cause*.

The script had derived from a non-fiction work, first published in 1944, by Dr. Robert M. Lindner. Ray was still struggling with the script, but thought that there was enough on paper to intrigue Brando with the role of the reckless, rebellious, and misunderstood Jim Stark. Ray was also aware that time was running out for Brando to realistically impersonate such a youthful character. With every month that passed, he was appearing less and less like a rebellious teen.

At a meeting with Ray, Brando became intrigued with the street gang aspects of the script, and agreed to study it. At around the same time, unknown to Irene Mayer Selznick, producer of the stage version of *A Streetcar Named Desire*, Brando had taken to riding every night with "The Eagles," a tough and rowdy motorcycle gang based in Brooklyn. Perhaps he was rehearsing for his future role in *The Wild One* (1953).

Details about the logistics of how he hooked up at regular intervals with this tightly knit group of hoods were provided by Brando's friend, Carlo Fiore.

He claimed that he had introduced Brando to the gang leader, Tony Medina, who at first was skeptical about allowing Brando inside his clique. Medina changed his mind, however, after Brando bought him one of the flashiest and most expensive motorcycles in New York. As additional "tribute," Brando also became a steady supplier of young girls for members of the gang.

As preparation for the milieu he wanted to depict on film, Ray was eager to learn all he could about gangs, and Brando asked and won approval from Medina to allow him to ride with The Eagles. Apparently, at no point was Medina informed that Ray was a film director. Later, in Hollywood, Ray would manage to hook himself up with a different gang, this one based in L.A.

One night at a location in New York State, the exact spot not known, Ray witnessed an extraordinary test of daring. During a game of "chicken," competing members of The Eagles raced their motorcycles toward the edge of a cliff. Both of the young men managed to stop before they, with their bikes, plunged off the edge. Ray was so inspired by this that he later incorporated it into *Rebel*, using cars instead of motorcycles.

Ray later said that Brando, too, had wanted to play chicken that night, but that he had persuaded him not to. "It's too risky," Ray said. "If you do, there might be another actor replacing you as Stanley Kowalski on stage tomorrow night."

Based on chronic problems with its script, *Rebel Without a Cause* simply did not get made in 1949, and it would not become the vehicle for Brando's screen debut.   But when the cameras rolled on the version of *Rebel* that was released, with fanfare, in 1955, it was James Dean who was cast in the star role.   By then, Brando was indeed far too old for the part. Ray later admitted, however, that at least some elements that made it into the final script, as interpreted by Jimmy, had been inspired by what he perceived as Brando's "personal character."

Fiore later remembered attending a screening of *Rebel Without a Cause* with Brando in 1955. "Bud sat through the entire film with a stone face, not saying a word," Fiore said. "After the show, we drove to a drive-in hamburger joint, where Bud ordered cheeseburgers with 'the works.' At this point he still hadn't told me what he thought of *Rebel*. Finally, the suspense was killing me. Losing my cool, I asked him, 'Well, what did you think of Dean? That kid is definitely living in your shadow.'"

"Marlon turned and looked at me like he didn't even know who James Dean was," Fiore recalled. "He didn't say anything at first. Finally, he mumbled, 'I plan to fuck Natalie Wood. She's now the first on my list of possible conquests in Hollywood.'"

"You've already fucked Dean," Fiore chided him. "Why not Sal Mineo? I hear he's gay as a goose."

"Yeah, that Mineo boy might get lucky too."

"I hear that big tit Jayne Mansfield was originally tested for the role of Judy before it went to Wood. Have you had her yet? Or is she on your waiting list?"

"Mansfield is too blonde for me," Brando said. "Besides I can have the real Marilyn anytime I want her. Why go for mock turtle soup when you can have the real turtle in the stew pot?"

"Good point," Fiore said.

Nothing else was ever said between them about either James Dean or *Rebel Without a Cause.*

Tough, hard to influence, and ferociously independent: Marlon Brando.

***

In 1949, after an extended visit to Paris, Brando flew back to New York, where he ignored literally dozens of offers from Hollywood for starring roles in various films. *[His agent, Jay Kanter, mailed the scripts to him, but learned, "He didn't read any of them."]*

Instead, he decided to make a public appearance at the Actors Studio. There, he was invited to say a few words. After his brilliant performances in both the stage and screen versions of *A Streetcar Named Desire,* for which he'd been nominated for an Oscar, Brando was idolized by most of the actors in Lee Strasberg's acting classes.

Marlon Brando in *The Wild One,* a film that made black leather, motorcycle drag, and hints of S&M hot, hip, and fashionable before anyone else figured it out.

By then, Jimmy had reconciled with Strasberg, having forgiven the acting coach for his harsh critique of his interpretation of *The Matador.*

Brando's "few words" turned into a long, drawn-out speech about stage acting versus screen acting.

At the back of the room sat a young man slouched down in his seat, so much so that his ass was hardly touching the bottom of the chair. Throughout Brando's speech, the young man stared at him "so intently I felt my skin burning," Brando later told Bobby Lewis, one of the founders of Actors Studio, "I don't think I've ever been looked at that way before," Brando said, "and I've been evaluated by the best of them, male and female."

From time to time, Brando would steal a glance at the young man, whom he found broodingly handsome, with a severe intensity combined with an appealing vulnerability. Brando immediately pegged the aspirant actor as a homosexual.

"He looked at me with such a childlike sincerity," Brando later told Lewis, "that I knew it must be love. What else?"

After the session, and after the other students had filed out of the room, Jimmy remained glued to his seat, still slouching, and still staring at Brando. As Brando approached him, he rose to his feet and extended his hand.

"I'm your greatest fan," he said to Brando. "Someday I want to become an actor just like you. Your style, everything."

As he said that, Brando continued holding onto Jimmy's hand, not returning it. "You can hold my hand all night long if you want to."

"Indeed I shall," Brando said. "Or should I have said, 'Indeed, I will.' I always confuse will and shall."

"I'm confused about a lot of things," Jimmy said. "Very confused. But not confused in my admiration for you."

"Since you seem to know who I am, who might you be?" Brando asked.

"James Dean. But you can call me Jimmy. Born in Marion, Indiana on February 8, 1931. Died April 17, 1967."

"You know the date of your death?" Brando asked. "How remarkable."

"I've always had this uncanny ability to predict deaths," Jimmy said.

"Do you know when I'm going to die?" Brando asked.

"You'll die on December 24, 2010," Jimmy said. "A very old man."

"Do you really plan to die so young?" Brando asked.

"I sure do," Jimmy said, snickering. "My motto is: Live fast, die young, and leave a beautiful corpse."

"If that's your intention," Brando said, "I'm sure you'll accomplish that lofty goal."

He stood looking into Jimmy's eyes for a long minute, maybe two minutes, maybe a lot more. As he would later recall the moment to Lewis, Brando said he wasn't certain of the time. Finally, he spoke to Jimmy. "I hope you understand what I'm about to do. I sometimes do this with men. I'm going to take you in my arms and give you a long, deep kiss. It may be the first time in your life you've ever been kissed, really kissed. My kiss will be just the beginning of a lot of other deep kisses that I'm going to give you in the months ahead." As he moved toward the young actor, Brando got so close he could smell Jimmy's breath. "All your dreams and fantasies about me are about to come true!"

***

In his autobiography, Brando concealed his romantically tortured involvement with Jimmy, suggesting that he met his young admirer—six years his junior—much later than he actually did. Lewis often saw Brando and Jimmy together during the winter of 1951.

At the time, Jimmy was being partially supported by Rogers Brackett, who wanted, despite Jimmy's resistance, a monogamous relationship. Perhaps to punish him, Jimmy described in intimate detail his various affairs with both men, including Brando, and women.

Alec Wilder and Stanley Haggart were each privy to the sexual involvement of Brando and Jimmy, as were Tennessee Williams and his lover, Frank Merlo. Later, each of those men, with additional information supplied by Lewis, relayed more or less the same accounts of the long-suppressed relationship between Jimmy and Brando.

In his autobiography, *Songs My Mother Taught Me*, Brando falsely claimed that he had been introduced to Jimmy by Elia Kazan on the set of *East of Eden*. According to the autobiography, Jimmy told Brando that he was "not only mimicking my acting but also what he believed was my lifestyle." In that statement, Brando was accurate. Only the date and place of the introduction were wrong.

Brackett claimed that according to Jimmy's own account, Brando took him back to his apartment and seduced him on the afternoon of their first meeting at Actors Studio. "I got to make love to Brando," Jimmy claimed, "which is something I've been longing to do ever since I first heard about him."

"He was completely in charge of our love-making," Jimmy revealed to Brackett. "He told me what he wanted, and I went along for the ride." Without Jimmy specifically saying so, it was obvious that Brando had sodomized his new young friend.

As in previous relationships, when Brando had walked the streets and attended clubs and cafes with Clifford Odets or Leonard Bernstein, he was soon "spotted everywhere with Jimmy Dean," claimed the actress and acting coach, Stella Adler. "I had many long talks with the two of them."

"They were definitely a couple," Wilder said. "Of course, the words 'sexual fidelity' would be unknown in each of their vocabularies. Jimmy and I used to sit and talk for hours in my room at the Algonquin Hotel. He kept me abreast of the affair. I really believe that Jimmy fell in love with Brando that year. As for Brando, I don't think he ever loved Jimmy. I met Brando only three times, and each time he was with Jimmy. In my opinion, Brando was in love with Brando."

"Jimmy tried to dress exactly like Brando," Wilder said. "With one notable exception. To keep warm in the winter, he wore a black bullfighter's cape slung

316

over his shoulders."

Jimmy frequently visited Stanley Haggart, especially when he was broke. Haggart at the time was the leading art director in New York for television commercials, and Jimmy wanted him to use his influence to get work for him. Brackett, too, helped Jimmy find work. But he would often disappear for weeks at a time, not returning at night to Brackett's apartment. "This would seriously piss off Rogers," in the words of Wilder, his most intimate friend. "When Rogers cut him off from jobs, Jimmy would go over to Stanley's."

"Jimmy never had any money in those days," Haggart said. "Sometimes I would lend him fifty dollars with no expectation of ever seeing the money again. Believe it or not, fifty dollars could actually buy something in those days. Even when Jimmy had less than two dollars in his pocket, Brando wouldn't lend him a cent. Jimmy said he felt that Brando deliberately wanted him lean and mean on the streets, looking for a handout."

Haggart said that Jimmy never phoned in advance before dropping by his apartment in the East Fifties. "He just arrived on the doorsteps. He always wanted me to make tapioca pudding for him. It was sort of a comfort food for him. He never came to see me unless he was depressed or broke. His manners were horrible. He'd put muddy feet up on my new sofa and would flick ashes on my Oriental carpet, never bothering to use an ashtray. He talked frequently about Brando and how frustrated he was in the relationship. I got the impression that Jimmy was engaged in a cat-and-mouse affair with Brando, with Brando being the cat, of course. Brando seemed to be toying with Jimmy for his own amusement. I think Brando was sadistically using Jimmy, who followed him around like a lovesick puppy with his tongue wagging."

"I sensed a terrible loneliness in Jimmy," Brackett said. "Whatever he wanted or needed, I felt I could not really provide, even though he shared my bed on many a winter's night. It was obvious to me that he preferred Brando's arms to mine. Even though he must have known that Jimmy was hopelessly in love with him that winter, Brando insisted on rubbing Jimmy's nose into his other affairs. Sometimes Brando would invite Jimmy over to watch as he fucked some pickup from the street. Jimmy told me that he'd spent many a night at Brando's watching like a *voyeur* as he made love to someone else. Jimmy claimed that Brando often invited him for 'sloppy seconds.' It wasn't a very happy relationship for Jimmy, and I was as jealous as a bitch in heat, because at least momentarily I'd fallen—and fallen big—for Jimmy. When Brando was out on one of his many dates, Jimmy would often stalk him, even following him home. On many a night Jimmy would stand beneath Brando's apartment house, looking up at his bedroom window as the lights went out, wanting to be in that bedroom himself. One very cold morning, Brando came downstairs in his pajamas and invited Jimmy, shivering in the cold, to come upstairs with him. But, I fear, those acts of kindness were the exception—not the rule."

Haggart cited occasional acts of generosity on the part of Brando. "When he found Jimmy half starved, Brando would sometimes invite him to a steak dinner in the Village. But these were very rare occasions. When Jimmy had no money at all, he told me that he would consent to blow-jobs in a men's toilet in Central Park to earn a few bucks. When he got money, he lived on chocolate milkshakes for energy. He claimed he could survive on a daily intake of milkshakes, although he complained of a runny stool because of the lack of solids in his diet. I fed him when he came to me, trying to give him some red meat and a garden salad, followed invariably by my tapioca pudding."

"Jimmy often spoke to me about his dreams of future stardom in Hollywood," Wilder said. "He vowed that he was going to keep imitating Brando in his acting style. Then, when he actually got to Hollywood, he wanted to star in all of the movies Brando turned down. 'I'm a natural for Brando's rejects,' he told me. Even though I urged him to forge his own style as an actor, he never listened."

One night at about two o'clock in the morning, Jimmy arrived at my apartment," Brackett said. "I hadn't seen him in days. He begged me to take him to an all-night diner where he could eat chili and beans like he used to when a boy in Indiana. Reluctantly I got dressed and went to the diner, even though I detest chili. He told me he was giving up his dream of a career as an actor. He said that Brando had told him that he could never make it as an actor and that he had no talent. Jimmy was sobbing between the beans. He claimed that his relationship had deteriorated and that Brando didn't want to see him again."

Ironically, at the time, Jimmy was hoping to land the role of Nels in the TV series, *I Remember Mama*. The same role, in the stage play, of course, had brought acclaim to Brando.

Back from the diner, Brackett felt that Jimmy was coming unglued. "He went to get his bongo drums. He always kept most of his possessions in my apartment. Back in the living room, he wanted to play the drums for an hour or two. At one point he pulled off all his clothing. I was shocked to see that he had burns on his chest. Jimmy told me that they were from cigarette burns by Brando. I was practically ready to call the police on this brutal son-of-a-bitch until Jimmy told me that he'd asked Brando to do that to him. For the first time in my life, I came to realize what a masochist Jimmy was—or was becoming."

While filming *The Last Resort [the film adaptation of Darwin Porter's best-selling novel,* Butterflies in Heat] in Key West in the 1970s, actress Barbara Baxley said that she had known both Jimmy and Brando during the Fifties.

According to Baxley, "I remember seeing Brando at a party in Greenwich Village. He knew that I was Jimmy's friend. I think these two guys had only known each other for a few weeks. Aware of our friendship, he came up to me. 'You'd better get your boy to a psychiatrist right away,' he told me. 'He's an emergency case. One crazed sicko! If you only knew what he wants me to do to him.'"

Already aware of the S&M implications of the Brando/Dean relationship, Baxley cautioned, "You don't have to participate if you don't want to. You could just walk away."

"That's just what I'm going to do with you right now," Brando said before retreating to the other end of the room.

"Self-destructive or not, Jimmy continued to see Brando even though I begged him not to," Baxley claimed.

Soon, word reached many of Brando's associates in Hollywood that he was having an affair with "The Mickey Mouse Marlon Brando," a description that Jimmy hated among all others. He still carried around a dangerous knife and on occasion, he'd threaten to kill whoever used that Mickey Mouse reference in front of him..

When shooting began in Hollywood of Brando's involvement in *Julius Caesar* (1953), Brando was rooming with his agent, Jay Kanter. When the Mexican actress, Movita Castenada, flew in, Kanter rented a house for Brando and his on-again, off-again "South of the Border" mistress in Laurel Canyon. But Brando was rarely at home, continuing with a wide number of affairs.

[Older than Brando, Castenada, or "Mo" as he called her, would become his second wife in 1960. She'd already had numerous affairs, beginning in 1935, when she had appeared with Clark Gable during his filming of Mutiny on the Bounty. *She later had an affair with Errol Flynn. She had once been married to Jack Doyle, the Irish heavyweight boxer and singer.*

Jimmy met "Mo" only once, when he'd visited Brando on the set of Desirée (1954), that cardboard costume drama which featured Brando as Napoléon. Jimmy talked to her briefly before she excused herself. "I've got to go to Marlon's dressing room. He called me here today so he can 'feck' me during the lunch break."

Before leaving, she said, "You're a cute kid. Young. I like that. Why don't you come over some night for one of my fabulous Mexican dinners?" She gave him her phone number, but he never called her.

Instead, he went to lunch with London-born Jean Simmons, who was starring op-

Movita Castenada: Fiery tempered, and with a gift for seducing A-list movie stars

319

posite Brando in Desirée. *He told the lovely star that Castenada had made a pass at him. "I'm not into mothers this year," he said. "Marlon can have his gypsy. I heard this Movita bitch was turning tricks when I was four years old."*

Before he left the set that day, he made a pass at Simmons, who rejected his advances. "I'm sure I'm missing out on something good. Perhaps I'll change my mind. Give me a raincheck."]

***

As the director of *Julius Caesar* (1953), Joseph Mankiewicz had assembled an all-star cast. Commenting wryly on the romantic imbroglios associated with his handsome male lead, Mankiewicz said, "Brando had his own star cast coming and going. I'll name them: Greer Garson, Pier Angeli, Rita Moreno, James Dean, Marilyn Monroe on occasion. Even Stewart Granger. Brando even let John Gielgud blow him."

Brando confided to Mankiewicz, "I don't want any of the motley crew I'm dating to pin me down." The director was astonished to hear such a distinguished group of actors and actresses referred to as a motley crew. "If a person wants an affair with me, he or she will have to learn my ground rules. I don't want to sound immodest, but I am, after all, Marlon Brando, a fucking movie star. That means I can have any star or starlet in Hollywood I more or less want. I can't really remember ever getting turned down. In relationships, I do the turning down. I'm the one who walks. No one walks out on me!"

Though stating that, he presented a different point of view to his producer, John Houseman. "Marlon is working his ass off," Mankiewicz claimed. "And it's a very talented and much fucked ass."

During the first week of shooting, Houseman showed up frequently on the set. Although originally, it had been his idea to cast Brando as Marc Antony, he later confided his bitter disappointment with Brando's acting ability to Mankiewicz. "I think our boy is awed by all this talent, especially Gielgud's," Houseman claimed. "He's a stuttering bumpkin only remotely acquainted with the English language."

Not wanting to interfere with Mankiewicz's direction, Gielgud modestly sought and obtained the director's permission to tutor Brando in Shakespearean speech patterns at night.

When Gielgud departed from the set, Mankiewicz turned to Houseman and said, "That British faggot wants to get into Marlon's blue jeans. Or at least see what's under the toga. I think he views these upcoming lessons as his golden opportunity. Gielgud, like that Dean boy, has developed a lovesick crush on Marlon."

***

In the year that *Julius Caesar* was released, Stanley Kramer offered Brando the lead in *The Wild One* (1953).

Brando told anybody who was interested that he'd turned down the film script when it was first offered. "I told Kramer I wasn't doing any motorcycle movies that year. 'Get Jimmy Dean,' I told him. 'He also rides a bike.'" As the script was continually weakened by mandates from the censors at the Breen office, Brando grew more and more disillusioned with the movie, becoming increasingly inarticulate, finally resorting to mumbling.

Finally, Kramer prevailed in getting Brando to change his mind. *The Wild One* became the original motorcycle film, a cult movie for young bikers, who imitated Brando's leather jacket and blue jeans.

As a fellow motorcycle rider, Jimmy followed suit, appearing on the street looking like one of Brando's bikers, even like Brando himself except for his size.

One fan later claimed that Brando's "sideburns, overt sexuality, and grooving to the jukebox invented the newly emerging Elvis Presley, whose name at first sounded like that of a Presbyterian deacon."

***

Although he loudly and frequently proclaimed that he hated parties, Brando was seen at quite a few of them, especially those in Greenwich Village during the making of *On the Waterfront* (1954). Norman Mailer threw a party and invited Brando, who showed up with Rita Moreno. "If a woman were married, you could almost guarantee it that Marlon would make a pass at her, even with Miss Moreno looking on. My wife was no exception."

One night at a party in Brooklyn, Brando brought as his "date," James Dean.

"How Brando could later proclaim he didn't meet Dean until he was starring in *East of Eden* for Kazan is beyond me," said Jimmy Schauffer, an out-of-work actor at that Brooklyn party. "All of us along Broadway knew that Dean and Brando were carrying on. It was the worst-kept secret. From what I observed that night, Brando was definitely in charge of the relationship. If he wanted something, perhaps a drink, he sent Dean to get it. When Brando was ready to go, he got up and without saying a word Dean tagged along like a puppydog after its master. We'd also heard rumors that there was more than a little S&M in that relationship. Guess who the S was?"

***

When Jimmy reached Hollywood, he found Clark Gable was no longer king, having surrendered the throne to Brando.

Soon, the press was linking Jimmy's *persona* to the already established image of Brando. *Photoplay* infuriated Jimmy by running their pictures side by side under the headline *THE BOY WHO'D LIKE TO BE BRANDO.* The columnist Sidney Skolsky adored Marilyn Monroe, but rarely had anything good to say about Jimmy. "The best way to describe him is to say that he is Marlon Brando seven years ago."

In a rare interview with Bob Thomas, the AP reporter, Jimmy claimed, "When a new actor emerges, he's always compared to a more established star. Once, Brando was compared to Monty Clift. Even John Barrymore was compared to the great Edwin Booth. Hell, let them compare me to W.C. Fields. Perhaps if I dressed in drag, I might be taken for Mae West herself."

"That boy sure had a wicked sense of humor," Thomas said. "I printed only part of the quote. Mae didn't like men dressing in drag to impersonate her."

In another column, Thomas wrote, "Dean told me that he was convinced that Brando hated him. Brando, however, indicated to me that this was not the case."

Photographer Ray Schatt in *James Dean: A Portrait,* wrote: "At times, he seems obsessed with Brando. Occasionally, for no apparent reason, he would begin quoting from *A Streetcar Named Desire.* One time, during a discussion of Method acting, he took off his shirt and ripped his undershirt to shreds, yelling, STELLA!' in an imitation of Brando as Stanley Kowalski calling for his wife."

Author Randall Riese claimed, "Granted, the similarities between Marlon Brando and James Dean were obvious. They both had an affinity for mumbling and motorcycles. They both played the recorder and bongo drums. They both belonged to the unruly school of fashion. They both wore scowls on their faces, boots on their feet, and *attitude* in their jeans. They were offered the same type of roles. Brando not only turned down *Rebel Without a Cause* back in 1947, but he also rejected Dean's role in *East of Eden*. Finally, and most significantly, they were both discovered by Elia Kazan."

William Zinser in *The New York Herald Tribune* in March of 1955 wrote: "James Dean inevitably will be compared to Marlon Brando, for Kazan stamped him with the same hesitant manner of speech, the same blind groping for love and security that he gave Brando in *On the Waterfront.*"

Christine White, who for a time had had a romantic involvement with Jimmy, later claimed that, "Jimmy was fixated on Marlon for a while. I was going to a party where Jimmy was not invited. He begged me to take him, but I didn't think the host would go for that. When I got home, Jimmy bled me for the most minute details about what Marlon did, what he said, how he walked, what he drank, and how he behaved."

Reporters and, in time, biographers, soon picked up on Jimmy's fascination with Brando. But they never knew, or at least didn't write about, the sexual link between the two lovers and rivals.

Charles Higham, in *Brando, The Unauthorized Biography,* wrote, "Jimmy fell in love with Marlon after viewing *The Wild One* and besieged him with phone calls."

Higham got it wrong, as he sometimes did. Jimmy was in love with Brando, but long before either of them ever heard of *The Wild One.* Not only that, Jimmy didn't have to pester Brando with phone calls: On many occasions, if he wanted to reach out to him, all he had to do was turn his head toward the face resting on the pillow beside him. Of course, Higham, and so many others, were misled by Brando's own statements about Dean in his autobiography, *Songs My Mother Taught Me.*

"Dean was never a friend of mine," Brando wrote. *[Perhaps not, Marlon, but he was your lover.]* "He had an *idée fixe* about me. Whatever I did, he did. He was always trying to get close to me. He used to call me up. I'd listen to him talking on the answering service. Asking for me, leaving messages. But I never spoke up. I never called him back." *[Really, Marlon, really...]*

Bill Gunn, Jimmy's African American friend, tried to put comparisons to Brando in perspective: "The *funk* of Jimmy was important. He bridged the jump we made, clear from the 1950s to the 1970s. Sure, he probably watched Brando and took things from him, but imitating someone is also a way to become yourself through an endorsement of yourself."

Gunn did admit that Brando and Jimmy were alike in one respect. "Both of them liked to play games. I was often the victim of one of Jimmy's practical jokes. Brando also liked to pull a 'fuck-you-stunt,' such as scratching his ass and pulling buggers from his nose at the same time."

"As an actor, I had no desire to imitate Brando," Jimmy claimed to a hometown reporter in Fairmount, Indiana. "I don't attempt imitation. Nevertheless, it is very difficult not to be impressed with Brando, not to carry the image of a highly successful actor. But that's as far as it goes. I feel within myself there are expressions just as valid, and I'll have a few years to develop my own style."

Of course, his prediction for his future did not happen.

Lee Strasberg of the Actors Studio weighed in with his view: "Brando and Dean are two totally different kinds of personalities. What was common at that time was the characters they played. I don't care what the authors may have intended, they brought onto the stage what we call the anti-hero, the person who cannot express himself, the person who is not a hero in the ordinary sense of the word."

Film historian John Francis Kreidl noted, "Jimmy arrived in Hollywood when the film industry was desperately struggling to stave off competition from the little black box. Americans were staying at home and watching television instead of going to the movies around twice a week, as they had before." At Warner Brothers, the search was on for the box office idols of the latter 1950s, and the studio focused on Jimmy as one of their best hopes for stardom. "Brando was getting a little long in the tooth," said one studio executive, "no longer convincing as a young rebel."

Robert Tysl, a Hollywood insider, claimed, "The campaign staged by Warners to brand Dean with Brando's old image was obvious and undeniable."

At parties, Jimmy became known for his devastating impressions of Brando. Not to be outdone, Brando at gatherings performed his impression of Jimmy. Hedda Hopper was at one party to witness his act. "If Jimmy had walked in and seen Brando's impression, he would flee from the camera forever and a day."

When Jimmy heard what Brando was doing, he retaliated. He topped Brando's act by doing his impression of Brando as Charlie Chaplin.

Hopper's rival, columnist Louella Parsons, saw Jimmy's Chaplin act. "I laughed so hilariously, "she said, "I pissed in my bloomers. I hadn't had such fun since I attended this fancy gathering where Mae West let a fart so big that it smothered Los Angeles in smog for two days and nights."

As Jimmy moved deeper into Hollywood, he increasingly resented the constant barrage of comparisons to Brando. When introduced to people, he warned them, "Don't give me that shit that I remind you of Marlon Brando. There's one god damn difference between us. I love bullfights, and he views them as cruelty to animals. I love a blood sport—the bloodier the better for my tastes." He still carried that vicious-looking knife he'd purchased in New York.

Warned in advance, gossips took to comparing Jimmy to Brando, but only behind his back.

Director Elia Kazan frankly admitted, "I do not like James Dean. He is obviously sick in the head. I don't know what is the matter with him. He got crazier as we moved ahead with our shooting schedule for *East of Eden.* But I'd rather not talk about him. He was not like Brando. Dean was a cripple inside. He was so sick and so twisted. Brando is not sick. He is merely troubled."

"Brando was clearly Dean's hero during the filming of our movie," Kazan said. "Everyone knew that. He dropped his voice to a cathedral hush when he spoke of Brando. I invited Brando to come to our set to meet Dean and to enjoy some hero worship." Kazan seemed completely ignorant that months earlier, Jimmy and Brando had become lovers, and that Jimmy had long been intimate with what the older actor called "my noble tool."

During Brando's visit to the set, neither he nor Jimmy gave any clues that they knew each other as David had known Bathsheba.

The gossipy author, Truman Capote, had been introduced to Jimmy through their mutual friend, Tennessee Williams. Around the time of Jimmy's death, he also interviewed Brando extensively in Japan when he was making *The Teahouse of the August Moon (1956)*.

Truman Capote insisted that "Marlon confessed everything to me in Tokyo."

He told Tennessee and others, "If there's one thing I know, it's dick. Neither Brando nor Dean were in the category of Milton Berle, Forrest Tucker, or John Ireland, not to mention Rock Hudson. But they performed well with what they had. I promised to write great roles for both of them. Tennessee used that promises as a seduction technique. Why not Little Me?"

"I also knew the deep dark secret they were hiding," Capote claimed. "Brando and Dean were lovers. Lovers isn't exactly the right word. From what I saw, there was no love there, only sex."

"Actually, Jimmy and Brando were sexually attracted to each other, but were also rivals—and at times, they positively seemed to hate each other," said William Bast. "It was the sort of relationship that Rhett Butler and Scarlett O'Hara had in *Gone With the Wind*. I watched as they glided through Hollywood pretending they were only casual acquaintances. They fooled a lot of people, mainly movie reporters."

Gary Carey wrote a biography of Marlon Brando, *The Only Contender*, in which he claimed, "James Dean was the most flagrant and successful of the Brando imitators. A surprising number of people who otherwise have good taste prefer Dean to Brando."

***

In 1954, Brando and Jimmy's relationship became one of the murkiest and most tangled romantic dramas offscreen in Hollywood, evocative of the steamy and contentious romantic roundelays of Arlene Dahl, Lana Turner, Lex Barker, and Fernando Lamas.

"What an embroglio," Bast said. "The convoluted affairs going on were a tangled whirlpool of churning, conflicting emotions, betrayals, and sexual attraction with both gay and straight sex."

The cast he was referring to included Brando, Jimmy, Pier Angeli, Ursula Andress, Vic Damone, and starlet Pat Hardy, with whom Jimmy had co-starred in his final teleplay, *The Unlighted Road.*

Brando dated both Andress and Angeli, both actresses also becoming involved with Jimmy. In fact, he once proclaimed Angeli as the love of his life.

Pat Hardy was also dating singer Vic Damone, who started dating Angeli when she was also sleeping with both Brando and Jimmy (not at the same time). Eventually, she would drop both actors and marry Damone.

Louella Parsons referred to it as "the love romp. Too bad I can't print all the gory details."

* * *

Shortly after Jimmy's death in 1955, Brando was offered two separate gigs; a film role in which he would impersonate Jimmy; and an offer to narrate a documentary about Jimmy's life and career. Ultimately, he rejected both possibilities. But during the time he was debating how to play it, he confided in Truman Capote, saying, "This glorifying of Dean is all wrong...he wasn't a hero. He was just a little lost boy trying to find himself. If a documentary ever got made, it should teach the truth about Dean so that his fans will stop worshipping him. I would cooperate in a film that told the truth, but neither of the scripts did that. They were a fantasy version of Dean. I see clearly what was happening. A cult was forming around the *faux* memory of this kid. He was not some mythical hero, just another pathetic figure wandering the sewers of Hollywood. At times, Dean was a madman with severe psychological problems. We should not glorify his insanity but expose it. In my view, Mr. James Dean should be placed in a back garage of long-abandoned vehicles."

Later, as the years went by, Brando named some other male stars of the time "who should join Jimmy Dean in the forgotten and dusty vaults of yesteryear: Robert Wagner, Tab Hunter, Jeffrey Hunter, Troy Donahue, Audie Murphy, George Hamilton, Peter Lawford, Sal Mineo, Ryan O'Neal, Robert Stack, Robert Hutton, Michael Wilding, and Gig Young, to name only a few. You might catch one of these jerks of yesterday on the late, late show if you're very, very drunk."

Guess who? A notorious example of Photoshopping that went through the internet to blogsites and commentators around the world. Many viewers thought it was authentic.

Chapter Ten

JIMMY TAKES MANHATTAN

Enraged, He Denounces Everyone at the Actors Studio

as a "Daisy Chain Faggot"

JIMMY GETS DOWN WITH EARTHA KITT, TRUMAN CAPOTE, A
MALE MUSICIAN IN HARLEM, "THE ONLY VIRGIN LEFT IN NYC,"
AND MANY, MANY OTHERS

Stopping Traffic, He Poses Nude as Adonis

on a Manhattan Sidewalk

Tennessee Williams claimed, "Long before *[the noted stage and opera director]* Frank Corsaro had to deal with the emotional demands of Bette Davis during the stage version of my play, *The Night of the Iguana* (1961), he was broken in by James Dean. Jimmy was a dynamo of human angst, and for a while, Corsaro was his mentor. Jimmy always created chaos on the dusty trail he left behind. In fact, if I ever write a play about him, I'll call it *Blossoms in the Dust.* But maybe that's too close to the title of an old Greer Garson movie..."

In June of 1953, Corsaro would cast Jimmy in *The Scarecrow.* Before that, he prevailed on Jimmy to return for more lessons at the Actors Studio, despite his unhappy memories associated with Lee Strasberg's savage attack on him, with the entire class watching, based on his interpretation of *The Matador.*

For months, Corsaro had been closely connected to Jimmy, pouring cultural enlightenment into his animated dialogues with him. Often, they spent quiet evenings together reading from the masterpieces of world literature, talking, and playing recordings of classical music. "He liked me because I was Italian," Corsaro said. "He told me I was very smart and a great director. We read poems together, listening to Italian opera. Those nights with me heightened his awareness. He was not well educated except for talking about *The Little Prince.* I think he'd read it fifty times. Sometimes, when reading a passage from it to me, he would burst into tears."

Jimmy's friend, John (aka Jonathan) Gilmore claimed that Jimmy intensely disliked not only Strasberg but the entire board of directors at the Actors Studio. Jimmy denounced Strasberg as an ugly man who kept no mirrors in his apartment so he would not have to confront his own image. He also made the claim that his fellow actors "either fuck or suck off" the Actors Studio's board members. "They don't like me, and I don't like them. Every time I hear Strasberg speak, nothing but shit comes out of his mouth. He's full of stodgy platitudes, and he farts out smelly opinions about acting."

"Strasberg's ideas are nothing more than ill-informed personal opinions," Jimmy said. "To quote Nietzche: 'It isn't that they are true, but only they're held up as being true.' Mostly, they are just so much hot air."

Yet according to Gilmore, "Despite those negative opinions, on other occasions he would express high praise for Strasberg."

John Stix, the head of the Board of Directors at Actors Studio, heard that Jimmy was going around New York claiming that his fellow board members "were nothing but a bunch of daisy-chain faggots."

According to Stix, "Jimmy's self-indulgence was not tolerated by Lee, even after his return to the studio. In class exercises, he did not allow Jimmy's defenses to protect him against criticism that all actors face. Jimmy disliked everyone there, except Kim Stanley and Geraldine Page, who babied him. They allowed more margins for his self-indulgences than anyone else did."

Eventually, after days spent summoning his courage and building up his walls of defense, Jimmy returned to the Actors Studio. At first, from a seat in the back row, he watched the proceedings, looking sullen. Gradually, he emerged from his cocoon.

In dialogues with Page and Kim Stanley, Strasberg said, "The Method, as you know, teaches an actor to utilize every emotion from his own life in creating a character on stage. Dean becomes confused about who he really is and the character he is playing. He approaches acting on a more personal level that the Method suggests. He tries to become in private the character he is portraying on stage."

Yet Page and Stanley recognized what Jimmy was trying to do, even if Strasberg didn't. "Lee was still hung up on the Method's emphasis on an actor relying on motivation and sense memory," Stanley said. "That had one major drawback. It did not recognize the concept that an actor can build a performance, create a strong character by perfecting individual moments. Jimmy became a master at doing that."

In her biography, *Lee Strasberg, The Imperfect Genius,* columnist Cindy Adams wrote: "Lee was drawn to anyone with a tic, perhaps because neurotics seem to have heightened sensitiveness. He loved gifted freaks, highly gifted freaks. He loved that negative-positive level of genius in the crazily, desperately talented Kim Stanley, Geraldine Page, and Jimmy Dean."

Actually, Strasberg wasn't as indifferent to Jimmy's acting as some studio members thought. "Dean has a basic honesty in every performance," Strasberg claimed. "Everything he does is commitment. When he pulls a hat down, it isn't just a mannerism. It is a gesture of defiance that comes from deep within."

At one point, Strasberg suggested that Dean appear in a bedroom scene with Carroll Baker, another emerging actress. "Dean seemed bursting out of himself with this animal vitality," Strasberg said. "Perhaps he was just horny. He demanded in his under-the-sheets scene with Baker that he actually penetrate her for greater sexual realism."

"I want to work her up to an actual climax, so the actors sitting out there cannot only see our movements up and down, but hear the sounds of our breathing and cries of joy."

"I turned him down," Strasberg said, "and I never consulted Baker with such an outrageous idea. You can carry Method acting just so far. I told Jimmy that in a Broadway play, which had two matinées a week, on Wednesday and Saturday, he'd have less sexual drive in the evening performance, where tickets cost more. You'd be experiencing your greater sexual thrill for the matinée crowd, and that doesn't seem fair for the higher-paying audience."

"Of course, I was tongue-in-cheek."

Jimmy would tell *The New York Times,* "Strasberg is an incredible man, a walking encyclopedia of fantastic insight." That was his public utterance. Privately he told friends such as William Bast and others, "Strasberg is a Jew cunt."

Once, during one of Marlon Brando's rare appearances at the studio, he shared a cup of coffee with Jimmy in a cafeteria nearby. He told Jimmy, "Strasberg tries to commercialize on his connection to me to promote the Actors Studio. He does the same thing with Marilyn Monroe. If you make it in Hollywood, he'll pull the same stunt with your name. I can just see the entrance a few years from now. Big blowups of MARLON BRANDO, MARILYN MONROE, and JAMES DEAN."

"Frankly, I loathe the man," Brando said. "Always have. My times at the studio have been very limited. Mostly while Strasberg was ranting about acting, I was casing the joint, checking out the goodies, deciding which lucky boy or gal I was going to fuck later that day."

"Of course, if Monty Clift ever walked in, I'd be out of Dodge in a minute," Brando said. "I can't stand Princess Tiny Meat. I'm sure that before it's all said and done, you in your memoirs will devote two chapters to me and perhaps a thin one to Clift."

Elia Kazan said, "Dean was scarcely at the Actors Studio. He came in only a few times. I remember him sitting in the front row, a surly mess. He never participated in anything."

Surely, Kazan knew that his remarks were not true. In both 1953 and 1954, preceding his Hollywood stardom, Jimmy appeared in several stage productions that were staffed, directed, and sponsored by the Actors Studio. Jack Garfein had already cast him in Calder Willingham's *End as a Man,* starring Ben Gazzara.

In May of 1953, Jimmy had also interpreted the small role of Konstantin Treplev in Anton Chekhov's *The Seagull.* As Konstantin, Jimmy was cast as a playwright who tries to commit suicide, succeeding on the second attempt. Based on his work in *The Seagull,* Jimmy said he learned far more from working with actor Joseph Anthony than he did in any acting class.

Born in 1912, Anthony had already starred on Broadway in *The Country Girl,* which was later made into a movie with Oscar-winning Grace Kelly, along with William Holden and Bing Crosby.

In time, Anthony would become one of the more prolific directors in the history of the American Theater, eventually being nominated for Tony Awards for his steerage of *The Most Happy Fella* (1957); Gore Vidal's *The Best Man* (1960); and *110 in the Shade* (1964).

Although *The Seagull* had been written in 1895, Jimmy said, "It still has meaning for modern audiences." The program stated that Constantin Stanislavski had directed the play in 1898 for the Moscow Art Theatre where it was hailed "as one of the greatest events in the history of the Russian theater and one of the greatest new developments in the history of world drama.'"

"Okay," Jimmy said, after reading that. "That's putting it on a little thick, but it's still a god damn piece of good work." He later told Corsaro that Strasberg had seen one of his performances, advising him "to play things closer to yourself."

"I got that advice from the master himself," Jimmy said. "God has spoken. Perhaps you'll tell me what in the fuck 'closer to myself' means?"

Corsaro was quoted as saying, "I think Strasberg misread Jimmy. He was a new and innovative talent sending out his own message. When the phone rang with Jimmy's message, Strasberg didn't pick up the receiver. I think, however, that in time, he came to understand Jimmy's unique talent better."

Jimmy Slits His Wrists

Rescue Comes in the Form of a Blonde Bombshell from Brooklyn

Broke, desolate, and insecure, Jimmy entered the Actors Studio—a high-ceilinged space at 432 West 44th Street, near Tenth Avenue. Originally conceived as a Greek Orthodox Church, it had been adapted into a theater with rehearsal space for acting exercises. Through its doors paraded what columnist Cindy Adams called "the chinchilla and caviar set," including Rock Hudson, Eva Gabor, Grace Kelly, or Leslie Caron. It became a theatrical Elizabeth Arden's."

Shelley Winters...Bitch Goddess

Jimmy had agreed to participate in another acting exercise in front of the class, something he had not done since his *The Matador* skit.

In the front row sat Lee Strasberg with a devoted supporter of the Actors Studio, Shelley Winters, that blonde bombshell from Brooklyn. At this point in her career, she was an established star, usually based in Los Angeles. She welcomed Jimmy back to the studio.

In the first of her two memoirs, Winters had published a picture of Jimmy with a caption that identified him as a man "who often played with knives both on and off the screen."

She recalled their first meeting in which he'd come into the studio wearing a big old overcoat, obviously purchased secondhand, typical of the type homeless men wore on the streets of the Bowery.

On stage for his performance, he removed the overcoat, revealing that he wore only a T-shirt and jeans. For his skit, he removed a switchblade knife from his pocket. As Winters noted, "Something reflected in his face revealed that he was reliving some horrible experience he'd had. He was acting out the role of a young man who had lost it all and wanted to get off the planet. He'd come to the end of his rainbow and found, not a pot of gold, but a stew of despair. His face seemed to signal that he did not have the strength to go on living."

He took his knife and held the blade up to his left wrist. Slowly, he began to make an incision as blood appeared. In horror, Winters realized that this was not pretend, but the real thing. She looked at Strasberg, who appeared dispassionate. When Jimmy then began to make an incision into his other wrist, Winters screamed and jumped up, fearing he was going to cut deeper.

"My God!" she later claimed. "He was actually committing suicide in front of the entire class. I could not believe it. I ran to the stage to stop him."

Confronting him, she struggled and forced him to drop the knife. Then she ripped off her scarf and applied it to his one of his wounded wrists. Finally, Strasberg got involved, handing her his large handkerchief, which she used to bind up the other wrist.

In the dressing room to which they'd retreated, Winters saw that the wounds were only superficial, and that there was no apparent urgent need to take him to a hospital.

At that point, Strasberg entered and scolded her. "Dean was portraying a boy who is unstable. He was obviously working through something as an actor. You may have stopped him from discovering the one thing within him that would have helped him in a future performance."

"Get the fuck out of here!" she screamed at him.

Sharing the seat with him in front of a dressing table, Winters noticed that Jimmy had bled onto her sable, for which he apologized. "He was weeping, and I found myself crying, too," she said. "He put an arm around me and kissed me consolingly."

He tried to explain why he'd attempted suicide on stage. "I want to fight this feeling I have of alienation because I feel nobody is for real. Perhaps it was a cry for help, for someone to come forward to save me." He looked into her eyes. "You were that someone."

"I invited him for some coffee," she said. "He put back on that awful overcoat and followed me. At table in a cafeteria, he appeared to be starving. He ordered three eggs with fried potatoes, toast, whatever."

"He seemed to have attached himself to me," she said. "I remembered the ancient Chinese proverb that if you save someone's life you are responsible for them."

She claimed that after breakfast, she could not shake him. He followed her out onto the street, where a limousine she'd rented for the day was waiting for her. In a few short hours, the chauffeur would take her to La Guardia for a flight to Los Angeles. "Even though I didn't invite Jimmy, he crawled into the back seat with me."

"When we got to the Plaza Hotel, he followed me upstairs on the elevator to my suite. I still had almost three hours before I left for the airport. One thing led to another. I felt he desperately wanted someone to love him. So it was more about loving him and holding him than it was about sex. Of course, there was that, too."

"Regrettably, he had to do most of the work, since I was in a back brace because of a recent car accident. Jimmy did not get the benefit of my usual gymnastic stunts."

At three o'clock that afternoon, he followed her downstairs, carrying his old airline bag with him. As she got into her limousine, he pleaded with her to take him along. "I said okay because his existence seemed so pointless and haphazard. No matter how much I quizzed him on the way to the airport, I never got a straight answer. He was obviously a very beautiful and gifted actor. In some way, he reminded me of Peter Pan, but without the joy, as if he had sprung directly from Never Never Land and would soon disappear back to it. He seemed to cling to me in some emotional way."

"I was so mixed up myself, I couldn't have done anything about helping him if I could. At the airport, I gave him twenty dollars and kissed him goodbye, telling him to get a room at the Y," she said. "I was afraid he wanted to get on the plane with me. I told the chauffeur to drive him back to Manhattan. As I left him, I saw tears forming in his eyes. When I looked back at him, it was one of the saddest, most forlorn faces I'd ever seen before."

[It almost came to be that Winters and Jimmy would work together. Briefly, George Stevens, who had directed her in A Place in the Sun, *considered her for the minor role of Vashti Snythe in* Giant, *but decided to hire Jane Withers instead.]*

I Was the Mirror Image of a God Damn Scarecrow"

—*James Dean*

The friendship between Frank Corsaro and Jimmy continued to deepen, although it had its ups and downs. At times, they would have an argument and not speak to each other for two or three weeks, but they always came back together again. After a spat, they'd meet at Jerry's Tavern for a spaghetti dinner, usually followed by an evening spent in the director's apartment listening to classical music.

Both of them seemed to believe in their respective destinies. Corsaro was firmly convinced that he was slated to become one of the major theater and opera directors in America, and that Jimmy would achieve stardom on both the stage and screen.

"At least Jimmy would sometimes believe in his future," Corsaro said. "At other times, he would plunge into deep despair, fearing he had only months to live."

"I've got to cram as much living as I can into the time I have left," Jimmy said.

According to Corsaro, "Jimmy had a lot of morbid thoughts which he expressed to me, even the possibility of committing suicide. I finally got him to go to a psychiatrist. He went for only three sessions. He told me, 'You sent me to a jerk.' He emerged from the sessions no saner than before. He was still taking out that switchblade and stabbing it into a wooden table or else my sofa."

In the spring of 1953, producers Terese Hayden and Liska March hired Corsaro to direct *The Scarecrow* at the Theater de Lys on Christopher Street in Greenwich Village. *[It eventually opened on June 16.]*

Sometimes called *The Glass of Truth,* the play was based on *Feathertop,* a short story by Nathaniel Hawthorne. Mercy MacKaye had adapted it as a play that was first performed at Harvard University in 1909.

Corsaro secured the services of three major stars: Patricia Neal, Eli Wallach, and his wife, Anne Jackson. Jimmy was hoping for one of the major roles and was very disappointed that he didn't get it.

Corsaro told Jimmy that he lacked the experience for one of the bigger roles and thereby had been assigned a non-speaking part, that of the mirror image of the scarecrow.

Jimmy's rival, Bradford Dillman, made his stage debut in it, cast as "Richard Talbot."

Angered, Jimmy threatened to drop out of the production entirely. *["You wouldn't give me a speaking role, yet you cast Dillman in my role. What experience has he had?"]* Corsaro asked to be forgiven and even promised to offer him a major role on Broadway in one of the plays he planned to direct. He would keep that promise.

Barbara Glenn, Jimmy's girlfriend at the time (one of many), was out of town. He wrote to her. "I accepted this thankless role because I think I can learn something from Frank. I'm getting a little stipend. With the money I'm going to buy me a new pair of shoes. I've worn out the leather on my old ones walking the streets of New York. I will also buy me a pair of pants. The one I'm wearing is so threadbare that my ass is almost showing. You know how dangerous it is for a good-looking guy like me to walk the streets of queer New York with his rosebud on display."

When producer Hayden sat through the first rehearsal, she complimented Jimmy to Corsaro. "The boy's physical grace will look beautiful as Lord Ravensbane's mirror image."

When Jimmy was introduced to Neal, she said she relished the challenge of playing an old woman—"and a witch at that."

In her autobiography, the actress remembered Jimmy. "There was a pleasant looking young man who excelled in a small dancing role. I was sure that James Dean had a great future ahead of him."

Her biographer, Stephen Michael Shearer, gave the best description of the play's convoluted plot. "It is the story of a female blacksmith Goody Rickby (Neal), who seeks revenge for having been spurned by Justice Gilead Merton (Milton Selzer). She makes a pact with Dick Dickon (Wallach), known as 'The Evil One,' and casts a spell that brings to life a Scarecrow to win the hand of Merton's daughter (Jackson)."

As a human, Lord Ravensbane (Douglas Watson), the scarecrow falls in love with the young girl and breaks his pact with Dickon. This dramatic acts brings about his death, but not before he has experienced, ever so briefly, the joy of life and love."

During his short time at the Actors Studio, Jimmy had developed great respect for the talents of the husband-and-wife acting team of Eli Wallach and Anne Jackson. He got to know them better during their work together on *The Scarecrow*. He had a dream that one day he, too, like Wallach, would marry a talented actress, and that together, they would perform on stage and screen. "If not Alfred Lunt and Lynn Fontanne, perhaps *Me and My Gal* could at least be Jessica Tandy and Hume Cronyn."

Wallace urged him to concentrate on becoming a stage actor. "Of course, if you need a paycheck, you might make a movie now and then. But the stage is the only real venue for an actor."

Years later, Wallace commented on the advice he had given Jimmy. "As a Method actor back then, I was almost evangelical in my promotion of it, as if reborn. I set out like a crusader trying to entice young actors into the fold, thinking they would bring fresh blood to the stage. I wanted to convert young Dean."

"I told Dean that stage acting is the most alive thing an actor can do. The

stage is a much higher level than film, a more satisfying medium. Movies, by comparison, are like calendar
art next to a great painting."

Wallace recognized that Jimmy was struggling to
survive as an actor, and he shared with him memories
of how "Anne and I started out. We found this dingy
little basement apartment in Greenwich Village for $35
a month. The bathroom was outside. We cooked on a
two-burner stove I got from a secondhand shop for ten
bucks."

Jackson joined Jimmy and her husband, recalling
days of working with him in the theater. Jimmy envied
them their various appearances in Tennessee Williams' plays, including *This
Property Is Condemned.* Rogers Brackett had taken Jimmy to see Wallach's
Tony-winning performance in Tennessee's *The Rose Tattoo,* opposite Maureen Stapleton.

Sometimes, Jackson joined Wallach and Jimmy, sharing her own memories of the theater. She recalled the time she'd visited backstage when Wallach
was appearing with Katherine Cornell in Shakespeare's *Antony and Cleopatra.*

"Charlton Heston was cast as Proculeius, a Roman general in Caesar's
army," Wallach said. "He wore this gray uniform with a short skirt. He asked
me if I didn't think he had beautiful legs to show off, suggesting that horny
women or gay men would buy tickets to the show to gape at his legs. He also
told me that he'd started out as a nude model, claiming that when he dropped
the robe to pose in the nude, there were sighs of desire heard from both the
men and women in the class."

"I told Chuck, 'If you're going to make it in the theater, there is no need
to be modest about your physical assets,'" Wallach said.

Patricia Neal Introduces Jimmy to His Mentor
(One of the Few Members of Hollywood's Old Guard Who Genuinely Liked Him)
GARY COOPER, THE MONTANA MULE

Ever since Marcus Dean, Jimmy's uncle, had taken him to see Gary Cooper
in *Sergeant York* (1941), the image of the ultimate all-American hero, nicknamed "Coop," had been implanted on his brain. To Jimmy, the lanky, handsome star was lean, laconic, and masculine, an image of inspiration to a small
boy growing up in the farmlands of Indiana.

To Jimmy, there was something real about the actor. "He had no bag of tricks," Jimmy said, "and none of the florid gestures of some other actors of his era."

As Jimmy rehearsed for his teleplays, he would remember Coop's speech patterns and his uncanny use of hesitancy, and his naturalness.

Without his uncle, Jimmy returned to the movie theater the next day to see for a second time Cooper portraying Alvin York, a backwoods turkey shooter who became America's most-decorated hero of World War I.

From that moment on, Jimmy never missed a Gary Cooper movie. He was especially enthralled with Cooper's superb portrayal of baseball star Lou Gehrig in *The Pride of the Yankees* (1942), or as the Ernest Hemingway character in *For Whom the Bell Tolls* (1943), in which he created a beautifully believable relationship with Ingrid Bergman.

When Jimmy met Patricia Neal in New York, he didn't tell her that he hadn't really understood the architect Cooper had portrayed opposite her in *The Fountainhead* (1949). But Cooper redeemed himself in Jimmy eyes when he was cast as the subtle and sympathetic sheriff, Will Cain, who must confront a coven of killer gunmen in *High Noon* (1952). Of course, Grace Kelly would be waiting for him at the end of the picture. "Grace Kelly—now that's something Coop and I have in common," Jimmy boasted to his friends.

Jimmy was aware, as were many a movie fan, that Cooper and Neal had begun a tormented affair when they'd co-starred together in *The Fountainhead,* even though he was married at the time to Veronica Balfe, whom he had nicknamed "Rocky." Neal was twenty-six at the time, and he was forty-six.

When Jimmy had lived with Rogers Brackett, and the producer had learned of Jimmy's fascination with Cooper, he brought Jimmy up on all the gossip. "What a cocksman that guy was, and bisexual at that," Brackett said.

Over lunch in Manhattan, Neal told Jimmy that she had accepted a marriage proposal from Roald Dahl, the British writer. With tears in her eyes, she also tossed a "bombshell" at him, revealing that Cooper had scheduled a brief visit to New York for their final goodbye before they parted forever. "He'll have very little time here, and he wants you to join us for dinner."

"I'm dying to meet him, but it sounds like you guys need some space all your own."

"We'll have that after he meets you," she said. "And you should know that there's a motive

Patricia Neal with Gary Cooper. Although they were acting together in a scene from *The Fountainhead*, their love was real, albeit thwarted.

337

to his madness. He's heard that Elia Kazan might cast you as the lead in *East of Eden*, and Coop thinks that the role of your mean and bitter father would be a choice role for him."

In anticipation of his dinner with Cooper and Neal, Jimmy got a haircut and wore his only suit. He wanted to look his best, but later confessed, "I was nervous as hell, but Coop put me at ease almost immediately. He'd made dozens of movies and won two Oscars—in fact, he was Hollywood royalty, a survivor of the Golden Age—yet he treated me like an equal worthy of respect."

Neal made no mention of what happened that night in her memoirs. But she described to Anne Bancroft [*a close friend of Darwin Porter and Stanley Haggart*] and others what happened that night: "I think Cooper was testing his chemistry with Jimmy. Coop and Jimmy could not have been more different as actors, yet they bonded. For reasons known only to him, Jimmy told Coop that he was inspired more by him than he was by either Monty Clift or Marlon Brando."

"You've always been my screen idol," Jimmy said. "Not those other fuckers."

As stated by Neal, "Right before my eyes, Jimmy and Coop seemed to develop a romance. Of course, you know I don't mean that in any sexual sense. These two men were from different generations and had divergent lives. But each seemed to sense that one lost soul was meeting and finding a sympathetic comrade in the other."

"Unlike Jimmy, Coop had actually read John Steinbeck's *East of Eden*, and both of them became animated about methodologies for the creating of a dynamic father-son confrontation on the screen."

"We've got to show love beyond the outward hostility," Cooper said to Jimmy. "We can do that."

"And I can show my love for you, too," Jimmy said. "You've meant so much to me. So tall, so handsome, so forthright."

"For a man of few words on the screen, Coop delivered quite a mouthful that night," Jimmy told Eli Wallach.

After a few hours, Jimmy politely excused himself, with the understanding that Coop and Neal needed time alone during their final night together.

Standing up, and towering over Jimmy, Coop extended his hand. Impulsively, Jimmy wrapped his arms around him and held him tightly for one long moment. Cooper responded with manly affection, even running his fingers through Jimmy's hair.

"For one brief moment, I saw a loving father holding his young son in his arms," Neal said. "It was a beautiful sight I'll never forget."

[Despite the onscreen suitability of Gary Cooper playing father to the character played by James Dean in East of Eden, *Elia Kazan had very different ideas.*

The austere, inflexible role of Adam, Jimmy's father, was awarded to Raymond Massey, a talented actor who was very different from Cooper.

"I'm so sorry Coop lost the role," Neal said. "He and Jimmy were heartbroken. Jimmy called me and was sobbing on the phone. He really wanted those moments onscreen with his idol."

Cooper called him at the end of the picture's filming to arrange a get-together in Hollywood. As such, he was one of the few golden age stars to welcome the newcomer, unlike Clark Gable and Cary Grant, who had each expressed contempt for him.

Even Jimmy Stewart turned against James Dean, ostensibly because they each competed for two of the same roles, despite the quarter-century difference in their ages. (Stewart was forty-seven, and Dean was twenty-three. They vied for the role of Jett Rink in Giant, *and for the part of aviator Charles Lindbergh in* The Spirit of St. Louis. *In the aftermath of Jimmy's rejection of the latter of those two roles, it was awarded to Stewart, who thus became the pilot who flew across the treacherous Atlantic to Paris.]*

When Jimmy and Cooper learned that they shared a passion for horseback riding, they sometimes went riding together on Saturdays.

"I got Kazan to arrange a screening of *East of Eden* for Coop and me," Jimmy said. "Later, over drinks, I asked Coop what he thought of my performance, and he told me I had all the elements of a really big star. As for Massey playing my father, he thought he was a shit."

"Massey played the role in the first dimension," Cooper said. "He should have shown more than contempt for his son. He should have conveyed a deep love, at least in a far and distant chamber of his heart. I would have reached down to show I really cared for Cal in spite of my neurotic behavior."

Jimmy later told Kazan, "That's not a bad appraisal coming from an actor who's supposed to be inarticulate."

He later related that one Saturday after a very long and tiring horseback ride, Cooper invited him for a steambath at his country club.

"We were bare-assed—now I know why Coop is called 'the Montana Mule.'" Jimmy told William Bast. "It was long, thick, floppy—and still soft. Those were some lucky guys and gals who got to make love with him."

"Unfortunately," Jimmy continued, "I cannot include my name on Coop's list of conquests. I would have been more than willing. If he'd played my father on the screen, it would have been a case of incest."

Jimmy's continuing fascination with Cooper was demonstrated during the filming of *Giant* in Texas. He admired the Stetson worn by actress Mercedes McCambridge. She told him that Cooper had given it to her after he'd worn it in three of his pictures.

"I thought it might be something like that," Jimmy said. "Your hat is the most authentic in the movie."

She later claimed that Jimmy made at least three unsuccessful attempts to steal it from her. "I was onto the little devil. I guarded that hat like it was the crown jewels."

When he heard the news of Jimmy's death, shortly after the filming of *Giant,* Cooper said, "I'm depressed, a bit morbid. What a loss. The roles he could have played."

Jimmy, of course, was not alive to see the last stand of America's hero. Cooper was at home battling cancer when James Stewart accepted an honorary Oscar on his behalf at the Academy Awards in April of 1961. Stewart chocked up, signaling to the world that one of its greatest stars was dying.

For Cooper, it was no longer *High Noon.* Midnight was fast approaching.

Gary Cooper died on May 13, 1961, about a month after being designated as recipient of that Oscar.

The first telegrams of condolence to his family came from President John F. Kennedy and Queen Elizabeth II of England.

Jimmy Misses a Bus Stop
WITH MARILYN MONROE

Albert Salmi, with his rugged good looks, brawny physique, and very masculine aura was a member of the cast of *The Scarecrow* who intrigued and physically attracted Jimmy. Like Jimmy, he was a Method actor and a member of Actors Studio.

The son of Finnish immigrants, he had been reared in Brooklyn. Four years older than Jimmy, he had joined the U.S. Army to fight during World War II.

During a rehearsal for *The Scarecrow,* Salmi's relationship with Jimmy deepened when he extended an invitation to join him in the East Village.

He wanted Jimmy to experience both an old-fashioned Turkish bathhouse and its Finnish counterpart, with the intention of demonstrating that the dry heat of a Finnish sauna was superior and more invigorating.

After testing each of them, the two young actors went to Stanley Haggart's apartment, to which Jimmy still had his private key. The next morning Haggart met both men, each attired in his underwear, and served them a Kansas-style farmhouse breakfast. Since it was a Sunday, they wanted to spend the rest of the day sunbathing on his rooftop terrace.

That evening over drinks in Haggart's living room, Jimmy asked Haggart—since he was considered an interpretive expert—to examine a sample of Salmi's handwriting.

Haggart later admitted to Alec Wilder and others that, "I didn't give an honest reading. Salmi appeared tame enough on the surface, but there was a dark streak, a touch of madness I intuited through the reading of his handwriting. He was capable of great violence, and the lines on his hand implied a horrible upcoming death. Jimmy seemed attracted to this reckless streak in Salmi, but I didn't tell either of them any of that."

"During the summer of 1953, the two of them made frequent use of my apartment, often sunbathing in the nude on my terrace. I jokingly told Jimmy that Salmi's real name should be 'salami.'"

"Jimmy sometimes complained to me that Salmi was a selfish brute in bed," Haggart said.

"When he's finished, he turns over and goes to sleep, leaving me panting and unsatisfied." Jimmy claimed.

Since both men were actors fully suited for portraying the same characters, they sometimes competed—alongside Paul Newman— for the same roles. Newman, along with a lot of other actors, too, especially desired the role of the rowdy cowpoke chasing after a stripper in William Inge's play, *Bus Stop.*

At first, Jimmy went after the role, planning to pursue Inge and to offer his body once again as a means of procuring the role. But then he read an item that Inge revealed to a journalist, perhaps as a means of concealing his sexual attraction to Jimmy.

"I don't want James Dean in one of my plays," Inge said. "His moods are unpredictable. He scares the pants right off me. What if in the middle of the play, this temperamental actor decides to tear up the script and write his own lines?"

Jimmy was deeply insulted and announced that he would not accept the role of Bo Decker even it was offered to him.

Ironically, the part eventually went to Salmi, appearing on Broadway at the same time opposite Jimmy's friend, Kim Stanley. She telephoned Jimmy and told him how disappointed she was that they wouldn't be working together.

Bus Stop opened to rave reviews at the Music Box Theater on May 23, 1953. Even Elvis Presley went to see it, seeking the movie role of the cowboy, but Col. Tom Parker, his manager, nixed the idea.

After that, Salmi was then offered the film role of *Bus Stop's* gauche and horny cowboy opposite Marilyn Monroe, but Salmi turned it down, proclaiming that he didn't like movie making. Eventually, the role of Bo in *Bus Stop's* film version went to Don Murray, who got rave reviews.

As for Salmi, during his road tour of the theatrical version of *Bus Stop,* he met and eventually married the former child actress Peggy Ann Garner, and ended his involvement with Jimmy. In 1963, the couple di-

June, 1955 edition of *Theatre Arts* magazine, promoting Albert Salmi with Kim Stanley as a washed-up stripper in the Broadway production of *Bus Stop*

vorced. The following year, Salmi married Roberta Pollock Taper. The couple had two daughters.

Eventually, Salmi moved to Washington State, where he lived in semi-retirement. He separated from his wife in 1990, but continued to harass and threaten her. Finally, on April 23 of that year, Salmi, suffering from a severe clinical depression, fatally shot his estranged wife. A few hours later, he put a fatal bullet to his own head.

Jimmy, of course, never lived to learn of Salmi's committing such violence.

"For God's Sake, You're Not Frank Sinatra—

AND DON'T GO TO HOLLYWOOD TRYING TO BECOME ANOTHER TAB HUNTER"

—ELI WALLACH TO JAMES DEAN

Jimmy would appear for a final time with Eli Wallach and Anne Jackson when he performed a dramatic reading at the Cherry Lane Theater in Greenwich Village on February 12, 1954. The New School of Social Research arranged for Howard Sackler to showcase Sophocles' tragedy, *Trachiniae,* a modern version with a provocative, free-wheeling translation by the crazed poet, Ezra Pound, who translated its title as *Women of Trachnis.*

Pound came up with his version of this classical Greek tragedy while a prisoner incarcerated at St. Elizabeth's Hospital in Washington, D.C. Here, he was held for twelve years, placed in Howard's Hall in a cell known as "Hell's Hole," with no window. He lived behind a thick steel door with nine peepholes through which psychiatrists could secretly observe him.

Jimmy knew nothing about Pound and went to the library to research his life. Born in the Idaho Territory in 1885, he graduated with a prestigious education from Hamilton College *[in Clinton, New York]* in 1905. Later, after spending years of what authorities defined as "collaboration with an enemy," he was defined as a traitor working against the interests of the United States.

In 1924, he'd moved to Italy, where he embraced Mussolini's fascism. From there, during World War II, he made radio broadcasts that attacked the Jews and Franklin D. Roosevelt. As a vicious anti-Semite, he supported the extermination policies of Adolf Hitler.

In 1945, he was arrested by Allied soldiers and sent as a prisoner to Washington, D.C., where he was incarcerated for years in a psychiatric asylum, producing poetry hailed by some academics as that of a troubled genius.

Jimmy found Pound's personal history fascinating, and was eager to work with Jackson and Wallach (whom he continued to admire) again. He also appeared with a distinguished New York actor, Joseph Sullivan, who had the fourth starring role. He was already well-known on Broadway, having starred in such productions as *The Country Girl,* a successful play that was later adapted into a movie starring Grace Kelly, who took the Oscar away from Judy Garland for her role in *A Star Is Born* (1954).

In the staging of this obscure ancient Greek play, Jimmy was cast as Hyllus, son of Herakles (Wallach) and Daianeira (Jackson). Onstage, he denounces his mother for murdering his father. *["Damn you, I wish you were dead."]* Devastated by her son's attack, she commits suicide. "Heavy stuff," was Jimmy's critique.

Wallach remembered that Jimmy was nervous during rehearsals, not about the Greek tragedy, but about a possible screen test for Elia Kazan who was casting *East of Eden* at around the same time.

Jimmy told Wallach that he didn't think he could go through with the test. "I hate being tested like a slave on the auction block. Frankly, I don't feel up to the role. What if I make an ass of myself and word gets out? I could be finished for future parts."

"You'll be great," Wallach assured him. "I used to vomit butterflies before going on. An actor who isn't nervous doesn't give a fuck."

"I've had a screen test before," he said. "I went out for the role of Curly in

Oklahoma!"

"For god's sake, boy," Wallach said. "Frank Sinatra was also offered the role, and so was Gordon MacCrae, but you're nothing like them. Be yourself."

"If you go to Hollywood, don't be another Tab Hunter," Wallach said. "One Tab is enough."

For Jimmy, the most lasting benefit of his appearance in *Women of Trachnis* involved his introduction by Howard Sackler to the musician, Leonard Rosenblum, who was composing the music for the play. Rosenblum, who later scored *East of Eden* and *Rebel Without a Cause,* would eventually become one of Jimmy's closest friends.

Rosenblum, who was gay, was immediately attracted to Jimmy. Sackler had warned him, "Dean's a tough kid. Sleeps on nails." Ironically, it was that very image that attracted Rosemblum, who liked to be dominated by a master.

Jimmy moved in with Rosenblum, and the two men became lovers. "He'll do anything I demand," Jimmy said. "One night I didn't want to get up and go to the toilet. I was too stoned. So I ordered the fucker to have a drink. He swallowed every drop, just as I commanded."

Jimmy eventually showed up at Jerry's Tavern for dinner with his new lover and S&M partner, shocking Jerry with his black leather jacket and boots. "My god," Jerry said. "He looked like a member of the Nazi SS."

When some of Jerry's Jewish guests complained, the owner told them that Jimmy was appearing in a World War II drama. When he asked Jimmy about it, he answered, "My new friend likes me to dress up like this. As a Jew, he imagines being assaulted, beaten, and raped by the Gestapo."

"You're bad, kid, but I really love you," Jerry said. "Try the lasagna. It's on the house tonight."

Sackler was very impressed with Jimmy's acting and promised to cast him in future plays he planned to direct. Regrettably, Jimmy would not be around to star in those roles.

Sackler would go on to direct plays across America, Europe, and South America. His best known work would become *The Great White Hope,* which opened as a play in 1967, and which was adapted into a film in 1970. Both the stage and film version (for which it generated Oscar nominations), starred James Earl Jones and Jane Alexander.

[Sackler died on October 12, 1982, in his studio on the island of Ibiza, one of the Balearic Islands off the Mediterranean coast of Spain. The cause of his death was never determined. His friends claimed that he was murdered.]

Jimmy, of course, ignored Eli Wallach's advice and moved to Hollywood, where he starred in *East of Eden.* But as soon as he could, he rushed back to New York and his Broadway friends, especially Frank Corsaro. This time, since offers were pouring in, he wasn't looking for work. He wanted to walk the streets of Manhattan again and visit his familiar haunts.

The first person he phoned after his return was Corsaro, who was organizing the production of a Broadway play entitled *A Hatful of Rain*. Honoring an earlier promise, he wanted Jimmy to star in either of two lead male roles.

During their reunion, Corsaro read aloud the play, authored by Michael V. Gazzo, to Jimmy.

A Hatful of Rain broke ground in that it was a candid and sympathetic portrayal of drug addiction. Corsaro defined it as "an unflinching portrait of a young, lower middle-class man struggling to break his drug habit."

"In other words, you want me to play a junkie?" Jimmy asked. "It's certainly got some pungent dialogue as this family struggles with its addict son."

Corsaro told Jimmy that he'd be ideal in the role of Johnny Pope, a veteran of the Korean War who, while recuperating from battle injuries in an Army hospital, became addicted to morphine. The script had another strong role too; that of Polo Pope, Johnny's brother who courageously lends strong support to his junkie sibling. Yet despite his status as Jimmy's mentor, Corsaro could not persuade his *protégé* to accept either role.

When the play eventually opened in November of 1955, about two months after Jimmy's death, on Broadway, Jimmy—had he lived—would probably have been jealous of the rave reviews his rival, Ben Gazzara, received for his performance alongside Shelley Winters and Tony Franciosa. Behind the scenes those latter two had "shacked up" (Winter's words) and later, in 1957, embarked on a tempestuous marriage.

Also in 1957, the script for *A Hatful of Rain* was adapted into a film. The role developed onstage by Gazzara went to Don Murray, and the Winters role was assigned to Eva Marie Saint. Franciosa repeated his stage role on the screen.

***

In the summer of 1954, Corsaro organized a production of August Strindberg's *Ghost Sonata [aka Spöksonaten]* at the Actors Studio. "I promised to give Jimmy the role of Arkenholz, the student with second sight," Corsaro said. "When he told me 'to go fuck myself,' I got so mad at him, I abandoned producing it altogether. He would have been terrific in the role. He and I had a silly argument about a rental I'd arranged for him in the studio of Jonathan Bates when he was out of town. We didn't speak until that autumn, when we made up once again."

***

[In the aftermath of Jimmy's tragic death in 1955, at least three key of his Actors Studio contacts weighed in with their opinions about his talents, and his accomplishments or lack thereof.

As expressed by Corsaro, "If Jimmy had lived, I was certain that he would have returned to the stage. He needed the sound of applause, something a movie star doesn't get. He needed a live audience, which he had the power to win over. How do you think his memory has survived after all these years if he lacked the ability to communicate to an audience.?"

Shelley Winters told Corsaro, "Marlon Brando and Jimmy certainly contributed to the itch-and-scratch school of acting. They were the chief graduates of the 'Dirty Fingernails School.' Also, the 'Torn Shirt School,' even the 'Smelly Armpits Academy.' They made wrinkled fatigues and dirty jeans their haute couture. *They also pioneered the inaudible school of acting, specializing in the slovenly and the rude. But let's ask ourselves the question: 'Why did we love them so?'"*

Months later, Corsaro shared his memories of Jimmy's return from the West Coast after his filming of East of Eden. *"He was drinking a lot of brandy when not swirling it around in a snifter. He was really on edge. He claimed that he'd 'managed' Kazan, although I doubted that. I don't think he was handling all his publicity very well. In fact, I think he was starting to believe his press."*

"He was a highly charged sexual son of a bitch," Corsaro said to Lee Strasberg. "A younger version of Brando, whom someone had labeled 'the brute with a girl's eyes.' Jimmy played the field with a delicate macho aura but with a feminine streak, too. He seemed to be uttering a contradiction—'Save me! Save me! But don't get near me.'"

"He lived in a complex, shadowy world. Emotionally, he remained the hustler he'd been in his early days in Hollywood and in New York, too, when he first hit town. A lot of his trouble stemmed from his androgyny. He wanted to celebrate it at the same time he wanted to eradicate it. His cruelty often arose from the inner turmoil raging within him."

In October of 1956, about a year after Jimmy's death, Strasberg addressed his class at the Actors Studio. "I have just seen James Dean in Giant," *he announced, "and I must say..." At that point, he choked up and began to cry. According to Strasberg, "When I got back home, the tears rained down. I cried from the pleasure and joy of watching his performance. I also cried for the waste, that awful waste of a great talent who never lived to show us just what he could do."*

Yet in the years to come, Strasberg would express views that were more negative about Jimmy. "Dean did not go far enough in his work, even in the latter stages, which is all we have to judge. He did not use enough of himself, which he kept buried in some secret dark hole. While he continued to forge ahead in getting work as an actor, he failed to make any progress that I was aware of. It seemed that he'd adopted this persona, and that he was going to stick with it."

In 1955, Jimmy launched a brief affair with Lee's daughter, the actress, Susan Strasberg. She once told Darwin Porter, "I didn't know if Jimmy were attracted to me as a woman, or else whether he was getting revenge on my father."]

James Dean vs. Tab Hunter

VYING FOR THE SAME ROLES, AND DATING THE SAME WOMEN
BUT DID THEY, OR DIDN'T THEY?

Leon Uris (1924-2003), a novelist best known for his bestselling historical fiction, had written a popular novel based on World War II, *Battle Cry*, and had also penned the screenplay for its adaptation into a film that was released in 1955. Raoul Walsh had been designated as its director. At the time, Walsh was one of the biggest directors in Hollywood, having helmed such actors as Humphrey Bogart and Errol Flynn.

Battle Cry was the story of the U.S. Marines, following them from boot camp in San Diego into combat at Guadalcanal in the Pacific, tracing their disparate cultural backgrounds as they build and manifest, through tragedy and sweat, an *esprit de corps*.

One of the best roles was that of PFC Danny Forrester, a sensitive young Marine who has a girlfriend but also indulges, during training, in an affair with an older woman.

William Orr, the son-in-law of Jack Warner, had tested some one hundred actors, including Paul Newman, but hadn't found anyone that suited his taste. John Kerr, Jimmy's former lover, had made one of the best tests, but Orr was also considering Robert Wagner for the role.

Elia Kazan called Orr and told him, "There is this hot young actor in New York who would make a great Danny. I think he's going to be a big star. His name is James Dean. Here's your chance to use him before his price soars."

Tab Hunter...American Adonis

The film was going to be shot in CinemaScope, which didn't interest Jimmy. Nor did the movie itself. But when he learned that his former acting coach, the rugged James Whitmore, had signed as one of its stars, he was lured into making a screen test.

Except for the role of Danny, the major parts had already been cast with actors who included Van Heflin in the key role of "High Pockets." He'd be backed up by Aldo Ray, Anne Francis, Dorothy Malone, Mona Freeman, and Jimmy's future nemesis, Raymond Massey.

"Most actors were watering at the mouth to play Danny," Orr said. "But not Dean. I figured he was just playing hard to get to make himself more desirable as an actor."

As his girlfriend in the test, Orr had selected an attractive young actress, Ruda Michelle (also known as Ruda Podemski). She was familiar with Jimmy, having spotted him from time to time back at Cromwell's Pharmacy, which she had often visited, carrying a sandwich in a paper bag, since she could afford only coffee.

When, in preparation for the screen test, she was formally introduced to Jimmy, he invited her to his small apartment in Manhattan. When she arrived there, she was startled to find him draped in a bullfighter's cape. He told her that it had belonged to the great matador, Sidney Franklin from Brooklyn. "That didn't sound like any bullfighter's name to me," Michelle said.

She later claimed that he didn't really want to rehearse their scene for the next day's test. Instead, he asked her to sit with him on his battered old sofa, telling her he wanted her to hear a recording of David Diamond's 1944 work for stringed orchestra, "Rounds." *[Modernist, melodic, and avant-garde, it's arguably the most popular work that Diamond ever composed.]*

"Sit close to me and don't be afraid," he told her. "I don't bite. Just listen to the sound of the music."

The evening passed, and unlike what she had expected, he made no attempt to seduce her.

Both of them arrived separately the next day for their screen test. Orr remembered it vividly: "Danny was supposed to be a cleancut, all American boy, but Dean came in with a three-day beard dressed in an old Army surplus jacket, a pair of dirty blue jeans, and wearing some shit-kicking boots, more appropriate for the wilds of rattlesnake country in West Texas."

Orr didn't expect the test to be successful, but he later claimed, "I was electrified by it."

As soon as he'd seen the results, he wrote to Jack Warner: "You will see from this test that even though James Dean is of dubious appearance, and there is a trace of the Brando school of acting, he is unique, certainly not a conventional actor. He brings more vitality to the role than a hundred actors

I've tested. He enjoys a fine reputation in New York as a most talented young man, perhaps a bit difficult to handle, but Walsh can get out his whip and, with that patch over his eye, beat some obedience into this unruly boy. Makeup, of course, can take care of his appearance."

Orr was very disappointed when his father-in-law, Jack Warner, rejected the idea of involving Jimmy in the film. "I couldn't believe it," Orr said. "Dean was fantastic in his test, but Jack decided to go for a name actor. At the time, Tab Hunter had a bit of a box office following, especially among teenage girls, even though he was gay as a goose. Warners lost out on a big opportunity in not casting Dean."

***

After they lost their respective roles in *Battle Cry,* Jimmy would have a final encounter with Ruda Michelle.

One afternoon in Hollywood, she spotted him coming toward her. He was wearing blue jeans and a T-shirt. He was accompanied by two beautiful teenage girls, each clad in a bathing suit, positioned on either side of him. Approaching her, he said, "Ruda, what are you doing here?"

"Hanging out looking for a job when not beaching it," she said.

He reached for her arm. "Come with me," he said, before telling those clinging girls to get lost.

She quickly wrapped her beach towel around her nearly nude body and wandered off with him. He seated her beside him in a yellow convertible and drove over to Warners. There, a secretary allowed them into William Orr's office.

Barging in, Jimmy said, "Bill, you darling man, I've found the perfect actress to play Judy in *Rebel Without a Cause*. You'd better give the part to her or else I might walk."

"Needless to say, I didn't get the role, which went to Natalie Wood," Michelle said. "And, before I forget, Jimmy changed his mind, forgave Orr, and indeed starred in the picture, as everybody in the world knows."

***

In Hollywood, Jimmy visited the set of *Battle Cry,* ostensibly for a reunion with James Whitmore, his former acting teacher. Whitmore welcomed him, though he told some of the cast that he suspected that Jimmy was really showing up just to see how Tab Hunter was doing in the role of Danny.

"There was a definite jealousy," Whitmore said. "All actors have it. I was so jealous of Spencer Tracy, I detested him."

In his memoir, *The Making of a Movie Star,* Hunter wrote, "Jimmy visited my dressing room several times during the making of *Battle Cry.* We'd also hang out on the steps outside talking between shots."

"I have no proof," Whitmore said, "but both the cast and crew gossiped about Jimmy and Tab. Tab was definitely gay, and Jimmy

Tab Hunter, weary from the rigors of war, in *Battle Cry.*

was bi, to say the least, so we assumed that when Jimmy disappeared into Tab's dressing room, it wasn't just to apply his makeup."

Motivated by dreams of becoming a Hollywood star, Jimmy took note of his competition, the so-called "Pretty Boy Pack." Led by Rock Hudson, Tony Curtis and Robert Wagner were "hot on my ass," as Jimmy so colorfully phrased it.

In the second tier of this cabal of young male actors was Tab himself, trailed by John Kerr, John Ericson, Steve Forrest, Jeffrey Hunter, and the doomed Robert Francis, who appeared in only four Hollywood films, all with military themes, before he died at the age of 25 in the crash of an airplane he was piloting.

Both Jimmy and Tab arrived in Hollywood just as the studios were getting rid of their contract players. During these tectonic shifts in the landscapes of Hollywood, even such stalwart Golden Age survivors as Humphrey Bogart and Clark Gable were sent out to pasture. Natalie Wood, Tab, and Jimmy were the last actors to be placed under contract to Warners.

Jimmy rejected a seven-year contract, and agreed to only a three-picture deal. As he told Tab, "I want to be a free agent, kiddo."

In contrast, Tab preferred the security of a long-term contract.

During one of Jimmy's visits to the set, a studio publicity photographer spotted the two of them chatting, and snapped pictures of the handsome young men together. "We were the polar opposites of America's youth culture captured together," Tab wrote.

Although Tab was called to the set, the

James Dean *(left)* with Tab Hunter, each a heartthrob of the 1950s, were rivals on the screen and with other lovers, too. But the question that's never been answered is, "Did they or didn't they do it?"

photographer wanted to get more pictures of them together. In response, "Jimmy flipped the bird at him," Tab said. "I knew that my friend, Dick Clayton, Jimmy's agent, had his hands full with him because he was unconventional and unpredictable. But he believed in Jimmy and thought he was well worth the trouble."

Clayton recalled going with Tab to deliver a contract to Jimmy on the set of *Rebel Without a Cause.* "It was being shot that night in the spooky mansion that had been the abode of Norma Desmond *[as portrayed by Gloria Swanson]* in *Sunset Blvd.* Jimmy and I hung out waiting for the crew to go through another setup."

In the months to come, Tab and Jimmy often dated the same rising starlets, including Natalie Wood, Terry Moore, and Lori Nelson. As a gay man, Tab did it for the sake of publicity, using the beautiful starlets as "arm candy." Hollywood insiders joked, "NATALIE WOULD BUT TAB WOULDN'T."

Both men doubled up on Tony Perkins, Jimmy having only a fling with him, Tab a fully blossomed romance that was whispered about all over Hollywood and later acknowledged by Tab in his memoirs.

Rumors were also rampant about the alleged affair of Tab and Jimmy, but so far as it is known, Tab never admitted to that.

Jimmy, however, did boast to a number of friends that, upon his arrival in Hollywood, "one of my goals is to fuck that pretty blonde to show him who's boss."

***

Battle Cry, which was released in 1955 to a disappointing box office, wasn't the only role that both Tab and Jimmy would compete for. That same year, a baseball-themed Broadway musical opened called *Damn Yankees,* the plot involving a Faustian bargain. *[The hero, Joe Hardy has offered to sell his soul to the devil if his team, the Washington Senators, can beat the New York Yankees.]* Stephen Douglass starred in the lead role of Joe Hardy. Warners acquired the film rights to the stage play, and briefly considered Jimmy for the romantic lead of the baseball hero, Joe Hardy.

At the last minute, however, they opted for Tab Hunter instead, backed up by Gwen Verdon, Satan's (reluctant) temptress, who demonstrates her seductive charms with "Whatever Lola

Tab Hunter, Gwen Verdon, in *Damn Yankees.* Jimmy was considered for Tab's role.

351

Wants." After the characters team up to thwart the devil's schemes, everything ends happily in the end.

Tab had just granted an interview to *Liberty* magazine in which he revealed, "I rebel against playing the teen-aged baby-faced 'boy next door' in my films. I'm twenty-six, and I'd rather play a murderer. So, guess what? I land my biggest 'boy next door' character to date, the role of naïve baseball hero, Joe Hardy."

In the movie roles he was assigned, Tab didn't always emerge the winner. Warners considered casting him, along with Debbie Reynolds, as the star of *Rebel Without a Cause,* a choice that would have "tamed" that picture considerably. Prompted by Jack Warner, *Rebel's* director Nicholas Ray evaluated the potential of those other actors: "Debbie and Tab are too anemic."

[Of course, the leads eventually went to Jimmy and Natalie Wood, but before Jimmy was cast as Jim Stark, both Robert Wagner and John Kerr were considered for the role.]

On the night Jimmy died, Dick Clayton, his agent, phoned Tab with the news: "Oh, my God!" Clayton shouted into the phone. "Jimmy's dead. He died in a car crash."

Tab later wrote, "Dick could hardly speak. He was devastated. Within days, he would suffer a bout of psychosomatic blindness caused by the trauma over Jimmy's death. His sight would return, but, frankly, I don't think he ever completely recovered from the shock, or the loss."

In the late 1950s, Clayton and Tab built a small house together in Palm Desert, California, near Palm Springs. Although they went on to other lovers, they remained friends for life. Clayton died of congestive heart failure in 2008 in Los Angeles at the age of ninety-three.

Jimmy Gets Musical

With the Avant-Garde Composer, David Diamond

"Jimmy had this thing for composers," Alec Wilder said. "Not for me, necessarily, but for other composers who were friends of mine. He must have been in love with David Diamond's music, certainly not that ugly mug of his."

"I knew David from our younger days in Rochester, New York. He'd won three Guggenheim Fellowships and became one of the pre-eminent composers of our generation. *Rounds,* released as a composition for strings in 1944, was his most popular piece, but he also wrote nearly a dozen symphonies."

"He was very gay and didn't give a damn who knew it," Wilder continued. "He later blamed homophobia and anti-Semitism for stalling his career. In time, he was shoved aside to some extent, eventually relegated to the forgotten generation of great American symphonists."

Composer David Diamond in the 1950s.

"A lot of Diamond's problems may have stemmed from what people called his difficult personality," Wilder said. "*The New York Times* quoted him as saying, 'I was a highly emotional young man, very honest in my behavior. I would say things in public that would cause a scene between me and, for instance, a conductor.'"

Diamond met Jimmy the night Wilder invited him to a Broadway rendition of *See the Jaguar*. Wilder had composed the music for the play.

In his diary, Diamond wrote, "Alec lured me to see what he called 'this wonderful boy you'll just love.' How true that was. This handsome young actor had to be seen to be believed. The play was a mess, like Brando in *Truckline Café*. But what this charming boy did really worked. He looked about fifteen and had a lot of Brando's mannerisms but with a wholly different sensibility. At curtain call, I had fallen madly in love with him. I had to have him."

In Diamond's diary appeared this entry from February 22, 1953: "My friend, Alec Wilder, introduced me to this charming young man. I think he has been studying at the Actors Studio with Elia Kazan. Very handsome, short, muscular. Has a provocative way of looking at you, then suddenly smiling. Said he loved my *Rounds;* that he plays it on his recorder. Works in TV. Now what was his name? Can't remember. His eyes are magnetic so he wears glasses, perhaps to hide the allure of his eyes."

Imagine Diamond's surprise three days later, when he discovered that he lived next door to this nameless youth at the Hotel Iroquois.

On their first date, Diamond took Jimmy to see Charlie Chaplin in his dramatic comedy, *Limelight (1952)*. "I couldn't believe it: Chaplin made Jimmy weep. I realized he was a very sensitive boy."

At the time, Diamond was teaching at the Juilliard School of Music, to which he escorted Jimmy and introduced him to his students. Jimmy told them he was the world's most expert bongo drum player.

On another occasion, Diamond introduced him to his friend and fellow composer, Leonard Bernstein. "Lennie, who had already seduced Brando, grabbed Jimmy, embraced him, and stuck his tongue down his throat. Later, I told Jimmy that he shouldn't get a swelled head. 'Lennie does that to every handsome young boy he meets.'"

"That afternoon, I introduced Jimmy to this emerging playwright I knew,

Edward Albee, in the lobby of the Algonquin. Jimmy also met Albee's companion, Bill Flanagan."

In his diary, Diamond wrote: "Jimmy feels more lonely than anything else. He seems to think I am famous and wants to get to know me, perhaps thinking I will advance his career in some way. I can't interpret his seductive signals. He hopes to get a break in the theater, so I guess he has to use every well-connected person he can. I'd bet a million on him if I had it. Only Marlon Brando has made me feel this way about an actor. Tonight, Jimmy has invited me to his room, ostensibly to listen to music. But I suspect he is going to offer his body to me."

For the first two hours, Jimmy lay on his bed as Diamond sat in a chair while they listened to the composer's music. Finally, Diamond told him that if he removed all his clothing, he could enjoy the music better.

"He looked at me with that seductive smile, then took off every piece of his clothing and lay down again for me to enjoy every inch of him. After a few minutes, he looked over at me and said, 'Take what you want.'"

"I approached him like a hungry puppy who had not been fed in three days."

Diamond later [inaccurately] stated to an interviewer that his relationship with Jimmy was platonic, "a sort of father-son thing. Jimmy is just not my type."

But he presented a different version to Wilder: "His pubic hair is a natural blonde, not like that of Marilyn Monroe. But I suspect you already know that, having lived for a while with him at the Algonquin. He likes for me to come over in the afternoon and help him with his bath, giving him a massage later. He lets me use my mouth during the massage."

"You are one lucky son of a bitch," Wilder said.

As Diamond described to Wilder: "Jimmy's breath is like a whiff from the gods, his tongue having the taste of nectar. Even his semen tastes sweet, as if it had a tablespoon of sugar in it. With his body spread out before me, it was a feast. He is Adonis reincarnate."

Alice Denham, the Playboy Centerfold
WHO SLEPT WITH THE LITERATI AND WITH JAMES DEAN

During the autumn of 1952, a strikingly beautiful, aspirant writer and model—Alice Denham—entered Jimmy's life. Unlike most of the "star-fuckers" who pursued movie actors, Denham's preference was for leading members of the literati. She had previously been involved in dalliances with both Norman Mailer and Philip Roth.

In time, she would sustain an affair with Hugh Hefner, who would eventually designate her as *Playboy's Playmate of the Month.*

The issue that featured her as its nude centerfold also included one of her short stories.

In 2006, she'd write a juicy tell-all entitled *Sleeping With the Bad Boys,* detailing her affairs in and out of the beds of the literary elite of the 1950s.

[Publishers Weekly *reviewed* Sleeping With the Bad Bays *like this: "Denham, an essayist, television writer and the only woman whose fiction and breasts have appeared in the same issue of Playboy, offers up a fast-paced memoir that chronicles how a pretty girl from suburban Washington ended up on a bar stool at the storied Lion's Head. Run-ins with notorious figures—Norman Mailer, Philip Roth, Marlon Brando, Hugh Hefner—pepper nearly every page,*

"NY in the 50s was like Paris in the 30s," said Alice Denham, who configured herself as a kiss-and-tell "groupie" to the literary hotties of the Beat Generation

though readers interested in the hot dirt promised by the flap copy will be disappointed, as the "bad boys" here come off as little more than horny juveniles, and Denham skimps on the steam when she sacks with, say, James Dean. Most of the narrative is consumed with her slow-out-of-the-gate literary career that limps along; as her peers became icons, Denham modeled until the gigs dried up, and then wrote freelance. Though Denham reveals little that isn't widely known (Roth is a perv, Mailer is a freak), the sheer number of names dropped and follies recounted make for a fast and fun read."]

Denham's friends included Christine White, with whom Jimmy had auditioned months before for the Actors Studio. In her memoirs, Denham surmised that they had had an affair, but what Denham didn't tell Jimmy was that White harbored "this powerful crush on Marlon Brando, his rival."

Jimmy eventually escorted Denham to a Broadway theater for a performance of *The Immoralist,* even after he'd dropped out of the show. *[Jimmy's disastrous involvement in that production is more fully explored in a later chapter of this book.]*

Denham remembered that after the show, she climbed the steps to his studio on the top floor of a brownstone on West 68th Street. After a discussion about bullfighting and Carson McCullers' novel, *The Heart Is a Lonely Hunter,* the two of them tumbled between his yellowing sheets.

Claiming that he was a tit man and that he liked to nuzzle, she later wrote:

"Jimmy had smooth, baby-smelling rosy white skin with very little hair except for a blondish brown patch around his privates. He was lightly muscled, and he smelled of vanilla. We fin-

gered and tugged. Then went to the core of the plot, the confrontation that twisted with escalating tension to the gory, grinding climax. Me first. He was skilled. Satisfied, we folded together. Jimmy was tender and considerate...We were lusty; we fit. His dimensions were neither disappointing nor thrilling. He was average, perhaps the only thing about him that was."

They arranged a final meeting in New York after his completion of *Rebel Without a Cause.* He was planning to rush to Texas for the filming of *Giant.*

"He bounced up the steps to my apartment. He seemed due for an appointment and told me he had 'No time now. Gotta run.' He kissed me lightly on the lips and rushed back down the stairs."

"So long, star," she called after him.

That was the last time she ever saw him.

Eartha Kitt

AFTER LESSONS WITH "DANCE EMPRESS" KATHERINE DUNHAM, JIMMY TANGOES WITH "THE MOST EXCITING WOMAN IN THE WORLD"

Orson Welles defined singer Eartha Kitt as "the most exciting woman in the world." From the cotton fields of South Carolina, she rose to become an international "voice artist, cabaret entertainer, dancer, and political activist. Around the time she developed "a special relationship with James Dean," she became famous for her recording of "C'est si bon," released in 1953, which became a worldwide hit.

In 1979, Kitt spent several months in Key West filming *The Last Resort,* based on Darwin Porter's radically outrageous novel, *Butterflies in Heat,* wherein she played a character inspired by a transsexual prostitute. One morning, when she wasn't needed on the set, she accepted an invitation to cruise aboard a private yacht along the Florida Keys with friends who included the co-author of this biography. During the hours spent at sea, she discussed her friendship with the doomed James Dean, often contradicting what she'd previously told the press.

"In its way, it was a love affair, filled with detours and complications," she claimed.

"Our love for each other just happened. I became his *confidante* and I taught him about stage presence. We were like soul brother and sister. I'm from the South, so a little incest was thrown into the brew."

"Jamie, that's what I called him, and I had a spiritual contact—rare in any relationship—whereby we could be with each other, just walking along the streets of New York, or in Central Park, without words being spoken between us for hours. But we knew what the other was thinking. Sometimes we could just look at each other and laugh at something we were sharing in our mental conversation."

In 1950, before Jimmy met her, Orson Welles had cast Kitt in her first starring role as Helen of Troy in *Dr. Faustus.* She achieved stardom after her Broadway exposure in *New Faces of 1952.*

During her difficult childhood in South Carolina, because of her *café au lait* skin, Kitt had been mocked as "Yaller Gal." She was of mixed blood, her mother being Cherokee and African, her father rumored to be a German.

She had fled to New York in 1943. Within two years, she was in the Broadway production of *Carib Song.* By the time Jimmy met her in the early 1950s, she had had six top hits, including "I Want to Be Evil."

When she learned that Jimmy wanted to take dance classes, she introduced him to her friend and mentor, Katherine Dunham, hailed at the time as "The Matriarch and Queen Mother of Black Dance."

Two views of Eartha Kitt, Jimmy's "soulmate." *Lower photo* as Catwoman, the feline opponent of Batman.

In her memoir, *I'm Still Here,* published in 1989, Kitt wrote: "There was never any desire for sex between Nat King Cole or James Dean and myself." She later admitted, "At least half of that statement was true. Both Jimmy and I had a strong sex drive." In her memoir, she also denied an affair with Welles, even though he claimed that he'd seduced her.

When queried about these contradictions, Kitt said, "Who says a gal has to tell the truth about her affairs?"

Kitt issued a warning to Jimmy about Dunham: "She's the queen of her beehive. She is a tolerant person unless you try to take one of her men away from her. If you do that, watch out. She's a grand lady. At some of her backers' auditions, Doris Duke might show up, along with the Rockefellers and the Vanderbilts. If you violate one of her rules, she'll fine you five dollars. Of course, you don't know what rule you violated, but you still have to pay the fine for some alleged wrong. I think she changes the rules daily."

Jimmy found Dunham intimidating. Born in Chicago in 1909, she was the daughter of a father descended from slaves from the Ivory Coast and Madagascar, and a French Canadian/Native American mother, who died when she was three. In Haiti, she had investigated Vodun rituals and later became a "Mabo," or a sort of high priestess of that (occult) religion.

In time, as a world-renowned expert on dance anthropology and African "ethnochoreography," she would teach stage movements to Gregory Peck, José Ferrer, Jennifer Jones, Shelley Winters, Sidney Poitier, Shirley MacLaine and her brother, Warren Beatty, and to the billionaire tobacco heiress, Doris Duke. Marlon Brando had been one of her star pupils. "Sometimes, he didn't dance, but played the bongo drums for my other dancers," Denham told Jimmy.

"I play the bongo drums myself," Jimmy replied.

Dunham was rich in experience and even richer in ego. After her Broadway debut in the

Dance anthropologist, "ethno-choreographer," and modern dance visionary, Katherine Dunham barefoot and onstage.

1930s, she'd become celebrated. In one revue, she had adorned herself with a birdcage on her head and a cigar in her mouth. One of her most famous roles was in the Broadway production of *Cabin in the Sky,* directed by George Balanchine and starring Ethel Waters with Dunham in the role of a temptress.

Jimmy was eager to learn about her connection to Brando.

"At first, I didn't think Marlon wanted to learn dance," Dunham said. "I thought he was drawn to my classes because they were filled with budding Lena Hornes in skimpy outfits that revealed everything. In time, he got around to fucking nearly every gal in my troupe, along with a few of the better hung boys. But mostly, he preferred my red hot mammas."

"In no time at all, Marlon learned the cakewalk and bebop dances, each of whose roots are from Africa," Dunham said. "He told me he didn't want to be a white boy dancer, but a black dancer, moving to the rhythms of drumbeats."

"That's what I want for myself, too," Jimmy said.

"You're lucky to be working with me," Dunham told him in the presence of Kitt. "In Chicago, the press calls me the hottest thing to hit town since Mrs. O'Leary's cow kicked over that bucket that started the Chicago fire."

"Marlon had no inhibitions," she said. "He was not one for false modesty. I teach my dancers they have to show off their bodies—a dancer can't come onstage clad in an overcoat. I once dressed him in a Tarzan loincloth with instructions not to wear a jockstrap. Jockstraps are not known in African dances. He came out with his buttocks exposed except for a string. When he danced, his loincloth flew up and showed us everything he had."

After two weeks of classes, Dunham told Jimmy, "You don't have enough nigger blood to be a real African dancer. By the way, I can say nigger but you can't. If you do, I'll cut off those little white balls of yours."

Later, she told Kitt, "Dean's a nice kid, but definitely not from deepest Africa. He is no Brando. Unlike Marlon, Dean didn't take a shine to me. He seems afraid to mess with a high-stepping black bitch like me. Frankly, I think I'm too much woman for him. He wouldn't know how to handle me. It takes a Mandingo for me."

***

As the days and weeks went by, Jimmy's friendship with Kitt deepened. "She became my tigress with a growl."

He told his newest friend, John Gilmore, that Kitt had mystical powers. "She's like a witch doctor. She has magic in her soul. She knows the answers to the mysteries of the ages."

"Jimmy and I were practically a debating society," she said. "He'd make some ridiculous statement just to hear me attack it. One time, he told me that he and I were descended from space invaders who arrived on earth thousands of years ago, fleeing from a soon-to-be extinct planet."

"You and I are different from most people because we are descended from those invaders," he told her. "One day, a team of archeologists will find their space capsule somewhere in the Sahara."

Sometimes, he'd arrive at her place and spend hours with her, just listening to recorded music. "At times, he was off in space, perhaps in that former planet from which he claimed we'd descended. When I knew he was coming over, I always went to Harlem and bought a lot of barbecued ribs from Louis Armstrong's favorite joint. Jimmy devoured them. Perhaps he did have some black blood in him after all, in spite of what Dunham claims."

Kitt was one of the few women with whom Jimmy felt free enough to discuss his sexuality, admitting to numerous affairs with men.

She lent a sympathetic ear. "Both of us are from a class of rejected people. Neither of us fits into society. If society really knew us, they'd reject us even more than they already do. We're oppressed, which leads to depression. Nothing in the world is more painful than rejection, and I've known my share of it—and I know you have, too. I'm straight, but I understand the gay impulse in men. Frankly, I think every man is a little bit gay, and that every woman has a lesbian streak."

She convinced him he was in metamorphosis. Ironically, at the time, he was performing a reading of Franz Kafka's drama *Metamorphosis*. "I won't be able to go home again to Indiana because I am no longer the farmboy who left it. That James Dean is dead."

"Been there, done that," she answered. "I'm not the little yaller gal who was raped by the white owner of the plantation where my mama and I worked in South Carolina. And of course, you're no longer a farmboy. You're an artist." She giggled and laughed with that growling purr of hers. "And sometimes you're the devil himself."

Eventually, Jimmy's liaison with Kitt would be played out against the backdrop of Hollywood.

***

Truman Capote once revealed to Stanley Haggart that he and their mutual friend, Tennessee Williams, had once seen Jimmy emoting on stage in a performance of Calder Willinghams' *End as a Man.*

And Tennessee had directly revealed to Haggart that he had once traveled to Philadelphia with the specific intention of seeing Jimmy in a tryout performance of *See the Jaguar.*

Addressing Haggart directly, Capote asked, "Do you think he could be had?"

Haggart answered, "Probably…Jimmy was a kept boy in Hollywood, sustained and paid for by my friend, Rogers Brackett. He was also a hustler, although he doesn't seem to be doing that anymore. Rather, he seems to be giving it away these days, and often at my apartment."

"Well, I'm going after him," Capote answered. "And, as you know, whatever Lola wants, Lola gets."

"You've got one advantage," Haggart said. "He loves your novel, *Other Voices, Other Rooms,* and he gives out copies of your short stories to people to read. He told Tennessee that you select words with the precision of a brain surgeon."

***

Two nights later, Capote returned to Haggart's apartment for a drink and to gossip. "I've met with Dean at this dump called Jerry's Tavern. He doesn't believe in dressing up. But I worked my magic on him. By the way, do you mind if I use that garden apartment tomorrow night? Right now, I have a lover staying with me, and I don't want him to think I have a cheating heart."

"Not you, Truman, never…" Haggart said. "But of course, you can. The back apartment is yours."

"I interpreted Dean as a rather sensitive boy," Capote said. "Far more than Brando, but not as much as Monty. He's full of anguish for reasons not known

360

to me. One day he'll probably be a character in one of my novels. I felt the same way about Dean that I did when I first met Monty. I sensed a blossoming artist in both men. Like Monty, Dean has all his sensibilities, but also all his flaws."

During the next month, Capote and Jimmy made use of Haggart's garden apartment. Since Jimmy had his own key, he came and went without getting involved with Haggart's frequent guests in the other rooms.

"They were Back Street Lovers," Haggart claimed.

Sometimes, Jimmy would visit without Capote," Haggart said. *"The Little Prince* remained his favorite movie, but Truman's *Other Voices, Other Rooms* ran a close second."

That novel, reviewed at the time as both notorious and shocking, had been published by Random House in 1948. Capote, then the country's most flagrant *enfant terrible,* had posed for a notorious portrait—photographed by Harold Halma—on the jacket's back cover. Halma captured him lying seductively on a sofa, emphasizing his petulant mouth, his baby bangs, his come-hither gaze, and his suggested availability as "bait" for molestation by older admirers.

The novel was the story of a precocious thirteen-year-old boy, Joel Knox, who is sent to live in a small hamlet in an Alabama backwater. Harper Lee later used Capote as the role model for Dill in her megaseller, *To Kill a Mockingbird.*

Months later, Capote carried around reviews of the novel, which he collectively called "the good, the bad, the ugly, and the raves." A reviewer at *Time* magazine claimed that the novel "made my flesh crawl." *Library Journal* advised librarians not to stock it. *The Nation* viewed it as "an apology for homosexuality. *The Chicago Tribune,* however, found it "as dazzling a phenomenon that has burst onto the literary scene in the last few years."

Capote told Haggart, Jimmy, and others of his friends that he wrote the novel "to exorcise my demons."

When Capote wasn't around, Jimmy told Haggart that he identified with the character of Joel. "In some ways, it mirrors my own sense of abandonment and my search for my father. I found aspects of myself in Joel, who seems to be going from an

Soem critics viewed Truman Capote's *Other Voices, Other Rooms* as a masterpiece. One attacker blasted it as "A fairy version of *Huckleberry Finn.*"

uncertain boyhood into a young man with a strong sense of himself and an acceptance of who he is, even his dark side. I think the book is about making peace with your own identity. At times, I want to stand up to the world and shout, 'Hello, suckers, I'm James Dean. Take me or leave me. I don't give a fuck."

One night over dinner with Haggart and Jimmy, Capote expressed how deeply he hated his mother. To toughen him up, she had enrolled him at St. John's Military Academy.

"From Day One, I knew I'd never be a functioning member of the U.S. military," Capote confided. "But my life among future soldiers had its advantages. I shared a dormitory with twenty other guys. Here is where I learned about dicks, finding out that they come in all shapes and sizes, cut and uncut. Men at the academy were at their sexual peak, and the only relief they had, other than whacking off, was for me to crawl between their sheets at night. I had a gay old time. It wasn't exactly what mother had in mind."

One morning after Capote left for an appointment at Random House, Jimmy, still in his briefs, had one of Haggart's home-cooked, farm-style breakfasts. "Don't get the idea that I'm sexually turned on by Capote," he said. "About five inches of pink meat is not my fantasy. I'm having sex with him because: *One*, I admire his writing, and *Two*, he's working on a novel that could be adapted into a screenplay with a leading role in it for me."

"Its main character is a café society hooker, Holly Golightly. She gets involved with this writer—played by me—who lives upstairs and who hasn't had anything published in five years. He's a kept boy, supported by this rich older woman."

"It sounds like it has possibilities," Haggart said.

"And do I ever know how to play a kept boy, thanks to your friend, Rogers," Jimmy said. "When I'm fucking Capote, I have to ask him to shut his trap. That babylike voice of his is such a turnoff. It sounds artificial to me, like some fourth grader whose voice never changed. It reminds me of a little boy trapped in a man's body."

"Don't be deceived by Truman's physicality," Haggart said. "He's stronger than he looks. When filming *Beat the Devil,* in Italy with Humphrey Bogart, he beat Bogie fair and square in an arm wrestling contest, and then, according to the terms of their agreement, Bogie had to submit to a blow-job because he'd lost. As for that 'unfinished novel,' don't assume that he's actually writing it. He often lies about such things."

"But he's told me events associated with every page of the novel," Jimmy said. "What I mean is, it's already written, at least in the fucker's head. But he doesn't have a title for it yet."

"That probably won't be a problem for him," Haggart said. "Tennessee and Truman are masters at churning out bizarre titles."

***

One night at a raucous and irreverent party in Key West, a drunken Capote showed up at the home of the designer, Danny Stirrup. "I've sucked off bigtime movie stars," he said later in the evening. "Errol Flynn, John Garfield...and did I name Rory Calhoun? I've also screwed around with Denham Fouts, the most famous male whore in the world, the favorite of the King of Greece. But despite all that, my greatest thrill (there was meat there for the poor) came from an air-conditioner repairman I met in Palm Springs."

"And ironically, my two major sexual disappointments were Gore Vidal and James Dean."

"It's too bad I don't like to go to bed with women," Capote replied. "I could have had any woman on the planet. Dietrich. Garbo. But I can't understand why anyone would want to go to bed with a woman. Boring. Just like Dean and Vidal."

Haggart, who was at the party, later said that he knew why Capote had turned on Jimmy. "Our friend just got tired of all the promises Capote kept making. He began to fear he wasn't going to carry through on a single one of them and was just stringing him along. He rejected further sexual advances from Truman. Jimmy had been handsome, charming, a great lover to Truman. Almost overnight, he went from that to the dullest lay of all time."

Capote had one final encounter with Jimmy at a party in Hollywood. He had just seen a screening of *East of Eden* when he approached Jimmy, who seemingly had been trying to avoid him. "I saw your picture, my dear," he said with a sneer of contempt, as if he'd just swallowed a bad oyster. "I fear you've been cast into the Brando mold. Of course, with just one picture under your belt, it's a little too early to rush to judgment. We'll have to see what you do in the future. You have a small but limited appeal that emerges now and then from all that Brando overlay. Don't you ever worry that he might sue you for impersonation? It's wrong to steal another actor's voice, his mannerisms, and his style. Perhaps in your next picture, you'll try to act like James Dean and not like Brando."

Jimmy glared at him. "Fuck off, faggot!" he said before moving quickly to the other side of the room, where he was surrounded by admirers.

Truman Capote...Ostentatiously vicious (including during his interchanges with Jimmy) and, in the end, tragic.

Capote never forgave Jimmy for his blunt sexual rejection of him. Even after Jimmy's death, he continued with his critiques. After seeing the knife fight in *Rebel Without a Cause,* he told *The New Yorker,* "Jimmy is the symbol of hot-headed youth, with a switchblade approach to life's little problems."

Years later, he even uttered a critique of Jimmy's short run in *The Immoralist.* "I knew Dean only because he knew Tennessee, and he was always hanging out with him and other friends of mine. So I inevitably kept running into him. He was hoping that Tennessee would write a powerful role for him, like he did for Brando. Alas, that would never happen. He certainly wasn't any good in the Gide play. To put it mildly, I never thought much of him as an actor. I don't think he had star quality."

Tennessee later commented on the Jimmy vs. Capote feud: "Jimmy once said to me, 'I want to ask you something. You, of all people, might know. Just who in hell invented Truman Capote?'"

Jimmy Discovers Arlene Sachs

"The Only Virgin Left in Manhattan"

Into Jimmy's life marched Arlene Sachs, a woman of some mystery who billed herself under different names depending on the era and venue she was publicizing. Her monikers included Tasha Martel, Arlene Martel, Arline Greta Sax, Arline Sax, and Arlene Sax.

An attractive Jewish girl from the Bronx, she would in time have affairs with everyone from Jimmy to Cary Grant.

At the age of seventeen, she was enrolled in Manhattan's High School of the performing arts, dreaming of stardom as an actress.

She'd seen Jimmy in the Kraft Television Theater's presentation of *A Long Time Till Dawn,* and was captivated by his image.

Somehow, she managed to get his phone number and used it to call him one evening. She explained that although she was a teenager, "I have a woman's desires." She also told him, "I'm very beautiful, and I want to be your girlfriend."

Intrigued by her audacity, he agreed to meet her the following day for coffee at the rooftop café of the Museum of Modern Art.

That very night, if reports are to be believed, he took her virginity at his studio. He admitted later that he didn't believe she was a virgin—"They don't exist in Manhattan"—until he saw blood on

Arlene Sachs...betrayed by Jimmy's cheating heart.

his sheets.

"I found the sex painful, and not at all enjoyable, so I wondered why people were so obsessed with it," she said. "But Jimmy was patient with me. I remembered he gave me my first orgasm, and then I began to feel what sex was all about. He broke me in. I started to enjoy it. He was very patient and considerate as a lover."

"Dining out for us often meant saving up for movie tickets and a bag of popcorn to share," she said. "Perhaps a hot dog to divide, if we were loaded. We sat in the balcony of Times Square theaters where, if the seat in front was empty, Jimmy would throw his legs across the back of it."

"I remember one night, he fell asleep watching Robert Mitchum and Jane Russell in *His Kind of Woman.* I had a hard time waking him up at the end of the picture. Then it was off to Jerry's."

"Once I got over the initial penetration, and on subsequent nights, Jimmy glided in smoothly," she wrote in an unpublished memoir. "I began to look forward to our rolls in the hay. I'm an Aries born in April, and he is an Aquarius born in February, so, as sexual partners, we were most compatible."

She later claimed that their subsequent dates were "boy-girl stuff," including strolls through Central Park, followed by long nights at his studio, where he played the bongo drums for her. "Or else, he put on classical music or read passages from *The Little Prince* to me, neither one of which I adored."

"I wanted him for myself, but that was not to be," she said. "One night I saw him at Jerry's talking to this very pretty girl," she said. "I followed him to his apartment. I stayed there looking up at his window. The lights went out after midnight. She had not left when I went home at three in the morning. I had to get up at seven to go to work. Not only that, but I heard from this guy I met on a casting call that Jimmy was also known for seducing other actors. So I learned painfully that he would never belong to me exclusively. Often, he would call me at three o'clock in the morning, since he suffered from insomnia and needed someone to pour out his feelings to. I was it. He'd talk for three or four hours."

Sachs had found a job as a hatcheck girl at Birdland, a venue for be-bop and jazz. She'd saved enough to rent an apartment for $35 a month.

One night, she invited Jimmy over for a home-cooked dinner. He asked if he could bring a friend, and she reluctantly said yes.

"He arrived with Barbara Glenn, who also wanted to be an actress," Sachs said. "He told me he was working with her on a scene for an audition."

"I left them to rehearse their scene when I went out to shop for diner," Sachs said. "When I got back with my pork chops and salad greens, I could almost smell the sex in the room. I knew he'd used our bed to fuck this girl. I stumbled into the kitchen with the groceries. My heart was broken. I wanted to vomit in the sink. Somehow, I managed to pull together a dinner, but I viewed his bringing Glenn here as an act of cruelty. I knew I could never trust him."

"In looking back, I believed he brought Glenn over to signal to me that our affair was over," Sachs said. "This was his way of telling me that he had moved on. Believe it or not, our friendship survived our affair. We became friends, not lovers."

He learned that she'd soon found another boyfriend, an actor named Don Miele, who was in his thirties. He was considered very temperamental and known as a rebel like Jimmy.

"One night, when I was entertaining Don, Jimmy phoned and wanted to come over," Sachs said. "I was afraid both men would get into a fight and said no. As it happened, Jimmy came by anyway.":

Like Jimmy, Miele was a member of the Actors Studio, and also like Jimmy, he rebelled. In Miele's case, the focus of his rage was Elia Kazan, who, from his niche at the Actors Studio, had delivered a verbal assault on Miele's acting.

To Sachs' surprise, the two actors bonded. Miele said that after Kazan had viciously attacked his acting, "I told him, 'You're nothing but a bunch of whores.'"

Kazan had responded, "You're a genius. Stick around."

To that, Miele had replied, "I may be a genius, but you're a second rate director." Then he had stormed out.

As the evening in Sachs' apartment progressed, and a third bottle of wine was consumed, Miele turned to Jimmy and said, "I hear you're a hot shot on Broadway, but that you had to give head to get there."

Sachs was amazed that Jimmy did not take offense. "If anything, they sat there on the sofa, laughing and talking like two lovers. I was afraid that Jimmy was going to steal my boyfriend."

The following night, Jimmy called to thank her and asked her for Miele's phone number. She pretended that she'd lost it.

"Are you really a homosexual?" she asked him.

"I'm a man," he answered, "but if the gay guys don't let up on me soon, I will begin to doubt that very seriously. They won't leave me alone. They bring me gifts. They offer me roles on television and in the theater."

One night, shortly after Sach's 18th birthday, she called Jimmy over for a party. She had invited about a dozen wannabe actors in for liquor, which they'd brought themselves. It was a mixed crowd of men and women. "I told Jimmy we were having an orgy, and I wanted to know if he would like to come over."

"I'll come over," he said, emphasizing the word "come."

She decided to play a gag on him, and her guests agreed. The girls took off their tops, the men pulled off their shirts, and some of them stripped down to their underwear before they collectively crawled beneath a pair of blankets.

The room was lit by candlelight, and Sachs left her door slightly ajar. Within twenty minutes, Jimmy entered and witnessed what he thought was an orgy in process.

"I couldn't believe it," Sachs said later. "Jimmy unzipped his jeans, took out his penis, and started to masturbate. I jumped up and turned on the lights and told Jimmy that it was all a joke. He didn't look the least bit surprised. Even with the lights on, he continued to jerk off and exploded onto the blanket, hitting one or two girls in the face. They screamed. I guess he had the last laugh that night."

Sometimes, even when they were dating, Jimmy could call this mysterious actor and make a date with him. One night he let her listen in. She heard a familiar voice tell Jimmy, "I want to cock you." He was basically begging Jimmy to come over.

"Who in hell was that?" Sachs asked after Jimmy put down the phone.

"That was Van Johnson, 'America's Sweetheart,' the idol of thousands of teenage girls."

[When he went to Hollywood, Jimmy would get far better acquainted with Johnson through their mutual friend, actor Kennan Wynn.]

***

In time, Sachs would become a member of the Actors Studio. There, she developed "intense relationships" with Sidney Lumet and Anthony Quinn.

She later claimed, "Tony was my first taste of a Mexican dick. He once was quoted as saying, 'A man's masculinity is never in his penis.' I would disagree with that, and so would Tony's many girlfriends: Ingrid Bergman, Rita Hayworth, Carole Lombard, Maureen O'Hara, Mae West, Shelley Winters, and even George Cukor."

"I went to bed with Tony only three times, and then it was over," Sachs said. "He told me that he had to move on because he wanted to impregnate every woman in the world."

Sachs never became a star, but she got a lot of work, appearing on Perry Mason dramas and even in an episode of *Star Trek*. She also played the evil witch on *Bewitched* and interpreted key roles in both *Hogan's Heroes* and *I Dream of Jeannie*.

At a Star Trek convention, she made an indiscreet comment, telling a fan, "I've known many men and three husbands. There's no argument that my two most famous lovers were James Dean and Cary Grant, two deeply troubled men. I shouldn't be saying this, but I had the feeling that, even though in bed with me, both of them would rather be getting screwed by some man."

During her courtship with Jimmy, Sachs escorted him to the studio of her friend, Ray Schatt, a photographer, with the suggestion that the budding actor might be a hot prospect for him to photograph.

Although Schatt specialized in photos of newsworthy personalities in the performing arts, at first, he was not impressed with Jimmy. Sachs told Schatt that Jimmy was appearing on Broadway in *The Immoralist* and that he "does this fantastic dance with scissors, which you really should shoot."

Schatt recalled, "I was baffled by this boy. He looked like some young man on the lam that she'd picked up wandering homeless in the Bowery. However, he suddenly sprang to life and did this incredible dance for us. It was an amazing feat. He had a radiance about him, a kind of glow. I'm not making this up. How can I put it? Jimmy danced into my heart that afternoon."

"He was a squinty little schlump of a person," Schatt later recalled. "I thought he was sort of ugly until he performed that dance around the room. He transitioned himself from a bum into an Adonis."

Beginning that afternoon, Jimmy and Schatt became close friends. Schatt eventually taught him some of the hands-on aspects of photography.

After Dennis Stock, Schatt became the second most-famous photographer to turn his camera on Jimmy, eventually churning out many iconic shots of the actor.

Even before his introduction to Jimmy, Schatt was a well-known photographer of theatrical personalities. His previous subjects had included Tennessee Williams, Geraldine Page, Rod Steiger, Patricia Neal, Elia Kazan, director Arthur Penn, Ben Gazzara, Paul Newman, Billie Holiday, Steve McQueen, and Marilyn Monroe.

But his photographs of Jimmy became his crowning achievement. Schatt was eventually designated as the official photographer of the Actors Studio.

He began snapping photos of Jimmy in February of 1954. Right from the beginning, he suspected that Jimmy was an exhibitionist. He would later find out just how much of an exhibitionist he was. "He told me that he worked out at a gym three or four times a week."

"I'm quite an attraction when I head for the showers," Jimmy said. "I figured the boys want a show, so I produce an erection. After all, they couldn't gauge the size of my dick if I kept it soft."

"Jimmy was a Method actor, and I soon recognized that theatrical instinct in him when I began to photograph him. I would direct and provoke scenes that became inspirational. But I knew my pictures must still be honest and interesting beyond the performance he was giving."

After their first meeting, Jimmy asked Schatt if he would follow him around and document his activities. "He also wanted to photograph *me*,"

Schatt confessed, "so I became his teacher."

"I immediately found out that his concentration was not to be counted on, which meant that our classes were somewhat unpredictable and by necessity changeable in form. However, when he was interested in participating, his energy was powerful. He had that greatest of intellectual qualities—curiosity about everything."

"Jimmy was always 'on,'" Schatt claimed. "I dubbed him Mr. Theater."

Soon, Jimmy was seen coming and going frequently from Schatt's studio.

"James Dean Is an Exhibitionist"

Claimed Ray Schatt, His "Torn Sweater" Photographer

Schatt's "Torn Sweater" photographic session with Jimmy remains one of the most celebrated and best set of photos of him ever snapped.

On December 29, 1954, Jimmy showed up at Schatt's studio wearing a yellow turtleneck sweater. He asked the photographer if he reminded him of Michelangelo's statue of David in Florence.

"A first, I thought that meant he wanted me to photograph him buck-ass naked," Schatt said. "But that wasn't the case. I shot him in this turtleneck. Only after I developed the pictures did I realize there was a tear in one of the sweater's shoulders. I hadn't spotted it before."

Life magazine rejected the pictures. In their editorial office, Frank D. Campion wanted "Shots that are more manly, not some actor impersonating Audrey Hepburn."

Despite the delay in their release, Schatt's "Torn Sweater" photos became among the most popular of all photographs of James Dean. In 1982, Delilah Books published *James Dean: A Portrait,* which included them. "He was still in that searching and scratching period of his life," Schatt said.

His photographs had great influence on how the world came to view James Dean.

"I came to love Jimmy as a friend," Schatt said. "But he was a crazy mother-fucker. Once, he took a chair from my studio and carried it downstairs. When I looked out my studio window, the lunatic was sitting on it, right in the middle of the avenue, almost daring cars to dodge him. That is, until he saw a cop coming, and then he hurried inside, leaving my chair."

"I wanted to spark up dull old New York today," Jimmy said. "Don't you sometimes get bored out of your mind and yearn for some action? I thought I might bring some life to the street, sitting out there casually smoking a cigarette, letting the cars brake to avoid killing me. I know I might have caused a death, maybe my own."

According to Schatt, "He also carried around a revolver, which he said had been a gift from Lynn Bari, a B-actress who was often cast as a gun moll in a lot of 1940s movies."

Jimmy told Schatt that he'd met Bari when he played a bit part in Hollywood on the film, *Has Anybody Seen My Gal?* He said he had only one bullet in the gun, which he planned to use to commit suicide should life prove too difficult for him.

"I don't think Jimmy was ever himself," Schatt said. "He was always impersonating someone. "One day, I had a party at my studio and invited such guests as his friend, Bill Gunn. At one point, after a few glasses of wine, Jimmy took out his two front teeth and passed them around. 'Wanna buy thum gold, man?' he asked my guests. 'I teed thum thoup.' *[translation: "Do you want to buy some gold? I need some soup."]* Then he launched into a bongo drum concert so loud no one could hear themselves talk. His desire to be noticed was almost pathological."

"He wanted to go just to restaurants patronized by people in the theater who were more likely to recognize him," Schatt claimed, "If nobody recognized him, he got pissed off."

"I know this sounds like a contradiction, but Jimmy was a loner who sought attention," Schatt said. "We used to eat at Louie's, this joint in the Village. But the lights were dim, and nobody recognized Jimmy, so he stopped going there."

"Even when we went to places where other actors gathered, he told me he still felt uncomfortable, because he was working and they were not," Schatt said.

"Jimmy wasn't afraid to strip down," Schatt said. "One day, I opened my door. He was standing there stark naked. Later, I heard that when he was making *East of Eden,* he came out of his dressing room without a stitch on and paraded around in front of cast and crew. The only other actor I'd heard who did that was Errol Flynn."

"There were also rumors that Jimmy would stand nude in the open doorway of his apartment while he was being sodomized," Schatt also revealed. "But that sounds just too far-fetched."

"Jimmy would do the damndest things," Schatt said. "One day he pulled off all his clothes in my studio and paraded out the door onto the sidewalk. I looked down from my window, and there he was, standing naked right on the sidewalk as cars slowed down to take a look and passers-by stopped to stare. He wasn't totally nude. He had on this porkpie hat that he wore for several weeks. I rushed down to the street with a blanket and wrapped it around him and brought him back upstairs. The next day, he walked the streets in a fruity Carmen Miranda headdress he'd picked up from somewhere."

"One day, Jimmy stripped down and wanted me to take some pictures," Schatt said. "He stretched out like one of those paintings that hung over the bar in a Gary Cooper Western movie—you know, of some nude woman. In this case, Jimmy placed his hand over his crotch and was giggling like a virgin as he pursed his lips and fluttered his eyes."

"I was often asked if he were gay or bisexual," Schatt said. "Well, maybe. His nuttiness and constant attempts at breaking the humdrum could have led him into anything."

Jimmy's agent, Jane Deacy, arranged for Howard Thompson of *The New York Times* to interview him. Jimmy didn't want the interview conducted within his private living quarters. "I don't want some god damn reporter knowing where and how I live."

He told the newsman that he'd gotten kicked out of UCLA because he'd "busted the faces of two fuckers who deserved it. I wasn't happy there. My father wanted me to study law. Can you imagine me as a lawyer?"

"To me, New York is a vital, thriving, throbbing city marching to its own drumbeat," he said. "The problem is that a cat like me can get lost in its maze. People are human beings in New York. In Hollywood, they are desensitized whores."

Thompson didn't print part of the interview.

***

The Schatt/Dean friendship eventually ended unhappily. When Jimmy finally attained the beginnings of some financial success, Schatt asked if he'd lend him the money for a new camera, which he badly need. Jimmy refused. "Who do you think I am, man? A god damn bank?"

Equally infuriating, he granted access to a rival photographer, and denied it to Schatt, who had befriended him for so long and taken so many pictures of him for free.

"I think he just used people," Schatt said. "He sucked up to them, got what he wanted, and then went on his way."

Months later, Schatt encountered Jimmy in Hollywood. "He no longer looked like something Michelangelo would want to sculpt. He had bags under his eyes from his insomnia. He could have passed for a consumptive romantic poet, a dying male version of Camille. The constant smoking had dimmed the luster of his skin. Four packages of Camels a day will do that to anybody. More than that, his soul seemed to be creeping out of his body, and all this inner misery was reflected on his face."

In later years, an embittered Schatt, during interviews he granted, demonstrated his increased disillusion about Jimmy, and expressed a certain contempt for the cult based on his former friend. "Every actor I photographed wanted to look like Jimmy Dean. The reputation spread that I had 'discovered' the boy, which was not true. For a time, I couldn't get rid of Steve McQueen who hung out at my studio. He had an obsession about Dean. He had me take a frontal nude of him. Frankly, I told him one day that he'd never make it as an actor. Was I wrong?"

"After seeing Jimmy in *The Immoralist,* I also told him what a lousy actor he was. My exact words were, 'You'll never amount to anything in the theater or the movies.' If truth be known, I still think Dean and McQueen were rotten actors."

Jimmy Kneels

IN HOMAGE TO A BLACK MUSICIAN

The most outrageous story ever told about James Dean topped any revelation made by Roy Schatt. Although it may be apocryphal, mention of it has been made in several books, and there are those who swore that it was true.

One night, back in the days when lots of upscale white people went late at night to Harlem for entertainment, Jimmy joined a party that included composers Leonard Rosenblum and Alec Wilder, along with Stanley Haggart and his artist friend, Woodrow ("Woody") Parrish-Martin.

[Almost forgotten today, the very gossipy Parrish-Martin was known in media and arts circles at the time for his then-iconoclastic views on set design and decorating. He enjoyed a minor degree of celebrity for his promotion of, among others, the then-novel Haitian school of painting and an avant-garde use of colors such as chartreuse and purple in his decorating schemes.]

"I met Jimmy a few times when he used Stanley's garden apartment," Parrish-Martin said. "I was told he was outrageous, but that night in Harlem, I saw evidence of it firsthand. Before we rode uptown together, Jimmy got into the taxi with his bongo drums. We had a hell of a time that night and stayed till the club closed at around two or three o'clock."

"At the club in Harlem, Jimmy joined the black musicians who let him play those blasted drums. There was a piano player there—a mulatto—who was strikingly handsome, with a Robert Taylor mustache. Jimmy had been fascinated by him all

An *avant-garde* arts arbiter of the 50s, with tales to tell: Woody Parrish-Martin.

evening. I thought he'd invite him home with him."

"We sat in front-row seats…all of us loved the jazz that the band was playing. As the night wore on, there were only about ten customers left in the club—everybody was drunk, including Jimmy. He approached this musician and bluntly asked, "Will you let me suck your cock?'"

"The piano player didn't look shocked at all," Parrish-Martin said. "I think a lot of white men, including Cole Porter and Monty Woolley, had gone down on him many times before. He simply unzipped his pants, pulled out his penis, masturbated it hard, and offered it to Jimmy. Then the kid got down on his knees and serviced him. It took him about ten minutes to reach climax, and we all sat there taking in the show. Management should have charged for the exhibition. It was well worth it."

"That night, I saw firsthand how good Jimmy was a deep throat artist. He'd been practicing on somebody, maybe Rock Hudson."

"After I moved out of Stanley's apartment, I never saw Dean again."

John Gilmore

"At Last, I've Found a Boy Prettier Than I Am"
—James Dean

Beating the pavements of Manhattan, looking for a gig, Jimmy encountered Ray Curry, another actor he'd met when he was an extra in Hollywood. Jimmy knew of a drugstore on West 47th Street that served fresh orange juice and "big muffins with all the butter patties you wanted." He invited Curry to go with him there.

At the counter, Jimmy noticed this young man sitting a few feet away. "Hot damn!" he said to Curry. "At last, I've seen a boy prettier than I am."

"Hey, I know this guy," Curry said. "He's Jonathan Gilmore [an actor/author later billed as John Gilmore]. "I'll introduce you."

Gilmore later recalled his memory of first seeing Jimmy in March of 1953, comparing him to a small scarecrow: "Dean lurched into the place and tripped over the doorsill, struggling to keep his balance. A shock of hair stood out like straw. His hands were jammed into the pockets of baggy gabardine trousers. A checked jacket hung on his frame like a sack with leather patches on the cuffs. He had the aura of a burlesque performer in vaudeville. He was hunched down into himself—almost shrinking and squinting through tortoise-framed glasses."

Later, Curry said, "It was a case of two soulmates coming together. These guys shared two passions: Bullfighting and motorcycle racing. Jonathan was actually reading a book on bullfighting when I introduced him to Jimmy."

A relationship with Gilmore was developed that afternoon that Gilmore would later write about in a trio of memoirs, including *Laid Bare, The Real James Dean* (1971); *The Hollywood Death Trap* (1997); and *Live Fast—Die Young: Remembering the Short Life of James Dean* (also 1997).

Many Dean biographers overlooked Gilmore's role in Jimmy's life, but he was a key figure. Even some of Jimmy's best friends were unaware of the bond between the two young actors.

Born in the charity ward of the Los Angeles General Hospital, Gilmore was four years younger than Jimmy. He became a child actor, even appearing in a movie with cowboy star Gene Autry and interpreting other bit parts at Republic Studios. John Hodiak and Ida Lupino, in time, became his mentors. Hodiak introduced him to Marilyn Monroe, about whom Gilmore would write a book, *Inside Marilyn Monroe* (2007).

At first, Gilmore and Jimmy were friends, not lovers. Sometimes, if Gilmore had ten dollars, he might lend Jimmy two. Both of them shared tips about the latest casting calls for Broadway plays. They would often meet at their favorite street corner, eating together at a drugstore counter where the food was cheap, greasy, and filling. In the beginning, they saw each other two or three times a week, often viewing films at rundown movie houses on Times Square.

It wasn't long before the subject of sex arose.

"Jimmy seemed obsessed with Marlon Brando and had this picture of him with a penis in his mouth." Gilmore said. *[That photo, replicated underground, was widely circulated at the time among the gay colonies of New York and Los Angeles.]* "In reference to Brando, Jimmy said, 'I learned that he often rolls over for guys and takes it up the ass.'"

At one point, Jimmy told Gilmore that he'd been seduced by some of the biggest stars in Hollywood. "As another pretty boy, you must have had your share of stars, too," he said.

Gilmore revealed that once, at a party in Hollywood at the Garden of Allah, he was only fifteen years old. "A drunken Tyrone Power came up to me and told me that I was one of the most beautiful boys he'd ever seen. He kissed me and wanted to kiss me again, trying to stick his tongue down in my mouth."

One night early in their relationship, Gilmore and Jimmy got smashed at Jerry's Tavern and later ended up in his apartment. Jimmy asked him if he'd

John Gilmore...kinky nights with James Dean

374

ever gone to bed with a producer or director when he'd worked in pictures in Hollywood.

"A couple of times," Gilmore said, "but I didn't like it."

According to Gilmore, Jimmy then asked him if he'd ever tasted "jizz."

Gilmore answered that he had, but that he had spit it out.

In a memoir, Gilmore wrote, "Jimmy put his hand behind my neck and pulled my face toward his, putting his lips on mine. I was the first time I've ever been really kissed by another guy."

"Can you be fucked?" Jimmy asked.

"Jesus, I don't think so."

Nibbling on his neck, Jimmy then tried to sodomize Gilmore. "At first, I tried to go down on him, but his cock was too big, and I choked. We tried to fuck, but it didn't work out exactly, as he wanted it to."

At some point, Jimmy had to withdraw without reaching climax. The session ended with Gilmore "Jacking Jimmy off with skin lotion."

In 1980, the gossip tabloid, *The Hollywood Star,* ran an article by Gilmore entitled "I Had Sex With James Dean." In it, Gilmore reported details he omitted from his books.

"Jimmy liked to be cuddled in bed. He liked to be held and he liked to be kissed."

On some occasions, Jimmy asked Gilmore if he'd dress up as a girl and let himself be escorted to parties as Jimmy's date.

Gilmore later wrote, "In time, I eventually felt as if I were Jimmy's mother, brother, and lover. We were bad guys playing bad boys while opening up the bisexual sides of our personalities...One sex scene between the two of us played out in black leather to the music of Edith Piaf. The sex was a game. Jimmy was obsessed with riding the black ship in hell, and for a time I was on board with him."

Jimmy seemed to view Gilmore as an unthreatening wastepaper basket. According to Gilmore, "Into it, he dumped his chaotic, erotic, and crazy ideas. We enjoyed poetry and bullfighting, bongo drums, girls (often the same ones). We had the same crummy friends, and we shared the same sleepless nights."

It wasn't just bullfighting they shared in common. Both of them had a mutual friend in singer Eartha Kitt. Jimmy told Gilmore that the singer was his *"café au lait* girlfriend."

They also knew a notorious Hollywood homosexual, Alfred de la Vega. "He sucked my cock," Jimmy said. "Did he do yours, too?"

"He wanted to," Gilmore answered.

In a memoir, Gilmore even described Jimmy and himself going to bed as a trio with an actress, Sharon Kingsley. "I pushed my cock into her, and she groaned and laughed a little, making a muffled sound because Jimmy's cock was in her mouth."

On another night, Jimmy wanted sex with Gilmore while wearing a black leather jacket. He gave Gilmore a pair of black lace panties "that I got off some chick," and begged his friend to put them on.

"Jimmy told me just to lie there and show him my stomach."

"I want to see if I get a hard-on by pretending you're this French whore."

"I was barelegged. But he wanted me to wear both a leather jacket and black panties. He kissed my legs and jacked off."

"We were sporadic friends," Gilmore claimed. "Our relationship was jumpy and spotty, but we'd connect like electric wires and it made sparks. He was drawn as if by magnet to what struck him as perverse. He saw me as a kind of teenage Rimbaud who didn't like anybody. He liked that about me."

[After Jimmy's death, Gilmore moved to Paris, where he stayed at the Beat Hotel, a 42-room flophouse at 9 Rue Gît-le-Cœur, in Paris's bohemian 6ᵗʰ arrondissement, notable as a residence for members of the Beat Poetry movement. There, he became friends with author and junkie William S. Burroughs, actress Brigitte Bardot, and the novelist Françoise Sagan.

Today, Gilmore is an author and a journalist, known for his iconoclastic Hollywood memoirs, true crime literature, and hard-boiled fiction. He wrote a shattering memoir of Elizabeth Short (aka the Black Dahlia) and her famous dismemberment, which ushered in a cult following for him. He also wrote The Garbage People *(1971) about Charles Manson and his psychotic family. Gilmore had known the butchered Sharon Tate. But of all his Hollywood stories, James Dean remained his favorite subject of memoir.]*

Jimmy Had a Question for Ronald Reagan About the Casting Couch—

"BACK IN 1947, DID YOU HAVE TO PUT OUT FOR JOHN VAN DRUTEN BEFORE HE GOT YOU THE PART IN THAT STUPID MOVIE YOU MADE WITH ELEANOR PARKER?"

"Because we were so young and pretty, John Gilmore and I sometimes competed for the same roles," Jimmy told his friend, Stanley Haggart.

Such was the case when the British playwright, John Van Druten, was involved in the casting for a Broadway play he had written, *I Am a Camera.*

[Van Druten's play had been inspired by Christopher Isherwood's Good-

bye to Berlin, *which was part of his* The Berlin Stories *collection. Isherwood had based his tales on his decadent and brutalizing experiences in the German capital during the early 1930s, when the Nazis were fighting to seize power.]*

The lead role of a young writer was based on Isherwood himself, who was gay. The play produced the character of Sally Bowles, the iconic "Come to the Cabaret" entertainer.

"I never told Jimmy about the part," Gilmore said. "I knew he might make inroads to Van Druten and go to be with him in order to get the role. I was up for it without yet having to go to bed with Van Druten, and was going to keep it that way."

Isherwood was in New York to meet with Van Druten and his lover, Walter Starcke, who was co-producer of the play based on his novel. Around the same time, Jimmy had dined with Tennessee Williams, a friend of both Jimmy and Isherwood. He told the playwright how he'd met Isherwood in Hollywood at Cecil Beaton's house. "Roddy McDowall and I did a sexual exhibition for some British expats," Jimmy confessed.

"I should have been invited," Tennessee said. "I could have worn my royal purple robes and impersonated the Queen of England."

Tennessee called Isherwood and set up a meeting with Jimmy the following night. In their cozy get-together, Isherwood remembered having been introduced to Jimmy before and complimented him on his performance in the sexual exhibition back at that private party in Hollywood.

"Don't embarrass me," Jimmy said. "It was a stupid thing to do. I'm older and wiser now. I've gone legit."

"My dear boy, I have done far more ridiculous things than that," Isherwood said.

It was arranged that Jimmy, the following evening, would pay a call at the apartment occupied by Starcke and Van Druten. Starcke had been the long-time lover of Van Druten ever since 1945, when he'd sent him a nude picture of himself.

Before going there, Jimmy was briefed on aspects of Van Druten's illustrious theatrical background. He was celebrated for plays filled with witty and urbane observations about contemporary life and society. *[After Van Druten moved to America from the U.K. and became a U.S. citizen, many of his plays were adapted into famous films such as* Old Acquaintance *(1943), with Bette Davis and Miriam Hopkins, and* The Voice of the Turtle *(1947), with Ronald Reagan and Eleanor Parker. Jimmy would later ask, "Before getting his part, did Reagan have to lie on Van Druten's casting couch like I did?"]*

That evening, confronting Jimmy, Starcke said, "Tennessee tells me it's not your first time at the rodeo. You know the rules by now, I'm sure."

"I know the rules, and I also know how to break them," Jimmy said.

"I hope you're obeying them tonight," Starcke said. "The male lead in *I Am a Camera* could make you the biggest star on Broadway. Let's adjourn to the bedroom. John gets lots of solicitations from young actors, and he insists I sample the merchandise before passing a guy on to him. Think of this as an audition. You're not the first stud to find himself in this position. Catherine the Great of Russia ordered her ladies-in-waiting to evaluate a stallion first-hand before recommending him to Her Majesty. John likes to follow Catherine's example."

"I see," was all that Jimmy said.

Later, after "interviews" with both Starcke and later, with Van Druten, Jimmy called Tennessee. "I have a sore ass," he complained. "That Starcke has a big dick. Van Druten came back to the apartment later, and gave me quite a workout, too. But with him, I got to be the top, which was easier for me."

Tennessee cautioned that Jimmy—despite the Starcke/Van Druten promises—still might not get the role. "Starcke and Van Druten, especially Starcke, are known for their broken promises. They've used and abused many an actor before throwing him out onto the street."

Tennessee was right about Van Druten and Starcke. Jimmy did not get the role. Neither did Gilmore. Another actor, William Prince, was cast. He had starred on stage with Katharine Hepburn in Shakespeare's *As You Like It.* In 1947, he'd been one of the founding members of Actors Studio.

Jimmy once met Prince, reporting later, "I was underwhelmed."

Had Jimmy gotten the role of Christopher Isherwood, he would have appeared on stage with Julie Harris before being cast opposite her in *East of Eden.* Harris was later assigned the film role in *I Am a Camera,* but the male role went to Laurence Harvey, who co-starred alongside Shelley Winters, playing a German woman who backs out of marrying a Jew.

In 1966, *I Am a Camera* was adapted into a Broadway musical, directed by Hal Prince, with music by John Kander, starring Jill Haworth, Bert Convy, and Lotte Lenya, Jack Gilford, and Joel Grey.

But the actress who made the character of Sally Bowles a household name was Liza Minnelli in the brilliant 1972 film musical retitled *Cabaret.* Directed by Bob Fosse, it starred Joel Grey and Michael York. Had he lived, Jimmy might have sought the York role and portrayed young Isherwood.

***

In 1959, Walter Starcke was living in Key West. His long-time companion, Van Druten had died two years before. In Key West, Starcke became friends with Darwin Porter, who at the time was the bureau chief in Key West for *The Miami Herald*.

At one point, Starcke asked Porter to help him write his memoirs. In pursuit of that goal, he articulated and dictated a long repertoire of "Broadway Babylon" anecdotes.

In anticipation of their compilation, Porter, as co-author, claimed, "Starcke's lurid *exposés* will reveal decadent, manipulative, and very lavender aspects of the Great White Way. Broadway's image as 'The Great White Way' wasn't a navigable highway. It was more akin to a fetid swamp.'"

One of Starcke's claims involved his "discovery" of Paul Newman. "He walked into my office in New York selling encyclopedias. I have this instinct about who's going to be a star and who isn't going to make it. I thought Newman was a living doll. I called the biggest agent in town and told him, 'You've got to meet this guy right now. What blue eyes! I haven't checked out his other body parts yet, but before sending him over, I will.'"

"Of course, Newman knew that my help came with a price," Starcke said. "No one ever accused him of being *naïve*. I didn't invent the casting couch, but I made good use of it."

"Steve McQueen was another actor who ended up on my casting couch," Starcke claimed. "Although I had predicted stardom for Newman, I didn't think McQueen was star material at all. Most of the actors I seduced eventually faded into oblivion. A few made it— Ralph Meeker, Marlon Brando, Monty Clift, and Tony Perkins. But the huge majority ending up selling vacuum cleaners or waiting tables."

"As for Dean, he was a little shit," Starcke claimed. "Just a hustler. But who am I to cast stones? That's how I got my start, too."

One of Broadway's most influential playwrights, notorious for pressuring young actors into sexually compromising positions, John Van Druten, depicted above, and his long-time companion and pimp...

Broadway impresario and new age guru, Walter Starcke.

Starcke eventually decided that his memoirs (previously dictated to Darwin Porter) were too seamy to ever publish.

Starcke later decided that the publication of his memoirs would be unwise and perhaps even dangerous. By that time, he had evolved into a spiritual leader, a guru *["You are what you create and you create who you are."]* who had authored a series of self-help books based on the mystical procedures and philosophies he had gleaned from one of his mentors, Joel Goldsmith, whose papers and writings he had inherited after Goldsmith's death.

Up until his death in 2011, Starcke spent the latter decades of his life developing New Age cult following, often from among twenty-somethings. It was then that he demanded that Porter destroy those extensive notes he'd written during the planning stages for his "Babylon-style" Broadway memoir.

"Do you understand me?" Starcke had said to Porter. "The indiscretions of my Broadway days would doom the development of my philosophies about spiritual development and heightened awareness of the human soul."

"Don't worry," Porter promised him at the time. "I'll assign all my notes to hell's fire."

Starcke didn't seem to realize that Porter had no intention of destroying the most scandalous material ever committed to paper about indiscretions and excesses associated with Broadway and its denizens after dark.

Chapter Eleven

TENNESSEE WILLIAMS

AMERICA'S MOST REVERED PLAYWRIGHT WANTS A SON
& INVITES JAMES DEAN TO BE THE FATHER

Auditioning Replacements for "The Horse,"
Tennessee Williams "Interviews" James Dean
as His Possible New Lover

TENNESSEE'S LOST MANUSCRIPT
THE YOUNG MAN (JIMMY DEAN) WHO TOOK A BITE OUT OF THE MOON

> "I've had sex with all four of America's most famous rebel actors: Marlon Brando, Monty Clift, Paul Newman, and James Dean."
>
> —*Tennessee Williams*

At several occasions, at parties and at private gatherings, Tennessee Williams and James Dean had circled each other before they eventually rendezvoused, early in 1954 with Elia Kazan and Eli Wallach, at a catered dinner within Tennessee's Manhattan apartment. The playwright's lover, Frank Merlo, away visiting relatives in his native Sicily, was conspicuously absent.

Tennessee had high praise for Jimmy's performance in *See the Jaguar*.

Afterward, although Jimmy and Tennessee each discussed their bonding with a number of friends, the extent of their relationship has remained unreported.

At that dinner, as witnessed by the other guests, Tennessee claimed, "I have always had a soft spot in my heart and a hard-on for most young actors. It seems that all of them play the waiting game, most often in vain, longing for that big part that might make them an overnight sensation. Marlon, as you know, found it in my creation of Stanley Kowalski in *Streetcar*."

"I've watched many an actor grow old without his dream ever coming true. But if my intuition hasn't betrayed me, I think this young man here, this Jimmy Dean, will be one of the chosen few upon whom the stars will shine ever so brightly."

Then he reached over and took Jimmy's hand in his. "Mr. Dean, you will find your role—in fact, I may be the one to write it for you, a part you were born to play, like it was your destiny. And I'm sure that when I do, Gadge here will direct it with his usual genius."

"I may be a little too drunk tonight to write such a play," Tennessee continued, "but I know I will summon my strength and create a memorable character."

Then he turned his attention to Wallach, who appeared jealous that he might be pushed aside after all the fine performances he'd delivered of *The Rose Tattoo [as a play, it had opened in 1951]*, and that Jimmy, and not himself, might emerge as Tennessee's new discovery.

"At this time in history, the Broadway stage is more liberal than the film industry in Hollywood," Tennessee said. "But there will come a day, I predict, when homosexuality will be depicted openly on both the stage and in films. Of course, movies have included prissy homosexuals like Edward

Spectacularly famous and sought-after at the time he met Jimmy, Tennessee Williams was fully aware that his endorsement of an actor for a role in one of his cutting-edge plays usually led to fame and glory. Marlon Brando, playing a key role in *A Streetcar Named Desire* had been one of his early *protégés*.

Everett Horton and that fussbudget, Franklin Pangborn, but that's not what I'm talking about; I'd like to depict a football hero as a homosexual."

Kazan seemed to agree with his point of view. He said he'd read Alfred Kinsey's *Sexual Behavior in the Human Male.* "Kinsey found that thirty-seven percent of males have had at least some homosexual encounters and experiences in their lifetimes. That should send a message to the shit psychiatrists who still define homosexuality as a mental illness."

"I'd be willing to depict a homosexual in a play," Wallach said, "that is, if the role is good enough."

[During this dialogue, Jimmy was fascinated. Later, during his filming of Rebel Without a Cause, *he was counseled for a brief period by Dr. Judd Marmor, the psychiatrist best known for his role in persuading the American Psychiatric Association to remove homosexuality from its* Diagnostic and Statistical Manual of Mental Disorders.*]*

True to Tennessee's prediction, Jimmy, cast as Jim Stark, would eventually appear in romantically compelling scenes with Sal Mineo, who interpreted his teenaged character as an obvious homosexual with an overpowering crush on Jimmy.

"If I write a role for a homosexual, I will do so with some subtlety," Tennessee said. "In other words, he won't be shown taking it up the ass. I prefer characters with certain sexual ambiguity. I believe that all characters, gay or straight, should end their performances with an aura of mystery about their futures. If you're a member of the audience who demands a road map about what will eventually happen to a character, then I'm not your playwright."

Once again, he turned to Jimmy and took his hand. "As a possible character both on and off the stage, I find you fascinating. You are nothing if not sexually ambiguous. There is an androgyny about you; you're completely unlike that brutal male Brando played in *Streetcar.* I'd even say that although his character was never seen by any audience, you might have played Blanche DuBois' doomed, and gay, husband."

Tennessee later revealed to his most enduring *confidante,* Maria Britneva *[later, Lady St. Just, aka Maria St. Just]* the ground rules he relayed to Jimmy that night after Wallach and Kazan left his dinner party:

He informed him that ever since he'd started having sex, he preferred to be sodomized. "But in December of 1953, I was horribly afflicted with thrombosed hemorrhoids as large as a hen's egg. I had to undergo the most painful operation of my life in New Orleans. I think that before he worked on me, that quack doctor performed medical experiments on Jews during the war. Ever since then, the thought of rectal penetration frightens me. I have therefore decided that the human mouth on a penis can be equally gratifying."

Later, Jimmy discussed details of his evening with Tennessee with Stanley

Haggart, who was also a friend of the playwright: "He's insatiable," Jimmy lamented. "Just insatiable. He wants to repeat everything again and again and again. If I see too much of him, I won't have any honey left for anybody else."

As the days and weeks went by, Jimmy—fearing that Tennessee was "auditioning" him for a role as his full-time lover—kept Haggart posted on the status of their "romance."

According to Haggart, "Jimmy, as was his nature, was out to get what

Long time companions and collaborators Frank Merlo *(left)* with Tennessee Williams, together at their home on Duncan Street in Key West.

he could get. He'd done that ever since he'd become an actor, and the pattern continued from Hollywood to New York and back to Hollywood again. And from what Tennessee told me, he was 'crazy about the boy.'"

Tennessee had nicknamed his Sicilian lover, Frank Merlo, "The Horse." From the beginning, their relationship was volatile. In the summer of 1952, Merlo left him. "Tennessee and I went our separate ways," Merlo told Darwin Porter.

Tennessee lamented his loss to Jimmy. "The Horse left me at one of the most desperate times of my life. I'd had two great successes, but the critics had turned on me, and I was insecure. I felt as alone as a man feels at the moment of death."

"I immediately asked myself if I could find someone else. Or could I live alone, without love, drifting from bed to bed? I was falling apart—and by the way, I had plenty of company. Almost everyone close to me was also falling apart, stricken with fatal diseases, or whatever. In the case of Maria, she had an abortion. There were other horror stories, too. I refer to that time as 'The Summer of the Long Knives.'"

Jimmy was made aware when Merlo eventually returned from Sicily for a reunion with his lover. But after that, he sometimes spent weeks at a time at their cottage in Key West, leaving Tennessee alone in New York. "When he came back, he displayed the charm of a porcupine—grouchy, sullen, irritable," Tennessee complained to Jimmy. "If I ever write a play about him, I'll entitle it, *Something Unspoken from the Distant Heart*."

During that period, Maria St. Just attended most of Tennessee's social gatherings. Although she and Jimmy deeply resented the other, they maintained a superficial politeness.

Before Jimmy's first dinner with Maria, Tennessee had issued a warning to him: "She has a savagely mordant sense of humor. Watch that it's not turned on you. She seems to say all the things that a discreet woman would not even think. And that tongue of hers: It'll either be turned on you viciously, or it will be lapping at your rosebud."

"She has a powerful sex drive, and has never been known to turn down a sexual advance. In fact, I sometimes have to curb her, like those ladies who lunch do to their poodles during their walks along Fifth Avenue. I have no doubt that if Maria had remained in Leningrad, she would by now have become a reincarnation of Catherine the Great."

Since it seemed that both of them had become the objects of Tennessee's current obsession, Jimmy set out to learn more about Maria.

[Maria Britneva was born in the Soviet Union in 1921, the daughter of one of the former Court physicians to the Tsar. Her father had fled from St. Petersburg during the 1917 revolution and was later murdered in one of the Soviet purges. With her mother, Maria emigrated to London, where she became a ballet dancer, living on whatever her mother could earn translating the plays of Chekhov for John Gielgud's acting troupe.

It was through Gielgud that she met Tennessee Williams, with whom she probably fell in love, later sublimating it into a devoted "amitié amoureuse," ferociously shielding him from sycophants and managing his chaotic domestic affairs. After moving to New York, she had studied at the Actors Studio, during which time, Tennessee had allowed her to interpret the role of Blanche DuBois in an Off-Broadway production of his play, A Streetcar Named Desire.

On July 25, 1956, she married Peter Grenfell, Lord St. Just, the wealthy son of Edward Grenfell, the British banking partner of J.P. Morgan.

Tennessee designated her in his will as the literary executor of his estate. It was rumored that he regretted that decision, and that as time went by, he was on the verge of eliminating her from his will completely, but he died before he filed the paperwork. By most accounts, Maria evolved into a tyrannically restrictive executrix, refusing requests from directors to produce many of Tennessee's more obscure plays, and systematically denying scholars' access to his private papers. Some scholars, however, have credited her ferocious territoriality as the means whereby Tennessee's literary reputation was salvaged from the dissipation of his drug excesses in the years before his death.]

Ferociously protective: Maria St. Just with Tennessee Williams

To his friends, Tennessee described Maria as "My Five O'Clock Angel. She's always waiting for me at that time of day when I could always count on her being on the other end of the phone as I described my emptiness after a day laboring on my typewriter. She is my friend, but also my court jester, *confidante,* cheerleader, dogsbody, and ultimately, the keeper of the flame."

Truman Capote had another view of her. He told Jimmy, "Tell her that if she sees me to stay clear, or else I will slap her tits and kick her down the stairs. You should see the crap she's written about me. *Quel bitch!* You tell her from me that she's a dreadful liar!"

Maria and Jimmy maintained an uneasy alliance, continuing to conceal their respective hostilities. She'd later express her view of him, merging it somehow into an anecdote about Montgomery Clift:

"Montgomery Clift was a friend of Tennessee. I visited him on a number of occasions when he was living with the torch singer, Libby Holman. There was something curiously intangible and inconclusive about Monty. But at least he wasn't as cracking a bore as James Dean, whom I met on a number of occasions with Tennessee. Dean simply sat there glumly, thinking no doubt about himself."

Jimmy later told Stanley Haggart, "I must be a god damn good actor because I've successfully managed to conceal my distaste for Maria. At least some of that is based on the weird idea Tennessee proposed for us the other night."

Tennessee had said: "I've been thinking for months about an element that's missing from my life—a son of my own. I don't think I'm capable of penetrating a woman to have an actual son the way nature intended, and I don't plan to adopt one. But I'm opposed to artificial insemination."

"How in hell, then, do you plan to have a son?" Jimmy asked.

"That's where *you* come in," Tennessee said. "I want you to seduce Maria in the missionary position—nothing kinky, just a straight fuck like the ones Richard Nixon gave Patricia, only twice in his life to produce two daughters."

"Of course, I could get 'The Horse' (Merlo) to fuck her, but I don't want a son with Sicilian blood. Actually, I want my son to have a Russian soul like Maria's, but to be imbued with all-American boy beauty like yourself. Hence, you're the perfect specimen."

"All right," Jimmy said, concealing his reluctance. "You name the time and place. I'm sure I'll score a home run my first time at bat."

"I, too, am certain of that," Tennessee said. "I noticed that your semen is extra thick and creamy, not watery like some guys emit. I think your sperm must be crawling with little baby-making gametes."

Later, Jimmy told Haggart, "Tennessee never mentioned that subject again. Nor did I. Having to do the dirty deed with that Russian bitch would have been one of the truly formidable challenges of my life, even though you know I love to fuck."

***

Whenever Frank Merlo, Tennessee's lover, was out of town *[in most cases because of trips he made to their shared home in Key West]* Tennessee's parties and social gatherings in Manhattan included James Dean.

At one of these events, Tennessee invited Jimmy to dinner with two of his favorite actresses, Geraldine Page and Maureen Stapleton, both from the Actors Studio.

Stapleton had already scored an enormous hit on Broadway appearing in *The Rose Tattoo* opposite Eli Wallach. Likewise, Page had appeared Off-Broadway in a successful revival of Tennessee's *Summer and Smoke.*

Before both actresses arrived at his apartment, Tennessee gave some coaching to each of them: "My secret for dealing with Jimmy involves talking to him as if you're addressing a wounded animal or a sick child."

Stapleton was the first to arrive. During the first moments of their reunion, Tennessee called her "Maw," and she called him "Paw."

"What is this Maw and Paw shit?" Jimmy asked.

"We named each other that in 1947, based on *The Egg and I,* the movie where Marjorie Main and Percy Kilbride played Ma and Pa Kettle," Stapleton said.

"How you guys identify with those hayseeds defies human imagination," Jimmy said.

When Page arrived a few minutes later, Tennessee complimented her on "the witchery" she'd brought to her role in *Summer and Smoke.*

"I'm so glad you approve," Page said. "I must confess that José Quintero told me that you didn't want me in the role. You knew, of course, that I can't guarantee box office. I hope it was my lack of box office clout and not a critique of my acting."

"At first, I thought your role demanded more power and technique than you possessed," Tennessee said. "But how wrong I was."

Later, when he went to answer a phone call from Tallulah Bankhead, Page spoke about

Maureen Stapleton and Eli Wallach exploring the entrapments of love and ego in Tennessee Williams' *The Rose Tattoo.*

what Elia Kazan had told her about Tennessee at the Actors Studio.

"He warned Tenn never to talk to an actor, and to never even consider being a director of one of his own plays. Gadge believed that Tenn's innate shyness and vagueness about everything would only confuse the actor."

Then she made a statement that completely astonished Jimmy. "Don't let anybody know I think this, but I believe that Tenn doesn't even read his plays after writing them. He doesn't know anything about them. You want to shake him and knock him on the head and say, 'Open up and let me talk to you.'"

At some point during the evening, the talk turned to two of Jimmy's rivals, Marlon Brando and Monty Clift, both of whom were well-known to Stapleton and Page.

"I've tried to place Jimmy here in the pantheon of gods that include Monty and Marlon," Stapleton said. "Of the two rebels, Monty is the aristocrat, Marlon the proletarian."

"But how do I fit in?" Jimmy asked.

"You, my dear, are the surly younger brother of the other two," Stapleton answered.

"If you get the right parts, you'll be the first modern teenager of the 1950s," Page accurately predicted, her prophecy coming true after his casting in *East of Eden* and *Rebel Without a Cause.* "The standards set by Mickey Rooney playing Andy Hardy are old-fashioned and corny," she said. "America in the 50s is far too sophisticated for that."

"I'm considering writing a play based on all our rebel males," Tennessee said. "Before I met Paul Newman, I thought Marlon Brando was the most beautiful male in the world. Before that, I used to cite Monty Clift, who has a beautiful face but a scrawny, hairy body."

"In other words, first I gave the crown to Monty, but then took it off his head and placed it on Marlon's. Then I passed it to Newman. But now, I must remove it from Newman's head and reposition it directly onto the glorious brow of one Jimmy Dean."

"I have a title for your play," Jimmy chimed in, impishly: *"The Fickle Heart."*

"Not bad," Tennessee said. "When I created Stanley Kowalski, I was intrigued with the beefy brutish type. But for Jimmy, I plan to write not about some muscle-bound lug, but about a very different young man, one who is lean, mean, and astonishingly beautiful. I want this new young boy to inspire sexual fantasies in women and in certain

Geraldine Page as a sexually and emotionally repressed *belle*, emoting with a hedonist in Tennessee's *Summer and Smoke.*

388

men of a distinct sexual preference."

"I hope I'll be worthy of the role," Jimmy said.

"All of us know you will," said Stapleton, who was drunk at this point.

"I conceived of Stanley Kowalski as a dandy, but not in the traditional sense of the word," Tennessee said. "He was a dandy in extreme masculine attire, using his magnificent body to intimidate others, both men and women. He could also bewilder with his moody silences. I wanted to portray Stanley with a latent fire burning inside him, but one ready to burst into flames at any minutes. One capable of rape. He demonstrated this every time he stood on the stage, stripped to the waist, with muscles rippling."

"Jimmy does not have the quality of the brute," Tennessee continued. "Nor would I want to create another Stanley Kowalski. Jimmy's part calls for more of the sexy sensitive."

"In my view, Monty, Marlon, and Jimmy are a modern sexual trinity. Rebel males who never integrated into society. They are the new, 1950s versions of Errol Flynn, Clark Gable, and John Garfield. Incidentally, after it was offered to him, Garfield rejected the role of Kowalski, claiming that it was 'too slight.'"

"What a fool," Jimmy said.

"As an actor, you are so very different from Newman," Tennessee said. "It takes a long time for him to work up to a character. He starts slowly, after hitting his mark, he becomes marvelous. On the other hand, you come on like dynamite the moment your image makes its entrance."

As Stapleton and Page were leaving, a drunken Tennessee kissed them goodbye at the door. "You know something? When I die, *The New York Times* will include a tantalizing detail in my obit. 'Tennessee Williams was the playwright who seduced each of the four most famous rebel males of the postwar stage and screen: Montgomery Clift, Marlon Brando, Paul Newman, and James Dean.'"

***

SURVIVING IN SHOW-BIZ
Handsome Playmates of a Decadent, Major-League Playwright

Left to right: Marlon Brando, Montgomery Clift, Paul Newman, James Dean

Tennessee was having lunch with the prominent Broadway director, Josh Logan, when James Dean was being discussed: "I realized that many people claim that Jimmy imitates Brando," Tennessee said. "But actually, I think both of them are imitating the mannerisms of Gadge *[Kazan]*."

In response, Logan said, "I hear that Gadge and Jimmy had a sort of father-son relationship during the making of *East of Eden*. If I had directed the boy, I would have visited his dressing room every morning and again at four o'clock every afternoon. On each occasion, I'd extract his honey. What sort of relationship do you have with the boy?"

Her husband, Paul, introduced his literarily brilliant, bohemian, and lesbian wife, Jane Bowles, to Cherifa (Amina Bakalia), a country woman working at the grain market in Tangier. Cherifa became Jane's publicly acknowledged live-in partner.

Jane, one of the most spectacularly eccentric (and later, unstable) writers in America, expressed something akin to adoration for James Dean.

"Like Gadge, it's a sort of father-and-son thing," Tennessee said. "But in this case, it's incestuous."

***

One night, to Jimmy, Tennessee poured out his frustration with Merlo.

"I have a spy in Key West, Danny Stirrup. He calls me every day and lets me know what 'The Horse' did the previous night. Frankie lays out all night in the taverns, returning to my house with two or three cars filled with Key West sailors. My house there has become a bordello and honky-tonk. 'The Horse' probably fucks with most of the sailor trade. He's also developed friendships with some local guys and gals, non-military. They're the dregs of life, each washed up on the shores of Key West after being run out of every town on the Eastern Seaboard. With apologies to Gertrude Stein, I call this motley crew 'the 'Afterbirth of the Lost Generation' crowd."

To his credit, Tennessee did at least try to get roles for Jimmy outside the orbit of his own plays.

In 1953, he introduced him to Jane Bowles, the American expatriate writer and playwright, during one of her visits to New York. Diagnosed in her later years as mentally unstable, she was the wife of composer Paul Bowles. Tennessee had defined her to Jimmy as the finest writer in the English language.

"Before you meet her, know that she has a unique sensibility," he said. "She's a charming woman, with a big, fat Moroccan Fatima lover back in Tangier. Jane is full of affection, so don't be alarmed if she expresses panic. At first, I thought her act was just theatrical, but now I know it is quite genuine. Jane and I both agree that our guardians will one day pack us off to the asylum."

After spending a few hours with them, Bowles and Jimmy became "like kindred spirits," in Tennessee's views. She ended the evening by telling him that there was a key role in her upcoming play, *In the Summer House,* and that she was going to recommend him to its producer Oliver Smith, himself a famous designer and director.

Subsequently Smith agreed to an audition, and Tennessee accompanied Jimmy to the theater. "Jimmy tried his best, really putting forth an effort, but Oliver told us that he was wrong for the role," Tennessee said. "Jimmy never could stand rejection very well, and he was bitterly disappointed."

On their way out of the theater, Jimmy grabbed Tennessee's arm and looked defiantly into his face. "Someday, when Oliver Smith isn't even a footnote in theatrical history, the whole god damn, mother-fucking world will know who James Dean is."

"I Don't Trust These Sons of Bitches"

—JAMES DEAN, IN REFERENCE TO ELIA KAZAN AND TENNESSEE WILLIAMS

In December of 1954, *East of Eden* was screened before a special audience that included such cultural luminaries as Josh Logan, Tennessee Williams, and Christopher Isherwood and his lover, Don Bachardy. Collectively, these men met later for drinks and dinner. Each was enthusiastic in his belief that a new star had risen in the Hollywood firmament.

"I was impressed with how he used his whole body, not just his face, to express emotion," Isherwood said. "At times, he looked like he was writhing in pain, and expressed that with his entire body. I mean, he appeared sort of twisted, rather spastic. In some scenes, he walked like a man crippled, not necessarily by his bones, but by life itself."

A few days later, Tennessee met with Elia Kazan, who had directed *East of Eden.* Kazan told him, "There was a scene where Jimmy had to show great anxiety. He was worried that he might not be able to pull it off. As a means of preparing for it, he told me he'd gone all day without taking a piss. When the cameras were turned on him, he was very uptight, perfect for the moment, even though he was about to piss his pants. He did the scene in just one take and then rushed to the toilet."

When Jimmy was with Tennessee, he expressed nothing but praise and support, but behind his back, he sometimes voiced a different set of opinions. During the filming of *East of Eden*, he wrote to his sometimes girlfriend, Barbara Glenn, with this:

"Gadge and Tennessee are very nice gentlemen, at least on the surface. But I wouldn't trust the sons of bitches as far as I could throw them. They can take advantage of an innocent, poor farm boy like me. God knows what unspeakable acts they'll force me to commit in order to enhance my screen career."

***

In Key West, Maria St. Just telephoned Darwin Porter and asked him to escort her to the local showing of *East of Eden.*

Before the movie had run for only forty-five minutes, she dramatically arose from her seat and loudly demanded: "Take me out of this damn place. I have never seen such a boring performance in my life. Dean is an impossible actor."

According to Porter, "Maria was almost psychotically jealous of anyone who got close to Tennessee, especially James Dean. She told unflattering stories about him and swore that he was a poseur, with absolutely no talent. She also detested Frankie Merlo, referring to him as a Sicilian peasant, common, uneducated, and ill bred. And she had a particular venom for Tennessee's lady friends, especially Anna Magnani. Frankie and Dean weren't the only objects of her contempt: She frequently threw poison darts at Vivien Leigh, Maureen Stapleton, and Tallulah Bankhead."

"Although she professed great love for Tennessee, she could also be scathingly critical of him. She especially disliked what she called the homosexual element in some of his plays."

Also according to Porter, "I agreed with Tennessee's assessment of her: Most women hated her, especially Tallulah, and few men knew what to think of her. Gore Vidal told us that he was afraid of her. 'She's such a forceful personality that at times, she just seems to envelop Tennessee,' Vidal said."

"That beak nose of hers was always turned up at people she considered inferior," Porter said. "She claimed that Dean still stunk of the barnyard and of the hogs he slopped."

Maria St. Just came in a small package and stood about 4 foot 9", but she was formidable, her face crowned by dark chestnut hair. Her eyes were not exactly brown. They were changeable, at time appearing a shade of gray like that of a foggy morning in November."

"She claimed that she had been Tennessee's inspiration for Maggie the Cat in *Cat on a Hot Tin Roof*," Porter said.

"She was constantly whining about money. She never had enough. She gave Tennessee emotional support, and he in turn had to give her financial aid. Behind her back, he always complained to friends about the money he was having to shell out."

Was the Character of Brick,

THE CLOSETED, DEEPLY TORMENTED ANTI-HERO OF TENNESSEE'S CAT ON A HOT TIN ROOF,

Inspired by James Dean?

In 1961, at a dinner party in Key West, Tennessee told his guests that he had used some of the character of James Dean in his literary construction of Brick, the closeted homosexual and former football hero in *Cat on a Hot Tin Roof.* Present at the party that night were Margaret Foresman, managing editor of *The Key West Citizen,* author James Kirkwood *[one of the creative forces behind the Broadway success of* A Chorus Line*],* and set designers Stanley Haggart and Danny Stirrup.

"In 1954, Jimmy was terrified and in agony over the possibility that, based on his increasing fame, his homosexual past might be exposed in the tabloids," Tennessee said. "He seemed deeply conflicted about that, with an anxiety I wove into Brick's character in my play."

"Jimmy kept asking me if I thought he were gay or not. I told him he didn't need to define things so harshly, and that with a certain finesse, he'd be able to lead a life in both worlds, as so many other movie stars did. 'Millions of men around the world are bisexual,' I assured him. But he didn't seem to want to accept that as a possibility."

[Revised countless times, the script of Cat on a Hot Tin Roof *established that Maggie the Cat had been jealous of her husband's inseparable friendship with Skipper, his "bromance" football buddy. Skipper had attempted to make love with Maggie as a means of proving his own heterosexuality and to establish that there were no romantic undercurrents associated with his friendship with Brick. Even before the opening act, it is established that Skipper was unable to consummate the sex act with Maggie, and that in the aftermath, he confessed to Brick his failed attempt at an adventure with his wife, and his undying love for Brick himself. Reacting to the news, Brick had rejected Skipper, who subsequently kills himself, thereby compelling the tormented and very conflicted Brick to descend into alcoholism and to desert Maggie's bed altogether.]*

Tennessee claimed that at length with Jimmy, he both discussed and analyzed the character of Brick, holding out to Jimmy the promise that he would eventually star in that role on Broadway when the play opened in the spring of 1955.

He said that the theme of the play had originated as a short story called *Three Against Grenada,* which was eventually retitled *Three Players of a Summer Game* and published in *The New Yorker.* It was the story of a young man who disappears behind a comforting veil of alcohol, eventually establishing his psychic residency at the bottom of a shot glass. As Tennessee put it, "Brick is like a man trying to finish a race with a sprained ankle."

"Kazan extensively refashioned my play," Tennessee said, "and rejected Jimmy for the role, even though he'd directed him so brilliantly in *East of Eden.* He still viewed Jimmy as an adolescent, and he wanted a more masculine figure to portray Brick, the former football star—hence the rugged Ben Gazzara."

"Three years later *[in 1958],* Brick's role in the film version went to Paul Newman, of course, and I was furious that the censors removed so many of the homosexual elements in my play. I accused all of them of sabotaging my work. Maybe Jimmy might have been perfect for the part. I don't know. I'm still blind with fury at the way *Cat* reached the screen."

Scenes from two different, world-famous productions of Tennessee Williams' blockbusting *Cat on a Hot Tin Roof.*

Upper photo: Ben Gazzara and Barbara Bel Geddes on Broadway in 1955, and *(lower photo)* Paul Newman with Elizabeth Taylor in the heavily censored Hollywood version of 1958.

Was the sexually frustrated female character of Maggie the Cat inspired by Tennessee's hellacious friend, Maria St. Just?

And was the repressed homosexual male inspired by James Dean?

Tennessee himself always said "yes."

Anna Magnani ("La Lupa")

EXTENDS A BOUDOIR INVITATION TO JIMMY

Tennessee and Jimmy were last seen in public in 1955 at the Crescendo Nightclub in Los Angeles. Tennessee escorted Anna Magnani, and Jimmy arrived with his latest girlfriend, Lilli Kardell, a nineteen-year-old Swedish actress who was under contract to Universal.

[Jimmy told Tennessee that he was intimidated by the idea of meeting Magnani. "She's an earth mother," Tennessee assured Jimmy. "Italians refer to her as La Lupa, the living she-wolf symbol of ancient Rome. She's volcanic, with a fiery temper, but she's also passionate and loving. I want her to star in the movie version of *The Rose Tattoo* opposite Burt Lancaster."

"Tallulah Bankhead, whom you know, and Anna Magnani are two of the most formidable women I've ever met," Tennessee confessed. "In most ways, they're completely different, except for one thing in common. They resent having to interrupt an animated conversation to answer a call of nature. Each of them will invite you into their bathroom while they go about their business. During their heaving and farting, you're asked to sit on the edge of their bathtubs as they continue their rapid dialogues."]

At the club, Tennessee escorted Kardell across the room to introduce her to a cluster of the Hollywood elite, leaving Magnani to interact with Jimmy.

Over drinks, she turned to him. "I hate fancy places like this. I don't know why Tennessee brought me here. He should have taken me to a place where the common people eat. I only relate to the people of the street."

"I'm with you, Miss Magnani," Jimmy replied.

"I hear you were raised on a farm, so you are one of the people of the earth, not some glamorous Hollywood boy who spends his entire day putting makeup on his face and gazing at his image in the mirror. If you've seen any of my movies, you know I appear on the screen without artifice, as a natural woman."

"Just meeting you for this brief moment, I realize why you are called the greatest actress in the world."

"You could show your appreciation for me in another way," Magnani said.

"Your wish, my command."

"After we get out of this dreadful place, I want you to return with me to my hotel and make love to me," she said. "I'll release you at dawn."

It is not known if Jimmy accepted that invitation. There is reason to believe that he did.

upper photo: Anna Magnani, "The She-Wolf of Rome"

lower photo: the 5-euro coin issued by the Italian government in her honor in 2008

During his filming of *Rebel Without a Cause,* Jimmy described Magnani to Natalie Wood, another actress who would appear in Tennessee Williams' dramas.

"Magnani's hair is the color of a raven," Jimmy said. "She has deep, dark shadows around her expressive eyes that speak of her tragic past. She's a little short and rather plump, but when she talks, she emerges as a Roman goddess who rose out of the earth. When amusing stories are told, Tennessee has this cackle last heard in a henhouse. Magnani has a loud laugh that comes from deep within her soul. It is overwhelming, but only if the tale being related reeks of gallows humor."

"My Orgy With Ganymede is Over"
—TENNESSEE WILLIAMS, IN A POSTMORTEM REFERENCE TO JAMES DEAN

There is some evidence that Tennessee, near the end of Jimmy's short life, became disenchanted with him, perhaps the result of Maria's constant negativity.

In front of guests in Key West, she loudly voiced her negative appraisal of James Dean:

"He is a compelling figure, and is so skillful in getting other people to come to his aid. His reckless behavior inspires others to try to save him from himself, but he really has no concern for anybody other than himself. He lives in a world of self-enchantment. His indifference to others is almost perverse. At times, he seems to have impulses of shocking cruelty. Tennessee, my dear, he will only hurt you in the end."

In 1955, a few days after Jimmy's tragic early death, Tennessee phoned Maria:

"My orgy with Ganymede is over. The greedy gods have carried his golden body to Olympus, where he has become the cupbearer for John Barrymore. Even in heaven, Barrymore has continued to drink heavily, inspiring the wrath of God who is powerless to wean him from the bottle and is therefore forced to keep him supplied with vintage Scotch. The kiss from Jimmy's lips still lingers on my own lips. The sensation is no longer of warm tenderness, but the cold hard mouth of the Grim Reaper, who will soon be bestowing the kiss of death on me."

***

Years after Jimmy's death, Tennessee claimed that he had written a play about Jimmy's life entitled *The Young Man Who Took a Bite Out of the Moon.* The only person who claimed to have read it, albeit as a rough draft, was Margaret Foresman. Managing Editor of the *Key West Citizen,* she had been a close friend of Tennessee's for many years, especially during the 1960s when "he seemed to live on drugs," as she recalled.

"It was clearly about James Dean," she said. "It was the story of a male hustler of great beauty who rose to sudden fame after drifting from one producer's bed to another director's bed. But he cannot handle fame and mass adulation."

A drugged Tennessee asked Foresman if she'd compose some descriptive "casting notes" for the character, with the understanding that they would be included with the drafts he was organizing for his literary agent, who would presumably send them on key players on Broadway.

She made a photocopy of the "thumbnail" she composed, based on her reading of the play:

"Indiana Hawke is a beautiful but conflicted young man. He is slowly being smothered by the bitch goddess, fame. He struggles for life, but is enveloped by a paranoia fed by past betrayals. Consumed by guilt, he uses others, especially producers and directors, but in the end, he fears that he is the one who has been used.

He is remorseful for the cruelty he has shown to those few strangers who showed him kindness, and he fears that the razzle-dazzle of his youthful glow is quickly fading. Unlike Dorian Gray, there is no portrait in a closet depicting his evil in lieu of having it embedded in his face. Instead, to his horror, he realizes that the evil is clearly etched into his looks.

He realized that he is misunderstood because he has tricked the world using gimmicks he's learned as an actor, and he's terrified that he has lost his talent and that his gimmickry has become obvious. The world which had once shone so brightly is now growing dark. He imagines that he is being pulled, without resources, out to sea, into the turbulent waters of a winter from which there will be no return."

Tennessee Discovers Christopher Jones

HIS VISION OF "THE NEW JAMES DEAN"

More than a decade after Jimmy's death, Shelley Winters invited Tennessee to escort her to a screening of a film in which she appeared, *Wild in the Streets* (1968).

[Reviewed at the time as "ridiculous and ludicrous," Wild in the Streets *survives as a cult classic of the counterculture 1960s. Nominated for an Academy Award (for best film editing), it presented an absurdist view of the culture wars of its era, especially issues associated with Vietnam.]*

Based on his screening of that film, Tennessee, from afar, fell madly in love with its star, Christopher Jones.

"He is one of the sexiest boys I've ever seen on the screen," Tennessee told Winters. "And those tight pants! He left little for my imagination. I predict Jones will be the next James Dean. There's a resemblance between Jimmy Dean and Christopher Jones: Each is a blonde, blue-eyed Adonis with farm boy sexuality."

"If the film rights are ever purchased for my play about Jimmy, this Jones Adonis would be the perfect vehicle for depicting him on the screen."

***

In the aftermath of Tennessee's death in 1983, none of the pages of his play about James Dean, nor any of its outlines or notes, were ever discovered among his possessions. Margaret Foresman told Tennessee's friends and acolytes, as well as the executrix to his estate, Maria St. Just, that he had taken them with him on a trip he made, alone, to Mexico, while the manuscript was still in progress.

"He was drunk a lot, and consuming large amounts of heavy drugs, and his behavior had become reckless," Foresman said. "He probably abandoned the manuscript in one of those seedy hotels, like the one he depicted in *Camino Real.*"

Three views of Christopher Jones. Although by temperament, they're very different men and very different actors, Tennessee Williams insisted, based on his only partially successful pur-suit, insisted that they looked almost the same.

Chapter Twelve

JAMES DEAN'S AFFAIR WITH
MONTY CLIFT

The Doomed Actor With the "Green Diamond" Eyes

REBEL ACTORS NEUROTICALLY FEUDING ON THEIR RESPECTIVE ROADS
TO SELF-DESTRUCTION

*On Stage, Jimmy Physically Attacks Libby Holman,
The Millionaire Torch Singer & Murderess*

"I don't understand it. I love men in bed, but I really love women."
—Montgomery Clift

"The guy acts like he has a Mix-Master up his ass, and doesn't want anyone to know it."
—Marlon Brando, in reference to Montgomery Clift

Author John Parker wrote, "It was at the Actors Studio during the winter of 1951-52 that Clift spotted Jimmy for the first time. Lee Strasberg told Clift, "This kid is an echo of you."

Clift said "I don't want to meet him. I find it unnerving to watch anyone whose work even in the remotest sense resembles my own."

During the development of his own style, it was evident to many members of the studio that Jimmy was mimicking both Clift and Brando. Jimmy wasn't exactly hiding the influence of these two older actors. He had started signing his name as "James Brando-Clift Dean."

He was a very determined man with one overriding goal: He wanted to be introduced to Clift, whom he had yet to encounter. But there was a problem: Clift did not want to meet Jimmy.

Dennis Hopper, Jimmy's future friend and co-star in *Rebel Without a Cause,* said, "Jimmy used to call Monty Clift when he was in New York and say, 'I'm a great actor, and you're my idol. I need to see you because I need to communicate.'"

Sometimes, Clift would pick up the phone and listen to Jimmy's voice, but say nothing. Eventually, the calls became so frequent that he had to change his number.

When Clift encountered Elia Kazan, the director told him, "Why don't you guys get together? Maybe both of you have something to gain from the other. He's a punk, but he has a *helluva* talent. He likes racing cars, waitresses, and waiters. He says you're his idol."

"I despise being idolized," Clift said. "I can't even walk down the streets of New York anymore without fans chasing after me. I no longer have my privacy. I don't need some puppy dog like James Dean following after me with his tongue hanging out."

As unflattering as it was, Kazan, as was his way, bluntly reported what Clift had said to Jimmy. "Better give up on your phone calls. You're beginning to really annoy him."

"That's too bad," Jimmy said. "But I know he'll change his mind after he meets me. I'll bet you he falls for me. We're the same breed. All the best actors come from the Midwest, me from Indiana, Clift and Brando from Nebraska. We grew up in the wide open spaces, not in the shadowy canyons of New York."

"That's true for you guys, but Mae West grew up in Brooklyn, and she has bigger balls that all three of you put together."

Three days later, when Kazan encountered Jimmy again, he told him that Brando had turned down the role of Cal Trask in *East of Eden.* "I had wanted to cast Brando as the evil brother, Clift as the good brother, Aron. Now I'm thinking that maybe you and Clift could play brothers. It's not an offer, so don't get too excited."

This gave new urgency to Jimmy's need for that long-hoped-for rendezvous with Clift.

Their meeting was arranged through a mutual friend and former lover of both men, the British actor, Roddy McDowall.

Clift had objected when McDowall pressured him to meet Jimmy. "Why should I? I don't need some punk kid in my life. What for?"

"C'mon, Monty," McDowall said. "The kid worships you. That should mean something to you."

"All right...Bring him over, but only if you must."

"If you don't like the kid, you can give him a quick blow-job, then kick him out on his ass. He's very cute. Of course, he doesn't have your male beauty. What man on the planet does?"

Two days later, Jimmy nervously accompanied McDowall to visit Clift.

Afterward, Clift told McDowall, "I expected some punk kid with attitude, but he seemed very humbled in my presence, very respectful."

"Did you go to bed with him after I left you guys?"

"You know I did," Clift said. "He's very good looking. He seemed to hold me in awe. I think he'd have done anything I wanted. Usually, my escort service sends me a guy whose dick is either an inch too short, or two inches too big. Dean was just the right fit. But first, we talked."

Jimmy would remember his first conversation with Clift, and reported it to others, omitting, of course, the sex act.

Clift complained to him about how the Actors Studio had used his name and image to promote itself, based on his success in such hit movies as *The Search [Best Actor Oscar nomination, 1948]; Red River [also 1948]*, co-starring John Wayne; *The Heiress [1949]; and A Place in the Sun [another Best Actor Oscar nomination, 1951]* and, more recently, *From Here to Eternity [yet another Best Actor nomination, 1953]*.

"Lee Strasberg is a charlatan," Clift had claimed during his conversation with Jimmy. "I never really trained at the Actors Studio. I had the same talent when I arrived as when I left. I never learned anything from Strasberg, and may have taught the fucker a thing or two. Now, I just drop in on special occasions. I'm at the point where I'm learning about the downside of fame."

"Like, for instance?" Jimmy asked.

"Once you're famous, each of your flaws and all of your weaknesses are exaggerated."

"Just what is a weakness of yours, if you forgive my asking."

"Self-destruction," Monty answered. "Same as you."

"But how do you know that about me? You've just met me!"

"It's etched on your face! It takes a doomed cat to know another one."

***

Later, in a follow-up visit, Clift told Jimmy that during the original planning stages of *East of Eden,* Elia Kazan had wanted Brando to interpret the film's meatiest role, that of Cal Trask; and that he'd envisioned Clift as Aron, Cal's rigid and sanctimonious brother.

"But I really wanted to play Cal, so I rejected the role Kazan had planned for me as Aron." Clift then continued, to Jimmy, "But you'd be great as Cal. Campaign for it."

"But you've rejected a lot of other hot roles recently. I heard that you even rejected the role of Joe Gillis in *Sunset Blvd.,* opposite Gloria Swanson," Jimmy said.

"William Holden took it, and, as you know, that was a huge break for his career."

"Why did you do that?"

"I didn't think I could be convincing making love to a woman twice my age," Clift said.

"But you're involved with Libby Holman, and she's at least sixteen years older than you, if a day," Jimmy answered.

[Clift's strongest emotional attachments were to women, notably Marilyn Monroe, Elizabeth Taylor, Myrna Loy, and Russian-born Mira Rostova, his long-time acting coach.]

Irrational anger suddenly flashed across Clift's face. "Why don't you shut your fucking trap about who else I'm involved with? Don't get the idea that my life centers around you. Get out!"

Less than a week later, Clift called Jimmy and apologized. "I'm touchy about certain subjects," he said. "Come on over tonight, and we'll have a make-up session."

***

The more time Jimmy spent with Clift, the more he began to imitate his mannerisms. Many future film critics, such as Lawrence Frascella, noted that, "Dean took the fragility and naturalism of Montgomery Clift and the rebelliousness and emotionally unbridled sexuality of Marlon Brando and created his own enlarged space for male behavior on the screen."

Sometimes, the comparisons were negative, as when Parker Tyler wrote: "James Dean is nothing but a homosexual parody of Marlon Brando.":

"I'd rather the comparison have been to Monty, not Brando," Jimmy said.

Clift, as he told Jimmy, resented being grouped with both Jimmy and

402

Brando as rebels. "I'm tired of all this rebel shit talk," he said. "I am neither a young rebel nor an old rebel, but more like an actor who tries to do his job with a maximum of conviction and sincerity."

One Sunday afternoon, Kazan had lunch with Clift and Jimmy. "I admire actors like you guys and Brando—men who don't insist on projecting a traditional masculine image. Lots of guys, and a lot of actors, have to constantly reaffirm their muscles, their fearlessness, their affluence, the strength of their erections. All three of you guys can appear vulnerable, almost like an open wound."

On the following Sunday afternoon, when Jimmy dropped in on Clift, he found film scripts scattered around his living room. "I can work and be unhappy, or I can stop working altogether and be unhappy," he told Jimmy. "For the time being, unless a great part comes up, I've chosen the latter, "

As Jimmy picked up and examined some of the scripts, he was amazed at the prominence and prestige of projects that Clift had interpreted as unsuitable, inappropriate or wrong for him. They included the role of Brick for the Broadway opening of Tennessee Williams' *Cat on a Hot Tin Roof.* He had also rejected the lead role in Elia Kazan's film, *On the Waterfront* (1954).

Clift also turned down *Friendly Persuasion,* William Wyler's gentle look at life among the Quakers. *[That choice role eventually went to Gary Cooper.]*

King Vidor had also offered Clift one of the lead roles in *War and Peace,* Tolstoy's sprawling Russian novel which was released as a film adaptation in 1956 with Henry Fonda, Audrey Hepburn, and Mel Ferrer.

Clift said, "All of these scripts are shit. There's nothing exceptional."

"I'd sure be glad to accept some of your sloppy seconds," Jimmy said.

"Paul Newman said the same thing," Clift said. "And you and Newman aren't even in the pecking order. Here's how it works: After I turn down a script, it immediately goes to Brando."

Jimmy engaged in repeated dialogues with Clift about his performance as the doomed young social climber in *A Place in the Sun* (1951) opposite Elizabeth Taylor. Complimenting Clift, he said, "No one ever depicted a troubled young man as great as you."

Clift confessed that for months, he had carried around a copy of a glowing review of that film, as written by critic Andrew Sarris. "It's the kind of review I dream about someone writing about me one day," Jimmy said.

He was referring to Sarris' observation that Elizabeth Taylor and Clift had been the focal points of the most beautiful couple in the history of cinema. "It was a sensuous experience to watch them respond to each other," Sarris wrote. "Those gigantic close-ups of them kissing was unnerving, sybaritic, like gorging on chocolate sundaes."

Later, one of Clift's biographers, Patricia Bosworth, wrote: "Then, of course, there was Monty's cruising swagger, which Brando and Dean picked up on. Few audiences in the 1950s were aware of the meaning of that androgynous swagger—it was very subtle and Monty did it for a few seconds in the film—but it was almost as if he were telling millions of women who swooned over him—'You think you're beautiful. Well, I'm beautiful, too, more beautiful than you. So who needs you?'"

Clift and Taylor, as they appeared together in *A Place in the Sun*, a blockbusting adaptation of Theodore Dreiser's *An American Tragedy.* They were breathlessly heralded as "the two most beautiful people in America."

Kazan, Tennessee Williams, and dozens of others, noted the weirdness and inappropriate behavior of both Jimmy and Clift. According to Kazan, "When it came to weirdness, Dean was an amateur; Monty, who was perhaps certifiably insane, had him beat. Brando might have been crazy, too but he at least hid his eccentricities better. Whenever he risked revealing too much through words, he evaded suspicions with acts that included mooning you."

Author Graham McCann wrote:

"Clift could behave as a child, trying to embarrass his parents. He would get drunk at parties and pass out on the floor, eat exclusively off other peoples' plates at dinner, drive his car at reckless speeds, and wander through movie executives' offices shouting expletives at no one in particular. It was a directionless rebellion, irrational and intensely repugnant. Sometimes, he would invite his friends to his room, and they would arrive to find him hanging from the window ledge by his fingertips thirteen floors above street level. It was a bewildering mixture of self-inflicted masochism, spoiled child attention-seeking, self-centeredness, and outrageous experimentation."

As time went by, whereas nearly every critic noted Jimmy's debt to Brando, many also acknowledged the debt he owned to Clift, particularly in how Jimmy found meaning and motion in the space between words, and then filled in nuances of emotion through small, sometimes minute gestures.

One night, Stanley Haggart invited both of the Clift brothers (Monty and Brooks), along with Jimmy, to a private dinner at his luxurious apartment. At the time, Brooks was at the center of a burgeoning career as an advertising executive who frequently employed Haggart as a set designer for the television ads produced by his ad agency.

After the other guests were assembled, it became obvious that Clift had failed to show up. As the evening progressed, over dinner, and after a few drinks, Brooks spoke candidly about his brother.

"My brother is a bisexual," Brooks maintained, "not a homosexual. He's already gotten two girls, each of whom I've met, pregnant. He was never exclusively one thing or the other. He swings back and forth. Both of us were raised in Europe, where homosexuality is more easily accepted, and he never felt ashamed about it until much later, after his adult years in the U.S."

"Monty dislikes effeminacy, and he used to ask with amazement why some straight men are so effete and why some gay men are so masculine."

Clift's physical attribute that most impressed Jimmy were his eyes, which Elizabeth Taylor likened to green diamonds. "When you look at me, you seem to have X-ray vision," Jimmy told him.

After Brooks left the party that night, Jimmy confessed to Haggart, "I'm not with Monty because of the sex. Actually, he's a lousy lay. He likes it rough. His kisses turn into bites that hurt and sometimes draw blood."

Haggart remembered several follow-up conversations with Jimmy about Clift, whom Haggart knew mainly through business links to his brother, Brooks.

"I find Monty more troubled than I am," Jimmy confessed. "But we're troubled in very different ways, and I'm not sure which ways. When we're together, we're nothing but a lot of confusion and contradictions."

"Monty lived his early life as a homosexual," Haggart said. "As a bisexual, he's a late bloomer. He has been known to go to female strip clubs, and he's had affairs with women. He lives in desperate fear that his homosexual meanderings will be exposed, something he believes would destroy his film career."

"He objects to having to hide his true identity and pretend to be something he's not," Haggart said. "Actually, he's an honest person with a high standard of ethics. He feels he's living a lie, and that disturbs him greatly."

"Well, maybe the same thing can be said for me, too," Jimmy said.

***

When Jimmy learned that Ruth and Augustus Goetz had written their screenplay for *The Heiress* with Clift in mind as the actor who would portray the weak-willed *arriviste*, he engaged the actor in some animated dialogues about how he'd interpreted the role.

[The Heiress (1949) had been inspired by a novel, Washington Square, *written by Henry James in 1881. At the time Jimmy was pumping Clift for information about it, the Ruth and Augustus Goetz were adapting André Gide's French-language novel,* The Immoralist, *into an English-language stage play, a role which had already been assigned to Jimmy.*

Jimmy had gone to see the film version of The Heiress *three times. In it,*

Clift played a gold-digger romancing a plain girl, as depicted by Olivia de Hav-
illand, despite the strident objections of her father (Ralph Richardson). More
than any other film, Clift's involvement in The Heiress *elevated him into a*
bona-fide movie star.]

"What is stardom like?" Jimmy asked.

"For one thing, I was presented to the Queen of England at a command performance," Clift said. "I stood between James Stewart and Tyrone Power. Power propositioned me. Stewart did not. I felt like a fool, but I received calls from both Marlene Dietrich and Noël Coward. Marlene propositioned me. So did Coward. I turned both of them down. Being famous is like belonging to a very exclusive club. Just ask Elizabeth Taylor. She once told me she couldn't remember a time when she wasn't famous."

As Jimmy moved deeper into Clift's world, Kazan issued a warning, urging him—even though he had initially encouraged it—to break off his relationship.

According to Kazan, "I ran into Dean after he'd spent a drugged out weekend with Clift. There were bags under his bloodshot eyes, and he looked like shit. He'd been smoking a lot of marijuana, and he'd consumed a lot of the pep pills he was getting from Clift. I felt that Dean was just one step from becoming a heavy abuser of drugs, and I knew that would destroy his career before it had even begun. I warned him that Clift might bring him down with him during his free fall, which seemed inevitable."

***

Through the intervention of Roddy McDowall, Jimmy was invited to Tree-tops, the lavish country estate of Libby Holman. It lay midway between Greenwich and Stamford, Connecticut. Its grounds were legendary for the one million daffodils whose cultivation had been organized by Holman. They greeted the arrival of spring with a riot of yellows.

McDowall was the only member of Clift's entourage that Holman liked. She referred to him as "Roduary," and he had nicknamed her "Lipsy." She was particularly amused by McDowall's humor, referring to it as "witty bitcheries."

It was only because of McDowall's urging that Holman re-

Olivia de Havilland and Montgomery Clift in *The Heiress*, adapted from a novella (*Washington Square*) by Henry James. The vehicle which propelled Montgomery Clift to stardom, it was one of Jimmy's favorite movies,

406

lented and allowed Jimmy to join the house party she had organized at her estate.

After her first introduction to Jimmy, she told him, "I have a venomous distaste for fakery, snobbery, egocentricity, fawning, pomp, social climbing, cleverness, and fashion. If you possess any of those qualities, you can leave at once. If you have none of those qualities, then a bedroom awaits you upstairs."

"I'm moving in," Jimmy answered.

When Alec Wilder heard that Jimmy wanted to visit Treetops, he called Libby and urged her to include him among her guests. He was one of her closest friends, and he'd promised he'd arrive "as a chaperone."

To round out the party, she also invited her sometimes lover, Tallulah Bankhead, but the star called with regrets. She encountered Wilder in the lobby of the Algonquin Hotel:

"When Libby isn't licking my pussy, she's always chasing after some young homosexual like Monty. Now perhaps Jimmy Dean. I predict she'll get him to fuck her before Sunday night. Libby and I go way, way back, and, as you know, Monty and I appeared on Broadway during the war in *The Skin of Our Teeth*. I've already bumped pussies with all three of them—Libby, Monty, and Jimmy. None of them is better than they should be. They're each rotten to the core."

Wilder characterized the mating of Holman with Clift as "a match made in hell." He was called "the dark Adonis," and she was a rather unattractive singer sixteen years older, with a face prematurely wrinkled because of excessive exposure to the sun.

Although Holman had insisted that she'd be able to cure Clift of his homosexuality, she continued to discreetly pursue lesbian affairs. Her biographer, Jon Bradshaw, described their coupling as "an extraordinary alliance: A young homosexual who claimed that he loved women, and a middle-aged millionairess with a latent penchant for women."

Wilder had been in the audience of a Broadway theater in 1929 when Libby got her first big break as a performer in a revue, *The Little Show,* which co-starred Clifton Webb and Fred Allen. Spectators were thrilled during her delivery of a simmering blues number, "Moanin' Low" by Ralph Rainger. After drawing a dozen curtain calls on opening night, she adopted it as her signature song. Wilder always remembered her appearance that night in a low-cut dress in a dark shade of *cerise*: "I think Libby virtually invented the strapless gown," he said about her, years later.

The day after her Broadway debut, columnist Walter Winchell proclaimed, "Broadway has a new star, a kid with misery chanting in her tropical voice."

"She's a freak," Wilder said: "So dramatic, such daring... She's got balls."
On the night of her opening, he had wandered backstage to meet her, and

from that night onward, they shared a "to-the-death" friendship.

Holman's life had followed a scandal-soaked variation of the rags-to-riches legend, thanks to her widely publicized affairs with various young men and women, including the modernist writer, Jane Bowles.

Her most famous longtime liaison was with DuPont heiress Louisa d'Andelot Carpenter. She also maintained a hot relationship with the doomed but legendary Hollywood star, Jeanne Eagels.

In time, Holman was pursued by Zachary Smith Reynolds, the closeted gay heir to the R.J. Reynolds tobacco company. Despite the seven-year difference in their ages, the couple married in 1931, over the ferocious objections of his mother.

Lesbian adventuress Libby Holman was Montgomery Clift's companion.

Reynolds was fatally shot at the couple's home in North Carolina under mysterious circumstances in 1932. A coroner's enquiry ruled that it was murder, and Holman was indicted. Motivated by their aversion to an enduring scandal, the powerful Reynolds family suppressed the case and eventually, Holman was freed, leaving North Carolina with $7 million, a staggeringly huge fortune during the depths of the Depression.

Libby immediately fled to Manhattan, where she became the *risqué* and *avant-garde* darling of café society.

Her friendly house party at Treetops, as described by Wilder, "developed cancer. Monty, formerly the estate's 'Golden Boy,' became jealous of

Libby's murdered husband and prey, tobacco heir Zachary Smith Reynolds.

Jimmy for moving in on his turf. Apparently, he spotted Jimmy leaving Libby's bedroom, partially undressed, at 3AM."

According to Wilder, "Monty, on occasion, had fucked Libby, but he didn't make a habit of it. She was rather oversexed and had to face weeks of dry spells with Monty. Libby was also jealous of Jimmy because she knew that he was sleeping with Monty. Frankly, Monty wanted to be relieved of having to service Libby. He had hoped that their romance would *segué* from a sexual relationship to a deep friendship, like the one he had established with Elizabeth Taylor."

A few weeks after her house party at Treetops, Holman accompanied Clift to the Actors Studio, where Jimmy was scheduled to perform in a skit with Kim Stanley. At the last minute, Stanley had called in sick, and Holman had agreed to learn the lines and perform the skit in the role of Jimmy's mother.

A fellow studio member, Billy La Massena, reported what happened that afternoon: "I saw Jimmy do a scene from *Caligula* that was hair-raisingly wonderful at first. I remember that he had on G.I. clothes. Libby Holman played his mother. In one scene he had to haul off and appear to kick her in the face. She was lying on the floor. The scene was so daring and real. Jimmy kicked her in the stomach real hard, and she screamed in pain. We thought he was seriously injuring her."

"Clift rushed onto the stage and shoved Jimmy backward. He fell on the floor. Then Clift rescued Holman. 'Are you a fucking lunatic?' Clift shouted at Jimmy. 'Get away from her and away from me. I don't want to see your fucking face again.'"

Holman told Wilder, "Dean is hysterically jealous of me. He knows Monty loves me more than he loves him, if he loves him at all. He wanted revenge on me. He used that god damn skit to act out his hostilities toward me. I didn't know how much he hated me until that afternoon. He's a dangerous little psycho, and Monty shouldn't let him get near any of us ever again."

Jimmy also expressed resentment, based on his belief that he was being used as a pawn associated with unresolved issues between Holman and Clift.

"After that, Jimmy's friendship with Monty flickered out like a firecracker on July 4th," Wilder said. "It was a violent parting. Two souls had come together seeking love and comfort and finding neither. After that, they pursued their separate paths to self-destruction. Monty, of course, took a hell of a lot longer to get there than Jimmy."

***

At the end of the summer of 1955, Holman and Clift were living together in her Manhattan brownstone as aftermath to their three-month tour together through Europe. One morning, he slept late, recovering from a hangover.

Abruptly, she shook him awake to tell him, "Jimmy Dean is dead! His car crashed in California. He was recklessly speeding in his silver Porsche."

Clift later confided to Bill Gunn, one of Jimmy's closest friends, "The instant I heard the news, I vomited. I don't know why."

***

Clift's own life was forever altered. On July 23, 1966, Elizabeth Taylor pressured him to attend a party at her hilltop house in Los Angeles during the course of her marriage to Michael Wilding. Clift's driver had been given the night off, so reluctantly, Clift agreed to maneuver his way, alone, up the steep hill to join Elizabeth with close friends who included Kevin McCarthy and Rock Hudson.

At the party, Clift drank bottles of rosé wine and took some "downers" before driving home, alone, in his car. Kevin McCarthy, driving his own car, left the party at the same time.

Clift soon lost control of his vehicle. His car went off the edge of an embankment, crashing into concrete pillars. The steering wheel shattered his face. Elizabeth Taylor remembered, when she recovered from the shock, repositioning one of his eyeballs back into the socket of his pulverized face.

He never really recovered. Plastic surgeons could never restore his former beauty.

Throughout the remainder of his life, he struggled through sinkholes of depression, drug addiction, alcoholism, and ongoing guilt about his homosexuality, a context which he never managed to accept with grace.

Kazan later recalled the shock he experienced upon seeing Clift after his recovery and its (unsuccessful) restorative surgeries. "His head had been knocked out of shape, and he didn't look like Monty Clift any more. He was no longer handsome, and there was a strained look about him—even, it seemed, in his effort to stand erect."

Robert LaGuardia, author of a respected biography, released in 1977, of the doomed actor, claimed that if Montgomery Clift had died after the release of *From Here to Eternity* (1953), at the age of thirty-two, he would have become an even greater cult figure than Dean.

As it was, a great deal of the world had forgotten about Clift before July 13, 1966, when he died.

Right before that, Elizabeth Taylor had persuaded Warner Brothers to hire him for a key role in the film adaptation of Carson McCullers' novel, *Reflections in a Golden Eye*. It had been arranged that he would interpret the role of a closeted, deeply tormented, army major. The part went to Brando.

It was later learned that his long time African American companion, Lorenzo James, had come into his bedroom to tell him that on *The Late Show*, *The Misfits* (1961) was being shown. That was the last movie that his co-stars Marilyn Monroe and Clark Gable ever made.

"Do you want to see it?" Lorenzo asked.

"Absolutely not!"

Those were Montgomery Clift's last known words.

Chapter Thirteen

IT COULDN'T BE LOVE: JAMES DEAN VS.

PAUL NEWMAN

Competing for the Same Roles, Sharing the Same Lovers

PIER ANGELI, SAL MINEO

"So help me God, every time I went to read for a part in New York, that son-of-a-bitch, James Dean, would be there. Every place I went, he went."
— Paul Newman to William Bast (1952)

"James Dean is dead. You can be the next James Dean!"
— Warners' executive to Paul Newman (1955)

"I think Dean would have surpassed Marlon Brando and me. He really could have gone for the classics."
— Paul Newman (1972)

As regards his appeal for casting in films, after the success of Marlon Brando, James Dean saw himself emerging with Paul Newman and Steve Mc-Queen as part of a cluster of similar "types."

As stated by Jimmy, "We were new kinds of heroes, the existential cowboy. My favorite philosopher, Elbert Hubbard, wrote, 'Geniuses always come in groups because groups produce the friction that generates light.'"

In September of 1952, Paul Newman shared many of the same dreams as Jimmy. Each of them had wanted entrance to the Actors Studio, and each was fantasizing about stardom on the stage and screen.

Later that autumn, with his wife, Jacqueline Witte, stashed away on Staten Island with their young son, Scott, Newman was enjoying a brief flirtation with a young actress, Sally Beckham.

Beckham's good looks made up for her lack of talent as an actress. Alongside Trevor Long, she had worked on a skit for presentation to the membership of Actors Studio, hoping that each of them would be accepted for membership. Three days before the audition, Long came down with the flu.

In desperation, Beckham asked Newman to play a scene with her from *Battle of Angels*, an early play by Tennessee Williams. He readily agreed, hoping to enter the august precincts of that school, too.

When he got there, Newman turned around to stare into the face of a broodingly handsome young man with an appealing vulnerability. On closer look, he seemed dangerous. Perhaps psychotic.

"Hi, I'm James Dean," he said. "Loved your performance. But you need to find your fire. If you'd get up there on stage with me, we could play a love scene in front of all these fuckers. You and me, emoting together, would set this whole studio on fire."

"I usually play love scenes with girls," Newman said defensively.

"Spice up your life with some variety," Jimmy said.

"Hey, pal, slow down," Newman said. "I'm just a country boy from Ohio. Back where I come from, we like to work up to things. First, a few harmless dates. Get to know each other a bit."

"Life's too short for that shit." Then he lit a cigarette and offered one to Newman. "A smoke? Shall I light for you?"

"No, I light my own."

"Stubborn little fucker, aren't you?" Jimmy said. "I love a challenge. I want to be the guy who breaks you in."

"Let's cool it a bit," Newman said. "The temperature's rising."

"Yeah, and that's an impressive hard-on rising in your pants. Somebody, and I know who, wants to fuck James Dean." Possessively, he linked his arm with Newman's. "Let's hit the sidewalk and give the queens a treat. The two prettiest boys in New York parading down the avenue. We'll have them salivating, but we'll have eyes only for each other. C'mon, Blue Eyes, let's get the hell out of here."

***

It wasn't until 6AM the following morning that Newman finally boarded the Staten Island Ferry for transit from Manhattan back to his apartment. He'd been out all night with Jimmy and hadn't called home. Whatever reception he got from Jackie is lost to history.

What isn't lost are some insights into the tortured relationship that Newman launched with Jimmy during the few years that remained until his death.

Jimmy, perhaps sadistically way, insisted in sharing details about his sexual trysts with his sometimes lover and patron, Rogers Brackett. It is only because Brackett in later life revealed the details of Jimmy's private life to many of his friends that we know about the Jimmy's links to Newman.

Portrait of Paul Newman with his "almost forgotten" first wife, Jackie Witte, "stashed"— as gossips had it— "way the hell out on Staten Island."

***

Newman was probably surprised when Jimmy took him to an address on West 38th Street near Fifth Avenue, Brackett's elegantly furnished retreat in a relatively posh neighborhood. Perhaps Newman imagined that the young actor would be living in a seedy hotel room. "I'm a kept boy," Jimmy explained. "It's not something I'm proud of, but it's what I'm doing for now. Hanging out with an older man is a learning experience in case I ever have to play a male whore on screen."

"I can play many roles, but I'd never accept the part of a male whore," Newman said with conviction. *[Apparently, he'd changed his mind by the time of his casting as hustler Chance Wayne in* Sweet Bird of Youth *by Tennessee Williams.]*

According to Brackett, "It's safe to assume that Jimmy was like no other lover Newman had known before or would know again. When the Indiana farm boy with the angelic face in the faded jeans met the pretty boy with the intense blue eyes from Shaker Heights, a volcano erupted...at least for a while.

Jimmy could never sustain such intensity for longer periods. Many of his relationships continued, but his love-making became more casual after his burning passions subsided."

"If Jimmy is to be believed," Brackett continued, "Newman fell madly in love with him, but from what I've heard, he's a level-headed guy who eventually came to his senses, but not before he embarked on that perilous journey as Jimmy's lover. I certainly sympathize with Newman. Following Jimmy around like a lovesick puppy is a descent into hell. I should know!"

From the very beginning of his relationship with Newman, Jimmy wanted to be in charge. He gave Newman a copy of *The Little Prince* by Antoine de Saint-Exupéry. Jimmy claimed he'd read it eighteen times—"and it changed my life."

Newman reacted differently. During one of his crossings from Manhattan to Staten Island on the ferry, Newman read its first chapter. Finding it silly and ridiculous, he tossed it into the sea.

During late afternoons of the period when their love affair was still torrid, Newman and Jimmy would meet at the Blue Ribbon Cafe, an actors' hangout in the Broadway district. Newman had usually finished his day's casting rounds, and Jimmy had often spent part of the day involved with some minor role in a television production.

One afternoon at the Blue Ribbon, Newman found Jimmy sitting in the corner, nursing a coffee and wearing a red baseball cap. On the table rested another red baseball cap. "Put it on," he ordered.

Newman tried on the cap, finding that it fitted. "From now on," Jimmy told him, "I want us to walk around in matching red baseball caps. It'll be a bond between us. Let people think what they will."

Newman not only wore the baseball cap that day, but was soon seen on the streets of New York walking with Jimmy, wearing his matching cap. Even after Jimmy's untimely death, Newman was spotted on the West Coast wearing that red baseball cap. And then one day he no longer wore it.

When Brackett returned to New York from one of his many trips to Chicago, Jimmy sadistically pointed out to him the stains of semen he'd exchanged with Newman on Brackett's bed. Jimmy seemed to take delight in describing in minute detail the sex he'd enjoyed while his sponsor was away. "I fucked him; he fucked me, and I taught him to swallow my spit just like you do," Jimmy claimed.

Brackett was always hurt and jealous, but at that point in their relationship, he was willing to hang on. "It was the price I paid for keeping Jimmy in my life."

"I am liberating that boy from Ohio," Jimmy told Brackett about Newman.

Jimmy and Newman shared endless long walks and deep, intense talks in the coffee houses of Greenwich Village, where they dared to dream impossible dreams. At one point, Jimmy suggested that Newman desert his family.

According to Jimmy's plan, both of them could set out hitchhiking from New York to Los Angeles. "I want to leave without a cent in our pockets," Jimmy claimed. "We'd be on the cutting edge. Live off the land, or as Tennessee Williams says, 'depend on the kindness of strangers.' Remember one thing: A pretty boy never has to go hungry."

"Are you suggesting we hustle?" Newman asked.

"Why not? Everybody in life, from the President of the United States to some housewife preparing dinner for her husband, is a hustler."

Apparently, Newman went through periods of enormous guilt about his neglect of his growing family. At some point it was rumored that Jackie found out about his relationship with Jimmy and demanded that he give it up.

Presumably, Newman agreed to her demands and promised to drop Jimmy, but he never did. If anything, he became more secretive than ever.

Their relationship continued even, or especially, after their migrations to Hollywood, even though they arrived there through very different means.

***

"Homosexual panic," as labeled by Newman's biographer, Lawrence J. Quirk, set in almost immediately after his first instance of "dirty sex" with Jimmy. But in spite of his misgivings, Newman would return again and again to Jimmy's side.

***

Brooks Clift, the relatively stable older brother of Monty Clift, met Newman after he'd been seeing Jimmy for two months.

According to Brooks, "When I first met Newman, he was struggling for his own identity, both as a man and as an actor. He had begun picking up some of my brother's mannerisms, many of which flowed into his acting style. Newman had tried being Brando, and later, he tried being Monty. I later learned he'd also taken up with James Dean. I think he wanted to draw upon their talent. It must have been difficult for him."

"When he went to Hollywood, Newman was at first pigeonholed as 'the second Brando,'" Brooks said. "Then, after a few pictures, he was referred to as the new Monty Clift. Then, he began competing with James Dean for parts. And aside from their professional rivalry, there was also this private thing going on between them. I suspect that Monty, Brando, and Dean hauled our squeaky clean Ohio Newman boy down a murky road unlike any he'd ever traveled before."

Brooks had said to Newman, "You and Jimmy are lining yourself up to become the heirs apparent to Monty and Brando. Good luck."

"Hell, man, I haven't completely decided that I even want to be a movie star," Newman responded.

"Cut the shit!" Brooks told him. "Every loser at the Actors Studio expresses a disdain for Hollywood. But just offer one of the fuckers a movie contract, and I bet you those Method farts will start salivating."

***

One afternoon, Jimmy invited Newman for a walk through Central Park. "I once had this diamondback rattler as a pet. When he grew too big, I released him behind that bush over there. Let's go over and see if he's still there."

"I don't cotton to diamondbacks," Newman said. Nevertheless, he followed Jimmy into the bushes.

There, concealed from passersby behind a screen of shrubbery, Jimmy grabbed Newman and pulled him close. "Kiss me," he commanded. Newman obliged, although he wasn't comfortable with this display of homoerotic love in a public park. Jimmy was an exhibitionist, Newman was not.

"I'd prefer this in some other place," Newman said. "Like in private."

"But I need it now," Jimmy protested.

Back on the park's main trail, Newman bought Jimmy a hot dog for lunch. After eating it, he impulsively turned to Newman, tugging at his arm. "Let's leave together this afternoon," he urged. "Drop everything. Leave everybody behind. I want to hitchhike with you back to Indiana."

"The last time you wanted to hitchhike, it was to Hollywood," Newman said.

"Fuck, Hollywood!" Jimmy claimed. "I'll never go there. I've changed my mind. I want out of the theater. Not that I was ever really in it. I want you with me. I know this old farm we can buy real cheap in Indiana. We'll make our living from the land. We'll be our own men. We won't have to listen to any more assholes telling us how to act."

"No way!" Newman said. "I'm not ready for that. I want to face the perils of a life in the theater. Sure, I'll make mistakes and be ridiculed, but I want to stay in the ring, keep on fighting."

"It's your choice," Jimmy said with despair. "Maybe I should follow your example. Stay here and become such a big success that Lee Strasberg one day will lick the dingleberries off my crack."

Later that afternoon Jimmy invited Newman to join him for his dance lessons with Eartha Kitt, who was giving twice-a-week lessons to Jimmy, whom she called "Jamie."

Ushering Newman and Jimmy into her studio, Eartha hugged and kissed Jimmy before planting a kiss on Newman's lips. Then she stood back and, with her cat-like eyes, surveyed the full figures of both men. "The two most beautiful white boys in New York, and Eartha's got 'em." When she spoke, her words had a purring intonation.

Embracing Jimmy again, she turned to Newman, "This is my soul brother. I'm his soul sister."

"She's my voodoo priestess," Jimmy said. "She even knows when I need to take a piss before I do."

Eartha Kitt, as a front-page feature in a 1950s Norwegian-language women's magazine.

In preparation for his dance rehearsal with Eartha, as Newman sat on the sofa, Jimmy stripped down to his underwear. As she moved with panther-like grace, Jimmy tried to stay with her, but he was awkward, not following the rhythm of the steps.

After their lesson, Jimmy and Eartha played a pair of conga timbo drums, treating Newman to a concert. He concluded that Jimmy was better as a drummer than he was as a dancer.

"Great concert, guys," Newman said when they'd finished.

Eartha rose to her feet, reaching for Jimmy's hand. Then she walked over to Newman and stared down at him. He rose to his feet. "At the end of our bongo music, Jamie and I like to adjourn to the bedroom."

"I got it," Newman said. "I'm out of here. Thanks for the entertainment."

"You don't get it," Jimmy said, reaching for his arm to detain him. "Eartha and I aren't opposed to a little company."

"You aren't against a little poontang, are you?" she asked.

"It'd be a new thing for me," Newman said. "And I'm ready to give it a try."

"Come along then," she said, taking his hand.

In the late 1970s, when Eartha was in Key West starring as Lola La Mour in a movie, *The Last Resort*, based on a novel (*Butterflies in Heat*) by Darwin Porter, she spent several long weekends with him. Porter was particularly interested in the juicy details she'd omitted from her various autobiographies. Although she talked of many things, some of her most tender memories were devoted to Newman and Jimmy.

"I had both of them that afternoon, and I came to the conclusion that white boys are SO delicious," she recalled. "I spread the word. The creators of *Hair* stole that line from me and used it as the title to one of their songs. I seduced Newman and Jamie on other occasions, too, but always separately, never again as a three-way. That afternoon in my studio in New York ranks as one of the most celestial experiences of my life. They transported me to heaven. I never knew that lovemaking could be that wonderful. Not bad for a yalla gal born in the cotton fields of South Carolina."

***

If both Newman and Joanne Woodward hadn't been cast in the Broadway production of *Picnic* (1953), their long-enduring love affair might never have blossomed. Years later, Woodward told an interviewer that, "Paul and I tried to run away from each other for five years."

The outspoken Rod Steiger called that remark "pure bullshit! They were like two drivers in hot rods playing chicken as they rushed toward each other for a head-on crash. They came together in a fiery explosion of emotions. Once Joanne had decided that she wanted Newman more than any other man, she set out to get him. That he had a wife stashed away somewhere didn't really seem to matter. But it mattered to Newman."

"I knew him well at the time," Steiger claimed. "The man had a conscience and a strong feeling of responsibility about his kids. Of course, that didn't stop him from having affairs with everybody else. From James Dean to Eartha Kitt, Newman tumbled head-on into an extremely

Paul Newman and Joanne Woodward in the CBS Playhouse 90 Teleplay, *The Eighty Yard Run* (1958).

complicated life. He was the Golden Boy of Broadway. Hell, he was so fucking beautiful. Everybody wanted him, and he was willing to share himself with both men and women, not just Joanne and Jackie, but Dean, too. Newman was so pretty I would have fucked him if he'd asked me to, and I'm about the straightest actor in the business. Marlon confided to me that he'd pounded Newman's ass on many an occasion. At one point Newman was more in love with James Dean than he was with either Joanne or Jackie."

"One day the Bitch Goddess of them all, Hollywood Herself, knocked on his dressing room door," Steiger said. "She'd come to claim Newman—a tasty morsel waiting to be devoured—as one of her victims. Few could resist her allure, not even old Rod Steiger himself."

Rod Steiger...witness to secret passions.

***

Knocking on Newman's door was Stephen Brill, an agent from Warner Brothers. He made an offer a cash-strapped actor could hardly refuse: a five-year contract at one thousand dollars a week.

Although tantalized by the money and fame of becoming a movie star, Newman cringed when he heard what was in store for him. "We at Warners think you can be groomed as a follow-up to Marlon Brando."

Later, that was changed to "the second James Dean."

***

During his casting of *On the Waterfront* (1954), Elia Kazan had considered both Newman and Joanne Woodward as the leading players.

Now, a year later, although he remained secretive about the casting of *East of Eden*, he once again considered that pairing. But seemingly every other day, he thought Jimmy and Julie Harris would bring more sensitivity to the roles.

Kazan was also considering Richard Davalos, a New York actor of Greek-American ancestry, for the lesser role of the brother Aron, with the understanding that either Jimmy or Newman would interpret the more prominent role of Cal Trask.

In a bizarre move, Kazan decided to bring both Jimmy and Newman together for a joint screen test. He wanted to analyze whatever chemistry existed between the two actors if he cast them as brothers.

When Newman received instructions to haul himself off to a sound stage in Brooklyn for his screen test, he thought that once again Monty Clift was looking after him, letting him have a chance at the bigger star's "rejects."

Eager for the role of Cal, Newman was alarmed when he encountered Jimmy in the studio testing for the same picture. Newman was even more alarmed when he learned that his screen test would be configured jointly and in tandem with Jimmy's.

For the occasion Newman appeared neatly dressed in a white shirt with a spotted bowtie. To give himself more of a rogue-like appearance, he placed a cigarette behind his left ear.

Wearing a casual blue sports shirt, Jimmy appeared more relaxed, with his glasses tucked into his shirt pocket.

Kazan didn't show up for the test, but delegated it to a young, inexperienced director. Part of its original sound track and film clips from that test remain today.

In the background you can hear the off-camera director calling to the actors, "Hey, you two queens, look this way!"

"I don't want to look at him," Newman says. "He's a sourpuss."

"I don't like him either," Jimmy answers.

The director then calls for the men to look directly into the camera. They each follow his instructions. Then the director calls out for them to look at each other. At this point, staring at each other face to face, they each break into laughter.

Jimmy moved toward Newman and said, "Kiss me!"

"Not here," Newman shot back. Impulsively, he pinched Jimmy's ass instead.

Then as the camera rolled, the director called out to Newman. "Do you think Jimmy will appeal to bobbysoxers?"

Newman appraised Jimmy from head to toe. "I don't know. Is he going to be a sex symbol? I don't usually go out with boys. With his looks, sure, I think they'll flip for him."

The test had been completely unscripted. Writing about it years later, Jimmy's biographer, David Dalton said:

Rivals by day, lovers by night, Paul Newman and James Dean test for roles in *East of Eden*. In the lower photo, James Dean appears on the left.

ªWhat determined the winner was the face: Both Jimmy and Newman were nascent icons, with features that were to become as easily recognizable as Christ, Mao, or Mickey Mouse. But in this test, Jimmy's enA tire countenance rippled with expression while the signals in Newman's eyes and mouth were almost vaudevillian numbers restricted to isolated parts of his face. NewA man's expressions were typecast into smile, frown, and cool stare, but Jimmy's face reA sisted and relaxed in alternating currents.º

After it was over, Jimmy seemed to

realize that the role of Cal was his. "Maybe we'll be cast as brothers," he told Newman. "It's a lesser part, but Aron is a strong role."

As Jimmy and Newman headed back to Manhattan from Brooklyn that day, Jimmy turned to him and smiled. "The day is not completely lost. Let's go to this brownstone where I'm living on West 68th Street. You can fuck me for the rest of the day. That's gotta mean something."

En route to his brownstone, Jimmy told Newman, "I ran into Marlon the other day. He asked about you. I told him that on some days I'm in love with him. On other days I'm in love with you. But I claimed you and I never made it. Marlon told me that he'd never made it with you either. Both of us knew we were lying."

Two days later Kazan called Newman with the bad news. "I've decided to go with Jimmy for the part of Cal. He came out better in the screen test."

"But what, then, about me playing Aron?" Newman asked, barely concealing his disappointment.

"I've given the part to Richard Davalos," Kazan said. "He's ten years younger than you."

"Are you saying I'm too old for Aron?" Newman asked. "Then give me Adam, the father's role. But, I'm warning you, you'll have to age me. I'm not that old."

"You're out of luck there too," Kazan said. "I gave that part to Raymond Massey."

"Okay," Newman said sarcastically, "then I'll play Aron's girlfriend in drag."

"Julie Harris has the part," Kazan said. "Your girlfriend, Woodward, would have been terrific in it, but Harris will be great. By the way, I saw her yesterday at the Actors Studio. She said she adores you."

"She's not my type," Newman said, putting down the phone.

***

Newman was up for another movie role in 1954 during the casting of *BatA tle Cry*, based on the Leon Uris novel about marines bonding in an *esprit de corps* during World War II. A key role was still available—that of a young soldier named Danny Forrester.

Bill Orr, the son-in-law of Jack Warner, conducted a joint screen test with both Newman and Joanne Woodward.

"They arrived with a preconceived idea of what they wanted to do in the scene," Orr said. "First they rolled around on a mattress and on the floor, and then they jumped up and engaged in a boxing match. Then they rolled around on a blanket. It had to be the worst screen test in the history of motion pictures. I suggested to Jack that he give the role of Danny to James Dean. Dean could pull this one off. Newman came off as a jerk."

On hearing this, Newman said, "Losing out to Jimmy I understand. But the world must never know that I lost the role to Tab Hunter. How could I ever live that down at the Actors Studio? Another God damn humiliation from Hollywood. Too fucking bad. My baby blues in CinemaScope would have lit up the screen."

Based on her screen test, Woodward also lost the role of the love-hungry Navy wife, the part going to Dorothy Malone.

After the bitter disappointment of losing out on three consecutive movie roles, Newman decided "to become another hired hand at Warner Brothers." He signed a contract, even though Geraldine Page warned him, "Hollywood will destroy you."

In advance of his departure, during goodbyes to Eartha Kitt, Newman told her, "Something tells me I've got to be free as a bird in Hollywood. It's not that I'm completely ducking my responsibilities. I told Jackie I'll send her a generous portion of my earnings. After all, I'm going to be making one thousand big ones a week."

During his farewells to Rod Steiger, Newman told him, "I'm not sure I'm the type of guy who wants to come home to face an angry wife every night, especially one who wants to know what I was doing the night before. I like to come home when roosters are crowing. Do you know how many propositions I get in the course of one day, mostly from women, but a ton from men too? Some of them I can't resist. Maybe I'm more like Marlon Brando than I thought. He told me he believes in sharing 'my noble tool' with the world."

Steiger later speculated that it was far more difficult for Newman to say goodbye to Joanne than it was to Jackie. "I don't know what really happened on their final night together," Steiger said. "But I bet the sheets caught on fire."

"On the way to Hollywood, I had anxieties about my age," Newman later told Geraldine Page. "Hell, Marlon made *The Men* (1950) before he was twenty-five, and Jimmy Dean, who's in his early 20s, is on the dawn of a huge film career. I'm pushing thirty. I know how youth-obsessed America is, and here I am, 'Daddy Newman,' trying to become the next hot stud."

"Brando inspires me," Newman said to Page. "Also Jimmy, to an extent. I want to be as wild as those rebels, Hollywood's new bad boy. For the first time, I want to shake Shaker Heights out of my bloodstream. A man like me would be a sucker not to live to the fullest, wife or no wife. Jackie insisted on marriage. She pushed me into it before I was ready."

***

422

Arriving in Hollywood for the first time, Newman checked into a seedy hotel near the Warners lot. "It was filled with hustlers, hookers, and drug dealers," he later recalled. "I didn't get much sleep. There were knocks on my door all night with offers."

On his first day at the studio, he was told he had to take a screen test before winning the role of a slave, Basil, in *The Silver Chalice*, a toga epic that Warners hoped would make as much money as did *Quo Vadis?* with Robert Taylor or *The Robe* with Richard Burton.

His test with Virginia Mayo, a former Samuel Goldwyn leading lady, and the star of the picture, was a disaster. Although Newman photographed beautifully, his acting was wooden.

Newman with Angeli in *The Silver Chalice*...shining offscreen as well.

When his screen test was shown to cigar-chomping executives at Warners, he was ordered to report to the studio's Hairdressing Department. "Mr. Kenneth," in charge of operations, already had his instructions in the form of a memo. "Make his hair blonder—not exactly Marilyn Monroe, but a cross between Alan Ladd and Tab Hunter."

[Kenneth Battelle (1927Æ2013) remained a leading celebrity hairdresser until his death. Tending to the public images, through their coiffures, of MarÆ ilyn Monroe, Audrey Hepburn, Brooke Astor, and Happy Rockefeller, he garÆ nered high profile fame for creating Jacqueline Kennedy's bouffant in 1961.]

Mr. Kenneth was a gossip, and he informed Newman, who was embarrassed when he heard it, that Jimmy had been Warner Brothers' first choice to play the young Greek sculptor, Basil. "Jimmy said he told Jack Warner that *The Silver Chalice* was a piece of shit and turned it down. That was certainly a wise choice. He's supposed to be terrific in *East of Eden*."

Studio chieftains asked Virginia Mayo to work seven days a week with Newman to prepare him for another attempt at a screen test.

"Paul was off on that rocky road to becoming a movie star," Mayo said, "and I warned him about some of the pitfalls. Frankly, I misjudged him. I thought he'd end up on that long list of pretty boys who emerged in the 50s never to be heard of again. Working with him during his first picture gave me no clue that he'd become such a big star—and a legendary one at that."

"This is religioso shit," Newman wrote to Woodward back in New York. "I was horrified, traumatized appearing before the camera in a cocktail dress to show off my skinny legs."

This dull, confused, and muddled film was shot against cheesy sets with the actors clad in bargain-basement wardrobes. Its plot, as conceived by Thomas B. Costain, had first been the framework of a bestselling novel. But Newman felt that Lester Samuels, writing the screenplay, had been inept.

[ºHow can I recite such laughable diaA logue?º he asked Virginia. He quoted a typical line to her: ºHelena, is it really you? What a joy!º]

Newman as an early Christian studmuffin, mauled by virtually every female in "this dud turkey of a script," *The Silver Chalice*. Above, his *inamorata* is the otherwise engaging Virginia Mayo.

Mayo was outfitted with vampiric eyebrows as Helena, Newman's *inamorata*.

Pier Angeli, as Deborra, was his other love interest. Also dyed blonde, Natalie Wood, with whom Newman would become involved in the future, played Helena as a child.

Nothing Newman did seemed to please Victor Saville. The director later said that, "Newman was just one of those troublemakers, anarchists, and eccentrics being shipped over like cattle from New York."

"Saville was a difficult bastard to put up with," Newman said.

"I introduced Newman to his co-star, Pier Angeli, at ten o'clock one morning on the Warners lot," Saville said. "By three o'clock that afternoon, I think he was hopelessly in love. As for Pier, I think she was still in love with Kirk Douglas, or perhaps Marlon Brando."

Frail, tiny, and undeniably lovely, this Italian actress—called "The Little Garbo"—had appeared in a pair of films in her native Italy before gaining prominence as a war bride in *Teresa* in 1951. The tabloids created a ballyhoo of a big romance between Pier and Kirk Douglas during their time together in 1952 shooting *The Story of Three Loves* with an all-star cast.

Unlike the hardened, career-driven "bitches" he'd met on Broadway and at the Actors Studio, Newman was enchanted by Pier's infectious laugh. He called her "virginal" and referred to her "refreshing innocence."

Actually she was anything but virginal. The Italian director, Vittorio De Sica, had introduced Pier—then known as Anna Maria Pierangeli—to Brando, hoping to cast them as a duo in his upcoming movie. Pier had confided to Mayo that she'd fallen in love with Brando, and that he'd "deflowered" her on a grassy knoll near Rome's Colosseum. "Then he went back to America and dumped me," Pier said.

Cast as Deborra, the Christian girl Newman marries in *The Silver Chalice*, Pier "looked radiant in Madonna blue with a gold circlet in her hair," in the words of her biographer Jane Allen. Forgetting about his wife or even Joanne, Newman fell hard for Pier, at least according to Mayo.

Although the singer, Vic Damone, was still a presence in Pier's life, she began to date Newman secretly. She even invited him to her family's home for an Italian Sunday dinner.

Newman at first enchanted Pier's ferociously protective mother, Enrica Pierangeli. But the day turned sour when Enrica learned that Newman "is not a Catholic. Not only that, but he has the Jew's blood in his veins." That night Enrica forbade her daughter ever to see him again, except on the set of *The Silver Chalice*.

After that, Newman was never seen in public with Pier outside the movie lot. Mayo noted that Pier spent long hours in Newman's dressing room, and "I could only assume they were having sex. Brando had already 'broken in' this angelic-looking little creature."

"I don't think there was any great love affair going on between them," Mayo claimed. "I know that seems to contradict what I said earlier about Newman falling hopelessly in love with Pier. Perhaps he did, but I think that the spell she cast over him lasted for only a few days. Newman was a very sensible young man, and he soon returned to reality."

"For the rest of the shoot, their romance was relatively harmless in spite of the sex," Mayo said. "She always seemed to have the giggles around him, and he was always playing tricks on her. Of course, there was the inevitable touching. They couldn't seem to keep their hands off each other. But I think even these two little lovesick puppies knew that theirs was an affair only of the moment. Nothing serious would come of it."

To further complicate matters, Jimmy, who was shooting *East of Eden* on a neighboring set on the Warners lot, strolled over to see Newman work. He introduced Jimmy to Pier. "We met the other day," Jimmy said.

"A romantic Romeo and Juliet legend was born that day between James Dean and Pier Angeli," Mayo said. "From what I observed, Pier and Jimmy were smitten with each other for a few weeks. The press and all those Dean biographers made far too much of this romance. If James Dean was in love with anybody on the set of *The Silver Chalice*, it was with Paul Newman."

***

If Newman ever resented Jimmy taking Pier from him, he apparently never revealed this to anyone. "What could he say anyway?" Mayo asked. "He was a married man with two kids back in the East somewhere."

Actually, during the shooting of *East of Eden*, Jimmy saw a lot more of Newman than he did of Pier. Whereas Enrica found Newman objectionable, she came to loathe Jimmy, who was rude and even downright hostile to her. "My daughter forced that horrible young man upon us until I put my foot down and ordered him out of our house forever," Enrica said. "But he was head over heels in love with my Anna Maria, although I began to hear stories about a wild homosexual streak in him."

Many biographers have suggested that the romance between Jimmy and Pier was platonic. Elia Kazan, the director of *East of Eden*, disagreed. "My bungalow was next to theirs. I could actually hear them making love through the thin walls. Jimmy was very vocal. Not a sound could be heard from Pier. The sex would usually end in a big argument. After one of these blow-ups, Jimmy always got drunk. I don't know how I ever finished the picture with him."

For his dates with Newman, Jimmy preferred some hamburger joint near a beach. He might be photographed in a tuxedo with Pier, but when he was with Newman he wore casual tight-fitting jeans, a T-shirt, and a black leather jacket, evocative of Brando's appearance in *The Wild One*.

A Sunday afternoon in Hollywood might find Newman and Jimmy riding horses in Griffin Park. At one point, Jimmy purchased matching gold friendship rings, and offered one to Newman. According to Rogers Brackett, Newman wore the ring for only a few days, before putting it away somewhere.

"When Hollywood wasn't gossiping about Pier and Jimmy, they were even more secretively gossiping about the strange friendship between Jimmy and Newman," Elia Kazan said. "I'm sure word got back to Joanne in New York. Even more devastating, I was told that word had also gotten back to Newman's wife, Jackie, and that she'd threatened to leave him and take his children if he didn't end his friendship with Jimmy."

"Newman refused to end the friendship, and the marriage puttered on," Kazan said. "But the bells were tolling, signaling the end of that marriage. Even so, it took a long time to die. I think the marriage ended long before the divorce finally came."

While he was making *The Silver Chalice*, Newman received a letter from Jackie. She told him that she was leaving the New York area and taking his son and daughter back to Wisconsin to live with her parents. His reaction to that move has never been revealed. "He had James Dean," Kazan said. "What did he need with a wife and kids? Newman was enjoying every moment of his bachelorhood, and wilder days were on the way when he moved over to the Château Marmont."

Sometimes Pier would defy her mother and ask Jimmy to take her to his favorite restaurant, the Villa Capri, a Los Angeles rendezvous for celebrities such as Frank Sinatra. Photographers and autograph seekers staked the place out.

When Newman wasn't needed on the set of *The Silver Chalice*, he strolled over to visit Jimmy on the *East of Eden* set. Increasingly, Jimmy was feuding with both Kazan and the co-star of the picture, the aging character actor Raymond Massey, who played his father.

Newman feared that Jimmy was becoming more and more anti-social. One afternoon when Kazan was showing some VIPs from New York around the set, Jimmy pulled out his penis and relieved his bladder right on the floor in front of an audience. "He didn't even bother to turn his back on us," Newman later said.

After urinating, Jimmy stormed off to his dressing room. When the VIPs had departed in shock from the set, Kazan walked over to Newman and put his arm around him.

"I made a big mistake in not casting you for the lead in this picture," Kazan said. "As a result, you're filming that shit next door. I don't know if I'm going to survive this film with Jimmy. And I thought Brando was difficult to work with. Jimmy is highly neurotic. Is psychotic the word? Yesterday it got so bad I kicked his ass. He won't speak his lines clearly. He questions my direction. He may not even be an actor at all. I turn the camera on him and what I get is this obviously sick young man coming apart right on film. He is so stupid, so very stupid. His face is that of a poet, so very beautiful. It registers his pain and desolation. Maybe the Academy will take that for great acting and award him an Oscar."

***

If there were any jealousy over the mutual involvement with Pier Angeli, it didn't manifest itself. In the weeks that followed Jimmy's breakup with Pier, the two men grew even closer, the most intimate they would ever become during the short history of their friendship.

With his $1,000-a-week paycheck, Newman could afford a motorcycle to match the one Jimmy rode up and down the southern coast of California.

Laguna Beach was their favorite spot for overnighting. One of Jimmy's favorite waterfront joints was called "The Point," and the two of them could be seen there every weekend. Sometimes late at night Newman, at Jimmy's urging, would strip naked and jump with him into the surf, where the waves crashed around them. After a midnight swim, Jimmy would make love to Newman on the moonlit sands.

Perhaps in a sadistic mode, Jimmy liked to give Brackett a detailed account of his sexual adventures, either one-on-one encounters or else his participation in orgies. He knew this would hurt him, as he was very jealous.

"Jimmy always felt he'd prostituted himself in front of me, and that I'd taken advantage of him when he was a struggling actor," Brackett said. "He felt he had to pay me back for that. I thought that once he became a movie star and was financially independent, I'd seen the last of him. But he always came back. The reason is simple: Perhaps without Jimmy really realizing it, I'd become the father figure he never had."

Jimmy invited Newman to spend many "wild, wild" weekends with him in Tijuana. One of his favorite cafes had a Western name, The Last Chance Saloon. A battered neon sign outlining the figure of a cowboy in chartreuse flickered invitingly over the door.

Instead of songs of Old Mexico, the café played country and western music. A long wooden bar ran the entire length of the saloon. On a small stage behind the bar, three nude women, each quite busty and overweight, performed lascivious dances.

As the lead dancer gyrated her massive hips, Jimmy told Newman, "Look at her squeezing those jugs like maracas." At the end of the number, the patrons, mostly men from California, shouted "*OlA!*" Pesos were thrown at the nude performers.

The act was followed by the appearance of two brown-skinned twins who looked no more than fourteen years old. They didn't dance but mostly rubbed their bodies together, rotating their pelvises, eventually leaning backwards as they rubbed their young vaginas together.

When the pesos landed on the floor, each girl turned the coins' edges, blocking them in some way from rolling along the floorboards. Straddling the money, they seemed to suck the coins into their bodies.

"We want those two," Jimmy instructed the manager. Then he turned to Newman. "We're gonna rent a room upstairs for an hour or two."

"Don't you think they're a bit young?"

"Nothing is too young for this cowpoke."

On another tequila-soaked weekend, Newman attended an orgy with Dean, at least according to the accounts told to Brackett. Smoke from marijuana competed with incense in a candlelit upstairs room painted a garish purple.

There must have been eighteen people at the orgy, almost equally divided between men and women. Four of the visitors were German tourists. "It was a night of gliding hands, shifting bodies," Jimmy relayed to Brackett. "If there was an empty orifice, something was plunged into it. Paul and I were the star attractions. Everybody had us that night."

"What a hot, pornographic movie that would have made," Brackett said, masking his pain.

En route back to Los Angeles, the actors stopped at a café for beer. "We don't have to go down to Tijuana for an orgy. You can always find one going on at the Château Marmont in Hollywood. I'll help you move there this weekend."

Years later, in summing up his own experiences with Jimmy, Newman left out the graphic details. "Brando was originally offered the lead in *Rebel WithA out a Cause*," he said, "but Jimmy was the true rebel. Brando could be outrageous in his behavior, but Dean was beyond outrageous. He was in orbit. As he entered the final months of his life, his amusements and diversions became more and more bizarre. Ordinary sexual diversions no longer held his attention. He began to move toward a dangerous new sexual frontier for his excitement. It was as if he knew he was going to die, and he wanted to squeeze decades of life into his final precious months."

***

After time in New York, Newman flew back to Los Angeles. There, he had a rendezvous with Jimmy on the set of *Rebel Without a Cause*, finding him more reckless and irresponsible than ever.

Appearing on the set to see him work, Newman encountered Natalie Wood, whom he hadn't seen since they'd appeared together in the ill-fated *The Silver Chalice*. Back then, he'd found the teenager had a "marvelous sense of mystery."

On the set of *Rebel*, she appeared far more sophisticated than her years. "I have ambitions to don a frilly gown by Don Loper and a silver blue mink and embrace Cary Grant in my arms before the camera," she said. "I desperately feel I'm ready to play sexy parts. Instead I wound up playing the younger version of Virginia Mayo in *Chalice*. In *Rebel*, I'm a teenager."

"And indeed you are," he told her, "but growing up very fast in front of my eyes." She seemed flirtatious with him. Later, he learned from Jimmy that he was not only seducing Natalie, but so was the film's director, Nicholas Ray.

On the way to see Jimmy, Newman met Ray who introduced him to Sal Mineo, the former delinquent youth from the Bronx who in 1951 had co-starred with Yul Brynner on Broadway in *The King and I*.

In a phone call to Newman, Jimmy told him that "Sal is a very sexy young man, very pretty, and mature for his age."

Years later in an apartment in Chelsea, in New York City, Mineo said, "at the time I met Newman, I was crazy in love with Jimmy, very sexually confused. I hardly paid attention to Newman that day, although I couldn't help but notice what a beautiful man he was. I heard he was married but dating Joanne Woodward. I naïvely assumed that Newman was hopelessly straight. How wrong I was. Frankly, I didn't think I would ever run into him again. But, wow, what an important role he'd play in my future."

According to Eartha Kitt, once Newman made it to Jimmy's dressing room, "those two guys picked up right where they left off. I'd bet my right nipple that Jamie had Newman's pants off in less than ten minutes. He told me that his passion for Newman was still as strong as before."

"But Jamie also told me that he was being pulled in a million different directions sexually," Eartha claimed. "He had his regular affairs at the time, especially with a young actor named Jack Simmons, for whom Jamie had gotten a small part in *Rebel*."

"Even so, he was still out on many a night searching for something new and different," Eartha said. "While shooting *Rebel*, his behavior became even more bizarre. On one occasion, he met this very sexy hustler who had only one arm. They were seen driving away in Jamie's new Porsche Speedster."

Somehow, when he wasn't sleeping with Wood, Mineo, Ray, or Simmons, Jimmy managed to fit Newman into his schedule.

Jimmy was also dating starlets, on orders of the studio. "There's a homosexual panic going on out here," he told Eartha and Newman. "Homosexual stars are being exposed. Rock Hudson is definitely not careful. He's getting too blatant. Word is reaching Jack Warner about my private life. Warner is insisting that I be seen out with girlfriends. Not just seen, but photographed."

"I can cum just so many times a day," Jimmy said. "Half of Hollywood wants my juice. They're sucking me dry out here. These blow-job artists make it hard for me to save up enough sperm for fucking."

"But you manage, don't you?" Newman said, smiling.

Jimmy flashed his own wicked grin. "You know me too well, man."

***

It was ironic that in the weeks right before his death, Jimmy was rehearsing during the day with Newman and making love to him at night. At long last their dream of co-starring together had come true. Both of them had been cast in *The Battler*, a teleplay based on an Ernest Hemingway story.

Producer Fred Coe, who rose out of the depths of Alligator, Mississippi, to become a prolific television, theater, and film producer, came up with the idea of casting them in the same teleplay. Coe was one of the major players in the Golden Age of television, having begun his career in 1945 when virtually no one had a TV set. He often relied on literary classics as a starting point for his teleplays.

Coe had been impressed with the dramatic potential of Ernest Hemingway's autobiographical "Nick Adams" stories, and his best friend, A.E. Hotchner, had agreed to write the teleplay for one of those stories, *The Battler*. In another touch of irony, Hotchner became Newman's best friend long after "Papa" had committed suicide.

The Battler was set to be aired on October 18, 1955 as part of NBC's Play-wright '56 series. Coe hired Arthur Penn as the director. He'd been a member of Joshua Logan's stage company and had attended the Los Angeles branch of Actors Studio. In time, Penn would direct eight different actors in Oscar-nominated performances, including Anne Bancroft, Warren Beatty, and Faye Dunaway.

Newman looked forward to working with Penn, although he soon realized that the director was not a sycophantic admirer of Lee Strasberg. "That guy ruined an entire generation of actors with that sense memory crap of his," Penn told Newman.

With his horn-rimmed glasses and a cigar perpetually in hand, Penn showed great sensitivity in working with Jimmy and Newman. "He knew how to handle an actor," Newman said. "He was not just a director, but a philosopher and an artist. He knew how to let whatever limited talent I had breathe and develop at its own pace. He wasn't a dictator like Otto Preminger with whom I'd regrettably work in the future."

Newman was set to play Hemingway's Nick Adams as a young man. The character was Hemingway's literary alter ego. Jimmy was miscast as an aging boxer with a damaged eye and that inevitable cauliflower ear.

One night around three o'clock in the morning, Jimmy woke Newman up. "What's the matter?" Newman asked, groggy with sleep.

"I just had a golden dream," Jimmy said, jumping out of the bed and dancing around the room. "It was great! I dreamed that you and I are about to become the two hottest shits ever to hit Tinseltown. James Dean and Paul Newman. We're going to win more Oscars, make bigger pictures, than all the farts who came before us. Years from now when everyone's forgotten Bogie as the fag in *Casablanca*, the world will be talking about James Dean and Paul Newman."

"Come back to bed," Newman said.

***

Marlon Brando did not seek out the press and did not like to talk to reporters. But when he did, his remarks were invariably controversial. He was particularly incensed when some critic, after seeing *East of Eden,* called Jimmy "not just another Elia Kazan actor, but one with far more depth and sensitivity than Brando himself."

Speaking on record, Brando said, "Dean has a certain talent. However, in *East of Eden*, he seems to be wearing my last year's wardrobe and using my last year's talent."

Jimmy's ego was weak and vulnerable, and his sense of self-esteem was

431

always shaky and so fragile he could collapse emotionally at only the slightest provocation.

Such was the case when Brando's remarks were relayed to him. Working with Jimmy in rehearsals for the Hemingway teleplay, *The Battler*, Newman claimed that "Jimmy practically had a nervous breakdown. He couldn't concentrate in rehearsals. At one point, he was shaking like a leaf in the wind. Marlon was a very bad boy. He must have known how devastating his remarks about Jimmy's talent would be. Maybe Marlon was trying to get back at some dumb critic and didn't consider how much Jimmy worshipped him."

"Marlon wanted both Jimmy and me to be our own men, our own style of actor," Newman said. "Maybe this was the way he had of cutting the umbilical cord with Jimmy. After all, Jimmy had been pursuing Marlon for years. Thank God Marlon didn't spill his bile over my body. I was too weak and vulnerable back then. An attack from Marlon on my own acting abilities would have shattered me."

"I must say Marlon always treated me with a certain respect, something he didn't always show Jimmy or another one of his rivals, Monty Clift," Newman claimed. "Even though they called me 'the second Brando,' and this must have pissed him off, he never made me the butt of his practical jokes. I also never became the victim of his sadism."

Meeting with Jimmy at Googies in Hollywood, Eartha Kitt and Newman had never seen him so bitter about Hollywood, "*Giant* is my last picture," he proclaimed. "I've decided this incestuous cesspool called Hollywood is not for me. Marilyn Monroe is the perfect personification of Hollywood. All false glamour. There is no reality to her. A man can go crazy here."

"Fuck Hollywood!" Jimmy said in a voice loud enough to be overheard at the next tables. "Fuck Jack Warner and his studio. So he made movies with Bette Davis and Joan Crawford. Big fucking deal. Who are they anyway? Davis was all about overacting and exaggerated mannerisms and Crawford is nothing but a self-created illusion. My greatest thrill in life would be to tie Warner down in a desert and crap over his face. Then I'd leave him to die in the desert, food for ravenous wolves."

"The best thing that could happen to Southern California is for an earthquake to come along and topple the whole fucking place into the Pacific Ocean like the lost continent of Atlantis," he said. "The whole town is filled with nothing but cocksuckers. I've stuffed my pecker into the mouths of some of the biggest producers and directors in Hollywood before those fuckers went home to give their wives and kids a big sloppy wet kiss. Those losers probably still had my semen in their rotten mouths."

"Rock Hudson couldn't get enough of my ass," he claimed, "when we started filming *Giant*. "He fucked me so much I thought his dick was going to fall off. Then he turned on me. Hudson is nothing but a piece of shit. There's nothing real about him. Like Marilyn, he's the perfect example of a Hollywood product. If Hollywood did not exist, Hudson would have been a truck driver getting blow-jobs at seedy truck stops."

That night Jimmy invited Newman to go with him for a midnight ride in the Hollywood Hills in his souped-up Porsche. He had another date and turned him down, but Eartha volunteered to go.

The next day she called Newman. "I wish I hadn't accepted Jamie's invitation. It was the nightmare ride of my life. I felt that he was committing suicide and trying to take me with him."

After she'd escaped from that death trap, she stood on the sidewalk, warning Jimmy. "This Porsche is going to be your coffin. I just feel it."

That was the last time she ever spoke to him or saw him again.

On September 30, 1955, Eartha called Newman. She'd just heard over the radio that Jimmy had died in a car crash. "That Porsche did indeed prove to be his coffin," she said sadly. "I'll never forgive Jamie for cheating me out of his presence in my life. No one else in the world understands me." She put down the phone.

Almost immediately another call came in. Still in shock, Newman picked up the phone. At first he thought it might be Eartha calling back, as she'd ended the call rather abruptly.

It was someone from Warner Brothers. Years later he tried to recall that phone call, but couldn't remember the name of the person calling. He thought it might have been Jack Warner himself, but he wasn't sure. "I was out of my mind at the time."

"Jimmy's gone but you're here, kid," the voice said. "Some actor has to fill his shoes. You probably didn't know this, but Jimmy was about to sign to do nine pictures in a row with us. All of those movies could star you. You'd be perfect. Here's the chance of a lifetime. It's a sad fact that Jimmy is dead, but we the living have to go on. Fuck all that talk about you being 'the second Brando.' If you're smart and play all the angles, and if you lick enough asses, you could be the next James Dean."

Newman put down the phone.

***

Based on the flood of public emotion which followed in the wake of Jimmy's death, Newman assumed that plans for the teleplay, *The Battler*, would be scrapped. But Fred Coe wanted it to be aired on schedule within three weeks of Jimmy's fatal crash. And he wanted Newman to take over Jimmy's role as the star of the teleplay.

Coe called Newman. "I have no one else who can learn the part at this late hour. It would be easy to get another actor to play the secondary role you were originally assigned, but at this point, only you can be the star. Let's face it: You know Jimmy's part better than he did."

Newman didn't want to change roles. "I can't do it emotionally," he told a mourning Eartha Kitt, who was suffering greatly at the loss of her soulmate. "If I accepted the lead, I'd be advancing my career at Jimmy's expense. Both of us loved him dearly. I can't—I won't—fill his shoes. Coe and Penn will have to get someone else."

Yet somehow, Eartha managed to convince Newman that filling in for their departed friend would be a way to honor his memory. "That heavy makeup that the role calls for will help everyone forget your reputation as a pretty boy." she said. "You'll have to survive purely on your acting skills, 'cause their makeup artists will make you look like a battered pug."

A.E. Hotchner, the teleplay's author, felt he had to apologize to Hemingway for pushing Newman into the lead role at the last minute. In a letter to Hemingway, he wrote, "We were forced to fill the part by risking young Newman in the lead." Papa Hemingway's reaction to Newman's performance that night in October is unknown.

"Suddenly, I agreed to play this punch drunk wreck of a man at fifty-five, a lean and hungry former champ," Newman said. "Since I was at the height of my so-called male beauty, it took the makeup boys hours to disfigure me."

Newman, as a prize-fighter, performing as a last-minute shoe-in for a role originally envisioned for James Dean.

In 1962 Newman would again portray *The Battler* when 20th Century Fox cast him in a big screen adaptation of that play, retitling it *Hemingway's Adventures of a Young Man*.

After the telecast, Coe took Newman out for a drink to congratulate him on his fine performance. A drunk in the bar had just seen Newman's TV portrayal of a boxer and challenged him to a fight. At first Newman tried to shrug him off, but the drunk was persistent. A brawl erupted, and Newman ended up with a black eye.

Two other industry insiders were watching the TV debut of Newman's telecast. One was the director, Robert Wise, the other a producer, Charles

Newman, in a remake of *The Battler*, released in 1962 as *Ernest Hemingway's Adventures of a Young Man*. The critics hated it.

Schnee. These two men had recently received an agreement from Jimmy to star as Rocky Graziano in his life story, *Somebody Up There Likes Me*. Both Wise and Schnee were devastated by the death of their potential star. But after watching Newman in *The Battler*, both the director and producer decided that Newman would be ideal in the role of Graziano.

Wise called Newman and arranged a meeting. Newman showed up with his black eye. "You didn't have to get makeup to give you a boxer's black eye," Schnee said.

"By the way," Wise said, "that's the best black eye I've ever seen the makeup department create."

"That's no black eye makeup," Newman said. "That's the real thing. I got into a bar fight."

"With that shiner, you've almost got the role," Wise said. "We know you can act. All we want you to do at this point is strip down and try these on." He held up a pair of scarlet boxing trunks with large gold bands on the sides. "We want to see how you're built," Wise said.

Hesitant to strip down to his underwear, Newman eyed Wise skeptically. "You're not gay, are you? I don't have to put out to get this part, do I?"

"I'm a pussy man myself," Wise said. "So is Schnee here."

Newman stripped down, and both Wise and Schnee found his physique well defined.

"You could be beefier, so go to the gym and puff yourself up every day," Wise said. "You've got the part, though."

"It'll make you a star," Schnee promised.

"We've also got great news for you," Wise said. "We've cast Pier Angeli as the girl. I heard you used to bang her before Jimmy took her away."

"Something like that," Newman muttered. He had reservations about Pier entering his life again.

He called Eartha and told her the news. "I think people are going to stop calling me the second Brando. Now they'll be calling me the second Jimmy. When will I ever become Paul Newman?"

"Don't worry, sweetcakes," Eartha said. "You'll need to worry only when some younger stud is billed as the second Paul Newman."

***

Newman once again came together with Pier Angeli, but their love affair, launched on the set of *The Silver Chalice*, had grown cold. She was distant, yet very kind and respectful of him. "We both loved James Dean, and we both lost him," she said to him privately. "Now I have Vic Damone and you have Joanne Woodward." He couldn't help but notice that she'd failed to mention his wife Jackie.

Both of them found it ironic that he was Jewish playing an Italian-American in the movie, and she, a bona fide Italian, was playing his Jewish girlfriend.

When he first encountered her, Pier was suffering from a broken ankle but mending quickly. She'd fallen down the stairs at her house. Until she recovered, he carried her in his arms to lunch and back. It was somewhere along the way that she seemed to fall in love with him again.

Their passion was rekindled when Wise flew them to New York to film scenes together on the East Side. "I'd never seen New York this cold before," Wise said. "In only a day or two, Newman was warming Pier's bed. Her plaster cast had been removed."

***

Mineo revealed to the Hollywood biographer, Lawrence J. Quirk, that during the making of *Somebody Up There Likes Me* (1956), he transferred the romantic attraction he'd developed for Jimmy onto Newman.

"I fell head over heels for the lug," he admitted years later. "Paul was not only manly, but kind and understanding. We used to talk about Jimmy a lot. Paul felt that Jimmy's death was a real loss, and we both missed him in different ways."

During his time appearing onstage in the radical play about prison life, *Fortune and Men's Eyes,* Sal Mineo confessed, "Both Paul and I knew what it was like to have Jimmy Dean make love to us. I can still feel his kisses on my body."

***

Long after Newman established his own film credits, and was no longer cites as "the next James Dean," so many other actors of the 1950s and beyond tried to take the title, each of them unsuccessfully. The list included Nick Adams, Edd Byrnes, Dennis Hopper, Dewey Martin, Rod McKuen, Sal Mineo, Don Murray, Tony Perkins, Philip Pine, Cliff Robertson, Dean Stockwell, and Elvis Presley.

Biographer Randall Riese wrote: "If Donald Turnupseed hadn't turned left on September 30, 1955, James Dean would have grown older and become Paul Newman—with a bit more edge and perhaps more passion. Likewise, if Dean had lived, Newman might not have become the Newman we know today. He might not have had the opportunity."

Chapter Fourteen

THE IMMORALIST

James Dean Opens on Broadway as an Arab
"He-Slut" With a Hundred Bitchy Tricks,
Including Blackmail

HATRED BACKSTAGE, AS
LOUIS JOURDAN & JIMMY EXCHANGE VENOM

"Working with this monster boy was my worst experience ever with an actor."

—Playwright Ruth Goetz, co-author of *The Immoralist*

"The Role Calls for a Feygele"

—Billy Rose

Billy Rose, the famous impresario and the-atrical showman, was set to bring André Gides's *The Immoralist* to Broadway. It was daring and *avant garde* for its era, relaying the tale of a long-suffering wife married to a homosexual who gets embroiled in a blackmail scheme after a sexual liaison with a scheming Arab boy.

The controversial French intellectual, ex-con, and commentator on sexuality and colonialism, André Gide.

Rose met with his director, Herman Shumlin. They had already agreed that Geraldine Page, Jimmy's friend, would play the lead role of the anguished wife of the closeted husband. The Arab boy was yet to be cast.

"For the husband, we'll need one of the famous *feygele* you know, faggots such as Brando, Monty Clift, or perhaps Tyrone Power. Perhaps a bisexual like Richard Burton."

"But where in the fuck are we going to get some kid to play the little Arab queer, that blackmailing, insolent, thieving, pervert who rents his ass to soldiers at the local barracks?"

"The kid has to be good looking," Shumlin said. "Enough for the soldier to want to fuck him. He could be slightly effeminate, but not too much so, since he is also athletic. Perhaps a swimmer's build. I've seen this one kid perform before. He's the only boy I know who can pull it off."

About the last person one might ever have expected Gide or his work to ever be linked to was the flamboyant Broadway impresario, Billy Rose, depicted above

...But as industry veterans have often said, "THAT'S SHOW BIZ!"

"Who is this God's gift to the stage?" Rose asked.

"His body is lilywhite but it can be darkened with makeup," Shumlin answered. "We don't want him too dark. We don't want to get into any interracial protests here. But from what I hear, the kid can take it up the ass and he's a Method actor, so he can use his personal experience to add authenticity to the role."

"Okay, okay," Rose said, impatiently. "Just who is this little queer?"

"His name is James Dean," Shumlin said.

"Never heard of the little fart."

"You will," Shumlin predicted.

***

Playwrights Ruth and Augustus Goetz had scored a hit when they adapted Henry James' novella, *Washington Square* into a play, *The Heiress*, which opened on Broadway in 1947. *[It was later adapted into a film, a box office hit, with triumphant act￼ing by Olivia de Havilland and Montgomery Clift.]*

A few years later, the playwrights decided to tackle a dramatization of André Gide's controversial novel, *The Immoralist.* The great and defiantly homosexual *avant￼garde* French writer had based his work in part on his own unconsummated marriage to Madeleine Rondeaux.

Set in French colonial Algeria at the turn of the 20th Century, the story is that of complex marital problems a young archeologist faces in the wake of his marriage to the most respectable woman in the Norman village where they lived. She cannot understand his coldness to her until he explains that he is a homosexual, with past scandals that return from time to time to haunt him. That revelation leads to his wife's descent into alcohol abuse, insanity, and death.

Homosexuality was a daring subject to dramatize, or even discuss, during the homophobic Eisenhower era. Many unsophisticated critics would refer to it in odious terms, one of them defining it as "the abominable crime," another labeling it as "an affliction.

Nonetheless, plays with homosexual themes had already begun creeping into mainstream Broadway venues. The New York-born theatrical showman Billy Rose had been impressed with the box office success of Robert Anderson's *Tea and Sympathy* (1953), whose theme involved a schoolboy falsely accused of homosexuality and the (supposedly successful) efforts of an older woman to alleviate his anxieties. Its male *ingenu* protagonist had been brilliantly portrayed by John Kerr, Jimmy's former lover. Perhaps with that in mind, Rose decided to apply his skills, as a producer, to a Broadway release of *The Immoralist.*

[Billy Rose was deep into a flamboyantly successful career. Once married (1929￼1938) to Fanny Brice, he was also a lyricist credited with such famous songs as ºMe and My Shadowº (1927), and ºIt's Only a Paper Moonº (1933).

Controversy had surrounded his staging of other plays he'd produced, includ⬜ ing Clifford Odets' Clash by Night *(1941), adapted eleven years later into a movie with Barbara Stanwyck and Marilyn Monroe; and* Carmen Jones *(1943), featuring George Bizet's opera score orchestrated for Broadway with per⬜ formances by an all black cast.]*

Actors who were considered for *The Immoralist's* lead character, Michael *[Michel in the original novel]*, included Marlon Brando, Montgomery Clift, and Tyrone Power. After each of them rejected it, it was assigned to Louis Jourdan.

Born in Marseille, he had made his American film debut in Alfred Hitchcock's *The Paradine Case* (1947) opposite Gregory Peck. Jourdan had also scored a hit in Max Ophüls *Letter from an Unknown Woman* (1948), appearing opposite Joan Fontaine.

The Immoralist's role of the morally upright, long-suffering wife was assigned to Geraldine Page, Jimmy's friend from the Actors Studio, who had previously scored a huge hit as Alma, the lonely spinster, in Tennessee Williams' *Summer and Smoke* (1948).

As director, Rose selected Herman Shumlin, one of the most respected names on Broadway. He was already known for his direction of plays which included *Watch on the Rhine* (1941), and Lillian Hellman's *The Little Foxes* (1939).

Rose fully understood that the role of the thieving teenaged pervert, Bachir, would be hard to cast. A blackmailing schemer, he rents out his body for sodomy to the (French) soldiers at the local barracks. He's also on the lookout for rich tourists he can ensnare in his web. Immediately, he recognizes Michael as a closeted homosexual and sets out to seduce him.

Jimmy's theatrical agent, Jane Deacy, had read the script and thought he would be ideal in the role. She arranged for him to show up at a reading before the play's director (Shumlin) and its co-author (Ruth Goetz).

Ruth recalled her first encounter with Jimmy. "He appeared in a ten-gallon hat and cowboy boots, a bright green vest, and jeans—he looked like a little Irishman, hardly ideal for playing an Arab boy. Then he read, and he was instinctively right, charming, but with a nasty, suggestive sexual undercurrent."

Shumlin agreed. "Dean was absolutely perfect for the role, once we applied some brown makeup and darkened his blonde hair. He perfectly combined the quality of pretend sweetness with a sinister kind of evil under his skin."

For $300 a week, he was offered the role with a run-of-the-play contract.

Rehearsals were at the old Ziegfeld Theater in Manhattan, where Jimmy reunited with Page.

Paul Hubner, one of the cast members, said, "We thought they were lovers. They were always hugging and kissing."

Jimmy denied it: "She's like a mother to me, very supportive. Would you fuck your mother? Wouldn't that make you a mother-fucker?"

Page seemed delighted with her role. "As an actress, it is a dream part for me. I get drunk. I go mad. And I die!"

"Louis and Jimmy hated each other on sight," Page said. "They had met before at Sarah Churchill's party, where Jourdan had appeared with his sometimes lover, Danny Kaye. Louis was a classically trained actor, and he detested Jimmy's Method approach. His style of acting was not really the Method, but it was Jimmy's way, which Louis—to his utmost frustration—could never really decipher."

Louis Jourdan with Leslie Caron in *Gigi* (1958).

During rehearsals, Page was the only player who understood Jimmy's way of approaching a role. "He had to work himself into the character, during which time he was slowly committing the script to memory. He would mutter and mumble, filling in the blank spaces with words not in the script."

Furious, Jourdan complained to Shumlin about this: "The jerk is uttering obscenities. He whimpers, he cries, he curses."

After he saw this photo of himself, French actor Louis Jourdan said, "I was voted the handsomest man in the world, but I should also have been voted the sexiest."

According to Page, "Jimmy is like a cat that jumps a great distance without the need to know how far he was to jump. I assured Louis that Jimmy would be perfect on opening night."

"Working with Dean, this monster boy, was the worst experience I ever had with an actor," Ruth Goetz said. "He was slovenly, always late, unspeakably detestable."

Alert to the eccentricities of artistic talent, Shumlin granted Jimmy free rein, letting him improvise wildly until he worked himself into the character. After a few days, he evolved into a sort of father figure for Jimmy. During a break in rehearsals, Jimmy was sometimes spotted resting his head on the director's shoulder.

***

Cast and crew eventually headed to Philadelphia for a week of tryouts at the Forrest Theater.

"I don't know from fairies," Rose told Ruth. "But I hear Jimmy's one, and the play is about fairies. So I'll sit through it and tell you what I think."

Consequently, Rose rode the train from New York to Philadelphia, and watched one of *The Immoralist's* dress rehearsals. Then, after conferring with Ruth and Augustus Goetz, he decided to fire Shumlin.

Although he was both respected and talented, and had directed many A-list stars, Shumlin had seemed reticent, even embarrassed, by the homosexual overtones of the play. In Rose's view, Shumlin was "skirting the issues associated with love that dare not speak its name."

Shumlin was dismissed immediately. As his replacement, Rose appointed Daniel Mann, another well-known director.

In front of Mann, before commuting back to New York, Rose articulated his opinion of Jimmy: "The kid has all these adolescent notions about being a man. He carries a switchblade and rides a motorcycle. A big fucking man, that one! I think he's mentally disturbed."

Bill Gunn, an African-American actor and playwright, had been cast as Jimmy's understudy. "I predicted fireworks would result from Mann's attempts to direct Jimmy, and, indeed, some Fourth of July blasts went off."

Soon after Mann's takeover of the play's direction, the other cast members, mainly Jourdan, expressed harsh appraisals of Jimmy and his work habits. Only Page took up for him.

During their first encounter, Mann told Jimmy, "I'm not going to sugar-tit you."

"Too bad, Jimmy replied, defiantly. "Most men claim my tits are sweeter than any honey a bee ever made."

"Forget everything you've ever learned from the Jewish Pope *[a reference to Lee Strasberg and the Actors Studio]* and listen to me," Mann demanded.

Then, much to Jimmy's annoyance, Mann set about revising the script, cutting out many of Bachir's lines.

"I think the bastard wants to write me out of the play," he complained to Page.

It can be argued that Daniel Mann (*aka*, Daniel Chugerman, *depicted above*) suffered more than any other director because of James Dean.

In his words: "I directed Shirley Booth, Burt Lancaster, Marlon Brando, and Elizabeth Taylor, but James Dean was my biggest headache. When Billy Rose, phoned me from New York about casting him, I told him, "That Dean's acting is like a fox trying to fuck a football. He's all around it, but he can't get into it."

From then on, Jimmy launched a war against Mann, at least when he wasn't battling with Jourdan.

Ruth said, "The battle raged through and included the final rehearsals. At times, Dean seemed to be performing in a play that he'd written himself, something that had nothing to do with my script."

According to Page, "One day, Jimmy stormed out of the theater, and we didn't think he was going to return. Finally, after a few hours, he showed up to discover Bill Gunn rehearsing Bachir's part with the other actors. This sobered Jimmy, and he was back in the role."

Mann wanted to fire him altogether until he discovered that from the beginning, he'd had a run-of-the-play contract, which meant that he would have to be paid whether he worked as a participating actor or not.

Rose told Mann, "If the little prick doesn't cut the shit, he walks, contract or no contract. Let him sue me."

Jimmy's big scene was the so-called "scissors dance," where moved sinuously, suggestively, even frenziedly, while brandishing a pair of scissors.

According to Gunn, "For the first time, I think Jimmy really listened to Mann's direction."

Mann had advised, "For this dance, imagine you're bouncing up and down on a very big cock. From what I hear, that is something you really know how to do."

As Gunn later said, "Jimmy was no Yvonne de Carlo, but his dance would become the highlight of the show."

Jimmy discussed his scissors dance with Page. "It was the strings I was snipping away, the strings that bound the Frenchman's character to the staid middle class morality of his early days in Normandy. The more I snipped and cut away with the scissors, the more I removed Michael from his hopeless respectability."

For the play's out-of-town opening in Philadelphia, Jimmy, as Bachir, appeared onstage with brown makeup and a seductive leer. From there, he attempted to entrap Michael with his sensual charm and that homoerotic scissors

Geraldine Page (*above, left*) claimed that Jimmy looked "the least like an Arab boy of anyone you could imagine. That face, that blonde hair. But he made us feel he was an Arab—not by his looks, but by his acting."

dance.

Ruth was amazed by the brilliance of Jimmy's performance that night. "Backstage, he'd been a terror, the most unprofessional actor ever. But that night, he was a pro, playing the role perfectly and winning the approval of most of the Philadelphia critics."

Jimmy's good behavior didn't last long. At a Wednesday matinee, to demonstrate his loathing for Jourdan, Jimmy upstaged him. During the French actor's execution of one of his key scenes, Jimmy reached into his pocket and took out an imaginary lollipop. Then he went through "pretend" motions of putting it in his mouth and vigorously sucking it.

When the curtain went down, Mann was furious. He chased Jimmy out through the stage door and into the street. He yelled, "If I get my hands on you, I'll kill you, you bastard punk."

The next day, Jimmy's friend, Martin Landau, called from New York. "How's it going, working with Jourdan?"

"He's great," Jimmy said in a mocking voice. Last night, he wasn't his usual wooden self. He even managed to raise both of his hands at the same time."

***

Cast and crew rode the train from Philadelphia back to New York to prepare for the play's opening night on Broadway at the Royale Theatre on February 8, 1954. Its big-time debut, coincidentally, occurred on Jimmy's 23rd birthday.

On opening night, fifteen minutes before the curtain, Jimmy, outfitted in full Arab makeup and drag, took off on his Triumph

"Louis Jourdan truly detested Jimmy, based partly on his behavior during rehearsals, but I adored him," said Geraldine Page, pictured above with Jourdan in a publicity photo for *The Immoralist*. "But it was hard to forgive him for walking out on the play after only two weeks, especially after getting such rave reviews. When he left, the play seemed to lose its power."

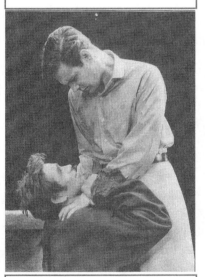

Louis Jourdan, onstage, with James Dean his bitter enemy, in *The Immoralist*. "We have a juvenile delinquent on our hands," he told the director.

motorcycle from an alley beside the theater.

Mann went into a frenzied panic, as did the rest of the cast and crew. Jimmy's understudy, Bill Gunn, was ordered to prep himself as a replacement.

"I had never seen such tension backstage," Page said. "Finally, at the last minute, Jimmy returned. I had been very patient with him, but this act to deliberately alarm everybody pissed me off, too."

Jimmy's destination, impetuously, even maniacally, pursued fifteen minutes before curtain time, had involved a meeting, bizarrely scheduled, with James McCarthy, a friend from his U.C.L.A. days. He told him, "I don't want to be a good actor. I want to be the best actor there is. I told you I'd take the big town someday. My moment arrives tonight."

Based on Jimmy's brilliant performance, after the descent of the opening night's final curtain Mann and Rose opted to forgive Jimmy's horrible behavior. "Jimmy wooed audiences, and Louis [Jourdan] didn't do badly either," Page said.

But although rumor and fact are hard to decipher at this point, Jimmy nonetheless released a shocker, virtually during the curtain's final descent. Still clad in his caftan, and with the understanding that he never wore underwear beneath his caftan, he curtsied like a girl.

Later, some members of the audience got a glimpse of just a flash of genitals as he curtsied; others maintained that only his upper thighs were visible. Confronted with this unexpectedly, it gave both Rose and Mann something else to be furious about, but when they realized what a hit Jimmy had been, they managed to control their tempers.

That very night, Jimmy would infuriate them even more when he officially and legally notified them of his plan to abandon his involvement in their play within fourteen days.

"It was his final 'fuck-you' to me and to everyone else in the play," Rose said. "I confronted him and we really went at it. I threatened him that if he did that, he'd never work another day on Broadway, and he didn't. 'You're a hit...Why throw it away?' I asked him."

Jimmy glared at Rose with fury. Then he spat on the floor. "Frankly, my dear, I don't give

James Dean performing the "Scissors Dance" onstage in *The Immoralist.*

His frequent mentor and supporter, James Sheldon, thought Jimmy was miscast. "The dirty, evil, seductive part he had down pat. But he was just too Indiana farmboy to be really convincing."

445

a damn."

Later, Rose commented, "Where have I heard that line before?"

After that evening's final curtain, Rod Steiger, a friend of Page at the time, was one of the first members of that night's audience to arrive backstage. "Jimmy is playing Bachir like a Manhattan faggot. He's not an Arab boy, but a hustler working Third Avenue."

Other immediate, informal appraisals were less caustic; in fact, most of them were raves.

Within a few hours, key members of the cast gathered at Sardi's to await that night's late-edition newspaper reviews. Nearly all of them, despite its homosexual context, reviewed the play and its performers favorably. Jimmy, however, came out by far as the best.

William Watkins of *The New York World‑Telegraph* wrote: "It is James Dean as the Arab houseboy who clearly and originally underlines the sleazy impertinence and the amoral opportunities which the husband must combat."

Walter Kerr in *The New York Herald Tribune* noted, "James Dean makes a colorfully insinuating scapegrace."

Brooks Atkinson in *The New York Times* referred to Jimmy's "insidious charm," and Richard Watts, Jr., of *The New York Post* found Jimmy "realistically unpleasant as the slimy one."

In the *Morning Telegraph,* George Freedley wrote: "James Dean gives the best masculine performance in the role of the Arab boy, a part which could easily have become extremely offensive with less good acting and direction."

Henry Hewes in the *Saturday Review* made a prophecy: "At the play's final curtain, one is left with the impression that Michael is a homosexual living ahead of his time, and that at some later date in the history of civilization, it will be possible for the abnormal to live undisguised and unapologetic within our society."

***

Jimmy's infuriating decision to abandon *The Immoralist* was catalyzed by Elia Kazan, who had dangled a pivotal role in his upcoming film *East of Eden*. The part that Kazan, and perhaps Destiny itself, had envisioned for Jimmy was that of Cal Trask, the rebellious and misunderstood younger brother, around whom the film revolved.

At the time, *East of Eden's* screenplay was being adapted from John Steinbeck's novel by Paul Osborne, author of *Portrait of Jennie*, a successful 1948 movie that had co-starred Joseph Cotten and Jennifer Jones.

Osborne had attended an out-of-town preview of *The Immoralist* and subsequently pleaded with Kazan that Jimmy would be perfect as Cal. Kazan, already familiar, through the Actors Studio, with Jimmy's reputation and potential, went to see *The Immoralist* too.

Ultimately, Kazan agreed with Osborne's assessment. "As I got to know Dean, I came to realize he was a shit, absolutely rotten to the core. He was a real cocker and an asshole. But he was the most perfect actor I knew for the part of Cal. All that Dean had to do was to play himself."

On February 23, 1954, Jimmy delivered his final performance on Broadway, never to return. Mann transferred his part to Philip Pine, who had previously worked with Jimmy in *See the Jaguar.* Pine remained with the play until it closed on May 1 of that same year.

"After I got the part, my daughter, Macyle, wouldn't speak to me for many days," Pine said. "She was a great fan of Jimmy's, and was mad at me for taking his role, even though I explained that Jimmy had quit and hadn't been fired."

Pine later expressed regret that *The Immoralist* didn't make him a movie star. "Jimmy and I had the same aspirations when we knew each other," he said. "In the end, that fickle goddess, Fame, decided to shine on him and not on me."

Before Jimmy flew away to Hollywood for *East of Eden,* he telephoned John Gilmore. "I'm going to L.A. for a job, but I can't tell you what it is. I'm sworn to secrecy. But I can tell you this: "I'm going to shake the shit out of Tinseltown."

In Hollywood, long after memories of the Broadway opening of *The Im☐ moralist* had faded, Beulah Roth encountered Rock Hudson and Louis Jourdan at a party. At the time, the two actors were engaged in a short-term affair.

She and her husband, Sanford Roth, the renowned photographer, had become close friends of Jimmy's during his short lifetime. "We more or less adopted him in the summer of 1955," she said.

"I asked the men what it was like working with Jimmy," she said. "Rock gave me 'that look,' and Jourdan told me with a Gallic chill, 'Never mention that boy's name in my presence ever again.'"

***

In the wake of her stage appearance in *The Immoralist,* Page would go on to enjoy a splendid film career. She was nominated seven times for a Best Actress Oscar before carrying one off for her role as Carrie Watts in *The Trip to Bountiful* (1985).

Having survived Jimmy, Daniel Mann went on to direct Burt Lancaster and Anna Magnani in *The Rose Tattoo* (1955); Susan Hayward in *I'll Cry Tomorrow* (1955); Marlon Brando in *The Teahouse of the August Moon* (1956); and Elizabeth Taylor in *BUtterfield 8* (1960).

As for Jimmy, based on his brief appearance in *The Immoralist,* he would be awarded a Tony as best newcomer of the year, and he would also win the Daniel Blum Award as Best Newcomer.

But as is the rule for actors, his involvement in the play did generate its share of bitchy, snarky comments: An out-of-town critic from Los Angeles, David Bettmann, wrote: "From what I hear of Mr. James Dean, I understand the character of the homosexual Arab boy is too close to his own personality to justify the term 'acting.'"

Struggling to get ahead as an actor, James Dean read whatever teleplay came along, if it contained a possible role in it for him. "I was an apprentice, and I took almost any crap."

Months before he went to Hollywood to feud with such film directors as Elia Kazan and George Stevens, Jimmy's rude and sometimes juvenile behavior alienated many directors in TV and on Broadway. This was best exemplified by his endless conflicts with Daniel Mann during rehearsals for *The Immoralist.*

Chapter Fifteen

EAST OF EDEN

Playing The Son of a Whore, A Star Is Born

JIMMY IRRITATES ELIA KAZAN AND INFURIATES RAYMOND MASSEY

His Oscar Nomination Positions Him in Direct Confrontation with
Hollywood's Old Guard

"And Cain went out from the presence of the Lord, and dwelt in the land of Nod, on the East of Eden."

—Genesis 4:16

"I could tell that Jimmy could be easily castrated, so I had to juggle his balls with great delicacy."

—Elia Kazan, Director of *East of Eden*

East of Eden has claimed an important niche in the history of cinema. Critic Marceau Devillers wrote: "Before Dean, the adolescent was portrayed as a psychological cypher—inferior, stupid, weak, or ignorant: the ultimate 'foil' to the older generation. With the advent of *East of Eden*, the adolescent became a person in his own right. *East of Eden* was a turning point in the history of the movies. Dean made the adolescent, with his complexities, his uneasiness, traits worthy of a hero."

It also transformed a young James Dean, with only one picture under his belt, into a superstar.

Screenwriter Paul Osborn had seen Jimmy in *The Immoralist,* and had been mesmerized by his performance. At the time, he was working on a screenplay, *East of Eden,* based on the novel by John Steinbeck. His most ambitious saga since *Grapes of Wrath,* it had been originally published in 1952 to rather lackluster sales.

East of Eden was the three-generation saga of the Trask and Hamilton families, archetypal settlers in California's Salinas Valley, following their evolution from the mid-19th century until the outbreak of World War I.

Because of the monumental size of Steinbook's original, Osborn could only base his screenplay on its final section, which *The New York Times* did not consider the best part. The screenplay condensed the saga into the story of one "bad" brother, Cal Trask, conflicting with his "good" brother, Aron. Both would vie for the love of a coquettish Abra, as played in the film by Julie Harris.

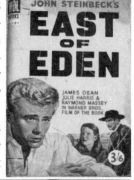

The hottest director in Hollywood at the time was Elia Kazan, who had scored a huge success with *On the Waterfront.* Based on that success, and on the fact that its male lead, Marlon Brando, had won an Oscar for his performance in it, Jack Warner had designated Kazan as both producer and director of *East of Eden.* It would be shot in CinemaScope and WarnerColor, with a musical score composed by Jimmy's intimate friend, Leonard Rosenman.

Osborn urged Kazan to attend a performance of *The Immoralist,* knowing that he was already familiar with Jimmy from their days together at the Actors Studio.

John Steinbeck...wants a quarter of the profits from the film version of the book he wrote.

Consequently, Kazan, too, was mesmerized watching Jimmy as the black-mailing homosexual Arab opposite Louis Jourdan and Geraldine Page.

The next day, he called Jane Deacy, Jimmy's agent, and asked that the actor come and visit him. She already knew that the role of Cal was up for grabs, and in reference to that, had placed a call to Kazan four days before, which he had not bothered to return.

"When Dean came in for an interview, he was a heap of twisted legs and denim rags, looking resentful for no particular reason," Kazan remembered. "I made him wait outside for half an hour, thinking that might drop that belligerent pose. When he walked in, I knew immediately that he was right for the role of Cal. He was guarded, sullen, suspicious, and he seemed to have a great deal of concealed emotion. He looked and spoke like a character in *East of Eden,* even though I learned later he had not read the novel."

"I also knew that making a picture with this guy would be a great challenge for me. I would have to cajole and comfort him. Need I say, pamper the baby and change his diapers. I would have to inspire him, challenge him, and, if the scene called for it, even provoke him to violence. And I'd have to indulge him. From what I'd heard, I might even have to let him suck my cock if it meant getting the picture made. My belief is that a director has to do any and everything to make a good film."

"After my interview, if it could be called that—Dean did not believe in communication—he invited me for a hair-raising, definitely hellraising, motorcycle ride through the canyons of Manhattan. That we survived that journey is miraculous. But obviously, I lived to tell about it."

"The next day, I took him to Steinbeck's apartment to see what he thought of him," Kazan said.

[The popular novelist had sold the movie rights to East of Eden *in 1952 for $125,000, a goodly price for a literary property at mid-century. He had also contracted for twenty-five percent of the profits.]*

Steinbeck reserved his opinion of Jimmy until he could deliver it discreetly and privately. He telephoned the director the next day to tell him, "He's a god damn snotty kid, but, by God, he *is* Cal. Good luck working with a shithead like that neurotic boy. Whereas before, I thought Clift and Brando would have been the ideal casting, I no longer believe that after meeting this Dean character."

***

Kazan invited Jimmy to fly with him to Los Angeles for a screen test, although he was virtually certain he'd get the role. A few hours before the scheduled departure of their flight, a long black limousine, with Kazan inside, pulled up in front of Jimmy's brownstone. Disheveled, Jimmy raced down the steps carrying two grocery bags filled with clothing and tied with string.

It was his first ride on an airplane, and Kazan noted with amusement that he spent most of the flight with his nose pressed against the glass of the window adjacent to his seat.

After their arrival in California, Jimmy asked Kazan if they could stop at a hospital where his father worked as a dental technician in a lab.

Kazan remained in the back of the limousine, and Winton Dean emerged ten minutes later. "I sensed the tension between those two," Kazan said. "I think Jimmy's father hated him. He did not seem impressed, either with the limo or with Dean's chance of starring in a major motion picture. He told me that he had wanted Jimmy to study law at U.C.L.A. They stood side by side without anything to say to each other. I ordered Jimmy into the car and we moved on."

"But at least I realized how deeply Dean could identify with the errant son, Cal, who was alienated from his father," Kazan said. "It would be a slice from his own life."

Because Kazan had already demonstrated his knack for Oscar-winning success, Jack Warner at Warner Brothers had more or less given him free rein in casting. Kazan had already alerted Warner that the role called for a nineteen-year-old-version of Brando or Monty Clift. He had also warned the studio boss that Jimmy was idiosyncratic and somewhat eccentric.

Warner's spies soon reported to him that Jimmy was extremely temperamental and hard to control. Kazan received a telegram from Warner. "I hope this Dean fellow isn't too odd. It's getting to the point now where if we make a picture with someone who is odd, the whole machine is thrown out of order, not to mention the expense to the studio as pictures fall behind schedules. You know it takes only one odd spark to make the motor miss. I am fed up with people who are too odd. But I'll take your word that you can control this little talented upstart."

Kazan dreaded introducing Jimmy to Warner. "He was used to such male stars as Errol Flynn, James Cagney, Humphrey Bogart, and Gary Cooper," Kazan said. "Now I show up at his doorstep with this fidgety kid from New York. Warner was pleasant enough, but skeptical of my judgment. As Jimmy waited for me outside, Warner kept me in his office."

"Is it true that this kid is a cocksucker?" he demanded to know.

"It's just a rumor," Kazan replied. He went on to assure him that the role called for a young man who could combine masculine virility with feminine softness and insecurity.

Over lunch in Warners' commissary, Kazan ordered Jimmy to drink a pint of cream every day to put on some weight and "for God's sake, get a suntan.

You're as pale as the Queen of England, and I want you to look like a healthy farmboy who works in the fields."

That afternoon, Jimmy's first reunion was with his former roommate, William Bast. Barging into his apartment, he gave Bast a deep and passionate kiss. "Come on, guy," he said. "Let's hit the road. I've rented a car. I've been cast in *East of Eden,* and Gadge *[Kazan]* wants me suntanned. Nut brown, please."

Bast seemed overjoyed for Jimmy and somehow managed to conceal his jealousy.

Within the hour, the two men were heading east to the Anza-Borrego Desert, an hour's drive from Palm Springs.

Bast had never seen Jimmy this enthusiastic. "When I was out here before, I took a lot of crap, kissed a lot of asses. No more! I danced to the fiddle of these Caligula wannabes, but not this time around. The bastards need me, they want me, and I'm gonna make them lick the dust off my boots."

At a small, rustic resort, they rented a modest cabin for a week. It contained two double beds and a private shower.

That night, over dinner, Jimmy told Bast, "I'm gonna fuck those Tinseltown bastards like they've never been fucked before."

Bast later concluded that he "knew that Jimmy had the tenacity of a Gila monster, but even a Gila monster has to roll over on his back to allow the poison in his jaws to flow."

"Hollywood hasn't changed," he told Bast. "It is still the same hostile, predatory place it always was, with a lot of hungry mouths looking for a pretty boy with a big cock."

That first night in their cabin, after the lights were off, Jimmy whispered to Bast, "Are you still awake?"

Bast later wrote, "*El momento de verdad* had arrived."

He answered Jimmy's siren call in the dark, crawling naked into his separate bed. He later told friends, "Then the inevitable happened. We made love all night. It was amazing it hadn't happened before. I mean, at our penthouse in Hollywood, we'd shared a double bed, and on many occasions, I'd felt Jimmy's erection pressing up against me. But this time, in his bed at that desert resort, that erection would do a lot more than 'press.'"

Jimmy's pursuit of a suntan, as demanded by Jack Warner and Kazan, evolved into a sort of honeymoon for the actor and actor turned writer. "I knew it wouldn't last," Bast said. "And as our lazy days went by, I feared a return to the real world, knowing I was bound to lose Jimmy to a dozen temptations, maybe more."

During their final day in the desert, Jimmy told Bast, "I am the sun."

"And so he was for me," Bast wrote in a memoir.

***

Back in Hollywood, Jimmy invited Bast to meet his agent, Dick Clayton. Jane Deacy did not have a West Coast Office, so she had designated Clayton, from the Famous Artists Corporation, to represent his and their movie interests.

Jimmy had known Clayton since the days they had appeared together in bit parts in *Sailor Beware!*

Clayton helped hammer out the details of Jimmy's movie contract with Warners. Finalized on April 7, 1954, it stipulated Jimmy's receipt of $1,000 a week during the shooting of *East of Eden.* To tide him over until the beginning of filming, the studio advanced him $700.

[In October of 1954, Warners renewed the contract with a six-month option. The contract was renewed again and expanded on April 2, 1955, into a long-term commitment. It called for him to earn $3,000 a week by his ninth film. However, from New York, Jane Deacy negotiated a better deal that would have granted him $100,000 for every film. "He was the hottest property we had," Jack Warner said. "We had big plans for him. I mean big plans."]

As an agent, Clayton would later represent such high-profile clients as Jane Fonda, Farrah Fawcett, Harrison Ford, Nick Nolte, and Angie Dickinson. For twenty-two years, he functioned as the personal manager of Burt Reynolds. In time, he would build and occupy a home with Jimmy's rival, Tab Hunter.

After signing the contract with Warner Brothers, as funneled through Clayton, Jimmy invited Bast as a visitor onto the studio lot. He introduced Bast to Kazan, with the boast that, "Gadge, you're shaking the hand of the best writer in Hollywood."

En route to the commissary for a meal together, Bast and Jimmy encountered Paul Newman, who was preparing himself for his leading role (one that Jimmy had previously rejected) in *The Silver Chalice.*

Newman told Bast, "Jimmy got the role of Cal that I wanted so bad I could taste it."

Despite their rivalry, Newman and Jimmy maintained an easy going relationship, almost like lovers, in the view of Bast, who suspected that some passion had flared between them back in New York. "They were just too god damn good looking for something not to have happened during the time they hung out together."

Over food, Newman attacked the script of *The Silver Chalice,* and their conversation remained pleasant until Newman said, "There isn't a single bastard in this lousy business who made it by himself. No matter who they are, someone was there to open the door for them."

454

Jimmy almost exploded in rage. Obviously, Newman had touched a nerve. "No one ever did anything for me. I did it myself. I don't owe nothing to nobody. Not a god damn cent," he said, slamming his fist against the tabletop.

Newman gracefully changed the subject. As he was leaving, he told Jimmy, "We'll meet at seven like we agreed."

That more or less confirmed Bast's suspicions that they were secret lovers.

***

Other "blasts from the past" (Jimmy's words), also reappeared in his life after his return to L.A. for *East of Eden.* One of them was Nick Adams, Jimmy's hustler buddy and sometimes lover.

Having heard that Jimmy was in L.A. and starring in a major-league movie, Adams arranged a reunion with him, through Bast. Access to Jimmy was getting more competitive, thanks to renewed competition from Bast and now, from Paul Newman.

"How can any guy compete with that fucking Paul Newman?" Adams asked.

Nevertheless, Jimmy agreed to see him from time to time, eventually promising him a role in his upcoming film.

Adams later said: "For most of the time, Jimmy was straight with himself. He'd never known the good life, and he wanted to know what it was like. He made his own way in life, and on his own terms. Whatever didn't fit into his new life, he dropped. I hoped it wasn't going to include me."

***

Dick Davalos was cast in *East of Eden* as Jimmy's "good" brother, Aron.

Before he was awarded the part, he, with Jimmy, submitted to a series of screen tests, in which Jimmy was paired alongside Joanne Woodward, even though Kazan, by this point, had more or less determined that Julie Harris would be the female lead.

"I remember rehearsing at his apartment the night before the screen test, and really assimilating our characters and developing our brotherly relationship as best we could," Davalos said. "I remember we were extremely tired the next day when we went to the studio."

Kazan later said to Harris, "I wonder if Davalos and Dean are tired from rehearsing all night, or from something else."

"Boys will be boys," Harris said, "especially if you have two handsome young men spending the night together. They do have strong urges at that age, you know."

"I remember it well," Kazan said.

On the Warner's lot, Jimmy survived both the screen tests and the wardrobe fittings, and even got a review from the boss himself, Jack Warner. Warner told the cinematographer assigned to *East of Eden*, Tim McCord, "Kazan brought this sad-eyed pretty boy with almond eyes and brown hair into my office. A rotten dresser. He's small—too short, really—slight, and looks as vulnerable as a lost puppy dog. God help us."

Warner had made a wise choice in his selection of McCord, whose almost monochrome cinematography captured the charm of an old-fashioned photo album from 1917, the year in which the story is set.

***

In the final lineup, top billing would go to Julie Harris in the lead role of Abra. In the beginning of the film, she is Aron's girlfriend, but later falls for Cal.

Raymond Massey was cast as the judgmental, puritanical, Bible-quoting father, Adam Trask, a lettuce farmer who clearly favors Aron. Jo Van Fleet plays Kate, who was once married to Adam but abandoned him and her two sons. She is now the deeply embittered owner of a bordello in a neighboring town.

The cast was augmented with Burl Ives as the sheriff; Albert Dekker as Will; and Barbara Baxley as a sadistic nurse. Months earlier, Jimmy had had a brief fling with Baxley when they each resided at the Iroquois Hotel in Manhattan.

On the set of *East of Eden,* she tried to renew their affair, but was brutally rejected by him. "Why do I need you now?" he responded. "Since I arrived in Hollywood, my phone's been ringing off the wall."

One by one, Jimmy met the cast. He already knew Harris from the Actors Studio in New York, and he had already prepared for and been evaluated in screen tests with Davalos.

***

Growing up in Grosse Pointe, Michigan, Harris had been enrolled for a year at the Yale School of Drama. In 1954, she'd won a Tony for her interpretation of Sally Bowles in the original

James Dean with Julie Harris, his brother's fiancé in *East of Eden.* Is their embrace an allegory for a biblical sin? *("Thou shalt not covet thy brother's wife")*

456

Broadway version of *I Am a Camera,* in which Jimmy had unsuccessfully competed for the role inspired by Christopher Isherwood. In time, Harris would receive ten Tony nominations.

She had made her screen debut in 1952, repeating her Broadway success as the lonely teenaged girl, Frankie, in the film adaptation of Carson McCullers' *The Member of the Wedding,* for which she was nominated for an Oscar as Best Actress.

A complicated triangle that gets increasingly complicated as the movie progresses: Dean *(left),* Davalos *(center)* and Harris *(right)*

Jimmy maintained fond memories of her. "Her voice was like the gentle rainfall on a summer night. Her eyes reflected the depths of her tender heart."

Harris later stated that "Jimmy and I were almost killed before filming began. One night he knocked on my door right after I'd arrived in Hollywood. He invited me to 'go for a spin' in the Hollywood Hills. He had just bought a new scarlet red MG."

"We rode into the night at top speed. At one point, he had trouble lighting a cigarette, and he almost ran off the road and down an embankment, which would have meant sudden death since it was so steep. I didn't dare lecture him. That would have made him go much faster. I let him do whatever his heart desired. He was the kind of man who did whatever he wanted to."

When he finally returned her to the pavement in front of her apartment, she gracefully turned down his invitation for a sleepover. "He was Tom Sawyer to me, a very wicked but adorable Tom Sawyer. He manipulated people, and he knew exactly what he was doing. He was mercurial, unpredictable, and very beguiling."

"I did not suffer the misfortune of falling in love with Jimmy," Harris said.

457

"It would have been a destructive relationship. Instead of seducing me, he went for Pier Angeli, who was starring in *The Silver Chalice* opposite that divine Paul Newman."

"Hollywood was nothing but a rumor factory. There was talk on the set that Paul and Pier were involved, and even that Paul and Jimmy were an item. I got left out of all these complicated sleeping arrangements."

"I remember Jimmy showing me this locket. In it, he had a lock of Pier's hair and a scrap from the dress she'd worn when he met her. It was all so romantic."

"But he was always upsetting Pier," Harris continued. "She was so prim and proper, so perfectly made up, and so well dressed. She invited friends of hers for lunch in the commissary so that they could meet Jimmy. He showed up without his shirt, his body smeared with a mechanic's grease. He wore a dirty pair of blue jeans with a big hole in the rear revealing bare skin and the fact that he wore no underwear. She burst into tears and went a week without speaking to him."

***

Richard ("Dick") Davalos, born in the Bronx a year before Jimmy and just as good looking, was of Finnish and Spanish descent. His career never lived up to its early promise. *[Coincidentally, he did play opposite Paul Newman as the convict, "Blind Dick," in* Cool Hand Luke *(1967), a role that might have gone to Jimmy had he lived.]*

Unlike Jimmy's flamboyantly non-conformist character, Cal, Davalos, as Aron, had to be sober, diligent, God-fearing, hard-working, humorless, and the obvious favorite of his moralistic father.

As part of a plan to improve their ability as actors to portray brothers, Kazan decided to house Davalos and Jimmy together as roommates in a one-room studio apartment across the street from the entrance to the Warner lot in Burbank.

Although there has never been any direct confirmation, word soon spread that Davalos and Jimmy were lovers.

According to Davalos, "As roommates, Jimmy and I became 'Cal & Aron' off screen. I was Mr. Goody Two-Shoes. Consistent with the character of Cal, Jimmy usually left our place in a mess, and I was always tidying up, *à la* Aron. Jimmy was very heavy into Cal."

"He asked me what my previous experience had been," Davalos said. "I told him I'd been an usher at the Trans-Lux Theater in Manhattan. But I let him know I'd beaten Newman out for the role."

"I beat Newman out for more than one role," Jimmy bragged.

On screen, Jimmy's scenes with Davalos carried a suggestion of latent homosexuality. One scene was so provocative that Jack Warner ordered that it be cut because of its hint of brotherly incest. Davalos was shown presumably nude in bed while Jimmy, wearing pants but shirtless, played a horn nearby. "The censors will never go for that," Warner said.

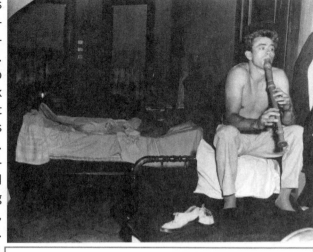

Many brothers have shared the same bedroom, but this sequence in *East of Eden* was ordered cut by Jack Warner even before it faced censorship. The studio mogul told Kazan, "They're half nude and look like they've been fucking all night."

After two weeks, Davalos told Kazan that he'd grown tired of Jimmy's constant mood swings and sloppiness, and moved out into better lodgings. After that, the rumor mill went into overdrive once again when the story spread that one night Jimmy "tried to rape the actor playing his brother."

"Working with Jimmy was a mind-blower," Davalos recalled years later. "We were so into those roles, me and Jimmy. Without going into too much detail, let me put it this way: It took me two years to get over working with him."

***

A Canadian actor from Toronto, veteran star Raymond Massey, born in 1896, was known for his stage-trained voice. He'd made his first stage appearance in London in 1922, and his first movie role, in *High Treason,* in 1927. His greatest Broadway triumph had been in Robert E. Sherwood's play, *Abe Lincoln in Illinois.* Later, he repeated his performance in the film adaptation, for which he was nominated for an Oscar as Best

Filial Anguish: James Dean, playing the less favored son, interacting with his screen father, Raymond Massey, who genuinely detested him.

Actor. He would go on to portray Lincoln again and again, and became so associated with the dead president that a fellow actor once quipped that Massey wouldn't ever be satisfied with his impersonation of Lincoln until someone assassinated him.

Right from the beginning, Jimmy and Massey detested each other with a hatred that might even have surpassed the on-Broadway loathing between Jimmy and Louis Jourdan.

"Ray couldn't stand the sight of the kid, dreading every day he had to do a scene with him," Kazan claimed. "He never knew what Jimmy was going to say or do. He knew only one thing to expect: Whatever Jimmy did would not be in the script."

"Our boy was fully aware of how much he was scorned by Ray," Kazan said. "He was sullen and surly around Ray, not disguising his contempt for the older actor. This was an antagonism I didn't try to heal. I almost encouraged it. It would make their portrayals of alienated father and son more effective."

During an especially bitter exchange, Jimmy yelled at Massey, "Gary Cooper wanted to play my father, but an old fart like you got the job, much to my regret."

According to Massey, "Dean approached everything with a chip on his shoulder. The Method had encouraged this truculent spirit. He never knew his lines before he walked onto the set, rarely had command of them when the camera rolled, and even if he had, he was inaudible. He went away alone after a scene was rehearsed. He would disappear and leave the rest of us to cool off in our chairs while he communed with himself somewhere out of sight."

In his memoir, *A Hundred Different Lives,* Massey wrote, "Simple technicalities, such as moving on cue and finding his mark, were beneath Dean's consideration."

[Coincidentally, Massey went on to become one of the leading contenders for the role of Uncle Bawley in Giant, *which meant he would have had to work with Jimmy again. Eventually, however, the part went to Chill Wills.]*

***

Troublemaker: Set in the rough-and-tumble boom years of early 20th-Century California, Jimmy, as Cal, is caught between the Sheriff, as played by Burl Ives *(left)*, and his morally obsessed father, Raymond Massey *(right)*.

Jo Van Fleet was a very talented, California-born theater and movie actress. Jimmy met her after she'd won a Tony for her portrayal of the abusive daughter-in-law in the 1953 Broadway adaptation of Horton Foote's teleplay *The Trip to Bountiful. [Its plot revolved around an elderly woman, played in 1953 by Lillian Gish, who lives with a daughter-in-law (Jo Van Fleet) who loathes her, and a weak-willed son who is afraid to defend her.]*

The role of Jimmy's prostitute mother in *East of Eden* was Van Fleet's first film role. *[After finishing it, she'd go on to star in* The Rose Tattoo *and* I'll Cry Tomorrow, *both released in 1955.]*

"I had always been told that Dean was a homosexual," Van Fleet said. "But I didn't get that impression. Word reached us that he strayed

In *East of Eden*, Jimmy learned that his mother, played by Jo Van Fleet *(depicted above)*, is the owner of a profitable bordello in a neighboring town. He desperately wants to connect with her, but until he virtually forces her to recognize him, she shuns him.

over to the set of *A Star is Born* to service Judy Garland. Pier Angeli also showed up almost every day, panting at the mouth."

***

Burl Ives, also known as a singer and banjo player, was cast in *Eden* as Sam, the town's tough, wise, and burly sheriff. Ives would later appear, brilliantly, as Big Daddy in the film version of Tennessee Williams' *Cat on a Hot Tin Roof* (1958), with Elizabeth Taylor and Paul Newman. In *Eden,* as a law enforcement agent, Ives is relatively benign. Consoling Jimmy, he gives him information and advice about his mother, who deserted him and his brother so long ago.

***

Cast as a secondary character named Will, Albert Dekker was a veteran actor from Brooklyn. He had previously appeared on Broadway as Willy Loman in Arthur Miller's *Death of a Salesman* and on the screen in such hits as the mad scientist in the 1940 horror film, *Dr. Cyclops*. Off screen, he'd entered politics, winning a seat in the California State Assembly, where he served from 1944 to 1946.

[Dekker, like Jimmy himself, was destined for a violent death. On May 5,

461

1968, under suspicious circumstances, Dekker was found dead, perhaps murdered, in his Hollywood home. Naked, his body was discovered in a bathtub. A noose had been tightened around his neck and attached, tautly, to a shower curtain rod. He had been blindfolded, his wrists were handcuffed, and a ball gag had been inserted into his mouth. Two hypodermic needles dangled from one arm, and his body had been covered with vulgarities that included the word FUCK scrawled upon his skin with red lipstick. Money and valuable equipment were missing, but there was no sign of forced entry.

Albert Dekker...He'd face a noose in his future.

Despite skepticism and widespread protests, the coroner ruled out the possibility of murder, claiming that Dekker's death had been the accidental aftereffect of autoerotic asphyxiation.]

***

Lois Smith who, like Jimmy, had studied at the Actors Studio, had snagged a small role as one of the "bar slaves" in Jo Van Fleet's bordello. Her character throws herself at Jimmy when he invades the forbidden premises. She was not the right weight before filming began, and lost many pounds, fast, by eating nothing but raw carrots, lettuce, an occasional slice of bread, and lots of black coffee.

Kazan had discovered her in New York based on her appearance in the Broadway comedy, *Time Out for Ginger* (1952). After the release of *East of Eden,* she was designated by *The Film Daily* as one of the industry's top juvenile actresses.

For a while, she stood a good chance of winning the *ingénue* role of Lux Benedict II in Jimmy's later film, *Giant* (released in 1956, after Jimmy's death), but the part eventually went to Carroll Baker. Smith did appear years later in *Five Easy Pieces* (1970) with Jack Nicholson.

***

On the set, Jimmy was frequently late for work, a result of his frequent late-night partying along the Sunset Strip. According to Kazan, "He didn't accept the fact that movie stars, when they're working, have to get up early. He started showing up looking like he needed a two-by-four to prop up the bags under his eyes—hardly the image of a California farmboy working the fields.

462

I demanded that he give up the nightlife, get to bed early, and look the god damn part."

During the course of filming, Kazan had ordered him not to ride his motorcycle. "Try to understand," Kazan told him. "If you're determined to kill yourself as a daredevil on the road, don't do it during the filming of *Eden*. Be as reckless as you want, but only after the film is wrapped."

As a means of chaperoning and "handling" him, Kazan ordered that Jimmy live in the bungalow he'd been assigned, an area positioned directly adjacent to his own bungalow on the Warners' lot. Jimmy's was luxuriously configured as a two-room suite, with its own kitchen and bathroom. It had once been occupied by Bette Davis when she reigned as the Queen of Warner Brothers. It had also been occupied by Errol Flynn, who, when he wasn't needed on the set, sometimes entertained three young girls there at the same time.

***

On May 15, 1954, Kazan ordered cast and crew, including Jimmy, to transfer to Mendocino, about 150 miles north of San Francisco, for the filming of some outdoor scenes. For a while, Jimmy lodged at the Little River Inn, but complained that the noise from early-morning trucks kept him awake. Consequently, during the remainder of his time there, he opted to sleep in a railroad car on the film set.

With a population of only 800 people, Mendocino warmly welcomed the film's cast and crew. Some of the local women prepared lavish meals for them. In gratitude for their hospitality, when the film was complete, Kazan arranged a special screening of *East of Eden* for them. Businesses shut down for the day.

One of the scenes filmed in Mendocino featured Jo Van Fleet, as Kate, at the local bank depositing the previous night's earnings from her whorehouse. The bank teller suggests that she sure did run a profitable enterprise to be saving so much money. In response, stone-faced, Kate emits a glacial chill.

After two days in Mendocino, both Davalos and Jimmy came down with severe cases of poison ivy. Kazan had to delay production until their skins healed.

On June 4, the cast and creed moved south to central California's town of Salinas. [*The home town of John Steinbeck, and known as "the salad bowl of the world," Salinas was and is the focal point for the production of huge amounts of lettuce, grapes, and vegetables. It was there that the famous scene associated with the failed attempt to freeze and transport lettuce was shot. One of the most memorable moments involved Jimmy dancing through his newly sprouted bean crop. It was not in the script, but Kazan gave him free reign. That creative freedom resulted in a clip that symbolized the epitome of enterprising youth, as represented by Cal.]*

Meanwhile, back in Burbank, set designers Malcolm Bert and James Base had been laboring to re-create the town of Salinas as it looked in 1917. For the carnival scene, a full-scale amusement park was erected, complete with an operable Ferris wheel.

In one of the most famous scenes in the movie, Harris and Jimmy take a ride on that wheel.

Kazan instructed Rosenman to craft the kind of musical score for the scene that might have prefaced "the birth of angels."

***

Pier Angeli visited Jimmy frequently on the set of *East of Eden.* From his dressing room immediately next door, separated from Jimmy's with only a thin wall, Kazan could hear them "boffing—that is, when they weren't arguing, which was most of the time. I hate to admit it, but I was glad when she ran off with Vic Damone. Now I had Jimmy where I wanted him on camera—alone and miserable."

"I noticed that with Angeli out of the picture, Rosenman was making long, extended visits to Jimmy's dressing room. I won't describe what I heard between those two queers."

***

After being invited onto the set by Kazan, Marlon Brando, on July 13, paid a visit to the set of *East of Eden.* His arrival came as a surprise and shock to Jimmy.

Most of the cast and crew weren't aware that Brando and Jimmy had become intimately acquainted in New York, and both actors promoted the myth that their paths had never crossed before.

Arriving late in the morning, Brando stayed around for the night shoot, eventually heading home at around 4AM.

A famous photo was snapped to document Brando's visit. Kazan appears dour, but Brando smiles into the camera, as Julie Harris stares adoringly at him. In the frame's far right stands a bewildered-looking Jimmy.

Because he'd received reports that Jimmy delivered onscreen performances that imitated his style, Brando wanted to see Jimmy at work.

"I'm directing him and he'll probably, based on my guidance, be a big hit," said Kazan. "The boy does have something. Call it star quality for lack of a better description. My deepest regret is that I'm not directing you in the movie.

Come on, fucker, it's the story of your life. You could play it brilliantly. You've lived it. The story of a young man abandoned by his mother—read that Dodie—and starved for the love of a rigid, puritanical bastard of a father—read that Marlon, Sr."

When Kazan called a break for lunch, Jimmy invited Brando into his dressing room. There, Brando warned him that by appearing in *East of Eden*, "You're courting fame, and nothing is more destructive than being famous. I can't walk down the

Kazan, Brando, Harris, and an absent-looking James Dean, on the set of *East of Eden*. Kazan later wrote that Jimmy "was shrunken and twisted in misery, staring off into the distance."

street any more but what I'm followed. I can't go see a movie any more but that a line of girls follow me into the theater. The other day, I went into a deli to order a hot pastrami on rye and a cream soda, and at least five faggots were suddenly behind me, yelling, 'Marlon, can we have your autograph?' You know what I did? I pulled down my jeans and mooned them. I told them, 'Autograph this, boys!" Write 'Marlon' on one cheek, and 'Brando' on the other."

Jimmy responded by telling Brando about a recent visit he'd received from Tennessee Williams, who was in town and working on the outline for a new play, *Cat on a Hot Tin Roof*. "He tried to persuade Kazan to direct the play on Broadway," Jimmy said. "But after he laid his eyes on me, he didn't have much time for Kazan. Tennessee told me he originally wanted you for the lead. It's the story of a repressed homosexual. Think you can handle it?"

"There's nothing repressed about me," Brando said.

"Perhaps," Jimmy said enigmatically. "Anyway, I invited Williams into my dressing room. I know he went down on you when you boys were on Cape Cod together. He was already a bit drunk when got here. But I took down my jeans and let him blow me. After that, he offered me the lead role in the Broadway production. I hear Kazan thinks *Cat* is going to be a major success. Bigger than *Streetcar*. Out with Brando. In with James Dean. The new boy on the block."

If Jimmy were trying to either provoke or anger Brando with that, he didn't succeed. Brando had already informed Tennessee that he planned to never venture onto a Broadway stage again, especially within the context of one of his plays. "We did it fine the first time, but once was enough for one life."

Brando is alleged to have told his best friend, Carlo Fiori, "I took Dean to his dressing room between takes and screwed him royally with my noble tool, just to show him who's boss, and still number one."

Kazan refuted what at the time was a widely prevalent concept that Jimmy, as an actor, was very similar to Brando. "Unlike Dean," he said, "Brando was a multi-talented person, a sort of stream of experience that could be tapped, then directed to flow as openly as if the actor were stripping himself psychologically and playing out, naked and vulnerable, before the world, the many facets of his personality."

"Dean, in contrast, had very little pliability. His vulnerability was hidden behind a facial hurt, one that he played again and again. There was a muted aggression that could give way at any moment to destructiveness."

According to Jimmy, "I don't think people should be subservient to movie idols, and I do not idolize Marlon Brando. *Brando!* If I imitate him subconsciously, I don't know about it, and if I do it consciously, I'd be a fool to admit it. I'd like to be a star in my own sense. I mean to be a very consummate actor, to have more difficult roles and to fill them to my satisfaction. But not to star on the basis of gold plating. A real star carries his own illumination and inward brightness."

***

Kazan interpreted Jimmy's performance as brilliant, a stunning presence, in the opening scene of *East of Eden.* He sat on a wooden sidewalk in the *faux,* studio-built town of Salinas, watching as his mother (Jo Van Fleet) walks by, without recognizing or acknowledging him, on his way to the bank.

In London's *Sunday Express,* Milton Shulman wrote, "Dean has the slouching grace of a tired cat and eyes that stare with the compelling magnetism of a deep and empty cave."

On the screen, he appears petulant, with jerky movements, his eyes frightened slits in the glare of the California sun. He's dressed in a babyknit sweater and a pair of white slacks, and looks five years

Veiled, and draped in black, Jo Van Fleet was cast in *East of Eden* as an aging whore. In this scene near the beginning of the film, she walks past her son, as played by James Dean, whom she deserted years ago. She's also walking into an Oscar win.

younger than his actual age of twenty-three.

Later in the film, he hurls a rock at his alienated mother's whorehouse before he's chased away by her bouncer.

Kazan claimed that "Jimmy arrived on the set every day very easily hurt. He was sensitive and bewildered. I worked with him to build up is confidence and then pointed him in the right direction and watched the kid go for the gold. One time, I had to get him loaded on Chianti to get the result I wanted on the screen."

"As filming progressed, he became increasingly difficult, not getting along with the cast, except for Harris." Kazan said. "At times, he was just impossible. He had this damn camera, and he could spend hours taking pictures of himself in the mirror."

As the shooting progressed, Jimmy began to show up later and later, and sometimes, even if he had reported on time, he would just disappear and no one could find him.

On one occasion, after a search, two of Kazan's grips found him in Judy Garland's dressing room on another part of Warners' lot, the one devoted to filming *A Star is Born* (1954). Coincidentally, the title of her film was the same as the label that the press had begun attributing to Jimmy.

He'd seduced Garland once before, along with his friend and lover, John Carlyle, who had been given a small role in *A Star is Born*. The handsome young actor would, years later and despite his gender preference as a gay man, would become Garland's companion and her sometimes lover.

Carlyle would later write a memoir about his involvement with the singer.

Escorted back to the set, Jimmy faced an angry director. "What was I to do?" Jimmy asked Kazan. "Judy wanted a little loving. You don't turn down *the* Judy Garland! No way!"

"He had a violent streak in him," Kazan said. "He seemed threatening, as if any minute he could turn into a serial killer. He was a little nuts, maybe a lot nuts. He was actually the Cal he projected in *Eden.*"

In one scene with Massey, Kazan was not getting the reaction he wanted from the expression on Massey's face. He came up with a plan, telling Jimmy to pick up a Bible and to start reading from it, but to throw in a lot of words to shock and offend Massey.

After Kazan quietly ordered the camera to focus on Massey, Jimmy picked up a Bible from a nearby table. "The Lord is my shepherd," Jimmy read, improvising. "I shall not suck cock, put anything up your ass, fuck you, shit, or piss on you, fucker," he said.

Massey exploded and stormed off the set. Kazan chased after him. "I will not play opposite this freak," Massey shouted at him. "Talk to my lawyers. I quit."

"Jimmy had gotten Ray mad, and I got the shot I wanted," Kazan said. "I explained to Massey that I had ordered Jimmy to do that. Finally, I persuaded him to come back to work."

Some sections of *East of Eden* were filmed in sequences that strayed from, or ignored, or weren't included in the original script. Examples included Jimmy's dance in the bean field, and his fetal-like posturing atop a rail car after his return from an anguished search for his brothel-keeping mother. Both of those were pure improvisations on Jimmy's part.

His most celebrated improvisation was when Cal's father rejects his gift of $5,000 (money earned from that bean crop). Osborn's script called for Jim to react by running away. Instead, he instinctively turned to Massey, and, in tears, embraced him. This scene, and Massey's shocked and embarrassed reaction, were retained within the final cut.

Kazan summed it up: "Dean will appeal to women who will want to mother him, and to faggots who will want to fuck him. I think he comes across as a mixture of autistic child and baby-faced psychotic."

After he'd seen the final cut, Kazan said, "I've never seen anything like it. Jimmy was that good, and that included Brando, whom I directed in *Streetcar*, and in *On the Waterfront*, as you well know."

At the end of filming, Kazan threw a wrap party. At its peak, after three intense months of shooting, Harris kept looking for Jimmy to say goodbye, but she could not find him. When the party was over, she went to his bungalow to see if he were there.

Inside, she found him crying: "What's the matter?" she asked. "You were wonderful in the picture."

"It's over," he sobbed. "All over."

She held him in her arms, forever remembering him as "a lost, lonely little boy."

***

Before the film's release, Hollywood was already treating Jimmy like a movie star. Word had gotten out. He told a reporter, "I guess I'm the flavor of the month."

"Someday, I'd like to follow in the footsteps of my great idol, Elia Kazan," Jimmy said. "You know, Kazan was an actor at Warner Brothers a number of years ago. Then he began to direct Broadway productions and went on to direct exceptional motion pictures."

Two weeks after filming shut down, Kazan credited Harris—through patience and empathy—for being more helpful than he had been as a director. "Without her, Dean would not have made it to the end."

Ted McCord later said, "With all this public buzz, Warners' publicity department latched onto Jimmy and began pumping out releases to the press."

One press agent told him, "You're already a movie star. One night you went to bed as a struggling, unknown actor. The next morning you woke up a golden prince. So now, you'll have to start acting and living like a prince.'"

"That's bullshit!" Jimmy responded. "I came out here to act, not to be a prince, not some social fop—and not a gilded dandelion."

"Maybe publicity is important," Jimmy said. "But I just can't make it, can't get with it. I've been told by a lot of guys that it works. The newspapers give you a big build-up. Something happens, they tear you down. Who needs it? What counts for the artist is performance—not publicity. Guys who don't know me already…they've already typed me as an odd ball."

"I probably should have a press agent. But I don't care what people write about me. I'll talk to the ones I like. The others can print whatever they please."

Columnist Mike Connolly asked Jimmy if he had lost anything during his process of becoming famous.

"I fought it for a long time. But after a while, I think I started learning what so many actors have already learned—something about that certain communicative power we have that so few people are privileged to have. We find that we can reach not only people with whom we work on the soundstages here in Hollywood, but people all over the world. And then we start thinking, 'I'm famous, all right, and I guess this is what I wanted, so now how do I face it?' And then the responsibilities come. And you have to fight against becoming egotistical."

William Bast had a front row seat as he watched Jimmy, now only his part-time lover, rise within the constellation of Hollywood. "It was a gradual disintegration, a splintering of an already multi-faceted personality into a fragmented jigsaw puzzle."

***

In January of 1955, Kazan arranged for the release of previews of *East of Eden* in Los Angeles. "The instant Jimmy appeared on the screen, hundreds of girls began to scream. They'd been waiting for him, it seemed. The response from the balcony reminded me of Niagara Falls spilling over. Their reaction spread to the audiences at other previews, and generated even more hysteria."

Movie reviews of *East of Eden* were suddenly being broadcast nationwide on the radio. "Jimmy Dean appears with innocence and emotional candor, having a look of evil at times, creating a screen image of fiery intensity."

After the preview, Jimmy summed up his public appeal as a movie star: "I guess Warner Brothers has discovered uranium."

During an interview with Harold Thompson of *The New York Times,* Jimmy said that he still had not read the Steinbeck novel. "The way I work, I'd much rather justify myself with the adaptation rather than the original source. I felt I wouldn't have any trouble—not too much, anyway—with this characterization once we started, because I think I understood Cal. I knew, too, that if I had any problems about the boy's background, I could straighten it out with Kazan."

The world premiere of *East of Eden* was scheduled for March 9, 1955 at the Astor Theater in Manhattan. It was configured as a benefit for the Actors Studio, eventually netting $34,000, and it was envisioned as a splashy, star-studded affair with Jimmy as the center of attention.

But he shocked and enraged his agent, Jane Deacy, by refusing to attend. "I can't handle the scene," was his excuse.

He also told his former girlfriend, Christine White, that he had no reason to go. "I know I was good. I don't need a lot of people embarrassing me by telling me how good I was."

At the premiere, Marilyn Monroe agreed to serve as an usher, thereby generating lots of publicity for herself. However, she upset the backers of the benefit by refusing to sing "Diamonds Are a Girl's Best Friend" at the post-screening party. Up until the last minute, she had promised that she would.

Other ushers at the premiere included Marlene Dietrich and Eva Marie Saint.

After the screening, key members of the cast, including Julie Harris and Kazan, gathered at Sardi's to await the reviews.

Time magazine referred to Jimmy as a product of the "tilted pelvis school of naturalistic acting. The picture is brilliant entertainment and more than that, it announces a new star, James Dean, whose prospects look as bright as any young actor's since Marlon Brando. He has the presence of a young lion and the same sense of danger about him."

The *Hollywood Reporter* wrote: "Dean is that rare thing, a young actor who is a great actor. The troubled eloquence with which he puts over the problems of misunderstood youth may lead to his being accepted by young audiences as a sort of symbol of their generation. He is no carbon copy of Marlon Brando. He is a completely individual screen personality."

Daily Variety weighed in on the Brando vs. Dean similarities: "Dean plays the lead character as though he was straight out of the Marlon Brando mold.

Just how flexible his talent is will have to be judged on future roles, although he has a basic appeal that manages to get through to the viewers despite carboning another's acting style."

Penelope Gillatt, in *The Observer,* wrote, "If ever an errant generation threw up an expression of itself, it was James Dean. Like Cain, he has the look of a fugitive and a vagabond on earth."

John McCarten of the *New Yorker,* found that "Jimmy looked like a miniature Gregory Peck," and the *Library Journal* hailed his performance as "one of the best of the year in a movie that is also one of the best of the year."

Even the fabled French director, François Truffaut, weighed in: "*East of Eden* is the first film to give us a Baudelarian hero, fascinated by vice and contrast, loving the family and hating the family at one and the same time. James Dean is a freshly plucked *'fleur du mal.'*"

With a hint of venom, Bosley Crowther of *The New York Times* raised objections: "*[James Dean is]* a mass of histrionic gingerbread. He scuffs his feet, he whirls, he pouts, he sputters, he leans against walls, he rolls his eyes, he swallows his words, he ambles slack-kneed—all like Marlon Brando used to do. Never have we seen a performer so clearly following another's style. Mr. Kazan should be spanked for allowing Dean to do such a sophomoric thing. *East of Eden* is a great, green iceberg, mammoth and imposing, but very cold."

In response to Crowther's critique, Pauline Kael of the *New Yorker* observed, "*The Times'* critic can always be counted on to miss the point."

Kazan said, "One reviewer seemed to catch on that Jimmy was full of piss, if not vinegar. He wrote that Jimmy looked like Baby Snooks reciting while waiting to go to the bathroom."

When William Bast saw the film, he said: "There was so much of Jimmy in that movie, so much of the young man I had known for so long and had grown to love as a friend, so much of the lost, tormented, searching, gentle, enthusiastic little boy, so much of the bitter, self-abusive, testing, vengeful monster."

Jimmy's stunning performance foreshadowed his iconic role as Jim Stark in his subsequent film, *Rebel Without a Cause.* Both Cal Trask and Jim Stark are angst-ridden, misunderstood outcasts, desperately craving approval from a deeply flawed father figures.

At the 1956 Academy Awards ceremony, less than a year after Jimmy's death, he received a posthumous nomination for Best Actor in a Leading Role for his performance in *East of Eden.* This was the first posthumous nomination for a male actor in the Academy's history.

[Jeanne Eagels had been the first actress to be nominated posthumously for her role in The Letter *(1929). The year it was released, she died of a drug overdose at the age of thirty-nine.)*

Jimmy had competed for the prize with some of the biggest names in Hollywood. His rivals that year included Frank Sinatra for *The Man With the Golden Arm;* Spencer Tracy for *Bad Day at Black Rock;* and James Cagney for *Love Me or Leave Me.* The award went to Ernest Borgnine for his performance in *Marty.*

Of the other actors in *Eden,* only Jo Van Fleet carried an Oscar home as Best Supporting Actress. Kazan was nominated as Best Director, but lost to Delbert Mann for *Marty.* Paul Osborn also received a nomination for Best Screenplay.

With the release of *East of Eden,* James Dean was on the dawn of international fame. In time, newer generations, many from the 21st Century, would focus their celebrity attentions onto only two movie stars from the 1950s, James Dean and Marilyn Monroe, virtually obliterating recognition of a forgotten galaxy of others. Both of them would end their young lives tragically and early.

Bast later speculated about what Jimmy would have said about all this posthumous attention:

"Hot damn! I'm a fucking legend!"

Chapter Sixteen

JAMES DEAN'S AFFAIR WITH
MARILYN MONROE

*How a Farm Boy from Indiana Seduced
the Sex Queen of Hollywood*

TOGETHER, THEY CLIMB THE SHOW-BIZ LADDER,
BUT FIND SOMETHING MISSING: A LONG & HAPPY LIFE

*From the Twisted Wreckage of their Ashes,
Icons Emerge to Enchant the World*

When the filming of *East of Eden* was finished, its female lead, Julie Harris, described the bond between Marilyn Monroe and Jimmy Dean: "Jimmy was charismatic and had a sexual attraction that was combined with a certain innocence," she said. "The same could be said of Marilyn Monroe. I think that combination was part of each of their appeals. They were curiously untouched by their sexuality and retained that certain innocence. It was inevitable that Jimmy and Marilyn would come together, however fleeting. I didn't mean that as a *double entendre.*"

The two future icons noticed each other at the premiere of Marlon Brando's *On the Waterfront* (1954). Shelley Winters, Marilyn's former roommate, escorted Marilyn to the premiere, and Jimmy arrived because of his association with Nicholas Ray, the director who wanted to cast him as the lead in his upcoming film, *Rebel Without a Cause.*

At that time, Winters said, "Jimmy was a nobody. I'd taken him to bed, and that was probably his claim to fame. But Marilyn was the newly crowned Queen of Hollywood. What did she need with a little runt like Jimmy Dean?

"Jimmy could not just come up to a big star like Marilyn and introduce himself, "Winters said. "But he made this insane attempt to attract her attention. I think his antics that night turned her off. After all, she could have anybody in Hollywood she wanted, man or woman. Marilyn batted for both teams. She didn't need this juvenile delinquent."

In her second memoir, *Shelley II: The Middle of My Century,* she wrote about Jimmy trying to attract Marilyn's attention after the premiere. As Shelley was driving her car, with Marilyn as a passenger, "Jimmy came roaring down the mountain on his motorcycle and started the deadly game of circling us. I was so angry at the kid. I was ready to run over him in my car. I kept honking at him, and he kept putting his brakes on right in front of me. He was laughing and enjoying the game. When we got to the Château Marmont, I quickly drove to the underground garage. Jimmy followed. Marilyn was rigid with fear, and I was ready to punch his lights out."

Winters and Marilyn had been invited to Ray's post-screening party at the hotel where he maintained a suite. Jimmy, too, was on the guest list.

As author Randall Riese described that evening: "Marilyn Monroe was everything Jimmy didn't like in a woman. She was an American blonde, obsessed with her own looks, and she was a movie star personified. In his view, she was decidedly not an actress of depth or conviction. As for James Dean, he was everything she didn't like in a man. He was a pretty boy and a punk, and she didn't have use for either. He was younger, and she preferred older. He was, despite his earnest aspirations, hardly an intellectual giant. He was considered to be an imitation of Brando—why did she need an imitation when she could (and *did*) have the real thing?"

At the party, according to Winters, neither Marilyn nor Jimmy made any attempt to meet each other. "They were like two boxers, each in their own corner of the boxing ring, sizing each other up," Winters said. "They treated each other like resentful siblings. This attitude continued throughout the night."

***

Marilyn's attitude toward Jimmy changed completely after she attended an advance screening of *East of Eden*. And eventually, for its premiere in Manhattan on March 9, 1955, she even agreed to volunteer as a celebrity usher at a special benefit premiere for the Actors Studio.

One day in Manhattan, they met at the Actors Studio. As she was heading inside, she ran into Marlon Brando, her sometimes lover, who was walking along with Jimmy. As she'd later relate to Winters, "My first impulse was to regret that I was not made up as Marilyn Monroe. I looked more like Norma Jeane. I had covered my matted hair with a scarf."

Jimmy was wearing his usual outfit of blue jeans, a white T-shirt, and jacket. Her gaze traveled from his crotch to his scuffed brown penny loafers before she met him eye to eye.

"Marilyn, meet this asshole who thinks he's a better actor than I am," Brando said. "I forget the kid's name."

"Hi, Marilyn," Jimmy said. "Wanna fuck? I'm James Dean."

Coming from anybody else, she might have been insulted. But the way Jimmy extended the invitation with a challenging grin made her giggle.

"How did you know what I want to do more than anything else on earth?" she asked. Then she looked skeptically at Brando. "I need to get it from somebody. I haven't been seeing much of this guy's noble tool, as he affectionately calls it."

"Neither have I," Jimmy said provocatively.

"Sorry, guys," Brando said, "I guess I find too many other holes to plug. Speaking of that, I'm late for an appointment. I won't tell you *voyeurs* with whom. Marilyn, do you mind if I dump Jimmy boy here on you?" He kissed both of them on the lips and left hurriedly, disappearing into the crowds on the street.

"'C'mon, doll," Jimmy said, taking her arm. "Forget this fucking Actors Studio. I'm taking you over to the Blue Ribbon Café. It's where all the out-of-work actors hang out."

"I'm out of work too," she said.

On the way there, he confided in her. "I hate that asshole Lee Strasberg.

He humiliated me one afternoon, and I've never forgiven him. I don't know why I don't boycott the place."

"What happened?" she asked.

"I was performing in front of the class," he said. "I came onstage in this bullfighter's black cape with a red lining. I'd adapted a scene from Barnaby Conrad's novel, *Matador*. When it was over, there was silence, as the jealous actors waited for the master's words. Guess what he told me? 'You failed to create a sense of being in an authentic place. You're not doing the work. You're acting, not being.'"

"Don't worry about it," she said. "*East of Eden* proved what a great actor you are. I can't wait to see your next pictures."

Seated at a table in the café, they attracted almost no attention from the other patrons. Only a handful of other tables were occupied.

"Where are you crashing?" he asked her.

"At the Waldorf Towers," she said. "Isn't that posh?"

"I guess so," he said, "as long as somebody else is picking up the bill. What's his name?" Rosenberg? Cohen? Katz?"

"Milton. Milton Greene," she said. "Jimmy, I didn't know you were so anti-Semitic."

"I'm not really," he said. "I guess their money is as good as anybody else's. Hey, I've got an idea. It's getting late. Why don't you invite me to your pad for an audition? I'm good. Really good."

"Audition?" she said, looking at him skeptically. "To tell you the truth, after seeing *Eden*, I want to star in a picture with you. I guess we might as well start practicing whatever chemistry we can generate together."

"You're on. You won't regret it. Fifty years from now, you'll be writing about me in your memoirs."

"But I've got a better idea than the Waldorf," she said. "Lee Strasberg, the man you hate, has given me the use of his cottage on Fire Island any time I want it. It's a bit chilly out there this time of year, but there's a fireplace and some electric heaters. We'll have the place to ourselves. Who wants to go to Fire Island at this time of year but crazy nuts like us? I've got a car. Why don't you forget whatever you planned for tonight and run away to our cottage by the sea?"

"I think that comes under the category of an invitation a guy can't refuse."

"If you don't mind my asking, what were you planning to do otherwise?"

"I was going to go to Tennessee Williams' apartment. He claims he's writing a play about a repressed homosexual and his hot-to-trot wife named Maggie the Cat. He thinks the part would be ideal for me. I think my audition will consist of an expert blow-job."

"Sounds like fun," she said. "But you'll delay that for a couple of days?"

476

"Yes!" he said. "And I'd much rather be getting blow-jobs from Marilyn Monroe than from Tennessee Williams."

"Those are about the most romantic words I've ever heard spoken to me."

***

Marilyn and Jimmy didn't arrive at the Strasberg cottage on Fire Island until the early evening. They rushed around trying to make the place livable, and he set ablaze the driftwood in the fireplace.

She rested a small suitcase on the floor of the living room. He had chosen not to bring a change of clothes. Before it got too late, she asked him if he'd walk along the beach with her. After searching in the closet, she found a parka for him.

The moonlight on the water's surface made it look like glass. Each of them stood silently, taking in the vast expanse of dark water.

Although it was cold, they sat down on the beach, huddling together. Neither of them said anything for a long time. She was the first to speak. "When I was a little girl, I would sit for hours just staring out at the sea. I felt that somewhere, someday, a sea captain, a beautiful, loving man, would want me. He'd take me away on a long voyage to a far and distant land."

Suddenly, they both became aware of the penetrating chill. She stood up and reached for him. Hand in hand, they walked back to the cottage, which, thanks to the driftwood fire, had become warmer.

She'd brought champagne with them in the car. It had already been chilled because of the cold weather. They sat on large cushions watching the flames. He had his arm around her. "I hardly know you, but I feel I've met my soulmate," she said.

"Me too, babe," he said. "From now on, it's just you and me."

"And all the storms at sea," she said. "You know there will be many of those."

For their dinner, she made ham sandwiches, and was eager to retreat under the blankets with him. She'd later confide, "Now I know why he's so desirable as a lover and why so many people, men and women, want him."

Exhausted, they clung to each other until each of them fell asleep.

They awoke to the chill of a late morning. He put on his jeans and a jacket, and she wore jeans, too, with a heavy sweater. When she said she wanted to cook his breakfast, he went outside to gather more firewood.

After breakfast, he looked into her eyes. "Let's call this our honeymoon cottage. When we get married, maybe we should book this cottage for a whole month, just the two of us."

"Jimmy, you're proposing!" she said. "Proposal accepted, but let's wait until autumn before we get hitched."

"That's okay with me, but I demand conjugal rights now."

The day was just beginning.

She would later refer to their two nights together on Fire Island as the most idyllic of her life. When she returned to the city, Winters called, eager for news. "I heard you ran away with Jimmy Dean. I want to know everything, a blow-by-blow description. Don't leave out the slightest detail, regardless of how revolting. Did he make you crush out a cigarette on his overused butt?"

"Shelley, please," she said. "He's not like that, and there was nothing kinky. He was very loving, very romantic. I've agreed to marry him one day."

"Please come to your senses, gal," Winters said. "You don't know what you're getting yourself into. Jimmy is a sicko."

"Maybe he was on his best behavior."

"What drugs are you taking?" Winters asked.

Brando called at around lunchtime and was equally discouraging. He, too, wanted a full report of what had happened. When she told him, he said, "Jimmy is my stalker and wants to be my clone. If you're not careful, when you guys return to Hollywood, you might find him parked in front of your place, smoking cigarette after cigarette until all hours, waiting for you to return home. You won't be able to get rid of him. He developed a fixation on me. In a way, it's kind of creepy."

"Oh, Marlon, you and Shelley are taking all this too seriously. Our romance will probably disappear like a summer cloud. But then again...Who knows?"

During the days and months that remained for them, Jimmy and Marilyn would sustain a love affair conducted more or less on the phone. But the time they'd spent together would forever be etched in her memory, even if "forever" wasn't far away for her....and even less so for him.

***

Early in 1955, Marilyn told Winters, "I'm miserable in Los Angeles, and I'm flying back to New York. I'm not working now, and there's more going on in New York."

She arrived in Manhattan in time to attend the benefit opening of *East of Eden*. As part of the razzmatazz associated with its release, its producers had arranged for superstars to function as ushers and "usherettes." When Marilyn learned that Marlene Dietrich and Eva Marie Saint had each volunteered to show ticket holders to their seats, she agreed to serve as an usherette, too.

The press was already hailing the event as the splashiest movie premiere of the year. As she told Walter Winchell, "A working girl needs to keep her name in the papers when she's off the screen."

Even though the studio and the film's other cast members were depending on Jimmy to show up, he called Marilyn three days before the event saying, "I know I promised, but I can't make the scene. I can't handle it. I'm flying to Los Angeles tonight."

"But it's your movie...and it's a benefit for a good cause," she pleaded with him.

"Fuck good causes," he shot back. "Don't you know by now that I'm a rebel without a cause?"

She begged him to change his mind, but after talking with him some more, she realized that he couldn't face the public.

She followed through, however, with her own commitment. Members of the audience that night were shocked to see Marilyn Monroe, one of the best-known stars in Hollywood, checking their tickets and guiding them to their seats.

At the end of the screening, Dietrich approached Monroe and kissed her on the lips, "Why not a repeat visit to my apartment tonight, you lovely child? Love is so much better the second time around."

***

In late spring of 1955, when the weather was warmer, Jimmy returned to New York. Once again, Marilyn invited him for a holiday at Lee Strasberg's retreat on Fire Island. He eagerly accepted.

Weatherwise, it remained windy and rainy throughout most of their stay, but they didn't seem to mind. "The sun is bad for my skin anyway," she claimed. Since it was during the week, and the weather was foul, the community was at low ebb.

She would again recall the experience to Winters, claiming, "Both of us tried to be completely honest with each other."

At one point, she asked him his real name. "I made up Marilyn Monroe. What about you?"

"My name is James Byron Dean."

"Wasn't that the name of a poet I've never read?"

"He was one of the romantic poets, I think," he said.

"Forgive me, but I think it would have been better if you'd billed yourself as James Byron. That would look better on a marquee. Dean reminds me of some stern schoolmaster with a ruler in his hand."

"It's too late now," he said. "In some ways, I preferred being anonymous. In New York I used to go to an all-night café and just sit there until dawn, talking to strangers. I learned that there are a lot of people in the world who—like us—regard life as pretty god damn frightening."

"Sometimes I'm so frightened I'm afraid to get up and face the day," she said.

"With all of our hang-ups, it's good that both of us drifted into acting. Acting is the most logical way for people's neuroses to manifest themselves."

Sometimes he kidded her about her image—and his, too. "I'm playing that 'little boy lost' for all it's worth, and I stole it from your 'little girl lost' act."

"Do you think behind that innocent victim image I'm a cold-hearted, calculating bitch?"

"I think both of us are bitches, using and manipulating people," he said. "Sex is our weapon. Now gimme a kiss and let's change the subject."

She was eager to hear stories about how it had been working with director Elia Kazan, her on-again, off-again lover. Responding, Jimmy said, "He flew with me to California to shoot *Eden*. It was my first time on a plane. I was frightened. He was amused when he saw my luggage: Two grocery bags tied with string."

"Elia is always promising to star me in one of his movies, but so far, nothing."

"It's nothing all right...nothing to look forward to, at least. Being directed by him is like getting zapped with electric shock treatments. Thank God for Julie Harris. Without her, I don't think I could have survived the picture."

They each complained about their low salaries. Jimmy had received only $1,000 a week for his work in *East of Eden,* and Marilyn had been paid only $1,250 a week, a total of $15,000, for her appearance in *Gentlemen Prefer Blondes.* In vivid contrast, Marilyn's co-star, Jane Russell, who was not a Fox player, got $150,000.

Marilyn and Jimmy were on a shared voyage of discovery with each other. They both suffered from insomnia. During their first night on Fire Island, they sat up talking until dawn.

Finally, they went to bed. When they awakened, at around noon, she tried to fix his breakfast. "I didn't expect you to be a great cook," he said, "but whether you are or not, I've survived in New York on a hot dog a day, if I could afford it."

They hadn't make love their first night there, but they did in the following afternoon, as she'd later relate to Winters, who seemed eager to hear every detail.

"He works hard to satisfy a woman," Marilyn said.

This time, her opinion differed from her first ap-

Marilyn Monroe and James Dean were in total agreement about one thing: Both of them felt they were working for "slave wages."

praisal of him as a lover. "You know he's bi, of course. He said that when he's fucking a man, he can maintain an erection until climax. But with women, he sometimes grows limp. He has to disconnect and masturbate himself hard again before entering again. I understand this, and was most sympathetic. Later, I asked him what he thought about when he jerked off. He told me, 'Sal Mineo, Natalie Wood, Pier Angeli, Nick Adams, and Eartha Kitt.'"

"That's not very flattering with the Love Goddess of the World lying underneath him," Winters said.

"I didn't get offended," Marilyn said, "considering all the men I've dreamed about while getting plugged by some slob. I even fantasize about Rudolf Valentino."

"He was another fag, too," Winters responded.

Marilyn revealed that once again, Jimmy and she had discussed "getting hitched." He told her, "Let's admit the truth: both of us need babysitters. Maybe if we got married, we could become each other's babysitters."

"It wouldn't work," she said. "We're both too destructive. Without meaning to, we'd end up destroying each other."

"Maybe you're right," he said. "In that case, let's just be fuck buddies."

As Marilyn told Winters, "Jimmy knows that I'm completely accepting of his personality. He even suggested that during our makeout sessions, he'd like to bring in a male friend. He said that 'While I'm fucking you, he could plug me. It'll make it more exciting for both of us.'"

"That sounds like fun," she told him. "I suspect that one of those guys you'd like to bring in is Marlon Brando?"

"Well, he's someone who knows how to have a good time."

She told Winters that Jimmy was almost as uninhibited as she was. "He has no false modesty. When he has to piss, he goes, regardless of where he's at. Half the time we walk around nude with each other. Once, he even helped me peroxide my pussy hairs."

"As two living sex symbols, Jimmy and I even discussed our body parts with each other," she told Winters. "He said he wished his penis was two inches longer and just a bit thicker."

"I guess all men wish that," she'd said to him. "As for me, I'm thinking of surgery to tighten my vagina and to enlarge my breasts. I'm planning to talk to two doctors in Los Angeles who specialize in such surgeries. I want a vagina as tight as an asshole. Men like to fuck assholes because of the tight fit, especially those who aren't well endowed. Peter Lawford told me that. I also want a forty inch bust like Kathryn Grayson over at MGM."

"I find it's more satisfying for me to fuck famous men that unknown ones," she said. "Because if they're nobodies, I find they can't handle the world's most seductive woman. Perhaps I intimidate them...But anyway, my fame makes their little weenies recede into their bodies. It's awful. I'm the greatest castrator in the Western World."

Jimmy told her that "If I become a big deal, Strasberg will probably try to exploit me the way he does Brando. Brando told me that he was trained by Stella Adler, and he was furious when Strasberg started taking credit for 'discovering' him. I'm sure that if you get more deeply involved in the Actors Studio, Strasberg will try to capitalize off your fame, too."

"I can just see the Actors Studio's entrance hall," she said. "There will probably be large blow-ups of me, flanked by you boys on both sides of me."

Jimmy was onto something that Barbara Leaming described in her biography of Marilyn: "Strasberg planned to take credit for his *protégée's* achievements. He wanted to be something more than Marilyn's instructor. When she was ready—and there was no telling when that might occur—he hoped to direct her as well. In short, he saw Marilyn as a vehicle to the success that had long and stubbornly eluded him. Marilyn would make it possible for Strasberg to direct the great productions of his dreams."

Strasberg wanted Marilyn—by now a well-established movie star—to perform before an audience of her peers at the Actors Studio. Her friend, Maureen Stapleton, had suggested a scene from Noël Coward's *Fallen Angels.* But Marilyn didn't like Coward as a writer, preferring instead a scene from Eugene O'Neill's *Anna Christie.* Greta Garbo had already immortalized that play's female lead onscreen in the movie adaptation of 1930.

"We ended up doing a scene from *Anna Christie,"* Stapleton said. "That wispy voice of hers seemed to carry all right, for all her worry about it. Afterward, we went out to a bar on Tenth Avenue, and celebrated having cheated death one more time."

To Winters, Marilyn claimed that Jimmy "was a lot of fun, and sometimes we played games designed to reveal our darkest secrets. In one game, we both had to name four very unlikely people we'd slept with. He named Barbara Hutton, Howard Hughes, Tallulah Bankhead, and J. Edgar Hoover."

"And who did you name, my dear?" Winters asked.

"You can guess one of them: Charlie Chaplin. But did you also know about Fidel Castro, Jimmy Hoffa, and Albert Einstein?"

"Oh, Marilyn, I never know when you're telling the truth or fantasizing," Winters said. "But knowing you as well as I do, I have to leave open the possibility that you're telling the truth. I know Charlie fucked you, because I was also fucking his son, Sydney. But the other three? It's hard for me to believe."

***

One day at the Actors Studio, Winters told Jimmy, "Marilyn told me you were a better lover than Brando. A more considerate one. I must say, I agree with her. She claims she likes a man who is kind and takes into account a woman's needs. She prefers that to brute sex."

"I don't like to be compared to Brando, both as an actor and certainly not as a lover," Jimmy snapped at her.

"Your cocks are different, but sometimes, you *do* look like him," Winters said.

Jimmy learned that Brando's own involvement with Marilyn was "stop and go," heating up and then cooling off, but never completely disappearing.

Despite what he revealed to a handful of close friends, Brando had little to say to interviewers about Marilyn and even less to reveal about Jimmy. In one interview, however, he admitted: "Marilyn was a sensitive, misunderstood person," he said, "and much more perceptive than was generally assumed. She had been beaten down, but had a strong intelligence—a keen intuition for the feelings of others, the most refined type of intelligence."

Marilyn herself made few public comments about Brando, but told Jimmy that she found him "very sweet and tender, not at all Stanley Kowalski, although he can on occasion be a brute."

To both Brando and Marilyn, Jimmy voiced his fear of getting permanently stuck with a youth image. "Something like that is dangerous for an actor. Youth, after all, is a passing thing. If you get stereotyped, there's nowhere to go but down. Take Shirley Temple, for example. The public didn't want to see her in grown-up roles. I don't want to be thirty-five, wearing extra-heavy makeup and still playing a troubled youth."

"Marilyn Is Too Old to Play a Baby Doll."

—*Elia Kazan*

After he'd directed Jimmy in *East of Eden*, Elia Kazan by chance encountered him one afternoon in Hollywood, and invited him for a drink. As they talked, he provocatively said, "I hear you've been chasing after my *puta.*"

"Exactly who is your *puta?*" Jimmy asked.

"Marilyn, on that rare occasion when she isn't screwing such august figures as Senator John Kennedy—or Frank Sinatra, Natasha Lytess [*her drama coach*], Brando, Sammy Davis, Jr., or George Jessel. Do you have all day? I can keep going till the last dog dies."

"With Marilyn and me, It's just a casual thing," Jimmy said.

"Who's a better fuck? Kazan asked, continuing his provocation. "Brando, Newman, or Marilyn?"

"Each has his or her own specialty," Jimmy said.

"You know, Joe Schenck, that old potentate at 20th Century Fox, was also her lover," Kazan said. "I can figure out the kind of love-making that went on between Marilyn and Joe. He told me he can't cut the mustard any more, but I guess his tongue can still devour a taste treat. He did give her some good advice, telling her, 'Don't be a scalp on some man's belt. Don't be a cuspidor. Don't be a damn garbage dump.'"

"I think she's both a baby and a woman," Jimmy said. "I don't know whether to bounce her on my knee or make love to her. Both of us aren't well educated, but she grabs bits and pieces of knowledge, yet has no real idea how to fit these tidbits of information into anything coherent. She's also an actress both on and off camera. When I do something that displeases her, she almost, but not quite, sheds a tear. She also makes her lips tremble. Then, after she's pulled that stunt, you give in to her."

"She does crazy little things," he continued. "One night at her place, a huge bouquet of flowers arrived from some admirer. She didn't have a vase for them, so she rested them in the water in her toilet bowl. When I had to take a wicked piss, I really watered them. The smell of urine and roses...absolutely intoxicating."

"For me, Marilyn is too obsessed with her body," Kazan said. "Johnny Hyde, a short little midget of a guy, was one of her first lovers. He's dead now, but one night, he told her she has a nigger's ass. That devastated her, and she's spent half of her life since then staring at her naked buttocks in the mirror."

"That's strange," Jimmy said. "She told me one night that she has black blood flowing through her veins. Actually, that turned me on. I'm not prejudiced."

"Don't you believe that," Kazan said. "She's no more octoroon than I am. She invents stuff about herself, especially her biography. She's of Norwegian descent, and people in that country are whiter than the Pillsbury dough boy."

"I was surprised she has so little money," Jimmy said. "Fox pays her starvation wages."

"I thought Hyde would leave her something in his will," Kazan said. "His estate came to $650,000. She got not a penny. She told me he left her six bath towels and sheets, but only three pillowcases. That's her reward for being his love goddess."

"About this love goddess shit," Jimmy said. "Marilyn and I are not ideally suited in bed. She has difficulty 'coming' with me. I don't have that problem with a lot of other guys and dolls."

"Don't worry about it," Kazan said. "Don't feel less a man. She has that trouble with nearly all of her lovers. She says she works hard to climax, but most of the time, her plumbing doesn't cooperate. I don't give a fuck. I'm more interested in getting my rocks off. I did find a way to work her up to a climax. I spank that ass of hers real hard. Somehow that unclogs her plumbing."

Then Kazan slammed down his drink. "Hell, let's stop talking this man-to-man crap. All I can say is that Marilyn needs a strong hand, so to speak. And both of you guys need a strong director."

"As for body parts, she has a complaint against me," Kazan said. "Ever since Joe DiMaggio, she's preferred uncut meat, which rule out all Jewish lovers and a lot of other men, too. Yes, Arthur Miller!"

[As regards Marilyn's opinion of Kazan, she once told Jimmy, "Gadge told me that I was great fun, but that I wasn't cut out to be anybody's wife. He had a wife and children back in New York, but he was seen out in public with me in Hollywood. We could always claim, if asked, that we were discussing a future film project. He told me that he had a European concept of fidelity within a marriage. In Europe, he said that most men were expected to have a mistress on the side, providing that they take good care of their wife and kids at home.]

Ordering another round of drinks, Kazan asked, "Do you think one day you'll become one of Marilyn's husbands?" Kazan asked.

Jimmy was very emphatic. "Never! We've talked about it. But it will never happen. Deep down, both of us know we are petulant children, even though at times we can act grown-up. We're desperate souls looking for that home we never found—just a pair of tumbling tumbleweeds."

"I don't know about Marilyn as a wife," Jimmy continued, "but I do know that she has this uncanny ability to bring out the finest qualities in a man. She's convinced me that by the time I reach my thirties, I'll be a great movie actor. She says I might be small in stature, but big in talent. 'You're a little guy,' she told me, 'but a big man under your skin.'"

"I haven't seen Marilyn lately," Kazan said. "What's cooking?"

"I suspect you'll be hearing from her any day now," Jimmy said. "She's heard that you're going to direct Tennessee's *Baby Doll*. She wants to be the doll."

He frowned. "She's too old. Baby Doll can be no more than nineteen, even younger. Besides, although I love her dearly, I don't think I could survive directing Marilyn in a film. I hear that Lee Strasberg arranges for his wife Paula to be a sort of co-director behind the scenes, for which she gets $2,500 a week. After every take, this cunt signals to Marilyn that it was okay—or else she has to reshoot it. I'd stand for that crap for about an hour."

"Another thing," Kazan said. "Marilyn has a time bomb inside her waiting to go off. Ignite her and she'll explode. I'd heard the horror stories. Fucking her is one thing, directing her is quite another. She wants approval more than anything, but she rarely gets it, except from her fans. She needs constant reassurance of her own worth. Yet she respects men who hold her in contempt because their estimate of her is similar to her own self-loathing."

**

During the course of Charles Feldman's affair with Marilyn Monroe, at a party the producer had hosted at his home, he had introduced her to Tennessee Williams. Feldman had played a key role in the production of *The Glass Menagerie.*

Ever on the lookout for her next gig, Marilyn had asked Tennessee, "Do you write plays with characters that I could play? You know, the dumb blonde?"

"I'm afraid not," he answered. "I was once hired by MGM to write what I called a 'celluloid brassiere' for Lana Turner, but I failed miserably. I fear I'd do the same for you. As regards the anguish I suffered trying to create a role for Miss Turner, I felt like an obstetrician delivering a mastodon from a beaver."

"With me it would be different," she cooed. "I once told Frank Sinatra that one day I'd like to star as Blanche DuBois in a revival of *A Streetcar Named Desire.* He mocked me."

"Oh, my dear, Miss DuBois was over the hill, and you look like you've merely begun to climb that hill."

"You just wait and see, Mr. Tennessee," she said. "One day, I'll be a very dramatic actress."

"May your dreams never die," he answered, as Feldman interrupted their chat.

"Jane Wyman is here, and she's asking for you," Feldman told Tennessee.

[Jane Wyman, the former Mrs. Ronald Reagan, was awarded a starring role in the film version of Tennessee's The Glass Menagerie *(1950).]*

**

Months later, Marilyn heard of a role in a Tennessee Williams play that she felt was tailor made for her. It was that of the title character in *Baby Doll,* the story of a child bride, bartered and sold by her corrupt father to a lecherous suitor, who spent her days curled up half-dressed in a crib, sucking her thumb, a Lolita-like virgin.

Denied sexual access to her, based on the terms of her contract, her frustrated new husband spies on her through a peephole drilled through the wall.

"If there's one thing I know how to do, it's suck," Marilyn told Feldman.

There was another strong role available: That of a Sicilian-American owner of a cotton gin that is taking business away from her husband's rival gin mill.

Marilyn told Feldman that in her opinion, that role should be offered first to Brando, then to James Dean.

Lobbying for the role, Marilyn called Kazan and set up a rendezvous. Afterwards, describing it to Winters, she said, "Our roll in the hay went okay, but I didn't do as well during the post-coital huddle. He didn't think I'd be suitable as Baby Doll."

What Kazan had told her was, "Do you really believe that the public will accept you as a virginal child-bride?"

"I'm an actress. Watch me go."

"Oh, please! No one will ever believe that Marilyn Monroe was a virgin...ever."

Furious at that remark, she had stormed out the door.

On the chance that Brando might be assigned the role of the Sicilian, she tried to enroll him in a scheme whereby he'd endorse her for the role of Baby Doll. And when that didn't work, she began to maneuver toward the source of the screenplay himself, Tennessee Williams, hoping that he might recognize her potential.

"After all," she told Winters. "We're not talking about me playing Blanche DuBois. We're talking about a sexy little baby doll. The whole world knows I'm America's baby doll."

Winters had reminded her that Tennessee "has the hots for Jimmy Dean," so Marilyn decided to include him in her meeting with the playwright. Fortunately, Jimmy was in New York at the time and available, especially when she told him that he might be considered for the choice role of Silva Baccaro, the competing Sicilian who tries to steal the sex kitten from her possessive husband.

In her scheme, Marilyn deliberately misled Jimmy by telling him that Brando wanted the role, but that the word was that Tennessee thought that "the two of us would make a better screen team."

Before their arrival at Tennessee's apartment, she described to Jimmy a sexy scene, perhaps as part of their audition process, they could play out under a blanket together. "It gets cold in Mississippi in winter. We're sitting on the front porch in a double wooden swing with a blanket over us. There's a lot of movement going on under the blanket. Our faces reveal all from the initial tongue-sucking kiss to the final climax reflected in the total ecstasy in our faces."

"I could go for that," he said. "We could make it one of the sexiest scenes ever put into a feature film, and we can do that without ever showing our asses."

She told him that Feldman had seen what the chief script reader at Warners had already said in his report. "*Baby Doll* has the potential of becoming the dirtiest feature film in the history of Warner Brothers. It is imbued with priapean detail that would have embarrassed Boccaccio."

"I don't know what 'priapean' means," he said.

"I didn't either, but I looked it up in the dictionary. Priapus was the Greek god of procreation, the personification of the erect penis."

"This film is sounding more and more like it's got the name of James Dean written all over it."

Since Kazan had objected, insisting that she was appropriate for the role, Tennessee remained her last hope. Jimmy later told Stanley Haggart, a friend of Tennessee, that he didn't know at the time that Marilyn had manipulated him. "I'm not blaming her," he said. "My whole life has been spent manipulating people."

"After our first drink at Tennessee's apartment, I could tell that Marilyn was not his conception of his baby doll. However, he did assure us that we would one day become known as the 'dynamic duo' of the screen."

Tennessee described to them his original concept for *Baby Doll:* "I saw her as an overweight bundle of horror, with fat arms, bulging calves, and thick ankles. But in my rewrite, she's beautiful and sexy, very blonde. It's not a part for Grace Kelly—in terms of breeding, Baby Doll is about as genteel as Paddy's Pig. She is touching but comic, a grotesquely witless creation, about as deep as a kitty-cat's pee."

Before the end of their interview, Tennessee had promised he'd use whatever influence he had to try to get the roles for them. Nonetheless, he felt that each of them might find it more rewarding to pursue the parts of Cherie and Bo in William Inge's upcoming film adaptation of *Bus Stop,* whose roles in the Broadway play had gone to Kim Stanley and Albert Salmi.

"I studied Tennessee carefully," Jimmy told Haggart. "Sometimes, when he had been giving me a blow-job, and if I had gotten overly excited, I had run my fingers through his hair. It was like feeling a nest of small, wet serpents. As he bid Marilyn goodbye, having invited me for a sleepover, he had that fat cat smile of deception, you know the one when the cat tells the mouse he's not going to be eaten. Marilyn believed his promise. I did not. He might be planning to recommend me for the role, but I think he had already agreed with Kazan that Marilyn was too old and not virginal enough for the part of Baby Doll."

***

Weeks later, Kazan still had not cast all of the actors he needed for *Baby Doll,* opting to delay his final choice until after he'd seen the early rushes of Jimmy's last film, *Giant.* To his surprise, he became fascinated by the performance of Carroll Baker, whom he knew, but only casually, from their time together at the Actors Studio.

He envisioned her as the perfect choice for the character of Baby Doll. Five years younger than Marilyn, she was twenty-four at the time.

In New York, Kazan arranged for an audition that included Baker alongside Karl Malden. He had already cast him as Baby Doll's lecherous and ferociously jealous husband.

Lee Strasberg, it is believed, tipped Marilyn off about what was about to happen.

She didn't want to make an appearance at the Studio alone, so she called Jimmy. She had already learned that the role he'd wanted, that of the Sicilian cotton gin owner, would probably be going to Eli Wallach.

A few moments before the beginning of her tryout, Baker learned that Marilyn had entered the studio and that she'd be watching from the audience. "I wish my breasts were as big as hers," Baker lamented.

Jimmy preferred to take a seat out front, and not accompany Marilyn onto the stage, where she greeted the other cast members, including Malden.

Marilyn's arrival was deeply unnerving: Baker's husband, Jack Garfein, had loudly predicted that if his wife did not succeed in the tryout, the role of Baby Doll would, based on box office clout and studio politics, almost certainly go to Marilyn as a last resort.

Baker remembered the Hollywood blonde goddess arriving, clad in a patterned scarf, a pink Angora sweater, and oversized sunglasses. "Her thin cotton pants might have been grafted onto her flesh. All eyes were on her. She pursed her lips and said. 'Hello Jack.' I was so jealous of her I could have killed her. She made the word 'Jack' sound positively obscene."

Baker later described Marilyn's mannerisms: "She was like a perpetual motion gel. If her hips weren't gyrating, she was winching

Karl Malden, pursuing carnal knowledge of "Baby Doll," Carroll Baker

with her shoulders, or else making that sucking fish-pucker mouth. Everything about her said, 'I'm yours.' I thought I smelled the fruity aroma of sex."

After having greeted all the key figures on the stage, Marilyn joined Jimmy in the third row of the audience to watch Baker emote with Malden. She sat motionless throughout their sketch, her face betraying no emotion. Jimmy kept glancing at her for a reaction, but got none.

At the end of the sketch, Tennessee, from a seat in the rear, jumped to his feet and came running toward the stage, bypassing Jimmy and Marilyn, as if they weren't there. "Baby," he gushed, rushing up to Baker. "You *are* my Baby Doll!"

Marilyn grabbed and then gripped Jimmy's hand He noticed she was on the verge of tears. "Let's get the fuck out of here," she hissed.

Outside on the street, a wind was blowing, and drops of rain were starting to fall. Marilyn got a cinder in her eye and reached into her purse for a handkerchief to help remove it.

After the cinder came out, Jimmy kissed her gently on the lips and took her arm. "Let's go. It's you and me, kid, against the wind."

***

Barbara Leaming, a respected Marilyn biographer, wrote: "Had she been directed by Kazan at that stage in her career, she probably would not have become as dependent on Strasberg. What need would there have been for him if it had been Kazan who enabled her to do her first important dramatic role? What need would there have been for Paula Strasberg, her acting coach? Had Marilyn done well in a film written by Tennessee Williams, quite possibly she would have been treated differently by the public, and even by the industry. And who could say what would have happened to Marilyn's relationship with Arthur Miller had she gone to Mississippi in November of 1955 with Kazan?"

***

Marilyn detested the scripts being offered to her, dismissing many of them as "another dumb blonde role."

One night over pillow talk, Frank Sinatra asked her if she'd co-star with him in a script about show business entitled *Pink Tights*. From the title, she gathered what kind of role it would be. After reading the script, she called Sinatra: "I want to escape the image of just a sex queen, and I'd like a more substantial role. I'm not going to do the picture."

"Listen, doll, you may think you're the only blonde in Hollywood, but they're a dime a dozen out here." Then he slammed down the phone on her.

Marilyn had attended a performance of Kim Stanley in the Broadway version of William Inge's *Bus Stop,* and was intrigued by the role of Cherie. For the dumb cowboy role of Bo, she thought first of Marlon Brando, although she'd heard that Elvis Presley also wanted the part. Again, she called Shelley Winters: "Isn't Marlon from Nebraska?"

"He sure is, babe," Winters answered.

"I hear Nebraska, or one of those states—maybe Montana—has a lot of cowboys," she said. "I bet Marlon would jump at the chance to be Bo opposite my Cherie."

"Any bet on our unpredictable Marlon is a risk," Winters said. "But why not give him a ring?"

Consequently, Marilyn reached him by phone. After some inaugural pleasantries, she made her pitch, beginning with "I'm getting some 4,000 fan letters a week, and many of them suggest that you and I make a movie together."

"I'm getting some 6,000 fan letters a week, and I don't recall any of them suggesting that. What makes you think our chemistry would work on screen?"

"It might not in just any film," she said, "but Bill Inge's *Bus Stop* would be ideal for the two of us."

"Are you kidding?" he asked. "I've appeared in Shakespeare on the screen. Now you're asking me to play a dumb cowboy chasing after a dumb blonde stripper?"

"It's a great part," she said. "You'd wipe up the screen. I can see an Oscar in your performance, and that's for sure."

"Okay, sugar," he said. "Come over tonight and we'll talk about it. At least I'll get a good fuck out of it."

"Oh, Marlon, how you talk."

Over dinner that night, Brando told her he was getting at least one film offer a day. "That shitbag, Louis B. Mayer, is gone at MGM, and Dore Schary is far more appreciative of me. He just told his brass to let me play Little Eva in *Uncle Tom's Cabin* if I want to. I think I'm going to settle for playing a Jap in *Teahouse of the August Moon.* That cowboy role in *Bus Stop* wouldn't mean anything for me."

"I convinced Marilyn that her pitch was hopeless," Brando later told his best friend, Carlo Fiore, when he reported on the incident. "But we made our own chemistry together in bed."

Brando bragged to Fiore that "I could take Marilyn from Arthur Miller in a minute if I wanted to. But my trouble is, I can't love anyone. I just can't. I know I should, but I don't trust a woman enough to fall in love with her...or a man, either, for that matter."

He noted that while Marilyn was going around professing "all this love for

Miller, she's screwing both Jimmy Dean and me, plus god only knows how many others. She's the Queen of the One-Night Stand."

The following night over spaghetti in a West Village tavern, Brando seemed jealous of Marilyn 's involvement with Jimmy. He spent much of the evening attacking him "for copying everything I do—the motorcycles, the jeans, the V-neck pullovers. As for those roles in *East of Eden* and *Rebel Without a Cause,* you know I was offered each of those parts before Jimmy got to fuck them up."

"I'm not so hard on him," Marilyn chimed in. "All of us begin by imitating someone. I used to go to any Lana Turner movie at noon and stay in the movie house until the midnight show. It's just a phase we go through."

"Not me," Brando said. "I'm an original."

"You're an original who's changing every actor's style in America—except for Clifton Webb's," she said. "Miss Priss."

"Dean and I have only one thing in common—and not just our Midwestern origins. Both of us had fathers who claimed that all actors are 'faggots and fairyboys.'"

"Well, aren't they?" Then she giggled provocatively.

"I'm not as hard on Dean as I pretend to be," Brando said. "Actually, he needs to be handled with loving care."

"It's getting late," she said. "Why don't we go back to your apartment, and let you do some loving care on *me?*."

"It's a deal," he said.

Jimmy Misses His Bus Stop

THE HORNY COWBOY VS. THE WASHED-UP STRIPPER

At this point in her career, Marilyn had virtually abandoned her dream of ever making a movie with Brando. He had been disdainful, even contemptuous, of the idea of co-starring with her in *Bus Stop,* a film that was eventually released in 1956.

However, in a call she placed to Inge, he told her he'd heard from Joshua Logan, the upcoming director of its film version, that "Brando must have changed his mind! He told Logan that he'd love to play Bo, and that it would be an unusual departure for him as an actor. Logan seems almost hysterically delighted to direct you and Brando."

"Marlon is such a bullshitter," Marilyn told Inge. "There's no way he's going to play Bo to my Cherie. If you call him back, you'll find he's not going to do the picture."

Having slept with him on many an occasion, Marilyn had come to realize that Brando was a man of many moods. Indeed, within a few days, Brando formally rejected the role of Bo.

For Marilyn, that meant that her second choice, James Dean, had suddenly morphed into her prime target. She called him and asked him over to where she was staying. She'd bought two copies of Inge's play, with the intention of setting up a private rehearsal.

She was so pleased at their reading that she told him, "You and I would be great together—you as a redneck clodhopper, far better than Brando could manage, even though he was born in Nebraska."

The next day, with Jimmy, Marilyn visited Inge at his apartment in an attempt to win his endorsement. Inge warned them that although he personally thought they'd be an ideal team, he had no say on who starred in the movie roles. He went on to admit that he had already discussed their candidacy for the roles with Tennessee, and that he had said they'd be wonderful together.

Inge told them that *Bus Stop* had originated as a one-act play entitled *People in the Wind,* and that he had rewritten and expanded it.

"I'll be frank," Marilyn told him. "When I first heard of it, I thought Cherie was going to be just another dumb blonde role. But I think she's a wonderful character. I see her as a girl who has never known a day of happiness in her whole life. She's been kicked around by men until this white knight arrives on a bus in the form of a rude, immature cowboy who's really dumb. But his love is genuine. And that's what wins Cherie's heart in the end."

"I think I'd be hot as Bo," Jimmy said. "An escape from 'troubled youth' associations."

After Marilyn and Jimmy's interactions with Inge, she formed a more empathetic and lasting relationship with the playwright than Jimmy did.

Ralph F. Voss, Inge's biographer,

Missing the **Bus (Stop)**

Don Murray (in the "dumb cowboy role" that was almost given to Jimmy) embraces MM playing Cherie, the washed-up, out-of-tempo-with-the-music stripper in the film version of *Bus Stop.*

493

wrote: "Inge and Monroe enjoyed a rapport that was probably based upon their mutual intelligence and his ability to sense the frustrations of a bright and spectacularly beautiful woman like Monroe and upon her realization that his interest and concern were genuine and not motivated by sexual desire. In years to come, their names were occasionally linked in the media as if they were romantically involved, but their relationship was no more than a friendship."

As for Jimmy, when he'd first contemplated the role of Bo, he had just completed the filming of *Giant,* and didn't want to rush into the portrayal of another western character. "I'm trying to escape the troubled youth image, but I don't want to be stuck in cowboy roles, either."

Eventually, however, he was won over by the character of Bo. "I think I could have had a lot of fun with him. And he's not at all like my Jett Rink character in *Giant.*"

Marilyn agreed. And whereas she lived to deliver a memorable performance in *Bus Stop,* Jimmy did not. The role of Bo eventually went to Don Murray.

***

During the filming of *Rebel Without a Cause* (1955), Jimmy learned that its director, Nicholas Ray, had been having an affair with Marilyn since the end of 1952. Ray had been telling her that he'd always wanted to direct her in a movie, and that he and his associates were making plans for its script, never written. Ray had inaugurated sexual advances toward her after meeting her on the set of *Gentlemen Prefer Blondes.*

Many of their sexual trysts transpired within Ray's suite at the Château Marmont. "I was a little surprised to learn about Marilyn and Nick," Jimmy told Stanley Haggart, who was spending time in Los Angeles producing TV commercials. "It seems that Marilyn and I are fucking the same dude."

Jimmy learned about the Ray/Monroe liaison from *Confidential* magazine, which had published a lurid *exposé* of their affair, claiming that Marilyn had been caught "balling" Ray in the back seat of a limousine.

Ray threatened to sue. He complained about it to Leonard Rosenman, who was composing the music for *Rebel Without a Cause.*

"But this isn't bad publicity for you," Rosenman said. "Thirty million guys in America want to plow Marilyn like you're doing, and at least some of them want to do Jimmy, too."

"I'll sue the sons of bitches," Ray said again. Then he paused. "But now that you've said all that, perhaps not."

For a while, Haggart's friend, Gore Vidal, was living at the Château Marmont near the bungalow rented by Ray. "You cannot imagine Ray's carnal adventures," he told Haggart. "On any given night, he might be seducing Dean, Sal Mineo, Natalie Wood, Jayne Mansfield, Dennis Hopper, or even Judy Holliday when she's not muff diving."

One of the genuinely historic hotels of Hollywood

"As for me, I want to meet his son, Tony," Vidal said. "He must be something else. Ray caught him in bed fucking his wife, Gloria Grahame. The kid had just turned thirteen. What a guy!"

***

Early one morning, Jimmy was still in bed in Ray's bungalow. They'd spent the night together. Ray had left early for the studio, but Jimmy wasn't needed until the next day. There came a knock on the door. Hung over, in his underwear, he staggered over to answer the door.

He was surprised to find Marilyn standing there in a fur and an evening gown. She'd obviously come directly from a night of partying at clubs along the Sunset Strip. She carried a bottle of chilled champagne with her. "I planned to drop in on Nick, but you'll do," she said to Jimmy. "I'm in need of a good fuck."

She walked into the room as if it were her second home.

As he'd later relay to Haggart when he went for a swim at his home in Laurel Canyon, "Whenever I finished with that succulent mouth of hers, Marilyn could always put me to sleep with that soothing voice she has. It's such a seductive tool. More than that of any woman I've met. Sound engineers capture its erotic whispers. She makes a man feel he's got big balls."

"She's got her flaws," Jimmy said. "Like me, she's too short, and her stomach is slightly pudgy from too much champagne. She shares her problems with me, her secret desires. I do the same with her. Otherwise, I tell people to fuck off when they ask too many personal questions."

"We had sex in Nick's bed, and he came home early that afternoon and caught us together."

"Did he threaten to fire you from *Rebel?*" Haggart asked.

"Not at all," Jimmy answered. "He pulled off his clothes and joined us in bed."

"Elizabeth Taylor Is a Hairy Ape"

—Marilyn Monroe

During the making of *Giant,* Jimmy saw very little of Marilyn, although they talked on the phone, usually late at night. She had as many troubles as he did.

She was particularly interested in any behind-the-scenes gossip from the set of *Giant,* especially if it concerned Elizabeth Taylor.

"I think Marilyn resents my making a movie with her," Jimmy told George Stevens. "She's very jealous of Elizabeth."

One night, Marilyn said, "I guess I should ask the $100,000 questions. Which one of you, Elizabeth or yourself, got to fuck Rock Hudson first?"

He laughed. "With Rock and me, it's been there, done that, long before *Giant.* But to answer your question, let me put it this way: Rock and I were assigned to live in the same house in Marfa, Texas. I got him first. But it wasn't a match made in heaven. Elizabeth finally got him, too. Sometimes, Rock is forced into delivering what he calls a few duty fucks."

"They're both big stars, as you know," Marilyn said, "and I hear that after *Giant* you're going to be right up there with them. I've been famously quoted as saying, 'I've sucked a lot of cock to get where I am today.' I don't know if I ever said that, but it's true. I'm sure you've been on many a casting couch, but for both of us, we won't have to do that anymore."

"We'll be able to pick and choose who we fuck, and ain't that grand?," he said. "In New York, I used to let guys blow me in the subway toilets for a dollar or two so I could buy a milkshake for some energy."

"On Santa Monica Boulevard, I'd give it away for just a hearty breakfast, which would last me for at least a day and a half before starvation set in," she answered.

George Stevens, who had directed Elizabeth in *A Place in the Sun* (1951), told Jimmy that "Marilyn resents Elizabeth's fame, beauty, and prestige. Their feud began when Elizabeth found out that Marilyn was fucking Nicky Hilton, her first husband. Frankly, I don't know what Marilyn saw in this jerk, except he's got money and a big dick. He was drunk most of the time he was married to Elizabeth. He used to beat her."

In a phone call one night, Marilyn seemed to have grown angry with Jimmy, because she'd read in the press that he had become extremely friendly with Elizabeth during the filming of *Giant.*

"I'm not surprised she went after you," Marilyn said. "Let's face it: She's got a voracious sexual appetite and the morals of a truck driver. Or else an alleycat. Sexually, she's supposed to be every man's dream, but I hear that unless she shaves constantly, she's hairy. One of her former lovers told me she even has hair growing between her breasts. Instead of her being mother's little dividend, she's mother's hairy ape. Did you know that she was born with hair all over her face?"

"Throughout her life, she's had everything handed to her. You and I had nothing. We had to fight every step of the way and make compromises. People have always taken advantage of us. She was virtually handed a career and everything else."

"Two nights later, Marilyn called Jimmy again and launched another barrage of attacks on Elizabeth.

"Did you know her eyebrows had to be reshaped into what is now called the Taylor arch?" Marilyn said. "Louis B. Mayer thought her nose was too thick at the bottom and ordered her to take care of it. How do I know all this? I must confess, I've had very private dealings with the source of this information. The same doctor who operated on her worked on my own nose and also gave me a chin implant."

"Well, dear one, beauty is, after all, an illusion," he answered. "As for me, I was born perfect."

"Yeah, right, except you need a surgeon who knowns how to make you a foot and a half taller."

"I resent that!" he yelled at her.

During the last phone call that he'd ever receive from Elia Kazan, the director said, "I can't believe it. You and Marilyn Monroe. A little Indiana farm boy who's also bedding the great Elizabeth Taylor. She's a story for another day. As far as Marilyn is concerned, to me, she's just a simple, decent-hearted gal that Hollywood keeps fucking over. Legs apart copulation has always been her way of saying thank you to anyone who ever gave her a break. But what in hell, kid, is Monroe doing with you?"

"Both of these ladies think I'm hot shit," Jimmy answered. "So eat your heart out, Gadge, ol' boy!"

***

Because of Jimmy's tragic car crash in September of 1955, the cinematic pairing of Jimmy with Marilyn, regrettably, remained a figment of their imaginations and never became a reality.

Ironically, they became closely linked in death as contemporaneous screen icons. Bars in remote outposts, sometimes as far away as Nigeria, still display images of James Dean and Marilyn Monroe.

During her third week of counseling with the psychiatrist, Dr. Ralph Greenson, she confessed that she planned, one day, to commit suicide. "I want to go out like James Dean, while I'm still young and beautiful. I want everything at my funeral to be white, very Mae Westy. All white satin in my coffin. White flowers. I want to be buried in a white *négligée* that's virtually see-through. Of course, I'll have my makeup man and my hairdresser make me camera ready. I want to leave a lasting memory to those who view my body. I want them to say, 'Marilyn Monroe was more beautiful in death than she was in life. Too bad they couldn't say that about poor Jimmy. I hear his body was mangled beyond recognition.'"

As Dean's biographer, Donald Spoto, put it: "At the end of the century, it is not outrageous to say that Dean and Monroe—even to those who have a low estimation of them—remain the most royal of deified Americans, if only because of the brilliant marketing strategies of their celebrity."

Jimmy's death mask at Princeton University has been placed beside those of Beethoven, Thackeray, and Keats; and Marilyn's image during the second decade of the 21st Century is bigger now than it was when she died.

* * *

During one of the last conversations Stanley Haggart had with Gore Vidal, the subject of Jimmy and Marilyn came up.

During their talk, Vidal said, "You know I've had reservations about both Monroe and Dean, as well as Mr. Elvis Presley, each doomed to die before their time. However, I must say that if a record shop, a clothing store, a diner, or a bar, wants to cloak itself in the glamor of 1950s Hollywood, a picture of one of these creatures on the wall will add to the establishment's youthful allure. Dean, of course, will be in that damn red jacket. That jacket will be manufactured for tomorrow's youth at least until 2080 when the world will no longer care about that unholy trio of mixed-up psychos."

"I don't think so," Haggart responded. "Elvis, Marilyn, and Jimmy will survive until the next Ice Age."

Social historian, celebrity novelist, and trenchant wit, Gore Vidal

A French advertising poster for Levi's jeans ("An American Masterpiece"), linking them to James Dean and Marilyn Monroe.

Chapter Seventeen

TALES FROM THE F.B.I.

J. EDGAR HOOVER

& HIS LOVER, CLYDE TOLSON

Hot on Jimmy Dean's "Tail"

JIMMY GETS CAUGHT SHOPLIFTING AND "RED-HANDED,"
YET MANAGES TO AVOID BLACKLISTING AND THE RED CHANNELS LIST

Unless He Submits to Their Closeted Desires
"Clyde & Eddie" Threaten to Ruin His Career

Until James Dean became involved with Marlon Brando and director Elia Kazan in the 1950s, the name of J. Edgar Hoover was of no special interest to the young boy growing up in Indiana. He knew that Hoover was the director of the F.B.I., and he'd seen some movies about that agency, but that was about it. Unlike many young boys of his era, he never had any fantasies of becoming a G-man.

But once he started discussing Hoover with Brando and Kazan, he discovered each of them had personal reasons for loathing "the ugly little toad," as Brando referred to him.

Brando warned him that Hoover could destroy an actor's career and he cited John Garfield as a case in point. Garfield was one of the few screen actors that Jimmy had admired in the 1940s, especially after he'd seen him opposite Lana Turner in *The Postman Always Rings Twice* (1946).

Jimmy also admired Garfield's reputation off screen, and he'd heard many tales of the women he'd seduced, including Joan Crawford, Hedy Lamarr, and Shelley Winters. Jimmy bragged to Brando and Kazan, "Garfield had nothing on me. I've bedded them, too."

"What about Ida Lupino and Ann Sheridan?" Kazan asked.

"You got me there."

"Garfield has also been known to seduce a man on occasion, if he's drunk enough," Kazan said. "Take Truman Capote, for example, back when he was much younger and a bit pretty."

"Been there, done that, too." Jimmy admitted.

The gossip columnist, Sheilah Graham, had summed up Garfield's lovemaking technique. "He was a demon lover. He died young and in bed with a woman. How fitting. He made love like a sexy puppy, huffing and puffing in quick gasps. Before intercourse, he preferred women to go on an around-the-world trip of his body."

"I can go along with Garfield on that around-the-world thing," Jimmy said. "But not the sexy puppy image. But women I seduce compare me to another animal: *El Toro.*"

"In their own estimation, all men are bulls," Kazan said. "Women usually tell a different story."

According to Kazan, Garfield's wife, Roberta Seidman, whom he'd married in 1935, had been a communist, but Garfield never was. Nonetheless, he was ordered to testify before the House Un-American Activities Committee during the Red Scare of the 1950s. During his time being grilled, the actor voiced his support for the First Amendment, which opposed government investigations of people's political beliefs.

Blackballed as a communist sympathizer, he remained a subject of invasive scrutiny even after the conclusion of his testimonies. His services as an actor were no longer in demand.

Before the committee, Garfield had claimed that he didn't know any communists in the film industry. He later hoped to redeem himself in an article he wrote entitled "I was a Sucker for the Left Hook," claiming he'd been duped by communist ideologies. The title of the article, of course, was a reference to movies that had cast him as a prizewinning boxer.

In May of 1952, during the peak of the Red Scare, the rebellious young actor died of a heart attack at the age of thirty-nine.

Jimmy didn't want what had afflicted Garfield to happen to him. He wasn't really afraid that it would, since he was almost completely apolitical. He hardly knew the difference between a Republican and a Democrat, much less a communist. When asked what he thought of President Eisenhower, Jimmy said, "I don't know what he does in the White House, but as a soldier, he sure put a lot of firecrackers up the asses of those god damn Nazi shitheads."

At the time Jimmy was hearing these stories about Hollywood's tormented conflicts with the FBI director, he had no idea that he would ever tangle with Hoover himself.

When he did, his involvement would have absolutely nothing to do with politics, but with sex.

WANTED BY THE FBI: HOOVER'S FILES ON

Marlon Brando & James Dean

GROW THICKER, LONGER, AND MORE INCRIMINATING

Hoover, an avid television watcher, especially crime dramas, had begun the compilation of a file on Jimmy when he first started seeing him in teleplays. His favorite was *The Dark, Dark Hour*, in which Jimmy, cast as a hoodlum, breaks into the home of a doctor (played by Ronald Reagan) and threatens to assassinate him if he doesn't remove a bullet from the body of his comrade, who had been shot during an earlier robbery.

According to reports, Hoover was intrigued by Jimmy.

Since 1946, based on political, not sexual reasons, he'd also amassed a growing and rather incriminating file on the communist/socialist leanings of Marlon Brando. Rumors about the Leftist sentiments of Brando had intensified when the actor had appeared on Broadway in the controversial appeal to radical Zionism written partially as propaganda by Ben Hecht, *A Flag is Born*.

Everyone connected to *A Flag is Born* was eventually evaluated by the F.B.I. as subversive to U.S. interests, not only its star, Paul Muni, but its director, Luther Adler, too.

Brando, self-styled as "the only *goy* in the cast," continued arousing the suspicions within the F.B.I, which, as demanded by Hoover, documented his civil rights clashes as well as his bisexual escapades.

At the close of the play, Brando traveled across the country raising money for Irgun, an anti-British group led by Menachem Begin *[later, Prime Minister of Israel (1977-1983)]* that advocated violence.

"I was a hot-headed terrorist back then," Brando said. "As I matured, I came to understand both sides, even the Arab point of view. I was a bit over the top, proclaiming in speeches that British troops blocking Jewish immigration to Palestine were committing greater atrocities than the Nazis. Blame it on my youth."

"I like Jews, and I fuck many of them for pleasure," Jimmy admitted. "About all I know of Arabs is that I played a homosexual Arab boy in *The Immoralist,* and I was a no good, blackmailing son of a bitch."

Even though Elia Kazan had directed Brando in his greatest hit at the time, *A Streetcar Named Desire,* the actor was very critical of his director.

Clyde Tolson *(left)* was J.Edgar's lover and personal assistant, and was called "the Gary Cooper of the F.B.I." Above, he is seen with Hoover, enjoying one of their favorite pastimes: Betting on the horses.

Clyde Tolson, J. Edgar Hoover, Guy Hottel, and an unidentified friend.

Like Brando, Kazan had been intensely investigated by the F.B.I. Its G-men turned up evidence that he "supported dangerous left-wing causes." He had been called before the House Un-American Activities Committee as a friendly witness, naming names. His collaboration and cooperation shocked Hollywood, soiled his reputation, and cost him the friendship of his liberal friends such as playwright Arthur Miller.

Brando at first didn't want anything more to do with Kazan after that, but the actor and the director obviously repaired their differences in time for Kazan to direct him in his Oscar-winning role in *On the Waterfront.*

[The F.B.I. investigation had determined that Kazan, from 1934 to 1936, had been a member of the Communist Party in New York. But later, according to the F.B.I. dossier, he had became disillusioned with the party, and turned against communism after the Hitler-Stalin pact. Consequently, his American communist friends turned against him.

As Kazan later told Miller, "I hate the communists and have for many years, and I don't feel right about giving up my career to defend them. That's why I'm naming names."]

Brando summed up Kazan's appearance before HUAC: "Gadge squealed like a ballsy pig on castration day."

***

What little is known about Jimmy's involvement with Hoover and his lover/assistant, Clyde Tolson, was gleaned from three sources, Guy Hotell, detective Fred Otash, and Stanley Haggart.

An F.B.I. agent himself, Hotell, for some twenty-five years, was the second-most-important man in Hoover's F.B.I., ranking just behind Tolson himself. A former football player at George Washington University, and known as "the stud" of the campus, Hotell often traveled with Tolson and Hoover on their many trips and vacations together, always remaining in the background.

F.B.I. agent Guy Hotell, Hoover's indiscreet henchman, "arranger," and pimp.

After a few months of working directly for "Clyde and Eddie" *[his nickname for J. Edgar]*, Hotell realized that one of his main duties was "arranging private hookups for these two guys who lived deep in the closet."

"'Pimp' is too nasty a word," Hotell said, "but Eddie and Clyde couldn't very well arrange sexual liaisons for themselves. They were too famous, especially Eddie. I spent a few nights with both of them when I was younger and had a full head of hair. But they later tired of me, and put me to work as an 'arranger.'"

They wanted me to accompany them on their vacations," Hotell claimed. "I tagged along, but unlike Clyde and Eddie, I was a lady killer with an oc-

Young Guy Hotell *(left)* with J. Edgar Hoover: "Just two guys on holiday together."

casional boy thrown in. When they were seducing some young man, I was most often banging some hot gal."

Eventually, Hoover got rid of Hotell when he became alcoholic and made a lot of indiscreet remarks around Washington.

After Hotell was booted, and, much later, when Hoover was conveniently dead, Hotell decided to write a best-selling tell-all about him. Through his prospective publisher, the writer James Kirkwood, Jr., was approached to ghost write the book for him. Kirkwood later won a Pulitzer Prize for his Broadway musical, *A Chorus Line.*

[A political investigation was an unusual detour for Kirkwood, who usually wrote light novels and plays, most often with a comic touch. An exception to this had been American Grotesque, *an account of the Clay Shaw/Jim Garrison affair in New Orleans. Garrison had vengefully charged Shaw, a respected business leader, with conspiracy in the assassination of President Kennedy, charges which later mushroomed into a horror story that unfairly ruined Shaw's life, bankrupted his businesses, and placed him at the mercy of the judicial system for decades.]*

American Grotesque was first published in 1968. Hotell had read it and been impressed by how it presented its information and premises. Consequently, Hotell and Kirkwood worked together on *The Gay Adventures of J. Edgar Hoover and Clyde Tolson.*

Regrettably, Kirkwood died of spinal cancer in 1989, and Hotell also died a few months later. The book was never published. However, author Darwin Porter had worked with Kirkwood, mostly on note tak-

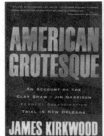

THE GAY ADVENTURES OF J. EDGAR HOOVER & CLYDE TOLSON

JAMES KIRKWOOD

Two inter-related books by James Kirkwood, only one of which (*American Grotesque*) was ever completed and published. Publication of the title depicted above on the right was delayed until 2012, when it reached the editors at Blood Moon Productions. After many amplifications from other sources, it emerged as the book displayed below.

Playwright and investigative journalist James Kirkwood, researching court records in Louisiana in the mid-60s.

J. EDGAR HOOVER & CLYDE TOLSON

INVESTIGATING THE SEXUAL SECRETS OF AMERICA'S MOST FAMOUS MEN AND WOMEN

BY DARWIN PORTER

504

ing and interviews, and he retained the material, which was later published by Blood Moon Productions as *J. Edgar Hoover & Clyde Tolson; Investigating the Sexual Secrets of America's Most Famous Men and Women.*

During extensive interviews, Hotell revealed that Hoover was fascinated "almost to the point of obsession" with the private lives of movie stars. Of special prominence were Marilyn Monroe, Elvis Presley, and James Dean.

"He even had three blow-ups of Dean hanging in his bathroom," Hotell asserted. He also told me that he had a porno clip that Dean had once made during his hungry days walking the streets of New York. I asked to see it, but he refused."

"He had seen most of Dean's teleplays, and Dean became his favorite TV star. He told me he thought Dean was not only cute, but sexy. He'd had him investigated, learning that he'd been a hustler. He suggested that I should arrange a session with Dean during their next trip to the West Coast."

"I don't want it presented that we're blackmailing him, but he needs to know that Clyde and I have stuff on him that is so damaging, it could ruin his movie star career before it even begins."

***

Fred Otash now enters the picture. Readers of Marilyn Monroe biographies are familiar with his name. He became Hollywood's most famous detective, especially in regards to aspects associated with her murder in the summer of 1962.

Otash had tangled with Hoover and Tolson long before anybody had ever heard of James Dean. One day at the Santa Anita Racetrack, he was caught doping a horse and was arrested. Hoover was at the track that day and had placed high bets on the mob's favorite horse. But the stricken horse, because of Otash's doping, didn't run.

Otash was discovered and hit with a felony conviction, which was later downgraded to a misdemeanor. He was given a suspended sentence, and the affair was later expunged from his record.

It was speculated that Otash got off lightly because he had incriminating evidence on Hoover. Lewis Rosenstiel, a multi-millionaire "philanthropist," who had links to mob bosses, handled the racetrack bets of Hoover and Tolson.

Susan Rosenstiel, Lew's estranged wife, called it "a sweetheart deal. Hoover liked to gamble. My husband would call up his boys and place the bet. If Hoover won, he collected the money. If he didn't, Lou covered his losses."

During the course of his friendship with Rosenstiel, Hoover discovered that he was a promiscuous homosexual who could "buy the best young men for sale" along the West Coast. He was also known for staging some of the best gay parties anywhere, flamboyant enough to rival those of Hoover's other friend, the Woolworth heir, Jimmy Donahue, a cousin of the heiress, Barbara Hutton.

Somewhere along the way, Otash learned of Hoover's link to Rosenstiel and the nefarious "back street dealing" between the two co-conspirators. It was said that Otash managed to evade charges in his future, including illegal wire-tapping, based on the incriminating information he had on the F.B.I. director.

Getting Busted: As a Shoplifter in a Food Market,

JIMMY GETS CAUGHT

Private detectives are supposed to keep silent about their revelations, except to their clients. But Otash often bragged of his inside knowledge.

Whenever he met a friend, he'd often begin his conversation by saying, "Did I tell you about the time...?" Then he'd relate a shocking incident from his vast repertoire. He once told columnist James Bacon one of his scandals. Of course, the journalist couldn't print it but privately gossiped about it.

One incident Otash related to Bacon allegedly occurred when he was a security guard at the Hollywood Ranch Market, which was experiencing a great deal of shoplifting. One afternoon, he caught James Dean stealing both a ham and a tinned caviar, "the expensive stuff, although he could afford to pay. It was my job to see that he was arrested. Charges were filed against him, but I learned later from someone in the police department that the case was mysteriously dropped. Someone important had intervened."

"Believe it or not, four months later I caught Dean stealing another ham at the market—no caviar this time," Otash claimed. "Instead of arresting him, I put the ham back on the rack and bought him some orange juice. I told him to cut out this shoplifting shit since he was making good money. But what I really wanted to know was who got him off on the last charge."

Private detective and movie fan, Fred Otash

"He looked at me with that smirky grin he had," Otash said. "'It was the most powerful man in America,'" he claimed. "'But I had to sing for my supper when I was driven in this big black limousine to La Jolla.'"

"As a detective, it didn't take me long to add two and two," Otash said. "I knew that Clyde Tolson and Hoover were staying in La Jolla at that time going to the race track. Suddenly, it made sense. Hoover could get anybody off from anything in those days, and Dean was his type. I'm also certain if you looked at that infamous book of Hoover's celebrity nudes, Dean posing with a big hard-on in that tree would be among his prized possessions. Some Dean biographers have written about the actor's claim to have been seduced by this 'bigwig in Washington.' It must have been Hoover. Eisenhower is definitely not a suspect."

***

Otash told Rosenstiel of Jimmy's shoplifting, and he no doubt relayed the information to Hoover. The F.B.I. director, ever ready to seize an opportunity, had Rosenstiel reach Jimmy to tell him that the F.B.I., in exchange for his cooperation, was willing to intervene to quash news of his shoplifting and potentially save his career from scandal and ruin.

Since Hoover already possessed scandalous material Jimmy, the news of his arrest for shoplifting "was another sword to hang over the kid's head," as Hoover told Rosenstiel. "Unless he's a fool, he'll cooperate. If he doesn't, he'll live to regret it."

Three days after his night with Hoover and Tolson, at La Jolla, Jimmy visited Stanley Haggart's home in Laurel Canyon, which had a private cottage and a swimming pool. Jimmy often liked to drop in to use the cottage and swim, nude, with a male companion.

Over drinks that afternoon, as the sun went down, Jimmy told Haggart of his rendezvous with Hoover and Tolson and how he had been driven in a limousine to La Jolla, where the two F.B.I. men were staying.

He revealed to Haggart what happened after he was introduced to Hoover and Tolson: "Within the hour, they made it clear that if I'd spend the weekend with them, and let them play with me, all the shoplifting charges would be dropped, but only if I promised to never shoplift again, and to pay like a normal everyday working slob after that. I agreed to everything, even though both of them were real turn-offs to me, especially that bulldog, Hoover."

"They sure got their money's worth out of me," Jimmy claimed. "I think before the end of that *loooooong* weekend, I must have shot off at least seven times. I didn't get my clothes back until Monday morning. They liked to see me lounging or swimming nude by the pool, and certainly in their bedroom."

"I was told that Hoover was a cross-dresser, but he didn't put on a gown that weekend. Thank god. And, as I said, I didn't wear anything at all. The worst part came when Hoover insisted I pose for some nudes. He told me that he already had a collection of nudes of me, plus a porno clip I'd made once when I was starving."

"Tolson told me, 'It's just our insurance that you'll keep your trap shut.'"

"I did my duty and was driven back to Hollywood," Jimmy said. "These guys kept their word. Any police charges against me were wiped clean. I understand that Hoover can even blackmail a president, much less a country boy like me."

Haggart shared the details of Jimmy's encounter with Hoover and Tolson with three other friends, one of whom was the gossipy Rogers Brackett, who spread the story around. "It was a hot topic of gossip for a while," Haggart said. "But many people were skeptical. Hoover and Jimmy Dean?—it was too incredible. But, given Hoover's track record, and his other involvements, it is entirely possible."

Jimmy's claim was given far greater credence when Scotty Bowers, a well-built, curly-haired blonde from southern Illinois, finally published his scandalous memoirs, some of which detailed time spent having sex with Hoover.

Issued by Grove Press in 2012, Bowers' biography was entitled *Full Service,* and it received the endorsement of Gore Vidal, who wrote that he had "known Scotty for the better part of a century and he doesn't lie."

The New York Times featured it in two different reviews.

In some respects, Bowers' testimonial about his sexual involvement with Hoover paralleled Jimmy's, except that Bowers was treated to a firsthand view of the F.B.I. director's cross-dressing too.

A slightly more detailed version of Bower's encounter with Hoover appeared in his original manuscript before it was slightly reduced in the published version.

"I Had Sex With J. Edgar Five Times that Weekend"

—Scotty Bowers

In 1945, at the end of World War II, Scotty Bowers moved to Los Angeles. Shortly thereafter, he opened Scott's Gas Station at the corner of Fairfax and Hollywood Boulevard. Within eight months, it had become the most popular gas station among gays in Hollywood.

Getting a lube job at Scotty's came to mean something else. He hired as many as a dozen young men to pump gas and to escort certain gentlemen callers into the back rooms. There, the car owners could perform fellatio on these handsome, strapping former servicemen, or else become passive recipients of sodomy. Scotty hired only "tops."

Among the many patrons of the gas station were director George Cukor and the very closeted Spencer Tracy. Robert Taylor often stopped by to get "filled up," and Tyrone Power took some of the young men home with him to "perform the down and dirties," in the words of one gas jockey hustler.

"Most of Scotty's men were gorgeous," or so claimed Vivien Leigh, who visited the gas station accompanied by her friend Cukor. Most of Scotty's men were bisexuals and could accommodate either gender. Sometimes one of the gas jockeys was hired for private sessions at the homes of a married couple. Stars seeking lesbian encounters could also find Scotty's services fulfilling.

In his investigation, author Paul Young quotes a source who claimed that "Scotty was smarter than some of his competitors. He refused to accept money from his boys or his clients. He'd only accept gifts: gold watches, silver trinkets, stocks, bonds, you name it. Some of his regular clients, who greatly appreciated his services, even went so far as to give him pieces of property."

The subject of many newspaper and magazine articles, Scotty, in his late 80s as of this writing, is a Hollywood legend. When not running his gas station, he moonlighted as a bartender at star-studded Hollywood parties where he met many of his admirers.

Over the years, various stars had need for his services including Katharine Hepburn ("no women with skin blemishes"), Cary Grant, Rock Hudson, Tennessee Williams, even the Duke and Duchess of Windsor. (She was a closeted lesbian, the former king a closeted homosexual.)

Scotty Bowers, a former Hollywood hustler and pimp, managed to reconfigure himself, late in his life, into a bestselling *raconteur.*

Late in life, Scotty wrote his long-overdue memoirs, called *Full Service*, a reference, of course, to the dual "services" provided by his filling station. The subtitle to his book is "Secrets, Sex, and High Society in Hollywood's Golden Age."

Arguably, the most shocking revelation in *Full Service* is the weekend Scotty spent in the company of J. Edgar Hoover. He recalled meeting a rich young doctor from La Jolla at a lavish party off Doheney Drive in Beverly Hills. In the book, the physician is referred to only as "Ted" (with the last name withheld).

Scotty bonded with this doctor, who invited him to take care of food and beverage arrangements at a party at his home in La Jolla two weeks hence.

Right on schedule, Scotty arrived in just fourteen days at an elegant, modern beachfront home where Ted, clad in a bathing suit, welcomed him. Scotty found his kitchen fully stocked with everything from caviar to lobster, so he soon realized that he was the choice hunk of meat on the menu that weekend.

After Scotty had showered and "slipped into something more comfortable," he noticed from his bedroom window a large black sedan pulling into the driveway, its windows dark tinted. A young chauffeur, around twenty-eight years old, emerged from behind the wheel to open the door for his passenger. Out emerged a stocky man in his mid-60s with thinning black hair. He wore dark glasses.

A few minutes later Scotty was introduced to the distinguished guest as "John." At the time, the face of J. Edgar Hoover was one of the most recognizable in the world. The FBI director and the handsome young driver disappeared for two hours behind the closed door of an upstairs bedroom, which contained a king-sized bed.

When J. Edgar and the driver, who was called "Rick," emerged from upstairs, Scotty noticed that he wore a shoulder holster with a revolver strapped to his well-muscled body. Apparently "Rick" was J. Edgar's bodyguard, perhaps a young agent at the FBI.

In his memoirs, Scotty wrote, "So the rumors were true." According to his account, sex began after an elegant dinner, Ted pairing off with Scotty, and J. Edgar disappearing inside the Blue Room upstairs with the young bodyguard.

"The evening didn't end there," Scotty said. "We swapped around a bit— no group sex, no gangbanging, no foursomes, no orgies. Everyone was one-on-one, with two couples going their separate ways" and having their separate sexual encounters.

He claimed that he had sex with J. Edgar five times that weekend and just as often with Ted. Both Ted and J. Edgar tried out Rick, but Scotty was not asked to sample his charms. In bed, Scotty claimed, J. Edgar was "a very pleasant and gentle man," unlike his public image, but he gave no more tantalizing details. Did they kiss? Was J. Edgar a top or bottom? How was the penis? Cut or uncut? Large? Average? Small?

During the weekend, Ted opened the locked door to a spare bedroom filled with a large wardrobe of women's clothing. Scotty claimed he was asked to serve Saturday night dinner in drag. He also said that J. Edgar appeared that evening in costly gowns, changing his selection of wardrobe two or three times that night.

On Monday morning, Scotty said goodbye to Ted, J. Edgar, and his young driver, as he headed back to Los Angeles. He wrote that Ted remained a client for years "but I never saw Hoover ever again."

Chapter Eighteen

JAMES DEAN AND THE WOOLWORTH HEIRESS

The "Five-and-Dime's Poor Little Rich Girl"

BARBARA HUTTON

LOVERS AND RACECAR DRIVERS JIMMY & BARBARA'S SON,

LANCE REVENTLOW

Together on the Fast Lane to Early Deaths

After a visit to New York, Jimmy returned to Hollywood in January of 1955. On his first night back, he headed for Googie's, his regular hangout. He didn't know who he would meet there: Vampira? Tony Perkins? Paul Newman?

What he did not expect was an encounter with one of the most famous—and richest—women in the world, as well known at the time as Hitler or Ernest Hemingway.

In another part of town, the Woolworth heiress, Barbara Hutton, had dined with her son, Lance Reventlow, and his date at the Brown Derby. After she bid Lance goodbye, her driver drove her back to the Beverly Hills Hotel, where she had rented Bungalow 6. On this particular night, she felt alone and abandoned. She envied the burgeoning romance of her son, despite her realization that the flame would flicker before dawn, when he would be off to his next conquest.

[Descended from robber barons, Barbara Hutton was called both "The Poor Little Rich Girl," because of her troubled life, or "The Million Dollar Baby." Author Truman Capote labeled her "the most incredible phenomenon of the century."

Her former companion, Philip Von Rensselaer, said, "She lived a gold-plated life. Her extravagance was fabled. She spent today's equivalent of $250 million in a decade. Her parties, clothes, jewelry, and furs—all flaunted during the Depression years—made her the envy of women around the world. Her romances with royalty and celebrities were widely publicized, as she went from tabloid headline to tabloid headline, most often with disastrous results."]

In Bungalow 6, Hutton found that the management of the Beverly Hills Hotel had left complimentary bottles of Pouilly-Fuissé and Château Lafite-Rothschild, along with a basket of lush tropical fruit. But she didn't want to drink alone. She had heard of a nearby hangout, Googie's, which was popular with young actors, a gathering place for what was called "The Hollywood Stars of Tomorrow."

In many ways, she felt she belonged to the past. Seized with an impulse, she called her driver, instructing him to take her there, a location adjacent to the famous Schwabs Drugstore. She wanted to take a look, perhaps to encounter the Errol Flynn or Cary Grant of

A catch-all rendezvous for jobs, lovers, pharmaceuticals, or trouble, Googie's sat adjacent to its equally famous counterpart, Schwabs, the most famous drugstore in Hollywood.

Both establishments were hangouts for Jimmy, but it was at Googie's that the second-richest woman in the world "discovered" Jimmy one night when she went slumming.

tomorrow.

She wore a mink coat, a diamond necklace, and a silvery gown she'd purchased from Chanel in Paris. As she entered the crowded, boisterous establishment, she was tempted to leave at once. It was not her kind of place, making her feel that at the age of forty-three, she was old enough to be the mother of every patron in the room.

The jukebox in the corner was playing a song by Jo Stafford. There was also a cigarette vending machine. The place had the aura of a bistro, with red-and-white checkered tablecloths resting on the too small tables.

The notorious life of Barbara Hutton has been the subject of many novels, films, and biographies. She led a lonely life in spite of the fact that she was surrounded by the rich and famous. She was a woman who enjoyed vast wealth and seven husbands (all of them disastrous). She lamented, "I never found lasting love."

She spotted only one empty table and headed there. On the way, she almost tripped on the outstretched legs of a rather sullen but handsome young man. He wore blue jeans and a black turtleneck, with dusty boots blocking access to the only available table. He stared at her through steel-rimmed glasses.

"Sorry," he said, rising to his feet, just as a young man and a woman sat down at that lone table. "Please join me?" he said. "I'm Jimmy Dean."

He eased her into a chair opposite him. "And I'm Barbara Hutton."

"Barbara Hutton!" he exclaimed. "In a place like this? So you're the lady who gets richer every time a register rings at Woolworth's."

"Well, not that directly," she said, looking up at the waiter who took her order for a glass of white wine.

"You don't know this," he said, "but I used to work for you. For a very brief time, I was employed at one of your five-and-dimes in L.A., demonstrating these new can openers. I wasn't very good at it, and I was fired."

"My dear boy, had I seen you, I would have immediately promoted you to general manager. Actually you don't look like a boy who should be forced to work at all. I'm amazed some eagle-eyed collector of pretty young boys hasn't kidnapped you and put you in a boudoir where you'd be permanently dressed in red silk pajamas, lying on the world's most expensive linen."

"I'm flattered."

"You could be the poster boy for the clean-cut all-American boy," she said.

"I'm not that clean-cut," he told her.

"I certainly am not either," she said. "If you read the newspapers, you know I've led a notorious life. Tallulah Bankhead once told me, 'Babe, you ended up with Lucrezia Borgia's poisonous heart, and you inherited Cleopatra's unsatisfied lust. Imagine taking on forty of her palace guards in just one night."

"That Tallulah," he said. "I know her.

"Is that *know* as in 'David knew Bathsheba?'" she asked.

"Something like that," he said. "But I'm not a kiss-and-tell guy."

"If you went for Tallulah, does that mean that I, too, have a chance?"

"The odds are in your favor, lady," he said.

Von Reventlow, sadist and opportunist, with Barbara.

"And what might you be doing now?" she asked.

"I'm an actor," he said. "I studied at U.C.L.A. I've already had my first break. I just completed a picture at Warners. I'm not famous now. But when the movie is released, I'll be a big deal in Hollywood."

"Who directed it?" she asked.

"Elia Kazan."

"Oh, the commie Jew," she said. "I never mess with people like that."

"I've heard of your son, Lance Reventlow," he said. "He's about five years younger than me, and he's very well known in car-racing circles. I share his enthusiasm for the sport."

"Then you must meet him sometime," she said. "You'll be discreet and not tell him where you met his mother."

"Of course," he answered. "You can count on

Rich, chic, decadent, and rancorously envied by virtually everyone during the Depression, Barbara Hutton is depicted above, in costume, at a party with the Duke of Buckingham in drag.

that. Frankly, I didn't think Googie's was your kind of place,"

"Tonight I'm slumming, which I've been known to do on occasions. I have a sense of adventure."

"I thought a famous lady like you would get all sorts of invitations in Hollywood," he said.

"I did tonight, but most of them were boring. I looked at them on my coffee table. I had my choice: a guest of Jack Warner, Joan Crawford, George Cukor, Jimmy Stewart, or Merle Oberon."

"Of the people named, I've had two of them," Jimmy said.

"My, for a little boy in blue jeans, you do make the rounds," she said. "I'm impressed...and not many things impress me anymore."

An entire two hours passed before Jimmy and Hutton left Googie's together. Out on the street, he told her to dismiss her chauffeur and hop onto the rear seat of his motorcycle.

"I'm up for that," she said. "A first for me."

"By the way, I hope you have a passkey if we go by a Woolworth's along the way," he said. "I need some razors and shaving cream. Maybe some after shave lotion."

"Tomorrow, if you give me your address, I'll ship you a year's supply."

They headed into the night on a hair-raising ride through the streets of Los Angeles, with her hair billowing in the wind. "If you pass this test, you can pass any test," he yelled back at her. She held tightly to his body.

After they returned to her hotel, he walked her to her bungalow. She didn't exactly invite him in, but he entered anyway, sitting down on her sofa and placing his booted feet on her coffee table. There, he spotted the two bottles of wine. "Let's knock off some of this grape juice. It doesn't look like the rotgut stuff I'm used to."

As Hutton's biographer, C. David Heymann, would write: "With Dean, Barbara felt oddly free, whimsical, aggressive yet feminine. His effect on her was agreeably bewildering."

As they talked, these two very different young man and middle-aged woman developed an amazing rapport. He seemed genuinely interested in her background, and for a while, she relished opening up and talking about her life, something she almost never did, even with close friends. As she'd later say, "Sometimes you can tell a stranger more than you can a close friend, who is more likely to judge you."

Heymann wrote; "Dean was blessed with a deep sense of curiosity. He seemed avidly interested in learning about Hutton's celebrated past, her friends, her poetry, her travels."

He might also have added, "and her marriages."

"Dean listened for long periods," Heymann claimed, "allowing her to develop her thoughts in an unhurried way."

At one point, Hutton quit talking about herself and asked him why he wanted to risk his life by riding a motorcycle so dangerously.

"I feel exhilarated taking wild chances," he said. "I'm pursuing what cyclists call the peak moment of intense excitement. Intense for its own sake, a dangerous thing that only men can feel, and can find only with each other."

"Are you a homosexual?" she asked.

"You can decide that for yourself later tonight when I crawl into bed with you," he said. "I have this philosophy of life. Real life means experience. That means experiencing everything without restrictions or moral restraints."

"That reminds me of this man I married in December and am planning to divorce in February," she said. "Porfirio Rubirosa, the Dominican playboy. During our brief marriage, he spent most of his time in bed with Zsa Zsa Gabor. The first time I saw him naked, I screamed in horror. It was something that belonged on a donkey. I much prefer the more modest penis of another of my previous husbands, Cary Grant. It wasn't too intimidating, and effective."

Jimmy Rejects Hutton's Offer to Become Her Toy Boy

Hutton recorded what happened next in her notebook, a document whose contents were later revealed to the press:

"It was late and he was drunk, and I was drunk, so I asked him to stay. He removed his shirt and pants and climbed into bed with me. I snuggled up next to him. He made love and then we made love again: It seemed the right and natural thing to do, although I couldn't help but wonder about his sexuality. He talked so fervently about men and adventure and masculinity. We talked and made love until long after the sun rose. In the morning, he ordered black coffee and scrambled eggs in the dining room."

What Hutton left out of her diary was that during breakfast, she made him an offer. With the understanding that she'd soon be divorcing Rubirosa, she wanted him to become a sort of toy boy. "My whole life, I had a dream that was not fulfilled, and that was to belong to someone and to some place," she said. "You could be that someone. I loved the way we could relate to each other. With me, you could set out to explore the world, sampling the best it has to offer. We'd live in palaces, on yachts, and I'd buy you the finest racing cars in the world. We'd attend all the races together. Summers in Deauville. Winters in Palm Beach. A hideaway in Hawaii. You'd meet kings, princes, and princesses, more movie stars than you know already, prime ministers, dictators. Your wardrobe would make Cary Grant green with envy, and you've read what a dresser he is."

"Sorry, Barbara, but as tempting as the offer is, I must turn it down," he said. "I'm the wrong guy for you. I can never belong to anybody, even myself. That's right: At times, I feel a stranger to myself. I've got to live out my destiny. And that is to be a god damn fucking movie star. I know how silly and shallow that is, but that is who I am. You were married to Grant, one of the biggest movie stars in the world, so you must have some idea of what I am talking about. I'm hardly proud of my dream, but I'm heading out to fulfill it anyway. I'm ready to face all the heartbreak, disillusionment, the glitter, the glamour, the phoniness—all for a bit of celluloid."

Concealing her disappointment, and almost holding back tears, Hutton later recorded in her notebook: "I watched as Jimmy climbed onto his motorcycle and disappeared around the bend. *Forever."*

***

Although Jimmy had rejected Hutton's very generous offer, he became intrigued at the idea of meeting and getting to know her son, Lance Reventlow. He was not only closer to Jimmy in age, but shared his enthusiasm for car racing. Jimmy had seen his picture in the tabloids, and found him "sexy, attractive, and perhaps susceptible to the charm of 'ol Jimmy Dean."

He'd heard plenty of stories about Lance. His home was dubbed "Camp Climax," because of the notorious orgies and daisy chains staged there, both gay and straight. Gossip columnist Louella Parsons had written that "Lance Reventlow invented the swinging jet set."

Somehow, Jimmy wanted to get connected with his lifestyle.

A few weeks after seducing his mother, Jimmy met Lance at a rally for racecar drivers, somewhere in the desert between Los Angeles and Palm Springs. The two handsome young men formed an instant attraction and friendship and went off to spend the weekend together at some remote little retreat on cactus-studded grounds.

As Jimmy later confessed to Stanley Haggart at his second home in Laurel Canyon, "What was I do to when meeting Barbara Hutton and Lance Reventlow? What would any red-blooded American boy do in those circumstances? I fucked both of them."

The relationship he formed with Lance would last until the final hour of Jimmy's life—*literally* that final hour. As Haggart recalled, "I'd known Jimmy for some time, both in New York and in Hollywood, but I'd never seen him take such interest in the backgrounds of anyone until he met Hutton and later, her son, Lance."

"They were so different from him, yet he bonded with them. He seemed to have the same curiosity about them that he'd have had if they'd been space aliens from Mars. He might have settled for a few hours of dialogue with Hutton, but, with Lance, he wanted to know everything. Out in the desert, Jimmy learned a lot about Lance's life, including its tragedies."

As Jimmy later told Haggart, "I'm more sexually compatible with Lance than I have ever been with anyone. But that doesn't mean we're setting up housekeeping together. Far from it. We're both too eager to have a lot of other experiences. Maybe when we've satisfied our curiosity elsewhere, we'll

Lance Reventlow was as much of a racing car enthusiast as James Dean

517

ride off into the desert right before the sun sets, and I mean that literally and symbolically. We'll become two old desert rats tearing up the desert in an old vehicle of some sort."

"Cary Grant Was More than My Stepfather.

He Was My Lover, Too."

—Lance Reventlow to Jimmy

Unlike Jimmy, Lance Reventlow was born in 1936 in a London townhouse into a life of spectacular wealth and privilege. Hutton may have been a kind and protective mother, but his father was a sadistic Prussian-Danish count, Court Heinrich Eberhard Erdmann Georg von Haugwitz-Reventlow.

Hutton had previously married (in 1933) a gold-digger, Alexis Mdivani, a self-styled Georgian prince whom she divorced in 1935, and who died that same year in a violent car accident

[In reference to Mdivani's death and the new man in Hutton's life, international headlines blared—THE PRINCE IS DEAD, LONG LIVE THE COUNT.]

Her marriage to her aristocrat, Count Reventlow, was marked by violence and deep humiliations. In Paris at the Ritz Hotel, he raped her on the floor of their suite. In her diary, she later wrote, "When he finished with me, he dragged me by the hair into the bathroom. 'You've always had an interest in scatology, Barbara. Now's your big change to experience it.' He forced me to sit on his lap while he excreted into the toilet. Then he locked me in the bathroom overnight."

Marriage to the Danish count would not only cost Hutton her U.S. citizenship, but a $4 million bundle. Their divorce was said to have given England "its greatest sensations since King Edward VIII renounced the throne eighteen months ago for the love of Mrs. Wallis Warfield Simpson." Their divorce decree wasn't finalized until March 6, 1941 since King Christian of Denmark had to sign it.

In the wake of the kidnapping of the Charles Lindbergh baby, Hutton hired security guards and a nanny to protect her son wherever he went. Almost monthly, she received ominous letters from deranged people threatening to kidnap Lance and hold him for ransom.

After divorcing her count, Hutton married Cary Grant at Lake Arrowhead, California, on July 8, 1942,

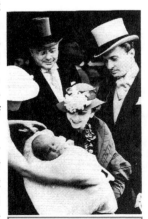

A supremely privileged childhood: Lance, 15 weeks old, after his christening.

during one of the darkest years of World War II. News of the event immediately redefined them, after Eleanor and Franklin D. Roosevelt, as the most famous couple in America. Almost immediately, the press nicknamed the couple "Cash 'n' Cary."

Lance was just six years old at the time his mother took another husband. Instead of resenting his stepfather, as many boys do in such circumstances, it was "love at first sight" between Lance and the handsome actor.

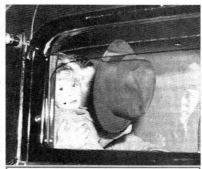
Lance, terrified, in 1939, after being spirited away from a crowd.

Guests at Hutton's mansion were astonished to see Lance running to greet Grant after his return from a hard day at the studio. The boy would plant a kiss on Grant's lips that "seemed to linger forever—much too long," in the opinion of one of Hutton's guests. He immediately wrote the count about this indiscretion, claiming that "I suspect something is going on here."

That opinion was reinforced when Grant would disappear upstairs with Lance for a long, leisurely bath that often stretched out for an hour or so. Hutton

Hutton with Grant as newlyweds...suffering and anguish lay in their futures.

would be furious when Grant would not even show up for dinner to join her fellow guests.

By his seventh year, Lance was calling Grant "General," and demanding that his mother's seamstress sew the words, "Lance Grant," into all his clothing. Under Grant's protective wing, Lance blossomed, telling the General all his secrets.

In the summer of 1944, Lance was sent to New York to live in an apartment with his father. It was a time of dreadful loneliness for the boy, who claimed his father would beat him so severely that he couldn't walk for a day.

Back in Hollywood, Grant told Elsa Maxwell: "Strange how the little chap has gotten under my skin. When he's away from us, I can never get him out of my mind."

Under threat of brutal beatings, the count forced the boy to reveal the most intimate details going on in the Grant/Hutton household. Breaking down in tears, Lance confessed to his father that Grant had "touched me down there." The count was well aware of Grant's homosexual lifestyle, whose de-

519

tails had been especially visible during the 1930s when Grant had lived openly with his gay lover, Randolph Scott. The couple had done little to conceal their romantic involvement with each other, even posing together for revealing pictures.

Infuriated, the count decided to take legal action. He was about to embark on what would become one of the most bitter custody battles in the history of café society.

In his dossier, the count charged that Grant had consistently used "foul language" around his son. Even more damaging, the count charged that Lance had told him that the movie star had "fondled my son in an inappropriate way." Reventlow lawyers eventually persuaded the count not to press that charge of child abuse, which would have made headlines around the world and possibly damaged Grant's stellar career for all time, as similar charges would have that effect upon Michael Jackson in the 90s. But the count demanded nonetheless that his son be prevented from speaking to Grant.

Fearful of a court ruling that could go against him, the count "kidnapped" his son and expatriated him to Canada. Eventually, lawyers persuaded the count to drop his charges and return Lance to Hutton and Grant, providing the heiress parted with $500,000. Back in Hollywood, Grant confessed to Elsa Maxwell, "Lance is the only thing holding this marriage together."

In 1945, after Hutton was reunited with her son, she launched divorce proceedings against Grant. After it was finalized, the couple agreed to be friends, and she asked Grant if he would continue his role as Lance's unofficial guardian. The actor readily agreed.

Lance discovered the world of Grand Prix motor racing at the age of 12, when Hutton, in 1947, married Prince Igor Troubetzkoy, who'd won the Targa Florio (a hysterical, haphazardly organized series of automobile races across the public roads of southern Italy) that year. From that moment on, car racing would dominate Lance's life until one day he suddenly abandoned it.

At the dawn of the 50s, Lance was growing up and becoming an attractive and sought-after young man. He stood six feet, had light brown hair, and an athletic build. Grant would often get angry at him if he chose to spend his weekends away from him.

As such, Grant would develop a bitter resentment of James Dean.

"Living Well Is the Best Revenge"

—*Barbara Hutton*

"I am earthbound," Lance told Jimmy one weekend in Tijuana, where they had gone to watch the bullfights. "Barbara lives among the pink clouds. I will never understand her—the spending binges, her love affairs, many with guys younger than me, her disastrous marriages, her incessant globe-trotting, never finding a place she likes."

During his private moments with Jimmy, Lance often talked so frequently about his mother that he seemed obsessed with her. "What chance did she have? Her mother committed suicide, and Barbara found the body. She was just seven years old when she became the richest girl in the world."

"As she grew up, and as those counter assistants toiled at Woolworth outlets ten hours a day, Barbara went shopping for husbands. She longed to be high born, so she set her sights on marrying a man with a title—hence, my father."

"Lance might think his mother strange, but he has a few weird moments, too," Jimmy told Stanley Haggart. "One night, he threw a hugely expensive drag party for some gay friends. All of us dressed up like gals. Lance, who dressed like Marie Antoinette, was showing off some necklace that had once belonged to her."

[Presented to Hutton as a wedding gift on the occasion of her (disastrous) first marriage in 1933, it was a necklace of 53 pearls that had been worn by Queen Marie Antoinette of France. Described in the press as "one of the rarest pieces of jewelry ever sold by Cartier," it was said to mark the beginning of her obsessive passion for pearls.]

"Barbara drives me up the wall," Lance said. "I get god damn tired of the fawning parasites around her. She collects a prince her, a sheik there, a military general, some English peers, a few tennis bums, and a lot of broken-down Hollywood rotters. She loves European titles. As for cash, no matter how much people hate her for it, she believes that if you've got it, flaunt it."

"One of her lovers told me that she was incapable of being satisfied. She demanded more and more. And a man can only give so much in a day and one long, hardworking night."

It is believed that Cary Grant learned about Lance's affair with Jimmy before Hutton did. He may have been the one who tipped her off, as both of them occasionally talked on the phone, mostly about their concerns for Lance.

When she heard about her son's affair with Jimmy, Hutton did not fly into the jealous rage that Grant had experienced. She'd been surrounded by homosexuals all her life, and had affairs with a few of them.

She had been far more shocked when she discovered a love letter that Lance had written to Grant. Even in her world of flamboyantly loose morals, she had deemed it inappropriate for her son to be sexually involved with her former husband.

Initially, though, she had raised no objections, telling he friend, the to-bacco heiress Doris Duke, "If Lance must be with a man, let it be Cary and not some of those hangers-on and race car bums he associates with."

As for Lance's sexual and emotional involvement with Jimmy, the hero of a distant one-night stand with her, she seemed tolerant: "Lance has trans-ferred his crush on Cary onto James Dean. I understand that, and in a way, it's an improvement. He's closer to Jimmy's own age. The relationship doesn't in-clude anything bordering on incest with his stepfather. Another thing, and I should know: Jimmy Dean is easy to love, and I think Lance will enjoy him."

By then, Hutton fully understood who James Dean, the movie star, was.

Was It Incestuous?

FEROCIOUSLY JEALOUS, CARY GRANT RESENTS JIMMY'S INFLUENCE ON "MY SON"

Cary Grant was adored by millions. For those who knew him, however, his glamorous facade concealed the tortured, closeted homosexual who lived behind that shield. The most revelatory statement about him was made by the actor himself. "There was no such thing as a Cary Grant until I invented him."

It seemed inevitable that Jimmy would meet Grant, and inevitable that Grant would want to "size up the competition."

As such, when all of them were involved in separate venues in or near Palm Springs (Grant was recuperating, alone, from Hollywood stress, and Lance and Jimmy were working one of the racecar rallies in the desert nearby), the older star asked Lance "to bring Jimmy by for a private dinner."

It was never firmly established, but Grant might have seen Jimmy, with-out actually meeting him, before that dinner. With Roddy McDowall, long be-fore he became famous, Jimmy had once been a porn performer at a raucous all-male party at the rented home of Cecil Beaton in Los Angeles. It had been attended mostly by British expatriates, including Noël Coward. Grant was ru-mored to have been among the spectators that drunken night, watching Jimmy perform.

Like every other insider in Hollywood, Jimmy had already heard plenty of rumors, mostly about Grant's long-enduring affair with Randolph Scott. Con-sequently Jimmy concluded that Grant must have been at least bisexual, based in part on Grant's marital histories with Virginia Cherrill, Barbara Hutton, and Betsy Drake. Grant was also said to have maintained affairs with Howard

Hughes, Gary Cooper, Noël Coward, Doris Duke, Cole Porter, Mae West, and Ginger Rogers. He was quoted as saying, "I think making love is the best form of exercise."

Over drinks, Jimmy and Grant did not get off on a good footing, partly because Grant insisted on delivering his opinions about one of his nemeses, Marlon Brando. He revealed that he had been one of the original "angels" who put up money

Randolph Scott *(left)* with Cary Grant. Both actors had lived together on or off for more than a decade of domestic bliss, interrupted by an occasional co-habitation with a woman.

for the Broadway version of *A Streetcar Named Desire.* "I was among the first on opening night to rush backstage to congratulate Marlon on his brilliant performance as Stanley Kowalski."

"I tried to be his friend," Grant said. "Months later, when he was in L.A., I invited him to join me for a weekend at the Fairmont Hotel in San Francisco. I thought we'd get to know each other better. I was more than generous, telling him that it was time for old guys like me to step aside and make way for younger upstarts such as himself and Montgomery Clift."

Jimmy later told Lance that he thought those words, although veiled, had been aimed directly at him, especially when Grant added, "and God knows what other actor jerks are waiting in the wings to take our places."

[From the subsequent gossip that emerged from that weekend at the Fairmont, it appeared that Grant made sexual advances to Brando and was rebuffed. That seemed to have contributed to some residue of bitterness in the older actor.]

Grant continued: "I expect that in the 1950s, movie audiences will want a very different type of talent from what was appealing in the 1930s and wartime 40s—hands-on, down-to-earth men like Spencer Tracy, Jimmy Stewart, Bogie, Edward G. Robinson, and me. You didn't have to be a pretty face back then. Now we have Tab Hunter. Need I go on?"

"Are you including me in that roster?" Jimmy asked.

"Since you brought it up, no, I am not," he said. "You're a different case. But I hope you don't mind a veteran actor giving you some advice. You're too much of a Brando clone, and that's not good for your career. He's better at playing Brando than you are. You really need to forge ahead and create your own identity on the screen. Like I did. I was an original, like Brando himself. I didn't imitate anybody else. In fact, tons of actors now imitate me, and in some cases, publicly ridicule me—Tony Curtis, for example with all those damn impressions of me he does, and that damn 'Judy, Judy, Judy." *[For more than fifty years, Grant impersonators attributed that repetition to Grant, since he was said to have uttered the line in one of his films.]*

"I'm sorry you have that opinion," Jimmy said, rising up from the sofa in Grant's suite. "I've decided I'm not hungry tonight." Then he looked over at Lance. "Come on, let's say good night. I have other plans for us."

"Don't go, Lance," Grant said.

This time, Lance did not obey Grant. He walked out with Jimmy.

***

Lance and Grant would later reconcile their differences, but Jimmy would never see Grant again.

The next day, Grant got in touch with Lance and urged him to drop Jimmy. "I don't know what you see in the lout. He's a total shit. A bad influence on you. Please get rid of him. You're too fine a person to hang out with riff-raff like that."

As Lance later said, "I didn't have to give Jimmy up. I was with him until the bitter end. Life gave up on him. Whether we would have remained friends, much less lovers, will never be known now."

Grant's hostility toward Brando and Jimmy once spilled over during an interview with a reporter: "I have no respect for this new breed of actors, especially those who pretend to be Method actors. What does that mean? A pair of dirty jeans, a lot of pot smoking, rampant sex, and a total lack of morals and decency."

"I hold these new idols of the screen in contempt. I detest their style of acting. Actually, it's not acting, it's posturing. That includes Brando and Monty Clift, and certainly that God awful James Dean. Under what haystack in Indiana did Jack Warner find that little devil?"

"My suggestion is to put Clift, Dean, and Brando in the same movie, and let them itch, scratch, mumble, and duke it out. When they've finished killing each other off, bring back Jimmy Stewart, Spencer, and me to start making some real movies instead of the garbage they're turning out now."

Whatever Happened to Lance Reventlow?

Like his friend and lover, James Dean, Lance—who continued his pursuit of race-car driving— would also suffer a fiery, violent, and youthful death.

In 1957, two years after Jimmy's death, he flew to Europe, where he purchased a Maserati, which he crashed soon thereafter. Amazingly, he escaped unharmed from the tangled wreckage.

Back in California, Lance established his own company, turning out Chevrolet-powered race cars, which he marketed as "Scarabs." He told his chief engineer, Phil Remington, "If Jimmy had lived, he'd be working right with me, turning out Scarabs. That is, when he wasn't making a great picture."

[During the lifetime of the company that produced them, four of the race-cars were spectacular failures and four were astonishing successes. Reaching their greatest fame and exposure in 1958, each was the brainchild of Lance Reventlow, then in his early 20s and his chief engineer, Phil Remington, both of whom were committed to the concept of an All-American racecar whose technical specifications would surpass those of anything produced in Europe at the time. To that effect, from the premises of an auto shop in West Los Angeles, he combined a 301-cubic-inch "overbored" adaptation of a Chevrolet V-8 that channeled power through a Corvette's four-speed gearbox. All of this, usually emblazoned in trademark colors of blue and white, were mounted onto a light aluminum chassis weighing only 127 pounds and sheathed with an aerodynamic and very expensive aluminum skin. Startup money for this dangerous, experimental, and horrendously expensive endeavor was almost certainly provided by Hutton. His mother had given him a $2 million trust fund, which he'd cashed in.]

With his Scarab, Lance won the 1958 Governor's Cup Race, and later a Grand Prix, using his low, shovel-nosed racer that outran Europe's long dominant Maseratis, Jaguars, and Ferraris. It was the Reventlow Scarab that competed in the 252-mile Nassau Trophy Race.

In 1960, perhaps to establish his heterosexual credentials, he asked the beautiful actress, Jill St. John, to marry him. When she accepted, he planted a spectacular ring—set with 100 diamonds—on her finger.

The marriage lasted for three turbulent years.

St. John was known for her high I.Q., but at her divorce hearing, she testified that Lance called her "stupid and incompetent" and insisted that she participate in dangerous sports.

The following year, he married Cheryl Holdridge, a former Mouseketeer in the Walt Disney's children's TV series, *The Mickey Mouse Club* (1955-1959). He showered her with mink coats and diamonds, but told Grant that she was still "in love with Elvis Presley."

In 1962, Lance visited his mother at her Japanese-style mansion in Cuernavaca, Mexico. Her cousin, Jimmy Donahue was there. Lance was in a belligerent mood, wanting to confront her with her many failures as a mother. He also found it offensive that she was shacked up with Lloyd Franklin, a man younger than Lance. Looking for his mother, Lance asked Donahue: "where's that drunken cunt of a mother of mine?"

Gossipy Donahue immediately reported to her what her son had said. That afternoon Barbara instructed her lawyers to cut off Lance "without a cent." That included his trust fund as well.

With almost no money, he sold his California home and bought a small place in Benedict Canyon. During this troubled time, Grant spent many a night just holding Lance in his arms to comfort him. As Grant later told Cukor, "It wasn't about sex—it was about love."

Lance recovered from his mother's belligerence. He told friends, "Regardless of what happens to me, Cary is always there for me."

In the last hour of his life, on July 24, 1972, Lance, who maintained a home in Aspen, set out with real estate brokers to examine the topography of a region of Colorado, near Aspen, that seemed ripe for the construction of a ski resort and hotel. He was a passenger, not the pilot, of a Cessna-206. The actual pilot was an inexperienced 27-year-old student pilot who flew into a blind canyon and stalled the aircraft. While trying to turn it around, the small plane plunged to the ground, killing Lance and the other men aboard.

Grant later told friends, "It was the single darkest day of my life." He experienced something akin to a nervous breakdown, but pulled himself together to fly to Aspen for the memorial service which had been organized by his widow, Cheryl.

The next few months were very hard on Grant, who entered a deep, dark depression that he tried—rather successfully—to conceal. Close friends said he was almost suicidal.

"He was my son," he told friends. "Don't even use the word 'step' in my presence. I will love that boy until the day I die. If I've known any joy in my life, it is the hours, days, and weeks I've spent with Lance. Just the two of us. If there is a God, he got jealous of such a bond—and had to take Lance from me. God succeeded in doing what James Dean failed to do."

The saddest picture Hutton ever saw was the wreckage of that Cessna-206 that had crashed onto that bleak mountainside outside Aspen, taking her only child, who died, estranged from her, at the age of thirty-six.

She later said, "Lance surrendered the greatest gift a young man can, an unfulfilled life. I wish I could have been a better mother to him. I will never smile again."

For the rest of her life, she obsessed over his death, somehow blaming herself for the accident. "I bear more guilt because of my cruelty to him than the pilot of that plane."

"After Lance's death, Barbara walked down a stairway to a dark gulf from which she never came back," Grant said.

Chapter Nineteen

THE BEAUTY AND THE BILLIONAIRE:
JAMES DEAN "AVIATES" WITH

HOWARD HUGHES
& TERRY MOORE

*Her "Alligator Love Call" Lures Jimmy
In and Out of Bed With "The American Emperor"*

AMERICA'S RICHEST ECCENTRIC DEMONSTRATES
WHAT UNLIMITED MONEY CAN DO IN HOLLYWOOD

As a new Hollywood agent, Dick Clayton was placing his hopes on what he called "my two stars of tomorrow. James Dean and Terry Moore are 'key race horses' in my stable of actors."

When Jimmy heard that, with a grin, he asked Clayton, "Am I a stud stallion or a pony?"

"What do *you* think?" Clayton answered.

Those two future stars met for the first time in Clayton's office early in 1954. At the time, Terry—an actress formed and nurtured by the entertainment industry since childhood—was farther along with her film career than Jimmy.

Terry Moore...
tickling Jimmy's nose.

[The petite, occasionally potty-mouthed Terry had been born in Los Angeles two years before Jimmy. As a child model, she had made her film debut in 1940 in Maryland, *in which she was billed under her real name of Helen Koford. The part called for a child actress who could stand up on a moving, barebacked horse, not fall off, and deliver lines convincingly as Walter Brennan's granddaughter.*

Later, with a new name, Judy Ford, she played a younger version of Ingrid Bergman in Gaslight *(1944).*

Her really big break had come as "Terry Moore" when she'd co-starred with Glenn Ford in the Columbia comedy, The Return of October *(1948). In that film, her character had to convey the belief that her kindly, recently deceased uncle had been reincarnated as a horse.*

It was this movie that brought her to the attention of the billionaire aviator and movie mogul, Howard Hughes. He would radically change and influence her life for all time.

Her first dramatic success had already happened before she'd met Jimmy. In 1952, she'd been cast as the young boarder whose shapeliness obsesses Burt Lancaster in Come Back Little Sheba, *based on a script by William Inge. The role earned her an Oscar nomination as Best Supporting Actress.*

Ultimately, it wasn't Terry, but Sheba's *star, Shirley Booth, who walked off with an Oscar (for Best Actress). Booth's performance as an ill-bred but good-natured housewife was reviewed as "plump, loveable, and possessed of a distinctively New York accent."]*

On that bright sunny day in 1954 in Clayton's office, slovenly dressed

Jimmy was asleep on a window seat. Terry walked over to him and slightly tickled his nose with the cord of a Venetian blind.

He jumped up and, then, to her surprise, he tackled her. Clayton's secretary was shocked to see them rolling over and over together on the floor. At first, she thought Jimmy was raping Terry, until she heard them giggling like schoolchildren.

Finally, he helped her to her feet, introducing himself as James Dean. "I know you," he said to her. "Elia Kazan directed me in *East of Eden*, and he told me all about you when he directed *Man on a Tightrope* (1953) with you in Germany."

"I hope he didn't tell you *all* about me," Terry said, half-jokingly, "at least not anything about when he tried to seduce me. He crawled in on my right, but within a few minutes, my mother—seemingly emerging from nowhere— crawled in on the other side."

"Oh no, such a sordid tale!" he said.

She would later remember her first impression of Jimmy in a memoir:

> *"As he hurried toward his destiny, he had to do everything now. Heaven could wait. Only it didn't. He had a devastating smile and a perky nose. His eyes, which peered out from behind thick glasses, sparkled when he laughed. His head appeared too large for his body and was emphasized by his springy hair that waved in all directions. His clothes were unkempt, as were his scarred motorcycle boots."*

That night, she invited him to her home for a family dinner, announcing to her mother, "Look what I found under a rock!" Jimmy didn't evoke any of Terry's previous pretty boy dates.

She was dating Hughes at the time, but he was away in Las Vegas. Jimmy ate heartily of the home-cooked meal. Then, sliding his chair back, he unfastened and partially unzipped his pants and let out a big belch. "I think that if my father hadn't been so stunned, he would have thrown him out the window," she said.

The next night, he accompanied Terry to a movie house screening *Man on a Tightrope.* The other stars included Fredric March, Gloria Grahame, and Adolphe Menjou. It was the story of a seedy traveling circus fleeing from Soviet-occupied Czechoslovakia to freedom in Bavaria. In several scenes, Terry had to ride circus horses and even an elephant. She had fallen off one of them, and—unable to rise from her position, prone on the ground—had to be rushed to a hospital in an ambulance. Prior to her fall, she'd been dizzy, and prone to early-morning nausea.

Two hours after her arrival at the hospital, she gave birth, prematurely, to a baby girl. All she remembered was the sound of a baby crying before she passed out. When she awakened, the baby was dead. The girl had lived for twelve hours, dying of septicemia.

After their first date, Jimmy more or less became Terry's shadow. He accompanied her to the Goldwyn Studios, where she did ballet stretches and *barre* work. Since he'd already trained with Katherine Dunham in New York, he joined her in the exercises.

Terry was a Mormon, and Jimmy put on his one blue suit, and even a tie, and escorted her to church. "He had a suit on, but he still wore those stinking old boots," she said.

She later said that Jimmy was sensitive about comparisons to Brando, a label that had haunted him since his days in New York. Before introducing him to her speech coach, Marie Stoddard, he warned her, "I don't want her to give me any shit about how I remind her of Brando. We dress as we please, and we ride motorcycles. Otherwise, the comparison ends there. Besides, my cock is longer than his."

He didn't reveal how he knew Brando's penile measurements.

Terry said to a friend that she saw through his act—"All that brooding, staring into his coffee at Googie's, mumbling if he spoke at all, acting strange, even hostile. Personally, I think all that posturing is premeditated. He's putting on an act to attract attention—that's all it is."

Early in his relationship with Terry, he wrote about her to Barbara Glenn, the girl he'd left waiting behind in New York.

"I like her, but she's a real bimbo. She's involved in this weird relationship with Howard Hughes. I don't get it. I can't imagine what the two of them do together, and I'm too afraid to ask. I'm told he screws both boys and girls. At least that's the poop running along the Hollywood grapevine."

Kazan remembered Terry in his memoirs, calling her "a gutsy little thing. She let it be known that she was the mistress of Howard Hughes, that plutocrat and scientific genius who made such a notable contribution to our war effort by designing the great, six-motored plywood seaplane, The Spruce Goose."

[Of course, Kazan was being sarcastic. Hughes's monstrous plane was an abject and very expensive failure, later widely ridiculed as his "folly." Cost overruns later led to Hughes' investigation by a Senate subcommittee.]

Kazan also wrote, "Hughes had been paying Terry's household bills, so she'd be available to him whenever he needed her."

When Hughes finally returned from Las Vegas, he took Terry out on his first night back. She told him about Jimmy. "That will serve you right for picking up strays. You might catch something. Who knows? You might not be able to get rid of it."

She had told Jimmy that when she first met Hughes, she found him repulsive, "But he grows on you."

During the fleeting few weeks they shared on-and-off (mostly off) together, Jimmy made an attempt to unlock the key to Hughes' personality, something that very few others had ever been able to decipher before.

At the time, many Hollywood insiders knew that despite Hughes' reputation as a womanizer, he maintained a discreet gay life, too.

Over the years, he'd been spotted dating such luminaries as Katharine Hepburn, Linda Darnell, Billie Dove, Ginger Rogers, Elizabeth Taylor, Lana Turner, Bette Davis, Marlene Dietrich, Tallulah Bankhead, Fay Wray, Gene Tierney, Carole Lombard, Norma Shearer, Hedy Lamarr, Rita Hayworth, Susan Hayward, Paulette Goddard, and Kathryn Grayson. Jean Harlow, Olivia de Havilland, and Marilyn Monroe were also among his conquests.

Among men, he dated from the A-list: Heartthrob Guy Madison, Randolph Scott, Gary Cooper, Errol Flynn, Tyrone Power, and Cary Grant, who eventually evolved into his closest friend.

Hughes liked to spy on the women he was seeing. When Ava Gardner learned that she was being trailed, she became so incensed that she hit him over the head with a heavy ashtray, knocking him unconscious.

Hughes' many conquests also included Barbara Hutton, who had been married to Cary Grant, Hughes' longtime lover.

When Jimmy found out about that, he said, "Been there, done that."

One night at Terry's house, Jimmy learned to recognize the sound of an "alligator love call." He heard it after Hughes telephoned Terry and talked to her for about an hour. She ended their call with a strange moaning sound.

Jimmy asked her "What in hell was that?"

She told him that she'd been fascinated by alligators and had read a book by an authority on reptiles (Ross Allen) and that "I have the distinction of having the only love call that could equal his. I can stand at the edge of a swamp that otherwise appears empty. I let out my mating call and alligators miraculously appear from nowhere."

[As noted by zoologists, during mating season, male alligators—despite their lack of vocal chords—emit sounds by inhaling air and then exhaling it in deep, rhythmical roars. These sounds attract females and warn other males to stay away. As documented on clips available on YouTube.com (keywords: alligator mating calls), the reptiles sometimes gather together in clusters for so-called "alligator dances," a feature of which is the soft, sometimes synchronized grunting, or "bellowing," described above.]

Hughes had heard her emulation of the reptilian love call and he had been intrigued. From then on, he tried to imitate the sound of alligator romance, and his attempt to replicate it had become their way of ending their phone calls.

Like Hughes, Jimmy, too, was intrigued and began to practice, even though whenever he sounded it off to his friends, they thought he had lost his mind.

William Bast claimed that it was "all too silly. Do you have dreams of having sex with an alligator? Don't lose your head over a 'gator.'"

Terry would later write a memoir entitled, *The Beauty and the Billionaire*, published in 1984, in which she detailed her relationship with Hughes. A few pages of it were devoted to Jimmy.

In it, she claimed that she began a relationship with the aviator in 1948, and that it lasted until 1956. Her most stunning revelation was her assertion that she married Hughes aboard a yacht cruising off the coast of Mexico in 1949. No evidence or documentation associated with that marriage has ever surfaced, but it is said that the Howard Hughes Estate made an undisclosed settlement on her, perhaps $350,000, in 1983, seven years after Hughes' death.

In her book, she depicted Hughes as a satyr, a sexually obsessive man who could never be faithful to just one person. She also claimed that he was a powerful lover, the best she had ever known.

When Jimmy first met Terry, she had ended her marriage to football hero Glenn Davis, who had previously been engaged to Elizabeth Taylor.

When Hughes had learned of the marriage, he had sent Terry, as a wedding present, a white bag filled with contraceptive diaphragms, for use during her honeymoon. He'd enclosed a note: "If you get pregnant, your nipples will turn brown instead of pretty pink, and you'll have stretch marks. In that case, I can never take you back."

***

As Jimmy and Terry's agent, Dick Clayton started to devise schemes to promote his new stars. At the time, "studio-arranged dates" were all the rage for stars under contract. Such unlikely pairings would match up a guy, Tab Hunter, for example, on a "date" with Debbie Reynolds, strictly for the production of photographs which would then be featured in fan magazines.

Columnist Sidney Skolsky was one of

Howard Hughes, the famous (and mentally unbalanced) aviator who flew both ways.

the first to write about this type of promotion. "The young Hollywood stars-to-be know that they have to attend every premiere, every party, and night-club opening. Always on hand are the likes of Tab Hunter, Zsa Zsa Gabor, and Terry Moore. That trio would go to the opening of an envelope."

Nicholas Ray, Jimmy's director in *Rebel Without a Cause,* later said, "Jimmy had contempt for the Hollywood scene. He shied away from social conventions and traditional manners. 'They represent disguise, like wearing a mask,' he once told me. 'I want to present myself as real and naked for all the world to see. No artifice.'"

He agreed to escort Terry to the September 22, 1954 premiere of *Sabrina,* starring Audrey Hepburn, Humphrey Bogart, and William Holden. One writer referred to Terry as "the reigning *piñata* of the Hollywood press." In a form-fitting sweater, with her breasts very prominent, she attracted the attention of photographers before they were known as *paparazzi.*

Whereas she basked in the glow of their flashbulbs, Jimmy, her escort, scowled and looked miserable in a tux.

The photographers snapping her picture asked, somewhat disdainfully, "Who's the guy with you?"

She claimed that they tried to edge Jimmy out of the frame, but that she held onto him tightly so that his image would be included in the media's coverage of the event. When one of the reporters thrust a microphone at them with a question, she answered for both of them, since Jimmy had nothing to say.

"In Jimmy's eyes, Brando was king, and he was out to steal his thunder," Terry claimed. "He just pretended he didn't want his picture taken. He liked having his picture taken so much he even photographed himself in the mirror. There were more photos taken of him during the early 1950s than any other star in Hollywood, with the exception of Marilyn Monroe and Elizabeth Taylor."

When pictures of Terry and Jimmy appeared in the morning press, one surprisingly bitchy caption read—THE MUTANT *[a reference to her prominent breasts and plasticity?]* MEETS THE HUMANOID.

Terry later said that her father was embarrassed the next day at his office, where his colleagues demanded, "Who was that creep with Terry at the premiere last

At the premiere of *Sabrina,* Terry Moore, in a form-fitting sweater, basked in the glow of the flashbulbs, but her escort, James Dean, unknown at the time, scowled, looking miserable in a tux.

night?"

"Within months, that so-called creep would be a Hollywood superstar with photographers shoving his dates aside to get a picture of him," she said.

Jimmy's public appearances with Terry did not escape the attention of the press. Columnist Sheilah Graham, former lover of the novelist F. Scott Fitzgerald, labeled Terry "the female James Dean."

[Ironically, when Jimmy started dating another starlet, Ursula Andress, Graham defined Andress as "the female Marlon Brando."]

"Why didn't she write about me?" Jimmy wanted to know. "I wouldn't mind being called the male Marilyn Monroe."

"It's because your tits aren't big enough," said Terry.

Word soon reached Hughes that Terry might be serious about Jimmy. Jealously, he ordered two of his spies to trail Jimmy and learn whatever information could be dug up from his past. Wherever he went, and without his knowledge, Jimmy had someone on his trail.

Hughes immediately learned that Jimmy was leading a bisexual life, enjoying women but also frequently involved in homosexual liaisons, too. The mogul was told that Jimmy's conquests had included Marlon Brando and Rock Hudson, and that during his days as a struggling actor, he'd hustled tricks along the edges of Santa Monica Blvd.

One night, Jimmy was driving back from Glendale with Terry, having attended the opening of *Red Garters,* a 1954 musical western spoof starring Rosemary Clooney. In a battered, junky-looking Chevrolet on its last legs, Hughes, who could have afforded the world's most expensive cars, trailed Jimmy's car for a few blocks until the actor had to stop for a red light. Then, Hughes deliberately rammed into the rear of Jimmy's car, although not seriously enough to do any major damage or bodily injury.

Hughes got out as Jimmy and Terry emerged from their car. Hughes shook Jimmy's hand and thanked him for "looking after Terry when I'm away."

He said that his business associate, Johnny Meyer, would show up in the morning and settle any damages to Jimmy's car—"and any emotional distress." Then he made a scribbled note of Jimmy's address and phone number before instructing Terry to get into his own car and telling her that he would return her safely to her home.

This, according to Meyer, "was Howard's way of introducing himself to Jimmy. I showed up the next day at Dean's place with a thousand-dollar bill. Howard also volunteered to buy Jimmy a new car instead of getting his rear bumper repaired. Dean rejected the offer. I told him, 'Why not? Howard's paying.' Apparently, Dean, unlike all the bimbos Howard hung with, had some integrity. How unusual for a young Hollywood actor. He may have nixed the car, but the little hustler didn't turn down the next temptation when Howard personally called him two days later. It was three o'clock in the morning."

Hughes wanted Jimmy to come to a remote neighborhood of industrial Los Angeles, which would be almost deserted at this hour of the morning. He said he'd send his assistant, Meyer, to drive him to the location where Hughes would be waiting for him in his battered old Chevrolet.

According to Meyer, "At first, Jimmy was reluctant, fearing he might be walking into some sort of trap. But his sense of adventure won out. At dawn, Jimmy was on Howard's plane to Acapulco for a boating trip and a holiday in the sun."

"So the kid could be bought after all," Meyer said. "Once a hustler, always a hustler."

As time went by, Jimmy began secretly rendezvousing for trysts with Hughes. As a couple, he and Terry faded from view.

INTERVIEW: BASKETBALL SUPERCOACH BOBBY KNIGHT

PLAYBOY

ENTERTAINMENT FOR MEN   AUGUST 1984 • $3.00

From Fifties Pinup to Eighties Knockout

Terry Moore Hughes

Howard Hughes's Ex Shows It All Off

Colorado Governor Richard Lamm Gives Us a Future Shock

A Viewer's Guide to the Olympics

Money, Sex and the American Couple

Years after the death of Howard Hughes (and perhaps because of him), life continued for Terry Moore.

In August of 1984, at the age of 55, this veteran survivor of show-biz solidified her reputation as a fun-loving, good-time gal by posing nude in *Playboy*.

***

[Terry would later work alongside Marilyn Monroe, Marlene Dietrich, Eva Marie Saint, and Anita Loose as a celebrity usher at the world premiere of East of Eden *in Manhattan. "Jimmy said he wasn't going to appear, shunning all that publicity," Terry said. "However, he got more write-ups by not showing up than he would have gotten if he'd made an appearance. Everybody was talking about a star not showing up at the world premiere of his debut movie."*

Sunny Shenanigans South of the Border

JIMMY DANCES NUDE FOR HOWARD HUGHES

With the understanding that Hughes would be away with Jimmy in Mexico for an undetermined number of days, Meyers was instructed to "babysit" (and spy on) Hughes' mistresses until Hughes returned. He was also to tell anyone who needed to know that Hughes had been summoned to Washington on urgent business involving TWA.

When Jimmy had protested that he didn't have time to pack anything in advance of their trip, Hughes told him not to worry. "They sell clothes in Mexico. They also sell toothbrushes, even toothpaste."

What happened in Mexico during the halcyon days of Hughes and Jimmy was later revealed by Hughes' playboy and bandleader friend, the Swiss-born former "swing-king" of Germany before he fled to Hollywood. Teddy Stauffer, an early promoter of the then-emerging resort of Acapulco, became more or less their host. Within that resort, he had arranged for them to stay at a luxurious villa known as "The New Discovery" which is exactly what Jimmy was for Hughes.

"I was asleep when Hughes arrived with this boy," Stauffer said. "At that time, Dean was a nobody. I thought he was just some trick. Howard was always with some trick, the gender not mattering so much to him. Later, I was shocked out of my mind when James Dean became such a big deal in Hollywood."

On the morning of their first day in Acapulco, Stauffer came to call on Hughes. "I found Howard fully dressed and talking on the phone by the pool," he said. "This young Dean boy was buck-ass naked, lounging on the other side of the pool, wearing only a pair of sunglasses."

"There were three bedrooms at the villa. Only one of them had been used—the beds in the other guest rooms were still freshly made. So, I knew that the two of them had connected. Dean seemed to have satisfied Howard's taste in young men, because he was fascinated by the boy."

"As for Dean, he seemed rather indifferent. He was unconventional for our aviator friend. As time passed, it became evident to me that Howard obviously liked Dean in bed, but that he wasn't that impressed when the boy delivered some opinion. Several of his utterances made Howard wince. When it came to ideas, no two men could have been more ill-matched. They were completely different personalities."

"There was also a big difference in their ages. I learned that Dean was born in 1931, and I already knew that Howard had come into this world before World War I. Howard was old enough to be Dean's father. It was also evident to me that Dean had no interest in Howard, other than his fame and money. He was just prostituting himself."

That night, Jimmy and Hughes dined with their host. According to Stauffer, "Dean really dug my cook's Mexican specialties, although Howard claimed that all this spicy food made him fart a lot and get the runs."

"One day, Howard took Dean flying above the western coast of Mexico," Stauffer said. "Another time, he rented a luxury yacht, with its crew, for a few days of sailing, landing in various seedy ports along the way. During his entire stay, when he wasn't otherwise naked, Dean wore Mexican clothes that Howard had bought him."

The kid seemed fascinated by bullfights, and Howard took him to some of the *corridas,* but I think Howard was just indulging him. I don't think the boss was that much interested in blood sports, but Jimmy was. He told us that he'd fought bulls in the ring, but both Howard and I thought that he was just bullshitting us."

"Frankly, I think Dean was just going along for a luxury vacation paid for by a man sometimes known as the U.S. Emperor."

"I'll always remember the final night when Howard asked me to join them," Stauffer said. "Dean was trying to polish off a bottle of tequila. At one point, he got really drunk and in front of us, he pulled off all his clothes. I had learned that he had studied dance with Katherine Dunham in New York. He performed this dance in front of us. I thought he was a lousy dancer, but Howard seemed to enjoy his cock bouncing up and down."

"Before the evening came to an end, Dean told us, 'Dream like you'll live forever, but live like you'll die tomorrow.'"

"Both Dean and Howard had tragic endings. But that statement about dying, at least in Dean's case, sure was prophetic."

Talking Dirty and Winging Low
WITH THE WORLD'S MOST FAMOUS AVIATOR

After their return to California, Jimmy never knew when Hughes would pop in, but it frequently occurred during the early hours of the morning, when he'd arrive on Jimmy's doorstep with the alligator love call.

"He had strange and weird ways," Jimmy told Stanley Haggart. Recalling his training as a former "leg man" for gossip columnist Hedda Hopper, Haggart pumped him for information he could learn about the private life of Hollywood's most perplexing airman, industrialist, and film mogul.

"I've begun to realize what an oddball he really is," Jimmy said. "One day he flew me to the Grand Canyon. I didn't even have time to get my wallet, expecting him to treat me to dinner, since I hadn't had anything to eat that day."

"After we admired the glories of the canyon, I was starving but had no money. Hughes reached into his pocket and found only a single dollar bill, enough to pay for a ham sandwich, which the two of us shared." Then, a smirk came over his face. "Of course, we couldn't afford mustard."

"He had strange ideas about food," Jimmy said. "I never knew what we were going to have for supper. One night, a waiter brought in a huge bucket of freshly made vanilla ice cream and about a quart of chocolate syrup—and that was it."

On another occasion, Hughes invited Jimmy to fly with him to Las Vegas where the younger man expected to be treated to ringside tables at all the best shows. "But that's not what happened," Jimmy said.

Airborne, and halfway to Las Vegas, Hughes suddenly announced that he had to return immediately to Los Angeles, and turned the plane around. A member of his staff had not packed three boxes of the brand of cookies he had ordered.

"You once told me I could buy clothes in Mexico," Jimmy said to him. "I'm sure you can get some pastry chef there to make any kind of cookie you want."

"That won't do," Hughes responded. "I have to have this certain type of cookie."

Jimmy later learned that Hughes had worked with one of his favorite chefs, perfecting a special kind of cookie with just the right amount of sugar and cinnamon. The butter it contained came from a specific breed of cow grazing in the pasturelands of California.

"Back at the airport, the boxes of cookies were retrieved from the back seat of a limousine," Jimmy said. "Once they were on board, we took off again for Vegas. I was looking forward to a good time. Boy, was I disappointed."

Once in Vegas and within Hughes' suite, Jimmy was subjected to eighteen solid hours of watching movies, reels of which had been sent over by Johnny Meyer. It is not known how many of these movies Jimmy slept through. Hughes had ordered him not to drink a lot, because he didn't want him going to the toilet in the middle of a screening.

Meyer had delivered such films as *Hell's Angels* with Jean Harlow; and *The Outlaw* with busty Jane Russell and Jack Buetel cast as Billy the Kid. *[Buetel became Hughes' long-term lover.]* Also shipped were *The Front Page* with Pat O'Brien; *Scarface* with Paul Muni; *Double Dynamite* with Frank Sinatra and Groucho Marx, and *Holiday Affair* with Robert Mitchum and Janet Leigh.

After many hours of film watching, Jimmy and Hughes retired to bed. "I thought that after that, he might want to read movie scripts. Guess what! The fucker read nothing but comic books. *Dick Tracy* was his favorite."

"He told me he never read any of the thousands of letters he received weekly unless they were from special friends. "I saw two of those special letters. One was from Elizabeth Taylor, the other from Cary Grant. Guess what? They were each annoying Hughes with requests for free rides on TWA planes. He told me he always allowed Ava Gardner to travel for free as well."

"There was one thing about Hughes that was a real turn-off," Jimmy said. "I don't think he bathed often, yet he was a fanatic about cleanliness. He had boxes of Kleenex around, wiping everything clean. And he'd never touch a doorknob himself—he always got someone else to open it. And in spite of his mania for hygiene, he sometimes smelled like an old goat."

During the days and nights Jimmy spent with Hughes, he learned how the mogul ran his empire. "I couldn't believe it! Hughes would sit for four or five hours—I'm not joking—on a toilet set calling people all over America. He had a phone installed in every one of his bathrooms. Sometimes, he'd read on the stool. At other times he watched TV, also installed in every bathroom. I was surprised that he likes to watch soap operas. Until I met him, I thought only bored housewives liked soap operas."

During some of their dialogues, Hughes shared his plans for the future with Jimmy, including his dream of moving to Florida and opening a large aircraft factory in the West Palm Beach area.

He continually urged Jimmy to transfer his interest in racing cars to airplanes.

Jimmy confessed he had a fear of flying, and that when Elia Kazan had taken him on his first plane ride (from New York to Los Angeles) "it was a real nail biter for me. I almost kissed the ground when we got to California."

Even though Jimmy resisted, Hughes kept demanding that he had to teach Jimmy how to pilot an airplane. He had selected a Cessna-140 to break Jimmy in as a pilot, promising him that if he'd learn how to fly it properly, he might give it to him as a gift.

"I never really got the hang of it," Jimmy later told Haggart. "I wish he'd offered me a custom-made racing car instead. I felt nervous up in the clouds. For all I knew, I might have a head-on crash with a god damn flying saucer."

"On the days when Hughes was busy, he turned me over to this flight instructor of his. I forget his name...Ray something. He was an older guy. Hughes said that when he was much younger, he'd been one of the stunt pilots he'd hired during the dangerous filming of *Hell's Angels*."

"Hughes would get impatient with me teaching me how to pilot a plane, but this Ray guy was most helpful. Whenever I made a mistake, he'd say, 'Let's try again.'"

"I never read a book on aviation, and I never intend to," Jimmy said. "But no one, not even Hughes or Ray, could explain to me what makes a plane stay up in the air."

"Hughes wanted me to try my hand at landing a plane," Jimmy said. "I was terrified that I'd crash it. He'd gone over the instructions countless times, but all I could remember was him shouting at me, 'Easy, easy, pull it back.'"

"'Pull what back?' I wanted to know."

"Easy does it, just a little bit more," Hughes yelled at him.

"It wasn't exactly a smooth landing," Jimmy said. "I hit the ground with a real bump and for a moment the plane jumped up in the air again, but I finally brought the fucker down. Anyone who thinks landing a plane is a piece of cake is crazy. Anything can go wrong. At least I brought the thing to a stop before we ran off the runway and into a nearby field."

"I had heard that a Cessna has been known to stall in mid-air, and I was afraid I might touch the wrong instrument, and we'd plunge to earth."

Hughes had told me that even if the plane caught fire, 'not to panic.' How in hell could I not panic? If anyone has the right to panic, it's when he's flying a plane and it catches on fire when you're up in space halfway to the moon."

"Hughes was a reckless son of a bitch," Jimmy said. "One afternoon, at some point after I'd been piloting for a while, never being any good at it, he wanted me to perform crazy things that only a stunt pilot with years of experience can pull off. I think the guy had a death wish. There was this thing about putting a plane into a tailspin—the less said about that, the better."

"Regardless of how rotten a pilot I was, Hughes never lost his cool. My god, even when he's in danger, that guy is as cool as a cucumber on an August day. Nothing seems to phase him. He'd been in crashes before, or so I heard, and had obviously lived to tell about it."

"You might call me the white knuckled terror of the air," he said.

Jimmy told Haggart that his most memorable time in the air was aboard one of Hughes' relatively large planes. "I didn't know one plane from another, but this mother fucker was big, and Hughes and I were the only passengers. He had a pilot and even a co-pilot manning the controls."

"When we took off, we got a snack served by this cute little waitress I'd like to make. I wonder if Hughes had made her. Probably he had."

"Way up in the clouds, Hughes did the strangest thing. He actually picked me up in his arms. He was a tall guy with long legs, and I'm a shortie. He carried me into a closed compartment near the back and locked the door behind us."

"My God, it was a bedroom with this quilt made of mink. Needless to say, I landed on that quilt, and he slowly took off my clothes before stripping down himself. Let's put it this way: It was my first airborne fuck. Before that afternoon, I'd never heard of such a thing as an airborne fuck. But it's recommended to anyone who wants it. But only if you can do in on mink, in a private bedroom, high up in the clouds."

The Weird and Wanton Ways of a Demented Billionaire

THE AMERICAN EMPEROR SHOWS JIMMY HIS HAREM

As Jimmy became more deeply involved with Hughes, he learned more and more about his sexual habits. Joan Crawford once proclaimed, "Hughes would fuck a tree."

"That wasn't exactly true," Jimmy said. "Oral sex was his favorite thing, both giving and receiving it."

"Howard would have five or six girls a day," said his former girlfriend Paulette Goddard, who was once married to Charlie Chaplin. "But it was kind of chaste because he did it only one way: Lip service."

Hughes told Jimmy that of all the movie star seductions he'd enjoyed in his life, Carole Lombard was the "Queen of Fellatio."

"Clark Gable was one lucky man during the time he got to be with her."

"Hughes claimed that he was a breast man," Jimmy said. "That's why he had cast Jane Russell in *The Outlaw.* He said she had 'the most beautiful pair of knockers he'd ever seen in his life."

He told Jimmy that he preferred "intermammary intercourse"—that is, making love by positioning and then rubbing his penis between a woman's breasts.

As Hughes' biographer Charles Higham wrote: "With men, he also preferred oral sex. He was a thoughtless, dispassionate lover, seeking only control. His sexual partners were not so much lovers as hostages, prisoners, or victims of his will. He had to dominate everything. His boyish, vulnerable charm, handsome, underfed, a lanky look, and an atmosphere of power and money captivated all of his sexual partners, but he left no echoes behind."

Higham also wrote: "Only his deafness, and a certain insecurity in his sexual performance, were blights on his existence. Yet he was impatient, restless, because there were people he couldn't buy. He was tortured by paranoia that was by no means unfounded."

One night in a rare confidential mood during pillow talk, Hughes confessed to Jimmy that he'd lost his virginity at the age of fifteen when his paternal uncle, Rupert Hughes, had seduced him. "He taught me how to perform oral sex, and it's been a favorite pastime of mine ever since, as you well know."

"He also revealed that his alltime sexual fantasy would involve having Elizabeth Taylor and her fellow Britisher, Jean Simmons, in bed with him at the same time. After a session with them, I would then like Stewart Granger to enter the room and strip down, so I could have him too. But the bastard is threatening to kill me if I don't stop pursuing Jean. They're married, you know."

Reviews for Hughes in the boudoir were mixed. Gambler "Jimmy the Greek" said, "In his heyday, Hughes boasted of deflowering two hundred virgins in Hollywood. He must have got them all."

But William Heller, the pioneer Hollywood publicist, claimed, "Two of Hughes' girlfriends told me he wasn't worth a dime as a lover. He was just no good in the sack. They said all he wanted to do was to look and fondle. He liked recently divorced women. For some odd reason, he referred to them as 'wet decks.'"

"I find that sex is so much better, so much more intense, with a new divorcée," he told Jimmy.

Hughes had installed each of his current mistresses in rented lodgings, and one night, he invited Jimmy on a tour through some of them. Collectively, he referred to this bevy of starlets as "my harem." He had within his employ about a half-dozen chauffeurs too. In addition to reporting back to Hughes details about the harem's betrayals or indiscretions, their duties included driving the women around on errands, such as shopping trips, during the course of their days.

"I hire only homosexuals as my drivers," Hughes said. "Once or twice I've been fooled. I recall one chauffeur who told me he was gay, but then he was caught fucking one of my starlets. I fired him instantly. Today, when I hire a chauffeur, I insist that he blow me. You can always tell the difference between a totally straight guy blowing you and a gay one."

Members of his harem were forbidden to go out with other men, although they sometimes managed to slip out for a date or two without Hughes' knowledge. Eventually, though, he caught them. He told Jimmy that his technique involved arriving unexpectedly at unpredictable times of the day or night.

On the night he included Jimmy on a tour of his harem, Hughes preferred to be his own driver.

"Within a period of about two and a half hours, we visited the homes of three really beautiful and sexy gals," Jimmy later told Haggart. "I was offered a drink at each house. Hughes drank nothing—not even a glass of water. We chatted briefly with a *puta,* and then moved on."

"I figured that at some point, Hughes would want to spend the night and perhaps engage me for a three-way. Nothing like that. After I finished my drink, he rose to his feet, told the starlet good night, and we were off to our next house."

"That left me and the gal unsatisfied, although I thought all of them would be willing to go to bed with me. I told Hughes that if he just wanted to watch, he could see me in action with a woman, but he turned down the idea."

Jimmy learned that Hughes insisted that every member of his harem be inspected by his personal doctor. Before he'd even touch one of them, Hughes checked their fingernails, insisting that they receive frequent manicures. He also controlled the diets of these women, creating menus heavy on carrots and broccoli, vegetables he insisted that they eat for both lunch and dinner.

On yet another night spent touring his harem, Hughes, with Jimmy, arrived at the home of a starlet who was in the process of entertaining a male guest. It was 2AM. Perhaps she had assumed that it was safe to slip a man into her bedroom at that hour.

"I don't remember the name of this girl," Jimmy said, "but she came to the door looking like she'd had a rough night. Like a bird dog, Hughes instantly sensed something and headed straight for her bedroom. I followed him. He yanked back the covers to expose a nude Nicky Hilton. Based on all that newspaper publicity during his marriage to Elizabeth Taylor, I recognized his face at once."

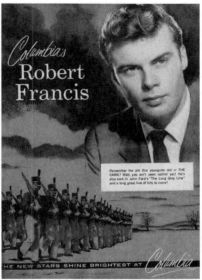

"Hughes was furious," Jimmy said. "He dragged Nicky out of the bed and through the living room, kicking him out the door, even though he was jaybird naked. Even in this agitated state, I was impressed with the hotel heir. He had a horse dick on him."

Later, Jimmy learned that one of the reasons Hughes detested Nicky was based on his affair—during the course of his marriage to Taylor—with Terry Moore.

"I never found out how a naked Nicky got home," Jimmy said. "But with that can of Budweiser between his legs, and those dangling balls, I'm sure he managed to hitch a ride in gay Beverly Hills."

***

Both Jimmy and the Aviator were men of changing moods. Hughes flew into

James Dean was not the only actor on whom Howard Hughes lavished money and obsessive attention. Another was Jimmy's competitor, the rising star known as Robert Francis.

Heavily promoted and publicized as a romantic heartthrob until his tragic early death in an airplane crash, Francis was the focal point of the poster depicted above. Its fine print reads like this:

"THE NEW STARS SHINE BRIGHT AT COLUMBIA: Remember the job this youngster did in THE CAINE? Well, you ain't seen nothin' yet! He's also sock in John Ford's *The Long Grey Line* and a long line of hits to come!"

Jimmy's life, and one day just flew out. He was later seen giving flying lessons to Robert Francis, the handsome, blonde-haired star who had captured a lifelong corps of fans after his appearance in *The Caine Mutiny* (1954) with Humphrey Bogart.

Rising star Francis was voted one of the most promising actors of 1954. His life would be cut short, violently and tragically, at the age of 25 on July 31, 1955 in the crash of the small airplane he was piloting.

***

Katy Jurado...from Gary Cooper to James Dean, and hugely famous as a movie star throughout Latin America.

During the peak of his involvement with Hughes, Jimmy, began to appear in public with some carefully arranged "studio dates." Most of them were harmless, ending with a fast good night and perhaps a kiss on the cheek.

Even if a date led to a seduction, there was rarely any lasting involvement.

One of Jimmy's most unlikely couplings was with the Mexican film star Katy Jurado, who was about seven years older than Jimmy. Born in Guadalajara, Mexico, she managed to launch herself—usually playing steamy *femmes fatales*—beginning in 1943, into both the Mexican and U.S. film industries.

In 1951, Budd Boetticher cast her in her first Hollywood film, *The Bull-fighter and the Lady*. Other producers became intrigued by her exotic beauty, and she soon followed in the footsteps of Dolores del Rio and Lupe Velez, two other Mexican actresses who played significant roles in Hollywood.

Jurado became the first Latin American actress nominated for an Oscar as Best Supporting Actress for her work in 1954's *The Broken Lance*. Today, she is best remembered for her role in the Gary Cooper classic, *High Noon* (1952), which she'd filmed around the time when Jimmy dated her two or three times.

Nicholas Ray asked Jimmy if he had gotten lucky.

"Maybe," he answered, enigmatically. "But I'll tell you one thing: The Montana Mule is a tough act to follow," a reference, of course, to his friend, "Coop."

***

Around the same time, another of Jimmy's foreign-born liaisons resulting from a "studio date" was with the French *ingénue*, Leslie Caron. She waltzed into and quickly out of his life after her appearance in her best-known film, *An American in Paris* (1951) opposite Gene Kelly. In time, she'd dance onscreen with Fred Astaire, Mikhail Baryshnikov, and Rudolf Nureyev.

Her emotional involvement with Jimmy was minor and fleeting, so it came as a surprise when she talked to the press the day after Jimmy died in 1955.

"I will never dance again," she vowed.

It was a vow expressed during her emotion of the moment, not a promise to be kept.

Even though her affair with him amounted to no more than a brief dalliance, she seemed emotionally shattered at news of his death. However, she recovered quickly.

Lori Nelson...Romantically linked by the tabloids to both James Dean and Tab Hunter, who supposedly competed for her attention.

***

As a studio date, actress/model and starlet Lori Nelson, who had emerged from Santa Fe, presented a context that was complicated at the time because she had been widely publicized by the Hollywood press as "Tab Hunter's girlfriend." In fact, her romantic involvement with Tab was more serious and long-lived than the brief encounter she had with Jimmy.

Jimmy's agent, Dick Clayton, arranged for Jimmy to escort her to a premiere.

Later she expressed nothing but compliments for him. "Jimmy was thoughtful about little things that count to a girl. You never had to open a car door—he did it for you. And you could count on other attentions which meant a lot."

Lori never explained what those "other attentions" were.

She had made her film debut in the 1952 Western, *Bend of the River,* and later appeared as "Rosie Kettle" in the film comedy, *Ma and Pa Kettle at the Fair.*

Lori admitted to Jimmy that her early life had been dominated by a series of beauty pageants and talent contests, the cumulative effects of which resulted, in 1950, in a seven-year contract with Universal when she was only seventeen. Although Tab was also dating Debbie Reynolds at the time, he and Lori became a hot item in the gossip columns. Reportedly, they were engaged to be married.

In his memoirs, Tab wrote: "More than once, I thought about bringing Lori home and introducing her to my mother, telling her that this is the girl I'm going to marry."

At the time of these marriage dialogues, Tab was involved in a torrid affair with Ronald Robertson, the well-known (male) figure skater. Tab admitted to Dick Clayton, "I'm confused about my sexual orientation."

Even though she probably knew better, Louella Parsons wrote about Tab's so-called "burning romance" with Lori.

In lieu of her blurb about Hunter's non-romance with Lori, Parsons would have preferred to run a different news item, preferably a "teaser" that might pique the interest of readers with hints about a possible marriage of Jimmy to any of the several starlets he was dating at the time.

In response to Parsons' coy queries about his marital plans, or lack thereof, Jimmy answered, "Lady, I'm not contemplating marriage to anyone...ever. You may not understand this, and I don't want you to print it, but the biggest affair I'm having is with myself. Call it a voyage of self-discovery."

In 2005, Blood Moon Productions issued the world's most comprehensive overview *(center photo)* of the Hollywood involvements of the eccentric billionaire aviator, Howard Hughes.

Chapter Twenty

WERE THEY REALLY STAR-CROSSED, LIKE ROMEO & JULIET?
JAMES DEAN & PIER ANGELI

Changing Partners With Ursula Andress

A TANGLED WEB OF HOLLYWOOD AFFAIRS
EVERYBODY SLEEPING WITH EVERYBODY ELSE'S LOVER

"In Pier Angeli, a nineteen-year-old Italian girl, Hollywood has found an actress who eludes the town's traditional classifications and whose unvarnished beauty and instinctive talent have already caused her to be called 'Little Garbo.'"
—Theodore Strass in *Colliers*, April, 1952

"It was fire & ice. She screwed half of Hollywood."
—James Dean, describing his affair with Pier Angeli

"I'm the father of that bambino—not Vic Damone!"
—James Dean

The much ballyhooed romance of James Dean and
Pier Angeli was a summer fling that began in the late
spring of 1955 and lasted until the autumn leaves
began to fall. Jimmy, of course, would die before the
end of that year's September.

His friend, John Gilmore, had been with him when
he met Pier on the Warner lot. He was shooting *East
of Eden,* and she had a role in *The Silver Chalice,* being
filmed on a nearby stage.

James Dean with Pier
Angeli...a sullen ro-
mance.

One day, she walked into the Warner commissary
with actor Jack Palance, who played the villain in *The
Silver Chalice,* which Jimmy referred to as "that fucking
religious thing." After Palance had turned down the lead role in favor of the
villain's, it had been assigned to Paul Newman, resulting in what he'd later define as "the most embarrassing flop of my life."

As Gilmore remembered it, Pier's first chat with Jimmy was awkward. He
managed to say that he didn't like living in Los Angeles and that he wanted to
return to New York as soon as possible. After she left, Jimmy told Gilmore,
"She's one stuck-up lady. But she's pretty."

In spite of their lackluster first meeting, Jimmy, within days, was dating
her. Warners was pleased with the consequent publicity because it would promote both of these new stars as well as their pictures.

"Perhaps now that I'm dating a respectable girl like Pier, maybe Sheilah
Graham will quit busting my balls and give me a decent writeup for a change."

"Jimmy pretended he hated publicity," according to Gilmore, "but the son
of a bitch loved it. As for Pier, she was publicity crazy. She devoured herself in
print like a fat lady swallowing chocolate drops."

When she wasn't needed on her film set, Pier became a constant visitor
to the set of *East of Eden.* Director Elia Kazan had a dressing room next to
Jimmy's, one with thin walls. From what he heard, he thought it sounded "like
Jimmy boy was giving this Italian gal multiple orgasms."

Many other times, however, he heard bitter arguments, mostly about
Pier's domineering mother, Enrica Pierangeli, who did not want her daughter
involved with "that rebel."

"I have never been interested in a boy as young as Jimmy," Pier told the
press. "I have always liked older men, finding them more interesting. They can
talk about something other than baseball and the jitterbug."

"He's a wonderful boy. He'll soon be twenty-four, and I'm twenty-one.
My mother lets me go out on dates. There's a joke going around Hollywood
that if a man dates me, he has to take my mother along as chaperone and also

my twin sister, Marisa Pavan."

Enrica's control over her daughter has been exaggerated by many other biographers. Obviously, as later events would show, she was not subject to her mother's total control. After her arrival in Hollywood, she'd had an affair with actor John Barrymore, Jr., and also with Eddie Fisher before Debbie Reynolds snatched him away.

At the time Jimmy began dating Pier, she was just coming down from a broken romance with Kirk Douglas, with whom she had filmed *The Story of Three Loves* (1953). The actor later said, "She had huge, dark eyes, and a refreshing innocence. She was virginal and had a beautiful body and an infectious laugh. I became enamored of her, this child that I could mold into the image I wanted, like Pygmalion."

Their relationship lasted for eighteen months. On night in Paris, Douglas had walked her back to her hotel, the very posh George V. He kissed her on the cheek.

"Will I see you tomorrow?" she asked.

"No, he replied. *"Domani è troppo tardi."* [*That was the name of her first film,* Tomorrow is Too Late *(1950).*]

Their romance ended at the entrance to the George V, leaving her heartbroken.

In Hollywood, she told a reporter, "I don't want to grow up. I just want to be young and have fun. I'm greedy for life, romance, and emotion, and that doesn't mean staying home every night and listening to my mother's lectures on morality. With my father dead, I'm the chief breadwinner in the family, and I don't intend to be pushed around."

Writer Stewart Stern wrote the script for Pier's first American film, *Teresa,* and was working on a screenplay for Jimmy's next film, *Rebel Without a Cause.* He said, "Jimmy's affair with Pier had to do with the child who resided in each of them. They played a game like a Hollywood fantasy."

Pier told Stern, as he later relayed to Nicholas Ray, "One of my greatest problems with Jimmy is that when he has to urinate, he'll do it anywhere regardless of where we are. He rarely bothers to make it all the way to a toilet."

Cal York, a gossip columnist, reported on Jimmy's romance with Pier:

"Woo-some Twosome: Some still say it's a publicity romance, but Cal knows a secret! Pier quietly bought Jimmy a gold wrist watch, a gold identification bracelet, and a miniature gold frame with her picture in it. No, they don't exactly go with his Levis and sweat shirt (the new school uniform!) but he was very pleased just the same. So help us, pretty Pier now wears a pearl ring on the second toe of her left foot! Cal tried to ask her if she was engaged—but the words just wouldn't come out!"

Pier told York, "I'm seeing a great deal of 'Jemmy,'" as she called him.

What Jimmy didn't know, and what might have ended the romance before it had really begun, was that Pier, after Kirk Douglas dumped her, had also launched an affair with Paul Newman, her co-star in *The Silver Chalice.*

As Deborra, she was Newman's love interest in the film. According to Virginia Mayo, the star of the movie, "Pier looked radiant in Madonna blue with a gold circlet in her hair. Forgetting about his wife, or even his other girlfriend, Joanne Woodward, Paul fell hard for Pier. He told me she was virginal. Paul could be so innocent. She wasn't virginal at all."

She had told Mayo that when she was fifteen, she'd been raped by an American soldier. A year later, she accused Marlon Brando of forcibly "deflowering her."

She had originally been discovered in Italy, by the director and actor, Vittorio De Sica. That led to her casting as his co-star in her first film, *Domani A troppo tardi.* "The moment I saw her, I knew I wanted her as my co-star," De Sica said. "That fragile body...That sensitive face..."

Their director was Leonide Moguy, who also cast her in her second picture, *Domani A un altro giorno (Tomorrow is another day).*

De Sica wanted to make a film co-starring Marlon Brando and Pier. Brando was in Rome at the time. He brought them together, and Brando invited Pier, then known as Anna Maria Pierangeli, on a date. Details are sparse, but Pier always claimed that Brando raped her after they made a nighttime visit to the Roman Colosseum. He asked to see it from the grassy knoll above. There, he forced himself on her. Despite her resistance, she was no match for his brute force. In tears, she later reported the incident to Da Sica.

***

Even though she'd made off with Eddie Fisher, Debbie Reynolds had become Pier's best friend and *confidante*. One afternoon, Pier phoned her: "Can you just imagine what is happening to me? I'm doing a balancing act, dating Jimmy Dean and Paul Newman, the two handsomest men in Hollywood."

"Lucky you," Reynolds reportedly said. "And I'm stuck with this Fisher guy, who seems to spend more time with Mike Todd than with

Pier Angeli with Paul Newman in a publicity shot for *Somebody Up There Likes Me.*

me."

Pier invited Newman to her home for Sunday dinner, where he met the formidable Enrica, who quickly ascertained that he was not a Catholic. Even worse, "Jew blood flows in his veins. I forbid you to see him again except for on the movie set."

"Paul's romance with Pier was relatively harmless," Mayo said. "Just two kids having fun. He soon returned to reality. After all, he had a wife and kids back on the East Coast, and was talking about getting a divorce so he could marry Joanne Woodward. Actually, I think he was relieved that Jimmy came onto the scene to take Pier away from him. And, since this is crazy Hollywood, the picture, of course, got more complicated. He was also slipping around and seeing Dean on the side."

The first time Jimmy had lunch alone with Pier, he invited Newman to join them, but he declined.

"I was shocked," Jimmy said. "Pier ordered a raw hamburger and two raw eggs. For her drink of choice, a glass filled with water. No wonder she was so little and petite. I'm short, but I towered over her. I don't think she was more than five feet, if that."

That night, Jimmy was introduced to Pier's twin, Marisa Pavan, who was also an actress. "There was strong sibling rivalry there," he said. "I mean, both of them were beautiful,

Two views of Marisa Pavan in Tennessee Williams' *The Rose Tattoo*. *Top photo*: With Ben Cooper, and *lower photo*, a "mother/daughter" shot with *La Lupa*, Anna Magnani.

Competition and rivalries for both romance and acting roles with her sister, Pier Angeli, was intense.

had the same look, though not identical twins. Ironically, at the time, Marisa was dating Vic Damone, who would, within weeks, marry Pier."

Pavan's breakthrough role came in Tennessee Williams' *The Rose Tattoo* (1955), in which she was cast as Anna Magnani's daughter. The role had first been offered to Pier, who was not available.

Pavan later received an Oscar nomination as Best Supporting Actress, but lost to Jo Van Fleet, who had played Jimmy's whorish mother in *East of Eden*.

[In 1956, a year after Jimmy died, Pavan married the French actor, JeanA Pierre Aumont, the former lover of Grace Kelly. (As Jimmy himself admitted from personal experience, ºGrace Kelly is a tough act to follow.º) Pavan was

still married to Aumont at the time of his death in 2001.]

Pavan was not charmed by Jimmy's *bragA gadocio,* as she phrased it. "He was rude to our mother. He'd just walk into our home without saying anything and put on our record player, playing the music really loud. When I pointed out the weakness of his film, *East of Eden,* he took grave offense. He couldn't stand criticism, and he screamed at me, calling me names."

As the days went by, the press wrote more and more about Jimmy's romance with Pier, which was still flourishing, even though both her sister and mother detested him.

"Jimmy is different," Pier told a reporter. "He loves music. He loves it from the heart the way I do. We have much to talk about. "It's wonderful to know such an understanding man."

Jean-Pierre Aumont in
The Cross of Lorraine (1943)
an MGM wartime film about the escape of French fighters from a Nazi prison camp.

Most of Jimmy's discarded gay lovers viewed the romance cynically. John Kerr told friends, "I'm sure their relationship is platonic, knowing Jimmy as I once did. He's dating Pier just to cover up his homosexuality."

Reporters continued to besiege Jimmy with questions about his possible engagement. He shrugged off such queries. "Who knows? Nothing compli-cated, just a nice girl for a change. I mean, you know, I can talk to her. She un-derstands. Nothing messy. Just an easy kind of friendly thing. I respect her. She's untouchable. We're members of totally different castes. She's the kind of girl you put on the shelf and look at. Anyway, her old lady doesn't like me. Can't say I blame her."

Slowly, Jimmy began to introduce Pier to his friends, including Gene Owen. She had taught acting when he was enrolled in Santa Monica College. "One Sunday, Jimmy and Pier arrived at our house as my husband and I were pack-ing to go to Europe. Pier urged us to include Italy in our itinerary. As soon as possible, she wanted to show Italy to Jimmy. She seemed to be deeply in love with him and he with her. I thought it was a solid romance."

Pier often spoke to him about her homeland and the deprivations her fam-ily had known in Rome after moving there from her native Sardinia. In Italy, she'd been known as Anna Maria Pierangeli.

De Sica introduced her to producer Fred Zinnemann, who had cast her in her first American film, *Teresa* (1951), with John Ericson and Rod Steiger, Jimmy's friend.

The screenwriter was Steward Stern, who would soon become a friend of

Jimmy's on the set of *Rebel Without a Cause.* He was a tall, dark, and sensitive man, a young cousin of Arthur M. Loew, Sr., president of Loew's International, the parent company of MGM.

In time, Stern also introduced the cinema heir, Arthur Loew, Jr., to both Marisa and Pier. "My relative was a real swinger, and I didn't want him to corrupt either of these girls."

As Sheilah Graham would later say, but couldn't put in her column, "Only in Hollywood, kids. After young Arthur had this widely publicized affair with Elizabeth Taylor, he took up with Pier Angeli. When Pier was out of the country, Marisa Pavan started to date him. He then got involved with the singer Eartha Kitt, but his family objected to the interracial aspects of that liaison. Guess what became unbelievable? After Arthur dumped Eartha, he shacked up with Jimmy Dean. As I said, 'Only in Hollywood, kids.'"

Meeting his friend, William Bast, Jimmy was asked, "Just what is going on here between you and Pier? I hear so many conflicting stories."

"You read too many gossip columns," Jimmy said. "Nothing is going on, absolutely nothing. What have you become? A stringer for Hedda Hopper? OK, if you must know, Pier and I are just fooling around. Nothing serious."

He did say, "She has the face of a Madonna in a Florentine fresco, not that I've ever seen a Florentine fresco except in a book. She dresses like an Italian princess. Her eagle-eyed mother detests me. She thinks I'm scruffy, a non-Catholic, and too crude for her immaculate daughter."

Jimmy might have accused Bast of reading too many gossip columns, but he read a few of them himself. "I learned more about Pier in the gossip columns that I did from her. As a protective mother, Enrica failed completely. Pier's been linked to too many men. Only the other day, I read she'd had this thing, perhaps a one-night stand, with Prince Mahmud Pahlavi, the brother of the Shah of Iran."

Helena Sorell, Pier's close friend, had been skeptical of the Angeli/Dean coupling since its debut. "Pier would flirt outrageously with any man in sight, even the waiter. If all the attention was not on Jimmy, he would pout worse than a small child."

One day on the Warner lot, Pier encountered Humphrey Bogart, who'd heard that she was dating Jimmy. "Why don't you suggest to your boyfriend that he take a bath once in a blue moon?" He then walked on.

During the filming of *East of Eden,* Jimmy told his co-star, Richard Davalos, "For better or worse, I intend to spend the rest of my life with Pier. We're going to buy a mansion in Beverly Hills and fill it with ten *bambini.* We'll have our honeymoon in Rome, where Pier claims she can arrange a visit with the pope. She wants me to become a Catholic."

On one occasion, he took Pier to meet his father, Winton, and his stepmother. For about an hour, the quartet sat together in the Dean living room, mostly in awkward and painful silence, although Winton asked his son how his front teeth were holding up.

When the deadly stillness of that hot summer afternoon in California became overbearing, Jimmy reached for Pier's hand. After a quick goodbye, he headed out the door, never to return.

A few weeks before her own death, Pier delivered a statement to the *National Enquirer* about that summer's involvement with Jimmy:

> *ªWe used to go to the California coast and stay there secretly in a cottage on a beach far away from all the prying eyes. We'd spend much of our time on the beach, sitting there or fooling around just like college kids. We would talk about ourselves and our problems, about the movies and acting, about life and life after death¼ We had a complete underA standing of each other¼Sometimes, we would just drive along and stop at a hamburger stand for a meal or go to a driveAn movie. It was all so innocent and so emphatic.º*

Nicholas Ray, director of *Rebel Without a Cause,* was fully aware of Jimmy's involvement with Pier. He said, "He is intensely determined not to love or be loved. He was fascinated, absorbed at times, with anything new— be it beautiful, bizarre, perverted or not so perverted, whatever. If a woman thought she was the only one in his life, she soon found out differently. He also had many men and women fall in love with him, including one of the most notorious homosexuals in Hollywood."

Ray refused to name the culprit, but actress Betsy Palmer, who once had a brief fling with Jimmy, thought she knew the answer.

"It was Liberace. I was with Jimmy one night when a call came in from Liberace in Las Vegas. He offered to give Jimmy $1,000 plus a round-trip, first-class ticket if he'd fly to join him in Las Vegas. He told Jimmy he'd already seduced Rock Hudson, and that he wanted him to be next. Later, Jimmy told me that Liberace wanted to go to bed with him even more than he wanted to go to bed with Brando, and that he then claimed, 'I'll get that one, too.'"

It is assumed that Jimmy never accepted Liberace's offer. Perhaps he would have back during his hustling days.

In a memoir, John Gilmore quoted one of Jimmy's observations about Pier. "She'd corner me with her dumb preoccupations because we'd just fucked. I thought I'd chase her away with what she said was my 'volcano of need,' but I'll tell you this—Miss Pizza's the one you can call a volcano—but there's no hot lava shooting out of her."

At the time that he was supposed to be having this torrid love affair with Pier, Jimmy showed up in Palm Desert at the vacation home shared by Tab Hunter and Jimmy's agent, Dick Clayton.

"Jimmy arrived in his new Porsche Spyder," Gilmore said. "He had this blonde pinup with him, some foreign starlet. He told everybody he didn't plan to spend the night."

"We don't have anything to talk about," Jimmy said, in reference to the starlet, "but she gives a great blowjob. My cock can go all the way into her empty head."

Some of the gossips who had promoted the so-called passionate romance of "Romeo and Juliet" began to have their doubts. It was even suggested that the "lovebirds" had an open relationship.

Pier was spotted showing up, alone, at the opening of singer Tony Martin at Ciro's, in Los Angeles. Before the evening was over, she was sitting and holding hands with another singer, Dean Martin, who, for some reason, had also arrived alone.

At seven o'clock the following morning, a doorman at Martin's hotel spotted Pier leaving his suite.

When she arrived back at her home, Enrica accepted her explanation that she'd been overly tired and had fallen asleep in her dressing room.

The following Saturday night, she went out with Jimmy, who did not return her until 4AM. Enrica was waiting with fury at the door, where she denounced Jimmy. "No decent Italian boyfriend would bring home a young girl at this hour."

"When in Rome, do as the Romans do," Jimmy told her. "Welcome to Hollywood. Here, we're lucky to bring a girl home before the sun comes up."

He later told Elia Kazan, "Nothing tastes better than forbidden fruit. Didn't Eve offer Adam some kind of fruit? An apple, I heard? But more likely it was a pomegranate, the ripest fruit growing in the Garden of Eden. It's juicier than an apple."

That afternoon, Enrica demanded and was granted an audience with Jack Warner. Not only had Jimmy brought her daughter home right before dawn, but during their long date, she had discovered a diaphragm in her daughter's bedroom.

"Pier is going to be a big star, and I don't want her life ruined by this Dean fellow. I want you to demand that he never see Pier again."

The following morning, Jimmy was summoned into Warner's office. "I want you to stop fucking that Italian broad or else I'll fire you from *East of Eden*. I even heard you're thinking of marrying her."

"Don't worry your pretty head about that," Jimmy told the studio mogul. "Signora Pierangeli wouldn't let me marry her precious daughter even if I were the pope."

For the next four days, Pier did not see Jimmy. During that interim, she was spotted at the Captain's Table, a Hollywood restaurant, dining with Donald O'Connor, who had recently made *Singin' in the Rain* (1952) with Gene

Kelly and Debbie Reynolds.

Columnist Mike Connolly spotted the odd couple, and wrote, "O'Connor was very quiet and very attentive to Angeli at a table in the darkest corner of the restaurant."

Hedda Hopper also spotted them yet another of their outings: "I have rarely seen a cuter couple than Donald O'Connor and Pier Angeli," she wrote in her column.

As it turned out, Jimmy was not alone during his exile from Pier. He was seen dating this curvy redhead, an extra from the set of *The Silver Chalice*. She had been "servicing" Paul Newman, who, wanting to get rid of her, had passed her on to Jimmy.

"Jane Doe *[not her real name, of course, but she didn't want her identity revealed]* said, "How many gals can say that they've been fucked by both Paul Newman and James Dean? Perhaps a few—Marilyn Monroe, for instance."

"Having had shack-ups with Scott Brady and Fernando Lamas," she continued, "I've known better-endowed men. But Newman and Dean were more than adequate for the job. But on that same set, I met my future husband, a cameraman. He's got them all beat, and we have three sons to prove it. I named them Paul, James, and Scott."

When Jimmy reunited with Pier, he said, "It was more exciting than ever because we had to slip around and see each other in offbeat joints. It became a joke with us, a sort of game, exciting because everybody thought we'd stopped seeing each other."

Pier was more serious, claiming, "He wanted me to love him unconditionally. But he wasn't able to love someone in return, that is, with any deep feeling for the other person. He wanted to be the beloved. He was a troubled boy who wanted to be loved very badly. I loved him as I had never loved anyone else in my life. I could not give him the enormous amount that he needed. It emptied me. There was no other way to be with Jimmy, except to love him and be emptied myself."

***

When *East of Eden* was wrapped in August of 1954, Jimmy told Pier good-bye and flew to New York where his agent, Jane Deacy, had arranged for him to star in *The Unlighted Road.* He had pleaded with Pier to accompany him, but she refused. Their relationship was beginning to fall apart.

Jimmy's composer friend, Leonard Rosenman, said, "Jimmy would get drunk on a couple of glasses of wine, and when he got loaded, he became very nasty, really mean. He underwent a complete personality change. I loved the guy, and I put up with it on many a night. But he had a real Dr. Jekyll and Mr.

Hyde personality. I mean, he'd get out of control. Often, he became vicious. Sometimes, he became violent and had a reputation for beating up his girlfriends. Perhaps he did this to Pier once too often. I think she had reached the point where she could take it no more."

"I don't mean to take up for Jimmy, but Pier was at fault, too," Rosenman said. "She wasn't some sweet hothouse flower, She had a very gloomy, dark side to her, and Jimmy told me about this. She also suffered great mental anguish and had a streak of cruelty.":

"Perhaps Jimmy did love her, but she'd go and flaunt affairs with other men, throwing them in his face. Many men, not just Jimmy, beat up their girlfriends or wives. I'm not forgiving Jimmy or any other men. These two volatile human beings would in the end kill themselves, Pier by descending into heavy drug abuse which led to her suicide."

During a reunion with Deacy, Jimmy told her that he was considering marrying Pier.

She urged him not to. "Do you want to be forever known as Mr. Pier Angeli? Surely, you don't want that."

He became cross with her. "Are you saying that you think her career will overpower my own? Thanks a lot."

"I hear she's always trying to control you," Deacy said. "Dick Clayton keeps me informed. And do you really want Enrica Pierangeli for a mother-in-law? Dick also told me that Pier wants you to become a Catholic. She's even got you wearing dark suits, white shirts, and a tie!"

Deacy had arranged for Jimmy to star in *The Unlighted Road* for the *Schlitz Playhouse of Stars.* Although he didn't know it at the time, this half-hour thriller, aired on May 6, 1955, would be his last television film.

His co-star was a pretty starlet, Pat Hardy, with whom he launched an affair. In another irony, she had been having an affair with Vic Damone.

One reporter picked up on this. "James Dean, the boy who was cooing it up with Pier Angeli before she switched to Vic Damone, has been seeing Pat Hardy, the girl who was mighty cozy with Vic until Pier came along. Sort of a change-partners deal."

There was another irony that the journalist didn't know about at the time. When she wasn't dating Jimmy or Damone, Hardy was also conducting an off-the-record affair with Marlon Brando.

Before he'd been drafted into the Army, Damone had sustained an affair with Elizabeth Taylor. In her column, Hedda Hopper had written: "Fickle Elizabeth Taylor has fallen in love again, this time with a handsome young crooner, Vic Damone, who is giving Frank Sinatra's fading career a push toward oblivion." *[Sinatra, of course, was furious.]*

"Vic was adorable," Elizabeth later said. "A dear man, but he was drafted, and I'm not the kind of woman who waits around."

[Born in Brooklyn in 1928, Vito Rocco Farinola, known for his melodic lyriA cism and impeccable enunciations, was three years older than Jimmy. As Vic Damone, he became a household word in America, singing such hits as ºMy Heart Cries for You,º and ºOn the Street Where You Live,º from My Fair Lady.

He became a serious rival of Sinatra, who very generously said, ºDamone has the best set of pipes in the business.º]

On the very day Jimmy flew to New York, Pier had a reunion with Damone at Warners. They'd had a brief romance before.

Ironically, she'd not yet run into him in Hollywood, even though her twin sister, Marisa Pavan, had been recently dating Damone too.

Pier and Damone had met in 1952 when she was in Munich filming *The Devil Makes Three.* At the time, he was stationed nearby with the U.S. Army, and he'd called Pier, asking her to appear as one of the players in a show he was producing for the servicemen at the base.

She agreed to make an appearance. Three days later, on stage, he was singing "September Song" to her, which led to their "heavy dating" for two months.

As she later admitted, "We danced a lot, had long talks, and enjoyed a lot of fun together. I had this electric sensation when I was around him. He was so cute, so very cute. But eventually, we went our separate ways. I had meant to call him until I heard Marisa may have been hot for him."

After having a drink with Damone, and reminiscing about their time together in Germany, Pier met him again at a Hollywood party that same evening. The next thing he knew, he was dining at the Pierangeli's family table presided over by Enrica.

When Marisa was confronted with Damone, her former date, being welcomed into her family circle as an escort for her sister, she had yet another reason to be jealous of her twin.

Enrica doted on Damone, finding him, "so handsome, so talented—I love his voice—so Italian, so respectable, and so Catholic."

She later told Pier, "and so heterosexual. Not a pervert like some of your other dates."

Before proposing marriage to Pier, Damone had not only very recently dated Marisa, but also Pier's major rival on the screen, the singing sensation Anna Maria Alberghetti. Anna was also dating Eddie Fisher when Pier wasn't out with him.

Damone was also seen out with Mona Freeman; Frank Sinatra's daughter, Nancy (Frank didn't like that); Maureen O'Hara (when she wasn't making a pirate film); Judy Spreckles; Sheela Fenton; and Joan Tyler.

Then, amid a flurry of tabloid speculation about Damone and his entanglements with Pier, Marisa, Anna Maria Alberghetti, and others of the women listed above, reports appeared that Damone was about to fly to New York with either Pat Hardy or Joan Tyler (claims differed), where they would announce their engagement. "Joan (Tyler) and I have kissed and made up," Damone told *Variety.*

Vic Damone...Stealing Frank Sinatra's fans and James Dean's girlfriend.

Then, within the week, Damone's engagement to Pier was announced.

Two days later, in New York, Jimmy read about Pier's engagement to Damone in Dorothy Kilgallen's newspaper column. He made no attempt to call her or to confront her.

Later, after Jimmy's return to Los Angeles, he phoned Pier, who agreed to meet with him. He later told Rosenman what happened: "She claimed Enrica was forcing her to marry Damone," Jimmy said. "But Damone wasn't the reason I beat the shit out of her that night. I found out that while I was in New York, she'd been fucking with Brando. I know Brando likes exotic foreign women, but I knew that he was fucking Pier only because I told him I was in love with her. Sometimes a gal can look so goddamn '*angeli*'—pardon the pun—and be nothing but a tramp."

"When Damone strips her down to fuck her, he'll discover she's black and blue. She'll probably tell him that a mad dog attacked her. Actually, I'm not a mad dog, but one cool cat. But if you get me riled up, watch out! I go from cool cat to Tigerman."

Enrica also reported that Jimmy—pumped up on liquor, pot, and amphetamines—sometimes struck Pier in anger. Even his friends used the words "erratic", "intense", and "impulsive" to describe him.

"I'm a serious-minded and intense little devil," Jimmy admitted. "I don't see how people can stay in the same room with me. I know I couldn't tolerate myself in the same room."

That confession was made to Elia Kazan.

Jimmy also told Rosenman, "I was shocked when I read about her engagement to Damone. I didn't see it coming. I figured that her family and friends got to her and changed her mind about me. Maybe she liked his singing better than mine."

Before the wedding, at the Villa Capri, Jimmy and Damone confronted one another. Jimmy was dining there with his new friend, Lew Bracker.

Recognizing Jimmy at a nearby table, the singer got up and made his way over to where Jimmy was sitting, extending his hand.

Jimmy refused it, just staring at him. "You may be marrying Pier," he said, "but she isn't yours. Never was, never will be."

Damone took a swing at Jimmy, but a waiter restrained him. Jimmy and Bracker got up and quickly left the restaurant.

Jimmy would meet Damone once again, months after the wedding, again at the Villa Capri.

***

When Jimmy escorted Terry Moore to the premiere of *Sabrina,* it led to press speculation about a break-up with Pier. Louella Parsons rushed into print, calling Jimmy's romance with Pier "as cold as an ice cube in Greenland."

Reporter Kendis Rochlen called Pier, asking if she and Jimmy had had a tiff.

"I was just too tired to go to the premiere," she claimed. "They're always such big productions, and I'd rather see the picture a few days later, when I can relax and eat popcorn. I've been terribly busy with dancing lessons and costume fittings for *Green Mansions.º*

[Pier never appeared in Green Mansions. *MGM decided to shelve it until 1958, when Mel Ferrer directed Tony Perkins, with Audrey Hepburn cast into the role originally slated for Pier.]*

Jimmy's last public outing with Pier was on September 29, 1954 at the world premiere of Judy Garland's "comeback picture," *A Star is Born.* Photographers were in a frenzy snapping their picture. Jimmy looked discontented, as if he wanted to escape the gala.

[It can be assumed that he didn't tell Pier that he'd previously been sexuA ally intimate with Garland.]

One reporter spotted Jimmy and Pier talking in a corner of the lobby with Clark Gable and Marlene Dietrich, who were apparently waiting for their respective companions to emerge from the toilets. Eavesdropping, the reporter heard Gable tell Dietrich, "Why, with my track record, haven't I gotten around to you yet?"

Pushed aside in the crowd, the reporter didn't hear Dietrich's response.

***

At St. Timothy's Catholic Church, on November 24, 1954, Pier and Vic Damone were married.

[Ironically, this would be the same church where seventeen years later, Pier would be buried after committing suicide by overdosing on sleeping pills.]

Some six-hundred star-studded guests showed up for the ceremony, in-

560

cluding her best friend, Debbie Reynolds. Other celebrities included Ann Blyth, Jack Benny (who had once seduced Jimmy), Cyd Charisse, Danny Thomas, and tap-dancing Ann Miller. Since Pier's father was dead, E.J. Mannix, president of MGM, gave the bride away.

A legend still persists that Jimmy, wearing a black leather jacket, was spotted across the street, astride his Harley-Davidson, as confetti rained down on the newlyweds as they emerged from the church. As photographers snapped away, the roar of the motorcycle engine could be heard by members of the wedding party.

As one reporter wrote, "Jimmy, looking like Marlon Brando in *The Wild One*, roared down the street and out of Pier's life forever."

Parts of that statement might not have been true.

Jimmy later told William Bast, "That wasn't me. As a bizarre joke, I hired someone to impersonate me, knowing that at that distance, no one could make out my face behind those goggles. Shame on you, Willie, for thinking I'd be so dumb, actually showing up myself. Surely you don't think I'm that dumb."

"Well, the rest of the world was taken in," Bast responded.

There was at least one eyewitness who claimed that Jimmy and Pier continued to see each other after the wedding. Joe Hyams, in his book, *Mislaid in Hollywood,* spotted Pier speeding past after leaving Jimmy's house when he was on the way there to interview him.

After Jimmy let him in, he found the actor looking distraught. "It's already done," he admitted in a choked voice. "Pier's going to have a baby. My kid. She was already pregnant with my baby when she stood on the altar exchanging wedding vows with Damone."

"I just sat there, not knowing what to say," Hyams said. "Jimmy started to cry. I held him in my arms. I hadn't held a man in my arms since the war."

Stanley Haggart continued to see Jimmy at his Laurel Canyon home. "He would often drop in. Sometimes, he'd be with a man, at other times, a woman. He never brought Pier by. He and some guy would go for a nude swim in the pool and later stay overnight in my little guest cottage."

"One night was different from the others," Haggart said.

Jimmy told him, "Pier's having a baby. It's my kid. I went out and bought some baby

"Marriage, Italian Style," as interpreted by Hollywood. Pier Angeli at her wedding to Vic Damone

clothes. Since I don't know its gender, I bought some blue duds for the boy, pink for the girl. If it's a girl, I want her named Mildred after my mother."

Jimmy, in a different mood, told John Gilmore, his friend, "I'm just putting on some broken heart act. Hell, Pier's screwed half the men in Hollywood. I should have figured she'd end up marrying some joker like Damone. Actually, he's sorta cute. I might fuck him myself one night if I'm horny enough."

"Fuck them both?" Jimmy said. "Who needs them? You find people who nobody need, and in a flash, they find each other."

When Jimmy encountered columnist Kendis Rochlen, he said, "Who gives a shit? I know how you can cure her from her new groom. Lock her up in a room with five-and-dime pictures of Damone plastered on all the walls. She'll break down the door and flee in horror."

Obviously Rochlen couldn't print his Damone's reaction, if she bothered to ask him for one.

Cal York wrote, "Jimmy makes no secret of the fact that he still hankers for angelic Miss Pizza, as he calls Pier."

"You might say I'm not exactly delighted that she married Vic," Jimmy said. "I've been dating Pat Hardy, and I'd say she seems a little hurt. My current girlfriend thought Damone was going to marry her. They were practically engaged."

In 1958, having realized that both Damone and Jimmy had moved on to other women, Hardy married actor Richard Egan. He is remembered today for appearing on screen with Elvis Presley in that singer's debut film, *Love Me Tender* (1956).

Jimmy told another reporter, "I've got this new girl in my life. It's a fast new Porsche Spyder Speedstar convertible."

***

On April 15, 1955, Jim and Lew Bracker were dining together once again at Villa Capri when Damone entered the restaurant. Their previous encounter had turned violent.

But this time, Damone seemed jubilant and conciliatory. Within minutes, he showed up at Jimmy's table with a bottle of champagne and three glasses. "I'm a father. I was hoping you'd drink a toast to my son."

Perry Damone, named after Perry Como, had entered the world on July 21, only eight months after Pier's marriage. Delivered by Caesarian section, he weighted eight pounds, thirteen ounces.

[Perry Damone, also known as Perry Farinola, died of lymphoma in 2014 after a successful career as a top-ranking radio broadcaster for the Phoenix, Arizona-based radio station 99.9 KEZ.]

With a smirk on his face, Jimmy said, "That's one kid I can definitely drink to."

After the toast, Damone moved on, never to see Jimmy again.

Bracker said, "I did not then, nor did I ever, ask Jimmy what he was intimating by his toast. But I drew my own conclusions."

According to Joe Hyams, Damone, two days later, had lunch with a former girlfriend and allegedly told her, "Pier's a mother all right. But it's not certain that I'm the father."

***

As many Hollywood insiders had predicted, Pier's marriage to Damone did not work out. They divorced in 1958. What followed was a series of bitter custody battles over their son, Perry, that would not be settled until 1965, when Pier got part-time custody.

She would marry musician Armando Trovajoli on February 14, 1962, that union lasting four years.

After his divorce, Damone would marry four more times, one of them an interracial union with singer Diahann Carroll.

An aging Damone entered into his final marriage in 1998 to fashion designer Rena Rowan. Although his first wife, Pier, had died penniless, Damone's current wife, in poor health after suffering a stroke in 2011, has an estate currently valued at $50 million.

Pier spent the final years of her life mostly wandering in Europe looking for work. Slowly, she descended into a twilight of drugs and alcohol. Another of Jimmy's girlfriends, Susan Strasberg, met with her in Rome, finding her "still beautiful, even with heavy makeup, although it didn't cover the strain of her features."

Arriving back in Hollywood, she had no money left. She moved in with her longtime friend, Helena Sorell, at 355 South McCarty Drive in Los Angeles.

She'd just been featured in *Addio Alexandra (1969)* an X-rated, English-language comedy filmed in Italy and released in the U.S. as *Love Me, Love My Wife.*

Desperate for some sort of comeback, she went to see her former lover, Marlon Brando, asking him to use his influence to get her cast as one of the wives of a Mafia don in his upcoming film, *The Godfather (1972).* He dismissed her, telling her he had no control over casting.

Pier was most candid in her final interview, telling the *National Enquirer:*

⁹Jimmy was the only man I've ever loved as deeply as a woman can love a man. I never loved either of my husbands the way I loved Jimmy. I tried to love my husbands, but it never lasted. I would wake up at night and find I had been dreaming about Jimmy. I would lie

Her former movie career but a memory, Pier died on September 10, 1971. Helena Sorrel found her dead in her apartment, where she'd consumed an overdose of phenobarbital. Pier Angeli was thirty-nine years old.

Jimmy's Affair With Ursula Andress

THE "BERNESE OBERLAND BEAUTY" WHO LATER BECAME FAMOUS AS THE LOVE OBJECT OF JAMES BOND, "007"

After his star-crossed affair with Pier Angeli, Jimmy began dating Ursula Andress, a Swiss-born actress newly arrived in Hollywood and hailed as "the female Marlon Brando." She was struggling to learn English, with some vague hope of making it as a Hollywood star. She had beauty and the physical assets, but lacked talent and never seemed to work hard to master the King's English.

Ursula became friendly with Dick Clayton, Jimmy's agent, who later said to Jimmy, "Ursula is going to be the screen's next Marlene Dietrich. Marlene's getting a bit long in the tooth."

An Ursula-with-Jimmy date was arranged.

She remembered it later: "He came by my house an hour late. He came in room like wild animal and smell of everything I don't like. He stalk through my house, then sit down like an animal. He just sat there and said nothing. When we did start to talk, we got into an argument about music. I knew then I had become an American. No European woman would argue with a man."

He took her to a jazz club on the Sunset Strip, where he sat with her for only about fifteen minutes. "He get up from table and play bongo drums with the band. I sat there an hour, got up, and went home. He came by an hour later. Ask me if I want to see motorcycle. We sit on sidewalk in front of this motorcycle and talk and talk and talk until 5AM. Then he get up and go home. No kiss."

Soon, she was seen riding around Hollywood on the back of his motorcycle. She was also spotted in fast-moving cars driven by him—in fact, she was with him on the day he purchased his silver Porsche that would cost him his life.

"I didn't know it at the time, but Jimmy was buying his coffin."

"I once ask Jimmy why he drives so fast," she said. "He told me, 'I've got to, since I'm not going to be around much longer.'"

"What does that mean?" she asked. "'You plan to commit suicide?' He said nothing."

"I go out with him, but we fight like cat and dog—no, two monsters," she said. "But we make up and have fun."

"Ursula has a mind of her own," Jimmy told Clayton. "She doesn't depend on a man to form an opinion."

When Jimmy met Ursula, she was only nineteen years old and had been imported from Europe after executives at Para-

Ursula Andress in *Dr. No* (1962)...Venus emerging from the ocean.

mount had become impressed with her beauty and presence during previews of the Italian film *The Loves of Casanova (1955),* originally released in Italy as *Le avventure di Giacomo Casanova.*

Instead of calling her "the female Marlon Brando," another reporter dubbed her "the female James Dean."

"She looked more like Brando than me," Jimmy said to Clayton. "Especially with that short, cropped hairdo and her pouting lips."

In contrast, composer Leonard Rosenman was struck by how much Ursula resembled Jimmy. "I came to believe that Jimmy's relationship with her was essentially narcissistic for both of them."

Jimmy later told Clayton, "Ursula is a real free spirt, she survives on almost no sleep. After a night out with her, I need matchsticks to prop my eyes open."

One night, having arrived to pick her up for a date, he immediately sensed her anxiety. "Oh, Jimmy, Jimmy," she said. "I make big mistake. I'm rushing to get ready. I made date with another man. He's waiting for me outside in this old, horrible car."

Jimmy looked outside her window, noticing a car parked under a streetlight. He recognized that "piece of junk" right away. "Could your date be Howard Hughes?" he asked.

"Jimmy, how did you know?"

"Never mind," he answered. He had no intention of telling Ursula that he and Hughes, and not that long ago, had been lovers.

She suggested to Jimmy that he join them for a night out on the town. For some perverse reason of his own, he happily agreed that it would be a fine idea.

Out on the sidewalk, she introduced Jimmy to Hughes, who did not acknowledge that he already knew him. "Pile into the front seat," he told Ursula.

She sat in the middle, with Jimmy on her right, while a stone-faced Hughes headed toward Malibu, where it had been prearranged that he'd take her to dinner.

Stopping at a traffic light on Santa Monica Boulevard, near a gas station, Hughes told Jimmy that he didn't have any cigarettes, and asked him if he'd go to the gas station and purchase a package for him from a vending machine.

Obediently, Jimmy got out of the car and walked toward the station. Midway there, he looked back. The traffic light had turned green. Hughes stepped on the gas and disappeared, with Ursula, into the night.

"That was the last I ever saw of the elusive Mr. Hughes, Jimmy told Clayton. I guess he has Robert Francis to play with instead."

* * *

Ursula and Jimmy spent time within his rental home, for which he paid $250 a month. He'd rented it from Nikko Romannhos, the *maître d'* at the Villa Capri.

In Sherman Oaks, the A-frame cottage resembled a modernized replica of a Bavarian hunting lodge. Downstairs was a seven-foot stone fireplace. Above it, configured as a kind of balcony, was a sleeping alcove. To reach it, Ursula and Jimmy had to climb a wooden ladder and pass through a trap door.

Sometimes, he took her to Villa Capri, where she always ordered a steak. He complained that she was driving him into bankruptcy. "Can't you settle for spaghetti and meatballs?"

The next week, he flew to Texas for the filming of scenes from his third and final picture, *Giant.* She suspected that while there, he'd be making love to both Rock Hudson and Elizabeth Taylor.

When the picture wrapped, he returned to Hollywood and to Ursula. But the relationship wasn't the same as it had been before.

"I tried to love him," she later said, "but it didn't work out. I was not ready for marriage to him, as he was too unstable. While he was away, I fell in love with this American Adonis, John Derek, the most beautiful male animal in Hollywood. Everybody, both men and women, was after him, but he was mine. I had to tell Jimmy the truth."

Lew Bracker, his friend, recalled, "Jimmy didn't miss too much of a beat when Ursula switched to John Derek. He wasn't even out of sorts and certainly not heartbroken. I think Jimmy knew that a split would happen sooner or later. As I look back, Jimmy never mentioned Ursula to me ever again. It was a seamless change."

***

The next actress Jimmy introduced to Bracket was starlet Lori Nelson, who was also dating Tab Hunter. "Lori was very girlish, Bracker said. "she was sweet and vanilla—not what Jimmy was interested in. She was all over Jimmy, oohing and cooing and telling him about her doll collection, her cutesy bedroom with dolls all over the bed and all over the room. This kind of conversation made Jimmy cringe."

***

Jimmy would see Ursula for a final time right before his tragic death. He stopped by in his Porsche and asked her to go to Salinas with him for a car race.

She turned him down. "You arrive at bad moment. John Derek is due any minute. Better go. He might get jealous."

Despite all that, she noticed that Jimmy was waiting around, as if he wanted to encounter Derek. When he pulled up in his car, he acknowledged Jimmy and shook his hand. He was all smiles. The two men seemed to bond.

Jimmy invited Derek for a spin in his Porsche. To Ursula's amazement, Derek accepted. Jimmy wanted to show his rival his ersatz "hunting lodge."

Jimmy had hoped to meet Derek ever since director Nicholas Ray told him that he had campaigned for the role of Jim Starck in the upcoming *Rebel WithA out a Cause*. Ray had, in fact, discovered Derek and had cast him with Humphrey Bogart in *Knock on Any Door* (1949). In that film, Derek played a killer, Nick Romano, appropriately nicknamed "Pretty Boy."

En route to his pad, Jimmy learned that even though Derek was dating Ursula, he was married at the time to Pati Behs, a Russian-born *prima* ballerina. Derek told Jimmy that his wife had uncovered the affair and was threatening to bring legal action

John Derek as a fighting priest in *The Leather Saint* (1956). Paul Douglas was in that film and is on the left.

against Ursula. Since she had arrived in the U.S. with a work visa, a lawyer had informed Behs that her litigation, if filed, might lead to Ursula's deportation on a morals charge.

A Jimmy's "hunting lodge," the actors had a few beers and talked about Ray and Hollywood.

Derek confessed that he'd gotten his start in Hollywood first as a male hustler and then by "lying on the casting couch of Henry Willson. I'm sure you've heard of him."

"I've met the creep," Jimmy said, "Wanted to get in my pants."

"He wanted more that getting in my pants," Derek said. "He took them off time and time again, getting his go damn pound of flesh before giving me some breaks. My real name was Derek Harris, but the fucker wanted to re-name me Dare Harris."

Four or five years after Jimmy's death, Otto Preminger cast Derek and Jimmy's gay friend, Sal Mineo, together in *Exodus* (1960). Derek told Mineo what happened at that hunting lodge during the final hours of Jimmy's life. "I'm not sure why, but I did this impulsive thing," Derek confessed. "After a few beers, I needed to go to the john. After I took a piss, I stripped off all my clothes. With a semi-erection, I walked back into Jimmy's living room naked."

"From the look on his face, I knew he wanted me. He got down on his knees and paid homage, giving me this terrific blow-job. He didn't seem to want to get off after I exploded."

"I knew he was a better actor than I would ever be," Derek candidly admitted to Mineo. "By the time he was old and gray, he would probably have won eight Oscars. But for those minutes in that hunting lodge, I was king, and he was my sex slave. It was a great ego trip for me. Although I'd spend the rest of my life chasing after beautiful women, the sex was really good."

"As far as I know," Derek told Mineo, "I was the last person on earth Jimmy had sex with. He died very soon after I met him. I was very sorry, so very sorry, even though we were rivals. I hoped that I had given him some pleasure. I called our time together *A Kiss Before Dying*. I stole that title from another picture I desperately wanted to star in. But the part I wanted went to Robert Wagner."

Contacted by the *Hollywood Reporter* in the aftermath of Jimmy's death, Ursula said, "If I had not broken off with him, he would not have committed suicide in that car. I tried to understand him, but I just couldn't make it work. I'm so sorry about how things turned out. Without meaning to, I think I led him to his suicide. That car crash was no accident."

[Derek would later marry Ursula, divorce, her, and wed Linda Evans, diA vorce her, and finally settle down with Bo Derek.

After Derek, Ursula had an eightАyear affair with the French actor, JeanА

Paul Belmondo, an actor sometimes defined as ªThe James Dean of France.º That was followed by a longtime liaison with actor Harry Hamlin, with whom she had a son.

Along the way, Ursula attracted other men, including Warren Beatty, Ryan O'Neal, and Fabio Testi.

Jimmy never got to see Ursula become a household name. Dr. No, the first of the James Bond thrillers, contained what became an iconic clip of her emergA ing from the sea, clad in her soonAtoÆbe famous white bikini. Cast in the role of Honeychile Ryder, she brought a smoldering presence to the film, becoming an almost overnight legend.

Even though she was paid only ten thousand dollars for her contribution to the film, her performance helped launch the Bond movies as a Hollywood staple. She later sold the bikini at an auction for $61,500.]

"My Two Beautiful Lovers, Marilyn & Jimmy,
WERE RIGHT—LEAVE THE STAGE WHEN YOU'RE LOOKING GOOD."
Ð Marlon Brando

Marlon Brando remained a fixture in Jimmy's life right up until the end. In one of the astonishing secrets of Hollywood, at least some of their rivalry and/or bonding—at least for a while—revolved around the women they were dating, Pier Angeli and Ursula Andress.

FLASHBACK: In 1951, when Pier arrived seeking stardom in Hollywood, fresh and optimistic after her film successes in Italy, she retained traumatizing memories of Brando's brutal "date rape" of her in 1950 on that grassy knoll overlooking the Roman Colosseum.

In 1953, MBM executives were considering joining Brando and Pier together as a screen duo in two separate projects—first, Antony and Cleopatra, and later, Romeo and Juliet.

[Neither film was made, although Brando would eventually appear, withA out Pier, in Julius Caesar (1953).]

But while they were still being considered, Brando called Pier with the news. At first, based on her memories, she refused to speak to him until she learned that starring roles in at least one and possibly two screen projects were being dangled before them.

Reluctantly, she agreed to meet with him as he pleaded with her "to forgive me for my past transgressions." He blamed her for his assault on her, claiming that it was "because you looked so god damn beautiful."

Brando later described Pier as "a mixture of child, waif, and minx," despite her ill-fated romance with Kirk Douglas.

After that, Brando showed up at the Pierangeli house for dinner, and even asked Enrica's permission to date her daughter. The mother agreed, providing that her twin sister, Marisa, accompany them.

The next morning, Brando arrived at the Pierangeli household driving a large truck. Loaded with bales of hay, he had borrowed it from another film set. He'd come up with a gimmicky idea for a hayride and picnic beside an obscure lake he'd located on an old map of California.

Along for the ride was Rita Moreno, whom he was dating, dancer/choreographer Jerome Robbins, and Phil Rhodes, Brando's makeup man. Pier and Marisa joined in the picnic, riding in the back with the bales of hay.

As it turned out, Brando never found the lake. He later learned that it had dried up. Instead, he located an idyllic spot in the country, and the show business crowd enjoyed their picnic there, except for the ants, which decided to join in the fun.

Within the next few weeks, Brando became a fixture around the Pierangeli household until Enrica finally trusted him with the responsibility of escorting her precious Pier out on a date without a chaperone.

Enrica was clearly charmed by Brando, who was constantly praising her home-cooked pasta. "He is the son I never had," she said. "He's so full of love and compassion." Apparently, she never learned that he had raped Pier in Rome.

With Pier seated beside him, Brando drove around Hollywood in the bullet-riddled car that had belonged to Bugsy Siegel. Brando was considering playing the gangster in a biopic based on his life.

To the degree that Enrica approved of Brando, she passionately disapproved of Jimmy.

On the set of Pier's movie, *The Silver Chalice,* its star, Virginia Mayo, said, "I had several talks with Pier between takes. She viewed it as a feather in her cap to be dating the two bad boys of Hollywood, Jimmy and Marlon. In spite of their dubious sexuality, those guys were in great demand from both men and women. When they weren't fooling around with Ursula Andress or Pier, they were probably making it with each other."

Actor Sam Gillman, who lived in Brando's home for several months, later revealed a shocking incident that took place in the "love triangle" flourishing among Brando, Jimmy, and Pier.

"I was never quite sure what his motive was, but Marlon set up an incident one night to broaden Pier's awareness of what some men do," Gilman said. "If anything, that night shoved her into the arms of Vic Damone."

In a perverse move, Brando made dates with both Jimmy and Pier on the same night. Jimmy had been invited two hours before Pier's arrival. Brando called Pier and told her he'd hurt his leg and that, because he'd been immobilized, he wouldn't be able to answer his door. He asked her to enter through his garden and to walk through the French doors opening directly into his living room.

Jimmy showed up for his date with Brando, not knowing that Pier was expected later. When she arrived at eight o'clock, she navigated her way through his garden and then, as instructed, directly into his living room. There she confronted an orgiastic scene that must have sent shock waves through her.

"On the living room sofa, a nude Marlon and Dean were having a hot sixty-nine," Gilman said. "I was in another room that night, but I heard Pier scream. She raced out, through the garden and back to her car. Welcome to Hollywood, gal."

As he expected, Brando read press reports of Pier's eventual break with Jimmy. "They wrote such bullshit about the end of the romance of those two. Take that story about Jimmy waiting across the street on his motorcycle during Pier's wedding ceremony. What a piece of crap! While Pier was marrying that Sinatra clone, Jimmy was probably somewhere else taking it up the ass. I should know."

Gilmore summed it up: "Pier wanted Marlon's noble tool, Dean's pecker, and Damone's Italian sausage."

***

As if his conquest of Jimmy's territory with Pier weren't enough, Brando set out to date Ursula Andress too. "I think Marlon wanted to show Jimmy who *the man* really was," said Gilman.

At the time, Ursula was sharing an apartment with Josanne Berenger, whom Brando had declared as "my one true love." In spite of that ardent declaration, he began dating Ursula after she moved into her own vine-covered cottage overlooking Sunset Boulevard.

Still living with him at the time, Gilman said that Ursula was a true *femme fatale*. "If Josanne wanted to hold onto Marlon, she should not have introduced him to Ursula. No woman with a boyfriend should ever introduce him to this Swiss bombshell. What a hottie!"

"One night, when Marlon had too much to drink," Gilman continued, "he confessed to me his ambition: that involved marrying either Ursula or Pier. He'd take one for a wife, the other for his mistress."

He also confessed something else to Gilman: "I know that Dean really goes for Ursula and Pier, and that is precisely why I'm interested in them, too. I want to show him up. If I told either of them to get rid of Jimmy tomorrow, she would. I like playing the game of love—it's a lot of fun. Rita Moreno's in love with me, too, plus countless others."

"I don't know if Jimmy ever found out, but Marlon wanted a sworn statement from both of these gals that he was a better lover than Dean," Gilman said. "He told me that although Jimmy might handle Pier, he wasn't man enough to handle Ursula. Frankly—and don't tell him I said this—I think Marlon isn't man enough for Ursula, either."

When Kazan heard of these entangled and interconnected romantic liaisons, he expressed an opinion of his own, telling Tennessee Williams, "I think Dean is in love with Marlon, and that he's dating these gals just to show how macho he was. Frankly, at one point, Marlon was ready to dump Dean until he heard that he was dating Pier and later Ursula. That aroused Marlon's sense of competition. Perhaps he wants to pay Dean back for all that press he's generating as the next Marlon Brando."

"For some reasons, those two very competitive men seem to want to date the same women," Tennessee said. "I heard that both of them are also dating Katy Jurado when she's not otherwise occupied with Gary Cooper. Marlon told me that Jimmy doesn't just want to imitate him, 'he wants to be me.'"

Even when Marlon was out on a date—most often with a woman—Dean sometimes stalked his prey," Gilmore claimed. "On his motorcycle, Dean would follow Marlon and his date in their car. If they went, say, to a Mexican restaurant—Dean would go there and sit alone at another table, drinking Tequila sunrises while he studied them. I was living with Marlon at the time, and overheard Dean's calls to him at three or four o'clock in the morning."

"Marlon told me that one groggy night, he was parked at a lookout on Mulholland Drive, making out with Natalie Wood. Suddenly, Dean appeared at the car window, staring in at them. When Natalie screamed, he ran away. Marlon said, 'I wasn't as spooked as Natalie was. Knowing Dean, I realize it was harmless—he's got a crush on me and he wants to see what I'm up to. I understand that. Lovers all over the world do that. So I can't blame Jimmy. Once he got a taste of my noble tool, he wants to own it. But it belongs to me. Only I will decide where to put it.'"

One night when Jimmy came to visit Brando, he kept him entertained by what Gilmore called a series of puckish tricks. "Like a Houdini, he disappeared into the bathroom and locked the door from the inside. Then he escaped through the lone window, yet managed to re-lock it, from the outside, after his escape. Marlon rushed to the front door to answer the bell. Dean was standing THERE, on the stoop. Marlon could never figure out how he pulled off that stunt."

Sometimes, Dean would put both a cigarette and a lit match in his mouth and put his lips together. He'd then open his mouth and the cigarette would be lit. and the match would still be burning. "It was amazing," Gilman said. "It drove Marlon wild."

"Dean and Marlon shared one bad boy trait in common," Gilman said. "When either of them had to take a piss, they found the nearest wall and urinated to their heart's content, regardless of who was looking on. When a wall wasn't available, they used a fire hydrant or a tree, like a dog."

Brando had another close friend, Carlo Fiore, who was sometimes present during his interactions with Jimmy. Once, he overheard the younger actor's praise for Brando's performance in *The Men* (1950).

"You were terrific," Jimmy said. "I didn't know what acting was until I saw you in that picture. You conveyed much with minimalism. Suddenly, I knew how to do it. Through you, I learned to show anguish. Unlike Bette Davis, who's in constant motion, you taught me the power of stillness. The use of outward serenity to convey internal turmoil was in complete opposition to most screen acting until you came along. Even the tiny flicker in your face conveys something, an emotional byproduct, an unrealized dream, an unfulfilled passion. It wasn't until I saw you in *The Men* that I decided to become a serious actor. It was the greatest moment of revelation of my entire life."

Both Fiore and Gilman agreed that all these pronouncements from Jimmy "was a form of ass-kissing."

"I think there was also a lot of ass-kissing, or whatever, of another sort going on with him in Marlon's bedroom," Gilman said.

One night, Jimmy took Brando for a spin in a new Alfa Romeo. Brando returned home two hours later, his face white, telling Gilman, "I think he has a death wish. He drives like he wants to die and take me with him. If I ever get into a car with him again, I'm going to take the wheel. Behind the wheel of a car, Jimmy boy is absolutely fearless."

Brando then confused Gilman with yet another pronouncement about Jimmy: "He wants to be loved, but he doesn't." Gilman was left to ponder that for himself.

"Don't fall in love with me," Jimmy warned Brando one night in front of Gilman. "When emotional demands are made on me, I collapse."

"Don't worry your pretty head about that," Brando said. "At least, you've revealed to me how to get rid of you in case that's my desire in the future."

When Jimmy left that night, Brando told Gilman, "There's a toughness to Dean that's only pretend. Actually, he needs to be nursed like a baby. Sometimes, when he's in need of a mother, I let him suckle at my breasts."

***

Director Robert Wise, for a time, thought Brando, an amateur boxer, would be ideal in the story of middleweight champ, Rocky Graziano in *SomeA body Up There Likes Me.* Brando considered the offer, but later rejected it. Wise, with revisions, then offered the role to Jimmy, despite his observation that he didn't have the hardened physique of a boxer.

Jimmy seemed thrilled with the offer, and subsequently, Brando agreed to train and work out with him in the ring.

"Frankly, I thought Marlon threw some killer punches at the kid when he wanted to punish him," Gilman said. "There was this undercurrent of hostility between these two guys. It was definitely a love-hate relationship."

After Jimmy's death, Paul Newman was shoehorned into the role of Graziano for a 1956 release. In a touch of Hollywood irony, the picture starred four of the late Jimmy Dean's lovers: Paul Newman, Pier Angeli, Steve McQueen, and Sal Mineo.

***

After Jimmy's filming of *East of Eden,* he paid a surprise visit to the gallery of a sculptor in West Hollywood, Kenneth Kendall to admire a sculpted head whose look had been inspired by Brando. Kendall later revealed that Jimmy was so impressed with the sculpture of Brando that "he almost devoured it, fondling it, loving it. He was totally fascinated."

While at the gallery, Jimmy asked to see Kendall's photos of Brando. "He went through my files one by one. At the end, he was very hesitant, but managed to blurt out a request."

"Would you sculpt me like you did Brando?" he asked.

Jimmy had not made a good first impression on Kendall. He'd shown up at the gallery looking slovenly—"a real turn-off to me."

However, the sculptor changed his mind when he saw Jimmy's performance in *East of Eden.* He called Jimmy and asked him to pose for him, and Jimmy seemed delighted.

Kendall's sculpture of Jimmy was later placed in Griffith Park in Los Angeles. By that time, however, its subject was dead.

***

Sam Gilman claimed that Brando's affair with Jimmy continued until the young actor's death. So did their rivalry.

Midway into the shoot of *Giant,* director George Stevens generated a genuine hysteria in Jimmy when he informed him that he had originally offered the role of Jett Rink to Brando.

"First, it was Marlon who turned me down," Stevens said. "Then I offered it to Montgomery Clift. He turned me down too."

"Guess I'm left with sloppy seconds," Jimmy said. Before storming off the set in anger, he told Stevens, "Or should I say sloppy thirds?"

"Hudson and Dean were thick as thieves for a few weeks there," Gilman said. "Marlon found their affair amusing, warning me that their romance wouldn't last. 'Rock is too square for our boy pervert,' Brando said."

"During his final months with Brando, Dean was out of control," Gilman said. "He arrived at Marlon's house at about three o'clock one morning. I let him in. He was threatening to kill himself if he didn't see Marlon. I woke up a sleepy Marlon who wandered downstairs naked. He conferred privately with Dean. Somehow Dean managed to persuade Marlon to drive away with him in the middle of the night. I hope Marlon was driving."

"I noticed that Dean would get drunk after only two glasses of vino. And he was one mean fucking drunk. Marlon would just sip a coke observing Dean like a boa constrictor sizing up a chicken to deep throat. Marlon needed to keep his sanity in order to control Dean later in the night. Under the influence of alcohol, Dean was a shit. He tried to physically assault Marlon on more than one occasion. Marlon never fought back. He was the stronger of the two, and he could have restrained or even destroyed Dean."

"I shouldn't mention this, and God will get me for it, but Marlon and Dean engaged in some very sick games together, especially near the end of Dean's short life," Gilman claimed. "Very S&M stuff. Marlon on occasion did engage in violence with some of his girlfriends, as has been widely reported. To my knowledge, he never got violent with any of his male lovers except with Dean. They played their dirty games with each other. It was like the two rivals brought out only the darkest side in each other. Many a night I heard Dean sobbing yet begging for more."

"Dean had a whole string of seduction mates, Gilman said. "To Marlon, I called them his little girlfriends and his little fairyboys. I can't speak for his whole life, but during the time he was dating Marlon, he also had a whole harem, both male and female, each one of whom seemed willing to do his bidding. He was banging some bitch one night, and the very next night getting fucked by some biker. I hear he liked only bikers who dressed like Marlon did in *The Wild One*.º

Jimmy's last night with Brando was a disaster," claimed Ronnie White, who hosted an all-male party in Malibu, which both Jimmy and Brando attended.

"Jimmy apparently had been drinking heavily all afternoon, and he came to the party stoned," White said. "Brando came in a little later. He was sober and ordered only a cranberry cocktail. Jimmy switched from liquor to pot. Then he and Brando got into a tiff, a sort of catfight."

In front of the other guests, Brando suddenly attacked Jimmy, accusing him of going out with women just to mask his homosexuality. "You and Tab Hunter just date for all this manufactured Hollywood publicity crap. You shamelessly court it. As for me, and unlike you guys, I have nothing to cover up. I am what I am, and I'm proud of it."

"Jimmy seemed on the verge of tears at this sudden attack from Brando," White said. "He ran out of the house and tried to hop onto his motorcycle, but Brando bolted from my living room and ran outside and stopped him, using force."

"I really believe that Jimmy that night would have committed suicide on that cycle. He was too far gone."

"Then Brando drove Jimmy home in his car," White said. "The next afternoon, a very hung-over Jimmy came to my house and retrieved his motorcycle. But he didn't come in and thank me for the party. I guess he wanted to forget it. The next thing I heard, he was dead."

***

In the wake of Jimmy's death, when the crowds died down, Brando, with Gilman, drove to the site of the young actor's fatal car crash.

Getting down on his knees, Brando surveyed the ground so recently soaked with blood.

Standing only a few feet away, Gilman heard Brando say, "Jimmy, I loved you more than I told you."

***

Years later, Brando told Gilman, "Jimmy went out in a blaze of glory. Marilyn Monroe disappeared from the scene just as her youthful beauty entered its final hours and those wrinkles inevitably appeared around her eyes. The trick in Hollywood is to die when you're young and still beautiful. I'll probably live to be 102. I'll look like an old bullfrog, wrinkled and fat, Stanley Kowalski in that sweaty T-shirt only a distant memory."

"But Jimmy will be eternally young: Cal Trask, Jim Stark, Jett Rink. Take my word for it, Sam. It's the lucky ones who fade from the scene while they've still got it."

"The Hollywood Hills are filled with former movie stars, both male and female, afraid to look in the mirror at the grotesques they've become. Marilyn got it right in that god damn song of hers. 'We all lose our charms in the end.' That is, those of us who stick around."

Chapter Twenty-One

JIMMY COMPETES WITH HIS "SOULMATE" (EARTHA KITT) FOR THE LOVE OF PLAYBOY, PRODUCER, & THEATER MOGUL

ARTHUR LOEW, JR.

How Vampira,
the Weirdest Television Personality of Her Era,
Lured (and Later, Cursed) Jimmy with Black Magic

Sammy Davis, Jr.
PULLS JIMMY TOWARD SATANISM & THE OCCULT

Jimmy's Affair With Van Johnson
America's (Male) Box Office Sweetheart of the 1940s

HOW PAUL NEWMAN
IN THE WAKE OF JIMMY'S DEATH, FILLED HIS SHOES,
BOTH ON THE SCREEN AND AS A BEDMATE FOR HIS FORMER LOVERS

"I'm hot shit," James Dean bragged on the phone to his friend, William Bast, who was still struggling to find his niche as a writer. "I guess I can now have any role I want in this town."

"Enjoy your moment," Bast said, trying to conceal his jealousy. "Hollywood is known for crowning princes, occasionally even kings. It's also known for dethroning them, sometimes after very short reigns. Then an actor's got to live with his fall from glory for the rest of his miserable days."

"What a downer you are," Jimmy charged, flashing anger. "Don't ruin my moment. Why don't you admit it? You're a failed actor. You'd love to be in my position." Then he slammed down the phone.

It would be several days before he spoke to Bast again.

But as he'd soon discover, Hollywood wasn't ready to give him any role he wanted.

Producer John Houseman had met him at a party, finding him an ideal choice to play the role of a mentally disturbed youth in an upcoming film, *The Cobweb.* It had been written by John Paxton, who had penned the script for Marlon Brando's *The Wild One* based on a novel by William Gibson.

At a lunch, Houseman handed Jimmy the rough draft of *The Cobweb's* script. Jimmy would later refer to it as "Grand Hotel in the Loony Bin." The plot dealt with a series of melodramatic events in a high-class mental institution. The role being discussed was that of Steven Holte, a troubled young designer with mental problems. Jimmy found the character "sweetly deranged. It's practically type casting," he said in a phone call to Houseman the next day.

Houseman arranged for Jimmy to drive, the following night, to the home of Vincente Minnelli, who was set to direct it. "I hope Judy Garland's former husband is not going to turn this into a musical."

"Have no fear," Houseman assured him. "He's equally good at dramas. He should know a lot about mental institutions, having been married to Judy."

Over drinks in Minnelli's living room, Jimmy told him that he had come very close to working with him before on *The Bad and the Beautiful* (1952), the film he'd directed with Lana Turner and Kirk Douglas. "George Bradshaw wanted to do something really daring. Instead of Lana catching Kirk with another woman, she goes to his house and discovers me in my panties coming out of Kirk's bedroom. It would have been ground-breaking."

"I'm aware of that and actually wanted to film it," Minnelli responded, but, of course, MGM nixed the idea as too daring. The Production Code just wouldn't have allowed it."

Minnelli had already nicknamed *The Cobweb* "our mental film," and told Jimmy that he was hoping for an all-star cast. "You'll get that chance to work with Lana after all. I've offered her a role along with Robert Taylor and Grace Kelly. Not bad. Three of the biggest stars in Hollywood...and you. The movie has a perverse fascination for me. I'm familiar with the psychiatric setting after all those years with Judy, including time at Menninger."

[The Menninger Clinic, a respected drug and alcohol rehabilitation center that at the time was located in Topeka, Kansas (and now located in Texas), had, for a while enrolled Judy Garland in one of its programs.]

Jimmy also said that he was looking forward to working with Susan Strasberg, daughter of Lee, who had been cast in the film as one of the mental institution's patients.

He was also impressed with the rest of the cast. "Fay Wray from *King Kong*. My God. And Adele Jergens. Ronald Reagan proposed marriage to her after Jane Wyman dumped him. Lillian Gish is also in *Cobweb*. What a dear. Do you know that she 'invented' the close-up?'"

the
COBWEB

RICHARD   LAUREN   CHARLES   GLORIA   LILLIAN
WIDMARK BACALL BOYER GRAHAME GISH

It was well known in Hollywood circles that Minnelli was gay, and, as Jimmy later admitted, "I was waiting for the inevitable invitation to his casting couch."

The next day, he phoned Bast to make up with him, and to tell him what had happened at Minnelli's home.

"Did he seduce you?" Bast asked.

"No, but his mouth was watering. I'm too big a star to lie on any more casting couches. I did wear a pair or tight jeans and no underwear to tempt him. His eyes kept darting to my crotch. I should have given the poor guy a break, but I held out. After all, I'd fucked Judy."

When Houseman phoned Jimmy the next day, he told him, "I talked to Vincente. He thinks you're perfect for the role. It's yours."

Jimmy phoned Bast again. "I got the part. And I got it without having some old guy suck my dick."

But Minnelli's dream cast didn't work out. Instead, he cast Richard Widmark, Lauren Bacall, and Gloria Grahame. Taylor and Turner had drifted on to make other pictures, and Kelly claimed she was exhausted after making four films virtually in a back-to-back row.

Jimmy was delighted to learn that Leonard Rosenman, one of his best friends, had signed to do the musical score.

He was also looking forward to meeting Gloria Grahame, who had been married to director Nicholas Ray until he caught her in bed with his thirteen-year-old son, Tony. And he was especially interested in a face-to-face with Lauren Bacall.

Humphrey Bogart and Bacall lived together in Benedict Canyon a few miles north of the Beverly Hills Hotel, in a ranch-style house that had been originally built for Hedy Lamarr.

Bacall called Jimmy and invited him over for a drink. She was aware that he'd played a brief role in *Deadline, U.S.A,* with her husband. But she didn't know that Bogie and Jimmy had had had several vicious encounters.

Jimmy brought along a recording of some of Rosenman's music to play for her, with the understanding that his friend had already been commissioned to compose a musical score for *The Cobweb.*

Lauren Bacall with Humphrey Bogart...a May to October affair.

Bacall would later tell Patricia Neal, who had worked with Jimmy before, "I found him charming and attractive. Unlike some of these punks in Hollywood today, he seems to appreciate an older woman. Actually, I'm only eight years older than he is."

"Many find Jimmy difficult, but I thought he was delightful," Neal said. "Coop *[Gary Cooper]* just adored him."

Neal also learned what happened later that night. "As we were listening to the music, Jimmy asked me to dance," Bacall said. "He held me very close, pressing his body against mine."

"All of a sudden, Bogie arrived home early and caught us dancing," Bacall said. "He'd been to the clinic. As you know, his health is failing. It was perfectly harmless. Maybe we kissed. I don't remember. Bogie went ballistic. He grabbed Jimmy by his neck and literally tossed him out the door on his ass."

Jimmy fared better with another member of the cast, Oscar Levant, who had signed to play the mother-fixated Mr. Capp. In the original novel, he was a homosexual. "Minnelli wants to leave the gay stuff in, but I'm sure MGM will object. Instead, he's having it rewritten. However, he's bringing all my neuroses and complexes into the plot, so I will, more or less, be playing myself."

Levant was an eccentric pianist known for his sharp tongue. His streams of barbed witticisms appealed to Jimmy's sense of humor. A friend of Levant's, Joan Collins, said, "Oscar and Dean were total opposites, but they got along fabulously, each relishing the other's unusualness."

Jimmy was drawn to Levant's music, but he also was impressed with him as an actor. He'd appeared in *Humoresque* (1946), with John Garfield and Joan Crawford and in such films as *An American in Paris* (1951) with Gene Kelly.

In his 1968 memoir, *The Importance of Being Oscar,* Levant wrote of another visit by Jimmy to his home.

"Jimmy Dean once spent a night until five in the morning talking to me about himself and his world. At that time, he was working on his biggest picture, Giant. *Arthur Loew, Jr. brought him to our house, along with Elizabeth Taylor, Michael Wilding, Joan Collins, and the producer of* Giant, *Henry Ginsberg. Arthur knew that one of my daughters was an ardent Jimmy Dean fan. It was a strange thing, but seeing my daughter's room filled with dozens of pictures of him in various poses did not seem to please Dean. On the contrary, it depressed him. He said he felt crushed under the weight of such adulation. He turned out to be a fascinating and intelligent young man who talked fluently about artists in music. And he was surprisingly knowledgeable about such recondite composers as Schönberg and Bartók."*

Two weeks later, Jimmy was disappointed when Warners refused to release him from his contract to film *The Cobweb*. He also was enraged to learn that John Kerr, his former lover and now his rival, had been assigned the role he'd wanted to play. To add to his fury, Kerr was being billed as "the new James Dean."

[After Jimmy's death, Bogie, nearing the final months of his own life, told the press: "The kid died at the right time. If he had lived, he'd never have been able to live up to his publicity.']

"It's Not the Whore Who Pays"

—James Dean to Rogers Brackett, a few months after their affair ended

In one of those embarrassing coincidences that occur too often in life, Jimmy, on a chance encounter on Third Avenue in New York, ran into Rogers Brackett, his former mentor and lover. Before Jimmy's rise to fame, Brackett had introduced him to important people in the industry and procured roles for him in teleplays.

But now, Brackett was no longer the powerful TV advertising executive he'd been during his heyday. He'd fallen on bad days and had taken to drinking. His bosses on Madison Avenue, who had been trying to peddle their products to typical American families, had been turned off by his numerous homosexual indiscretions.

Jimmy had also heard stories about how Brackett was going around taking credit "as the man who discovered James Dean," and he resented that. Now that he was a movie star, and fully aware that there were aspects of his past that it would be wise to conceal, he did not want to acknowledge the role that Brackett had played in his past.

Brackett explained his financial predicament to Jimmy, and then, with a twinge of desperation, asked to borrow $10,000 from him, a sum he promised to pay back with interest.

"I didn't know it was the whore who paid," Jimmy said. "I thought it was the other way around."

"I no longer need a mother hen cackling over me," Jimmy said. "Now, struggling young actors turn to me, asking me to get them work. I've learned that to get where I want, I've had to fly over some badlands. That explains my involvement with you. I've flown over those badlands and landed in green pastures."

At the time, Brackett was living in Stanley Haggart's garden apartment, the setting of many of Jimmy's former sexual trysts. Haggart was grateful for the artwork commissions that Brackett had directed his way during his tenure as a powerful TV producer.

When the composer, Alec Wilder, still Brackett's best friend, heard about Jimmy's treatment of him, he scolded him. "Rogers should sue you for overdue payment of all the money he's extended to you," Wilder said.

"He got his pound of flesh from me," Jimmy countered.

Wilder later wrote, "I read Jimmy the riot act when he came by the Algonquin. His treatment of Rogers was dreadful. Nowhere in any of Jimmy's publicity was Rogers' name even mentioned, and he had done so much for Jimmy."

"I told him that what he had done was morally wrong, and that he owed Rogers an apology. Jimmy replied that he couldn't do it, so I drafted the letter for Jimmy, and then demanded that he rewrite it in his own handwriting."

The following evening, I invited both Rogers and Jimmy to come by the hotel," Wilder said. "The three of us had a very pleasant, giddy time. But the damage had been done. As far as I know, they never saw each other again."

Brackett related to Haggart how painful and embarrassing his final goodbye to Jimmy had been, and how he'd tried to put a good face on it. "Frankly, I was humiliated and heartbroken."

"I wanted so much more from Jimmy," Brackett told Haggart. "I wanted him to love me."

"You must have gotten some enjoyment out of it, because you kept going back for more," Haggart said. "Everybody wants more out of a relationship, but, as you know, we so rarely get that. As for me, I take what I can get—and move on. You have to do that, too."

After Brackett had moved out and away from Haggart, Jimmy came by to visit. Unlike Wilder, Haggart didn't denounce Jimmy for his cavalier attitude to Brackett.

"Rogers was silly to think you could love him back," Haggart said. "He's been around Hollywood and New York long enough not to be so naïve."

"When Rogers used to seduce me, I closed my eyes and imagined it was someone else," Jimmy confessed. "I know Rogers is going around spreading this shit about his having discovered me in that damn parking lot. Should the jockey take credit for the speed of the race horse? I think not!"

RANDOM ACTS OF KINDNESS
Jimmy's "Affair of the Heart" with Toni Lee

One of Jimmy's most bizarre friendships was with entertainer Toni Lee, who later wrote a book, *A Kind of Loving* (1970), about her involvement with him.

A popular vocalist, she had appeared on the TV shows of Mike Douglas, Johnny Carson, and Steve Allen, and was a familiar fixture in nightclubs, attracting jazz fans and pop lovers across the country.

Whenever the beautiful brunette swung into a song, no one in the audience seemed to know that she had had the misfortune of losing a leg in a motorcycle smash-up when she was nineteen.

For her public appearances, she wore a prosthetic leg and long, floor-length dresses.

Jimmy and Lee had fallen into the habit of ending their respective late night venues with breakfast at Googie's. Each had noticed the other, but had not yet spoken.

One evening, both of them entered Googie's, each alone but virtually at the same moment, for a late night supper. Four actors were sitting at a nearby table, loudly unaware that Lee had come in. They were discussing possible dates to escort to the premiere of Judy Garland's *A Star Is Born*.

One of the actors said, "Too bad we have to show up with a girl. Will the day ever come when we can be escorted by our boyfriends?"

"Why not take Toni Lee?" one of the actors suggested.

Both Lee and Jimmy overheard the answer. "For a premiere this important, do you think I'd want to show up with a one-legged woman?"

Humiliated, Lee quickly exited from the

Toni later wrote of her friendship with Jimmy, describing "the ominous, almost occult portents of their first meeting, and the quick, warm relationship that grew between them."

restaurant.

She later revealed in her memoirs that about two hours before dawn, she'd heard her doorbell ring. When she stumbled to the door, she found it was a man she recognized from Googie's. Although they'd never spoken, she'd seen him many times before, and somehow, he'd gotten her address.

"Hi, I'm James Dean," he said. "You know, from Googie's?"

She was wearing a robe, and he said, "I want you to take off your clothes."

"What?" she asked, thinking that she might have misunderstood him.

"Your clothes," he said. "Take them off!"

To her own utter amazement, she claimed that she obeyed his request and stripped. "I didn't have that fake leg attached," she said. "Jimmy kneeled down in front of me and ran his fingers over the scars on my stump. He went over the scars one by one, very delicately with his fingers. At the end of his inspection, he gently rained down little kisses on my stump."

"Don't listen to those jerks at Googie's," he said. "You are beautiful. Forget those morons. Now, get dressed."

She told him that for a few months after the accident, she'd kept her deformed, scarred, unusable, and withered leg, "But it looked so hideous, I went to a surgeon and had him cut it off."

After their unusual introduction, she said that in the weeks to come, she grew used to Jimmy ringing her doorbell at three or four o'clock in the morning. According to her, it was a friendship, not an affair.

"We'd have long talks, which always ended with his reassurance that I was beautiful. Later, I'd prepare raisin toast and hot chocolate for his breakfast."

"Over and over, he kept telling me I was beautiful until I came to believe it," she said.

"You've got a good mind," he said. "Use it! Develop your insight so you can look behind their words and see why people say them. Learning to appreciate people—that's hard, but important. But first, learn to appreciate yourself. Because you're very special, very special indeed. So don't be smothered under all the ugliness of Hollywood."

One night at Googie's, Jimmy and Lee shared a chance encounter with his friend, William Bast, who also wrote about it in his own memoir. Bast didn't know that Lee was a well-known entertainer in her own right. At the time, she was a blonde in her late twenties, as he remembered it.

"The talk was of motorcycles," Bast said, "I asked her if she were a cyclist like Jimmy."

"I was, but I had to give it up," she said. "I lost a leg. With that, she swung out into the aisle to show me that her leg had been amputated at the knee. Only then did I notice the crutches tucked discreetly beside her, against the wall."

584

After their brief three-way conversation, she disappeared into the night with Jimmy, accepting his offer of a ride home on his cycle.

The next time Bast saw Lee at Googie's, she was alone. "We talked about Jimmy."

"He's the greatest guy in this whole god damn town," she told Bast. "He's got real guts. Most of the creeps in Hollywood are afraid to even look at my leg. Not Jimmy. He wanted to know all about it."

Bast asked her about her sex life.

"Not many guys get their kicks fucking a one-legged woman," she said.

Actually, Lee was living at the time with six handsome young men, each an actor, in an apartment. She prided herself for being able to hobble around on one leg carrying hot chocolate without spilling it. Her six cohorts often rubbed her stump, and she claimed that the rubbing was her greatest joy in life.

Lee also related a dramatic incident that took place one night with Jimmy. She met him at Googie's when he was with photographer Dennis Stock and his date. It was agreed that all of them would go to this Hollywood party. They would go first to Stock's place, with the understanding that Jimmy would park his motorcycle there, and that he'd then be driven to the party by Lee, who would drive her own car, following behind Stock in his.

On the way to his house, Stock suddenly slammed on his brakes when a kid ran out in front of his car. Reactively, Lee slammed on her brakes, too. On his motorcycle behind her, Jimmy pressed hard on his brakes, but not fast enough. He was hurled off his bike and, literally under her car.

"I got out of my car, screaming," Lee said. "I feared I'd killed him."

Jimmy crawled up off the tarmac, groaning in pain, but smiling to signal that he wasn't bodily harmed.

"I begged him that night to sell that damn bike," she said. "Time and time again, I begged him, telling him he was going to kill himself on it. "

One night, he showed up, telling her he'd sold his cycle. "My new transportation is this shiny new Porsche," he said.

"In it, you'll be much safer," she assured him.

Jimmy often dropped by," she said, "because two of his friends, Nick Adams and Dennis Hopper, lived next door. Nick and I didn't get along. Sometimes, we'd go out to Googie's, even Villa Capri. But often, we stayed in my apartment. He'd read from passages in *Lord Chesterfields's Letters to His Son*, which seemed to be his favorite literature after *The Little Prince*."

Jimmy turned me in the right direction in my life, as a friend, not a lover, although we had a kind of loving."

The last time she saw him, in September of 1955, he was heading to the car races in Salinas, and he invited her to go along. He was traveling with his mechanic, but he said he also had a station wagon. You'll be comfortable in it, and we can tow the Porsche behind us."

She told him she couldn't go because she had a gig coming up, but "I'll see you when you get back from Salinas," she promised him.

"Of course, as the world knows," she said, "Jimmy never came back."

Satanic Rites

WITH SAMMY DAVIS, JR.

One night, Sammy Davis, Jr. was dining at Villa Capri, Jimmy's favorite restaurant, with Dean Martin and Peter Lawford. The leader of the "Rat Pack," Frank Sinatra, wasn't there that night, which was just as well. He didn't like Jimmy, whose career was soaring at a time when Sinatra's was bottoming out.

Sammy went over to introduce himself to Jimmy and invite him to a party. He also ordered the *maître-d'* to deliver a bottle of champagne to Jimmy and his date.

After that night, Jimmy and Sammy started seeing each other, mostly at parties.

Unlike many young men of his generation, Jimmy had no prejudice against African-Americans. He'd studied dance with Katherine Dunham in New York, and Eartha Kitt was one of his best friends, along with writer Bill Gunn and Cyril Jackson, who taught him how to play the bongo drums.

Jimmy told composer Alec Wilder, "I have a lot to learn from black culture—the music, the dance. Those cats known how to have a good time. They know how to forget their cares and woes, at least for a few hours."

John Gilmore, Jimmy's friend, remembered one Sunday afternoon visiting Sammy when he was living at his grandmother's house, as hard as that is to believe.

Jimmy invited Sammy for a spin on his motorcycle through the surrounding hills, careening around corners at record-breaking speed. Back in front of his grandmother's house, Sammy climbed off. "Wow!" he said. "Wow, man, what a fucking gas!"

His grandmother invited them to stay for lunch, the featured staple of which would be a ham-based stew bubbling on the stove. Sammy served a bottle of wine Dean Martin had given him.

Retro chic: Jimmy's favorite restaurant, The Villa Capri, in the 1950s.

They ended up that night at a club, "with the hottest chicks in town."

As Gilmore recalled, "Jimmy was beating the bongos—stoned out of his mind. Sammy danced and shook the maracas at the hi-fi speakers, while other people seemed to arrive out of nowhere, thickening the group like chunks of starch in his grandmother's stew."

By midnight, Sammy was throwing his arms around Jimmy, proclaiming, "This is the *cat* I love! The *one* I love!"

Then Sammy and Jimmy kissed each other passionately.

Still stoned the next day, Jimmy wanted to return to Sammy's, but when he called "grandma," he learned that Sammy had gone to Palm Springs.

He came up with another idea. Back home, Jimmy wanted to dress up as a chick, with a big blonde wig and red high heels, and with makeup like a Parisian whore.

He wanted Gilmore to be his "stud date" at the Tropical Village, the gay bar at Santa Monica.

***

One night, once again at the Villa Capri, Jimmy dined with Sammy and Eartha Kitt. During that dinner, she told an amusing story of how she'd met Sammy when she was appearing on Broadway in *New Faces of 1952.*

"He was standing near the stage manager's door, and I took him for an errand boy, and demanded that he bring me a cup of coffee. Sammy went to get the coffee. When he got back to my dressing room and handed it to me, he told me that someday he'd be a bigger star than I would ever be."

Both entertainers laughed at the memory of that (embarrassing) incident.

Later on, Sammy got serious, telling them that at parties, he often stood in the corner, looking at Tony Curtis or Robert Wagner across a crowded room. "Female fans nearly dropped dead at the sight of them."

His left eye was gone *[he had lost it in a car accident in 1954]* and a deep, dark socket was left in its place. Its eyelid was lower than the eyelid of the remaining eye.

"Sammy always looked like he's been in a terrible fight, perhaps with a knife," Eartha said.

"He's a beautiful man to me," Jimmy claimed, not really meaning it.

"As a boy growing up, the fear of rejection always crawled beneath my black hide," Sammy said. "I had an overbite, really crooked teeth. Before I became a celebrity, it was almost impossible to get a girl without paying for some poontang. Now, I'm sought out by gals, often blonde bimbos, but they're usually there just to meet Frankie or Deano—or else to help me spend my money."

Eartha and Jimmy were quick to assure Sammy that they loved him for himself.

"Yeah, but you two don't put out," he answered. "I wish you would. I'd take both of you on at the same time."

"You can't complain too much," Jimmy said. "Marilyn Monroe, Kim Novak, and Ava Gardner, from what I've heard. Not bad, not bad at all."

One night when Sammy and Jimmy were out by themselves, he'd asked him why one fingernail was painted red. "That's a signal to other Satanists. I'm a Satanist, you know. We use the red nail as a signal to each other," Sammy said. "Actually, I'm on the edge of that cult. I'm

Sammy Davis, Jr. onstage...He attended Satanist orgies with James Dean and "did our thing" in view of other devil worshippers.

not into all that shit about devil worship. I'm in it for the sexual kicks, and there's plenty of that."

Jimmy wanted to attend a Satanist orgy, and the following week, Sammy escorted him to a gathering of devil worshippers, where sexual acts among the participants were always part of the ritual. Details are sketchy, but rumors still persist that Jimmy, in front of others, fellated Sammy at the orgy. He'd performed a similar stunt at a late-night jazz club in Harlem, so the rumors were met with some belief.

As Sammy later told Lawford, "It was the right night. There was a full moon. Jimmy was stoned out of his mind. There were no limits about what he could or could not do. He did. I admired him for that. What a little devil!"

"Our friendship was just starting to blossom," Sammy said after Jimmy's death. He regretted that he hadn't approached Jimmy sooner at parties.

"I didn't take too much notice of him when I spotted him a few times in 1954," he said. "He was always in the corner somewhere looking depressed and sulky. If someone approached him, he would look up and say, 'I want to act.' And then he would slump back into his own world."

"Hollywood hardly touched him as a person. It was to our eternal shame as a community that we passed him off as a bit of a slob. He was difficult to talk to, but we should have tried harder."

He also said, "I finally broke through his barrier, and was well on my way to having a new best friend...but then I lost him."

Sammy once wrote, "James Dean was more than a phenomenon or even a legend. He was far more than a cinematic genius who could act his balls off."

He was simply the greatest screen experience of all time. The fact that he was cut off in his prime is unfortunate, but irrelevant. The three films he left us will stand as their own monument. He remains indestructible. In only three films, he ruined the careers of hundreds of other aspiring actors who tried to follow him."

In a subsequent memoir, published after the death of Marilyn Monroe, Sammy drew a parallel between the two icons: "Unlike Jimmy Dean, who never realized his real potential, Marilyn became prematurely spent as an actress because she was never allowed the artistic freedom she craved. After *Some Like It Hot,* she went into decline. She even began to lose her international clout at the box office. Jimmy, on the other hand, faced possibly a series of some of the greatest motion pictures ever to be made."

Sammy would also respond to one of the most vicious posthumous attacks on Jimmy ever made. It occurred in October of 1956 and was the opinion of show business biographer Maurice Zolotow, wrote it. His article was headlined "Jimmy Dean Should Be Nobody's Idol—The Late Actor Was Sadistic, Uncouth, Arrogant, Cruel, & a Filthy Slob."

"He was surly, ill-tempered, brutal, without any element of kindness, sensitivity, consideration for other, or romantic passion. He was physically dirty. He hated to bathe, have his hair cut, shave, or put on clean clothes. He smelled so rankly that actresses working with him in close contact found him unbearable."

Zolotov also asked, "What's so great and beautiful about stepping on the gas, blowing your horn, and speeding down a public highway like a maniac?"

Sammy shot back, "I don't give a fuck how some of these assholes criticize Dean. He did his number and he did it better than anybody else in the world."

Lance Reventlow

HOW THE INSECURE, MUCH-ABUSED SON OF BARBARA HUTTON, ONE OF THE RICHEST WOMEN IN THE WORLD, RACED WITH JIMMY TO THE FINISH LINE

For the most part, Jimmy and Lance Reventlow, son of the heiress, Barbara Hutton, went their separate ways, but they got together whenever they could to resume their affair.

They not only made love, but attended car races and fussed over their vehicles, discussing the merits of one racecar over another. Mostly, they were concerned with how fast a car could go.

When they weren't together, Jimmy and Lance sometimes talked on the phone during the early morning hours. One of their conversations lasted for four hours.

Lance told him, "I never know what continent my mother is on."

Bruce Kessler, Jimmy learned, was Lance's closest friend. His father, Jack Kessler, had founded Rose Marie Swimwear. "His wife, Nina, was like a surrogate mother to me."

Jimmy also found out that Lance's friends were radically different from Hutton's. He preferred the company of Ronnie Burns, son of George Burns and Gracie Allen, or that of Julie Payne, daughter of actor John Payne. Lance also liked to hang out with Gary Crosby, the abused son of Bing, or Chick Daigh, a race car driver.

"Lance was never true to one person," Jimmy recalled, although he was dating Jill St. John and planning to marry her. "He gave her a diamond engagement ring that stretched from knuckle to knuckle," Jimmy said.

"Like Jimmy, Lance, too, had dropped out of college, after attending only one semester at Pomona College. "I'm interested in car racing," He said. "Why do I need an education?"

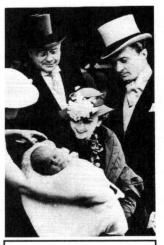

Lance told Jimmy that when he reached twenty-one, based on the complicated lineage of his abusive Danish father and American-born mother, he was offered the choice of citizenship, either American, Danish, or British. "I thought it over for twenty seconds and decided to go the Yankee Doodle Dandy route."

Jimmy often came and went from Lance's house, which was a modest one on North Knoll Drive in Benedict Canyon. "He was having financial problems because his mother had cut him off at one point."

There, Jimmy met Dudley Walker, Cary Grant's former valet, who organized and managed Lance's bills when he was solvent. "I never had any sense of money," Lance told Jimmy, "Other than how to spend it. That, I know."

Barbara Hutton holds her fifteen-week old son, Lance in her arms as her father *(left)* looks on and her husband, Count Reventlow *(right)*, seems to approve.

A photographer caught this troubled family leaving their London townhouse for the boy's baptism in the Chapel of Marlborough.

Jimmy was fascinated by Lance's fleet of cars, nine in all. His friend offered him the use of any of them "at any time."

"I have a Mercedes for running errands," Lance

told Jimmy. "A Jaguar for a hot date, and a Rolls-Royce for special events."

"For car racing, I prefer a Porsche like you have, or a Maserati, perhaps a Cooper-Climax. And just for the hell of it, I keep an old, beat-up Chevy like Howard Hughes drives around in."

Once, Jimmy invited Lance for a drive in the first Porsche he'd purchased. "He was like a kid who'd been given the greatest of all Christmas gifts, even though he had to pay for it," Lance said. "He was excited by it, and wanted me to admire it, too. Sometimes, with me in the passenger seat, he would take me on a reckless drive through the Hollywood Hills. He treated those curvy roads like a race track. Finally, I told him I didn't like being in the passenger seat, preferring to be behind the wheel where I belonged. 'You can sit in the damn passenger seat and be my bitch,' I told him."

"For Jimmy, the Porsche was a symbol that demonstrated that he'd arrived as a star, but it was more than that: It was a token of his new-found freedom, and his defiance of the system."

Jimmy and Lance frequently attended major car races together, after which they'd slip away to some retreat as a means of continuing what Jimmy defined as "our male bonding."

He rarely discussed Lance, even with his closest friends, other than to say, "He's a very special guy, very special."

Lance was the first person Jimmy invited for a spin in "The Little Bastard," the nickname he'd given his newly purchased Silver Porsche Spyder.

At one point, he even let Lance take the wheel "to get the feel of it," as they headed east to Little River, California, three miles north of Mendocino.

When they got there, they checked into the Little River Inn, an establishment, built in 1853, which had housed Jimmy and the cast of *East of Eden* during its filming less

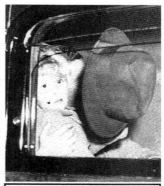

Lance was the by-product of a marriage for which his mother, Barbara Hutton, had renounced her citizenship to become the wife of a Danish count. It was a bitter marriage, leading to endless custody fights over Lance.

A terrified Lance is seen in this photograph from October of 1939, when a bodyguard, Bobby Sweeney, shielded his own face – not that of the three-year old – as reporters stared into the limousine.

Lance was later removed from the car and put aboard the *Conte di Savoia* to sail across the Atlantic.

On scooters far too small for them, Bruce Kessler *(left)* goes for a ride with his best friend, Lance Reventlow,

than a year before. *[Jimmy stayed in room #8 within what is now a California State landmark.]*

On May 1, 1955, they drove to Minter Field in Bakersfield, where Jimmy placed third behind Marion Playan in an MG Speck and John Kunstle driving a Panhard Devin.

That same month, on Memorial Day, they participated in the Santa Barbara Road Races, Jimmy entering the small car, "Under 1,500 cc Production Event," moving up to fourth place before he blew a piston on his four-cylinder Porsche.

Lance Reventlow, *depicted above,* and James Dean were destined to die in fiery crashes—Jimmy in a racecar and Reventlow in a small airplane.

Now, in anticipation of Jimmy's last race with Lance, both of them were heading in separate vehicles for Salinas, where Jimmy planned to debut his newest Porsche 550 Spyder. But whereas Lance made it to Salinas, Jimmy never did.

As for Lance, after his safe and relatively uneventful arrival in Salinas, where he heard about Jimmy's death, he said, "My god, I just had this awful feeling. The next crash has my name on it."

[Except for its timing, Lance's premonition of his own death was more or less accurate. But it wasn't until 1972 that he died in a fiery crash in a small airplane.]

Jimmy's Relationship with

Van Johnson

America's Favorite (Gay) Boy Next Door

During the final year of Jimmy's life, he entered into an unlikely friendship with character actor Keenan Wynn, son of the famous vaudeville comedian, Ed Wynn. That bonding would ultimately lead to him to Van Johnson, Wynn's best friend and lover.

Jimmy's friendship with Wynn began on Thanksgiving Day, 1954, when a mutual friend brought him to the Wynn home for a festive dinner. Jimmy had just completed *East of Eden.*

Wynn and his wife, the former Shirley Hudson, greeted Jimmy like a member of the family. Wynn had previously been married to the former stage actress, Eve ("Evie") Lynn Abbott. Following their divorce in 1947, Wynn turned

Evie over to Johnson as part of an arranged, studio-sanctioned marriage to camouflage the popular actor's homosexuality.

Over dinner, Jimmy learned that Wynn shared his fascination with motorcycles. Within days, the veteran actor was teaching him how to navigate open terrain and hills on a cycle.

Keenan Wynn...a three-way with Van Johnson and James Dean.

Gradually, Wynn became one of Jimmy's closest friends, and he set out to learn what he could about him. A New Yorker, Wynn had grown up in a theatrical family that had settled in Hollywood in 1934. In time, he'd appear in hundreds of films and on TV. When Jimmy met him, he was a contract player for MGM, and had recently filmed *Battle Circus* (1953).

Jimmy admired Wynn's versatility as an actor, as he could play almost any part except romantic leading men. His *forte* was affable sidekicks, shifty schemers, sad sacks, villains, con men, and simpletons. He'd gotten his start in Hollywood performing stunt work for Joan Crawford in *Chained* (1934).

"People thought they were watching Crawford perform those dangerous maneuvers, but it really was *moi* in drag," he told Jimmy.

Within a week, Jimmy was introduced to Johnson, a tall, freckle-faced, strawberry blonde actor who'd been a major box office attraction in the 1940s.

When MGM's major male stars, such as Clark Gable, Robert Taylor, Robert Montgomery, and James Stewart were shipped off to war, Johnson had shot to stardom as "The Boy Next Door," often appearing in films with June Allyson as the male half of a screen team billed as "America's Sweethearts."

During the wartime absence of Clark Gable and Robert Taylor (both of whom had entered the armed services) Johnson was featured in frothy romantic comedies with MGM's A-list movie queens, especially Lana Turner and Esther Williams.

Jimmy didn't like those kinds of pictures, although he'd admired Johnson in the military courtroom drama, *The Caine Mutiny* (1954), in which he'd played an unsympathetic character opposite Humphrey Bogart.

As a kid, Jimmy had seen Johnson in his first hit, *A Guy Named Joe* (1943), co-starring Spencer Tracy and Irene Dunne.

"Spence had the hots for me," Johnson confessed to Jimmy. "He even demanded that production on the picture be delayed until I recovered from a horrible car accident."

"Tracy went for me, too," Jimmy said.

"I'm not at all surprised," Johnson said. "I could go for you, too."

For many months, Jimmy had known that Johnson had wanted to seduce him. When she was dating Jimmy, actress Betsy Palmer, while eavesdropping, had overheard Johnson telling Jimmy during a phone conversation, "I want to cock you."

"I hope you don't fall for all that 'boy next door' crap from MGM's publicists," Johnson said. "If those bobbysoxers in the 40s ever learned that I was a cock-sucker, my career would end overnight."

Johnson's marriage was fraught with difficulties, and he ended up referring to his wife as, "The Dragon Lady."

Van Johnson...the actor known as the male half, alongside June Allyson, of the couple billed during the 1940s as "America's Sweethearts."

Ed Wynn, Keenan's father, once said, "I can't keep things straight—pardon the pun. Evie loves Keenan, Keenan loves Evie, Van loves Keenan, Keenan loves Van."

Evie eventually divorced Johnson, and she later discussed her marriages, respectively, to Wynn and to Johnson: "MGM had to protect its big star from all those rumors about his sexual preference. Unfortunately, I was selected as 'It,' the one Johnson should marry. Louis B. Mayer, who had the morals of a cockroach, said that if I didn't marry Van, he wouldn't renew Keenan's contract."

There was some urgency for a quick marriage. Screenwriter/playwright Arthur Laurents, in his autobiography, claimed that "Van had been caught one time too many 'performing' in a men's urinal."

Jimmy would later tell Eartha Kitt, "Van is a perfect illustration of the fantasy world that Hollywood projects. Golden boys are actually cocksuckers, *femme fatales* are muff-divers, and America's hero, John Wayne, has a small dick."

He also discussed his involvement with Wynn and Johnson to William Bast. He claimed that he had sat in the Johnson living room for three hours, before their host finally extended an invitation for Keenan and him to retire with him to the bedroom.

"What happened?" Bast asked.

"To cut to the chase, and I don't want to give a blow-by-blow description, we did a lot of fondling of genitals and exchanging of spit. Van then sucked me off while Keenan fucked him. Then Keenan serviced Van, as I lay back on the pillow, smoking a cigarette."

"At around three in the morning, I was half awake, and one of them—I don't know which—was messing around with my ass. I didn't bother to find out if it was Van or Keenan. What did it matter at that point?"

How "Hollywood Royal," Arthur Loew, Jr.
FELL INTO BED WITH JAMES DEAN

The "usually heterosexual" Arthur Loew, Jr. was a surprise choice as Jimmy's last male lover. Born in 1925, he was seven years older than Jimmy.

His maternal grandfather, Adolph Zukor, had founded Paramount Pictures, and his paternal grandfather, Marcus Loew, had launched both Metro-Goldwyn-Mayer and the Loew's theater chain. His father, Arthur Loew, Sr., had once been president of MGM.

Loew Junior was a minor film producer, turning out such B-list pictures as *Teresa* (1950), with Jimmy's future girlfriend, Pier Angeli; *Penelope* (1966) with Natalie Wood, Jimmy's co-star in *Rebel Without a Cause;* and later, after Jimmy's death, *The Rack* (1956), starring Paul Newman.

During Arthur's production of *Teresa,* he began dating one of its stars, Pier Angeli, but within weeks, he'd switched his romantic interest to her twin sister, Marisa Pavan.

One afternoon, Arthur arrived at the Pierangeli household in Brentwood to retrieve Marisa for a date. On lawn chairs in the distance, he spotted Pier and a young man, each of them holding a script.

"Who is that guy?" Arthur asked Marisa.

"Don't disturb them," she answered. "Pier is rehearsing with this actor, James Dean."

"Who in hell is James Dean?" he asked.

"He's this fabulous actor from New York."

"Never heard of him," Arthur said.

"You will," she predicted.

Arthur may not have heard of Jimmy, but Jimmy had never heard of him, either.

Unlike his illustrious and hardworking ancestors, and despite brief work stints as a drama critic and sports reporter, Arthur was a playboy who only

Arthur Loew, Jr.

dabbled in the occasional production of films. He was better known for a widely publicized romance with Elizabeth Taylor. Later, he dated Joan Collins, but she broke it off, having defined their relationship as "too platonic."

Arthur had just ended an affair (which had included an engagement) to Jimmy's closest female friend, Eartha Kitt.

Amazingly, despite their friendship, Eartha had never described the depth of her relationship with Arthur. In fact, she had barely, if ever—at least to Jimmy—mentioned him at all.

Their love affair had ended horribly: The Loew family had ferociously objected to their heir's association with a woman of color, and relentlessly pressured him to end it, which he did. At the time of Jimmy's association with Arthur, Eartha was far away, on singing engagements in Manhattan.

That day, in the Pierangeli's living room, Arthur asked Marisa, "Who is this shit out in the yard? So he can't be disturbed while rehearsing? Who in hell does he think he is? Laurence Olivier?"

Within two months, Keenan Wynn, one of Arthur's closest friends, arrived with Jimmy at Arthur's house on Miller Drive. Jimmy's apartment at 1741 Sunset Plaza Drive, was nearby.

When Keenan introduced him to Arthur, he remembered the sight of him rehearsing with Pier. Also sitting in the room was Rod Steiger, Jimmy's actor friend from New York, who had already assured Arthur that Jimmy was one of the best actors performing in teleplays in Manhattan.

"Arthur was prepared to dislike Jimmy," Steiger said. "But when they started to talk, it was love at first sight. I had already warned Arthur that Jimmy had to be handled with kid gloves or else he might explode into a temper fit."

"Both Arthur and Jimmy had a wicked sense of humor, and they really got off on each other," Steiger said. "Keenan and I found ourselves sitting and talking with each other, as those two lovebirds played the mating game. They did everything that night except fuck, and, for all I know, they did that, too, after I left."

Steiger had departed an hour earlier. As the evening wound down, Wynn turned to Jimmy. "It's time for us to hit the road, kid, and ride our machines down those winding roads."

He later told Van Johnson and others, "Jimmy did something wild and impulsive. At the door, after I said good night to Arthur, Jimmy locked him in a tight embrace and gave him a kiss. Not a peck on the cheek. I hadn't seen a kiss like that since Toomey kissed Wyman."

[Wynn was recalling Regis Toomey and Jane Wyman in a 1941 movie, You're in the Army Now. *Their kiss was the longest up to that point in cinematic history, lasting three minutes and five seconds, or four percent of the film's duration.]*

"The last words I heard was Arthur telling Jimmy, 'I'll see you tomorrow night at seven,'" Wynn recalled.

After that, Jimmy practically moved into Arthur's household. Originally, the maid had prepared the guest room for him, but later discovered that the bed had never been slept in. Only the sheets on Arthur's bed had been used.

Even before Arthur met Jimmy, he virtually threw open his doors every night at five o'clock for "sundowners," as part an ongoing house party that attracted *tout* Hollywood.

On any given night, you might hear Judy Garland accompanied on the piano by Oscar Levant. Perhaps a drunken Errol Flynn would show up, a few hours later trying to bang out a melody on the piano with his erect penis.

Marilyn Monroe dropped by on occasion, as did Desi Arnaz and Lucille Ball, as well as Kirk Douglas, Eddie Fisher, James Mason, and Danny Kaye. Guests were likely to include Paulette Goddard, Jane Powell, June Allyson, Ginger Rogers, Ethel Merman, and Debbie Reynolds.

Jimmy soon learned that Arthur was having a sometimes affair with Susan Strasberg, the daughter of Lee Strasberg of the Actors Studio. It was at Arthur's house one night that he met Susan, with whom, he too, would launch a brief fling before he made *Giant*.

Jimmy was impressed with Arthur's light-hearted, charming style, and his outgoing personality. As he noted one night, "He could even keep Milton Berle in stiches."

He was surprised to learn that Stewart Stern, who at the time was writing the filmscript for *Rebel Without a Cause,* was Arthur's cousin. "Unlike his cousin, Arthur, Stern was bookish and always very serious," Jimmy said.

Elizabeth Taylor and Paul Newman were also among Arthur's friends, as were Farley Granger and Shelley Winters. Beginning in the late 1940s, much of young Hollywood had started to gather at Arthur's house to watch "Uncle Miltie" (Milton Berle) on *The Texaco Star Theater*. At the time, Arthur possessed one of the few television sets in Los Angeles.

One night at Arthur's house, Jimmy met Janet Leigh, who told him "After Elizabeth (Taylor) finished with Arthur, she turned him over to me. That was before Tony Curtis."

"One night, Arthur introduced me to his friend, Sammy Davis, Jr," Leigh continued. "Sammy told me I hadn't lived until I'd had a black dick buried deep inside me."

"That Sammy!" Jimmy said, not wanting to reveal anything.

Often, after a date with Pier, Jimmy would arrive at Arthur's house to spend the night. Sometimes, they preferred to dine at home; at other times, they went out for dinner. Since Jimmy wasn't properly dressed for such clubs as Mocambo's, where Arthur had more-or-less permanent and direct access to his favorite table, the two men went together to offbeat places, the type with sawdust and beer spilled on the floor.

Two months later, Jimmy ran into Steiger, who asked him, "How are things going between you and Arthur?"

"Great, man, just great."

"Until he met you, I always thought he was straight," Steiger said.

"All men are straight until they meet the formidable James Dean."

One night, Jimmy invited Arthur and his cousin, Stewart Stern, to a preview of *East of Eden.* Neither man had seen Jimmy perform in anything, not even any of his teleplays.

Jimmy himself had not seen the complete cut until he attended this sneak preview.

In his biography of James Dean, Venable Herndon described what happened after Arthur became aware of his friend's success and talent as a film star:

"It was an overwhelming experience," Arthur said. "So beautiful, so fantastic. It must have been like the first night someone went to see John Barrymore perform in Hamlet. *It was such an awakening, an eye opener. Here was this guy I'd been palling around with for quite a while, yet I had no idea who he really was."*

After the screening, the three of them [Arthur, Steiger, and Jimmy] went to a bar in the Valley. As Arthur later told Steiger, "Jimmy was still my best buddy, but I no longer related to him just as a bedmate to keep my feet warm at night, but as a star. *A Star is Born*, starring James Dean instead of Judy."

"He pulled no star act with me, however," Arthur said. "He was still the crazy, lovable, yet infuriating guy he always was one night when Walter Pidgeon came by. I was driving him *[Pidgeon]* to dinner. I exited through the gate at the end of my driveway and headed out onto the street. Suddenly, blinding lights almost caused me to have an accident. I fully expected a head-on collision."

Later, he learned that both Jimmy and Keenan Wynn had trained their motorcycle lights onto him and were roaring at high speeds directly into the front of his oncoming car. Before they collided, both men swerved their bikes to the left and right, respectively, of Arthur's vehicle, each of them yelling at the top of their lungs.

"Later, when Jimmy dropped by, I really lit into him," Arthur said. "Fun is fun, but all of us could have been killed. I blamed the stunt on Keenan, who should have known better."

"Jimmy was this terrific personality," Arthur said. "A real cuckoo. It was very informal at my place, a house party atmosphere. Lots of people unless we wanted to be alone. No stiff cocktail party atmosphere, as is so often seen in

Hollywood."

Jimmy later told Bast about the wildest, most intimate party presumably his host ever gave. Guests included Artie Shaw (the musician, who at one time or another married both Ava Gardner and Lana Turner), Errol Flynn, and Robert Mitchum.

"Mitchum and I got stoned. Mitchum went into the kitchen and pulled off all his clothes and covered his chest with catsup. 'I'm a raw hamburger,'" he told us."

Then, according to Jimmy, who relayed it to Bast, Flynn immediately took advantage and got down on his knees, and begin fellating Mitchum. Shaw provided the musical accompaniment to the act.

Robert Mitchum...do you want catsup with this raw hamburger?

While all this was going on, Jimmy went upstairs and emerged in a gown and high heels borrowed from the wardrobe of Arthur's mother.

"Then I did my best Mae West impersonation," Jimmy told Bast.

Suddenly, the doorbell rang and rang, followed by a loud pounding on the door. "It's the police," a strong, masculine voice yelled out. A fully dressed Arthur answered the door.

As Jimmy recalled, "The world's best-looking and most macho policeman stood there. He looked like a Viking god. Think Sterling Hayden in a movie from the early '40s."

But instead of a raid, the policeman told Arthur he'd been summoned to investigate a burglary, reportedly still in progress, in the neighborhood.

"Fuck the robbery," a drunken Arthur told the cop. "You can arrest Mitchum for pot and indecent exposure, Jimmy for speeding, and Flynn for stashing away a thirteen-year-old girl in one of my bedrooms upstairs. As for Artie Shaw here, make it bigamy. He married Ava Gardner before divorcing Lana Turner."

"The cop seemed like a real regular guy, so Arthur invited him to join the party," Jimmy said. "The robbery in progress was forgotten. After a few drinks, the cop told us he'd really come to Hollywood to be a male stripper at private parties. And that he'd like to try out his act on us."

"Piece by piece, his clothing came off, beginning with that gun. He really put on an act for us. Finally, when he showed it hard, Errol reached for it, and using it as a rudder, guided him into one of the downstairs bedrooms. Neither of them was seen again until a few hours later."

"Then the cop stood at the door, in uniform, fully dressed," Jimmy said.

"Thanks for the party, guys," he said. "Real Hollywood stuff, the type I was told went on here, but hadn't hooked up with until tonight."

Jimmy Steals Arthur Loew from Eartha Kitt

Arthur Loew, Jr. had not only been previously involved in romances with Pier Angeli and her sister, Marisa Pavan, but he'd also had a torrid affair with Eartha Kitt. The black singer was still Jimmy's best woman friend and "soul-mate."

"Jamie was always full of surprises," Eartha told the co-author of this book, Darwin Porter, one night in Key West when she was filming the film adaptation, *The Last Resort,* of his novel, *Butterflies in Heat.*

"I'd been cut off from Arthur, and I was hoping for a reconciliation. I called at two o'clock in the morning on a private line that fed directly into his bedroom. Then, I got the shock of my life. Jamie was in bed with the man I still loved."

In her memoirs, she wrote, "I still felt that the love Arthur and I had for each other was stronger than any outside influence. I still believed he'd stand up to the Loew family, who opposed any possibility of an interracial marriage between us."

In desperation early one morning, she'd put through a call to him, hoping he had changed his mind about her. "Perhaps I wanted him to say, 'I love you too much to let anything come between us.'"

"When Jamie came onto the phone, I felt like I was about to have a heart attack," Eartha said years later in Key West. "I knew him so well. I could tell by his voice that it wasn't a case of two men bunking together. I knew they were lovers. Jamie was loving the one man on earth I most desired. At first, my reaction was, how could he do this to me? I wanted to kill him. But I told my heart to settle down. After all, I'd rather Jamie be making love to Arthur than for him to be in bed with some blonde floozie like Jayne Mansfield."

Eartha Kitt with Arthur Loew, Jr.
A photographer captured the tension building between them over pressure from his powerful family about their interracial coupling.

"Knowing I had caught him

600

red-handed, Jamie told me that Arthur was in the tub taking a long hot bath."

He said, "The whole Loew family has moved in. Everyone is unhappy and very cold, and no one says much of anything to each other."

"Arthur has been very quiet," he went on. "He stays in his room most of the time, drinking throughout most of the day. The only person he lets into his bedroom is me. I offer what comfort I can. The operators at MGM warned me to not let any calls from you get through to him. His mother is here. This afternoon, she told me that her son would marry you only over her dead body."

"That article about you and Arthur in *Confidential* really blew the lid off," Jimmy told her, speaking in a very soft voice. "His mother told him that if he married you, it would mean the death of his grandfather. He's in his seventies and has suffered two recent stokes. He's confined to his suite at the Waldorf Astoria in New York. The pressure is really on Arthur."

"The one man I want to be the father of my child is being emotionally blackmailed," Eartha responded. "I wish he'd defend his position like a man who's not afraid to reach out for his happiness."

"Take care of him, Jamie," she said, trying to conceal the jealousy in her voice. "I still love him, you know. And I love you, too."

"I will, and I know you must be heartsick and filled with anger and frustration. Please don't turn on me. The friendship that Arthur and I developed just happened. It was just one of those things."

"It's always just one of those things," she said. "Sounds like a refrain from a song by Cole Porter." Then she hung up.

The next morning, Mrs. Arthur Loew, Sr. confronted Jimmy when he was in the study listening to music. "Please understand this," she said to him. "I know about you and my son, and I want it kept very quiet, very discreet. My family has a reputation to maintain. Forgive me for saying this, but I'd much rather that Arthur be secretly involved with a faggot than publicly married to a nigger woman."

***

Back in Hollywood, Eartha checked into a suite at the Sunset Towers. Later, with two escorts, both of them black and both of them jazz performers, they went to Ciro's for dinner.

She later wrote that as she was ordering food, "the hair on the back of my neck began to send messages. I knew that *he* was there. I could feel *him*. He was coming closer. Or was I going mad?"

It was Arthur. He looked down at her, telling her he was hosting a late night party, and asked her and her friends if they'd like to drop in.

She didn't commit herself, but later, with her escorts, she drove to his house.

"It was Jamie who opened the door," she said. "We fell into each other's arms, but something was different. 'What have they done to you? I feel your spirit is gone.'"

He laughed. "Ah, Kitt, you're on one of your voodoo trips again."

Soon after her arrival, she retreated from the guests in the living room, heading to her favorite part of the house, Arthur's study. He followed her and joined her on the sofa. Without saying a word, he took her hand.

In about ten minutes, Judy Garland entered the study, followed by Jimmy. She stood, confrontationally, in front of Arthur. "You bastard! You are so much in love with this girl you can't see straight, and you're too fucking weak to do anything about it. Arthur, when in the fuck are you going to grow up and be your own fucking man?"

Then, she stormed out of the room. Arthur jumped up and followed her. Jimmy noticed that the two of them became engaged in an animated conversation outside the door. He sat down on the sofa with Eartha and took her hand.

Two hours later, it was time to go. Jimmy walked Eartha to the door, where her escorts awaited her. Arthur was there, kissing Garland good night.

He turned to Eartha. "Sunset Towers, right? I'll call you tomorrow." Although he had kissed Garland goodbye, he had only shaken Eartha's hand.

The next day, that call from him never came in.

Two days later, Jimmy called her and invited her to Arthur's home on Miller Drive. He was at the door to let her in. Arthur was nowhere to be seen. He asked her to go with him in his Porsche to retrieve some records, including some of her own recordings, from his own residence.

When they got back, Arthur still had not appeared. "Give him time, Kitt," he said. "He's got to get rid of a lot of shit that he's been trying to get over for years. You know, family stuff. He's trying, but you've got to give him time."

"With this encouragement, Jamie and I parted," she later wrote in her memoirs.

She left the next day for Las Vegas, where she was performing in a show.

The following Sunday, she was in Las Vegas, in her dressing room. A chorus girl came in and announced, "I just heard over the radio that James Dean is dead in a car crash."

Eartha later wrote about her reaction. "I mourn you, Jamie, not so much for your death, but for cheating me out of your presence in my life. How dare you cheat me of that? You took the only friend I had, my one true friend. Jamie, you cheated me. I won't let you leave me. I will hold your spirit with me. You won't leave me, Jamie. *Ever!*"

She later admitted, "I fell to pieces. Jamie was long gone. So was Arthur.

Forever.

***

In 1956, Arthur Loew, Jr. established the James Dean Memorial Fund at the Actors Studio in honor of his former friend.

***

In 1959, Eartha was dining with her friend, Jack Dunaway, in Hollywood. "Oh, did you hear?" he asked her. "Arthur Loew just married Tyrone Power's widow. She was three months pregnant. It was the right thing to do."

He was referring to actress Deborah Ann Minardos, who Arthur married and then divorced within the same year.]

Vampira

GLAMOUR GHOUL OF TV REVEALS SECRETS FROM THE MORGUE

"Nicolas Ray, the director, told me that James Dean was 'intensely determined not to be loved—or to love.' Jimmy himself told me that the only success is immortality. In that he succeeded brilliantly. In spite of his small oeuvre of only three pictures, the world remembers him and not dozens of guys who made more than fifty movies."

—Vampira

If you were alive and living in Los Angeles in 1954, you knew who Vampira was. Resembling a more sexually alluring version of Morticia Addams, she appeared on the then-new medium of television like an exotic voodoo priestess.

Born Maila Elizabeth Syrjäniemi in Finland in 1922 (some sources say 1921), she emigrated to the United States and adopted the last name of her famous uncle, Olympic runner Paavo Nurmi, emerging as Maila Nurmi.

Although she failed as an actress, in 1944 she'd been cast on Broadway with Mae West in a play Mae had written, *Catherine Was Great*. It was produced, incidentally, by Elizabeth Taylor's future husband, Mike Todd. West, fearing that the younger girl was upstaging her, booted her out of the play.

Migrating to Hollywood, Maila supported herself by posing for pinup photographs in men's magazines such as *Gala*.

After several more failed attempts at acting, she hit it lucky. Attending a

603

masquerade ball, she dressed as a female vampire, complete with ghoulish white makeup, evoking a Charles Addams cartoon. She won first place in costume design.

A TV producer at station KABC spotted her and offered her the role of television hostess for a series of horror films they were going to run. She gladly agreed and officially changed her stage name to "Vampira."

During her brief reign, Vampira ruled the night, terrorizing audiences with her just-risen-from-the-coffin appearances, many of them configured as introductions to blood-sucking horror movies.

Her series ran for 16 episodes in 1954, with frequent reruns throughout the rest of the decade. For each of them, Vampira made a spectacular entrance amid dusty spider webs and dry ice fog. As the camera zoomed in on her vampire-deadly face, she'd let out a piercing scream before introducing the movie of the night. Usually, she reclined seductively on a skull-encrusted Victorian sofa.

An exotic & campy cult celebrity from the early days of television: Maila Elizabeth Syrjäniemi, *aka* Maila Nurmi, *aka* VAMPIRA.

Like a Zombie-mate of Bela Lugosi, she accessorized herself with all the trappings of Fright Night. Her drag included long, heavily painted fingernails in midnight black, with a mane of raven-colored hair, and a big-busted, slim-waisted, black-as-night outfit set off with fishnet hosiery.

Her eyes were heavily mascara-ed which contrasted with her blood-red lipstick. In character as a vampire-inspired sex kitten driven by a powerful thirst for fresh blood, she introduced such films as *Devil Bat's Daughter* and *Revenge of the Zombies*.

[In 1989, she lost a $10 million lawsuit in which she had charged that Cassandra Peterson's late-night hostess "Elvira" had pirated her character.]

She was an overnight sensation and

Vampira...Mae West viewed her as too much competition.

developed a campy cult following thanks partly to a ghastly appearance that made her look like she'd just emerged from a haunted coffin.

When she wasn't emoting in front of a TV camera, Vampira became a kind of "Mother Confessor" to the Bad Boys of Hollywood, notably and most famously James Dean, her on-again, off-again lover. She also hovered over Paul Newman and Tony Perkins, and was privy to their off-the-record romance with each other.

In that punitive era, these secretly bisexual men found it difficult to talk—with the noteworthy exception of Vampira— to a woman and make her privy to their affairs. Vampira, or so it is said, gave birth to the term "fag hag."

Googie's, that zippy, populuxe-style coffee house where stars gathered on Sunset Strip, was a major venue during the last summer of Jimmy's life. A new woman was about to enter the scene.

Vampira arrived nightly at Googies, emerging from a long black hearse, which she'd purchased from a funeral home. She called it "The Black Death."

Nurmi recalled meeting Jimmy. "One night, he walked into Googie's, and I was devastated by his male beauty and those blue eyes. He was a bit short, and I'd been seduced by men with more buffed bodies, but the kid had something, and I wanted a part of it. I thought he was a knock-out."

"I was coming down from an affair with Brando, who had just kicked me out on my ass after only three nights, and I was shopping for some fresh new meat to devour. However, I suspected that one of the pretty boys at Googie's would get him before I had my chance. How right I was. His name was Tony Perkins."

Nurmi would later claim that during that fateful summer, Jimmy, his close friend, Jack Simmons, and herself became almost a part of a "love triangle. We were almost never separate."

That, of course, was a gross exaggeration, although for a while, they did form an intense relationship, mainly because of their shared interest in the occult.

"Sometimes, I went home to my husband...what's his name...I forget."

Nurmi only pretended she didn't know the name of her husband. Dean Reisner was a former child actor in silent films, and he later became a screen writer, penning the script of *Dirty Harry.* Newman turned it down, the career-making role going to Clint Eastwood.

"Jack, Jimmy, and I would stay together at Schwabs Drugstore until it closed, later moving next door to Googie's," she said. "After midnight, we'd wander off to some experience, perhaps unmentionable."

"When I first met Jimmy, I was the star, and he was completely unknown. Fans of Vampira would push him aside to get to me. He'd be lost in a sea of what he called 'asses and elbows.'"

He referred to Vampira as "the Witch."

"But during our relationship, our positions changed. Fans pushed me aside to get to him."

Jimmy held court almost nightly at Googie's, sometimes lingering till long after the sun came up. Vampira was always there among his devoted listeners.

Almost nightly at some point he would speak about the implacability of his upcoming death. "Live fast, die young," was his motto.

Both Jimmy and Vampira shared the same ghoulish humor. For a publicity photo, Vampira once wandered through a local cemetery, announcing to the press that "I'm attending my own funeral."

Vampira cultivated a devoted following of campy gay men in the 50s, and many of them often performed free favors for her just for the privilege of being in her company. One man arranged her hair; another designed outfits for her, and one, Freddie Brandell, drove her around Hollywood, without charge, in his car, a luxurious Cadillac, a gift from his rich father.

At the peak of her fame, Vampira had at least eight gay boys on call. Each of them was introduced to Jimmy, and each developed a crush on the sexily handsome and increasingly famous young actor.

Dean referred to the boys as "flamers," and rejected each of their invitations for sex.

Freddie, who himself would die in a car crash in 1966, developed the most overwhelming crush of them all on Jimmy. He told Vampira, "I'm gonna have him if it's the last thing I do on this earth. I'm mad about the boy."

Jimmy would abuse Freddie, send him on stupid errands, or even give him his dirty underwear to wash. Vampira protested the abuse. "Girly boy loves it," Jimmy told her. "He'd even eat my shit if I asked him to."

In some respects, Vampira agreed with that.

She claimed that she was surprised by how intensely Newman bonded with Tony Perkins and Jimmy Dean. "Tony and Jimmy were wild boys," she claimed. "They should have been put away somewhere. They were such tormented souls. In contrast, Paul seemed only mildly disturbed, but he drank a lot. It was a difficult time for him. He couldn't make up his mind if he wanted to be straight or gay. I think Paul was basically straight, and had a great love for women. But back in those days, a good-looking gay guy could get him into bed."

"I dated Tony, but he always took me home early, usually at nine o'clock, and I had to settle for a kiss on the cheek. With Jimmy, I saw some action."

"One night I took Jimmy to meet my friends at the Maleficarum Coven, the oldest coven of witches in Los Angeles."

Jimmy was only momentarily intrigued with these witches, later telling author Joe Hyams, "It's all a bunch of cow pies, but weird and kind of fascinating."

Once, Vampira and Jimmy attended a ghoulish Hollywood party of witches and warlocks. She came dressed in her Vampira drag, and he came as Boris Karloff impersonating Frankenstein.

"Even after Jimmy became a star and could afford to treat us once in a while, he would pay only his part of the check—nothing else," Nurmi said. "He was a real miser."

"The first time Jimmy invited me back to his apartment, I was shocked to see a noose hanging from the ceiling," Vampira said.

"He told me he kept it there in case he wanted to commit suicide in the middle of the night. Of course, who was I to be surprised? At the time, I was driving around in a funeral hearse. I also noted that he kept a lot of books on black magic scattered around the room. One night he threw a party. What a motley crew of friends he had. A lot of bongo players and dope smokers, and a lot of 'actors' who had never acted in anything. Dope, dope, and more dope—that's all that crowd was interested in. Jimmy could have had any beautiful woman in Hollywood, but he was sleeping with guys."

"He was also going through his amputee period, dating this ugly woman who had only one leg. Jimmy told me that she was the leader of a gang of beatnik thieves who made their living robbing the homes of rich movie stars. That night, Jimmy stripped down to his underwear and rubbed her stump. To judge from the rising bulge in his underwear, that turned him on big time."

[This unidentified woman, of course, was not Toni Lee, the well-known entertainer. It was another amputee with whom Jimmy became involved.]

In her way, Vampira loved Jimmy, but was aware of his dark side, "which was darker than the black nail polish and black gown I wore to introduce those horror movies," she said. "I agreed with Elia Kazan, who claimed that Dean 'was a punk but a helluva talent.' He also said that 'Dean liked cars, waitresses—and waiters.' Sometimes, though, he dated high on the hog."

"Jimmy even managed to seduce Marlon Brando, Paul Newman, Steve McQueen, and Merv Griffin. Even Howard Hughes found out what his underwear was hiding, but had to pay for it."

"He often took me out and around as his date," Vampira said. "One night we showed up at a party in Malibu. Jimmy encountered a former lover, who denounced him in front of everybody, claiming he dated women only for publicity. 'Nobody in his right mind thinks you're straight,' the queen shouted at him."

By now, Jimmy was used to having that accusation hurled at him.

Sometimes, Nurmi, with Simmons, would ride together in "The Black Death," while Jimmy would precede them on his motorcycle. "He was reckless," she said, "riding with his hands held above his head and gyrating his hips like in an old Carmen Miranda movie. I thought he might be killed instantly, since another vehicle was likely to run into him. I just knew he was going to kill himself one day, sooner than later."

In addition to Simmons, Newman and Perkins were also fixtures in Jimmy's life. "Tony was carrying on with Jimmy, even though he was involved in a torrid romance with Tab Hunter, I think," Vampira said.

Jimmy revealed his affair with Tony to William Bast. "He's tall and skinny, but he's got a decent sized cock. He's so god damn shy. When he tries to talk and relate to people, he practically gets lockjaw. When he does speak up, he glances nervously around the room. He doesn't speak words, he spits them out. Late at night, though, he opens his trap and I can't get him to shut up. I'll wake up and find he's still talking. What a contradiction."

"His favorite form of sex involves dressing me in black and having me slip in through his bedroom window as 'The Kissing Bandit' before I rape him, violently, biting his lip as I do until I draw blood."

Television director James Sheldon, one of Jimmy's closest friends from his days in New York, once asked Tony why he didn't date starlets for publicity purposes.

"If a pill existed that would make me like women, I'd grind it into the ground with my foot," he said.

In the spring of 1955, director William Wyler wanted Jimmy to play a supporting role in *Friendly Persuasion,* Jessamyn West's affectionate book about conscience-torn Quakers during the Civil War. Jimmy was excited to work with Gary Cooper, but since *East of Eden* had made him a star, he was advised by Dick Clayton not to accept this or any other supporting roles.

"I'm so glad he didn't," Tony said. "I got the part. It made me a star, too. I got an Oscar nomination."

According to Nurmi, "Jimmy and I often ended our night at Googie's just as Paul and Tony were beginning their day. We'd be wasted and Paul and Tony would come in all bright eyed and bushy tailed. Tony would order a dozen prunes and a glass of freshly squeezed orange juice, but Paul wanted the works, bacon and eggs. On some mornings, he even ordered a greasy cheeseburger for breakfast."

"Even though I knew the boys were bed-hopping like rabbits in those days, they seemed devoted to each other," she said. "Tony would tell us goodbye and then hitch a ride down Sunset Strip.

Tony Perkins...inviting rape.

He always got picked up right away. No sooner did that sexy young stud stick out his thumb than we could hear the screech of brakes from some gay male eager to pick him up and give him a ride to the studio . . . or whatever."

Nurmi remembered one evening when Jimmy, Tony, and Paul all went with her to Googie's. "Paul and Jimmy climbed up on a soapbox that night. Jimmy said he was not going to become some performing monkey for the studio machine. Paul also claimed that he was not going to be turned into some paper doll created by a studio. 'Surface glamour doesn't interest me at all,' Paul said. 'These Hollywood stars can have all the false glamour they want. The estates in Beverly Hills. The swimming pools. Their fancy cars. Of course, the easy sex isn't bad.'"

Jimmy agreed with him.

"Tony shocked Jimmy and Paul when he took a different view," Nurmi claimed. "'I'm going to climb the ladder of success out here,' Tony vowed. 'Go to the right parties, meet all the VIPs. I want to be a movie star and enjoy all the trappings. You guys can ride your motorcycles into the desert and hang out with rattlesnakes. Not me. I want to drink champagne with the big boys.' At that point, Jimmy took his glass of freshly squeezed orange juice and slowly drizzled it over Tony's head."

"Tony never fell for Jimmy," she said. "If he was in love with anyone, it might be Tab. I'm sure he enjoyed sex with Jimmy, but as we found out later, Tony wanted to be James Dean, or at least 'the next James Dean.' He perhaps figured that by seducing him, some of Jimmy's talent would be passed on through semen."

"On separate occasions, Tony managed to entice Paul and Jimmy to walk barefoot with him from the Château Marmont along the entire length of Sunset Strip to Doheny," Nurmi claimed.

"Those guys were before their time. In the 60s, thousands of hippies were walking barefoot along the Strip. Perhaps those boys launched a future fad."

"The boys had their secrets," Nurmi said. "Tony was a tormented soul who really wanted to go straight, but he was screwing around with guys all the time. It was hopeless. Paul was the straightest of the bunch. But in those days, he had a wild streak of adventure in him and could be had. I knew Jimmy had already had him. They were rivals, though."

"Whereas Paul tried to suppress his dark side, Jimmy wanted to explore his, and that included lots of gay sex. Paul and Jimmy also took out their adventurous side through car racing, flirting with death."

"All the boys back then were going through a period of sexual experimentation. Hollywood pretty boys were fucking each other, occasionally screwing gals, and going to orgies. What a glorious time that was—the Eisenhower 50s."

Jimmy later denied it, but Nurmi on at least three occasions managed to lure him into her bed, draped in black sheets. "Frankly, I don't think Jimmy's prick was up for it at the time we bonded. I fear I didn't turn him on with my witch act."

***

Freddie Brandell had not given up on his scheme to seduce Jimmy. One night, a ghoulish opportunity arose that this schemer soon set into motion.

He remembered the pictures, published in *Life,* that Dennis Stock had taken of Jimmy. Some of them depicted him posed in a coffin—a display model in a general store back in Fairmount, Indiana.

Vampira's career as a TV ghoul had suffered from some recent bumps and grinds. When her show was canceled, although none of them accepted, she approached some of its competitors in the hopes that they'd pick it up.

As it happened, her friend and "gopher," Freddie, who was hoping for a career as a studio publicist despite the fact that it was going nowhere, convinced Vampira that her sagging career could be saved through a publicity scheme he had devised.

"We'll have Dean lying in a coffin, pretending to be dead, and you'll hover over him, looking like the most glamorous vampire who ever invaded a cemetery."

At first Jimmy was reluctant, but one night, after a liberal consumption of drink and drugs, he agreed to it. Freddie drove them and a photographer to a funeral home owned by the uncle of one of his friends. There were no dead bodies there on the night of this ghoulish party's arrival.

Before Jimmy agreed to crawl into the casket and lie down, pretending to be dead, Freddie offered him a final drink. The young actor made a big mistake in downing the drink in one gulp.

Inside the coffin, Jimmy jokingly sat up, in emulation of a corpse rising from the dead, but finally drifted off into a coma on the satin upholstery inside the casket. Vampira just assumed he had fallen asleep.

She had another appointment, and asked Freddie if he'd hang around and drive Jimmy home. Planting a kiss on Jimmy's lips, she left the funeral parlor accompanied by the photographer.

The next afternoon Freddie, told Vampira what he'd done the night before. Before Dean got inside that casket, Freddie had slipped him a vodka-based Mickey Finn. Not knowing the drink was drugged, he drank all of it, fast.

"After you and that guy left, I went and opened the back door and let in four of our friends," Freddie confessed. "Jimmy was knocked out, and we were sure that he'd remain that way for a long time. We lifted him from the coffin and placed him on a mortuary slab where we stripped off every piece of his clothing."

As Vampira listened in horror, Freddie told her more. "As you know, Jimmy has denied us any sex for a hell of a long time, even though all the guys have been panting for him. Unconscious on that marble slab, he could deny us nothing. We did everything we could think of, sexually speaking, before the rooster crowed. We left him lying on that slab to be discovered by the mortician in the morning. I hope he realized that Jimmy was still alive and didn't embalm him."

Vampira let out one of her famous screams and slapped Freddie's face. "You little fool! Don't you know each of you guys could get ten years or more for a stunt like that? Get out! I never want to see you or any of your so-called friends again. All of you are sick. Sick!"

She immediately called the photographer and told him to destroy all the negatives. She didn't want a picture with her in it to be used in evidence in case a trial was later held and the boys' rape of Jimmy exposed in open court.

***

After several months, Jimmy tired of Nurmi and had nothing good to say about her to gossipy Hedda Hopper, who published his comments.

"I don't go out with witches, and I dig dating cartoons even less," Jimmy claimed. "I have never taken her out, and I should like to clear that up. I resent her exploiting our acquaintance for publicity."

"I have a fairly adequate knowledge of the occult," he said. "I have studied *The Golden Bough* and the writings of the Marquis de Sade. I was interested to find out if this girl was obsessed by satanic forces. She knew absolutely nothing. I found her a novice with no true interest in the occult, except her Vampira makeup."

Biographer David Dalton wrote: "Vampira cut off all her hair in a last attempt to get Jimmy Dean's attention, but he would not respond to her trick-or-treat threats. Finally, she actually cast a spell on him! *'Oh, Ye Powers of Mwuetsi Moon Men, Come to My aid!'*

Dalton continued: "She drew Oola-Oola signed with thrice-charmed ashes. Snakes and lizards! She was using black magic against Dean! She administered the dreaded rites of the eight-by-ten glossy, cutting out his eyes and ears from the photographs with a little gold dagger, incanted fiendish curses (*"by the Fates of Ghastly Guchkakunda!"*), made a black-and-white voodoo doll to represent his body and performed the macabre ceremonies in her room, which was said to resemble some witch doctor's shack back in Haiti."

In one of Hollywood's tragic ironies, a few weeks later, on September 30,

1955, Dean suffered a broken neck, and subsequent death, during a car accident while recklessly driving his Porsche near Salinas, California. His ruined body was placed in a coffin at the Kuehl Funeral Home on Spring Street in Paso Robles, California, for shipment to Indiana. This coffin would be the final one.

Shorly after Jimmy's death, Nurmi posed for a postcard photo depicting herself sitting beside an open grave. The inscription read: "Come and join me!"

Published less than a week after Jimmy died, and interpreted as a nuanced but clearly implied reference to his violent and unexpected death, her campaign catalyzed a backlash of protests. In Vampira's words, "Letters from Jimmy's fans poured in by the tons."

Later, Liberace hired Vampira to appear in Las Vegas as a minor part of his nightclub act. She told him, "You're the only person in show business who has been nice to me since Jimmy died. I liked Jimmy so very much. It was the little things. I gave him a Tokyo-made ear picker, so he'd quit using those damn toothpicks to clean his ears."

In Vegas, Liberace told her that he'd tried to offer Jimmy money, as a means of enticing him to visit him in Nevada, but he never would fly out to see me."

Three years after Dean's tragic death at the age of twenty-four, Vampira met with director Elia Kazan to discuss the actor's growing legend. "I don't like it," Kazan said. "His fans are glorifying a Dean that never existed. They see him as a little waif brutalized by Hollywood. He was a sicko with talent. He hated everybody, mostly himself. I'd call him a half-baked pudding of hatred. If you actually tasted that pudding, it was poison."

In 1959, Vampira made one last attempt at stardom when director Ed Wood, who made the most ridiculous movies ever filmed, cast her alongside Bela Lugosi ("Count Dracula") in the *schlocky*, not-even-funny-enough-to-be-camp *Plan 9 from Outer Space*. Critics have, since then, defined it as "the worst film of all time." It was the last film Lugosi ever made—an inglorious end to a fabulous and otherwise leg-

In the immediate aftermath of Jimmy's death, Vampira, the ghoulish neurotic of the night, shamelessly tried to twist it into a tasteless publicity stunt for herself. In this replica of a postcard she distributed, she poses in front of an open grave, with the implication that she's inviting him to join her during her "walks with the living dead."

The tasteless prank backfired, provoking massive outrage from Jimmy's fans.

endary career.

In 1994, when the historic reality of Vampira had evolved into a cultish and very campy icon brought back to the screen, she was too old to play herself in *Ed Wood*, Tim Burton's tribute to the F-movie director. It starred Johnny Depp. Vampira was portrayed by the Goth-inspired Lisa Marie Smith, a model and actress from New Jersey who billed herself simply as "Lisa Marie." *[No, not the one associated with Elvis Presley and Michael Jackson.]*

In 2006, two years before her death, Vampira's life story, or at least a heavily edited version of it, would be relayed in a documentary by Kevin Sean Michaels entitled *Vampira: The Movie*.

She never benefited financially from her fame. In later life—almost destitute—she sold handmade jewelry. At her lowest point, she lived in a garage and became a cleaning woman in a restaurant.

Unlike her friend, James Dean, who died young, Vampira would not meet the Grim Reaper until January 10, 2008, in Los Angeles. She'd lived a turbulent, unhappy life before finally—at the age of 85—releasing her last breath.

In her later years, she proclaimed, "The world doesn't have much use for a broken-down old fag hag. Where are all my golden boys of the 50s? Of course, they were sleeping with each other and rarely gave me a tumble, but I loved them all the same."

His Late, Late Show: Jimmy Hangs Out on Sunset Strip With
"Unsavory Aliens of the Night"

During the last summer of his life, James Dean moved into an apartment on Sunset Plaza Drive, overlooking Sunset Strip. Rogers Brackett had brought him to this street when he was the producer's kept boy. He could now thumb his nose at Brackett and pay his own rent. "Now, Brackett runs from his landlord, who's demanding back rent."

Googie's remained Jimmy's favorite hangout. When Bast spotted him there with the gay actor, Tony Perkins, Jimmy stopped to acknowledge him and introduce a former lover (Bast) to a new lover (Perkins).

"Tony and I have been hanging out with a lot of spooks," Jimmy said. "I'll give you a ring some night."

Bast stood watching as Tony and Jimmy wandered off together into the night.

The "spooks" Jimmy referred to were no doubt members of what the press called "The Night Watch." After midnight, these young men and women, on the fringe of show business, convened at Googie's. Bast described them as "the lonely, the alienated, and the disenfranchised, trying to meet other kindred souls."

Newspapers made outrageous claims against the coven, labeling them "Satanists who practice the black arts, including eating both excrement and human flesh."

The Warners publicity department was horrified that Jimmy's name would be dragged into this group, which was becoming increasingly notorious and was under scrutiny by the police.

"Jimmy was not the man I had known and loved," Bast claimed. "He was dealing with the darker side of his personality and, for a time at least, found comfort with these unsavory aliens of the night. When I dared ask him about that during another encounter, he told me he had an answer.

"I like bad people," he said. "I guess because I'm so god damn curious about what makes them bad."

As Jimmy moved into the final weeks of his life, he saw less and less of Bast, who was writing teleplays. Their long ago sexual contact in the California desert never blossomed into a love affair. Jimmy had turned elsewhere.

Finally, that day in late September that Bast had long anticipated had arrived. Jimmy was killed in a car crash on the road to Salinas.

Bast later wrote, "I'd spent much of the time of the past five years, between the time we met and the time he died, in his thrall. I couldn't have guessed then that I would spend the next five decades in his shadow."

Throughout the rest of his life, Bast, in spite of his own accomplishments as a writer, would be famous for having known James Dean. Fueling that fame would be his authorship of two books and a TV movie focusing on details associated with the life of his former friend.

As the years passed, Bast's statements about Jimmy grew increasingly ambivalent and bitter. Friends sometimes interpreted his unflattering comments about Jimmy as "traitorous."

He told the press, "In real life, Jimmy was not an extraordinary person. If anything, he was rather bothersome." On *Entertainment Tonight,* Bast defined Jimmy as "cocky and arrogant."

Yet it was his very association with Jimmy that made Bast famous in certain circles. "Dean was very, very shrewd in the way he used people. He knew what he was doing. To get where he got, he kissed a lot of asses, and he hated himself for that."

For the rest of his life, whenever Bast was introduced to people, they more or less asked the

Sir John Gielgud..."Were you and Jimmy lovers?"

same question.

On the Left Bank of Paris at an all-male party in the 1950s, Bast met John Gielgud.

"Ah, yes, William Bast," Gielgud said. "The young man who knew James Dean. Tell me, my dear, were you lovers? I had Brando, but never Dean."

In his final known comment about Jimmy, Bast told his remaining friends, "When one dines with the devil, it's best to use a very long spoon. Of course, I loved him. There is no denying that. Not a day goes by but what I don't wonder what it would have been like, had I moved in with him again, this time as his lover. Could I have trusted him with my love, my devotion, my life? I doubted it then, and I doubt it still, but the biggest question persists. Would I really have risked it, for better or worse, at least to find out if it would have worked?

Jimmy's Newest Best Pal & Confidant Exposes Him to
Life in the Straight World

During the final year of his life, Jimmy bonded with Lee Bracker, a well-dressed insurance agent.

In the Warner Commissary, Leonard Rosenman, one of Jimmy's closest friends, brought the two men together. Bracker was married, the father of two girls, Alison and Lesley.

Two young men of the mid-century came together, and within a week or so, they were "best pals and confidants."

Their friendship did not begin all at once. It evolved gradually, beginning one night when Jimmy arrived, unannounced at the Rosenman home. He discovered that the couple were out, and that Bracker had volunteered to babysit for them.

Jimmy decided to stick around, and they talked for hours, discovering their mutual interests.

Before the night was over, Jimmy had intrigued Bracker with Porsches and car racing.

A friendship was formed that would last until Jimmy's death. Bracker and Jimmy would soon be meeting at night, arriving in separate vehicles at the top of Mulholland Drive "to go for a spin," in whichever of the several cars Jimmy was driving at the time, since there wouldn't be many cars on the road at that hour.

Bracker was straight, and he made it clear in a personal memoir, published in 2013, that his relationship with Jimmy had nothing to do with sex. He was of the opinion that Jimmy's homosexual life ended when he arrived in Hollywood to film *East of Eden.*

Jimmy was an expert at keeping various facets of his life separated, especially when he was with his straight friends.

It was Bracker who accompanied Jimmy when he went to

Lew Bracker with James Dean...call it a "bromance."

purchase his infamous Porsche Spyder 550, little knowing that it would become his friend's coffin. Coincidentally, Bracker, the week before Jimmy's death, in his capacity as an insurance salesman, drew up an insurance policy on his life.

[James Dean died without leaving a will. Even though he'd made only one payment on his insurance policy, the company owed Jimmy's heir $100,000. It is not known who Jimmy would have selected as an heir to his estate.

In the absence of any specific instructions designating a beneficiary, Winton Dean, Jimmy's father, received the policy's the entire benefit. It was ironic that he'd given Jimmy so little money—almost none—and he ended up profiting from his son's death.]

Two days before, Jimmy had confronted Bracker, telling him, "you and I have got to get married."

"To each other?" Bracker asked in astonishment.

"We both have to get married to women and have families. That's what we both want. That's what we both need."

"He never talked to me like a man worried about cutting life short," Bracker later wrote.

Slowly, Bracker came to know his new friend, who was becoming more famous every day. "Jimmy would be bothered when someone would say he was mean and disrespectful. Actually, he wasn't. They took silence to mean he cared little or nothing for them. They didn't have the insight, or didn't care to exercise that insight, in knowing that he was a shy boy that just didn't know how to approach them. Instead of making an attempt to approach him, they just wrote him off."

Some of Jimmy's closest friends, who knew about his relationship with Bracker, felt he was in love with his new friend, who shared so many of his mutual interests.

"Stanley Haggart had that view: "I never met Bracker, but the way Jimmy talked about him made me aware of just how strong his feelings were for this man. But Jimmy was no fool. He was completely aware that Bracker didn't go that route, and I doubt if he ever made a pass at him. He didn't want to ruin what he saw as an important new figure in his life. Of course, Jimmy wouldn't be the first gay man who fell in love with a straight man."

From all reports, Bracker and Jimmy enjoyed many a "crazy, fun-filled day" in the bittersweet and halcyon summer of 1955, as Jimmy's life edged toward a cliff.

Bracker recalled hanging out with Jimmy beside a swimming pool one hot afternoon, inventing a parody of a "swords-and-sandals" movie with a Biblical theme. "We had Mary having an affair with Joseph and getting her pregnant," Bracker said. "They decided to hit the road because no one believed that cockamamie story about an Immaculate Conception. During their journey to Bethlehem, Joseph tried to tune out Mary's kvetching."

In their contrived scheme for a screenplay, Joseph suddenly flashes on a moneymaking scheme: "From this *mensch,* we can make a living. Look what Moses did with the burning bush tale and that slab of stone with ten scratches on it. I'm broke and can't afford a room. I'll find a barn; you'll have my boy, and I'll round up a few goat and pigs. And I'll get three guys from Central Casting with costumes borrowed from Hope and Crosby's *Road to Morocco* movie. We'll be in business."

Before his fateful trip to Salinas, Jimmy stopped by Bracker's house and pleaded with him to accompany him to the car races. Bracker refused, preferring to stay home for what he called "My most pleasurable pastime, a USC football game."

The last time Bracker saw Jimmy was when Jimmy, rebuffed, called back to him during his exit, "Okay, it's your funeral."

In his memoir, Bracker related how dazed he'd become when he received news about Jimmy's sudden death. As the years went by, he summed up his involvement with Jimmy by writing, "His physical presence in my life has ended, but our friendship continues."

JIMMY ON THE FAST TRACK WITH A
Hot Brunette from Sweden

In January of 1955, as Jimmy experienced a California winter, his romantic life with women consisted mostly of a series of "chicks picked up at Googie's," as he confessed to William Bast. On the mornings after his adventures, he usually didn't bother to remember the name of his conquest of the previous evening.

As he complained to Bast, "Sex with these mannequins isn't turning me on. These gals really aren't interested in me. The want to brag about fucking James Dean, the new movie star."

Just when he was about to give up on women, Lilli Kardell came into his life. When Jimmy started dating her, virtually no one in Hollywood had heard of her.

She was beautiful and Swedish. She had come to Hollywood to become the next Greta Garbo or Ingrid Bergman, both of whom had also been from Sweden.

She had been discovered by a Stockholm-based agent working for RKO films. As a secretary, she'd been employed because she had a good command of English, which she'd been taught in school.

Lilli Kardell...Jimmy's last female flame.

Soon, at the age of eighteen, she was "shipped" to Hollywood. Her diary recorded that she met Jimmy on February 19, 1955, early in the year he died.

Ironically, Kardell was introduced to him by Arthur Loew, Jr., his male lover. The Swede and the farm boy from Indiana would soon become engaged in an affair that would endure through his last summer.

Author Joe Hyams described Kardell as, "The quintessential starlet, a pretty brunette with almond-shaped eyes and a big bosom. She was good-natured, forgiving, and generous with her favors. She was also dedicated to the craft of acting. Before seeing Jimmy at night, she took singing, dancing, and diction lessons during the day."

Soon, Jack Simmons, Jimmy's closest and most faithful male companion, met Kardell. "Lilli was quite bovine," he said. "Jimmy and I called her 'The Cat Lady.'"

[As the Cat Lady, she must have been more "feline" than "bovine."]

Author Donald Spoto claimed, "Kardell could have passed for a reverse image of Jimmy himself. They wore their hair similarly, they wore matching bathing suits, and they favored black leisure outfits. As with Pier Angeli, he favored exotic foreign ladies to escort out in public, following the example of Marlon Brando."

At their first public outing, Jimmy and Kardell were accompanied by Tennessee Williams and Anna Magnani.

While the women were at table, Tennessee had a brief chat with Jimmy at the bar. Later, to Darwin Porter, in Key West, Tennessee recalled that evening: "I asked Jimmy if he were in love with this young Swede. Had she made off with his fickle and most unreliable heart?"

"Tenn," he answered. "You know me well enough to know by now that I'm a deceitful lover, not to be trusted out of one's sight. I'm sure you once fell in love with me, and I'm equally certain I broke your heart. That's what I do. When biographers record my life story years from now, I'm sure at least one of them will entitle their bio, *James Dean, The Heartbreaker.*"

"I've never really loved anybody in my life," Jimmy confessed to the playwright. "I tried to have an affair with myself, but that didn't work out. As for Lilli, I'm just hanging out for the sex, and sometimes, even that bores me. I hate to confess this, but my greatest sex has been with myself. I failed in an affair with myself, but the sex is great."

"I know what you mean," Tennessee said. "Masturbation is, after all, one of life's pleasures when one's sexual partners prove unreliable."

Jimmy held up his right hand. "This is my most reliable sex partner. This hand never fails me. I'm sure she'll be there servicing me when I'm old and gray."

"*If* you ever become old and gray," Tennessee said. "Time herself, that relentless bitch who destroys all of us, both mentally and physically, will never claim you. You'll outrun her, I'm sure."

"Does that mean you're predicting an early death for me?" he asked.

"You know in your heart that's how your story will end."

***

For his first trip out of town with Kardell, Jimmy drove her to Palm Springs for a car race at a track alongside the foreboding concrete runway of the Palm Springs Airport, the arrival point for many visiting celebrities from Hollywood. To Kardell, Jimmy cut a dashing figure, dressed in black racing coveralls with a black-and-white checkered cap. Before the beginning of the race, he told her, "I know I'm going to win. I can feel it in my bones."

She reminded him to be careful. "Bones can be broken!"

It was late March, but the noonday sun already made the desert resort feel like August.

About twenty cars were competing, driven by such ace drivers as Ken Miles and Cy Yedor, along a grueling 2.3 mile track. The starting positions were drawn by lot, and Jimmy was "seriously pissed off" at his car's subsequent placement in the fourth row at the rear. "I've been assigned to the fucking boondocks," he complained.

The moment the flag went down, he jammed his foot on the accelerator and took off, zooming past cars who had been assigned better starting positions. He cut wide around them on the outside, almost scraping the left door of a driver from San Diego. "The fucker almost killed me," that driver complained in a formal protest he later filed against Jimmy.

As the first quarter-mile was reached, Jimmy had moved up to fifth position. Never letting his foot leave the accelerator, he was leading the pack at the end of the hazardous first lap. His Porsche could go no faster than one-hundred miles an hour. His aim was to beat Yedor and Miles in their MG Specials.

To his disappointment, Jimmy ended the race in third position. However, judges, on a technicality, disqualified Miles, so Jimmy was moved up to second place. That meant he would carry off the Silver Trophy. "I should have won the gold," he complained to Kardell.

"On the track, I learn about both people and myself," he told her.

"Speed fascinated Jimmy," Kardell said. "He loved it so much, it would ultimately lead to his death. It was not just some passing fancy, but an all-consuming passion."

After the race, Kardell and Jimmy got into a tiff, perhaps because she was seen having a drink with the dashingly handsome Robert Evans, who would later, from 1967 to '73, be in charge of production at Paramount.

"What are you doing with him?" Jimmy later asked her, angrily. "I hear he got his start selling jockstraps in New York."

[Evans would later marry actress Ali McGraw, who would eventually divorce him—with disastrous consequences for her movie career— to marry Steve McQueen.]

In her diary, Kardell wrote: "Jimmy and I were angry at one another. Idiotic evening. Finished with myself drunk, and sleeping in a rented car."

The two made up the following day, and he took her to the Shadow Mountain Resort and Golf Club in nearby Palm Desert to celebrate his victory. There had been two races.

In one of them, he came in first, beating out several veteran drivers.

Miles, an English driver, told the press, "Dean is a reckless daredevil, even if he doesn't give a fuck for his own life, he should not try to kill the other drivers. Car racing is not a bullfight, his other favorite sport. The bloody little punk just doesn't get that."

[Miles would later die in an accident during a car race in Riverside, California.]

In her diary, Kardell recorded details about the second night of their weekend together. "Terrible atmosphere between us. He behaved in a ridiculous fashion and ignored me completely and flirted with other girls. Finally, we reconciled, and he drove me back to Los Angeles. He slept a little, and we made love. Everything is well between us now. I hope."

Jimmy spent the following night in the bed of Arthur Loew, Jr., on Miller Drive, where he'd been given the keys to come and go as he wished.

Kardell later described what it was like being "Jimmy's girl."

"He would all of a sudden just leave and go away and find some buddy of his and start talking about cars. He would be gone for half an hour or more. He was very moody. He could one minute be very deep in thought about something, and then snap out of it, and in the next minute, he'd be on the floor dancing and making some joke, and it was just no use getting mad at him for that kind of thing, because that just didn't do any good. You just had to understand—that was the way he was."

In April, while Jimmy was filming *Rebel Without a Cause,* he came down with the flu. Both Maila Nurmi (Vampira) and Kardell took turns bringing him hot soup and making hot tea for him.

When he recovered, he did not date Kardell exclusively. Not only was he involved sexually with certain members of the cast from *Rebel,* he was also seen on occasion with April Channing, a Broadway showgirl, and with Dana Wynter, who had arrived in Hollywood from her native London, hoping to make it in American pictures. Lucy Marlow, who had had a small role in Judy Garland's *A Star Is Born,* was also seen on his arm, as was Julie Robinson, a dancer with Katherine Dunham's troupe. Jimmy publicly referred to Robinson as "my mambo instructor."

In August of 1955, perhaps against Jimmy's wishes, Kardell talked to a reporter from *Modern Screen.* "Jimmy is an ice man. Some of the things he does, it is because he is youthful. It takes time to handle fame. But he really is very kind. They tell me he doesn't smile enough. Not true. He smiles much. He has a good sense of humor."

As that summer of 1955 came to its inevitable end, Kardell perhaps realized how hopeless any long-term commitment from Jimmy would be. She began dating other men, especially after Jimmy left for Texas to shoot *Giant.*

On September 30, 1955, she wrote in her diary: "Jimmy Dean, my only love, died on his way to Salinas for the races. Auto crash. Please take care of him, God, and let him be happier now than before. I can only hope that I will find Jimmy in some other person. My thoughts will always be with you, Jimmy. Goodbye forever. I love you, and will never forget you and the memories we shared."

[Kardell never found Jimmy in another person. In 1958, she married an insurance executive, but the relationship ended disastrously. Alleging cruelty, she divorced him after less than a year. Her next engagement was to an actor as dif-

Troy Donahue...No replacement for James Dean.

ferent from Jimmy as a mongoose is from a snake. She began an affair with Troy Donahue, that handsome blonde pin-up who became a cardboard fixture in films during the late 1950s and early 60s before his Hollywood fame flickered and died. Ironically, he once made a film called Live Fast, Die Young, *which is the most-used epitaph applied to Jimmy.*

It was rumored that Donahue's motivation for hooking up with Kardell was entirely based on the fact that she'd once been "Jimmy's girl."

Donahue and Kardell never married. One night, she was rushed to the Cedars of Lebanon Hospital, suffering from a severe beating. When she recovered, she sued Donahue for $60,000 for assault and battery. The case was settled out of court.]

Actors Eager to Fill the Shoes of
JAMES DEAN

In the wake of the death of James Dean, studios both in the United States and Europe would market some emerging actor as "The New James Dean."

Of all the inheritors of the throne, Christopher Jones, who for a while was married to Susan Strasberg, came the closest to physically resembling Jimmy, based on his blonde hair and slender yet strapping physicality. He reigned briefly in the 1960s as the reincarnation of Jimmy.

For a while, the extraordinarily handsome Maxwell Caulfield, who once appeared frontally nude in a play in New York, was also promoted as another James Dean. Caulfield's well-muscled physique elicited more praise than his acting in any film he made. He was truly a rebel without a good movie role.

In West Germany, the bisexual Horst Buchholz was hailed as the next James Dean. He was known for his brooding intensity, his tousled hair, and his sexy appeal. He wasn't really Jimmy, although he did wrap his car around a tree one day. Unlike Jimmy, he survived.

For a period in the 60s, Alain Delon was sometimes marketed as "The James Dean of France." He rose to stardom in *Purple Noon* (1960), a Franco-Italian production based on Patricia Highsmith's *The Talented Mr. Ripley.*

In the immediate aftermath of Jimmy's death in 1955, the executives at Paramount decided that Tony Perkins, Jimmy's sometimes lover, should be defined as their reincarnation of James Dean. Alert

Maxwell Caulfield...Perhaps the body of a Greek god was not enough.

to the public hysteria that followed in the wake of Jimmy's death, the studio wanted someone to pick up his mantle. Tony seemed their best candidate.

Along with many others, Paul Newman was taken aback by the false claims that Tony Perkins was making about the closeness of his relationship with Jimmy. He even asserted to reporters from fan magazines that he and Jimmy had roomed together in his apartment on Sunset Plaza Drive, which was not true.

Jack Simmons, who had actually been Jimmy's roommate, was very resentful. "No one can replace Jimmy Dean," he said. "Certainly not Tony Perkins. Jimmy was all internal and driven, while Perkins is sort of mechanical, physically plotted, and contrived. There is no comparison to Jimmy, except in Perkins' own head."

Alain Delon...The French had their own James Dean.

Tony Perkins, as he appeared in *Psycho.*

Photoplay magazine disagreed: "We need an actor to fill the shoes of James Dean. Tony Perkins is an ideal candidate to fill those shoes. He does offbeat things like Dean and makes good copy."

Ultimately, it wasn't Perkins, but Newman who moved in to take over roles that had been slated and conceived for Jimmy. The first of the lot was a boxing picture, *Somebody Up There Likes Me* (1956), the cinematic saga of Rocky Graziano.

Newman complained to Rod Steiger, "Whereas Perkins is courting it, I'm having this new James Dean image thrust upon me. I'm the unwilling actor taking over his roles both in the movies and on TV. When will the newspapers stop making these stupid comparisons between Jimmy and me?"

"When the next Paul Newman comes along," the veteran actor told him, cynically.

In *Somebody Up There Likes Me,* Newman found himself co-starring with two of Jimmy's former lovers, each of them of different genders—Sal Mineo and Pier Angeli. Newman himself had already been sexually intimate with Pier during their work together in *The Silver Chalice.*

When they came together on the set, she said to him, "We both loved Jimmy, and now we've lost him. Fortunately, I have Vic Damone, and you have Joanne Woodward."

Both of them found it ironic that in *The Silver Chalice,* Newman was a Jew playing an Italian-American, and she, a *bona fide* Italian, was playing his Jewish girlfriend.

When Newman had first encountered her, she was suffering from a broken ankle, the result of a fall in the stairwell of her home. Until she recovered, he sometimes carried her between her dressing room and lunch in the studio commissary.

After he'd done that two days in a row, he lingered for a few hours after their return to her dressing room, since neither of them was due that afternoon on the set.

When an assistant came to summon Pier to the set, he found Newman in his jockey shorts with Pier, together in the shower.

"The first day Newman met Sal Mineo on the set, the young man was still mourning the loss of his friend. Mineo had been cast in *Somebody* as Graziano's friend, Romolo.

Fourteen years older than the Bronx-born Sicilian-American, Newman congratulated him on his Oscar nomination for *Rebel Without a Cause.* "I thought you and Dean were terrific," he said. "I'm sorry he's gone."

"Not as sorry as I am," Mineo said, appearing on the verge of tears. "I noticed you work out every day. I'd like to join you"

Aware of Mineo's gender preference, Newman warned him, "Okay, but working out is all we're going to do. I don't intend to replace Dean in your life."

At the gym, the two men worked out for more than 90 minutes before Mineo joined Newman in the shower. "You can look, but don't touch!"

"I promise."

As Mineo later confessed, "I didn't keep my promise. As Paul was showering, before he knew what was happening, he found me on my knees. He told me to leave him alone, but I didn't. Finally, he said, 'Go for it, kid. I'm too far gone to stop you.'"

Getting sudsy with Sal Mineo.

Chapter Twenty-Two

REBEL WITHOUT A CAUSE

"YOU'RE TEARING ME APART!" JIMMY SCREAMS, IGNITING THE ANGST OF TEENAGERS EVERYWHERE

Live Fast, Die Young and Violently

THE JINXED CURSE OF *REBEL:* NICK ADAMS, SAL MINEO, & NATALIE WOOD

"Who's Sleeping with Jimmy Tonight?"

Long before he met Jimmy, director Nicholas Ray had filmed *They Live by Night (1949)*, co-starring Farley Granger and Cathy O'Donnell, a *film noir* story of teenage lovers fleeing from the law.

Since then, he had wanted to create another "youth-in-angst" saga. Originally entitled The *Blind Run*, it was later renamed *Rebel Without a Cause*.

In the late 1940s, he'd screen tested Marlon Brando for the role, but never got a green light to film a script inspired by a case study researched and written by Dr. Robert Lindner, *Rebel Without A Cause: The Hypnoanalysis Of A Criminal Psychopath*. It had been researched during his stint as a staff psychiatrist at the Federal Penitentiary in Lewisberg, Pennsylvania. Warners had acquired the film rights to Lindner's book back in 1943, but the property just languished on the shelf until it was reactivated in 1954, an era when juvenile delinquency was making headlines across the country.

Ray had just filmed what became one of the most notorious westerns of all time, *Johnny Guitar* (1954), co-starring Joan Crawford and Mercedes McCambridge. "I fucked Crawford and got to suck off Scott Brady, who is very well hung," Ray later told Jimmy Dean shortly after they met. "I got to see Sterling Hayden, a Viking god, in the nude, and what a whopper, but he made it clear to me he was off limits."

Ray went through two distinguished writers, Leon Uris and Irving Shulman, rejecting each of their scripts.

Ray finally hired Stewart Stern, the cousin of Jimmy's lover, Arthur Loew, Jr. He'd written the script for Pier Angeli's debut film, *Teresa* (1951). In Stern's version of the script, seventeen-year-old Jim Stark is the new kid on the block, arriving at Dawson High, where he is immediately men-

Rebel's 1949 predecessor--noir, with a focus on juvenile delinquents, with direction by Nick Ray and starring bobbysox heartthrob Farley Granger.

Nicholas Ray's film project had impressively scholastic origins: written by the resident psychiatrist at a Federal penitentiary, it was subtitled, *The Hypnoanalysis of a Criminal Psychpath*.

When James Dean was cast into the male lead, his enemies and detractors made note of the original title.

aced by a tough gang.

"We get going with a bang," Ray said. "Stark gets into trouble with the cops, the girl next door snubs him, and a young homosexual develops a crush on him."

It was a screening in New York of *East of Eden* that had convinced Ray that Jimmy would make the ideal Jim Stark. He immediately got in touch with Jimmy's New York agent, Jane Deacy, and a meeting was scheduled.

The two men bonded almost from the first. Although Jimmy had already turned twenty-four, Ray thought he looked young enough to pass for a teenager.

"Jim Stark and Jimmy shared one thing in common," Ray said. "Both of them wanted to belong, yet feared belonging. Dean understood the character, and Stark's conflict of violent eagerness and mistrust, the intensity of his desires, his fear, all of which could make him at times arrogant and egocentric. I felt Dean could capture the character behind all this and depict Stark's desperate vulnerability."

Ray spent two weeks in New York with Jimmy, concluding that he encapsulated many of Jim Stark's characteristics, as laid out in the script. "He was both the boy and the man, the gay and the straight, the tender and the violent."

Ray told Elia Kazan, "I lived for a while with Jimmy in that little apartment of his, cluttered with books and other junk, including a matador's cape on the wall. We went to a lot of movies. We got drunk a lot. Jimmy let me fuck him...a lot. He was better than my former wife, that whore, Gloria Grahame."

"Actually, I needed Dean to help me flesh in Stark's character and bring him to life on the screen. The script had not been fully developed. I wanted Dean to probe his own experiences in life and apply them when needed."

As Ray told Kazan, who had helmed Jimmy in *East of Eden,* "You know I walk on both sides of the sidewalk. I not only screwed Jimmy in New York, and I plan to take director's privilege and keep plugging him as long as we're making *Rebel.* I'm looking forward to it."

"I'd rather fuck Marilyn Monroe, which I do," Kazan said.

After returning to Los Angeles, Jimmy hit some of the rougher streets, hanging out with alienated young men and often with their "gang molls," as he called their girlfriends. "They wore leather jackets and roamed the streets at night, looking for a faggot to beat up. Not all of them were poor. Some were from rich families. Boy, those guys scared me. One night, I got gang raped by three guys. But I'm not going to go into that." *[He made this revelation to Ray, who had already flown back to Hollywood.]*

Jimmy signed on to the film shortly before Christmas of 1954. At the time, he had serious reservations about it, interpreting it as a Grade B movie typical of the type being cranked out by producer Roger Corman.

Originally, Stern had told Jimmy that he envisioned *Rebel* "as a modern version of *Peter Pan,* three troubled kids inventing a world of their own. I want to say something about the nature of loneliness."

"I set for myself a big goal," Stern said. "Within a period of only twenty-four hours, I wanted to tell the story of a young generation coming into maturity."

Stern later said, "It was obvious to me that Jimmy did not want to play the role I wrote. He wanted to play himself."

Before shooting began, Ray asked Jimmy about his draft status. "I was rejected for bad eyes, flat feet, and butt plugging."

For his work on the film, Jimmy would receive only $12,500.

[That compared with 20ᵗʰ Century Fox giving Marilyn Monroe $15,000 for her co-starring role in Gentlemen Prefer Blondes *(1953).*

[The James Dean Foundation takes in $6 million annually, including licensing agreements for such products as jogging suits, T-shirts, pillowcases, and sunglasses. In Japan, a customer can buy a life-size mannequin of Dean to take to bed for whatever pleasure one desires.]

*** *** ***

Author Gore Vidal was living at the Château Marmont with his longtime companion, Howard Austen. His friend, Paul Newman, had turned him onto the place. Grace Kelly occupied one of its bungalows, as did Nicholas Ray. One Sunday, Vidal met Ray by the pool, where he introduced himself, thinking that perhaps he might buy one of the film scripts he was writing at the time.

Within thirty minutes, Vidal and Ray argued, Vidal maintaining that the scriptwriter was more vital to the film than its director. Ray responded with, "If it's all in the script, why film it?"

Despite their disagreement, Ray invited Vidal to a party that he was hosting later in his bungalow. He told Vidal that he was casting a film called *The Blind Run* about juvenile delinquents and starring James Dean.

Nicholas Ray in 1961. Gore Vidal described him as "a silver haired, chain-smoking *auteur* cursed with a romantic nature and a taste for vice."

"I've seen Dean before," Vidal said. "At the Actors Studio. He's always hanging around sucking up to Tennessee Williams, hoping he'll write another great part like he did for Brando."

Vidal attended the party with every intention of

"putting the make on Dean." But it didn't work out that way. "I found him ar-rogant and insulting to me. What a prick he was. We hated each other on sight."

Vidal later described his negative impression of Dean to Ray: "The first thing he said to me was, 'I never heard of you.' He knew damn well who I was. I should have told him, 'I never heard of you, either, punk.'"

"Since you and Dean didn't hit it off, I'll introduce you to Dennis Hopper," Ray said. "He's just getting started as an actor. And he's available—that is, if you're not a size queen."

Searching for Judy

ITS OUTCOME WAS DECIDED ON RAY'S CASTING COUCH

After Jimmy's casting as the male lead was finalized, Ray set about hiring the rest of the ensemble. The film's other most important role was that of Judy.

As a juvenile delinquent, she comes from a cold home and perhaps is in love with her father, who can't stand for her to kiss him. Her character yearns for a utopian family that includes Jim and herself as central figures.

Jimmy's friend, Lew Bracker, left the impression in a memoir that starlet Lori Nelson had not made a favorable impression on Jimmy when they dated briefly. Actually, Jimmy may have been more impressed with her than Bracker thought. He recommended that Ray consider Lori for the role of Judy. His rec-ommendation was backed up by an onslaught of letters from the Lori Nelson Fan Club, pleading with Ray to cast their favorite star as Judy.

For a very brief period, Ray considered Margaret O'Brien, the former child actress of the 1940s, for the role. As a child, she had enthralled audiences of the World War II era, eventually replacing the fast- ma-turing (and increasingly syrupy) Shirley Temple as America's favorite pre-adolescent.

After MGM let her go after she turned twelve, she complained to the press, "The public can't accept me with a bosom."

Jimmy had seen her in only one film. When she was seven, she had played Judy Garland's sister, Tootie, in *Meet Me in St. Louis* (1944).

When Ray auditioned Margaret, he asked her what she thought of her parents. "I love them," she

Margaret O'Brien as Tootie...adorable, but not right for the portrayal of a teenage trollop.

answered. That was not the response he wanted. "Judy is alienated from her parents," Ray said.

Jimmy told him, "I can't emote with Little Tootie. Instead of Margaret, why not Shirley Temple?" he asked sarcastically. "Seriously, perhaps you'll consider Carroll Baker."

Margaret O'Brien was out the door.

Jimmy pursued Baker, whom he knew from the Actors Studio. When she was contemplating a role in *Giant,* he approached her. "I'm going to do another film before *Giant.* The script is crap, but the characters are good. I think you'd be perfect

Unconvincing as Juvenile Delinquents: Debbie Reynolds with Carleton Carpenter singing and dancing "Aba-Dabba Honeymoon"

in the female lead of Judy. The director, Nick Ray, is a good guy. I'll take you to him, I bet his tongue is hanging out at the prospect of getting you. I've already pitched you for the lead."

Baker, however, was also rejected by Ray.

Ray told Jimmy that MGM "is trying to push Debbie Reynolds onto me. I guess they don't have anything for her to do. If it's a musical, she'd have been perfect."

"I've met her," Jimmy said. "She's the least likely juvenile delinquent in Hollywood. Maybe you could recycle 'Abba-Daba Honeymoon.'"

[Relentlessly cheerful, and written and first recorded in 1914, "Aba-Daba Honeymoon" became a nationwide hit in 1950 when it was reprised in Two Weeks with Love *(1950) as a song-and-soft shoe dance by Debbie Reynolds, Carleton Carpenter, and a banjo-strumming ensemble of Edwardian-era singers and dancers.]*

Jayne Mansfield
JIMMY VS. THE "RELENTLESSLY PINK"
WORKING MAN'S MARILYN MONROE

The next candidate for the role of Judy was Jayne Mansfield, whose widely publicized superstructure famously measured 40"-24"-36".

Jimmy said, "As Judy, she would be 'busting' out all over."

The studio was pushing Jayne onto Ray, who defined the idea of casting her as "the most outlandish suggestion of the decade."

Actually, Mansfield as Judy was not as outlandish as, in retrospect, it appears. *Rebel* had originally been conceived as a cheap and fast-produced black-and-white juvenile delinquent film of the genre so popular in the 1950s. Some of those featured Jayne's major rival at the time, Mamie Van Doren, whose quickie genre flicks later included *Untamed Youth* (1957)

As the script for *Rebel* had originally been conceived, the film would have opened with sixteen-year-old Judy being arrested for solicitation. That episode was later "tamed," rewritten to depict being disciplined at the police station for breaking curfew.

Actually, Ray was secretly dating Mansfield at the time, and over pillow talk, she was urging him to cast her as Judy. She agreed to a screen test, but the director later confessed, "I didn't put any film in the camera. I knew at the time I was never going to use her."

Ray was also engaged at the time in "carnal adventures" with Shelley Winters, who recalled that his bungalow at the studio was "surrounded by night-blooming jasmine." Also seen coming and going from that bungalow were two other blondes, Marilyn Monroe and Judy Holliday.

When Jimmy learned that Ray was dropping Jayne, both as a girlfriend and as a candidate for the role of Judy, he said, "Wait one night before telling her. Give me her number. I want to call her and tell her that I'd like to test the chemistry between Jim Stark and Judy."

"Okay, buster," Ray responded. "But you'll owe me one. You'll get Jayne's ass, and I'll get yours."

Dubbed "The Working Man's Marilyn Monroe," Jayne seemed only too eager to welcome Jimmy into her home. She'd cleared the house of family members and servants so that she could entertain him in private.

He later reported to Ray, "As you know from banging Jayne, she's more of a cinematic sight gag

Jayne Mansfield as a cover girl in March, 1965, and...

Jayne Mansfield as Queen Deianira in *Amori di Erole* (*The Loves of Hercules*), released in 1960. Four months pregnant at the time of this photo, she insisted that Hercules be played by her husband, muscleman Mickey Hargitay.

Outside Italy, where it was filmed, it was released as *Hercules vs. the Hydra* as a late-night TV teleplay.

than an actress, but she sure is bosomy and breathy. She *cooed* and *aaahed* her way through the night, especially when I plugged her. She greeted me at the door in an ivory-colored see-through *négligée*. She didn't walk toward me, she sashayed."

"I couldn't wait to sink my teeth into those pink nipples of hers. She served me dinner. All her décor is pink and heart-shaped. Cupids everywhere. She even dyes the mashed potatoes pink. Naturally, the drink was pink champagne."

"I detest the color pink," she told him. "But it's important for my image. Men want women pink, helpless, and to do a lot of deep breathing. When I was first told about how sex worked, I laughed and then I cried. I just couldn't see the point of it. Fortunately, I've changed."

"After our romp in her pink bed with its pink sheets, she told me that she just knew that she could play 'that trollop Judy,' even though I'm a good girl."

"If you get the part, we'll have to change the title," he said. "Make it *Rebel With a Cause.*"

"And what might that be?" she asked.

"To bang Suzi every night." *[She had already told him that she'd nicknamed her vagina Suzi.]*

After that encounter, Jimmy never saw Mansfield again and, needless to say, she didn't get the role of Judy.

"I'm Going to Marry James Dean"

—Natalie Wood

Ray might have gone for Carroll Baker had not a sixteen-year-old brunette, a ferociously competitive former child actress, entered the fray.

Her name was Natalie Wood.

She had worked with Jimmy before in the teleplay, *I'm a Fool,* based on a plot by Sherwood Anderson, and more fully described in Chapter Eight of this biography. *I'm a Fool* was eventually broadcast in November of 1954 through television's General Electric Theater, hosted by Ronald Reagan.

After her first viewing of *East of Eden,* Natalie exited from Hollywood's Egyptian Theater exclaiming to her girlfriend, "I'm going to marry that Jimmy Dean!"

"I felt an instant link to Judy," Natalie said. "I just had to take the role to express something inside of me. Up until *Rebel,* I had been a child actress, or else

Natalie Wood is seen emoting with James Dean in *Rebel Without a Cause.* When she read the script, she said, "I am Judy. The story mirrors themes from my own rebellious teen years."

playing an *ingénue*. Judy was real, a gutsy character. The prospect of bringing her to the screen with Jimmy thrilled me."

As she admitted, she stalked Ray, trying to get the role. "Nick still saw me as a child actress in pigtails," she lamented. "I knew I had to convince him I was grown up. Actually, I was only sixteen, but I had the desires of a woman."

"Then one night, I was involved in a car accident with Dennis Hopper, who would also get cast in *Rebel.* Ever since Nick Adams, who was also cast in the picture, took my virginity, I'd been carrying on with both of them. Dennis and I had this car accident, and I was rushed to the hospital, injured."

"I ordered the nurse to call Ray at once and get his ass over here," she said. "I wanted him to see me in my condition. He looked me over. I was a wild juvenile delinquent out speeding in a car with my lover. 'Now do I get the part?' I demanded of him. He thought about it a minute, and then said, 'You are our Judy.'"

"Ray not only gave me the part," she told Jimmy. "He's also fucking me. Is there a man who doesn't desire a sixteen-year-old girl?"

She revealed, "Nick took me to a tiny candlelit restaurant where the table-cloths were pink. We drank pink champagne. Jayne Mansfield had nothing on him when it comes to pink. Incidentally, pink is my favorite color."

"He then took me back to his suite at the Château Marmont, where he seduced me. He told me, 'I want to make love to you.' That was so romantic. Most of you young guys tell a gal, 'I want to screw you. How about it?'"

"Nick might be an old man, but some guys are still sexy after forty," she said. "And he sure knows how to deliver the goods. "He's a thirty-minute man in the saddle. Poor Dennis seems to shoot off just as he's putting it in."

Later, she would tell her friends that she and Jimmy shared some of the same men: Arthur Loew, Jr., Nick Adams, Dennis Hopper, Steve McQueen, and Lance Reventlow. She included Tab Hunter in that list as well, although in his case, despite rumors, it's unclear whether he was actually involved with Jimmy.

Jack Simmons

"THE HAWK" GLIDES INTO JIMMY'S LIFE

Jack Simmons had come to Hollywood to become a movie star, or at least a screen actor. John Gilmore remembered his hook nose. "Everybody called him 'The Hawk.' He had a reputation as one of the most notorious faggots of Hollywood."

The first time Gilmore met Simmons, he was dancing with Rock Hudson at a gay bar in Santa Monica, the Tropical Village, and wearing a tight-fitting pink bikini. Gilmore wrote that Simmons was "a reject, a pitiful fringe-nut in Hollywood's substratum, who captured Jimmy's interest with his unwavering, doglike devotion." Jack would later claim that Jimmy was the only love of his life."

Author Donald Spoto wrote: "For years, the Dean-Simmons friendship was the subject of considerable pornographic imagination. Both men died without uttering a word about the specifics of their relationship, and, as the old maxim runs, no one held the lamp. Most people in the social circle saw the devotion as one-sided. It was a case of the adoring Jack, the acolyte to a diffident Jimmy, who made him a kind of hip valet."

Faye Nuell Mayo, Natalie's stand-in on *Rebel,* claimed, "Simmons adored Jimmy, but how seriously Jimmy took him was really unclear to everybody."

Jack Simmons *(left)*, told friends that he was going to pursue James Dean, get him, and then spend the rest of his life doing whatever he wanted him to do.

Based on events that later unfolded, only the first two parts of Jack's plan ever came to be.

Simmons was the best friend of Maila Nurmi (Vampira), and it had been through her that he had met Jimmy.

Biographer Paul Alexander wrote: "When Jimmy returned to Hollywood, he and Jack Simmons became romantically involved. More than likely, it was Jack who made himself available to Jimmy, for he had seen pictures of Jimmy in the newspapers and had gone to see *East of Eden.*"

Jack told friends that he was going to pursue Jimmy, get him, then spend the rest of his life doing whatever Jimmy wanted him to do. Based on events that later unfolded, only the first two parts of Jack's plan came true.

Jimmy told William Bast that when they first met, he considered Simmons "a pest. He wants to have sex with me, but I keep turning him down. I'm not remotely attracted to the kid sexually. He keeps telling everybody that sooner or later, he's going to kiss me."

Simmons did not take Jimmy's rejection as his final word. He remained undaunted in his pursuit.

Vampira learned and later talked about the intimate details of their relationship: "When Jimmy found out that Jack imposed no limits on what he would do sexually, Jimmy reappraised him. They had a lot of sex. Jack told me about it. But it wasn't the usual kind of sex."

"With Jack, Jimmy began to live out his darker fantasies. He was very abusive to Jack and put him through all sorts of hideous, disgusting scenes, things no human should do to another. And Jack took it."

"I don't want to go into the graphics, but surely, you can use your imagination. Bondage was the more vanilla stuff Jack went through."

Jimmy used his influence to get Simmons cast in a teleplay, *The Dark, Dark Hour,* which also starred Ronald Reagan.

Jimmy got Ray to agree to a screen test that would include Simmons and himself as a means of evaluating his suitability as Plato. It was a disaster.

The venue was the stage set for *A Streetcar Named Desire,* which had not yet been dismantled. The stairway to the Kowalski apartment in New Orleans was still there. Jimmy couldn't resist running up those steps, bellowing like Brando did in both the stage and movie versions, *"STELLA-A-A-A-A!"*

"I couldn't believe what happened next," Ray said. "Suddenly, Simmons followed Jimmy up the steps, and the two men disappeared behind a screen. We heard them giggling, followed by two golden streams of urine raining down from one of the flat's windows. It turned out these jokers were having a pissing contest to see which stream could reach the greatest height. Jimmy said he won the contest, but how would I know?"

He later told Ray, "Jack was nervous, and I figured pissing might relax him before the test."

"The boy just couldn't act," Ray said. "But he was a real pisser."

Ray rejected Simmons for the role of Plato. According to Stewart Stern, "In my script, I wanted to present Jim Stark and Plato in gay overtones. But Simmons was a bit much. It would have made Plato's relationship with Jim Stark too obvious, just too much."

After Simmons was rejected as Plato, Jimmy managed to get him cast as Moose, one of the gang members.

During the filming of *Rebel,* Simmons lived with Jimmy at his apartment on Sunset Plaza Drive.

Simmons was absolutely devoted to and committed to Jimmy, but he finally dropped him altogether.

Columnist Sidney Skolsky wrote: "Wherever Jimmy goes, Simmons was sure to follow. If Jimmy wants coffee, he gets it. A sandwich, Simmons gets it. He also runs interference for Jimmy, keeping people away if Jimmy doesn't want to see them."

Decades later, Simmons would break down and sob at the mention of Jimmy's name. He claimed that he had not only lost his "one true love," but his soul as well.

Sal Mineo

MAKES PORNOGRAPHIC LOVE TO JIMMY IN FULL VIEW OF NICK RAY

For weeks, Sal Mineo, in avid pursuit of the role of Plato, had pursued Ray.

Mineo was the veteran of two Broadway shows, including *The King and I* (during the course of which Yul Brynner had molested him backstage) and Tennessee Williams' *The Rose Tattoo.* Despite his status as a fifteen-year-old, he was nonetheless fully immersed in homosexuality. "I matured early in the Bronx, especially one part of me."

At the time, he was already a film industry veteran, having appeared in two movies, *Six Bridges to Cross,* and *The Private War of Major Benson,* both released in 1955.

Ray kept rejecting him as Plato, claiming, "I don't see any possible chemistry between you and Dean."

But finally, he relented, inviting both Jimmy and Mineo to his lodgings at the Château Marmont.

Mineo arrived wearing pegged pants, a skinny tie, and a jacket. Jimmy showed up in jeans and a T-shirt. "They were from different planets," Ray said.

Mineo later revealed what happened that late Sunday afternoon.

"At first, Jimmy and I were awkward, and I gave a bad first reading of the script. Perhaps Ray was right: We had no sexual chemistry. But I was determined to play Plato, and begged for a chance to do it over. Ray tried to get us to relax with each other. Instead of reading the script, we were told to improvise."

"Suddenly, Jimmy and I were talking to each other, and he was fascinated to learn I'd been a street kid from the Bronx. We relaxed—and how! He even started to wrestle me, which ended up in a long, passionate kiss. We stripped down to our underwear and continued to wrestle some more until both of us got erections. Off came our panties."

"Right in front of Ray, I came on to Jimmy like gangbusters. Ray was all eyes. Jimmy and I really went at it. When I looked over at our director, he'd whipped it out and was jerking off. I got the role of

Three views of Sal Mineo, America's first (onscreen) gay teenager.

636

Plato, and I later got Ray. But by then, I was already in love with Jimmy."

Something happened during the making of *Rebel*, Mineo said. "It was as close as you could get to a spiritual experience. Jimmy was the focus of all of it. Everything that happened was a result of his presence."

During the first week of his involvement with *Rebel*, Jimmy told Mineo that he couldn't sleep and that he was overcome with a nervous anxiety. He went to three sessions with a psychiatrist. "This headshrinker told me to love my father. What a stupid assignment! I could have told him that fifteen years ago. The fucker should have tried to love my father himself."

"Whatever's inside me makes me what I am. Cut me open and take it out, and let in the light, and it might kill my acting talent. Tennessee Williams calls it 'creative malady.' Sometimes, it's the wackos who create the greatest art. Make them normal, and they may lose that neurosis that drives them to create in the first place."

Natalie's double on *Rebel*, Faye Nuell Mayo, also became aware of Jimmy's anxiety, and she thought she knew what might help to relieve his tension. She invited him to attend a class where Kenpō karate was taught.

He attended only one class and didn't like it. He told her, "Instead of a karate chop, I prefer to stick to my own kind of fighting. A finger with a sharp nail in the eyeball, and a castrating kick in the balls."

Casting Issues:

A Henpecked Husband, A Domineering Tarantula of a Mother, A Cardboard 1950 Sitcom Mom, & an Incestuous Father

After players for *Rebel's* three leading characters had been cast, Ray set about hiring actors for the secondary roles, including Jim Backus and Marsha Hunt.

[Marsha Hunt, hailing from Chicago, was known as "Hollywood's most unfortunate also-rans." Attractive, and with alluring eyes, she spend most of her career under contract for MGM, making B-list pictures, or as a supporting player in such movies as Pride and Prejudice *(1940) playing one of Greer Garson's sisters.*

Regrettably, during the early 1950s, she came under fire from Senator Joseph McCarthy, who claimed she was a communist. When Ray cast her in 1955, she had not worked in three years because of her inclusion on the Red Channels list.

637

When she arrived on the set of Rebel, *she announced to Jimmy, "Here's what's left of Marsha Hunt after all those witch hunters in Washington finished with me."*

Ray, also a champion of left-wing positions, wanted her for the role of Jim Stark's henpecking mother until a phone call came in from Jack Warner, asking him to get rid of her and to cast Ann Doran instead.]

***

Doran, once marketed as "The Yellow Rose of Amarillo, Texas," was cast as Jimmy's domineering mother. As a hard-core shrew and a major league emotional blackmailer, her character reminds Jim Stark that, "I almost died giving birth to you."

[In time, Doran, a genuine Hollywood workhorse, would appear in some five-hundred motion pictures.]

In an unlikely friendship, Jimmy bonded with

At the police station, Mrs. Stark, as portrayed by Ann Doran, grips her son in a suffocating embrace.

her, although she claimed that he almost killed her after they'd first met. He had invited her for a ride on his motorcycle.

Jim Backus, cast as Jim Stark's father, warned her, "Jimmy Dean is opinionated, and he'll tell you how to act."

"Just let him try it!" she responded.

Backus was right. After his first rehearsal with Doran, Jimmy attempted to tell her how to play it.

"Listen, junior," she said, icily. "I've been around a long time, and you're new. Don't tell me how to do it. Let me make my own mistakes."

Despite their early confrontation, the two actors bonded, and soon he was referring to her as "Mom."

Prior to his casting as Jimmy's henpecked

A McCarthy-Era Tragedy: One of the candidates favored by Ray for the role of Jimmy's mother was Marsha Hunt, whose involvement on Broadway in *The Devil's Disciple* earned her a place on the cover of the March 6, 1950 of LIFE magazine.

Despite her competency in more than 50 film roles in the late 30s and 40s, her blacklisting by the film industry for her political views cost her the role of James Dean's mother in *Rebel Without a Cause*, and virtually every other film role for which she applied throughout the rest of her working years.

screen father, Jim Backus, beginning in 1949, had been known mainly as the voice of the cartoon character, "Mr. Magoo." Later, he was indelibly association with his characterization of a wealthy, out-of-his-depth eccentric, Thurston Howell III, on the widely syndicated TV sitcom, *Gilligan's Island* (1964-1967)

He was astonished to see Jimmy directing the picture. "Never in the history of motion pictures had an inexperienced 24-year-old become, in essence, a co-director, especially with one as established as Nicholas Ray. He gave Jimmy full reign."

Judy's parents were to be played by William Hopper and Rochelle Hudson. Hopper had appeared in more than 80 feature films during the 1930s and 1940s, although he'd obtained his greatest fame as Paul Drake to Raymond Burr's *Perry Mason* in a TV series (1957-1966). Although married, Hopper pursed a closeted homosexual lifestyle. Stanley Haggart, Jimmy's friend, had known Hopper back in the 1930s.

"Bill appeared in more than ten films with Ronald Reagan," Haggart said. "He had a big crush on Reagan, but apparently, he never scored, even though they shared a bedroom together on location. He got to see Reagan in the nude—and that's about it."

"Alas," Hopper said. "Ronnie was saving it for Lana Turner or Susan Hayward."

In *Rebel*, Rochelle Hudson was hired to portray Natalie Wood's mother. A star in the 1930s, she'd

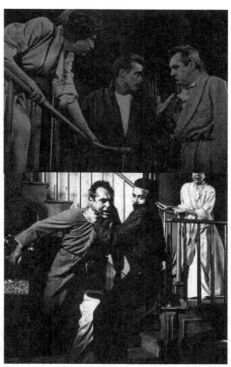

Cast against type, character actor Jim Backus appeared with James Dean in one of the most iconic scenes of *Rebel Without a Cause*.

As the cameras rolled, Jimmy shocked Backus by accelerating their confrontation, unannounced and unrehearsed, into a fistfight, as Ann Doran (Jimmy's film mother), looks on.

Blinkered, naive, uncomprehending 1950s-era domestic hell: William Hopper and Rochelle Hudson, portraying Judy's parents.

begun making pictures when she was sixteen as an attractive *ingénue.* She'd already appeared in such films as *She Done Him Wrong* (1933) with Mae West and Cary Grant, and she had starred as Claudette Colbert's daughter in *Imitation of Life* (1934). Jimmy knew nothing of her movie career, but wanted to hear about her espionage work for Naval intelligence when she was stationed in Central America during World War II.

For Hudson, a woman who'd starred in major movies, her role in *Rebel* wasn't much. One reviewer noted, "She is nothing but a cardboard cutout of a 1950s sitcom mom."

As juvenile delinquents, Ray rounded up a cast that included Corey Allen, Beverly Long, Frank Mazzola, Steffi Sidney, Jack Simmons, and Dennis Hopper.

For a while, Steffi Sidney held out the hope that she might be cast as Judy. However, Ray decided instead to give her the lesser role of Millie, one of the "gang molls." Steffi was the daughter of the famous Hollywood columnist Sidney Skolsky, who had written extensively about Jimmy. His "office" was Schwab's Drugstore, where Jimmy often hung out.

According to Steffi, "My character always carried a hairbrush with her, and I was a very insecure girl who desperately wanted to belong to the gang."

Some of the other cast members resented her, charging nepotism, claiming that Steffi got the part only because of her influential father. The same charge was leveled against William Hopper, son of Hedda Hopper, who was cast as Natalie's angry father.

Steffi was disappointed with *Rebel's* final cut. "My scenes were eliminated. I was left with one line and a sneeze."

She said that the first time she saw Jimmy, which was during a wardrobe test, "He came up to me, and he just swaggered, and then he hit me real hard. I thought, 'Why in hell did he do that to me?' The next time he wandered over, I said, 'What, you're not going to hit me again?' He said, 'No, no, my name is Jimmy Dean.'"

MORE THAN A BROMANCE:
Dennis Hopper

Of all the gang members, only Dennis Hopper was being groomed for stardom at Warners. "I tried to get to know Jimmy. I started by saying 'hello.' No answer. He wouldn't talk to people on the set. He would go into his dressing room. He would be into himself, into his thing. He'd lock himself away."

"Finally, about halfway through filming, during a break in the nighttime filming of 'the chickie run' scene, I grabbed him and threw him into the car. I said, 'Look, I want to be an actor, too, and I wanna know what you're doing, what your secret is."

Dennis wrote those words in *James Dean: The First American Teenager.* After that night, the ice was broken, and they became intimate friends.

Cast as "Goon," Dennis was four years younger than Jimmy and looked even younger. Like Jimmy, he had grown up in the Middle West, in his case, Kansas. He told Jimmy, "When I was a kid, I used to get off sniffing gasoline from my grandfather's truck."

"There will never be another man like Dean," Dennis said after his friend died. "In a strange way, I had a closer friendship with him than most men have with each other. It wasn't the kind of friendship where you say, 'Let's go out and tear up the town.' Sometimes, we'd just have a quiet dinner together and share our darkest secrets. Also, Jimmy and I were into peyote and grass before anybody else caught on."

Peter Winkler, who wrote a biography of Dennis Hopper *(depicted above)*, said, "It is difficult to overstate the importance of James Dean's influence and the impact it had on Hopper's life. He once spoke of Dean as if recalling the love of his life."

"I was with him almost every day for the last eight months of his life," Hopper claimed. "I was haunted by his death, which had been the greatest emotional shock of my life. When he died, I felt cheated. I had my dreams tied up with him. His death blew my mind."

When pressed about whether his relationship with Jimmy turned sexual, he said, "What in the fuck do you think? How much do I have to spell it out? Do you want a blow-by-blow description?"

Movie historian David Thomson wrote, "Dennis Hopper was an ardent young man fatally unlucky to cross the path of James Dean—in *Rebel Without a Cause* and *Giant.* He believed he was the heir to something. He knew he wanted to act, and he believed that rebellion was some proof of his artistic integrity. Much of Hollywood found Hopper a pain in the ass, strident, staring, and monotonous."

***

Corey Allen was cast as the gang's leader, "Buzz," who tangles with Jimmy in an ego-driven conflict that ends in a knife fight.

He claimed, "I was twenty, inexperienced, and I had a very high kind of voice. I felt unmasculine. I was awed to be working with Jimmy after seeing him in *East of Eden.* When I met him, we got off on a bad start. I came up to him where he was sitting, surrounded by a bunch of kids fawning over him. I told him I was going to be his adversary in *Rebel*. Without looking up, he said, 'Yeah, hi.' And then he turned back to chatting with those adoring kids."

Three years younger than Jimmy, Allen bore an amazing resemblance to a young Marlon Brando. "On the second day, when Jimmy talked to me and looked at me, I felt that instead of indifference, he was really turned on by me. He felt I looked like either Brando's son or else his younger brother. He brought that up time and time again."

James Dean with Corey Allen: "Gay directors were known for 'auditioning' young actors on the casting couch. But in the case of Jimmy, he auditioned me."

Ray warned Allen not to get carried away and to try to imitate Jimmy's style.

To that, Allen responded, "Jimmy was like a kind of black hole, with magnetism so great that nothing can go in the other direction."

Ray recruited a real, "from the streets" gang leader, Frank Mazzola, to play "Crunch," a member of the gang in *Rebel*. As a child, he had worked on the Bogie film, *Casablanca*. At Hollywood High, he'd led the Athenians, the most infamous gang in the city.

"Our major activity was strolling the streets at night, trying to pick a fight with some punk," he said. "We were real tough guys, football players, boxers. One time, I punched this guy and threw him out of a second-story window. He survived, with a few broken bones."

"I played the right-hand man to Buzz, the leader of the pack, but I should have been the Big Cheese."

Mazzola got to know Jimmy and even took him shopping to show him how a contemporary teenager dressed. "Jimmy was allowed to attend secret meetings of the Athenians. Sometimes he'd spar with me, but mostly we just hung out. He was a good basketball player."

Beverly Long had been in the Pepsi Cola commercial that's acknowledged today as Jimmy's first appearance on TV, and was said to have dated him for a while.

Long was cast as Helen, a tough, pony-tailed blonde bimbo.

"You never knew what Jimmy's attitude would be," she said. "In the morning, he might speak to you, then again, he might not. He could look right through you like you didn't exist."

"I was easy prey for his off-color jokes. One time, in one scene, while he was repairing a slit tire that Buzz had slashed, Dean handed me the tire iron. 'Ever felt a thing so hard in your life?' he asked me. He could twist and turn anything into an off-color joke."

Dennis said, "Jimmy captured the moment of youth, that moment where we're desperately trying to find ourselves."

Mineo went a step farther: "Jimmy started the youth movement."

"Me Tarzan, You Jimmy"

—Johnny Weissmuller

Two weeks before actual shooting began on *Rebel,* Jimmy mysteriously disappeared. There were rumors that he'd been kidnapped by a gang of gay bikers, and that they were repeatedly sodomizing him at some remote desert outpost.

Jack Warner phoned Jimmy's West Coast agent, Dick Clayton, threatening him. "If that bastard kid doesn't show up in the next forty-eight hours, I'm firing him from the picture and replacing him with Robert Wagner, if he's available. If he's not, then maybe John Kerr."

Thinking he might not return, Ray considered recasting Dennis Hopper as Jim Stark.

"It would have been my first big break," Dennis reflected, years later. "Alas, it was not meant to be. Thank god that *Easy Rider* later came along."

Jimmy's mystery trip out of Hollywood may have had something to do with a casual chat he'd had with Stewart Stern, who was still revising the script. He wanted to signal to the world that Plato was gay, but not in any obvious way that would incite censors to cut it.

He came up with the idea of Plato opening his locker at school. Inside their own lockers, the other boys often attached publicity photographs of their favorite pinup queens.

"I wanted Plato to post a really handsome picture of his favorite hunk of beef. That will show viewers what turns him on."

Jimmy said that during his teenage years in Indiana, he had decorated the walls of his bedroom with pictures of screen Tarzan, Johnny Weissmuller.

"Why don't you call him?" Stern asked.

"Maybe he wouldn't even talk to me," Jimmy replied.

"Wise up, kid," Stern said. "You're now a god damn movie star. One of the privileges of being a hot-shot star is that you can get to meet almost anyone you want. As I said, ring him up. I bet he'd meet with you any time you wanted."

"Maybe I'll just do that," Jimmy said. "See if the real thing lives up to my schoolboy crush."

Jimmy's friend, Stanley Haggart, who had sometimes granted him access to one of his apartments in New York, and also to his guest cottage in Laurel Canyon for his sexual trysts, knew what Jimmy was up to.

According to Haggart, "Just out of the blue, Jimmy, in New York, phoned and asked if he could come by with a friend. I told him that would be fine. When he showed up with this mysterious friend, I was shocked. It was the film industry's most famous Tarzan, Johnny Weissmuller. If Jimmy was known for anything, it was for his 'odd couple' matings."

"He later explained that as a kid, he had long fantasized about Tarzan in his loincloth."

"I understand that," Haggart said. "I collected pictures of John Gilbert." He welcomed both of them, and even fed them a late night supper with champagne.

Jimmy claimed that he'd met his screen idol at his favorite restaurant, the Villa Capri. The owner had given the Austria-born former athlete permission to let out his ear-splitting jungle yell any time he came in for dinner. Weissmuller would thump his chest and bellow that maniacal yell.

"I tried to imitate that yell as a kid," Jimmy said. "But it never came out right."

As it turned out, Weissmuller was an amusing guest, not at all as inarticulate as Tarzan.

"Jimmy and I discovered we have something in common," he said. "We've both fucked Joan Crawford and Tallulah Bankhead. Tallulah once told me, '*Dahling!* You are the kind of man a woman like me must shanghai and keep under lock and key until both of us are entirely spent. Prepare for a leave of at least ten days.'"

Weissmuller went on to relay other amusing stories based on his early days in Hollywood, some of them were spent traveling on promotional tours for the *Tarzan* series.

"In Texas, during World War II, I was at a bond rally. I was auctioned off, presumably to deliver the Tarzan yell in private. The highest bidder was willing to pay $50,000. Some sources say only $5,000. But it was $50,000 big ones. A rich Texas oilman was the highest bidder."

Weissmuller with Frances Gifford in *Tarzan Triumphs* (RKO-1943).

"He invited me for dinner in his hotel suite, and I went," Weissmuller said. "When I got there, a lobster and Texas steak dinner, with lots of champagne, was sent up."

"After dinner, my host told me, 'I don't give a damn about that Tarzan yell. I'm not going to pay that kind of money for some yell. I brought you up here to find out what's under that loincloth. Incidentally, you'll soon find out that I'm the best cocksucker in Texas.'"

"In case Johnny doesn't show it tonight," a drunken Jimmy said, "It's ten inches, but the final inch is pure foreskin."

"When I first arrived on the MGM lot," Weissmuller said, "I was sent for a costume fitting. This fucking sissy handed me a feathery-looking G-string and asked me if I knew how to climb a tree. He tried to fit this damn G-string on me. No way. I demanded a heavy duty jock strap."

"Johnny wasn't what I was expecting," Haggart said, later. "He was the last actor in Hollywood I thought Jimmy would hang out with. Most of Johnny's references were far more sophisticated that that *'Me Tarzan*, you Jane' crap."

"As an art director on TV, I often had to fit stars into their outfits when the budget didn't allow for a wardrobe master (or mistress). Johnny spotted some old fashion magazines in my living room. Before he left, that night, he asked me if he could take some of my old editions of *Vogue*. I agreed, of course."

"He surprised me by telling me that *Vogue* was one of his favorite magazines. He also thanked me for my lavish dinner, telling me with meals like that, he was going to have to come up with new devices to cover his expanding waistline."

"Johnny wasn't the Tarzan that both Jimmy and I had once fantasized about from back in the late 1930s and '40s," Haggart said. "After all, he was born in 1904 and was older than I was. Even so, he was still the hot stud that no one in a gay bar would turn down."

[Johnny Weissmuller lived until 1984. His last screen appearance was in Won Ton Ton, the Dog Who Saved Hollywood *(1976).]*

***

In Los Angeles, Stewart Stern picked up his phone at about two o'clock in the morning. Jimmy was on the other end of the line, calling from New York, where he'd stashed himself away, without per-

Vogue magazine had a most unlikely reader, the super macho Austrian athlete and screen Tarzan, Johnny Weissmuller, depicted above, reading the magazine.

mission, from *Rebel,* its director, and its scheduling.

Stern warned him that if he didn't fly back to Los Angeles at once, Warner was going to replace him with another actor. "You'll be suspended. Without pay. Your career will be ruined."

"I want to come back, but I'm frightened," Jimmy said. He sounded drugged. "I don't think I can play Jim Stark—and I don't trust Nicholas Ray as a director.

Stern entreated him to return. "Jimmy, we're ready to begin shooting. I've tried to fashion all my rewrites around Jim Stark, based on you. You can do it. You haven't seen the final script. It's Jimmy Dean! God damn it, you can play yourself, can't you?"

Two days later, at around midnight, Jimmy showed up on Ray's doorstep at the Château Marmont. "He just walked in," the director said, "and had absolutely no excuse for his running away. He wanted to spend the weekend in bed with me, making love until I forgave him. The kid got his wish."

Jimmy Rages
THROUGH SOME OF THE MOST ICONIC FILM SEQUENCES IN THE HISTORY OF CINEMA

At last, after almost a decade of delays, *Rebel Without a Cause* was set to go before the cameras. All sorts of problems had already been resolved, including censorship by Warners, casting problems, even Jimmy's mysterious disappearance.

Ray wanted a very dramatic opening, and both he and Jimmy worked together to create something unusual, even stunning, to launch their movie.

As the title and opening credits of *Rebel Without a Cause* are flashed across the screen, a drunken Jim Stark lies on the sidewalk intoxicated, whimsically playing with a toy monkey. The scene might not have worked, but Jimmy made it memorable. The toy monkey was his idea.

Within a week of shooting in black and white, Jack Warner halted the production after reading the acclaim that Jimmy's performance had generated for *East of Eden.* "We've got a star on our hands," he told Ray. "There's big box office here. We're going to shoot the damn picture in color."

Consequently, costume designer Moss Mabry scrambled to redesign Jimmy's wardrobe, replacing Jim Stark's original black leather jacket with a red nylon windbreaker. It became one of the most enduring costumes in film history, rivaled—among male stars, at least—by Charlie Chaplin's bowler and Humphrey Bogart's trenchcoat.

[Mabry dressed not only Jimmy and the other stars of Rebel, *but would go on to design Elizabeth Taylor's outfits in* Giant, *for which he received an Oscar nomination in 1956.]*

During the filming of *Rebel,* Jimmy's reputation from *East of Eden* grew rapidly, as did his fan base. Letters poured in from across America, including bags of mail from gay men. Many other handsome, well-built male stars, including Rock Hudson, also received gay fan letters, but none with the volume of what was sent to Jimmy.

As regards Jimmy's friends, journalist George Scullin noted some changes: "He collected a group of sycophants who performed what gaucheries they could think of—party crashing, drunken binges, drug excesses, and offending for the sake of offending. What a pack of bastards!"

Early in *Rebel,* three troubled teenagers, as portrayed by Jimmy, Natalie, and Sal Mineo meet, at random and for unrelated transgressions at the local police station.

[In that scene, a drunken Jim Stark slams his fist into the side of a desk with a force greater than what the script had called for. When the scene was over, Jimmy was rushed to the hospital, since Ray feared he'd broken some bones. As it turned out, he was only badly bruised. "Too much Method acting," Ray told him.]

Plato (Mineo), a mentally disturbed youth, had been hauled into the station for killing a litter of puppies for reasons he cannot explain. Judy was there for having violated some unexplained curfew.

Later, all three encounter each other again on the first day of school. As the camera focuses on Plato, an object of derision and ridicule by his peers, Mineo opens his locker to reveal a handsome publicity photo of his movie idol, Alan Ladd. Based on this cinematic clue, whereas gays across America immediately recognized Plato as one of their own, straight audiences of that day hardly took notice of the signal being (discreetly) projected.

In Manhattan, years later, Jay Garon, a notoriously well-known literary and film rights agent, proposed that Mineo write a memoir, for which Mineo would receive an advance of $40,000. Garon designated his client, Darwin Porter, co-author of this book, as its ghost writer.

According to Mineo, as relayed to Porter, "Late one night, after *Rebel* was released, I got a call from Alan Ladd." Mineo said. "He sounded drunk.

"Thanks, kid," he said, "for using my picture as your dreamboat in that locker scene in *Rebel.* I need all the publicity I can get."

"They wanted me to use Burt Lancaster, but I went for you," Mineo said. "My all-time favorite."

"As a reward, I'd like any fantasy you might have to come true tonight. I'm home alone if you care to drop in."

"Did you accept the invitation?" Porter asked.

"What do you think?" Mineo replied. "I'll tell you this much. Alan was not short all over."

[Since the early 1940s, Hollywood insiders knew that Alan Ladd led a secret bisexual lifestyle.]

Mineo's autobiography collapsed when he refused to out himself as a homosexual. Without that revelation, no publisher wanted a "vanilla view" of his life.

"I just couldn't break all those female hearts, who sent me all those adoring letters in the 1950s," Mineo said. "The money would sure have been nice, though."

Alan Ladd...Plato's "dreamboat."

***

"The repressive censorship of films, originating in the 1930s, was on life support when *Rebel Without a Cause* was made," Ray said. "But it would have been an even more powerful film if the original script had been used."

He was referring to the underlying homosexual context of the dynamic between Plato and Jim Stark. "Homosexuality was still the love that dared no speak its name on the screen. And Judy was supposed to be a teenaged trollop. But we gave in to the demands of the censor, much to my regret."

"Jimmy wanted to do other, more daring scenes that were not in the script. In one episode, he wanted to be shown lying in bed on his belly, with his naked ass showing. Of course, in a few years to come, such a scene would be considered typical, but not in 1955. European films had already broken through most of these taboos, but Hollywood was slow to catch on."

"I watched Jimmy and Sal fall in love right on camera," Ray recalled. "Jimmy even issued a director's cue to Sal, telling him, 'Pretend you want to run your fingers through my hair, but you're too shy. Make believe you want to throw yourself in my arms and kiss me passionately. I want Nick to film us kissing and see what the blue noses say about that. They're all mother fuckers anyway. Art should not be censored. Neither should love. It's all right for films to depict men brutally killing each other. But to love a man? That's out!"

So spoke James Dean.

Rebel, in addition to same-sex attraction, contained very oblique references to yet another theme of forbidden love too—incest.

Stern's script called for William Hopper and Natalie's characters to suggest an undercurrent of incest. An early version had called for her to sit on his lap, as she'd done for years in her capacity as his adolescent daughter. Without getting embarrassingly graphic, Stern had hoped to portray Hopper becoming sexually aroused, with the understanding that when he ultimately rejected her, it would be as a punishment for his own sexual feelings toward her.

In a pivotal scene that made the final cut, when Judy repeatedly tries to kiss her father, Hopper, with barely concealed fury, rebuffs her, saying "You're getting too old for that kind of stuff, kiddo." In reaction, she kisses him anyway, receiving a vicious slap in response. As her mother passively (and naïvely) observes this dynamic, Judy, sobbing, storms out of the house.

***

Based on the rave reviews being generated for *East of Eden,* Jimmy felt entitled to direct the other actors. Consequently, he instructed Dennis Hopper, "Don't act like you're smoking a cigarette. Smoke it! When you know there's something more that should go into a character, and you're not sure what it is, you just have to go after it! Walk on a tightrope!"

Jim Backus, in his own words, was Jimmy's "henpecked father in an apron, mentally flabby and shillyshally."

"He was a self-deprecating weakling of a man whose wife had long ago cut off his balls," he claimed.

"I wish my character had been rewritten. I felt that, like my Mr. Magoo, Mr. Stark was also a cartoon character, not three-dimensional at all. I struggled to do the best I could, but the fault was with the script."

"Actually, I never knew it would become such a legendary picture," Backus said. "We started out to make a sort of *Ozzie and Harriet* sitcom with venom until Dean suddenly became an overnight sensation on our hands."

***

Rebel's soon-to-be-famous knife fight (Jim Stark vs. Buzz) was shot at the Griffith Planetarium, high in the hills above the Hollywood Bowl. With Jimmy and Corey Allen, Ray attempted to film the scene eight times, but none of them looked realistic. Finally, the two young actors got it right, although at one point, Allen's switchblade slashed the skin of Jimmy's throat. Although it was a surface wound, the cut drew blood.

Genuinely alarmed, and in his capacity as the film's director, Ray yelled "cut" and frantically summoned the on-site nurse.

Bleeding from the throat, Jimmy denounced Ray for halting the action. "Just when we were getting real, you fucked it up, you bastard!"

The cast had rarely, if ever, heard an actor address his director like that.

The nurse bandaged Jimmy, and he didn't need to go to the hospital. After that, Ray instructed Rod Amate, a young stuntman, to double for Jimmy during the scene's final moments, with the understanding that his face would not be visible.

When Method acting gets out of hand: the knife fight in *Rebel*.

Amate would also double for Jimmy in his souped-up '46 Ford for the "chickie run" scene.

Days before the knife fight scene, Jimmy and Allen had each been carefully coached and rehearsed by "Mushy" Callahan, a former welterweight boxing champion, and a former street fighter.

***

Rebel's most hair-raising scene involved the infamous "chickie run." As a means of flaunting their nerves of steel (or their "yellow bellies," depending on the outcome) Buzz confronts and challenges Jim Stark to a deadly and motorized game of "chicken." Each of them agrees to race (stolen) cars to the edge of a cliff. The "coward" will be defined as the one who loses his nerve and jumps out first.

Allen was one of the longest-lived members of *Rebel's* cast, surviving many of film's other actors by decades, until his death in 2010. It took him years to be able to discuss the events that transpired between Jimmy and himself.

"He was practically directing the picture himself," Allen said in his last interview. "Late one afternoon, he asked me if I'd ride off with him for the weekend. I didn't want to, so I turned him down. He almost begged me to change my mind, and I finally gave in to him. I didn't want to antagonize him. He invited me to this rental home he had, which looked like a hunting lodge."

"I'd heard stories that he was gay, so I suspected what was coming. I was straight, and I felt that all I had to do was let him blow me. But after some weed and a few drinks, he made his request very explicit: 'I want you to ride me like you're Brando's son,' Jimmy said. 'Really fuck the hell out of me.' Believe it or not, I actually enjoyed it. Very tight. Great sex, I stayed all weekend, and he did things to me like no gal ever did. I don't want to get specific, but there are some things a whore might do, but in most cases, not a girlfriend."

"Before the end of the weekend, he told me what he really wanted from me as an actor during the final moments of the chickie run. He wanted me to convey that under different circumstances, instead of enemies, we might have been lovers. I understood that, and I tried my best to convey that on the night we shot the scene."

"The character I played turned to him and said, 'You know something? I like you.'"

"Why do we do this?" Jim Stark asks.

Allen, as Buzz, answers, "We gotta do something, don't we?"

"It was a tender moment between the two men, one of whom will careen in his car off the cliff, crashing to a fiery death onto the rocky beach below. "I get my jacket caught, and can't escape from my car in time. Those were my final words to Jim Stark. My character has only moments to live."

When Jimmy jumps from his car before it plunges over the cliff, he was supposed to land on a mattress, with the understanding that as a prop and safety device, it would not be shown on camera. He ordered the prop man to take it away. "Okay, kid," the man said. "It's okay with me if you want to bust your nuts. But it's the same mattress Errol Flynn used to land on out of camera range in one of his swashbuckling movies. It came from Warner's prop department."

"I said to move the god damn thing!" Jimmy ordered.

Allen later said, "That scene became iconic. It was a classic, the underlying question of each generation. 'Here we are. What do we do?'"

After Buzz disappeared over the cliff and burst into flames on the beach, Judy (almost unbelievably and perhaps opportunistically) shifts the focus of her love away from the deceased gang leader and onto Jim Stark.

Another classic scene occurred after the death of Buzz, when Jimmy returns home to confront his parents, as played by Doran and Backus. He wants to go to the police and tell them the whole story.

Years after Jimmy's death Doran, with a sense of admiration for his raw, intuitive talent as an actor, noted how Jimmy prepared for one of his scenes: "He'd drop to the floor in a fetal position for the longest time, chin and knees together, but still on his feet. He'd get as close to the floor as he could without lying on it. Finally came this weak little whistle from him, and he stood up, ready to do the scene, which he'd do in a single take."

A big scene between Backus and Jimmy, with his mother looking on, occurs at the foot of a staircase. "A boy—a kid—was killed tonight!" Jim cries. He wants to report the incident to the police, but Mrs. Stark aggressively opposes that. "A foolish decision like that could wreck your whole life!"

In response, Jimmy pleads with his father: "Dad, stand up for me!"

At that point, Jimmy broke from the script and devised the action on his own. Backus wasn't prepared for what happened next: Jimmy leaped at him like a wild animal released from its cage. He grabbed the beefy actor by his lapels and dragged him down the stairs and across the living room. The violence continued at a whirlwind pace as he threw Backus onto a chair, which fell over backward. Jimmy than wrapped his hands around Backus' throat in a choke hold.

"He choked me until I thought I was a goner," Backus said.

Doran, as Mrs. Stark, screamed, "You're killing him! Do you want to kill your own father?"

The screenplay's author, Stern, said, "I didn't mean for the scene to be that violent. In my script, I expressed my own feelings about my own father. I wanted him wiped out, but I also wanted him saved."

As one critic wrote, "In that dramatic scene, James Dean channels a young generation's frustration and emotional claustrophobia."

***

Near the end of the film, a decaying mansion became the setting for the most evocative scene in the movie. It involved Jim Stark, Judy, and Plato in a kind of love triangle, with Jimmy as the object of the others' affections. It laid the groundwork for the film's tragic ending.

It was Stern who came up with the idea of renting it. Located at the intersection of Wilshire and Crenshaw Boulevards, and owned by J. Paul Getty, one of the era's richest oilmen, it was slated for demolition. Its cinematic fame had derived from its setting as the home of the demented movie queen, Norma Desmond, as portrayed by Gloria Swanson, in *Sunset Blvd.* (1950).

Desperately, Stern and Ray tried to contact the oil magnate so that they could film there. They finally reached him, and he agreed, charging them only $250 a day. "I bet that's what he pays for a lobster cocktail," Ray said.

Dating from the flapper age of the mid-1920s, the mansion, with its Mediterranean-style porticoes, pool, balustrades, and gardens, had been built by William O. Jenkins, the sugar magnate. Its swimming pool was especially famous, thanks to the fact

The "love triangle" in *Rebel* was filmed within the decaying mansion, just before its demolition, which had been the setting for many of the scenes within *Sunset Blvd.*

In the photo above, Gloria Swanson, playing the demented movie star, Norma Desmond, delivers her most memorable closeup.

that in *Sunset Blvd.,* William Holden's body had fallen into it after the abandoned egomaniac (Norma) fatally shot him.

It had been dubbed "The Phantom House," because for many years, no one had lived there.

After Getty granted his approval for the building's use as Ray's film set, the director said, "I'm ready to film our Walpurgis Night."

[In Germanic folklore, Walpurgisnacht, *the night of April 30th (May Day's eve), is when witches congregate on the Brocken mountain in north-central Germany, and conduct sexual revels with their gods in anticipation of the arrival of Spring.]*

Walpurgisnacht

"ALL THOSE KIDS IN *REBEL* WERE SLEEPING WITH EACH OTHER.
GENDER DIDN'T MATTER—
AND NICK RAY WAS SEXUALLY INVOLVED WITH MOST OF THEM"
—Ann Doran

Celebrity psychic John Cohan was a friend and confidant of Hollywood stars for decades, including such luminaries as Elizabeth Taylor. In 2008, he shared some of those celebrity secrets in a memoir, *Catch a Falling Star.*

Cohan was privy to many of the behind-the-scenes dramas associated with the lives of Jimmy's two co-stars, Natalie Wood and Sal Mineo. Cohan also became close to Nick Adams.

Adams would later reveal that he had "an insatiable lust" for Jimmy and, later, for Elvis Presley, who befriended him after Jimmy died.

Natalie said that when she came together again with Jimmy in 1955, after having made a teleplay with him the year before, "I was older and more grown up, and I knew a lot more about sex than I did when we first met."

"I liked talking to him more than to anybody else I knew. My whole life seemed to change completely when he walked in. I was in incredible awe of him. I also thought he was the sexiest boy I'd ever met. Of course, I said the same thing about this guy named Robert Wagner."

One afternoon, Jimmy told Natalie that in the real world, each of them lived a variation of the alienation that was represented by the characters they were playing, Jim Stark and Judy.

Columnist Hedda Hopper wrote: During the making of *Rebel Without a Cause,* Natalie Wood fell hard for James Dean."

Even though he stole scenes from her, Natalie claimed that, "Working with Jimmy is pulsating, as he generates a theatrical electricity. Anyone playing with him can't help but feel his tempo and drive. Even if he doesn't have a line to speak, I feel he's talking to me. I can tell by the way he looks, the movement of his hands, the slight motion of his facial muscles. I've never felt so excited with an actor as I do with him."

"It's great working with her," Jimmy said. "Gone are the pigtails. No more bobbysox. She has pep, real vitality, and all the attributes of a powerful performer. I'm sure that in her future, she'll play such roles as a whore."

In reference to what happened over the course of the next few weeks, author Gore Vidal—who, like Ray, was living at the Château Marmont at the time—made several very clear assertions in his memoir, *Palimpsest*. "Nick Ray was openly having an affair with the adolescent Sal Mineo while the sallow James Dean skulked in and out, unrecognizable behind thick glasses that distorted myopic eyes. Ray would soon be embroiled in a different affair with a sixteen-year-old girl, Natalie Wood herself. He was forty-three at the time."

Beverly Long said, "Dennis Hopper was terribly in love with Natalie, too, and he was heartbroken when he found out that she was also sleeping with Ray and Jimmy."

Natalie told Cohan that it was Nick Adams who took her virginity at the suggestion of her mother.

She approached Adams when he came over one evening to pick up Natalie. Her mother told him, "I want you to teach Natalie the ways of the world. I'm afraid that if you don't, she might be broken in by that queer guy, Jimmy Dean. That fellow is really weird. You're not. I trust you with my daughter."

Natalie showed Cohan her deformed wrist. "I have to wear bracelets to cover it on camera." She shared her fears and anxieties with him. "After I moved on from child roles, I didn't know who in hell I was or what they wanted from me. I'm talking about agents, producers, directors, and other actors."

In *Rebel,* Jimmy gave Natalie her first screen kiss. "We did a lot of practicing off screen so we'd be camera ready," she said, giggling.

"I played my first love scene with Jimmy," Natalie said. "He seemed like a great nonconformist, a great rebel, but really, he was only eccentric."

She also said that Jack Simmons was always trying to find out if Jimmy were having sex with her.

She was still curious to know if Simmons was also having sex with Jimmy. He told her, "I won't say no, and I won't say yes. I love and worship Jimmy."

During filming, Natalie developed this powerful crush on Jimmy, and was always ready to accept his invitation to his dressing room any time he wanted to seduce her.

"He was so inspiring," she said to Cohan. "Always patient and kind. He didn't act like a movie star at all."

"After our lovemaking, he gave me advice as an actress, very good suggestions. He was very critical of his own work, and never satisfied with a performance he'd just given. He worried about how every scene would turn out. He also had the ability to make his co-stars look great, too."

She also told Cohan that during the making of *Rebel,* she was resentful that she and Mineo had to be supervised by a welfare worker because both of them were underage, and as such, their working hours, based on California State law, were limited. They were also given lessons by a tutor. "I was trying to play a grown-up, and I was embarrassed to be treated like a child. So was Sal."

***

Sal Mineo was also a friend and client of Cohan, who said, "During the filming of *Rebel Without a Cause,* the young Bronx-born actor had a hot and heavy affair with Jimmy. In one scene, Ray had the two young men kissing, but, in the uptight 1950s, when homosexuality could not even be mentioned on the screen, that segment was cut by the censors. 'The world wasn't ready to see two young men kissing,' Mineo said."

Mineo told Cohan, "Natalie was real competition for me. I was madly in love with Jimmy and so was she. Before she was cast in *Rebel,* she told me that she must have seen *East of Eden* fifty times. Even if she were exaggerating, she'd seen it a hell of a lot."

[Ray confronted Natalie years after Jimmy died. "You're telling the magazines and even friends that you and Jimmy did not have sex. Is that true?"

"Come on, Nick," she said. "I can tell the innocents that, but not you. You know I've spent many nights with Jimmy. What did you think we did? Hold hands? Frankly, I much prefer Robert Wagner's cock to Jimmy's, but we did go at it more times than I can remember. Sometimes, Jimmy liked to hurt his partner, and be hurt, and I don't go in for that."]

"Both Natalie and I adored Jimmy," Mineo claimed. "If he didn't give me a warm embrace when we met on the set in the morning, I was a wreck for the day. Actually, I wanted to kiss him any time I was around him, but there were always people about. I waited for him to call me into the privacy of his dressing room. That guy was some swell kisser, among other attributes."

Jimmy's friend, John Gilmore, paid a visit to the set. Between takes, the two actors amused themselves by naming the producers and directors who had put the make on them.

During Gilmore's visit to the set, he became aware that Jimmy was having an affair with Mineo. "I knew something was going on. We headed for lunch in the commissary, and Mineo was walking ahead of us. Jimmy stepped up and pinched the right cheek of his ass. Mineo jumped. He was startled. But when he realized it was Jimmy, his big brown eyes lit up. His face flushed red, and he giggled, beaming in awe at his top."

Another friend of Jimmy's, William Bast, learned graphic details about Jimmy's affair with Mineo. "Sal may be just a kid, but he's got nine inches of Italian sausage that no butcher has ever tampered with," Jimmy claimed.

"The nights Jimmy could spare for me were the most delightful of my life," Mineo confessed. "I had never been penetrated before he did the job. Up to then, only oral sex. It hurt at first, but he made me take it, and I came to love it. He told me I had to endure the initial pain to prove my love for him. I did, and soon that pain turned into the greatest sexual thrill of my life."

Mineo also told Cohan that before filming began on the flirtatious scene in the mansion with Jimmy and Natalie, Ray had coached him on how to play the scene. "Both Natalie and I were instructed to look at Jimmy like we were in love with him. That wasn't hard to do. Both of us were already in love with Jimmy, especially yours truly. We played the scene like he was 'Lucky Pierre,' and we couldn't wait to discover his erotic zones."

Mineo talked to Cohan about what it was like working with Jimmy. "Rehearsing with him kept us on our toes. Without warning, he'd throw in different lines and improvise scenes. Frankly, I didn't know at first what all the fuss about Jimmy was about, until I went to the first screening. He was great. He was sitting just behind me in the theater, and at least half a dozen times, I turned to look back at him. He was giving that grin of his and almost blushing, looking down at the floor between his legs."

Mineo confessed that off screen, as lovers, Jimmy experimented with S&M, and that, on occasion, urged lovers to crush out their cigarette butts on his ass. He wanted to keep his chest and back free from burn marks in the event that he had to strip before the camera. "Jimmy wanted some kinky stuff, but I told him to get it elsewhere," Mineo said. "I wasn't into doing stuff like that. I just liked regular gay sex."

John Cohan, survivor of decades in the entertainment industry, is a psychic and confidant to celebrities, as depicted on the cover of his 2008 memoir.

In the wake of Jimmy's fatal crash, a coroner examined his body, inch by inch, making a note of the "constellation of kerotoid scars" he discovered.

Mineo described a bizarre and heretofore unreported event that happened to Jimmy and himself during the making of *Rebel:* Before the beginning of filming, Jimmy had hung out with a street gang from the south side of Los Angeles, hoping to absorb enough atmosphere to convincingly portray Jim Stark.

At one point, Mineo and Jimmy were abducted and taken to an abandoned warehouse in South Los Angeles. One biker accused Jimmy of not only giving him crabs, but a venereal disease too.

"We were saved by a miracle," Mineo said. "Jimmy was allowed to call this doctor friend who agreed to cure the biker of both afflictions. Of course, getting rid of crabs was a lot easier than VD."

Jimmy also made a $5,000 payment to the bikers. Mineo believed that, "If he hadn't done that, I expect that both of us might have gotten a switch-blade embedded in our guts."

[Nightly in that part of L.A., bikers and members of their gangs were routinely murdered, especially during their turf wars.]

As related by Mineo to Cohan, one night, Jimmy invited him to his rented home, the one that evoked a hunting lodge, and came up with a surprising idea. According to Mineo, "He wanted me to save a sample of my sperm, frozen in a capsule for the later impregnation of the right woman. The plan was, that when Jimmy found the right carrier, he would pay for her to have my baby, which he would later adopt. Back in the 50s, this was a radical idea."

"Jimmy also told me that he'd had his own sperm stored away for future use," Porter said. He wouldn't tell me where the sperm was stored, but it was at some clinic."

[Shortly before Mineo was murdered in 1976, he told Cohan that "I'm the father of a child somewhere, but I don't know where he is today."]

Jimmy's on-again, off-again affair with Mineo would continue after both of them were cast in *Giant.* "Instead of Natalie and Nick Adams, I had to compete with Elizabeth Taylor and Rock Hudson, at least in the beginning. Elizabeth continued to adore Jimmy until the end of his short life, but by the end of filming, Rock hated him and turned to me for sexual relief."

"Mineo denied that he and Jimmy were lovers, at least at first," Ray said. "Why not? It would have ruined his career. But his comments were hogwash. I'd seen them make love in my suite. They were great at it."

***

As the years went by, Mineo became more open about his sexuality. During one of his last interviews, he told *The New York Times,* "I was in incredible awe of James Dean. I was fascinated by him. I think it was sexual to some extent, but I had no understanding of affection between men. I really gave him hero worship, and I recognized later what it was, but the feeling then was that I couldn't wait just to get near him. It was only years later that I understood I was incredibly in love with him."

Mineo recalled his death scene toward the end of *Rebel,* when he is shot by a policeman after he ran out of the Planetarium with a gun. It was not loaded. Jim Stark had removed the bullets.

"I wanted to do the scene over and over because he was grieving over losing me, and I was thrilled to be loved like that by someone. If you watch the scene, you realize he seemed genuinely moved, and I felt loved. After that, he was very protective of me. For the rest of the time, he didn't want me out of his sight. He was always there for me. Alas, it didn't last."

As Mineo related to Cohan, "Both Natalie and I had the hots for Jimmy, both on and off the screen. But, according to the Production Code, for my sin, I had to get bumped off in the end. In those days, if a 'queer' was depicted in a novel, or whatever, he has to die at the end. I was fatally shot by the cops. Faggots aren't supposed to go on living, much less loving."

***

Dennis Hopper, on the set of *Giant,* bragged to Jimmy about the conquests he had made, even at a young age. "I don't think there's a starlet walking that I can't screw," he boasted. "Actually, I prefer to give head to a beautiful woman rather than fuck her."

In time, Dennis would have A-list conquests such as Ursula Andress, Jimmy's former girlfriend, and Joan Collins. But when Jimmy met him, he was involved in an affair with Natalie.

He later confided to Jimmy, "A day after I met Natalie—Ray introduced us—the little bitch phoned and asked if I'd go out with her. She told me I was very good looking, and that she wanted me to fuck her. I found out that Nick Adams had broken her in. Back in Kansas, women weren't this aggressive. The following night, we drove up to Mulholland Drive and made love. I think she wanted to get into her character of Judy, who in the first script, was sexually promiscuous."

"I got into terrible problems with Ray," Dennis said, "because we were both fucking Natalie. Her parents were starting to figure that out. Nick snitched on me to them. I was furious at the bastard."

Perhaps to get back at Dennis for his pursuit of Natalie, Ray decided to set him up with his neighbor at the Château Marmont, author Gore Vidal. As a means of engineering the hookup, Ray lied to Dennis, telling him that Vidal was writing the script for a major motion picture that might contain an Oscar-winning lead role for him.

"Hopper went for it," Vidal later told Tennessee Williams and others.

"He arrived all innocent and wide-eyed, dewey eyed, really," Vidal said. "For dinner, he drove me to his favorite pizza joint in his new red Austin convertible he purchased with money he'd made in the movies."

"When I got him home, he objected to getting fucked, but he endured it anyway," Vidal said. "I told him to think of God, country, and the lead role in the hottest new movie property coming up. He endured it, but then wanted me to blow him. I told him I'd owe him one."

"There was no movie contract," Vidal said. "The kid had to learn that you don't trust people like Gore Vidal or Nicholas Ray."

***

Despite his sexual involvements with a number of men—namely Simmons, Ray, Dennis Hopper, and Mineo—Jimmy continued his dating of women. Once, he invited the Swedish starlet, Lilli Kardell, to the set of *Rebel* to watch a scene being shot.

Natalie seemed jealous of her, especially when Kardell informed her that Jimmy had escorted her to the bullfights in Tijuana the previous weekend. "Later, in our hotel, he stripped naked at the foot of the bed and told me to pretend that I was the bull. Then he got an erection and jumped on top of me, plunging his sword deep into the gut of the 'bull.'"

***

Beverly Long, cast as Helen, one of *Rebel's* "gang molls," noted how "Nick Adams was always sucking up to Jimmy, desperately trying to be his best friend. They had been roomies."

Adams had serious competition from Jack Simmons. He was ready to hop into Jimmy's bed, or Natalie's bed, whoever summoned him. Sometimes, it was Ray himself.

"I had the feeling that Jimmy knew that Adams was sucking up to him," Long said.

At the time of filming, Adams was rooming with Dennis Hopper. Jimmy with a certain derision referred to them as "Big Dick and Little Dick." *[The chronically indiscreet shock jock, radio star Howard Stern, once asserted, on the air, that "Dennis Hopper's got one the size of an elevator button."]*

One day at lunch, Adams was dining with Jimmy in the commissary. Jimmy looked up and saw that a publicity picture of himself had been on the wall where an equivalent likeness of Dennis Morgan had once hung.

"Morgan out, Dean in," he told Adams. "I can't stand publicity." He jumped up, grabbed the photo from the wall, and smashed its protective glass by hurling it to the floor. Then he stormed out of the dining room.

Ironically, George Stevens, who later directed Jimmy in *Giant,* summoned Adams to a recording studio after Jimmy's death. When Jimmy played Jett Rink, an old man in a drunken banquet scene, his voice had not recorded properly. Nick Adams was the best imitator.

"I stuffed my cheeks with chewing gum to produce Jimmy's exact sound," Adams later explained.

Natalie claimed that "Nick Adams wanted to be my lover, Jimmy's lover, and Ray's lover, but what he really wanted was to become Jimmy's replacement, adored by millions. Alas, dreams often are only to be dreamed."

***

One night in his apartment, Jimmy told Jack Simmons, "I really like Natalie, and I want to be friends with her, perhaps star in another movie with her. But I'm growing bored with her schoolgirl crush on me—in fact, I find it intolerable. I have this plan. It's inspired by something really shitty that Marlon Brando did to Pier Angeli to break off their affair."

Independently, and as confirmation of that, Natalie also discussed some of the shocking provocations that ended her romantic fantasies about Jimmy.

As they moved deeper into their relationship, he began to taunt and tease her. One day, when she was studying her lines from a script, he walked over to her, whipped out his penis, and urinated on her pages.

At first, she was forgiving, dismissing it with, "He's just a Method actor trying to work himself up to play Jim Stark before the camera. That act was something that Stark, an alienated outsider, might do."

His provocations of her continued: Almost daily, Jimmy began to chastise Natalie for being "too Hollywood," accusing her of coveting the trappings of stardom and longing to become as famous as Marilyn Monroe.

As part of this ongoing campaign, Jimmy invited Natalie to visit his rented home—the one that resembled a Bavarian hunting lodge. "I'll be upstairs on the balcony—just call up to me and come in. The door will be unlocked."

That night, however, he wasn't waiting for her on his balcony, but downstairs on the ground floor, entertaining Mineo. Shortly before her scheduled arrival, Jimmy stripped off his clothes and ordered Mineo to do the same. They were kissing and fondling each other when Natalie's car drove up. Mineo was ready to reach for his clothes, but Jimmy held him down and forcibly penetrated him, imprisoning him.

From the driveway, Natalie called up to the (otherwise empty) balcony and, as instructed, opened the front door without knocking. She screamed in horror at the sight of her (naked) lover sodomizing Mineo. In tears, she fled from the scene.

The next day on the set, Jimmy approached her. "Stop your dreaming about me. I'll never marry you."

Holding back her tears, she ran toward her dressing room.

Love knows many faces in *Rebel Without a Cause.* Alienated from their own families, and although tragedy was about to strike, Sal Mineo *(left)*, Jimmy, and Natalie Wood created an ersatz family all on their own.

***

In years to come, usually during conversations with a girlfriend, Natalie would become very graphic during discussions of the various merits (or lack thereof) of her lovers and their respective endowments.

"Nick (Adams) had the biggest, Dennis (Hopper) had the smallest, and Jimmy was somewhere in between. Nick Ray was far more than average. When it came to kissing, Jimmy sure beat Elvis Presley. Nicky Hilton was a beer can. I don't know why Elizabeth (Taylor) divorced him. Steve McQueen was a dud in bed, but he told friends I was lousy in bed, too. Frankly, he just didn't inspire me. When it comes to giving out a prize the length of Oscar, the Academy should present a statuette to John Ireland. What a man! Oh, and Frank Sinatra should at least get a Supporting Player award."

Natalie had this X-rated conversation with gossipy Shelley Winters, who had also seduced both Jimmy Dean and John Ireland.

***

Jimmy dreaded the end of shooting of *Rebel Without a Cause.* After his involvement in its filming ended, he lingered on the set for a conversation with Ray, telling him, "Never has an acting job taken so much out of me. I put everything I had into that film."

"Jimmy and I were alone," Ray said. "We wandered about and didn't want to admit it, but it was all over. Finally, I said to him, "Let's go. We've got nothing more to do here.""

"We kissed each other passionately. Then he climbed onto his motorcycle, and I got behind the wheel of my car. We rode toward Hollywood Boulevard. He spread himself like a flying angel on the cycle, with his feet up on the back mudguard, his arms outstretched. With that reckless maneuver, he sped off with a roar."

Jimmy never lived to read his reviews.

***

Doran later said that about a week after the film was wrapped, she heard someone calling up to her bedroom window at three o'clock one morning: "Mom! Mom!"

She looked down to see that her porch light was dimly illuminating Jimmy standing in her front yard.

"It's your son, Jimmy!" he called up to her after she raised the window.

"He was drunk," she said. She let him in and poured some black coffee into him "as he spoke of his fears and talked about his dreadful loneliness."

***

The last time Steffi Sidney saw Jimmy was when he came into the Villa Capri, right before his death.

Frank Sinatra had thrown a party there. A few months before, he had mocked Jimmy, but now he'd apparently accepted him as a member of the Hollywood elite. Jimmy staggered in, obviously drunk.

He stopped first at the table of his friend, Sammy Davis, Jr., before heading to the men's toilet, trailing behind Sinatra.

When he emerged, his fly was open. "You could see his dick, as he wore no underwear," Davis said. "He complained to me: 'I stood at the urinal beside Sinatra. And now I'm jealous. His dick is bigger than mine.'"

"Then he made his way over to Sidney's table, and put his arm around her. His hair had been shaved back from his forehead so he'd resemble a more accurate rendition of the aged character he'd portray at the end of *Giant.*"

"You know, Steff," he said. "We've never had our picture taken together. Let's go for it." He summoned the on-site photographer, who snapped several pictures of them, shooting Jimmy, for the most part, from the waist up.

He placed one arm around her, holding a cigarette in one hand, and rubbing his belly with the other.

[The ironies associated with that photo was that eight-by-ten glossies of Jimmy with Steffi arrived at her house on the morning of September 30, 1955. Jimmy would be dead in the afternoon of that same day.]

662

***

It was on that September 30, 1955, in New York that Natalie Wood was dining with Sal Mineo, Nick Adams, and Dick Davalos, who had portrayed Jimmy's tormented older brother in *East of Eden*. All of them talked about Jimmy, and how he flirted so dangerously with death. To a person, they agreed that he would probably die one day in a car crash.

Before the end of their dinner, news reached them that Jimmy had died in a car crash on a lonely road in California on his way to Salinas.

***

Rebel Without a Cause was released on October 3, 1955. Jimmy had died just a few days before, on September 30. For the most part, Jimmy's performance elicited rave reviews.

Author Lawrence Frascella wrote: "Ray and Company offers up a romantic, charismatic, sexually charged archetype—a heroic ideal of what being a teenager might mean in *Rebel Without a Cause*. The film took teenagers as seriously as they took themselves."

Writing for *Esquire*, Joy Williamson said: "*Rebel's* appeal is obvious. We were watching the intense, doomed performance of a dead youth, a myth, the myth of those who would wish to see themselves dead without dying. Dean was dead, pre-dead, dead upon our discovery of him. His vivid presence projected a fathomless absence. It was thrilling."

Film historian Jeanine Basinger wrote: "*Rebel* hits home because the teens in it understood their situation at a level the adults could not even imagine. The film is true emotionally, setting up the world of teenagers as a separate universe. It treated their pain seriously, respecting it, instead of turning it into the subject of a cute little comedy about growing up."

Arthur Knight in *Saturday Review* said: "The late James Dean reveals completely the talent

seen in his *East of Eden* performance. Gone are the Brando mannerisms, gone the obvious Kazan touch. He stands as a remarkable talent, and he was cut down, it would seem, by the very passions he exposed so tellingly in this strange and forceful picture."

William K. Zinsser, in *The New York Herald Tribune,* said: "The movie is written and acted so ineptly, directed so sluggishly, that all names but one will be omitted. The exception is James Dean, the gifted young actor. His rare talent and appealing personality shine through, even in this turgid melodrama."

Wanda Hale, of *The New York Daily News,* interpreted the picture like this: "As an honest, purposeful drama of juvenile hardness and violence, it doesn't measure up. Nonetheless, Dean gives a fine, sensitive performance of the unhappy teenager, tormented by the knowledge of his emotional instability."

Variety asserted, "As a farewell performance, James Dean leaves behind, with this film, genuine artistic regret, for here was a talent which might have touched the heights."

Milton Schulman, in London's *Sunday Express,* wrote: "Again, one is impressed by the effects of powerful emotions so harnessed and controlled that if it were not carefully rationed, it would explode."

Bosley Crowther, in *The New York Times,* delivered his usual attack on Jimmy's performances, leveling the familiar charge that he imitated Marlon Brando in his characterization of Jim Stark. "This imitation grows monotonous at some point," he lamented.

Alan Brien, in London's *Evening Standard,* wrote, "James Dean, alas, is dead. But his ghost on the screen in what was only his second film will remain among the immortals of cinema."

Dilys Powell, in London's *Sunday Times,* claimed, "There has been no player of his or any other generation to rival James Dean's interpretation of the desperation of youth."

The novelist, William Faulkner, weighed in, too: "*Rebel Without a Cause* will remain a masterpiece, because it is the only American cinema's Greek tragedy."

***

When the Academy Awards announced its Oscar nominations, it came as a surprise that Mineo was nominated as Best Supporting Actor and Natalie was nominated as Best Supporting Actress. Both of them lost to Jack Lemmon in *Mister Rogers* and to Jo Van Fleet in *East of Eden.*

Jimmy was not nominated, presumably because he'd already been nominated for *East of Eden.*

James Dean's Effect on Elvis Presley

AND HOW IT LED TO THE MURDER OF NICK ADAMS

Elvis Presley was fascinated with James Dean and would endlessly watch *Rebel Without a Cause.* So when he got to Hollywood, he sought out and befriended Nick Adams, who had been Jimmy's friend.

After only a few weeks, Nick became best friend to Elvis, launching a troubled relationship that witnesses claimed turned sexual. Nick himself loudly proclaimed that he'd had affairs both with Jimmy and later with Elvis.

Their bromance began when Elvis accepted an offer to be Nick's "date" for a preview of the film *The Last Wagon* (1956).

Nick was known as a "star-fucker." His closest friends said he'd go to bed with any star – male or female – who might advance his career. Rock Hudson. Director John Ford. Natalie Wood. James Dean. Elvis Presley. It didn't matter to Nick as long as the fuckee was a star or even better, a director.

In the words of Albert Goldman, Nick was "forever selling himself: a property which, to hear him tell it, was nothing less than sensational—'the greatest little actor to hit this town in years.' In fact, he had very little going for him in terms of looks or talent or professional experience. He was just another poor kid from the sticks who had grown up dreaming of the silver screen."

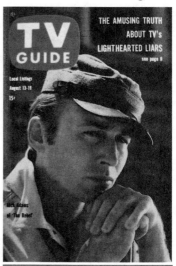

The handsome, blonde-haired actor became the fourth member of the doomed young crew of *Rebel Without a Cause* who would die young and violently.

In death, he joined the actual stars: James Dean (died September 30, 1955), Sal Mineo (February 12, 1976), and Natalie Wood (November 29, 1981).

Born on July 10, 1931, in the gritty coal-mining town of Nanticoke, Pennsylvania, actor Nick (whose name at the time of his birth was Nicholas Aloysius Adamshock) was the son of Ukrainian immigrants.

A close bond between Elvis and Nick Adams was established on the first night they met. Nick told Natalie Wood, "Elvis is going to replace Jimmy in my life."

Nick Adams' greatest success came when he was cast in a TV series about a Confederate soldier, Johnny Yuma, nicknamed *The Rebel.* Even though it became wildly popular, it was pulled after two seasons, based on studio politics.

Right from the beginning, Nick offered his services to Elvis: Friendship, a guide to "Inside Hollywood," a bosom companion, a homosexual lover. "Whatever it is you want, I've got it ... and plenty of it," Nick told Elvis. "If you want to meet movie stars, I know them. Want to fuck Natalie Wood? I can set it up." And so he did.

When Elvis arrived in Hollywood in 1956 to make *Love Me Tender*, the mega-star fell in love with his co-star, Debra Paget. She gave him his blue suede shoes and told him to keep on walking.

Elvis asked Nick to show him Hollywood, and Nick readily agreed. When Elvis and Nick met, "the chemistry exploded" between them and an instant friendship developed.

Within a week, as Nick later told another lover, Sal Mineo, Nick and Elvis were sleeping together. Elvis preferred oral sex and mutual masturbation. Penetration, apparently, was never an option between them.

In those days Elvis could drive his white Cadillac all over Los Angeles with Nick beside him. There was never any fear of molestation from fans. Fan magazines of that era were quick to pick up on this new friendship. However, they misinterpreted its real purpose and accused Nick of riding on Elvis' coattails to promote his own career. (Previously, the same accusations had been leveled about Nick when he developed his friendship with Jimmy.)

Nick took Elvis to the same places he'd frequented with Jimmy, including the old Villa Capri when it was on McCadden Place. They were seen dining frequently at Googie's Restaurant on Sunset Boulevard. Elvis wanted to know what foods Jimmy had liked, and he asked for the same dishes.

When Elvis had to return to Graceland, he left Nick an airplane ticket. To avoid suspicion, Nick flew to Tennessee two days later, telling friends that he was going to New York to seek work on the stage.

Sometimes at Graceland, Elvis would have a lover's quarrel with Nick, and Nick would be forced to sleep in a room with Vester Presley, Elvis's uncle.

A tabloid ran a story that Nick and Elvis shared the same bed at Graceland. When that news

By the time Elvis Presley *(right)* got to Hollywood, James Dean was dead. The singer had wanted to bond with Jimmy and become his most intimate friend. He even wanted to play him on the screen. In lieu of Jimmy, Elvis "settled" for Nick Adams, based on the assumption that Nick—for a while, at least—had been Jimmy's best friend.

broke, Elvis—ever sensitive to charges of homosexuality—ordered that a cot be brought into his bedroom. He told friends that Nick slept on the cot and not in the same bed with him, which—according to the hired help—was not true. A maid later told the press that the covers on that cot were never turned down the mornings after Nick slept over with Elvis.

Late at night, Elvis and Nick would be seen together on the streets of Memphis, riding their twin Harley Davidson motorcycles.

Elvis's girlfriend, June Juanico, claimed that when she dated Elvis all he ever did was talk about Nick Adams.

To legitimatize their relationship, Elvis hired Nick to accompany him on cross-country tours. Nick came out first to warm up the audience by doing his impressions of the famous actors he'd learned to mimic as a kid, notably Cagney and Bogart. Elvis warned Nick not to allow them to get trapped alone together by a photographer. Elvis always insisted that he be photographed with some pretty young girl in the picture, most often a fan. On several occasions that pretty little girl was Natalie herself.

In the hotel suites they co-inhabited during their tours, Elvis also insisted that Nick walk around in a pair of tight-fitting white jockey shorts, arranged so that his pubic hairs would peep out. He confessed to Nick that this was his ultimate turn-on.

"Elvis was into oral sex and enjoyed getting a blow-job more than intercourse," Dennis Miller, a former friend and companion, confirmed. Nick later claimed that while Elvis was watching a sci-fi flick, *Queen of Outer Space [a campy 1958 bomb co-starring Zsa Zsa Gabor]* he was "getting head" from Nick.

Nick later revealed some of Elvis's sexual secrets, claiming that the star was uncircumcised. Nick went on to assert that Elvis had told him that during sexual intercourse with a woman, or even masturbating, his tight foreskin would often tear, causing him to bleed.

Elvis constantly bragged to Nick about his conquests with women. But he claimed that

Years after Jimmy's death, Nick Adams was still a working actor in Hollywood. He's depicted in the upper photo as he appeared in *Hell is for Heroes* (1962).

he could not have sex with a woman who had borne a child. "Fucking a woman who's given birth is like plowing your dick into a tub of fat," Elvis said. "She's too loose to provide any enjoyment for a man."

In the months following Jimmy's death, Nick learned that Robert Altman was going to film *The James Dean Story*. Elvis was excited and intrigued, eventually lobbying to portray his hero on film. "This would be my greatest achievement," Elvis told Nick.

Elvis was bitterly disappointed when he learned that Altman had decided to configure the film as a documentary with still photographs, film clips, and narration by everyone from Natalie Wood to Clark Gable (of all people).

Nonetheless, Elvis persisted, insisting that he wanted to be the narrator, for which he agreed to appear free. Altman wanted Marlon Brando for the job, but he turned down the job, which eventually went to Martin Gabel instead. *[The most sardonic moment in the documentary, released in 1957, occurred when the filmmakers inserted a commercial of Jimmy, with Gig Young, wherein he urged viewers to drive safely. As a promotional device, Warner Brothers hired Nick to travel to Marion, Indiana (James Dean's birthplace) for the premier of the Altman film. On site, Nick visited Jimmy's aunt and uncle, Marcus and Ortense Winslow.]*

***

At Graceland, Elvis became obsessed that "I look like a faggot on film." Night after night he sat with Nick watching his own movies. He asked Nick to warn him if he were "making any limp-wrist moves like one of those god-damn effeminate swishes." To his male friends, Elvis, in spite of his own nocturnal adventures, often attacked "swishes" or "faggots," never wanting to be identified with them in any way.

When Nick pointed out some scenes where Elvis raised his wrist limply, Elvis would go into a rage and denounce Nick. At one time Elvis got so angry that he ordered Nick from Graceland and tore up his return ticket home. But the next day he forgave his friend and welcomed him back.

Elvis's manager, Colonel Tom Parker, handled the Elvis/Nick affair calmly. "At least he's not impregnating another gal and leaving me to abort another brat."

Col. Parker appreciated Nick's support of Elvis after the death of his mother, Gladys Presley, on August 14, 1958. "Nicky Admas [sic] came out to be with Elvis last Week wich [sic] was so very kind of him to be there with his friend."

During his period of mourning, Elvis locked himself in his darkened bedroom with Nick for three days and nights, refusing to eat or to see anyone else. Nick later claimed that Elvis talked for days about Gladys. Nick recorded all that he'd learned in journals which he'd been keeping ever since he arrived in Hollywood.

At one point he revealed Elvis's darkest secret to both Natalie and to Rock Hudson, suggesting that he feared "Elvis's relationship with Gladys was incestuous."

Afraid that news of Elvis's homosexuality would leak out, the Colonel spread stories about what a stud Elvis was, even linking him to the stripper Tempest Storm, whom previously Elvis had seduced.

Elvis told his stepmother, Dee Presley, that he'd slept with more than 1,000 women before marrying Priscilla. Over the years he claimed to have had sex with everyone from the British sexpot Diana Dors to the American sexpot, Jayne Mansfield, even Cybill Shepherd, Nancy Sinatra, Connie Stevens, Tuesday Weld, Mary Ann Mobley, and Ann-Margret, among countless others.

In 2012, Nick Adam's daughter, Allyson Adams, published a posthumous overview of her father' relationship with Elvis. Some readers interpreted it as a "whitewash."

Susan King of *The Los Angeles Times* wrote, "*The Rebel and the King* chronicles Adams' and Presley's adventures...with a youthful exuberance and innocence."

With all his commissions, ancillary deals, and trinket sales, Col. Parker was actually making more money—an outrageous 50% split—than Elvis himself.

In the words of biographer David Bret, Col. Parker had a "Svengali-like grip over Elvis because he continually threatened to reveal that Elvis had romanced Nick Adams."

Every time Elvis would get fed up with the colonel's larceny and try to fire him, Parker would threaten to blackmail him. Only after Elvis's death did revelations about his bisexuality appear in print, notably in Dee Presley's memoir, *The Intimate Life and Death of Elvis Presley.*

Nick's luck turned when a producer, Andrew J. Fenady, created a character for Nick to play in a TV series. It was Johnny Yuma, a young ex-Confederate soldier who helps restore law and order as he roamed the West after the Civil War. The series became known as *The Rebel,* and premiered on October 4, 1959.

It didn't occur overnight, but eventually, Nick Adams became a household word throughout America. No more did columnists refer to him as "The

Leech," and even today, many viewers from the Age of Sputnik can remember the catchy jingle that opened each episode of the series. But in spite of its success, ABC canceled the series after two seasons. Nick was bitterly disappointed. He'd spent all his money.

Somewhere along the way, Nick's straight side asserted itself. On May 10, 1959 he married Carol Nugent, a former child actress. They would have two children—Allyson Lee, born February 23, 1960, and a son, Jeb Stuart, born April 10, 1961.

Ultimately Nick had a devastating effect on Elvis. He was the man who introduced Elvis to drugs, supplying him with his first bennies.

On the verge of bankruptcy, Nick flew to Graceland for a meeting with Elvis. Their passion for each other had long ago cooled.

Nick arrived drunk for his showdown with Elvis. Alone in Elvis's bedroom, Nick demanded that the star give him a check for $100,000 for all the services rendered over the years.

Elvis was drugged. He accused Nick of being "The Leech," applying the exact same words used by tabloid columnists during the late 50s and 60s. Elvis refused to give him any money, even his return fare to Los Angeles.

At that point, Nick made a fatal mistake. He threatened Elvis, claiming that he was going to write a tell-all memoir. Throughout the course of his star-fucking career, he'd kept extensive journals, even describing the pornographic details of sexual bouts with both male and female stars. Nick used to tell friends, "I take the advice of Mae West. Keep a diary while you're young, because it will keep you when you get old."

The exact details of Nick's final confrontation with Elvis aren't known, but when Elvis steadfastly refused to "give you one buck, you bastard," Nick delivered his final, perhaps fatal, threat. He warned Elvis that he was not only going to write about their affair, but tell all the secrets he'd learned about Elvis and Gladys during the three days and nights he'd spent with Elvis in the wake of his mother's death.

Col. Parker "threw a fit" when he heard that Nick was writing about his affair with Elvis. "He's joining those tabloid vultures," the colonel told his confidants. "This is only speculation, but I'm not sure that boy has much longer to live."

***

Nick Adams found peace at last on February 6, 1968. His dead body was discovered by his lawyer, Ervin Roeder, at his house in Coldwater Canyon. It was propped in a sitting position against the bedroom wall. An autopsy revealed that he had overdosed on a cocktail of the anti-anxiety medications

Paraldehyde and Promazine. A coroner's report determined that the death was "accidental, suicidal and undetermined." But persistent reports of foul play continue to this day. There was no suicide note.

Roeder called the police at once. When they arrived fifteen minutes later, Nick's body was removed on a stretcher and placed in an ambulance. As this was being done, the house was searched. There were no signs of a robbery, and the police even noted some loose cash and two valuable rings on a nearby nightstand.

When Roeder searched through Nick's desk, he reported that the manuscript of the *exposé* which Nick had been working on was nowhere to be found. Even more significant were Nick's journals, which were also missing. He'd kept them for years. Nick's tape recordings were also missing, even his typewriter, a cherished gift from James Dean.

An autopsy performed that night by the L.A. County Coroner revealed that Nick's body contained a massive dose of the sedative paraldehyde. The drug had acted in lethal concert with the tranquilizer Promazine. But no paraldehyde container was found in the house. A chemical cousin of formaldehyde, paraldehyde had been prescribed by Nick's brother, a doctor, Andrew Adams.

Dr. Thomas Noguchi, "coroner to the stars," finally concluded on March 3, 1968, that, "The mode of death is certified as accidental suicide and undetermined." What was not said was that at first Nick's death had been ruled a homicide.

The case would become fodder for a legend. The tabloids went wild, speculating that Nick's so-called suicide was actually murder.

One of his closest friends was the Oscar-winning actor Broderick Crawford. "Nick was very outspoken to me in the weeks before his death," Crawford said. "He told me about the memoir he was writing about Elvis and James Dean. I warned him that if Col. Parker found out about it, 'You're dead meat, kid.' But no one could tell Nick anything. Until my dying grave, I'll believe that Parker ordered Nick killed."

A fellow actor, Forrest Tucker, agreed with him. "In the weeks before his death, Nick told me that he feared bodily harm from Parker. He also told me that he kept two guns in the house just in case of a break-in. When the police searched the house, no weapons of any kind were found. Whoever broke in to steal the incriminating journals and manuscript even took

Adams' house on El Roble Lane in Los Angeles, where police found him dead. The unsavory circumstances of his death were never clearly explained.

his Johnny Reb cap. Nick always told me he wanted to be buried in that cap one day. I just hope that hip gyrator, Elvis, had nothing to do with this."

"Absolutely, it wasn't suicide," Robert Conrad, Nick's closest friend, was quoted as saying. "We were so close that if he'd intended that, I'd have known about it. Murder? I don't know. It could be foul play."

Jeb Adams, Nick's son, claimed in 1992 that he was "99.99% sure" that his dad had been murdered.

His revelations about James Dean and Elvis Presley have, as of this date, never been published. The whereabouts of his manuscript are not known. Perhaps it was destroyed.

Only a few graying fans, mostly homosexual men, still visit the grave site of Nick Adams. He was buried near his birthplace in Berwick, Pennsylvania. The restless son of immigrant parents from the Ukraine, he always maintained a burning ambition to become a movie star, "The New James Dean."

After a brief success, his career began to slip into oblivion. Faced with mounting bills, he played the dangerous card of blackmail. That move probably cost him his life.

Chapter Twenty-Three

HOW A SHORT, NEARSIGHTED FARMBOY FROM INDIANA BECAME A

GIANT

ALONG WITH HOLLYWOOD SUPERSTARS
ELIZABETH TAYLOR AND ROCK HUDSON

A Lesbian Author, a Gay Leading Man,
a Sultry, Bed-Hopping Beauty, and a Bisexual Rebel
Bring a Sprawling Saga of Texas to the Screen

JIMMY DISCOVERS THE RATTLESNAKE-EATING COWBOYS OF TEXAS,
WHERE MEN BOAST THAT THEY'VE ALL GOT SOMETHING BIG

Hollywood was abuzz with the news that director George Stevens was going to make the all-star spectacular film epic of the year, the screen adaptation of Edna Ferber's best-selling 1952 novel, *Giant*, set in the Lone Star State.

The novel had enthralled thousands of Americans, but not many Texans. As John Barkham in *The New York Times* wrote: "Miss Ferber makes it very clear that she doesn't like the Texas she writes about, and it's a cinch that when Texans read about what she has written about them, they won't like Miss Ferber either."

In reference to a saga that sprawled across three generations of sweeping historical changes, critic Robert Tanitch wrote: "The Lone Star State was turned into a symbol, a *giant* symbol, for all that was the least estimable in America: It's money-grabbing materialism, its thick-skinned self-interest, its profligacy and vulgarity, its low-browism, its snobbery and racism, its narrow-mindedness, its self-satisfied isolationism, and its spiritual impoverishment."

Set for release in 1956, Warner Brothers had budgeted it at five and a half million dollars, a staggering sum of money in the Eisenhower era.

In July of 2002, when the US Postal Service issued an 83¢ stamp honoring the literary legacy of Edna Ferber, collectors realized that, based on a printing plate error, some were missing the blue, black, and ocher-colored ink that would otherwise have been included in their print runs.

The value of those judged as "aberrant" immediately shot up to around $500 each, and the recognition quotient of Edna Ferber skyrocketed.

Now at the peak of his acclaim, California-born George Stevens was a deeply respected kind of Renaissance figure with a career that had included stints as a director, producer, screenwriter, and cinematographer. As the head of the U.S. Army Signal Corps in World War II, he'd taken newsreels of the Allied landings on the bloody beaches of Normandy. Later, he filmed the liberation by U.S. troops of the notorious concentration camp of Dachau.

He'd already won the Best Director Oscar for his 1951 *A Place in the Sun,* and was Oscar-nominated for his 1953 Western, *Shane.*

The trio of leads that Stevens would focus on first included Bick Benedict, patriarch of what becomes an oil dynasty and his wife, Leslie Benedict; and his employee, an upstart ranchhand-turned-wildcatter, Jett Rink. *Giant* also contained many lesser roles for which established stars would compete.

Bick is a strapping, tall, and handsome Texan, the owner of the sprawling Reata Ranch that's almost the size of the state of New Hampshire. The cattle baron is proud and a bit of a chauvinist in that he treats women like second-class citizens, perhaps granting Mexicans third-class status.

The film opens when he's in Maryland with the intention of purchasing a champion black stallion. There, he falls for the beautiful and somewhat calculating Leslie on her father's horse farm. Unlike most of the women he had known, she's intelligent and a bit of a liberated woman, rather strong willed and high-spirited. Ignoring certain warning signs, he is spellbound by her beauty, marries her, and hauls her back to his sterile, arid, and searingly overheated ranch.

George Stevens, perplexed, possibly based on an issue associated with James Dean.

She's appalled at some of the conditions she finds there, including the Jim Crow class distinction between rich and poor and the horrible treatment of Mexicans.

A lesser role, but one far more colorful was that of a poor local rancher, Jett Rink, who works for the Benedict family. Edna Ferber described him as "a character threatening sexual danger. He was a brute, a savage, dirty, belligerent, irresponsible, sadistic, a sullen, loutish kind of boy, who bore a grudge against the world."

"He was all right when he behaves himself," she wrote. "But when he drinks, he goes kind of crazy. He's a kind of genius, Jett is. He'll probably end up a billionaire—or in the electric chair. Put him in a car and he goes crazy."

It was almost as if she were describing James Dean.

When Jimmy heard through his lover, Arthur Loew, Jr., that the role of Jett Rink "might suit you as tight as a rubber on your dick," he rushed out and bought the paperback edition of *Giant,* which he read cover to cover in three days. He later told Loew, "That's me, boy. I'm Jett Rink. If I grab that role, I can escape being typecast as a sinister adolescent."

Loew promised to approach Stevens and to pitch him for the role of Jett. To Jimmy's dismay, he learned that the director had already sent the script to Marlon Brando. Once again, these two Method actors would each be in consideration for the same role. Brando sent the script back, rejecting the part as "too small."

Stevens also considered Charlton Heston, Cornel Wilde, Anthony Quinn,

675

Jack Palance, and Gordon McCrae for the role of Jett.

Right before reaching his final decision, Stevens came up with the idea of putting Richard Burton into the role as a "hell-raising wildcatter" in love with Bick Benedict's wife, Leslie.

As it turned out, Burton was not available. "It would have been a challenge to me as an actor," he said. "Having a Welshman speak with a Texas drawl."

[Later, after Burton learned that Elizabeth Taylor had been cast as Leslie, he ran into Stevens one night at Chasens in Los Angeles. In the men's room, he whispered, "I'm sorry I wasn't free to play Jett Rink. It would have given me a chance to introduce Elizabeth Taylor to my Welsh dick.]

After losing Burton for the role, Stevens offered it to Alan Ladd, who, unknown to the director at the time, was despondent to the point of suicide, and drinking heavily. He dreaded facing the camera, and was undergoing a lot of personal hell, including fear of a blackmail attempt from one of his hustler lovers, who was threatening to tell all to *Confidential* unless he surrendered $10,000 in cash.

Stevens had gotten along smoothly with Ladd during the filming of their 1953 blockbuster, *Shane*. With that in mind, he sent him the first draft of the script for *Giant*.

Ladd read the script that night and eagerly telephoned Stevens the next morning. "I'm your Bick Benedict!"

Stevens was aghast. He hadn't told Ladd that he wanted him for the lesser role of Jett.

"There's no way in hell I could make a midget like Ladd play a tall, strapping Texan," Stevens told his aides. "Stand him on crates to make him taller?"

Stevens got back to Ladd with, "No, no, Alan, I want you to play Jett Rink!"

"I'm not going to play that shit," Ladd said. "A flamboyantly corrupt Texas

Had Richard Burton accepted the role of Jett Rink in *Giant*, his affair with Elizabeth Taylor might have begun years before he co-starred with her, (*as depicted above*) as Marc Antony in *Cleopatra*.

"Lightning didn't strike twice," said Alan Ladd. He was referring to my "idiotic decision" to reject the role of Jett Rink in *Giant*. Ladd had scored a big hit when George Stevens cast him in the Western, *Shane (see above)*.

oil millionaire who begins life as a dirty little punk? Not for me, buddy."

He hung up on Stevens, but two years later, he told a reporter, "Turning down the role that went to James Dean was one of the biggest mistakes of my career."

What Ladd had rejected, James Stewart went for in a very big way, even though Jett Rink would be a radical departure from the good guys he usually played on screen. Perhaps that change of pace was the reason he wanted to star as *Giant's* corrupt ranch hand.

Nothing illustrated "New Hollywood" vs. "Old Hollywood" better than the rivalry for roles between James Dean and James Stewart. Stevens called it "The Battle of the Two Jimmy's."

Stewart was pushing fifty (actually forty-seven years old) when he campaigned for the role of Jett Rink. From the beginning, Stevens didn't want him. "If he were twenty years younger, he could have handled it with that drawl of his, his beanpole physique, and his shy, gulping manner," Stevens said. "Being in a Western was no problem. He'd come to personify the American West as much as John Wayne. I could make a younger actor old with makeup, but there was no way I could make Stewart a young man—even with all the makeup in the world."

"It was one of my greatest embarrassments to have to call Stewart and turn him down for the role," Stevens said. "After all, he was one of the greatest of all screen actors. I didn't feel so bad for him, however. After all, he'd just had a hit opposite Grace Kelly in Alfred Hitchcock's *Rear Window* (1954)."

"I finally decided the role should go to Dean," Sevens said. "The guy had been hounding me for days to get that juicy part. I called him to tell him to transform himself into a Texas ranger. 'The role is yours,' I promised him."

Stevens believed that Jimmy would be ideal in the opening scenes, when Jett Rink was a young rancher. But since he has to age into a drunken, battered 45-year-old for the film's final scenes, the director worried that he might not pull them off, even with heavy makeup and graying hair.

Actually, he'd been aware of Jimmy's acting ever since he'd watched his teleplay, *A Long Time Till Dawn.* He told a reporter, "It was the first time that I ever watched anxiously during the credits so I could find out who this brilliant, sensitive actor was."

After Stevens had *East of Eden* screened for him, he congratulated Elia Kazan. "I found the kid's performance mesmerizing," Stevens said. "I was sorry I lost your boy, Brando. I'd wanted him to play Jett Rink. But getting Dean might be even better."

"Working with Jimmy will be an experience you'll carry with you to your grave," Kazan said. "I'll say no more."

"Don't Fall In Love With Me"

—*Grace Kelly to James Dean*

After Jimmy agreed to play Jett, Stevens turned his attention to casting the two other leads, Bick and Leslie Benedict.

Producer Henry Ginsberg , in a phone call to Stevens, recommended Marlene Dietrich for the role.

"Are you out of your mind?" Stevens responded. "As far as it is known, Marlene was born in 1901, or maybe even in the 1890s. She'd be perfect if we adapted Leslie as a grandmother, and if we rewrote the character as a German. The answer is 'no.' She's too old, and too Teutonic."

Jennifer Jones, with the understanding that she'd have to age from a young bride to an older woman during the course of the film, was the first to personally lobby Stevens for the juicy female lead.

More than a decade before, Jones had won an Oscar for the somewhat sappy religious tear-jerker, *The Song of Bernadette* (1943). She promised Stevens that if he'd give her the role of Leslie Benedict, she would win another Oscar—"and put your big movie on the map."

He thought she was "too syrupy" for the role, his mind set on Audrey Hepburn. Flying to New York in July of 1954, he visited the petite actress, who was appearing at the time on Broadway in *Ondine*.

Almost from the beginning, Hepburn and Stevens disagreed over the in-

What Might Have Been: Actresses considered for the role of Leslie Benedict included TOO GLAM! Marlene Dietrich (depicted in 1951 in *No Highway in the Sky*; TOO PIOUS AFTER *SONG OF BERNADETTE!* Jennifer Jones, as she appeared with Gregory Peck in *Duel in the Sun* (1946); and the very cosmopolitan but NOT PARTICULARLY CONVINCING AS A RANCH HAND, Audrey Hepburn.

terpretation of the role. She wasn't really interested, anyway, telling Stevens, "I hear Texans eat rattlesnake for breakfast."

Within a week, Hepburn was no longer in the running.

His telephone kept ringing throughout the rest of the year. He decided that Eva Marie Saint would be perfect for the role, only to learn that she was pregnant with a baby due in April.

Stevens then began to focus on Grace Kelly, who had just made such hits as *Dial M For Murder* (1954) with Ray Milland, and *Rear Window* (also 1954) with James Stewart. Her interpretation of the female lead in *The Country Girl* (1955) with William Holden and Bing Crosby would later be awarded with an Oscar.

Grace Kelly in her very-fashionable, much-reviewed-by-fashion-writers black dress, as she appeared in *Rear Window*.

Jimmy's lover, Arthur Loew, Jr., through his direct pipeline to the executives at MGM, learned that Grace had wanted the role of Leslie so badly that she was willing to go on suspension, refusing to show up for the filming of *Jeremy Rodock* with the aging Spencer Tracy.

As all of this was happening, Jimmy was spending many of his nights in Nicholas Ray's suite at the Château Marmont, a venue that was by now so familiar to him that management seemed to think he was a permanent resident.

By coincidence, he learned that Grace was living within a bungalow at the same hotel. He hadn't seen her since their previous encounter in New York.

Ray noted a smirk on Jimmy's face. "Don't tell me you've bedded her, you little devil!"

"Something like that," Jimmy said. "My dream might be coming true. Starring in a movie with Grace Kelly."

The next morning found Jimmy, in a bathing suit, beside the hotel's swimming pool, from a position with an unobstructed view of the door to Grace's bungalow.

When she emerged from her quarters, she was putting on a pair of white gloves as she headed toward the lobby. "Hi Gracie!" Jimmy called out to her as he emerged from the pool. [*"I imagined I was a male version of Esther Williams, trying to look as sexy as possible," he later told Ray.*]

She kissed him on the lips as he wrapped himself in a giant bath towel.

"Well," he said. "What have we here? The most beautiful girl in New York is now the most gorgeous gal in Hollywood."

"I'm glad you think so," she said. "Now I hope the world will agree with you."

"They will, I predict," he said.

"I'm terribly rushed right now," she said. "and I'm running late. Perhaps we'll get together sometime."

Fearing that he was losing her forever, he said, "I just heard from Arthur Loew. MGM is considering lending you out for *Giant.* And Stevens has more or less given me the third lead of Jett Rink."

Grace stopped in her tracks, focusing on him with renewed interest.

"Is that so? Then by all means, we must get together. Are you free to drop by my bungalow at four tomorrow afternoon?"

"I'll be there with my Stetson and some Texas cowboy boots," he promised.

She gave him another gentle kiss on the lips. "I will hold my breath until you're on my doorstep."

Over pillow talk, late the following afternoon, she shared her anxieties with him. "I'm afraid to go on a location shoot in the Texas desert. I'm a city girl."

"Don't worry," he assured her. "You'll have me to protect you."

"I'll consider that, but only on one condition," she said.

"What might that be, princess?" he asked, ironically referring to her as "princess" long before she actually became one.

"That you don't fall in love with me. Too many men fall in love with me."

Over the next ten days, Jimmy paid four visits to Grace's bungalow. Once, he invited her to lunch in the Hollywood Hills, at a restaurant with a scenic view. Although she seemed serenely cool with his driving, back at the bungalow, she admitted, "That's the last time for that. I was terrified every time you came to a curve in the road. This psychic, Frank Andrews, once told me that I'd be killed one day in a car crash."

Jimmy admitted to Ray, "I've had to deny you and everybody else sex because I've been saving it for Grace."

But one afternoon, Jimmy learned that he was paying his last visit to Grace's bungalow. She told him that she was not going to play Leslie in *Giant.* "MGM is not going to lend me out. Another thing, I learned that George Stevens really doesn't want me in the role. He prefers Elizabeth Taylor."

She went on to tell him something else. "I want you to understand," she said. "My dance card is very full. You're sweet, cuddly, and adorable. I'll always have the fondest memories of you. Got to run now." Then she gave him a gentle farewell kiss on the lips.

That night, Jimmy told Ray what had happened. He didn't seem surprised. "I was a bit taken aback that Grace took up with you in the first place. She's known to prefer older men. Established stars. You're just small fry."

"But unlike some of those grandfathers, I can always produce a reliable erection."

The next afternoon, Jimmy, at the pool, was joined by his least favorite author, Gore Vidal. "I heard Grace has given you the brush-off."

"You might call it that," Jimmy said.

"Well, she'll be doing another picture, and she's sure to have an affair with her leading man. Just think of it: Gary Cooper, Ray Milland, William Holden, Bing Crosby, James Stewart. She refused to make a movie with Spencer Tracy, but I hear he's fucking her anyway. Now she's going to star in a movie with Cary Grant. Oh, did I leave out Clark Gable from *Mogambo?*"

As Jimmy was exiting from the pool area later that afternoon, he spotted Grace heading for her bungalow. When the face of the man who was accompanying her came into view, he recognized that it was the much married actor, David Niven.

[More than six months after Jimmy's death, Grace abdicated her throne as Queen of Hollywood to become a mere Princess of Monaco, based on her (relentlessly publicized) marriage to Prince Rainier.

She would eventually die in a car crash at the age of fifty-two in September of 1982.]

***

During several tense weeks, Elizabeth knew that the role she coveted, that of Leslie in *Giant*, was almost beyond her reach. George Stevens, who had directed her so brilliantly in *A Place in the Sun*, "seemed to want every other actress in Hollywood, but considered me chopped liver, I guess," Elizabeth told her husband, Michael Wilding. "But I want that part, and I'm going for it. Imagine a script that calls for me to transform myself from a beautiful young bride to a grandmother. Oscar, you've got Elizabeth Taylor's name written on your ass!"

When it became clear that Grace Kelly would not be available, Elizabeth jumped with joy and headed for Benny Thau's office to beg him to have MGM lend her services to Warner Brothers.

There was still one problem: MGM didn't want to lend her. "I had to go on a sitdown strike...well, almost," she said to a reporter. "Dare I say blackmail in certain quarters? No, don't print that...it wasn't exactly blackmail."

Then, she engaged in a big brawl with Thau. "I think he wanted me to play Lassie's mother—or some such shit—in a sequel."

She finally won out, "but my bruises were black. I got no extra money. MGM took it all for the loan-out."

When at last they become convinced that Elizabeth was the right actress for the part, the executives at Warner Brothers offered $250,000 for her services, even though her contract called for her to make only $100,000 a year from MGM at the time. MGM pocketed the difference.

***

Once she signed for the role of Leslie, Elizabeth insisted that "the only actor to play Jett Rink is Monty Clift."

Knowing what a good actor he was, Stevens went along with her proposal until Warner's insurance underwriters advised Jack Warner that "Clift is just too god damn risky. We won't insure him."

Stevens, even at this early stage in the compilation of *Giant,* was already hearing rumbling suspicions that Jimmy might carry some baggage with him. As expressed so colorfully by biographer David Brett: "Jimmy was already being hailed as a lost cause, a cock-hungry schizophrenic, a pre-'Brat Pack' *prima donna*, whose only truly happy, but not entirely sane moments occurred when he was creating merry hell."

Stevens was forced to delay the filming of *Giant* to accommodate his three big stars. Elizabeth was pregnant; Hudson needed to finish shooting *All That Heaven Allows* with Jane Wyman; and Jimmy still had scenes to shoot for *Rebel Without a Cause.*

How Hollywood's Fading Matinee Idols Schemed for the Role of Texas Patriarch
Bick Benedict
And How It Was Eventually Awarded to the Macho and Charming
Rock Hudson

During his selection of candidates for the male lead, the character of Bick Benedict, Stevens was bombarded with phone calls from William Holden, Gary Cooper, and Clark Gable. At least a dozen other Hollywood males also made their voices heard.

Lying on different massage boards at their gym, John Wayne told Forrest Tucker, "I'm gonna play Bick Benedict."

"Like hell you are," Tucker responded, lying nude on his board. "The role calls for a big dick." Then he ripped the towel off Wayne. "As you can plainly see, my Moby Dick is six times the size of yours."

Sterling Hayden said: "Forrest Tucker is too drunk to play the part. I'm the right size to play Benedict...in all departments."

Robert Mitchum said: "I've practically got the role of Bick Benedict sewn up! Stevens has always had a hard-on for me. I can just see billboards across America: *ROBERT MITCHUM AND ELIZABETH TAYLOR STARRING IN GIANT WITH JAMES DEAN.*"

William Holden, as the doomed writer, Joe Gillis, in the 1950 movie that made him a star, *Sunset Blvd.*, starring Gloria Swanson as Norma Desmond.

Mitchum had also been considered for the role of Jett Rink

Late one afternoon, a call came in from Ross Hunter, the producer of *Magnificent Obsession* (1954), starring Rock Hudson and Jane Wyman. "I want you to consider Rock for this part. He's going to become the biggest macho male star since Gable."

Universal, however, didn't want to lend Hudson, rushing him instead into another soapy tearjerker with Wyman, *All That Heaven Allows* (1955). But when it became clear that Hudson could fulfill his obligations to both films, he persuaded Warners to let him star in *Giant.* "I had to

"With a chest like I used to have, I didn't mind going topless in a movie," said Robert Mitchum, pictured here in the 1962 *Cape Fear.* "I was considered for both Jett Rink *and* Bick Benedict."

let a lot of guys at Universal suck my cock to get the role of Bick," he later told Elizabeth.

Before deciding on Hudson, Stevens had more or less made up his mind that the role of Bick Benedict should go to William Holden. Hudson later recalled that on the day the announcement was made that he would be the male star of *Giant*, he entered the studio sauna nude, only to discover an equally nude Holden sitting on a slab of marble.

Hudson would describe the incident's irony to Elizabeth: "Here I was, the new star of Hollywood, confronting an aging star with my better body, a bigger dick, and a more awesome presence. I felt embarrassed for Holden."

Some Hollywood historians have suggested that the casting of *Giant,* more than that of any other picture, represented "a changing of the guard in Hollywood," based on the fact that box office champions of yesterday [*James Stew-*

art, Clark Gable, Robert Mitchum, John Wayne, Sterling Hayden, Gary Cooper, and William Holden] were rejected in favor of new, postwar stars such as James Dean and Rock Hudson.

Mean-Spirited Jimmy and Confidential Magazine
HOW THE MALE LEAD IN GIANT WAS DANGLED BEFORE PAUL NEWMAN

Newly arrived in Hollywood for the filming of *The Rack [a war drama based on a play by Rod Serling and released in 1956]*, Paul Newman invited Jimmy for an afternoon swim at the Château Marmont. Newman was anxious to learn about how filming was progressing on *Rebel Without a Cause.*

Jimmy told him that Warner Brothers was cracking down on the script, especially as regards the implied homosexual attraction between his character that of Plato. "Sal and I are playing a trick on them. I told him to look at me with moonglow eyes. It'll be obvious to audiences that he's in love with me."

He also claimed that he had been lobbying to get Mineo cast in the role of a Mexican soldier in *Giant.* "If I'm going to be shipped off to a remote outpost in Texas, I'll need a fuckmate with me. I can't take a chance of finding someone on the hoof there."

"Don't you think Sal is a bit young for you?" Newman asked.

"I take the position of the Emperor Caligula," Jimmy answered. "As long as they're out of the womb."

Later, Jimmy asked him to go with him to a car race, but Newman turned him down, pleading another engagement.

"When I'm racing, it's a more powerful thrill than any drug," Jimmy claimed. "I feel like I'm not of this earth. I feel like a real man. I answer to no one. I'm in control of my universe."

Newman, too, seemed intrigued by car racing, promising, "Sooner than later, I bet we'll be racing together, maybe even competing for the gold."

Although the two men didn't notice her, Susan Strasberg, daughter of Lee Strasberg of the Actors Studio, was checking into the Château Marmont with her mother, Paula.

She later recalled seeing the two actors in their bathing suits. "They both had slender bodies, not beefed up, but perfect in every way, like Michelangelo's *David.* They had thick hair, Paul's being wavier. Paul had this habit of touching his finger to his nose when talk got a little rough. I saw him do that a lot at the Actors Studio. Lying on a pad side by side, they were the epitome of male beauty. I understood why men turn gay. Each of them could have posed for a Renaissance painter, perhaps Leonardo da Vinci, not just Michelangelo."

The next weekend, Newman did agree to drive down the Pacific coast for a weekend at a roadside motel outside Laguna Beach. After a night of heavy drinking, they went back to their motel and fell into bed together, too tired to make love. As Jimmy would later tell Nicholas Ray, "We were too exhausted and too intoxicated that night, but came the rosy glow of dawn, we made up for it."

Over lunch that day, Jimmy promised Newman that, "I'm going to do everything in my power to get you cast as Bick Benedict in *Giant*. We didn't get to work together in *East of Eden,* but the two of us will be dynamite on the screen together. Both of us can take turns fucking Elizabeth Taylor."

Ex-con and bisexual, Rory Calhoun, depicted above, was sacrificed and savaged by *Confidential* magazine and a conspiracy of Hollywood agents and casting directors.

"I don't understand," Newman said. "I've heard that George Stevens has already cast Rock Hudson."

"Don't let that worry you," Jimmy said. "The shit's about to hit the fan. I've heard that *Confidential* has been on Rock's tail for some time. They're going to expose him as a homo. Rock is certain to be fired from *Giant* before shooting begins. It's all over for him. The part will make your career after that *Silver Chalice* shit."

[At the last minute, Henry Willson, Hudson's agent, made a deal to expose (and sacrifice) another of his stars, Rory Calhoun, in lieu of his bigger, more profitable client, Rock Hudson. Consequently, it was revealed that Calhoun had spent time in prison years before becoming a Hollywood star.

Hudson stayed in the cast of Giant, *and Newman went on to star in the boxing saga,* Somebody Up There Likes Me *(1956), cast as Rocky Graziano. The role had been earmarked for Jimmy, but his fatal car crash abruptly ended that dream.]*

As a western star, Paul Newman survived his rejection for the role of Bick Benedict in *Giant*, moving on to play the male lead in *Hud*, depicted above.

685

Susan Strasberg Aborts Jimmy's Kid

The sixteen-year-old actress, Susan Strasberg, had long admired James Dean. In her memoirs, *Bittersweet,* published in 1980, she wrote: "He fascinated me. He epitomized an iconoclastic approach to life, opposed to the more measured, intellectual cadences I was accustomed to."

She also said that during her stay at the Château Marmont, "Nick Ray, Jimmy, my mother, Paula, and I used to go out for dinner. Jimmy borrowed one of Nick's jackets, which made him look like a little boy dressed in his father's clothes."

Soon, Jimmy and Susan were dating without their chaperones. *The Hollywood Reporter* took notice. "James Dean courts Susan Strasberg in jeans, a dirty pair at that, a leather jacket, and scruffy cowboy boots. Susan is as happy as if he had dressed in a tuxedo."

The couple were seen at dives on Sunset Strip.

She was in Hollywood because Vincente Minnelli had cast her in *The Cobweb* (1955), which Jimmy was to have starred in. His role went to John Kerr, his rival and former lover. The other stars included Charles Boyer, Richard Widmark, Lillian Gish, Lauren Bacall, Gloria Grahame, and Oscar Levant, who had become Jimmy's friend.

Jimmy was anxious to learn how the shoot was going.

Susan claimed, "I'm cast as a hypersensitive, paranoid teenager. Call it type casting."

One morning, Susan introduced Jimmy to the former silent screen great, Lillian Gish. He told her that he'd once appeared in a teleplay with her sister, Dorothy.

"Of course you did, my dear," Gish responded. "I was offered the role, but turned it down. When it was shown on television, I had another engagement."

Two days later, Susan claimed that she had one big scene in *The Cobweb.* "I was a nervous wreck. I went out to take a breath of fresh air. As I was standing there, gasping for breath, Jimmy roared up on his motorcycle."

"I came to take you for a ride," he said. "Hop on!"

"I can't leave. I'm due back on the set in a little while."

"It won't take that long," he said. "It'll relax you."

"I really want to," she said, "but I don't know."

"Then shit, do it!" he commanded. "C'mon!"

She later recalled, "I wasn't used to hearing the word shit used around my family."

Soon, she was on the cycle behind him, holding on for life. "The wind whipped my hair over my face, stinging me. I leaned closer, my face buried in his leather jacket."

The next morning, Jimmy awakened early and paraded out from Ray's suite in his briefs, jumping into the pool, perhaps hoping it would wake him up.

He became aware that there was another swimmer in the water. When her head surfaced, he realized he was staring into the face of Greta Garbo. He'd heard from Ray that she was in residence at the Château Marmont, occupying one of the penthouses.

"Morning," he called to her. "I'm Jimmy Dean."

"And I'm Harriet Brown," she said, rather coldly, swimming away.

"That was the extent of my conversation with Miss Garbo," he later told Ray.

***

For reasons rather obvious, Susan left out the behind-the-scenes details of her brief fling with James Dean.

Years later, in New York in the 1970s, Darwin Porter escorted her to a number of gala events, often followed by dinner at Joe Allen's, where she preferred to go.

Gradually, she confided in him why she couldn't write about her brief affair with Jimmy. She relayed how he took her to his rental property that looked like a hunting lodge, in the Hollywood Hills. "He took my virginity. I didn't like it. Messy stuff, but he told me that the next time would be easier, smoother, and better."

"He was right. I almost fell in love with him before he disappeared from my life. As the weeks went by, and he was away making *Giant,* I became pregnant. My mother denounced me and threatened to have Jimmy killed. She told me that my father must not find out. Vincente Minnelli knew this doctor. I had an abortion. Lee never found out."

Many biographers have assumed it was lyricist Richard Adler who took Susan's virginity. "I misled them. I told them that Richard was my first love affair. There's a difference between a love affair and losing your virginity. After Jimmy, there were so many other men—Cary Grant, Richard Burton, Warren Beatty, even Marcello Mastroianni."

Ten years after her seduction by Jimmy, Susan married actor Christopher Jones. Six months later, she gave birth to his child, Jennifer Robin. Ironically, Jones had long ago been labeled as "The New James Dean."

In *Bittersweet,* she quoted Jones' opinion of Jimmy.

"He was a great actor. A fucking saint. That's why he had to die so young."

"Chris was more obsessed with Jimmy than I was. In his private little study, he had at least six pictures of Jimmy on the wall. He looked more like Jimmy than all the other imposters wanting to carry Jimmy's banner after his death.

Chris wore his rebel badge with pride, and, like Jimmy, was a war with society. He started out with such promise. But there was this damn thing called drugs."

"As the years have gone by, I've had two regrets. First, I didn't have Jimmy's kid. I was also up for the Luz Benedict II in *Giant.* For a while, I thought I had it wrapped up. I was looking forward to going on location with Jimmy. The last time I saw him, he dropped by our bungalow. One of my saddest moments was when he told me the role I had coveted had gone to Carroll Baker."

Ramon Novarro Vs. Jett Rink

"BEN HUR WANTS MY HONEY"

—James Dean

Ramon Novarro, the Mexican-American actor once promoted by MGM as the greatest Latin Lover of the Silent Screen, attempted to come out of retirement to play a minor role in *Giant,* that of an itinerant rancher, "Old Polo." He had thrilled audiences in the 1920s, reaching the peak of his fame in *Ben Hur* (released in 1925).

At a luncheon in the Warners commissary, director George Stevens introduced Novarro to Jimmy. The long-faded matinee idol "wanted desperately to meet this Jimmy boy."

After a quick drink, Stevens departed, leaving the two actors, one from yesterday, one of them contemporary, to talk privately.

Judging from his references, Novarro had heard that Jimmy was gay, and he wanted to share some advice about how a studio was likely to handle, if necessary, the possibility of a gay actor's exposure.

During Novarro's heyday, Louis B. Mayer, the MGM mogul, had wanted him to enter into what was known as a "lavender marriage" as a vehicle that might squash rumors that he was gay. "He tried to force me into a loveless marriage, but I refused, even when he told me he'd line me up with a lesbian star at MGM. He did not name her. I think it might have been Nazimova."

"I stubbornly refused. I've heard that such a marriage is now being forced upon Rock Hudson."

The lunch went quickly, but Jimmy was not

Mexican-American silent film star Ramon Novarro. "I was a bathing suit beauty," he said.

turned on by Novarro's adoration, especially when he told him, "I like to enjoy young men, such as yourself, who reward me with their honey." Then he invited Jimmy to visit him at his residence that evening at eight o'clock.

Jimmy agreed, writing down Novarro's contact information.

Escorting the aging actor to his car, Jimmy gave him a passionate kiss on the lips, telling him, "I can't wait. I won't wear underwear."

Ramon Novarro as Ben-Hur in 1925.
Both he and James Dean had only one thing in common: Each of them would meet violent deaths.

Apparently, Novarro was waiting at his home at eight o'clock and beyond. Surely by midnight, he'd realized that Jimmy had been putting him on, with no intention of ever showing up.

Jimmy later told Stevens about Novarro's come-on.

"You shouldn't play games with an old queen," Stevens chastised him. "He was a big star worthy of respect. Didn't you see Norma Desmond in *Sunset Blvd.?* One day you, too, may be a fading star being humiliated by young men. However, in your case, maybe not. You might not live that long."

To add insult to his injury, Stevens had to call Novarro later that afternoon to inform him that he'd decided to give the role of Old Polo to character actor Alexander Scourby.

[On October 30, 1968, Novarro picked up two brothers, Tom and Paul Ferguson, thinking they were hustlers with whom he could have sex for pay. However, they had another motive in mind. Someone had told them that the fading star kept a huge stash of money at his home.

As the evening progressed, Novarro wanted them to come into his bedroom one by one to extract their "honey." Paul had another plan: He and his brother tortured Novarro for several hours, trying to get him to reveal where the loot was hidden, but there was no stash of money in the house. The brothers had been misinformed.

After the two perpetrators left the building, Novarro died of asphyxiation, choking on a mixture of his own vomit and blood.

The Ferguson brothers were later caught and sentenced to long prison terms, but released on probation in the mid-1970s. They were later sent back to prison on unrelated crimes.

After his final release, Tom committed suicide in 2005 by cutting his throat in a Motel 6.]

Angela Lansbury & Joan Collins

CONSIDERED, BUT REJECTED. WERE THEY "TOO BRITISH?"

Susan Strasberg and Ramon Novarro were not the only actors rejected for lesser roles in *Giant*. Two of the most talented actresses in the entertainment industry were also turned down.

Stevens had long been fascinated by the acting skills of British star Angela Lansbury, who had fled the London Blitz to come to America in 1940. He first saw her in *Gaslight* (1944), in which, at the age of eighteen, she had played a cockney maid, adding spunk to this film with Ingrid Bergman and Charles Boyer. She won an Oscar as Best Supporting Actress in her American debut. Amazingly, she was also nominated the following year for Best Supporting Actress. She was cast as Sibyl Vane, the music hall singer in the adaptation of Oscar Wilde's *The Picture of Dorian Gray* (1945).

For a while, Stevens thought she might play Rock Hudson's butch sister, Luz Benedict. He finally decided, however, that in spite of her talent, she would not be convincing "as a Texas broad." Instead, he opted for Mercedes McCambridge, figuring that she was more "dyke-like," citing her performance opposite Joan Crawford in *Johnny Guitar* (1954).

After that, still intrigued with her potential, he considered her for the lesser role of Vashti Snythe, a plump, uncouth heiress, but eventually assigned it to Jane Withers instead.

After her second rejection, with a touch of bitterness, Lansbury was quoted as saying, "I thought in America it was three strikes and you're out, not two strikes."

For a brief time, Stevens considered casting one of the most talented Puerto Ricans, Rita Moreno, in the role of Juana, a Mexican girl who marries Dennis Hopper, son of Bick and Leslie Benedict. But at the last minute, he opted for the beautiful Mexican actress, Elsa Cárdenas, instead.

[Actually, the role was too small for a performer of Moreno's talent. She would go on to win all four major American entertainment awards, including an Oscar, a Grammy, a Tony, and an Emmy.]

Joan Collins, the sultry British brunette, was also under consideration by Stevens for a role in *Giant,*

Angela Lansbury...Not butch enough.

mainly as a backup possibility in the event something happened to Elizabeth Taylor that prevented her from performing her duties.

When Elizabeth came through, the offer was never pitched to Collins. Ironically, she later became the bewigged, bejeweled, bitch goddess of the hit TV series, *Dynasty* (1981-89), which— along with its competitor, *Dallas* (1978-91)— were said to have been inspired by *Giant.*

Collins met Jimmy at a small dinner party in the San Fernando Valley. He later said, "I was with Ursula Andress that night, but I found Joan a hot little number. I staked her out for a big seduction in my immediate future."

He never revealed if he fulfilled his sexual fantasy with Collins.

Collins remembered him in one of her memoirs: "He was intense, moody, and had incredible charisma. He was short, myopic, not good looking in life, really. You know who he was like? A young, better-looking Woody Allen. He had the same qualities of shyness, uncertainty, and insecurity."

"I was particularly energized by his eyes, which were a deep, piercing blue and could change instantly from a look of sullen brooding to an expression of extreme mischievousness. He was quite short for a film actor and had longish, blonde, wavy hair."

Joan Collins was considered as an alternative choice to star in two of Elizabeth Taylor's most famous movies: *Giant* and *Cleopatra.*

***

At long last, Stevens rounded up what he called his "Texas posse," with supporting roles going to Mercedes McCambridge, Carroll Baker, Jane Withers, Chill Wills, Nick Adams, Dennis Hopper, Rodney Taylor, Earl Holliman, and Sal Mineo. Mineo told his gay friends, "With Hudson and Dean in the cast, I expect to get my ass pounded a lot."

Warner Brothers summoned a press conference to introduce the stars of its upcoming Texas saga to reporters.

Jimmy was the last to arrive, appearing in a threadbare red flannel shirt, tattered boots, dirty blue jeans, a Stetson, and a large silver buckle on a cowhide belt that he claimed had once belonged to Roy Rogers. A cigarette drooped from the corner of his mouth, and he wore very dark sunglasses which he refused to take off for reporters. He claimed, "I had a hell of a fucking night, and I've got bags under my eyes."

When Jimmy was introduced to Elizabeth Taylor, he was rude to her. He had a good reason to dislike her. She was still demanding that Stevens replace him with Montgomery Clift in the role of Jett Rink.

Leonard Rosenman, the composer of the musical scores for both *East of Eden* and *Rebel Without a Cause,* and who had been Jimmy's sometimes lover back in New York, had not been able to get him on the phone in Hollywood. He decided to show up at the press conference, hoping to get a chance for a conversation. He wanted Jimmy to recommend him to George Stevens as a composer for *Giant.*

"I was shocked," he later said. "Jimmy practically didn't even acknowledge me. We'd never had an argument. But it was like he didn't even know me, and I had been one of his best friends."

"He told me he could not recommend me as a candidate for the composition of music for *Giant.* Dimitri Tijomkin got the job. I sensed that Jimmy had really changed, not gone Hollywood exactly. But he had become a big star—at least he was acting like one."

"He claimed he hated Hollywood and detested the press conference, but the fucker actually got off on all the attention."

"It's like this," Rosenman said. "In the land of the blind, even a one-eyed king stands out. In Hollywood, Dean could stand out as a New York intellectual, a regular Arthur Miller. After all, what was his competition? Bimbo starlets and directors and producers who used to be gas jockeys filling up your tank, or else attendants in wash rooms handing out towels."

Hollywood's Hottest New Star
JIMMY SUDDENLY RECEIVES DOZENS OF OFFERS FOR MOVIE ROLES

During the last month of his life, Jimmy was the most sought-after actor in Hollywood. Virtually every major studio wanted to cast him in some film, but in almost every case, Jack Warner was unwilling to lend out his most prestigious star. Some examples of the many offers swirling around him are elucidated below:

***

Both Marlon Brando and Jimmy were seen together one night at the Villa Capri, sharing a table and talking about the 1954 release of *The Egyptian*. Brando had turned down the role before it was sent to Jimmy, who also rejected it. The role was that of Sinuhe, a physician in the ancient Egyptian court, who sustains an affair with one of the Pharoah's mistresses.

In this intimate scene from *Giant*, Jett Rink (Dean) is secretly in love with Leslie (Elizabeth Taylor), who is married to his boss, Bick Benedict. He conveys his longing for her with his eyes.

Director Michael Curtiz cast Edmund Purdom instead. In the final version, he appeared opposite Jean Simmons, Victor Mature, Gene Tierney, and Peter Ustinov.

***

Producer Lew Kerner wanted Jimmy to play the title role of *Studs Lonigan*. Its script would be based on the trilogy of Studs Lonigan novels by James T. Farrell, which today are ranked by Modern Library as one of the one hundred best English language novels of the 20th Century.

At the time of the Great Depression, Farrell set out to expose the evils of capitalism. Studs deteriorates from a tough, adventurous teenager to an embittered, physically shattered alcoholic.

During Jimmy's short lifetime, the project never got off the ground, but in 1960, it was adapted into a minor movie featuring a young Jack Nicholson in one of his first film roles. In 1979, it was adapted once again into a TV series starring Harry Hamlin.

***

Billy Wilder wanted Jimmy to play the aviator Charles Lindbergh in *The Spirit of St. Louis,* set for release in 1957. The script was to depict the thirty-three hour transatlantic flight of the young aviator in his monoplane crossing the Atlantic. Setting a world's record, he landed at Le Bourget in Paris on May 21, 1927, when it seemed that most of Paris turned out to give him a tumultuous welcome.

Even though he was the right age to play Lindbergh, and vaguely resembled him, Jimmy rejected the role.

At the time, although he was forty-seven years old, and Lindbergh at the time of his crossing was twenty-five, James Stewart was also vigorously campaigning for the role. He went on a diet, dyed his hair, and worked out every day, trying to beef up his beanpole physique.

In this still from *The Spirit of St. Louis*, a "too old for the part" James Stewart impersonates the twenty-something Charles Lindbergh in a role originally rejected by James Dean.

Jimmy had objected to the script because he wanted more spice in it. He wished to insert a scene showing Lindbergh picking up a waitress in a diner to seduce her before taking off from New Jersey. "It might have been his last chance for a good fuck," Jimmy told Wilder.

He also wanted some scenes of a younger Lindbergh in flashbacks, before any footage depicting his transatlantic success, as well as an overview of his reaction to the kidnapping of his child in 1932.

"The audience has to understand the character," Jimmy lectured Wilder, "or else I'll be reduced to looking out at the clouds until I get to Paris."

He later said, "I just couldn't see myself sitting up there for thirty-three hours in that airplane, pissing in a jar."

[If circumstances had been different, Stewart and Jimmy might have worked together on the same film, East of Eden. *For a while, Elia Kazan considered casting the veteran actor in the role of Jimmy's stern, puritanical father. But the role went to the more suitably cast Raymond Massey. Jimmy told Kazan, "Stewart is too lovable a character to play the mean father role.]*

Wilder briefly considered casting Jimmy's rival, John Kerr, in the role before finally giving in to Stewart. Upon its release, *The Spirit of St. Louis*—made for $6 million—was massively promoted as the saga of a hero who became the first person in history who was in New Jersey one day and in Paris the next. In spite of the hype, the movie failed at the box office, although some critics cited Stewart's "boyishness."

***

Jimmy was shopping around for a heroic sports hero to show his versatility. He had agreed to star as Rocky Graziano in the boxing film, *Somebody Up There Likes Me,* but died before the picture was made. In the aftermath, the role went to Paul Newman.

***

Jimmy also gave serious consideration to starring in *Fear Strikes Out,* the story of the mentally disturbed baseball player, Jim Piersall, who cracked under the pressure of a domineering father. Piersall was the baseball center fielder who played seventeen seasons in the Major League from 1950 to 1967.

Tony Perkins, as an emotionally unbalanced baseball player, a role rejected by James Dean, in *Fear Strikes Out.*

The movie would deal with the baseball great's bipolar disorder, not a subject guaranteed to lure 1950s audiences to their local movie houses. In 1957, the role went to Tony Perkins, Jimmy's rival and sometimes lover, still being billed as "The New James Dean."

***

After *Giant*, Jimmy didn't want to be cast in another Western, although he was vastly intrigued at the thought of playing Billy the Kid, which had been brought to the screen many times, even by Robert Taylor. Instead of some idolized figure from the Old West, Jimmy wanted to play him as a baby-faced, cold-blooded killer.

At the Château Marmont, Gore Vidal told him that he was working on a very different script. All of his reading about Billy the Kid had convinced him that the bandit was a homosexual.

Once again, Jimmy's death would prevent him from taking a role he truly wanted to play. And once again, the role went to Paul Newman. Word buzzed around Hollywood that Newman was going to "play Gore Vidal's fag cowboy."

Newman seemingly went through very few struggles about playing a subtly gay role. He once said, "Ever since I was a kid, I've never been able to understand attacks on the gay

Paul Newman in a role offered to but rejected by James Dean, *The Left Handed Gun.*

695

community."

Even Vidal's title, *The Left Handed Gun,* was a code for being gay. *[The historical figure of Billy the Kid, born Henry McCarty, also known as William H. Bonney (1859 – 1881), was actually right-handed.]*

Jack Warner objected to Vidal's script. "When movie-goers hear that Newman is going gay, they'll stay away from the theaters in droves."

Leslie A Stevens III was called in to revise Vidal's script, turning *Billy the Kid* from a repressed homosexual into more of a surrogate father-son drama with a Freudian subtext.

Newman later referred to the revised version, released in 1958, as *"The Left Handed Jockstrap."*

Arthur Penn, a young Turk from TV land, directed the picture. He later claimed that "Paul Method-acted his way through the entire film. At one point, he curls up in a ball on the floor, a scene and acting style that was pure James Dean."

Newman confided to Fred Coe, the producer, "I feel Dean could have done a better job than me. That thought is driving me crazy, leading to an extra three beers every night."

Edna Ferber Doesn't Like Texas

AND THEY DON'T LIKE HER

Born in 1885 in Kalamazoo, Michigan, Edna Ferber was a best-selling novelist and playwright, author of such celebrated works as *So Big* (1924); *Show Boat* (1926), *Cimarron* (1929), and *Giant* (1952). The daughter of a Hungarian-born Jewish storekeeper, she was a lesbian who never married.

Ivan Moffat and Fred Guiol were assigned the difficult task of reducing her 447-page novel into a 178-page script, which they completed in April of 1955.

Before tackling it, they read various comments from critics about her novel. John Barkham in *The New York Times* noted, "Miss Ferber makes it very clear she doesn't like the Texas she writes about, and it's a cinch that when Texans read about what she

Edna Ferber with James Dean, unconvincingly made up to resemble an aging Jett Rink. Note his new hairline.

696

has written about them, they won't like her either."

Marghanita Laski in the *Spectator* claimed that "Edna Ferber can always be relied on for a good story interwoven with fascinating information and sound moral judgments on the shortcomings as well as the virtues of her country and its history."

Moffat was a British screenwriter and the grandson of the famous Edwardian actor and theatrical producer, Sir Herbert Beerbohm Tree (1852-1917). *[A brilliant actor long associated with London's Haymarket Theatre, and an influential visionary in the entertainment industry of his day, he arranged some of the first filmed versions of segments of Shakespearean plays.]*

As such, Moffat was an odd choice as author of a screenplay about Texas. He'd met George Stevens in World War II during his filming of the activities of the U.S. Army in Europe. After the war, Moffat followed Stevens to Hollywood, assisting him at Paramount.

There, he became known for his high-profile affairs, notably with Elizabeth Taylor and later with Lady Caroline Blackwood. His gay friend, author Christopher Isherwood, said, "He's so pretty and bright-eyed, it's no wonder he's in bed with some woman every night."

Another odd choice to adapt Ferber to the screen was Guiol, who had worked at the Hal Roach Studios for several years and was known for directing many of the Laurel and Hardy movies. Although a sort of "odd couple" writing team, Moffat and Guiol would be nominated for an Academy Award for Best Adapted Screenplay of 1955.

Although many films had already been adapted from novels by Edna Ferber, the first time she actually visited a movie set was in Marfa, Texas.

She arrived there in time to see Elizabeth emoting in front of the camera. She later interpreted that day's depiction of Leslie as "simpering." When the completed film was finally released, she did not approve of her, but kept quiet, because her contract called for her to share in the profits.

During Ferber's second day on the set, she met Jimmy. In a memoir, *A Kind of Magic,* she wrote: "He was an original. Impish, compelling, magnetic, utterly winning one moment, obnoxious the next. Definitely gifted, frequently maddening."

She sized him up, telling him, "Your profile is startlingly like that of John Barrymore, but then, I know your motorcycle racing or one thing or another will fix that."

Before she flew out of Texas, Jimmy took a picture of her. Days before he died, he was working on a sculpture of her back at his studio in Hollywood.

***

Just an hour after completing his post-recording of *Rebel Without a Cause,* Jimmy, in early June of 1955, was aboard a train headed to Marfa in the high desert of the Trans-Pecos of West Texas. Founded in the early 1880s as a waterstop, the bleak little outpost was located between the Davis mountain range and Big Bend National Park.

The Benedict Mansion, a studio prop, under construction on the Evans Ranch in Marfa.

What he found when he got there was a drought-stricken town where daytime temperatures sometimes rose to 120° F. It was a three-hour drive from El Paso, and some sixty miles north of the Mexican border.

The cast and crew of *Giant* had swelled the population of Marfa to 3,000. Many locals rented their homes to them and camped out in tents during the filming.

On Main Street stood one hotel and two movie houses, each showing Mexican films. Technicians had produced the façade of a three-story Victorian mansion, the abode of the Benedicts. It had been built in Burbank and shipped east to Texas. Since Marfa lies in a part of West Texas without oil wells, Warners had to erect derricks that gushed *ersatz* crude.

George Stevens set about creating harmony in the town by employing some 200 locals, thereby easing tensions between the town and its invaders. The local newspaper, *The Big Sentinel,* had denounced Ferber's novel, defining it as "superficial and derogatory to Texans."

For the big barbecue scene, Stevens invited a lot of Texas millionaires to participate, winning their support, since they wanted to see themselves in the film, not realizing that it was mocking and satirizing them.

One of the cast members, crusty Chill Wills, knew Marfa well, having made a film there in 1950 called *High Lonesome,* in which he co-starred with John Drew Barrymore.

During the course of *Giant's* 198 minutes, it moves through the rise and failing fortunes of Texans, with side detours into moral dissipation, racism, miscegenation, the oppression of women, oil well conflicts, and the changing social scenario of Texas itself. The movie's subplot involves the war between the longtime Texas aristocracy and the *nouveau riche* wildcatters whose oil wells have "come in big."

For Elizabeth, after suffering through all those "rubbish" movies at MGM, *Giant* became a milestone in her life. Other than being saddled with a husband she didn't want, her biggest problem involved having to postpone her flourishing romance with Kevin McClory, a production assistant to Mike Todd, who would become her next husband.

"I'll Never Work With the Cocky Little Bastard Ever Again"

—Director George Stevens, in reference to James Dean

Ever since he'd seen *A Place in the Sun* (1951), with Montgomery Clift and Elizabeth Taylor, Jimmy had nothing but praise for Stevens, its director. Before heading for Texas, he told the press: "George Stevens is the greatest director of them all, even better than Elia Kazan. He was born to make movies. Hollywood can, on occasion, make a great movie. I have a feeling that *Giant* will be up there with the best of them."

[Alas, after the first week of working with Stevens, he would have a radically different opinion.]

"Stevens is so real, so unassuming," Jimmy went on. "You'll be talking to him, thinking he missed your point and then—bang!—he has it."

For the first two weeks of shooting, the location was in Charlottesville, Virginia, where Bick (Rock Hudson) meets and falls in love with his future bride, Leslie (Elizabeth Taylor). Jimmy stayed behind in Texas, working with Bob Hinkle, his dialogue coach. Hinkle was also teaching him rope tricks.

In just two weeks, Jimmy seemed to have mastered the Texas drawl and its "lock-hipped swagger of a wrangler." On weekends, he and Hinkle headed for the enveloping desert to shoot jack rabbits and coyotes.

Nicknamed "Texas Bob," Hinkle had grown up in Brownsville, Texas, at the state's southernmost tip. "We were so poor, we could afford only a tumbleweed for a pet," Hinkle claimed. Early stints in show business had included gigs as a rodeo rider and a diction coach. During the course of the shooting, he trained not only Jimmy, but Rock Hudson in the subtleties of portraying a "Texan."

For some fifty years, Hinkle remained active in show business as a diction coach, a director, a friend of movie stars, and

Pat Hinkle taught Jimmy how to walk and talk, Texan style.

occasionally, a film producer. In 1963, Paul Newman asked him "to do for me what you did for Dean in *Giant.*" At the time, Newman was preparing for his award-winning role in *Hud,* co-starring with Patricia Neal and Melvyn Douglas.

After his return from filming the Maryland (as shot in Virginia) segments of *Giant,* Stevens learned that Jimmy had slipped away and had competed in a racecar rally in Bakersfield, California. In that race, Jack Drummond, a thirty-year-old ace driver, had been killed.

Horrified at the implications of that, Stevens demanded that Jimmy "Give up car racing until this picture is wrapped. Then you can kill your fool self."

"I don't have a death wish," Jimmy protested. "I'm not risking my life, since I have too much to live for. There are too many things I want to do in this one life."

Before *Giant*, Stevens had worked with some of the biggest names in Hollywood, including Katharine Hepburn and Spencer Tracy in *Woman of the Year* (1942); with Cary Grant and Jean Arthur in *Talk of the Town* (also 1942); and Alan Ladd and Jean Arthur in *Shane* (1953).

Stevens was well acquainted with Elizabeth, having directed her in 1951's *A Place in the Sun,* but he'd never helmed Hudson or Jimmy. He found Hudson relatively compliant, "always on the mark, always knowing his dialogue, and carrying out my instructions perfectly."

In contrast, he found his working relationship with Jimmy much more difficult, defining it as a "rapport of challenge."

Stevens was a perfectionist, demanding that a small scene be reshot sometimes as many as fifty times. Several times, Jimmy shouted back at him, "I got the god damn thing right on the first take."

[Weeks later, when Stevens was editing the final version, he realized that he'd shot 25,000 feet of film, and used only 7,500 feet of it, ultimately producing a movie with a running time of 198 minutes.

In a memo to Jack Warner, Stevens complained about Jimmy, citing his "tardiness, his unmanageableness, his soaring resistance to reasonable demands, differing from what I have in mind, and his depleting the morale of the entire company. My impression is that is a George Stevens Production, not a James Dean Production."

In protest, Jimmy said, "I can't get my ideas of Jett Rink over to Stevens. I know Jett better than Stevens does. He just won't listen to me. He's trying to keep me from making a truly great picture instead of a mediocre Western."

"The cocky little bastard accuses me of interfering with his work," Stevens claimed. "I accuse him of jeopardizing my movie. I'm the son of a bitch running this show, not some snot-nosed cocksucker from Indiana who takes it up the ass."

Eartha Kitt remembered desperate phone calls from Marfa during the wee hours of the morning. "Jamie sounded like he was going out of his mind. He felt that Stevens was sacrificing his character and devoting all his attention to Rock Hudson or to Elizabeth Taylor, who had star billing over him."

"He told me that *Giant* was too big in an artificial way," Stevens said. "He wanted his interpretation as an old man to be quite different from what it was turning out to be."

It would have been interesting to view an aging Jett Rink the way Jimmy wanted to play him. As it turned out, his interpretation of Jett Rink as a drunken senior citizen was his weakest characterization, eliciting the harshest criticism.

During another call, Jimmy complained to Eartha about Hudson. "How can I create a character working with someone so plastic? I feel nothing from him. I also have no support from Elizabeth in her later incarnation as she's maturing. They are not maturing with me. They are the same from beginning to end; only their hair has been grayed. You can't be an old person by aging your face with makeup and by putting some gray stripes in your hair. You have to imagine old. You have to become old."

***

After the first two weeks of filming, Stevens said, "Dean never understands that Jett Rink is only part of the film, not the central figure. In his first two movies, he was the primary focus. But I have two other stars: Rock Hudson and Elizabeth Taylor."

When Stevens attacked Jimmy's performance in front of cast and crew, the actor became very sullen, addressing the director as "Fatso." He also began to show up late, once going an entire day without making an appearance and holding up production which, of course, ran up costs for Warners.

Reflecting later on the turmoil he suffered from Jimmy, Stevens said, "All in all, it was a headache to work with him. He was always pulling and hauling, and he had developed this cultivated, designed irresponsibility. It's tough on you, he seemed to imply, but I've got to do it my way. From the director's point of view, this is not the most delightful sort of fellow to work with. Anyway, he delivered his performance, and he cracked himself up, and I can't say I'm happy about all that's happening about that. There are some people involved in it who don't show up well."

[When Stevens saw the final cut of Giant, *he said, "I made the right decision in casting Dean, the little bastard, as Jett Rink. But he'll never appear in another picture that I'll direct.]*

"Rock Hudson Is Giving Me a Sore Ass"

—James Dean

Because of the severe housing shortage in Marfa, only a few members of the cast were granted the privilege of living alone, privately and without roommates, in a house of their own. The best of the rented homes went to Elizabeth Taylor. Her husband, Michael Wilding, remained, for the most part, in California with their children.

Jimmy was assigned lodgings in a rented house that he shared with Rock Hudson and Chill Wills. Wills had his own bedroom, and Hudson and Jimmy would sleep in a small room with twin beds. The building's only bathroom was shared by all three of them.

When Jimmy arrived there, he introduced himself to Wills, who invited him for a beer in the kitchen. He wasn't familiar with the career of this actor and set out to learn what he could.

The folksy, shaggy-haired actor had gotten his start singing in medicine and minstrel shows before abandoning them and heading to Hollywood.

Soon, he was appearing as a sidekick cowboy in Westerns or else as a backwoods rustic equivalent to the role he'd been assigned in *The Yearling* (1946) with Gregory Peck and Jane Wyman. That same year, he appeared as a roughshod but good-natured "diamond in the rough" with Judy Garland in *The Harvey Girls.*

[He would go on to become the voice of Francis, the Talking Mule, in that series of pictures starring Donald O'Connor. Our favorite? Francis Joins the WACs (1954).]

In his raspy, homespun voice, Wills enthralled Jimmy with tales of growing up in Texas, the effect of which deepened his understanding of the character he was playing.

As they talked, Jimmy felt he was getting close to understanding the mentality of a dyed-in-the-wool Texan. Wills had been born in Seagoville (now a suburb of Dallas) in the hot summer of 1903. His views had never changed from those learned growing up. As Jimmy later said, "I liked him for some strange reason, but he was to the right of Joseph Goebbels, hating

Chill Wills in 1953. He was the roommate of Rock Hudson and James Dean in shared quarters in Marfa, Texas. "I heard a lot...a hell of a lot." Later, he took Jimmy and Dennis Hopper "on a jaybird naked cruise off the coast of Catalina."

what he called 'niggers, Mexicans, Hollywood Jews, and Indians.'"

[In spite of their deeply divided views of the world, some sort of bond was formed. "He is about the most amusing old redneck I've ever met," Jimmy later said.

In fact, back in Hollywood, Wills invited Jimmy and Dennis Hopper for a weekend of charter fishing off the coast of Catalina Island. "During our sail, those two boys, out at sea, walked around jaybird naked. By the time it came for them to retreat to their bunks at night, I was too drunk to care what they were up to. I retreated to my own cabin to sleep it off.]

Wills would later describe to Forrest Tucker and John Wayne, among others, what it was like living in small quarters with James Dean and Rock Hudson. "The walls were paper thin. For the first week or so, those two pretty boys were as happy as a pig in shit. Those creaky bedsprings got a lot of workout."

[In 1987, Elizabeth Taylor told Star *magazine that, "In the beginning, I thought Rock and Jimmy were two lovebirds. When I was with the both of them, I felt like an uncomfortable third party. But that was to change very soon.]*

"Jimmy and Rock were two such very different kind of men and polar opposites as actors," she said." It seemed inevitable that their fucking would soon turn to feuding. It was a short honeymoon before war was declared. Jimmy moved out."

On the day he left, he told Wills, "Hudson is trying to queer me and make me his bitch. My ass is sore. He's too big."

Jimmy may have resented the enormous buildup that Warners was giving Hudson. One press release trumpeted, "The prize acting plum of the year, one which has often been reported in the grasp of a number of Hollywood's top male stars, goes to a dark horse who has never once been mentioned in the spirited competition. Hudson will be co-starring with the beautiful Elizabeth Taylor, with newcomer James Dean in a small supporting role."

Jimmy almost detested Stevens on sight, but Hudson seemed to adore him. Or, as Jimmy said, "He follows Stevens around like a lovesick puppy."

During their filming of *Giant*, Rock appeared on the cover of *Life* magazine, headlined as "Hollywood's Most Handsome

Elizabeth Taylor and Rock Hudson as man and wife in Texas. For a brief time, they were also off-screen lovers. Later in life, a drunken Elizabeth once said, "Occasionally, Rock delivered a mercy fuck to a woman."

Bachelor."

Life speculated about why the twenty-nine-year-old had never gotten married, telling its readers that it was about time he explained to his fans why.

At times, Jimmy found Rock very troubled. Somehow, a blackmailer had obtained sexually explicit photographs of him and was demanding a lot of money, more than Hudson had.

Jimmy and Hudson had completely different approaches to acting. Jimmy was from the Marlon Brando/ Monty Clift/ Rod Steiger/ Eli Wallach school of (Method) acting, and Hudson was from the "erotic hunk of beefcake academy" whose members also included Tab Hunter, John Derek, and Guy Madison.

The very urbane, very handsome, very charming Rock Hudson

When Jimmy was forced to act out a scene with Hudson, he referred to his colleague as "a lump of dead wood." In retaliation, Hudson called Jimmy "that little scruff."

When Hudson got to know Elizabeth more intimately, he confessed to her, "I want sex, real man-on-man sex, but I don't go in for this kinky stuff. Dean wants to get into that claw-footed, old timey bathtub we have, and then he begs me to piss on him. He also likes me to burn his ass with my cigarette butt—shit like that. I'm not into all this sicko crap."

Hudson would later tell Elizabeth, "Dean is the kind of guy who could make mad, passionate love with you one minute. Then, after he shoots off, he starts complaining about your acting. It's amazing."

***

Instead of spending time with Hudson, Jimmy bonded with Jane Withers. She had beat out more established stars to get the role in *Giant* of Vashti Snythe. Withers had worked as a child actress since the age of three. Less than a decade later, at the age of eleven

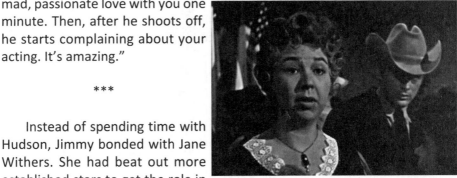

The former child star, Jane Withers, was cast as a *nouveau riche* oil heiress, Vashti Snythe, in *Giant*, a role that several other aging actresses also wanted. On screen, Jimmy eyes her skeptically, but off-screen, she became his "mother confessor."

and twelve, she emerged as one of Hollywood's top box office stars of 1937 and 1938.

At the time that Jimmy met her, she was divorcing a rich Texas oilman, William P. Moss, Jr., with whom she had produced three children.

[Oddly enough, her greatest fame would come in the 1960s and early 70s, based on her TV commercials for Comet as "Josephine the Plumber."]

During the Marfa shoot, Withers turned her rented lodgings into a kind of USO-inspired social center. Inviting cast and crew to hang out there at night. She played records, organized games, and served refreshments, but didn't allow liquor or poker.

She recalled that Jimmy would sit in his parked car across the street from her house. "He'd wait until my eleven o'clock curfew, when I kicked everybody out. Then he'd come in alone and talk to me until two or three o'clock in the morning. That certainly interfered with my sleep when I had a 4AM call on the set."

"I think that in some way, I helped Jimmy get over his negative attitude toward life," she said. "He became my Number Three son. We sometimes read the Bible together."

[Long after Jimmy died, Withers appeared in a DVD documentary about his life, revealing that she owned this favorite pink shirt he wore off screen nearly all the time. He didn't want it washed, fearing that it would lose its vibrancy. "It was pretty rank, so he let me wash it for him. I did this often. In fact, before he left for Salinas on that fateful day of September 30, 1955, he came by house and dropped off the pink shirt for me to wash. He told me he'd drop by and pick it up when he returned from Salinas. That pink shirt is still hanging in my closet."]

Sal Mineo

ADIOS! TO REBEL WITHOUT A CAUSE AND JIMMY, HOLA! TO GIANT AND TO THE ROCK

Jimmy had campaigned for Stevens to cast his sometimes lover, Sal Mineo, in the small role of Angel Obregon II, the son of poor Mexican immigrants. Jimmy said, "Sal has the look of the angels." The director agreed and gave Mineo the small but key role. *[Mineo had no scenes with Jimmy onscreen.]* They'd been lovers on the set of *Rebel Without a Cause,* and the Italian-American actor retained powerful emotions. He had bought a rebuilt Mercury like the car his idol had driven in *Rebel.* He had also taken to wearing a red jacket similar to the one Jimmy had worn in it.

"My father made coffins, hand-finishing them for the Bronx Casket Company, where he was a hand-finisher and later, a foreman," Mineo said years later, in Manhattan, to Darwin Porter. "Near the end of *Giant,* I join the Army and leave Texas, only to be sent back in a coffin. Since my dad made coffins, I tried to get Stevens to use one of his since it was my coffin in the film, but he turned down my offer."

Sal Mineo was cast as a U.S. soldier in Giant. returning from war in a coffin. Like James Dean, in real life, he would meet a violent end. At 9:30PM February 12, 1976, a paramedic noted in his report that Sal Mineo's murder had been committed in an alley at the rear of his Manhattan apartment. He had died from a single stab wound to the middle of his chest, apparently part of a garden-variety mugging unrelated to his status as a movie celebrity.

"I did not have to go to Texas because my scenes were shot at Warners in Burbank. But I went there anyway, to see what was happening and with the intention of shacking up with either Jimmy or Rock—or maybe both, if I got lucky."

"When I got there, I found out that Jimmy had moved out of the house with Rock, and that big, muscular son of a bitch was looking for another boy ass. I volunteered and he got mine."

"I didn't think I had a chance, because the rumor was that he preferred tall, blonde-haired and muscular guys who looked liked Steve Reeves. Here I was, a 5'8", raven-haired 120-pound, olive-skinned WOP from the Bronx."

"But he really came on to me and invited me to spend the night with him in a bed recently vacated by Jimmy. What a pounding I got that night! He nearly split me open, and I loved it. I got to spend two of the most glorious weeks of my life in bed with Rock until he discovered this cowboy in Marfa. Into that little bedroom went the cowboy. Out went Sal Mineo."

"Jimmy broke off his friendship with me when he heard I'd slept with Rock. We later made up. I'd planned to get involved with him again, since we'd been cast together in the boxing movie, *Somebody Up There Likes Me.* Of course, that was not to happen. Into my life walked Paul Newman instead."

"The last time I saw Jimmy, I almost didn't recognize him," Mineo said. "It was on the Warners lot. I was coming out of the commissary as he was going in. This old man with gray hair, a mustache, and hunched shoulders passed me by. Well, almost passed me by. He stopped and groped my salami. I was about to punch him out when I saw through the makeup. It was Jimmy. He grabbed me and embraced me. He promised to call me real soon."

"It was a day in late September. That phone call never came in. The next thing I heard, he was dead."

Biff Beaufort, a Hot Local Cowboy, Is Reconfigured as "Sage Durango"

BASED ON JIMMY'S ADVICE, HE RIDES INTO THE SUNSET TOWARD HENRY WILLSON'S DREAM FACTORY

After Hudson, Jimmy was soon shacking up with a tall, blonde-haired, handsome cowboy he'd presumably met through Pat Hinkle.

Biff Beaufort had drifted down from Wyoming, where he'd gotten into some trouble with the law. Jimmy was immediately attracted to the 6'4" rodeo rider.

It was reported that he borrowed some of Beaufort's characteristics for his portrayal of Jett Rink.

Whenever they could get away, they drove off to a battered-looking shack about ten miles from Marfa. Otherwise, they lived together in the town's only hotel.

Jimmy spoke little about his relationship with Beaufort, except to tell about one of the most romantic nights he'd ever spent in his life.

It was a clear night when two horses took Jimmy and the cowboy to a scenic outlook on the outskirts of town. Perhaps that was the night Beaufort shared his dream with Jimmy, and that involved becoming a Hollywood star. "I'm bigger and better looking than Rock Hudson," he bragged.

Actually, he wanted Jimmy to promise to take him back to Hollywood after the filming of *Giant*. Jimmy didn't really want to do that, as he had other plans.

Hollywood Dreams
May They Rest in Peace:

Whatever Happened to
Biff Beaufort, *aka*
SAGE DURANGO?

He had an idea. One night, he asked Beaufort to put on a pair of tight-fitting briefs. He told him to get them wet in the bathtub, thereby making them semi-transparent. Then Jimmy photographed him, "bulging out" of those briefs.

He sent the photograph to Henry Willson in Hollywood. At the time, Willson was "dating," (of all people) Margaret Truman, the daughter of the former U.S. president Harry S Truman.

Five days later, Willson responded, sending Beaufort a one-way train ticket to Los Angeles and a money order for five hundred dollars. Willson wrote, "I've already changed his name: Instead of Biff Beaufort, why not Sage Durango?"

The re-christened cowboy spent his last night in Texas in Jimmy's arms before riding a train to Los Angeles.

With only weeks to live, Jimmy never heard of him after that.

Oil Baron, Glenn McCarthy

JIMMY FLIES TO HOUSTON WITH THE KING OF TEXAS

"I've flown to this hellhole of Marfa just to size you up," said the big, burly Texan who stood before Jimmy, looking him up and down. "That asshole, George Stevens, must have been on something when he cast a little runt like you to play me on the screen. Hell, I'm bigger than the State of Texas itself. You look like the kind of pretty boy a whore might ask, 'Are you in yet?'"

"Thanks for the buildup. I'm James Dean. Just who in hell are you?

"I'm Glenn McCarthy, the King of Texas. In case you didn't know, that pussy-eater, Edna Ferber, based Jett Rink on me."

Jimmy did some sizing up too. Indiana didn't produce men like McCarthy. His eyes were hidden behind the darkest sunglasses Jimmy had ever seen. He wore a gleaming leather jacket with a leopard-patterned ascot. On his pinkie rested a diamond ring which Jimmy thought might have been the Hope Diamond.

[McCarthy's nickname was "Diamond Glenn.]

"Listen, Buddy, you don't have to be big in person to look big on the screen," Jimmy answered.

"Guess you're right, kid," McCarthy said. "After all, everything's blown up thirty feet or so, isn't it?"

In the late 1940s, much of America knew who McCarthy was, as he ranked up there with that coven of billionaire Texas oilmen such as H.L. Hunt, Clint Murchison, and Hugh Roy Cullen.

As a wildcatter, McCarthy drilled himself a fortune of "black gold," built the massive and legendary Shamrock Hotel in Houston, and then, in time, faded into obscurity, a relatively forgotten figure.

He was called "Texas Crude, a stereotype of the raw, hard-living, bourbon-swilling, damn-the-torpedoes, Texas oil millionaire," as one reporter defined him.

Author Bryon Burrough wrote that McCarthy rubbed shoulders with the likes of Howard Hughes, another Texan billionaire, and such movie stars as Errol Flynn and John Wayne, "drinking and brawling his way from Buffalo Bayou to Sunset Boulevard." At the peak of his fame in the late 1940s, he was depicted on the cover of *Time* magazine.

Jimmy was almost stunned by the larger-than-life creature who stood before him, now, in Marfa. Then, welcoming the chance to study the character he was depicting on film, he accepted McCarthy's invitation to fly with him to Houston for a weekend at the Shamrock Hotel. *[Ironically, although McCarthy had built and widely publicized it, at this stage in his fortunes, he was no longer in full control of its management.]*

Oil baron Glenn McCarthy on his 15,000-acre ranch near Uvalde, Texas, about 80 miles west of San Antonio.

Before the end of their time together, Jimmy had learned plenty about McCarthy, perhaps more than he needed to know. McCarthy enthralled him with stories of his wildcat days, when he was known as the hottest oil finder, and biggest risk taker, in Texas.

"I owned 15,000 acres of West Texas prairie outside Uvalde," McCarthy boasted. "Hell, Rock Hudson as Bick Benedict could also be playing me, but he's not wild enough like you are, kid. I've heard stories about you. I hope it's just a rumor that you suck cock."

"But if you are," he continued, "you've come to the state where the men have the biggest dicks in America. At a urinal, I stood next to Lyndon Johnson. He called his 'Jumbo.' We sized each other up. I had him beat, but not by much."

Arriving at the Shamrock, Jimmy was ushered

James Dean in a detail from a scene in *Giant*.

709

into the gray-granite, eighteen-story hotel. He stood in awe at the sight of the cavernous lobby covered with Honduran mahogany. "It's called the Lone Star State's answer to the Taj Mahal," McCarthy said.

"I felt like a king riding the elevator up to the top floor of this colossus where I was installed in the guest bedroom of McCarthy's suite."

Two hours later, the two men descended together to the lavish bar, where McCarthy treated him to what he called "Kentucky bourbon a century old."

"No one makes bourbon like Kentuckians," he said. "It's got that special flavor. I hear they piss into the mash for that zippy tang."

Over drinks, McCarthy amused Jimmy with stories of the spectacular opening of the Shamrock in March of 1949, when dignitaries flew in from all over Europe and North America. He said he rented the entire fourteen cars of the Santa Fe Railway, renaming it "The Shamrock Special" as it hauled movie stars to Houston from Los Angeles for the hotel's lavishly publicized gala opening.

It was disastrous. "I invited two-thousand people and about another five-thousand showed up, storming all over the place and disrupting everything. It became a raging stampede, Texas-style."

The press described it as "a gaudy, diamond-strewn, chaotic metaphor for the New Texas of the vulgar *nouveau riche.*"

"I personally checked in my first guest, Frank Sinatra," McCarthy said. "Later that night, I arranged for him to fuck Miss Texas."

To beef up the entertainment, he also staged the premiere of a movie. Because nothing recent was available at the time, he decided to finance his own, arranging for a scriptwriter to turn out a sad story of a young girl who wants to raise two baby lambs. "I cast Natalie Wood in the part when she was still a child star, long before you got to mess with her in *Rebel Without a Cause.* Walter Brennan was her co-star."

[It was a low-budget affair for RKO, one that extolled the virtues of Heartland values and 4-H clubs. The love interest was provided by Robert Paige and Marguerite Chapman, a glamorous brunette. It wasn't shot in Texas, but near the Feather River outside Sacramento.]

"Natalie had a special plate at her dining table every night for her pet Chihuahua. Her left wrist got broken when we shot this dramatic scene of her crossing a collapsing bridge in a thunderstorm, a stunt that went wrong. Her mother didn't get a doctor for her. I hear that even today, her left wrist is misshapen. But you'd know more about that than I do. If you go for young poontang like I do, I'm sure you've banged her. Which reminds me—I've invited two sixteen-year-olds to join us. I married a sixteen-year-old, and I've been addicted to sixteen-year-old pussy ever since."

McCarthy also claimed that he started the tradition of Texas oilmen marrying movie stars. "I invited Joan Crawford to christen my *Flying Shamrock* with a bottle of the world's most expensive champagne. I bought a P38 fighter plane and spent another $50,000 upgrading it. Later that day, I fucked Crawford high in the clouds. My Errol Flynn mustache tickled her twat when I went down on her."

"She wanted to marry me," he said. "But I turned her down. We got a lot of publicity in the papers."

[He went on to cite a long list of other oil tycoons from Texas who had "married Hollywood." Oil magnate Bill Moss had married Jane Withers. After their divorce, Moss wed Ann Miller. Howard Lee married Hedy Lamarr. After Lee dumped her, he married Gene Tierney. Dallas oilman Buddy Ferguson married Greer Garson.]

Later, back in Marfa, Jimmy omitted details about what happened that night in Houston with the underaged prostitutes whose services McCarthy had arranged. He did, however, tell Stevens, "Glenn McCarthy sure knows how to show a guy a good time. I'll never be the same again. Finally, I had to tell him to quit sending up any more *putas.* Enough is enough."

Mercedes McCambridge

"THE MEANEST, MOST MACHO WOMAN IN TEXAS"

Jimmy bonded with yet another member of the cast, Mercedes McCambridge. Nicholas Ray had shown Jimmy a film he'd directed, the campy *Johnny Guitar* (1954) with Mercedes and Joan Crawford.

McCambridge, cast as Bick's butchy sister, harboring a deep-seated hatred for Bick's wife (Taylor), had won a Best Supporting Actress Oscar for her debut performance in *All the King's Men* (1949) opposite Broderick Crawford.

"My character in *Giant* liked Jett Rink," she said. "We bonded both on and off the screen. It's true, he was a little bastard, but an amusing one. My role was small, but I was nominated for an Oscar as Best Supporting actress once again. I didn't last long in the picture, as I was mangled to death by a mean horse."

There were two bars in Marfa, and she and Jimmy often hung out in both of them every night

In reference to her autobiography, Mercedes McCambridge wrote, "I wanted to call the book *Life Is a Bitch*, but my publisher wouldn't let me. Jimmy, however, liked what I wanted to entitle my memories."

711

for a while. She told him stories about growing up in Joliet, Illinois and her work in radio before arriving on Broadway for a role in *A Place of Her Own*. A critic said, "She attracted attention with her tight-lipped performance with her cold, demanding eyes."

She discussed working with Broderick Crawford in *All the King's Men*. "Believe it or not, that tough, burly, macho bastard was gay as a goose. He would really have gone for you."

She also told him that Joan Crawford was "a mean, tipsy, powerful rotten egg lady. She put the make on me. When I didn't want to lick her pussy, she turned on me."

Night after night, Mercedes drank too much, and Jimmy would have to drag her back to the hotel. "Mercedes would down bourbon after bourbon until she passed out. Quite a gal. I liked her. She told it like it was, and spared no one."

Pretending to be Texans, and although most of the crew didn't like them, Mercedes McCambridge and James Dean became friends on the set of *Giant*. Midway through the filming, she fell off a horse and suffered lacerations to her face.

She said, "Jimmy wanted to be patted like a little dog. He was the runt of a litter of thoroughbreds, and you could feel the loneliness beating its way out of him."

In her memoir, *The Quality of Mercy*, she wrote: "While he was playing Jett Rink, he was inseparable from Jett Rink. He did not become Jett Rink, but Jett Rink was his constant companion."

[September 30, 1955, occurred near the end of Mercedes's stay at a remote resort in the California desert. Its accommodations had plumbing, but no access to radios or newspapers. As she was driving back to Los Angeles, she stopped at a gas station in the little town of Cholame, where she spotted what used to be a shiny silver Porsche, now a mass of wreckage.

She inquired about it from the gas station attendant.

"Oh, didn't you know?" he asked. "James Dean was driving it. He was killed. It's been all over the news!"

She gasped. "I didn't know."]

Rock Hudson and Jimmy Dean
In and Out of Elizabeth Taylor's Bed
Jimmy Exposes Himself to 250 Rubber Neckers

Elizabeth recalled, "In Texas, Rock and I hit it off right away. The heat, humidity, and dust in Marfa were so thoroughly oppressive we had to bolster our spirits any way we could. So we stayed out drinking all night and luckily were young enough and resilient enough to go straight to the set in the morning with fresh complexions and with no bags under our eyes. During our toots, we concocted the best drink I've ever tasted—a chocolate martini made with vodka, Hershey's syrup, and Kahlua. How we survived, I'll never know."

"Rock and Elizabeth were like kids again," claimed Stevens. "They indulged in a kind of baby talk, and they liked to play pranks on each other, tossing water at each other from our rapidly dwindling supply."

She told her assistant, Dick Hanley, "Rock has become my second best friend—no one will replace Monty as Number One."

In Texas, Hudson and Elizabeth discovered nachos, devouring them along with a massive consumption of alcohol. "Then they staged belch-and-fart contests," Dennis Hooper said.

On the set of *Giant*, Elizabeth had to battle her weight problem. All those chocolate martinis she consumed with Hudson were obviously fattening. But Stevens complained that she compounded the problem with her midnight snacks, which consisted of homemade vanilla ice cream drenched in fudge and peanut butter, preceded by a series of mayonnaise sandwiches, "which I just adore."

For about ten nights, Hudson seduced Elizabeth. Actually, she was the aggressor. She'd later tell Roddy McDowall something he already knew: "Rock is really endowed, and I mean *really*. As a lover, he's very efficient and eager to get on with it. For me, it's over before it begins. We've decided to be great friends, not lovers. No woman will ever succeed in igniting his enthusiasm in bed, and of that, I'm certain."

During the filming of *Giant*, Rock Hudson provided emotional support for Elizabeth Taylor. She was distraught, as her marriage to Michael Wilding was crumbling. According to Hudson, "She is very extreme in her likes and dislikes. If she likes, she loves. If she doesn't like, she loathes. She liked me."

***

In the beginning, Jimmy was leary of Elizabeth, mainly because she'd lobbied to have Monty Clift designated as Jett Rink. Yet he was attracted to her. One hot afternoon between set-ups, he confided to Chill Wills one of his sexual fantasies. "In World War II, I heard women wore a shade of lipstick called Victory Red. My greatest turn-on would be to have three women, their mouths painted with that lipstick, each give me a blow-job—Elizabeth Taylor, Tallulah Bankhead, and Edith Piaf."

[Wills agreed on Elizabeth, but didn't know who Bankhead and Piaf were.]

Elizabeth confided to Hanley, "Jimmy and I, in Texas, were at first rather suspicious of each other. We circled each other like two animals of prey. I was just another Hollywood star to him, all bosom and no brains. To me, he was a would-be intellectual New York Method actor. We were not prepared to dig each other at all."

Stevens later referred to the June 3rd filming of Jimmy's first scenes with Elizabeth as "a day that will live in infamy in the annals of cinema history." They were filmed on an open set at the Worth Evans Ranch, which Stevens had temporarily rented. It was the site of the famous scene where Jimmy was depicted with a rifle hoisted over his shoulders—he called it "my crucifixion pose."

Elizabeth Taylor as Leslie Benedict calls on Jett Rink (Jimmy) for tea. The sexual tension between them inflamed the hot Texas afternoon.

James Dean had difficulty filming this "crucifixion" scene with Elizabeth. To ease his tension, "I took the most famous piss in the history of cinema, with all of Marfa looking on."

Time and time again, he flubbed his lines. Watching the proceedings, Dennis Hopper said, "That was one nervous queen. He was fucking up big time with another Queen (i.e., Elizabeth) of Hollywood."

In front of at least 250 onlookers, Jimmy ruined take after take by freezing up. A total of sixteen shots failed. Suddenly, he broke from the set and walked over to a wire fence in front of the assembled population of Marfa, some of whom included children who had skipped school to attend this first ceremonial film shoot. As everyone looked on, he unzipped his jeans and hauled out his penis. Hopper claimed it looked about four inches soft. Shock waves were heard from the crowd as he took what he called "a horse piss."

He later told Hedda Hopper, "I knew that if I could piss in front of some two thousand *(sic)* people, I could do anything. I'm a Method actor." Then he returned to the set and did the scene perfectly in one take. When it was over, he turned to Elizabeth: "I'm cool, man. It's cool."

When Jimmy saw this picture of himself as a Texan cowboy, he proclaimed, "This is the sexiest photo I've ever posed for. I could go for me myself."

Eventually, they developed a friendship. "One night, he arrived at my house. He seemed engulfed in loneliness. We talked for hours. He loved our Siamese cats, and I gave him one of them. I knew he wanted something that belonged to him, something of his own, so I gave him a kitten. He cried when he accepted my gift."

Jimmy seemed to dote on Marcus, the Siamese cat, but later gave the animal away. When asked why, he said, "I lead such a strange and unpredictable life that some night, I might never come home again. Then what would happen to Marcus?"

"After a while, we found we were just two human beings, and we became intimate friends," Elizabeth said. "There was sex in the beginning, but none of that kinky shit that Rock talked about."

"But, as in the case with Rock, Jimmy and I decided that we could hold each other to protect each other from the cold winds, but as friends, not as lovers."

Perhaps as an emulation of Rock's relationship with Elizabeth, Jimmy engaged in playful games with her. "Two kids on the playground," Stevens called their intimacy.

However, during their moments of manic giddiness, he had a tendency to go too far. One day, he grabbed Elizabeth, picked her up off her feet, and turned her upside down so that her skirt fell over her head, exposing her "unmentionable" regions to photographers.

As she later told Stevens, "Fortunately, unlike Marilyn Monroe on most occasions, I wore my panties that day, or else my twat would be hanging on every bathroom wall in every man's toilet in America."

To Elizabeth, Jimmy always remained a mystery, but she came to love him. "Sometimes, Jimmy and I would sit up until three in the morning, talking, and he would tell me about his past life, his conflicts, and some of his loves and tragedies. And the next day it was almost as if he didn't want to recognize me, or to remember that he had revealed so much of himself the night before. And so he would pass me and ignore me, or just give me a cursory nod of the head. And then it took him a day or two to become my friend again. I found all that hard to understand."

As regards his military record, or lack thereof, he told Elizabeth, "I would have been shot down by some yellow boy in Korea, but I escaped the draft."

Shortly before his death, he was said to have confided his most painful secrets to Elizabeth, sordid details of his life he shared with no other. One of these was revealed after Elizabeth's death in 2011 by writer Kevin Sessums in *The Daily Beast.* Elizabeth had granted Sessums an interview in 1997.

"I'm going to tell you something, but it's off the record until I die," she told Sessums. "When Jimmy was eleven, he began to be molested by his minister. I think that haunted him the rest of his life. In fact, I know it did."

[His biographers have long suspected there was a sexual relationship with the Rev. James DeWeerd, a Wesleyan pastor in Fairmount, Indiana, who had a penchant for young boys. For more on this, refer to Chapter Four of this biography.]

When Hudson learned that Elizabeth was having an affair with Jimmy, he jokingly asked her, "Did he piss on you, or did you piss on him?"

"Let's just call it a tinkle-winkle," she said, perhaps jokingly.

***

Stevens had a closeup view of the shifting alliances and shifting romances of his major stars throughout the production of his film. Some of them later revealed some enticing details:

"George always had to have a patsy to pick on throughout every one of his films," Elizabeth claimed. "On *Giant,* it was both Jimmy and me. Actually, Rock and I speculated that George secretly had the hots for Jimmy. Whenever he thought Jimmy wasn't looking, he was always eying him like a lovesick schoolgirl. One scalding hot afternoon, when Jimmy didn't show up for work, George told Rock and me, 'I should punish the little bastard and make him suck my dick.'"

"George and I staged some epic battles under that hot sun," Elizabeth said. "Our biggest fight was when he wanted me to wear those thick brogue shoes and a long 'grandma-in-the-wilderness' skirt, plus a man's battered old cowboy hat. I attacked him for trying to force this ludicrous getup on me. I told him, 'What are you trying to do? Make me look like a lesbian in drag? I'm Elizabeth Taylor, in case you forgot it.'"

At first, Jimmy and Carroll Baker sat together whispering conspiratorially. "Our main diversion was making fun of Rock and Elizabeth," Baker later said. "We were cruel and cutting."

Baker was popular both as a sex symbol and also as a dramatic actress. She and Jimmy were the same age. She had beautiful features, striking blonde hair (not dyed), and a slight Southern drawl, despite her birth in Pennsylvania. A year later, *Baby Doll* (1956) earned her some screen notoriety, thanks to Tennessee Williams and Elia Kazan.

Carroll Baker, cast as Luz Benedict, daughter of the characters played by Rock Hudson and Elizabeth Taylor in the multi-generational saga, *Giant*.

Unaware of Jimmy's past, Baker, at first, didn't believe that he was a homosexual. She thought that the rumors about him being gay had begun on the set of *Giant* when he began to hang out with a "posse" of Texas cowboys. Unknown to the cast, these cowboys were gay, as were many men in the Old West. They rode together, slept together in bunks, bathed together, gave each other massages, including paying special attention to their buttocks, which were sore from riding too long in the saddle. And they made love at night.

"Jimmy desperately wanted to be a part of that *camaraderie*," McCambridge said. "He talked openly about it to me. He'd heard that I was a lesbian, so I guess he felt his secrets would be safe with me."

An aging, lecherous Jett Rink (Jimmy) courts Luz Benedict (Carroll Baker), the daughter of his bitter rival.

Author Randall Riese wrote; "During the shoot of the bar scene in which Jett Rink proposes marriage to Luz, Jimmy slid one of his hands under the table and allegedly assaulted Carroll between her legs in a schoolboy fit of one-upmanship."

After the release of her 1956 picture, *Baby Doll*, Carroll was absurdly billed as "The Female James Dean."

Baker admitted that Jimmy worked hard to pick up the speech patterns of Jett Rink. "He listened to the cowboys' speech patterns and watched their mannerisms. He not only learned to ride and wore those slant-heeled cowboy boots," she said, 'but he walked with the bow-legged gait of a man born in the saddle."

***

717

During their first two weeks in Marfa, whereas Elizabeth and Hudson spent nearly every evening together, Jimmy was frequently seen bonding with Baker, whom he'd known from the Actors Studio in New York.

Hudson constantly complained to Elizabeth about Stevens. "He gives Dean all the close-ups, and I'm left out in the cold."

In one scene in *Giant*, Dennis Hopper, depicted above, has a push-shove altercation with Jett Rink (Jimmy). Gossip columnists later reported that Hopper was sent to a local hospital for treatment of injuries sustained during that onscreen fight with Jimmy.

Elizabeth and Hudson feared that Jimmy was stealing the picture. Both actors set out to woo Baker into their cabal. In that, they succeeded, and subsequently, Jimmy stopped speaking to her, feeling betrayed.

"Dean got the ultimate revenge," Baker said. "He succeeded in stealing Elizabeth from Rock and me. The dirty rat wanted Elizabeth for himself, and I went into a state of mourning. Elizabeth went off every evening with Jimmy, ignoring Rock and me. The tables had turned."

During the final three weeks of the shoot, Elizabeth temporarily deserted both Hudson and Baker. *[Her friendship with Hudson would be recharged after Jimmy's untimely death.]*

The film's cast and crew were shown the daily rushes in a battered old movie theater that had closed down with the coming of television. Most of the participants preferred to sit on the theater's ground floor, but Elizabeth and Jimmy usually retreated to the balcony where they were alone. She brought popcorn from her house to share with him.

"They were like two lovebirds," Chill Wills said. "I never could figure out these switch-hitters. One night, Jimmy is taking it up the ass, and on another night, he's pounding pussy. You figure."

Throughout the filming of *Giant*, Elizabeth was plagued with various illnesses, some of which required hospitalization. The first of her health emergencies began in July of 1955, when she developed a severe sore throat and could not deliver her lines. That was almost immediately followed by a bladder infection and thrombophlebitis, a blood clot in a vein of her left leg. She blamed its flare-up on Stevens for "making me wear those tight breeches."

Dr. John Davis examined her and asserted that she suffered from "a congenital anomaly of the spine." To alleviate the pain in her lower back caused by a dysfunctional sciatic nerve, she took heavy doses of Novocaine.

One scene in *Giant* called for Elizabeth "to do a lot of jumping and twisting on a bed." Her always-sensitive back exploded in pain again, as she suffered a ruptured intervertebral disc. She was shot with Novocaine and

Hydrocortisone and also given Demerol and Meticorten. "I was a god damn walking pharmacy," she claimed.

Stevens didn't believe in any of her illnesses, calling them "psychosomatic." On August 12, she returned to the set on crutches.

"Elizabeth Plans to Divorce You and Marry Me"

—James Dean to Michael Wilding

On the set of *Giant* in Texas, a studio underling rushed Elizabeth the latest edition of *Confidential* magazine, which ran the headline: *WHEN LIZ TAYLOR'S AWAY, MIKE WILL PLAY.* It detailed the night Michael Wilding picked up two female strippers at a club in Hollywood and brought them back to the home he shared with Elizabeth in Beverly Hills. In the scandal's aftermath, Elizabeth told Stevens, "Whether it's true or not, a woman can't let an indiscretion break up a marriage."

Of course, considering the dramas of her own affairs, she was in no position to chastise Wilding.

Flying to Texas with their two sons to check up on Elizabeth, Wilding was greeted with a blaring headline—*MICHAEL WORRIED ABOUT LIZ AND ROCK.*

When Wilding with their children arrived in Marfa, he went to find Elizabeth, perhaps to remind her she was a wife and mother. Not finding her, he was told that she was last seen driving off with a young man.

"Where in hell do you drive to in this one-horse town?" he asked.

Instead of Elizabeth and Hudson, Wilding encountered Jimmy. "I have to be very frank with you," Jimmy told Wilding. "I've fallen in love with your wife. She's going to divorce you—and marry me. But, remember, you had your chance. Now it's my turn."

Wilding was so amazed by and skeptical of this that he told Stewart Granger back in Hollywood, "I could only conclude that Jimmy was poking me in the ribs. He could not have been serious. Elizabeth will no more marry James Dean than I'll marry the Queen Mother!"

On his first night in Marfa, Wilding was allowed to stay at Elizabeth's rented home, but she didn't return that night.

Nick Adams, Jimmy's longtime lover, had arrived in Marfa, and Stevens spread the rumor that Jimmy had fixed Elizabeth up with Adams. "He's living proof that big things come in small packages," Jimmy told Elizabeth.

Knowing that Wilding would be alone that evening for dinner, Jimmy brought over some West Texas chili and cold beer.

Over the chili, Wilding pointedly asked Jimmy, "Your plans to marry Elizabeth shocked me. I was told you were strictly homo."

"Depending on how much rain falls on any given night, I can go either way—male or female," he answered. "What does it really matter, come to think of it? Sometimes I reward people who do favors for me with sex. I recently flew to Key West to fuck Tennessee Williams. I virtually made him sign a blood oath that he would lobby to get me to play the male lead in all the future adaptations of his plays."

"Smart career move, dear boy," Wilding told him.

At the end of their chili supper, Jimmy said, "Elizabeth is likely to be engaged for the rest of the evening. In that case, would you like to go back to my place and fuck me instead?"

"A tempting offer, but I'm the babysitter tonight," Wilding said. "Give me a rain check."

Wilding claimed that he was still in love with Elizabeth, "but I found the daily tremors of living with such a volcanic creature more and more difficult. After my failure to make it as a star in Hollywood, I felt like James Mason in that role of a has-been in *A Star Is Born*."

Elizabeth and Wilding quarreled throughout his stay in Marfa, and he soon flew from El Paso back to Los Angeles, taking their two sons with him.

"By then, I knew the marriage was all but over," he said. "All that remained was bringing down the final curtain."

***

After he returned from Marfa to Los Angeles, *The Hollywood Reporter* interviewed Rock Hudson, who said: "I didn't like James particularly. Chill Wills and I lived together in a rented house for a while. Dean was hard to be around. He hated George Stevens, didn't think he was a good director, and he was always angry and full of contempt. He never smiled. He was sulky, and he had no manners. He was rough to do a scene with for reasons that only an actor can appreciate. While doing a scene, in the giving and taking, he was just a taker. He would suck everything out and never give back."

Back in Hollywood, Elizabeth continued her friendship with Jimmy, and also "recharged the batteries in my love for Rock, who was going through a troubling time and needed me."

As influenced by his agent, Henry Willson, Hudson agreed to marry Phyllis Gates, his lesbian secretary. Willson had helped to arrange the marriage based on the fear of exposure of Hudson's homosexuality in *Confidential* magazine.

"Michael and I visited Jimmy at least three times at his little house in San Fernando Valley, and he came to see us," Elizabeth said. "He seemed engulfed in loneliness The first time he invited us for dinner, he heated up two cans of beans—and that was that. We sat and talked and listened to his music."

On another night, Jimmy invited Elizabeth for a ride in the pride of his life, a new Porsche Spyder nicknamed "Little Bastard."

He took her for a spin through Beverly Hills and rode up and down Sunset Boulevard. He turned left onto Hollywood Boulevard, passing Grauman's Chinese Theater. When they passed the theater with its cement casts of the hands and feet of the stars, he told her he was considering having a cast of his erect cock made in the cement instead.

The next day, he dropped in at her home to tell her goodbye, claiming that he was driving his Porsche, accompanied with a friend, to the road race at Salinas. The date was September 30, 1955.

"Whatever you do, Jimmy, be safe—just be safe," she cautioned him.

***

The night before his farewell to Elizabeth, he'd received a similar warning from another big star. Quite by chance, he encountered the British actor, Alec Guinness, whose work he admired, at the Villa Capri. He had seen Guinness in *Kind Hearts and Coronets* (1949), in which he'd played eight different roles, and also in *The Lavender Hill Mob* (1951), for which he'd received an Oscar nomination for Best Actor.

Before inviting Guinness to dinner, Jimmy was eager to show off his new Porsche.

Guinness remembered that night in his memoirs: "The sports car looked sinister to me, although it had a large bunch of red carnations resting on its bonnet. I heard myself in a voice I could hardly recognize as my own, 'Please, never get in it! It looks like a death trap."

***

At Warner Brothers in Burbank, Stevens invited some of his stars, including Elizabeth, Hudson, and Baker, to watch the rushes for *Giant*. At one point, there was an urgent ringing of the telephone. Stevens got up to answer it.

Then the cast heard him say, *"No! My god! When? Are you sure?"*

As Baker remembered it, "The picture froze. The lights shot up. We turned and looked at George. The phone dangled in his hand. He was white and motionless. Death was present in that room. 'There's been a car crash,' he said. 'Jimmy Dean has been killed.'"

Within the hour, Elizabeth heard all the painful details.

After Jimmy's death, she went into hysterics and had to be hospitalized for five days.

Communal Grieving and Mass Hysteria:
The Cinematic Premiere of Giant
SCENES TORN FROM THE PAGES OF THE DAY OF THE LOCUST

In Los Angeles, Elizabeth, along with Rock Hudson and George Stevens, pressed their hands and footprints into the freshly poured cement in the forecourt of Grauman's Chinese Theater.

The premiere of *Giant* was announced for this same theater on October 7. Before arriving, Mike Todd and Elizabeth had drinks with Debbie Reynolds and Eddie Fisher.

[At this time, Elizabeth was divorcing Michael Wilding and had fallen in love with producer Todd, whom she would marry in February of 1957. Todd was the best friend of Fisher. The two couples often spent evenings together.]

Todd escorted Elizabeth to the Los Angeles premiere. Rock Hudson arrived with his new wife, Phyllis Gates. They were followed by Clark Gable escorting Joan Crawford, and Tab Hunter with Natalie Wood on his arm.

Late in October, a few weeks later, Todd and Elizabeth flew to Manhattan for the respective New York premieres of both *Giant* and *Around the World in 80 Days*.

By then, a weird cult had formed around the image of the late James Dean. Thousands of his fanatical fans believed that he had not died, but that he was going to make an appearance at the New York premiere of a movie that had helped to make him famous.

Shortly before the screening, Stevens hosted a reception for the film's cast. The director warned everyone that there might be a problem associated with security at the premiere. The New York Police Department had assigned extra men to the premises, and wooden barriers had been erected to restrain the throngs. Fears involved the possibility of a riot because of the hysteria engulfing the fans, mostly those who had come to worship the deceased actor.

Hudson was among the first to arrive. The identity of his date for the evening—Tallulah Bankhead—came as a surprise. She had gone to bed with him the night before. Hudson called such seductions of older female stars "mercy fucks."

She told a reporter from NBC, "I'm here tonight, darling, because of this divine young man, Rock Hudson, who is a giant in every conceivable way."

In advance of the premiere at New York City's Roxy Theater, Todd had presented Elizabeth with a pair of ten-thousand-dollar diamond earrings. The crowd outside the theater grew and grew until it stretched for several blocks. As Elizabeth and Todd emerged from their long black limousine, a roar went up as fans pushed against the police barricades.

Before the beginning of filming, it was clearly understood that James Dean had third billing in *Giant*, the leads defined as Elizabeth Taylor and Rock Hudson. But by the time *Giant* opened across the nation, Jimmy's posthumous fame had grown to such an extent that marquees, such as this one in Chicago, gave him star billing.

Carroll Baker and her husband, director Jack Garfein—a Holocaust survivor for whom she had converted to Judaism—walked directly behind Elizabeth and Todd. As Baker remembered it, "The fanatic Dean cult were nearest the red-carpet aisle leading into the entrance. Those closest to us were thrashing against the barriers, letting out menacing, eerie cries; they had red, distorted, lunatic-like faces. The sight of them filled me with revulsion a moment before the premonition of danger gripped me."

In front of them, Todd, too, was aware of the danger, and he was shoving photographers and reporters aside to make a pathway to safety for Elizabeth. It was as if he was trying to create a tunnel for her to escape.

Baker then described the pandemonium that followed. "There was an explosion of human bodies across the barricades and a stampede of howling maniacs trampling each other and rushing the actors."

Photographers were knocked down along with their cameras. Some of the fans even knocked over police officers, whose caps often went flying through the air. Jane Withers was nearly trampled to death.

The fans tore at Elizabeth, grabbing her hair and trying to rip off pieces of her gown. Todd yelled at them, "Stand back."

A screech went up. "My earring!" shouted Elizabeth. "I've lost one of my earrings!"

"Forget the god damn earrings." Todd shouted at her. "I'll buy you another pair."

The manager of the Roxy appeared, and ushered Elizabeth and Todd into his office, where he offered them a brandy to steady their nerves. Bankhead had retreated to the women's room, and Hudson joined Elizabeth. His shirt was in shreds, and his jacket had disappeared, along with his wallet.

Giant became the highest grossing film in the history of Warners until the 1978 release of *Superman*.

Bouquets and Brickbats for the Surly Ranch Hand Who Becomes a Corrupt Oil

Giant

Most of the reviews generated after the premieres were raves. Posthumously, Jimmy was singled out for special praise. And, as with all movies, there were occasional attacks.

Isabel Quigly in the *Spectator* claimed, "James Dean more than fulfills his early promise. Small and cocky, writhing, with self-consciousness, with guile, with the pangs of poverty, ignorance, social ineptitude, the quintessence of everything youthful, impossible, impressionable, frustrated, and gauche—and yet a 'personality,' someone that matters beyond his pathetic presence—his performance in the first half (later, he is asked to grow old, and cannot manage it), would make *Giant* worth seeing, even if it were five hours long."

Lindsay Anderson in *New Statesman and Nation* delivered this: "The acting is moderately adequate by Rock Hudson, good by Elizabeth Taylor, and virtuoso by James Dean, whose Jett Rink is a willful and brilliant variation on the character he made his own, and died for—the baffled, violent adolescent, rejected by the world he rejects. The middle-aged Jett Rink he could not manage: a matured, hopelessly corrupt character was beyond him."

Fred Majdalany in the *London Daily Mail* wrote: "He was one of the very few genuine personalities to come up since the war."

Time magazine stated: "He created the finest piece of atmospheric acting seen on the screen since Marlon Brando and Rod Steiger did their 'brother' scene in *On the Waterfront.*"

Walter O'Hearn in the *Montreal Star* said: "James Dean may well have been the most promising young actor of this generation."

Edwin Schallert, in the *Los Angeles Times,* found Jimmy "in the championship class."

In *The Houston Post,* George Christian claimed: "James Dean's talent glows like an oilfield flare."

Variety believed: "The film only proves what a promising talent has been lost. Dean delivers an outstanding portrayal. It's a sock performance."

Hollis Alpert in the *Saturday Review* wrote: "It's Dean, Dean, Dean. This young man has caused a mass hysteria at least equal to that caused by Valentino."

"James Dean's depiction of the amoral, reckless, animal-like young ranch had will not only excite his admirers into frenzy, it will make the most sedate onlooker understand why a James Dean cult ever came into existence." So wrote Herbert Kupferberg of *The New York Herald Tribune.*

Perhaps to honor Jimmy in his death, Bosley Crowther of *The New York Times* actually penned a favorable review: "The late James Dean makes the malignant role of the surly ranch hand who become an oil baron the most tangy and corrosive in the film. He plays the curious villain with a stylized spookiness—a sly sort of offbeat languor and slur of language—that concentrates spite."

Paula Rotha, in *Films and Filming,* cast a dour note: "I found Dean so mannered and exhibitionistic as to be repellent in a way not, perhaps, intended by the role. It is a calculated, erratic, and unsubtle performance lacking the depth of his promising work in *East of Eden* under Kazan."

In the *Sunday Express,* Milton Shulman came down hard on Jimmy: "As a middle-aged, power-crazed megalomaniac, his limitations are seriously revealed. Looking like a small-time watch salesman, inarticulateness maddeningly reduces the character to an unintelligible throttle of grunts that arouses neither sympathy nor repugnance. It is a pity that he died before he had learned to correct the mistakes he made in *Giant.*"

Paul Dehn in the *News Chronicle* said: "Mr. Dean, with his realistic gulps, hesitations, and strangled tardiloquence, is ill-suited to the sort of 'literary' dialogue which calls for articulate declamation rather than a manneristic mumble."

Courtland Phipps in *Films in Review,* attacked "the loutish and malicious petulance which present-day teenagers profess to admire. Dean made the young Jett Rink such a boor not even a wife more neurotic than one Miss Taylor was portraying could have thought him attractive."

Giant

"A CENTURY OF STORMY PASSIONS, DEEP HUMAN UNDERSTANDING, AND LOVE, ALWAYS LOVE, POWERFUL, UNQUESTIONING, CONSTANT."

—Giant, *as described in Warners' promotional material*

Almost no critic attacked the camera work of William C. Mellor, one of the leading cinematographers of his era, who took the great open spaces of Texas, its skyline, its panoramic vistas and cactus-studded deserts, with oil derricks "masturbating" what's under the earth, bringing them to eruption.

Mellor had previously won an Oscar for his camerawork on Stevens' *A Place in the Sun* (1951). Future awards would include an Oscar for his work on *The Diary of Anne Frank* (1959), and an Oscar nomination for his work on Mark Robson's *Peyton Place* in 1957.

He died suddenly in 1963 while filming Stevens' *The Greatest Story Ever Told.*

At the time of the Academy Awards in the spring of 1956, *Giant* was a strong contender for an impressive string of other awards as well. It was nominated for Best Picture; Stevens for Best Director; both Jimmy and Hudson for Best Actor; and Mercedes McCambridge for Best Supporting Actress. Only the director, George Stevens, won.

Ironically, the award for Best Picture that year went to Michael Todd for *Around the World in 80 Days*. He would become Elizabeth's third husband.

Many critics claimed that Dean would have won if he'd been nominated as Best Supporting Actor, which he really was. He and Hudson split each other's votes.

As it turned out, Anthony Quinn won that year as Best Supporting Actor for his performance in *Lust for Life,* and the Best Actor Oscar went to Yul Brynner for *The King and I.* Also nominated for Best Actor, along with Jimmy and Hudson, were Kirk Douglas for *Lust for Life* and Sir Laurence Olivier for *Richard III.*

Pictured above is the last major scene James Dean ever filmed. Portraying the oil millionaire, Jett Rink, at a banquet in his honor attended by the elite of Texas, he gets drunk and hostile, embarassing himself, and emptying the room.

He finally collapses onto the banquet's head table, an inglorious end to Jett Rink and perhaps, symbolically, to James Dean, too.

Epilogue

DEATH IN THE AFTERNOON

During the last months of the life of James Dean, and in spite of a budding career about to explode into bloom, friends of the actor reported that he had a death wish. "He was obsessed with death," claimed Maila Nurmi (TV's Vampira). "He once told me he wanted to die because that was the only way he'd ever know any peace."

"All the signs were there," reported William Bast. "Even the noose he always kept hanging in any bedroom he occupied."

His favorite literary passage was from Ernest Hemingway's saga about bullfighting, *Death in the Afternoon:* "The only place where you could see life and death—that is, violent death now that the wars were over—was in the bullring."

Composer Leonard Rosenman said, "Jimmy saw death as a challenge."

Elizabeth Taylor revealed that Jimmy had told her "I will never live to reach thirty."

Nearly every friend who rode in a car with him reported that even for casual errands, he drove at frenetic, death-defying speeds.

Repeatedly warned about the dangers of this, he responded, "What better way to die than in a car crash? It's fast and it's clean, and you go out in a blaze of glory."

***

On September 19, 1955, Jimmy was walking along Hollywood Boulevard, when he ran into Rolf Wütherich, a 28-year-old German mechanic whom he'd met at the Bakersfield Races on May 1, a month after Rolf had arrived in the United States.

This former glider pilot and paratrooper for the *Luftwaffe* was one of the world's leading experts on racecars, especially if it were a Porsche.

In 1949, emerging from the ruins of a country devastated by World War II, he'd joined the Porsche factory in Germany as part of their racing department. He was eventually transferred to California as a field engineer for Johnny von Neumann's Competition Motors racecar distributorship in Hollywood.

In early September, the outlet had received five new "state-of-the-art" Porsche 550 Spyders, with the understanding that these high-maintenance, limited edition vehicles were to be offered for sale only to "privateer racers."

The two racing aficionados talked cars over cups of coffee at a café on Hollywood Boulevard. Before they parted, Rolf had convinced Jimmy to trade in his old Porsche for one of the new Spyders, "which can go a hell of a lot faster than the Model T you're driving, perhaps reaching 140mph."

Rolf Wütherrich in 1954 at the Le Mans races *(top photo)* and *(lower photo)* in 1966, "more or less" recovered from his injuries more than a decade before

Two days later, on September 21, the Spyder was Jimmy's, but only after Van Neumann had gotten him to agree to let Rolf accompany him to any race as his mechanic. Jimmy accepted the deal and Rolf agreed to go with him to the Salinas Road Races scheduled for October 1-2.

On Friday morning, September 30, his last day on earth, Jimmy arrived at Competition Motors, where Rolf convinced him that both of them should—personally and together—drive the Porsche to Salinas, a 300-mile journey, for "break-in miles" before the races. Originally, Jimmy's plan involved towing it on a trailer hitched to a 1955 Ford Country Squire station wagon, into which he'd invited several of his friends, all of whom turned him down.

"You need 'seat time,' behind the wheel to get the feel of this baby," Rolf told him.

That day, before leaving Hollywood for the last time, Jimmy and Rolf had coffee and donuts at the Hollywood Ranch Market on Vine Street, across from

Competition Motors.

It was 1:15PM PST when the two men departed, Rolf later claiming that "Jimmy's nerves were frayed."

By 2PM, Jimmy was photographed at a Mobil station at the corner of Ventura and Beverly Glen Boulevards in Sherman Oaks. He left there at 2:15PM, heading north along CA Rt. 99 and then over "The Grapevine" Highway in the direction of Bakersfield.

As later reported by Rolf, these two racing enthusiasts discussed their upcoming dream competing at racing events in Europe, particularly at venues in the South of France.

Following them in the station wagon, with the trailer, were Bill Hickman a movie stunt man, and Sanford Roth, Jimmy's close friend, a professional photographer who planned a photo shoot of him at the race for *Colliers* magazine.

Years later, Rolf recalled that fateful afternoon: "Jimmy was brimming over with happiness. We had such great plans. He was so affectionate with me, I got the feeling that the might be falling in love with me. Far more than being an actor, he wanted to be the world's championship car racer. Somehow, I became a part of his fantasy, a part of his dreams."

"Alas, the Devil must have been listening to our plans and wanted to destroy our future happiness," Rolf claimed.

[After their crash later that day, Rolf would spend a month at a Los Angeles hospital recovering from a double fractured jaw and major femur and hip injuries. For the next six months, he endured separate surgeries at three-week intervals, and became emotionally scarred in ways that became increasingly obvious throughout the rest of his life.

Later, in Europe, despite his physical pain and violent outbursts, he became a navigator for the Porsche factories at the Monte Carlo Rallye. For eighteen years after that, he worked for Porsche in Germany, drifting into alcoholism and sometimes threatening suicide. He ended up in a psychiatric ward.

In July of 1981, he was intoxicated and driving through Kupferzell, in what was then known as the Bundesrepublik Deutschland (i.e., West Germany).

For their "date with destiny," Rolf Wütherrich and James Dean set out in newly purchased Porsche Spyder. Their lives would be changed forever. Jimmy's would be ended, and Rolf would be physically and emotionally scarred for the years that remained for him before his own tragic and violent death.

There, perhaps in a suicide attempt, he lost control of his vehicle and crashed into a wall, dying instantly.

Like Jimmy, more than a quarter-century before, he had to be extricated from the wreckage. He was fifty-three years old.]

* * *

Once upon the open road to Salinas, and with no cars around them, Jimmy began to speed, referring to his new Porsche as "a torpedo on wheels." He was wearing sunglasses and had tossed his *Rebel Without a Cause* red jacket into the back. Rolf later reported that he actually said, "It's a wonderful world after all. I'm doing what I always wanted to do."

Suddenly, he heard the sounds of a police siren. At 3:30PM O.V. Hunter, a California Highway Patrolman, pulled Jimmy over at Mettler Station on Wheeler Ridge, just south of Bakersfield. He issued a ticket, asserting that Jimmy was doing 65mph in a 55mph zone.

Soon, amid a landscape of arid, scrub-covered desert, Jimmy and Rolf were on what was known as "The Racer's Road" to Salinas. As they neared Blackwell's Corner, Jimmy slowed down when he spotted the gray Mercedes-Benz 300 SL Coupe belonging to Lance Reventlow, son of the Woolworth heiress Barbara Hutton.

The two men had agreed to stay together that night at a private home Lance had arranged for them in Salinas. Lance was accompanied at the time with a fellow racecar driver, Bruce Kessler.

Over sandwiches and coffee, Lance and Jimmy discussed their upcoming plans to escape to his private lodge in Sun Valley, Idaho.

Kessler had wandered off with Rolf to inspect their respective cars.

Jimmy estimated how long it would take to reach Paso Robles, where they were to have dinner together in a steak restaurant before retiring for the night.

At 5:12PM, Jimmy and Lance were seen locked in a tight embrace before climbing into their cars. At 5:15PM, Jimmy drove with Rolf out of Blackwell's Corner, heading west on CA Route 45. Paso Robles lay sixty miles in the distance.

Rolf reported that Jimmy drove recklessly, accelerating his Porsche and dangerously passing other cars as he made his way to the Polonio Pass and the "Antelope Grade," heading for the Y-shaped intersection of Routes 41 and 46. Its location was a mile east of the small town of Cholame.

[In 1955, what is now identified as Route 46 was known as Route 466. At the time, Route 41 and 466 were two-lane roads (i.e., with traffic moving on single lanes in each direction) with narrow shoulders.]

Before taking off, Rolf had warned Jimmy that the low-slung, aluminum-skinned, pale gray Porsche might be hard to see in certain lights. At 5:43 PM, the sun was setting, but Jimmy hadn't yet turned on his lights.

Anxious to get to Paso Robles and his rendezvous with Lance, Jimmy stepped on the gas, testing his Porsche to see if it indeed could reach a maximum speed of 140mph. The speedometer registered 85mph. At a junction coming up, he slowed down to 65mph.

Also heading for the "Y" intersection was Donald Turnupseed, a twenty-three year old Cal Poly (California Polytechnic State University) student who had never heard of James Dean. He was driving to the little town of Tulare to spend the weekend with his parents, and was motoring recklessly as if he were late for some rendezvous.

Only two minutes before their gut-wrenching crash, he was heading east, blowing his horn as he passed two other cars. They included a 1948 Mercury Sedan driven by Earle Requa, and a 1952 Dodge pickup with Tom Frederick behind the wheel.

Also speeding toward the junction were Jimmy and Rolf. Jimmy zoomed west, passing a car driven by John R. White of Los Angeles, who was traveling with his wife and son. "Look at the god damn maniac go," White said.

On route 46, at the "Y" junction, Turnupseed slowed down to make a left turn onto Route 41 and then moved suddenly into the intersection. His car's radio, at high volume, was blasting out Doris Day's rendition of "Sentimental Journey."

In the distance, Jimmy spotted a two-toned black-and-white 1950 Ford Sedan. Neither vehicles slowed down. Jimmy's last words to Rolf were, "He's gotta see us. He's gotta stop!"

Without signaling, Turnupseed turned into Jimmy's right-of-way. Jimmy's position was just thirty yards away from the intersection.

Behind Turnupseed, also approaching the "Y", was the Hord family, with father, wife, and son sitting in the front seat, three abreast. Ken Hord, the son, called out, "Jesus Christ, Dad, look at that son of a bitch coming our way!" Later, in an analysis of the events, he said, "To

Donald Turnupseed's Ford, from which, amazingly, he emerged unscathed—at least physically.

avoid a crash, my father just yanked our car to the right and went off the road into a barbed wire fence."

Panicking, with seconds before the inevitable, Jimmy slammed on his brakes as Rolf screamed, "We're going to die!"

Then, Jimmy made a desperate, split-second decision to "power steer" his Porsche into a side-stepping racecar maneuver that drivers use on the track during attempts to steer around another car. Unfortunately, the clock had run out. It was too late, and the maneuver failed.

Tom Frederick, a twenty-eight-year-old beekeeper, said, "In my pickup, I was right on Turnupseed's tail. I was next to him, passing him on the right, when the Porsche hit the Ford with a sound that could probably be

heard a mile or two away. It was like a bomb. A part of the Porsche went sailing over my pickup."

Earle Requa's Mercury was also headed toward the intersection. His wife, Edith, screamed "Look out!" as a car flew through the air. Requa brought his car to an abrupt stop near Turnupseed's bashed-in Ford. Its driver was sitting behind the wheel, bloodied and dazed, but still alive. The driver's-side door had been flung open.

The lightweight and aerodynamic Porsche had been hurled more than fifty feet through the air, hitting the earth but "leaping up" again three times before ramming into a telephone pole.

Rolf was thrown fifteen yards from the scene of the accident, landing with a sickening thud on the tarmac of the highway.

When an ambulance arrived, two attendants found Jimmy's mangled body within the wreckage, trapped behind the splintered steering column. His remains were pulled from the metal that entrapped it. Limp and covered with blood, he had fractured bones and a broken neck. His forehead was caved in, as was his chest.

He had died upon impact.

Weeks later, in a hospital, Rolf gradually emerged from his leaden haze. He remembered not only Jimmy's last words, but his last sounds as well.

"I heard a soft cry that came from deep within his throat. It was the cry of a little boy wanting his mother...or a man facing his God."

***

The local radio station, KPRL, was the first to broadcast the news. Within thirty minutes, the events surrounding Jimmy's death were flashed around the world, radio and television stations interrupting their broadcasts with bulletins. Newspapers going to bed remade their frontpages.

James Dean, aged twenty-four years, seven months, and twenty-two days, passed into history.

A legend was born.

Acknowledgments

The data in this biography of James Dean was compiled over a period of half a century. Sometimes, years would pass with nothing added to the dossier. In other cases, bountiful harvests of information would appear, suddenly and unexpectedly.

In particular, seven sources were so enormously helpful that they were singled out on this book's dedication page. They included Stanley Haggart, Rogers Brackett, Alec Wilder, Nicholas Ray, William Bast, Eartha Kitt, and Geraldine Page.

And in addition to those seven, there were hundreds of others.

***

Over the years, virtually anyone who ever knew or worked with James Dean had an opinion about him, and usually didn't mind sharing it. Understandably, some of them didn't want to be named.

Our task, as developers of this project, involved tracking down all these comments, including those gathered from secondary sources. All of these are acknowledged as they were cited.

Much of the insider information about Dean's days in television came from Stanley Haggart, who was a TV producer and art director in the 1950s. He knew many of the producers, directors, and actors who worked with Dean, and many of them had tales to tell. Before his death in 1980, Haggart, in collaboration with Darwin Porter, recorded most of the fruits of his labors into a manuscript tentatively entitled *James Dean: What Becomes a Legend the Most?* Although it was never completed, many of the revelations appearing in this book about Dean's convoluted life during his TV years derived from that original source.

Whereas some of the sources cited within these acknowledgments are well-known personalities (Rock Hudson, for example), others with memories and opinions about him flickered for a moment in the public eye and then faded from the scene. Those sources, of course, were the hardest to track down.

But regardless of their "celebrity quotient," everyone whose memories were included in this book articulated some distinctly personal reactions to

James Dean: good, horrible, or indifferent. Some sources delivered only a paragraph; others could talk about him for hours. Some of them waited until the beginning of the 21st Century, when they had little to lose, before relaying what really happened.

We extend our apologies to those who were left off this list. Our gratitude remains, however, even if it's not expressed.

WITH RESPECT AND APPRECIATION TO THE FOLLOWING SOURCES,
WHETHER THEY'RE LIVING OR DEAD

Many Thanks

Nick Adams, Stella Adler, Eddie Albert, Ben Alcock, Corey Allen, Ursula Andress, Pier Angeli, Ted Avery, Lemuel Ayers, Jim Backus, Carroll Baker, Margaret Baker, Tallulah Bankhead, Marshall Barer, Lynn Bari, James Barton, Kenneth Battelle, Barbara Baxley, Ed Begley, James Bellah, Lee Bergere, Richard Bishop, Humphrey Bogart, George Bradshaw, Freddie Brandell, Pat Breslin, "Mushy" Callahan, Truman Capote, John Carlyle, John Carradine, John Cohan, Bill Claxton, Dick Clayton, Monty Clift, Brooks Clift, Fred Coe, Joan Collins, Mike Connolly, William Corrigan, Frank Corsaro, Cheryl Crawford, Hume Cronyn, George Cukor, Ray Curry, Paul Darlow, Sammy Davis, Jr., Vittorio De Sica, Jean Deacy, Alice Denham, John Derek, James DeWeerd, David Diamond, Marlene Dietrich, Vincent J. Donehue, Ann Doran, Kirk Douglas, Isabelle Draesmer, Mark Ducus, Dick Dunlap, Mildred Dunnock, Jerry Fairbanks, Edna Ferber, Carlo Fiore, Constance Ford, Margaret Foresman, Jack Garfein, Ben Gazzara, John Gilmore, Sam Gilmore, Dorothy Gish, Barbara Glenn, Ruth Goetz, Michael Gordon, Sheilah Graham, Lee Grant, Merv Griffin, Bill Gunn, Walter Hampden, Louis Thomas Hardin, Pat Hardy, Matt Harlib, Julie Harris, Terese Hayden, William Heller, Franklin Heller, George Roy Hill, Hedda Hopper, Dennis Hopper, William Hopper, Rock Hudson, Marsha Hunt, Barbara Hutton (her diaries), William Inge, Christopher Isherwood, Anne Jackson, Erskine Johnson, Louis Jourdan, Lilli Kardell, Kurt Kasznar, Elia Kazan, Arthur Kennedy, Dorothy Kilgallen, Archer King, Martin Kingsley, Toni Lee (aka Toni Lee Scott), Peggy Lee, Oscar Levant, Ralph Levy, Ralph Levy, Bobby Lewis, Arthur Loew, Jr., Beverly Long, Sidney Lumet, Gene Lyons, Moss Mabry, Karl Malden, Daniel Mann, E. G. Marshall, Billy Massena, Virginia Mayo, Frank Mazzola, Andrew McCullough, Clyde McCullough, Roddy

McDowall, Maggie McNamara, Don Medford, Johnny Meyer, Ruda Michelle, Wilson Millar, Samuel Miller, Martin Milner, Terry Moore, Adeline Nall, Richard Nash, Patricia Neal, Lori Nelson, Ralph Nelson, John Paul Nickell, Maila Nurmi (Vampira), Barbara O'Neil, William Orr, Fred Otash, Gene Owen, Betsy Palmer, Terry Parks, Robert Pastene, Marisa Pavan, John Peyser, Arthur Pierson, Philip Pine, Donald Pressman, Nicholas Ray, William Redfield, Lance Reventlow, Kendis Rochen, Stuart Rosenberg, Leonard Rosenblum, Beulah Roth, Arlene Sachs, Howard Sackler, Ray Schatt, Jimmy Schauffer, Rod Serling, James Sheldon, Elizabeth Sheridan, Herman Shumlin, Steffi Sidney, Jack Simmons, Sidney Skolsky, Rusty Slocum, Helena Sorell, Maria St. Just, Kim Stanley, Maureen Stapleton, Teddy Stauffer, Rod Steiger, Stewart Stern, George Stevens, Robert Stevens, John Stix, Dennis Stock, Lee Strasberg, Susan Strasberg, David Swift, Jessica Tandy, Vaughn Taylor, Dean J. Taylor, Tom Tryon, Forrest Tucker, Gore Vidal, Eli Wallach, Clifton Webb, Ronnie White, Miles White, James Whitmore, Tennessee Williams, Calder Willingham, Chill Wills, Beverly Wills, John Wills, Henry Willson, Robert Wise, Jane Withers, Natalie Wood, Cal York, and Maurice Zolotow.

REST IN PEACE
JAMES DEAN
(1931–1955)

DARWIN PORTER

As an intense and precocious nine-year-old, **Darwin Porter** began meeting movie stars, TV personalities, politicians, and singers through his vivacious and attractive mother, Hazel, an eccentric but charismatic Southern girl who had lost her husband in World War II. Migrating from the Depression-ravaged valleys of western North Carolina to Miami Beach during its most ebullient heyday, Hazel became a stylist, wardrobe mistress, and personal assistant to the vaudeville *comedienne* Sophie Tucker, the bawdy and irrepressible "Last of the Red Hot Mamas."

Virtually every show-biz celebrity who visited Miami Beach paid a call on "Miss Sophie," and Darwin as a pre-teen loosely and indulgently supervised by his mother, was regularly dazzled by the likes of Judy Garland, Dinah Shore, Veronica Lake, Linda Darnell, Martha Raye, and Ronald Reagan, who arrived to pay his respects to Miss Sophie with a young blonde starlet on the rise— Marilyn Monroe.

After graduation from the University of Miami, Darwin was commissioned with the opening of a bureau of *The Miami Herald* in Key West (Florida), where he took frequent morning walks with retired U.S. president Harry S Truman during his vacations in what had functioned as his "Winter White House." He also got to know, sometimes very well, various celebrities "slumming" their way through off-the-record holidays in the orbit of then-resident Tennessee Williams. Celebrities hanging out in the jaded and very permissive arts environment of Key West during those days included Tallulah Bankhead, Cary Grant, Tony Curtis, the stepfather of Richard Burton, a gaggle of show-biz and publishing moguls, and the once-notorious stripper, Bettie Page.

For about a decade in New York, Darwin worked in television journalism and advertising with his long-time partner, the journalist, art director, and distinguished arts-industry socialite Stanley Mills Haggart. Haggart was a close friend of James Dean, who often used his apartment in Manhattan or his guest cottage and swimming pool in Laurel Canyon in Hollywood.

Stanley (as an art director) and Darwin (as a writer and assistant), worked as freelance agents within the then-emerging medium of television. Jointly, they helped produce TV commercials that included testimonials from Joan Crawford (then feverishly promoting Pepsi-Cola); Ronald Reagan (General Electric); and Debbie Reynolds (Singer sewing machines). Other personalities appearing within their televised pitches included Louis Armstrong, Lena Horne, and Arlene Dahl, each of them hawking a commercial product.

Many of the Haggart/Porter commissions derived from TV producer Rogers Brackett, who "discovered" James Dean, fell desperately in love with him, mentored him, paid his bills, and introduced him to casting directors throughout the entertainment industry. Testimonies from Brackett appear frequently within the context of this book.

Stanley and Darwin were also close friends with Brooks Clift, the relatively stable older brother of Montgomery Clift. A well-positioned executive at Grey Advertising, an entity responsible for the production of TV commercials during the medium's early heyday, Brooks also contributed many stories and points of view about James Dean that made their way into this book.

Additional anecdotes derived from Haggart and Porter's friendship with the composer, Alec Wilder, who had housed James Dean during his early days in Manhattan, who introduced him to some of the insiders within the then-emerging medium of television.

During his youth, Stanley had flourished as an insider in early Hollywood as a "leg man" and source of information for Hedda Hopper, the fabled gossip columnist. On his nightly "investigative" rounds, Stanley was most often accompanied by Hedda's son, William Hopper, a close friend of Ronald Reagan's. Hopper, later cast as Natalie Wood's dysfunctional father in *Rebel Without a Cause,* continued his long-standing tradition of gossipy conversations with Stanley, who transmitted many of his tales onward to Darwin.

When Stanley wasn't dishing newsy revelations to Hedda, he had worked as a Powers model, and been cast as a romantic lead opposite Silent-era film star Mae Murray. He had also been intimate, live-in companion of superstar Randolph Scott before Scott became emotionally involved with Cary Grant; and a man-about-town who archived gossip from everybody who mattered back when the movie colony was small, accessible, and confident that details about their tribal rites would absolutely never be reported in the press. Over the years, Stanley's vast cornucopia of inside Hollywood information was passed on to Darwin, who amplified it with copious interviews and research of his own.

After Stanley's death in 1980, Darwin inherited a treasure trove of memoirs, notes, and interviews detailing Stanley's early adventures in Hollywood, including in-depth recitations of scandals that even Hopper during her heyday was afraid to publish. Most legal and journalistic standards back then interpreted those oral histories as "unprintable." Times, of course, changed.

Beginning in the early 1960s, Darwin joined forces with the then-fledgling Arthur Frommer organization, playing a key role in researching and writing more than 50 titles and defining the style and values that later emerged as the world's leading travel accessories, **The Frommer Guides,** with particular emphasis on Europe, California, New England, and the Caribbean. Between the creation and updating of hundreds of editions of detailed travel guides to England, France, Italy, Spain, Portugal, Austria, Hungary, Germany, Switzerland, the Caribbean, and California, he continued to interview and discuss the triumphs, feuds, and frustrations of celebrities, many by then reclusive, whom he either sought out or encountered randomly as part of his extensive travels. Ava Gardner, Lana Turner, and Broderick Crawford were particularly insightful.

One day when Darwin was living in Tangier as part of an assignment associated with *Frommer's Morocco*, he walked into an opium den to discover Marlene Dietrich sitting alone in a corner. Even Miss Dietrich had an opinion about James Dean.

Darwin has also ghost written books for celebrities (who shall go nameless!) as well as a series of novels. His first, *Butterflies in Heat*, became a cult classic and was adapted into a film, *Tropic of Desire*, starring Eartha Kitt, who had been James Dean's *confidante* and "soul sister." During its filming in Key West, Eartha transmitted many of the tales generated by her friendship with Dean on to Darwin.

Since then, Darwin has penned more than thirty uncensored, unvarnished, and unauthorized Hollywood biographies, many of them award-winners, on subjects who have included Bill and Hillary Clinton, Peter O'Toole, Marlon Brando; Merv Griffin; Katharine Hepburn; Howard Hughes; Humphrey Bogart; Michael Jackson; Paul Newman; Steve McQueen; Marilyn Monroe; Elizabeth Taylor; Frank Sinatra; John F. Kennedy; Vivien Leigh; Laurence Olivier; the notorious porn star Linda Lovelace; Anne Bancroft; Sophie Tucker; Veronica Lake; Lucille Lortel; Greta Keller; Tamara Geva; all three of the fabulous Gabor sisters; plus Tennessee Williams, Gore Vidal, Truman Capote, Jacqueline Kennedy Onassis, Jane Wyman, and Ronald and Nancy Reagan.

As a departure from his usual repertoire, Darwin also wrote the controversial *J. Edgar Hoover & Clyde Tolson: Investigating the Sexual Secrets of America's Most Famous Men and Women*, a book about celebrity, voyeurism, political and sexual repression, and blackmail within the highest circles of the U.S. government.

He has also co-authored, in league with Danforth Prince, four *Hollywood Babylon* anthologies, plus four separate volumes of film critiques, reviews, and commentary.

His biographies, over the years, have won at least a dozen First Prize or runner-up awards at literary festivals in cities which include Boston, New York, Los Angeles, Hollywood, San Francisco, and Paris.

Darwin can be heard at regular intervals as a radio and television commentator, "dishing" celebrities, pop culture, politics, and scandal.

A resident of New York City, Darwin is currently at work on *Donald Trump, The Man Who Would Be King*. He is also a Hollywood columnist.

DANFORTH PRINCE

The co-author of this book, **Danforth Prince** is president and founder of Blood Moon Productions, a firm devoted to salvaging, compiling, and marketing the oral histories of America's entertainment industry.

Prince launched his career in journalism in the 1970s at the Paris Bureau of *The New York Times.* In the early '80s, he joined Darwin Porter in developing first editions of many of the titles within *The Frommer Guides.* Together, they reviewed and articulated the travel scenes of more than 50 nations, most of them within Europe and The Caribbean. Authoritative and comprehensive, they were perceived, before the collapse of the travel industry in the aftermath of the Great Recession of 2008, as best-selling "travel bibles" for millions of readers.

Prince, in collaboration with Porter, is also the co-author of several award-winning celebrity biographies, each configured as a title within Blood Moon's Babylon series. These have included *Hollywood Babylon—It's Back!; Hollywood Babylon Strikes Again; The Kennedys: All the Gossip Unfit to Print; Frank Sinatra, The Boudoir Singer, Elizabeth Taylor: There is Nothing Like a Dame; Pink Triangle: The Feuds and Private Lives of Tennessee Williams, Gore Vidal, Truman Capote, and Members of their Entourages*; and *Jacqueline Kennedy Onassis: A Life Beyond Her Wildest Dreams.* More recent efforts include *Peter O'Toole—Hellraiser, Sexual Outlaw, Irish Rebel;* and *Bill & Hillary—So This Is That Thing Called Love.*

Prince is also the co-author, of four books on film criticism, three of which won honors at regional bookfests in Los Angeles and San Francisco.

Prince, a graduate of Hamilton College and a native of Easton and Bethlehem, Pennsylvania, is the president and founder of the Georgia Literary Association (1996), and of the Porter and Prince Corporation (1983) which has produced dozens of titles for Simon & Schuster, Prentice Hall, and John Wiley & Sons. In 2011, he was named "Publisher of the Year" by a consortium of literary critics and marketers spearheaded by the J.M. Northern Media Group.

Publishing in collaboration with the National Book Network *(www.NBN-Books.com)*, he has electronically documented some of the controversies associated with his stewardship of Blood Moon in at least 50 documentaries, book trailers, public speeches, and TV or radio interviews. Most of these are available on **YouTube.com** and **Facebook** *(keywords: "Danforth Prince" or "Blood Moon Productions")*; on **Twitter** *(#BloodyandLunar);* or by clicking on **BloodMoonProductions.com**.

WHAT IS BLOOD MOON PRODUCTIONS?

"Blood Moon, in case you don't know, is a small publishing house on Staten Island that cranks out Hollywood gossip books, about two or three a year, usually of five-, six-, or 700-page length, chocked with stories and pictures about people who used to consume the imaginations of the American public, back when we actually had a public imagination. That is, when people were really interested in each other, rather than in Apple 'devices.' In other words, back when we had vices, not devices."

—The Huffington Post

Want to see us, up close and personal?
Consider staying with us during your next trip to New York City.

Magnolia House

A reasonably priced "AirBNB.com" Bed and Breakfast Inn specializing in literary nostaligia, pop culture, and the book trades. Elegant, historic, & comfortable, it's a historically important building in the landmark neighborhood of Saint George, Staten Island, a ten-minute walk from the departure point of the ferryboat to Manhattan.

As stated by its resident manager, Danforth Prince, "Magnolia House results from my 30-year role as co-author of many titles, and many editions, of **The Frommer Guides**, each of which included evaluations of the bed and breakfast inns of Europe. Whereas I'm still writing travel articles and celebrity *exposés* from the upper floors of this building, its 'showcase rooms' now operate as a client-indulgent B&B loaded with mementos from the early days of the Frommer Guides, 'the Golden Age of Travel,' and souvenirs from Blood Moon's associations with Broadway, Hollywood, and the Entertainment Industry."

"Edgy media associations have always been part of the Magnolia House experience," Prince continued. "Previous guests have included **Tennessee Williams** (*"Magnolia House reminds me of Blanche DuBois' lost plantation, Bellereve!"*); golden age film personality **Joan Blondell** (a close friend of celebrity biographer and co-owner, **Darwin Porter**); **Lucille Lortel** (the philanthropic but very temperamental Queen of Off-Broadway); the very outspoken **Jolie Gabor** (mother of the three "Bombshells from Budapest" otherwise known as **Zsa Zsa, Eva, and Magda**); and a host of other stars, *starlettes*, and *demi-mondains* of all descriptions and persuasions."

For photographs, testimonials from previous guests, and information about availabilities and reservations, click on **www.MagnoliaHouseSaintGeorge.com**. Otherwise, contact DanforthPrince@gmail.com.

Magnolia House
Saint George

is the site where we produce
Blood Moon's Award-Winning

ENTERTAINMENT ABOUT
HOW AMERICA INTERPRETS
ITS CELEBRITIES

MagnoliaHouseSaintGeorge.com

LOVE TRIANGLE

Ronald Reagan, Jane Wyman, & Nancy Davis

Unique in the history of publishing, this scandalous triple biography focuses on the Hollywood indiscretions of former U.S. president Ronald Reagan and his two wives. A proud and Presidential addition to Blood Moon's Babylon series, it digs deep into what these three young and attractive movie stars were doing decades before two of them took over the Free World.

***

As reviewed by Diane Donovan, Senior Reviewer at the California Bookwatch section of the Midwest Book Review: *"Love Triangle: Ronald Reagan, Jane Wyman & Nancy Davis may find its way onto many a Republican Reagan fan's reading shelf; but those who expect another Reagan celebration will be surprised: this is lurid Hollywood exposé writing at its best, and outlines the truths surrounding one of the most provocative industry scandals in the world.*

"There are already so many biographies of the Reagans on the market that one might expect similar mile-markers from this: be prepared for shock and awe; because Love Triangle doesn't take your ordinary approach to biography and describes a love triangle that eventually bumped a major Hollywood movie star from the possibility of being First Lady and replaced her with a lesser-known Grade B actress (Nancy Davis).

"From politics and betrayal to romance, infidelity, and sordid affairs, Love Triangle is a steamy, eye-opening story that blows the lid off of the Reagan illusion to raise eyebrows on both sides of the big screen.

"Black and white photos liberally pepper an account of the careers of all three and the lasting shock of their stormy relationships in a delightful pursuit especially recommended for any who relish Hollywood gossip."

***

In 2015, LOVE TRIANGLE, Blood Moon Productions' overview of the early dramas associated with Ronald Reagan's scandal-soaked career in Hollywood, was designated by the Awards Committee of the **HOLLYWOOD BOOK FESTIVAL** as Runner-Up to Best Biography of the Year.

LOVE TRIANGLE: Ronald Reagan, Jane Wyman, & Nancy Davis

Darwin Porter & Danforth Prince

Hot, scandalous, and loaded with information the Reagans never wanted you to know.

Softcover, 6" x 9", with hundreds of photos.   ISBN 978-1-936003-41-9

CONFUSED ABOUT HOW TO INTERPRET THEIR RAUCOUS PAST? THIS UNCENSORED TALE ABOUT A LOVE AFFAIR THAT CHANGED THE COURSE OF POLITICS AND THE PLANET IS RE-QUIRED READING FOR ANYONE INVOLVED IN THE POLITICAL SLUGFESTS AND INCENDIARY WARS OF **THE CLINTONS.**

Bill & Hillary
So This Is That Thing Called Love

As defined by Diane Donovan, Senior Reviewer at the *Midwest Book Review* and *California Bookwatch*:

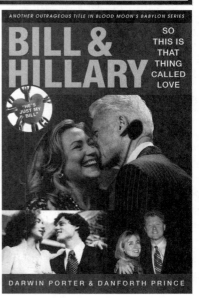

"This is both a biographical coverage of the Clintons and a political exposé; a detailed, weighty exploration that traces the couple's social and political evolution, from how each entered the political arena to their White House years under Bill Clinton's presidency.

"Containing gossip, scandal, and biographical sketches, it delves deeply into the news and politics of its times, presenting enough historical background to fully explore the underlying controversies affecting the Clinton family and their choices.

"Sidebars of information and black and white photos liberally peppered throughout the account offer visual reinforcement to the exploration, lending it the feel and tone of both a gossip column and political piece - something that probes not just Clinton interactions but the D.C. political milieu as a whole.

"The result may appear weighty, sporting over five hundred pages, but is an absorbing, top recommendation for readers of both biographical and political pieces who will thoroughly enjoy this spirited, lively, and thought-provoking analysis, which arrives in perfect time for Hillary's presidential run."

***

Shortly after its release in December of 2015, this book received a literary award (Runner-up to Best Biography of the Year) from the New England Book Festival. As stated by a spokesperson for the Awards, "The New England Book Festival is an annual competition honoring excellence in books, with particular focus on projects that deserve closer attention from the academic community. Congratulations to Blood Moon and its authors, especially Darwin Porter, for his highly entertaining analysis of Clinton's double-barreled presidential regime, and the sometimes hysterical over-reaction of their enemies."

Available Everywhere Now
BILL & HILLARY—SO THIS IS THAT THING CALLED LOVE
Softcover, with photos. ISBN 978-1-936003-47-1

THOSE GLAMOROUS GABORS

Zsa Zsa! We Love You!

Bombshells from Budapest, by Darwin Porter

Zsa Zsa, Eva, and Magda Gabor transferred their glittery dreams and gold-digging ambitions from the twilight of the Austro-Hungarian Empire to Hollywood. There, more effectively than any army, these Bombshells from Budapest broke hearts, amassed fortunes, lovers, and A-list husbands, and amused millions of *voyeurs* through the medium of television, movies, and the social registers. In this astonishing "triple-play" biography, designated "Best Biography of the Year" by the Hollywood Book Festival, Blood Moon lifts the "mink-and-diamond" curtain on this amazing trio of blood-related sisters, whose complicated intrigues have never been fully explored before.

"**You will never be Ga-bored...this book gives new meaning to the term compelling.** Be warned, *Those Glamorous Gabors* is both an epic and a pip. Not since *Gone With the Wind* have so many characters on the printed page been forced to run for their lives for one reason or another. And Scarlett making a dress out of the curtains is nothing compared to what a Gabor will do when she needs to scrap together an outfit for a movie premiere or late-night outing.

"For those not up to speed, Jolie Tilleman came from a family of jewelers and therefore came by her love for the shiny stones honestly, perhaps genetically. She married Vilmos Gabor somewhere around World War 1 (exact dates, especially birth dates, are always somewhat vague in order to establish plausible deniability later on) and they were soon blessed with three daughters: **Magda**, the oldest, whose hair, sadly, was naturally brown, although it would turn quite red in America; **Zsa Zsa** (born 'Sari') a natural blond who at a very young age exhibited the desire for fame with none of the talents usually associated with achievement, excepting beauty and a natural wit; and **Eva**, the youngest and blondest of the girls, who after seeing Grace Moore perform at the National Theater, decided that she wanted to be an actress and that she would one day move to Hollywood to become a star.

"Given that the Gabor family at that time lived in Budapest, Hungary, at the period of time between the World Wars, that Hollywood dream seemed a distant one indeed. The story—the riches to rags to riches to rags to riches again myth of survival against all odds as the four women, because of their Jewish heritage, flee Europe with only the minks on their backs and what jewels they could smuggle along with them in their *decolletage*, only to have to battle afresh for their places in the vicious Hollywood pecking order—gives new meaning to the term 'compelling.' The reader, as if he were witnessing a particularly gore-drenched traffic accident, is incapable of looking away."

—New York Review of Books

Softcover, 730 pages, with hundreds of photos   ISBN 978-1-936003-35-8

BLOOD MOON
Productions, Ltd.